.NET Common Language Runtime

Kevin Burton

SAMS

Unleashed

.NET Common Language Runtime Unleashed

International Standard Book Number: 0-672-32124-6

Library of Congress Catalog Card Number: 00-111067

Printed in the United States of America

First Printing: April 2002

05 04 03 02 4 3 2 1

Trademarks

All terms mentioned in this book that are known to be trademarks or service marks have been appropriately capitalized. Sams Publishing cannot attest to the accuracy of this information. Use of a term in this book should not be regarded as affecting the validity of any trademark or service mark.

Warning and Disclaimer

Every effort has been made to make this book as complete and as accurate as possible, but no warranty or fitness is implied. The information provided is on an "as is" basis.

Associate Publisher
Rochelle Kronzek

Development Editor
Songlin Qiu

Managing Editor
Matt Purcell

Project Editor
George E. Nedeff

Copy Editor
Karen A. Gill

Indexer
Larry Sweazy

Proofreader
Plan-it Publishing

Technical Editor
Mike Deihl

Team Coordinator
Denni Bannister

Interior Designer
Gary Adair

Cover Designer
Aren Howell

Page Layout
Michelle Mitchell
Mark Walchle

Contents at a Glance

Table of Contents

B .NET Framework Class Libraries 835

Foreword

Walking down the aisle of your favorite bookstore, you will find numerous books covering various aspects of Microsoft's new .NET strategy. But unlike most of those books, *.NET Common Language Runtime Unleashed* focuses squarely on the Common Language Runtime (CLR). Regardless of the language you use or the type of application you are building, *.NET Common Language Runtime Unleashed* offers a rare insight into how your application and the CLR operate. It offers a perspective that nearly every developer who is using the CLR will find valuable.

What exactly is the CLR? I've spent the past four years explaining that to thousands of developers. From a technical perspective, four key aspects of the CLR make it interesting: the type system (covered in Chapter 2, "The Common Language Runtime—The Language and the Type System"), the execution environment (covered in Chapters 3, "The Common Language Runtime—Overview of the Runtime Environment" and 5, "Intermediate Language Basics"), the deployment model (covered in Chapter 6, "Publishing Applications"), and the security system (covered in Chapter 16, ".NET Security"). But from the more practical perspective, the CLR is all about simplicity, making it easier to design, build, integrate, and deploy safe and economical business solutions.

In the years leading up to the development of the CLR, application complexity was growing by leaps and bounds. Each year, a new set of technologies was introduced that added to the complexity of solving business problems. Each new technology added value, but the cumulative effect of all these technological additions became insurmountable for most application developers. Building a typical application was beginning to require a team of highly paid software specialists. The days of programming as a hobby were becoming a distant memory.

Several groups within and outside of Microsoft made attempts to build abstractions over the complexity. MFC, ATL, and Visual Basic 6.0 did a fantastic job of hiding details in exchange for greater developer productivity. But in the end, no single tool, language, or framework could solve every problem. The tools that were designed to make development simpler only contributed to the technology explosion.

To truly simplify development, nothing short of a revolution would suffice. It would take dedication and commitment to come up with a solution that addressed the problem at the most fundamental levels. The solution wouldn't be easy, it wouldn't happen overnight, and certain tradeoffs would be downright painful to face. Some folks would embrace the idea of a fundamental change, whereas others would remain skeptical.

The CLR is a result of that dedication and commitment to making development easier. Creating the CLR was a monumental effort lasting more than four years and requiring the personal devotion of thousands of professional software developers. It sprouted from the vision of a handful of individuals at Microsoft who believed that a better, more productive way to develop software existed, and it grew into the foundation for an entirely new software platform.

Simplicity takes on many forms. It means doing away with some of the complexities that developers have reluctantly learned to live with over time—things like having to define types in IDL as well as the language you use to implement those types, having to deal with various incarnations of common data types like strings and dates, and having to assign globally unique identifiers (GUIDs) to every new data type you define. It also means offloading some of the more mundane coding chores like having to manage object lifetime on your own and having to add code to support late binding or serialization.

The CLR takes a new approach to simplification. It starts at the lowest level by introducing a language-neutral type system that makes type definitions ubiquitous. A type defined using the common type system can be used by a variety of programming languages. More importantly, those languages that target the CLR use the type system natively, thereby eliminating type incompatibilities and unnecessary data transformations. The common type system makes every type look familiar to every type of developer regardless of how the type was created. The common type is the single most important feature of the CLR. Understanding the value of a common type system is key to understanding why the CLR is so important.

Because all types are defined with a common type system, the CLR's execution environment is able to offer a number of runtime services to the objects that a program creates. Services such as lifetime management, dynamic inspection, late-binding support, serialization, and remoting are all made possible by the common type system. Each service that the CLR provides is one less piece of code that developers have to provide and one fewer source of potential bugs.

Another aspect of simplicity involves deployment. In fact, the single biggest cost in building applications today is often the cost of deploying the application to an enterprise. In large organizations, the deployment cost can easily outweigh the cost of actually developing the application. The challenge in deployment is managing the pieces of code that are shared among several applications. As new applications are installed, the shared code is often overwritten with a newer but subtly incompatible version of the shared code. These incompatibilities often lead to problems with other applications that share the same component (a situation commonly referred to as *DLL Hell*).

The CLR addresses deployment headaches in several ways. It captures precise details about the shared code on which an application depends. This information (metadata) allows the CLR to identify exactly the code on which an application depends. This precise binding information along with the ability to have multiple versions of shared components installed on the same machine makes application binding much more resilient. It allows multiple applications that depend on different versions of a shared component to coexist peacefully on a user's machine. It also allows developers to evolve types over time without being overly constrained with maintaining backward compatibility.

Concerns about security are a way of life, and software is no different. Security requirements are different for various applications. Application developers need a system that allows them to build highly secure applications and the trivial utilities that know nothing of security. What's difficult is that security isn't an on/off switch; developers also need to be able to build applications with varying degrees of security (partially trusted applications). Key to the CLR security model is the notion that code, as well as users, can have an identity and that decisions of trust made at execution time can be based on the identity of the code and the user. This model is much different from older models that were based solely on the user identity. This model also differs from the Authenticode model, which only comes into play when code is being installed on a user machine.

What is the CLR? It takes much more than a 90 minute presentation to answer that question. About the best way to understand the CLR is to read the rest of this book. As you read it, you should get a sense for what the CLR really is. It's not just another new technology; it's the culmination of years of effort targeted squarely at simplifying the development process. Going forward, Microsoft has made some bold changes in the way people will build applications. Adopting this new platform will present its own challenges, but it is Microsoft's hope that history will judge the CLR as the start of a new era—an era where application development became easy again and people started programming just for the fun of it.

Enjoy!

Dennis Angeline
Lead Program Manager
Common Language Runtime
Microsoft Corporation

About the Author

Ronald Kevin Burton has been around software development for almost 20 years. He has worked with small and efficient real-time executive programs for controlling the flow of communications data in a communications system. He participated in a team to build critical flight-control software, and has worked on Cyber, Unix, VAX/VMS, OS/9, VxWorks, Windows NT, and Windows 2000 systems. Kevin built complex real-time systems that analyzed images and provided feedback to the user, as well as custom software to augment the operation of an electron microscope. Currently, Kevin is working on building cutting edge systems to automate the production and distribution of news broadcasts. He sees the .NET Framework as the next evolution of software development and is excited about being part of that movement. Kevin can be reached at `Kevin.Burton@inewsroom.com`.

Dedication

To my wife, Becky, and my four children, Sarah, Ann Marie, Michael, and Rose.

Acknowledgments

First, I would like to thank Shelley Kronzek, Executive Editor at Sams Publishing, who started me on this journey and provided needed support through the project. Songlin Qiu, Mike Diehl, Karen Gill, and George Nedeff were also key to the success of this book as they provided an unending stream of feedback on my writing.

General thanks to the personnel at Microsoft who made sure that I understood the material. Thanks, too, to Mahesh Prakriya for coordinating my introduction to the CLR team and for providing much needed feedback. Jim Miller and Jim Hogg patiently fielded each of my questions on the organization and architecture of the assembly metadata. Jim Hogg stepped in at various levels, but I particularly remember his contributions to the chapters on debugging and profiling. Thanks to Dennis Angeline, whose expertise and overall vision of the interop services within .NET was very much appreciated. Steve Pratshner supplied me with much needed information on the interaction of COM components and the CLR. He also provided a good deal of assistance in helping me understand deployment and building a host for the CLR. Steve also responded to many questions that I had about remoting and AppDomains. Brad Abrams seemed to have some insight into just about all aspects of the .NET Framework and very enthusiastically shared what he could or referred me to the most qualified person. When it came down to testing some of my interop applications, Sonja Keserovic stepped in to provide much needed assistance.

Sanjay Bhansali not only provided me with a one-on-one tutorial of threading .NET style, but he also gave me assistance when my misunderstanding caused my applications to break. Christopher Brumme provided advice and feedback on threading issues. Eric E. Arneson shared information about some of the lesser-known members of the **`ThreadPool`** class.

Lance Olson and Tom Kaiser provided samples to help me understand the peer-to-peer networking in .NET. They also were able to spend some time reviewing my chapter on networking. Alexei Vopilov was patient while I tried to understand **`SocketPermissions`**.

Loren Kohnfelder was always responsive to my security-related questions. This topic required some extra effort on Loren's part for it to sink in for me, and his patience was very much appreciated. Brian Pratt was able to supply me with some valuable feedback on network security. Jian Lee stepped up to answer some specific questions about code that did not seem to work correctly.

Piet Obermeyer provided my first introduction to .NET remoting and spent a good deal of time helping me form a basis of understanding. Jonathan Hawkins was responsive with specific questions that I had about remoting. His enthusiasm for the technology could be felt even through e-mail.

Jayanth Rajan provided much needed information about AppDomains in the context of reflection. Dario Russi gave me much of his time discussing reflection while I was at Microsoft and has provided much needed feedback since.

Shri Borde provided a much needed review of my chapter on exceptions. Raja Krishnaswamy took on the task of reviewing the three chapters on interoperation and provided invaluable feedback. Adam Nathan was helpful in resolving some problems that I was having with COM interop. Ralph Squallace reviewed my chapter on threading and provided a good deal of e-mail feedback. Mei-Chin Tsai was able to take time from a busy schedule and provide me with feedback on my chapter on reflection. Dan Takacs also provided thorough feedback after reviewing a rough draft of my chapter on reflection. Jim Warner gave some tips after having reviewed my chapters on profiling and debugging.

Thanks to Keith Ballinger, Scott Berry, Arthur Bierer, Kit George, Shaykat Chaudhuri, Bret Grinslade, Brian Grunkemeyer, Paul Harrington, Abhi Khune, Anthony Moore, and Kris Stanton. They were there to answer important queries that were holding me up.

Finally, thanks to Matt Lyons' for his contribution to the chapter on security. Matt provided a very thorough review.

Tell Us What You Think!

As the reader of this book, *you* are our most important critic and commentator. We value your opinion and want to know what we're doing right, what we could do better, what areas you'd like to see us publish in, and any other words of wisdom you're willing to pass our way.

As an Associate Publisher for Sams Publishing, I welcome your comments. You can fax, e-mail, or write me directly to let me know what you did or didn't like about this book—as well as what we can do to make our books stronger.

Please note that I cannot help you with technical problems related to the topic of this book, and that due to the high volume of mail I receive, I might not be able to reply to every message.

When you write, please be sure to include this book's title and author as well as your name and phone or fax number. I will carefully review your comments and share them with the author and editors who worked on the book.

Fax: 317-581-4770

E-mail: `feedback@samspublishing.com`

Mail: Rochelle Kronzek
Associate Publisher
Sams Publishing
201 West 103rd Street
Indianapolis, IN 46290 USA

Introduction

Jim Miller, Program Manager for the Common Language Runtime (CLR) at Microsoft, when interviewed by Robert Hess, defined the CLR as follows in *The .NET Show* (`http://msdn.microsoft.com/theshow/Episode020/Transcripttext.asp`):

> **Robert Hess:** So what exactly is the CLR? If I want to talk [about] it as an object, what would you define it as?
>
> **Jim Miller:** Well, it is hard to define as a single thing. It is a combination of things. It is a file format that is used for transferring files between systems that are using the .NET framework, essentially. It is the programming goo inside there that lets your program run. It is the thing that takes the way your program has been compiled into this Intermediate Language, and actually turns that into machine code and… executes it, plus all the support services that you need while it's running… Memory management services, exception handling services, compilation services, reflection services—[the CLR] encompasses all of those pieces, but just up the sort of the very lowest level to bring you up to essentially the level you would have been at, let's say, if you were doing programming in C with just the minimal runtime, no libraries above it. The libraries above it are part of what we call the framework, and that's sort of the next level of the system.

Whether you are running code derived from VB, C#, managed C++, JScript, or any of the other 15–20 languages supported by the .NET Framework, you are using the facilities and services of the CLR. The CLR provides services that promise to move software development into the 21st century. The CLR provides a whole new way of developing software. This book provides you with the information and samples you need to quickly apply and use the CLR to its fullest potential.

This Book's Intended Audience

This book is primarily targeted toward software engineers who require a thorough understanding of the underpinnings of the .NET Framework. It is intended to assist those engineers who understand the vision of a managed environment and believe that it is one of the primary means by which software productivity will rise to the next level. It is targeted toward those engineers who believe that although the .NET Framework frees the programmer from many mundane tasks, it does not replace the need for true understanding of the platform and tools upon which he or she is developing software.

What You Need to Know Prior to Reading This Book

This book makes many assumptions about the experience you need prior to reading this book. In some chapters, this is more true than others. If you have experience programming in threads, you will better appreciate the chapter on threading. If you have experience with peer-to-peer networking, you will better appreciate the chapter on networking. If you have experience with trying to lock down your system and security, you will better appreciate the chapter on security. If you have attempted to make your application global, you will better appreciate the chapter on globalization and localization. All readers who have experience developing software undoubtedly have experience debugging and profiling it. In this case, you certainly will appreciate the chapters on profiling and debugging. Finally, if you have experience in developing Java code, you will certainly be able to appreciate Appendix D, "The Common Language Runtime as Compared to the Java Virtual Machine." You will be able to appreciate the examples and the principles of the Common Language Runtime more if you have experience in developing traditional or unmanaged code. If you find that you need to understand the CLR and what it can do for your company and you are a little short on experience but are well motivated, the concepts presented should not be overwhelming.

Appendix A contains a brief tutorial on C#. If you cannot read and understand C#, then much of the sample code will not be clear. If the overview in Appendix A is insufficient for your understanding, you should seek some familiarity with C# before reading this book.

Scattered throughout this book are samples from other languages, such as VB, C++, JScript, Java, Perl, J#, and so forth. Usually, these samples are presented in the context of comparing another language's implementation with a C# implementation. If you do not understand all of the syntax of the language, try to see a pattern between that language and C#.

What You Will Learn from This Book

There is so much to learn and grasp in this book that it might seem overwhelming. Read the book once cover to cover and then refer back to it often. Download the samples for each chapter, formulate theories about different runtime scenarios that are not specifically covered by the sample, modify the sample, and try it. In other words, use this book as a starting point in your quest for understanding. If you have an immediate need for understanding in one subject or another, don't hesitate to jump to that chapter and study it and the samples thoroughly. Keep in mind, however, that some background material might be required to understand a particular chapter out of context. If this is the case, refer to the appropriate chapter. If you approach the book in this manner, you will gain the following:

- Understanding of .NET Types and the Common Type System (CTS)
- .NET Assembly metadata structure and layout
- COM/COM+ interoperation with .NET components
- Legacy integration with Win32 DLL's through P/Invoke
- CLR memory/resource management
- Management and use of threads in a .NET environment
- Ability to build high-performance peer-to-peer networking applications
- Use of remoting for next generation distributed computing
- Flexible application interaction with `events` and `delegates`
- Integration of .NET error handling into your application with exceptions
- Building and maintaining a secure application with .NET security
- Dynamic discovery of type information through .NET reflection
- Targeting of an international audience using .NET globalization/localization tools
- Debugging of a .NET application
- Profiling of a .NET application
- Overview of key C# syntax and design issues
- Overview of .NET framework libraries
- Hosting of your own CLR
- A comparison of the CLR and JVM

Software Needed to Complete the Examples Provided with This Book

Most of the samples in this book require the latest version of the .NET Framework SDK. For most of the samples in the book, it is assumed that Visual Studio .NET has also been successfully installed. Appendix D requires the installation of the latest version of the Java SDK from Sun Microsystems. The appropriate URL to a download site is provided in the text. A couple of small examples are written in Perl and a few more are written in J#. Installing these languages is certainly required to compile and run the samples. It is also possible to skip actually building these samples and just glean what you can from the source. Doing so will not detract too much from your overall understanding of the CLR and the concepts presented.

How This Book Is Organized

This book is divided into four parts. Part I establishes the architecture around the CLR and the operating environment that the CLR creates for your application. Part II introduces the assembly and how it is organized and used in the runtime environment. This part also discusses the assembly as a standard unit of deployment within the .Net Framework. Part III discusses various services that the CLR offers an application and how best to take advantage of those services. Part IV contains five Appendixes that offer supplemental information you might find useful.

- **Part I: .NET Framework and the CLR Fundamentals**—The chapters that make up Part I describe the .NET Architecture. This part describes the Common Type System (CTS) and the Common Language System (CLS) that allow multiple high-level languages to efficiently and completely interoperate with each other.
  - Chapter 1—This chapter introduces the idea of managed code and some of the benefits that are available from managed code—in particular, the CLR.
  - Chapter 2—This chapter describes the types that make up the .NET Framework and how the CLR manipulates these types and your application.
  - Chapter 3—This chapter presents an overview of the runtime environment in which your .NET application runs. It provides a step-by-step overview of how an assembly is loaded in preparation to be executed.
- **Part II: Components of the CLR**—The Assembly can be thought of as self-describing code. The data that describes the data is known as metadata. Part II describes the metadata in an assembly and how it is organized. It also has a description of the Intermediate Language (IL) that is part of every assembly. Finally, this part describes how to install an assembly.
  - Chapter 4—This chapter focuses not only on the types of metadata that are contained in an assembly, but also provides two unmanaged methods for accessing the metadata within an assembly.

- Chapter 5—This chapter provides enough information about the various opcodes that comprise IL to make you at least IL literate. You will undoubtedly be constantly referring to the IL code that is generated by the high-level language compiler of your choice.
- Chapter 6—This chapter focuses on tools and ensure that what is built and tested is what is finally delivered to the customer. Nothing is more frustrating than having code that you have thoroughly debugged blow up at a customer's site.

- **Part III: Runtime Services Provided by the CLR**—The remainder of the book describes each of the services that the CLR offers. Along with the description are examples of how you can take full advantage of these services to make your application more portable, more secure, and more maintainable.
  - Chapter 7—Win32 has been around for quite some time now. There is such a large body of code that has been developed that some means was required from within a .NET component to access these legacy libraries and APIs. The .NET facility to do this is platform invoke, or P/Invoke.
  - Chapter 8—Another type of software that is at least as ubiquitous as Win32 DLLs is COM components. To ensure that traditional COM components do not need to be ported or simply thrown away, the .NET Framework provides a method to import the type library information from a COM type library and build a wrapper around the component.
  - Chapter 9—This chapter shows you how to make a .NET component usable from within unmanaged code as a COM component.
  - Chapter 10—This chapter shows how the CLR manages memory allocation and deallocation using an efficient garbage collection algorithm. This chapter also discusses how you can most efficiently manage resources that are not memory related, as well as hooks that are available for you to step in and modify the management of resources.
  - Chapter 11—This chapter focuses on the facilities that are available for manipulating and using threads. Threads are abstracted by the .NET Framework into a logical thread that is encapsulated by the Thread class.
  - Chapter 12—This chapter illustrates how you can use networking support in your application to develop a fast and efficient peer-to-peer network solution. Networking as presented in the System.Net namespace is not a service directly provided by the CLR; however, networking is at the base of most of the .NET Framework and certainly key in XML Web Services and Remoting.

- Chapter 13—This chapter seeks to remove much of the mystery behind remoting so that you can fully use the remoting services in your application. Because a remoting application is so ingrained into much of the .NET Framework and because much of its functionality is so automatic, it is often described as “magic happens here.”
- Chapter 14—This chapter details how you can use and extend the event model of the .NET Framework in your application. Windows has long been an event-driven environment. The CLR brings the event model into the core of the runtime with events and delegates.
- Chapter 15—This chapter details what exceptions are and how they can be used and extended. One of the main drawbacks of the Win32 APIs and with programming in general is the lack of a cohesive and uniform method for handling errors and exceptional conditions. The CLR again brings exception handling into the core of the operating environment.
- Chapter 16—This chapter address some of the key security features that the CLR brings to the table, mainly under the headings of code access security and role access security. With a new debilitating virus being created virtually every day, security is important to all persons who are using or developing software.
- Chapter 17—This chapter focuses on accessing the metadata from the runtime through reflection. Reflection allows for the discovery and creation of metadata at runtime as opposed to statically analyzing an assembly.
- Chapter 18—This chapter focuses on how to use the information that is provided in the metadata to build a global and localized application. The CLR considers an application to be global from the start.
- Chapter 19—This chapter details the tools that you will need to debug your .NET application. Because of .NET’s unique runtime environment, debugging a .NET application requires some specialized tools.
- Chapter 20—This chapter focuses on tools that are available to profile your .NET application so that you can fine-tune it. A .NET application uses memory and disk space much like any other application. However, a .NET application also supports JIT compilation, garbage collection, and security checks that are specific to a .NET application.

- **Part IV: Appendixes**—The Appendixes are provided as background information for this book. Each Appendix supplies information that is considered important, but that is either out of the scope of this book or is not applicable to all readers.

- Appendix A—This Appendix provides a brief overview of some C# constructs that will act as either a reminder or as a base level of understanding so that the samples are more readily understood. The samples are written in C# throughout this book.
- Appendix B—This Appendix provides a broad overview of the libraries and classes that are at your disposal as part of the .NET Framework SDK.
- Appendix C—This Appendix presents a discussion of how you can build your own host for the CLR.
- Appendix D—This Appendix provides a brief comparison of the JVM and the CLR from a programmer's perspective.
- Appendix E—This Appendix lists additional resources that are considered important to concepts developed in this book.

The Sams Web Site for This Book

The chapter-by-chapter code files that are described in this book are available on the Sams Web site at `http://www.samspublishing.com/`. Enter this book's ISBN (0672321246) in the Search box and click Search. When the book's title is displayed, click it to go to a page where you can download all the code. The code can be downloaded on a chapter-by-chapter basis.

Conventions Used in This Book

The following typographic conventions are used in this book:

- Code lines, commands, statements, variables, file drives, programming functions, APIs, directories, and any text you type or see onscreen appears in a `monospace` typeface. **`Bold monospace`** typeface is used to designate classes and namespaces that are part of the .NET Framework class libraries.
- Placeholders in syntax descriptions appear in an *`italic monospace`* typeface. Replace the placeholder with the actual filename, parameter, or whatever element it represents.
- *Italic* is used to highlight technical terms when they are being defined.
- The ➥ icon is used before a line of code that is really a continuation of the preceding line. If you see ➥ before a line of code, remember that it's part of the line immediately above it. This is not part of the code, just a book's convention.
- This book also contains Notes, Tips, and Cautions to help you spot important or useful information more quickly. Some of these are helpful shortcuts to help you work more efficiently.

.NET Framework and the CLR Fundamentals

PART I

IN THIS PART

CHAPTER 1

Introduction to a Managed Environment

In This Chapter

This revolution has been long in coming. Visual Basic programmers have known it for years. Java came along and converted many others. The fact of the matter is that it is hard to develop quality software that targets your market and is robust enough to be useable. It seems to be perfectly acceptable to allow the operating system and the related services to manage the memory space of your program. Talking about virtual memory and virtual devices seems perfectly natural.

All except the people who develop device drivers and real-time systems have come to realize that it is not in their best interest to try to develop software that handles what the operating system handles for them. It is also perfectly acceptable and recommended that you use a commercial database rather than developing your own. Unless you are in the business of developing databases, you cannot remain competitive for very long by spending precious resources on developing software that is not part of your core business.

When these technologies were new, many believed that they could do a better job, or because it was "not invented here," it was not to be trusted. The revolution of today requires a similar shift in your thinking. The reason that you don't develop your own database or your own memory management techniques is that these problems have already been solved in a way that is probably better and certainly cheaper than developing solutions on your own. Adopting the .NET Framework requires a similar mindset.

The .NET Framework is a completely new way of developing software. It is interesting that many of the same objections that were heard when the last revolution occurred are again being voiced. The last revolution was when software development moved from physical memory, interrupts, and dedicated processing to virtual memory, events, and multiprocessing. This chapter is written to give you an idea of the benefits that a managed environment can provide you and your users. Although it is true that you will have to give up a certain amount of control, the additional functionality and flexibility more than makes up for the loss of control. This chapter focuses on some of the reasons that you should take advantage of the .NET Framework.

Brief History of the CLR

The CLR started around 1997. By then, COM had been around for a while and was due for a makeover. Work was begun on MTS and building a more comprehensive type system for COM+ to make COM more universally accessible from a wider array of languages. At the same time, Microsoft wanted to somehow unify the many different code management schemes. Visual Basic, FoxPro, and later J++ all had different mechanisms to manage code. Although each had its strengths and weakness, it was desirable strictly from a code-management point of view to merge the code management methodologies.

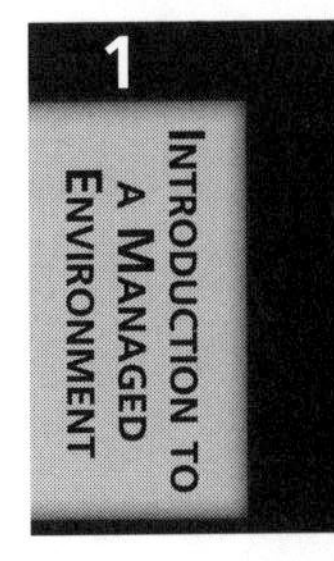

Intermediate Language (IL) specifically can trace its roots to Microsoft P-Code. A key design consideration was that the code had to be designed for compilation at the beginning. IL was never considered for a possible interpreted language. It was always assumed that this code would be compiled somehow.

As the COM3 project grew, it ended up pulling people from most of Microsoft. The name changed from COM3 to COR to COM+ 2.0 (was in parallel with COM+ 1.0) to NGWS and finally to .NET.

Overview of the Managed Runtime Environment

Adopting the .NET Framework programming model is beneficial in many ways. It is a simple model that places at its core the Common Language Runtime (CLR). Figure 1.1 shows a simple block diagram of the .NET Framework.

FIGURE 1.1
.NET Framework block diagram.

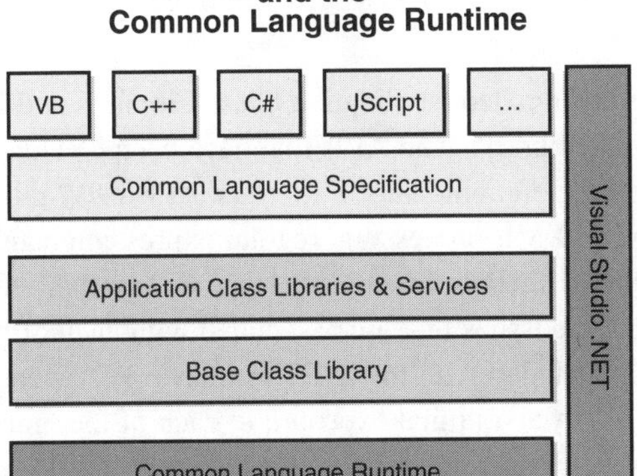

On the right of this figure is Visual Studio .NET. This is obviously an important part of the .NET Framework because it provides a means for the programmer to access the framework at any level. A programmer can use Visual Studio .NET to write code in many supported managed languages, or he can bypass the CLR altogether and write unmanaged code with Visual Studio .NET. With all of the hoopla over .NET, it is important to know that you always have a way out. You can always write unmanaged code if you want or need to. Increasingly fewer situations warrant "dropping down" to unmanaged code, but the option is available.

On the left in the figure, you can see the four languages that Microsoft has announced it will provide support for "out of the box." The ellipsis signifies the other significant and growing set of languages that support the Common Language Specification (CLS) and are full participants in the .NET Framework.

The CLS is the glue that holds all of the languages together. Chapter 2, "The Common Language Runtime—The Language and the Type System," goes into more detail on specific types that are defined within the CLS, called the Common Type System (CTS). The CLS is a statement of rules that allow each language to interoperate. For example, the CLS guarantees that Visual Basic's idea of an integer is the same as C#. Because the two languages agree on the format of the data, they can transparently share the data. Of course, it is much more complicated than this because the CLS defines not only type information, but also method invocation, error handling, and so forth.

One of the important results of a language that adheres to the guidelines set forth in the CLS is that it becomes a full-fledged member of the .NET Framework. You can define a class in Visual Basic and use it in C#. A method that is defined in C# can be called by Visual Basic or any other language that adheres to the CLS. After an API is learned in one language, then using that API in any other CLS-compliant language is virtually the same.

Figure 1.1 shows a middle layer called Application Class Libraries and Services. This layer represents the rich set of libraries and APIs that have been created to support virtually all aspects of programming. Graphical user interface APIs or Windows.Forms, database APIs through ADO.NET, XML processing, regular expression handling, and so forth are all part of this layer. Although this middle layer is important, this book does not spend much time addressing the issues that are associated with each of the areas represented by the class libraries included with the .NET Framework. Appendix B, ".NET Framework Class Libraries," gives minimal exposure to each of the more prominent classes and namespaces in the class libraries.

Figure 1.2 shows the execution model of the .NET Framework.

On the far right of this figure, you can see how some languages (C++ for example) can either generate managed or unmanaged code. For example, you can compile C++ source as unmanaged code, which generates native CPU instructions and directly interacts with the OS. This is how you traditionally develop code. You develop a program in C or C++, compile it, and that is what your application becomes. Although certain problems are best handled in this manner (such as device drivers and real-time applications), these programs bypass the CLR and cannot take advantage of the services that the CLR offers.

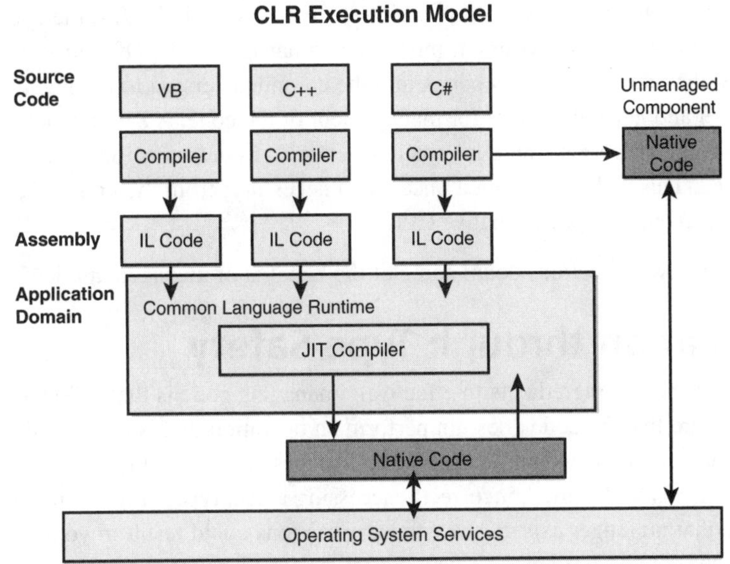

FIGURE 1.2
.NET Framework execution model.

The middle portion of this figure is what is important as far as the CLR is concerned. Instead of generating native code, each compiler generates IL instructions. Java has a separate program that executes Java byte-code generated by the Java compiler. Microsoft has integrated the IL instructions into the Portable Executable (PE) format that has been used for Windows applications for some time now. After you compile your program, your application will either be an .EXE or a .DLL that, based on the filename and extension, is indistinguishable from every other .EXE or .DLL in your system. If you run one of these .EXE files, it will appear to run just like any other .EXE on your system. This compiled code is called an *assembly*, and it is the standard unit of deployment within the .NET Framework. The way that an assembly is loaded and run, the way that it masquerades as a PE file, and an overview of the IL instructions to which your source is compiled are detailed in Chapters 2 through 5. These chapters provide much more detail on an assembly.

The CLR loads an assembly into what is called an *application domain*, or just *AppDomain*. This is where your program is actually executed. One of the first tasks of the CLR is to convert the IL code that was generated by one of the language compilers into native code that can be run on the native CPU. This conversion process happens on a method by method basis. Upon entering a new method, the IL code is converted into native code and then executed. This process is known as *Just-In-Time (JIT)* compiling.

After a method has been compiled into native code with the JIT, the code runs at full speed on the native processor, much like unmanaged code. Of course, when the JIT compiles the method, it places hooks into the compiled version to maintain the execution model and generally allow for management of the code. A key distinction between this and other platforms where intermediate code is processed is that this code is not interpreted. This code is compiled once when necessary; from then on, the code runs with all of the capabilities of the native CPU.

The following sections detail some of the benefits of managed applications.

Isolation through Type Safety

One of the key ingredients to effectively managing code is that safeguards be put in place to ensure that the code does not perform an operation that is unexpected. Typical unexpected operations would be attempting to access an element of an array that is outside the bounds of the array, incorrectly accessing a data type, or accessing a field in a data type that no longer exists. All of these operations could result in your program crashing or your data becoming corrupted. A core aspect of the CLR and the CLS-compliant languages that produce IL code that the CLR runs is type safety. A given type is only allowed to perform a discrete set of operations that is appropriate for that type. It is impossible to convert or cast an object into a value that is not compatible. It is also impossible to access a character as an integer because pointers are not allowed and because such an operation would be disallowed by throwing an exception such as `InvalidCastException`. The code is rigorously checked to ensure that the types that the code is manipulating are safe. Figure 1.3 shows a set diagram that illustrates type safety within the .NET Framework.

FIGURE 1.3
.NET Framework type safety.

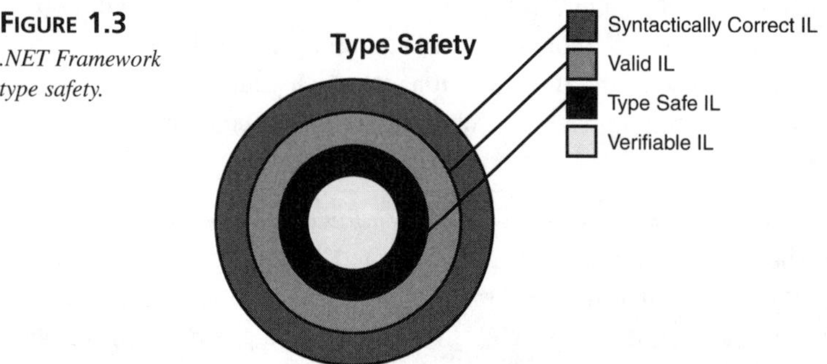

The outer ring depicts all possible sets of IL code that a compiler could generate. This ring represents all the code that has the correct opcode that is within the defined set of IL instructions followed by a correct operand. The next ring designates all the code that is valid IL. For example, although it might be syntactically correct to have an opcode followed by four bytes for the operand, it might not be valid unless the four bytes represent a valid token. Details of the IL instruction set can be found in Chapter 5, "Intermediate Language Basics." The next inner ring represents code that is type safe. This code manages and manipulates types in a safe manner. Only operations that correspond to the type are allowed, and conversion between types is carefully controlled. The last ring represents verifiable type safe code. This code can be proven to be type safe. Notice that just because code cannot be proven to be type safe does not mean it is not type safe. However, all code that can be verified as type safe is type safe. For example all C++ code is not verifiable. This does not mean that all C++ code is not type safe; with C++ code, it is up to the programmer to verify that the code that is being written is type safe. A similar situation holds true for C# code that is compiled with `/unsafe` and uses unsafe methods.

For code to be verifiably type safe, it must pass a strict set of rules. These rules include verifying type safe flow control, initializing variables, checking stack state, verifying type compatibility, and checking the construction of the .NET version of function pointers called `delegates` (covered in Chapter 14, "`Delegates` and `Events`"). A utility called *`PEverify`* runs a verification algorithm on an assembly. Types that are a part of the .NET Framework are covered in greater detail in Chapter 2.

The CLR runs these verification checks at runtime if it is determined that the code is verifiable. The key benefit that is gained with all this concern about type safety is that the .NET Framework can use a lightweight version of a process, the application domain, to isolate each running program. This isolation ensures that an application running in one application domain will not interfere with an application running in another. The overall system benefit is that the system can now support more logical processes as application domains than it could with physical processes with the same level of isolation.

Complete Security

Type safety plays a key role in building a secure application. If you were to poll the IT managers around the world to find out the number one cause for their systems being compromised, you would find that buffer overruns were high on the list. A type safe program does not access memory that is not within the respective types, so a type safe program cannot have a buffer overrun.

Part of the management of your code is to prevent unauthorized users from using the code (role-based security) and to prevent the code from performing operations that it was not designed to perform (code-based security). As further detailed in Chapter 16, ".NET Security," the CLR allows for tight control over the managed code that can lead to a secure application. Security checks in the past amounted to assigning permission to run certain programs. The CLR performs dynamic security checks, such as walking the stack to check for inadequate permission in the call chain before performing an operation. This kind of security is not possible with unmanaged code unless the individual programmer built that into the application. One of the primary goals in developing a managed runtime environment was to allow a user to download a piece of code from the Internet, run it, and know that it was safe.

Traditional security was built on the idea that you would attach permissions to objects and grant authenticated users permissions to perform operations on those objects. These systems were good at doing this task. One problem with that model was that permission was granted to a user and not the code. As an administrator, you could accidentally run a program from the Internet that reformatted your hard drive. If you were only a guest on the system with minimal permissions, however, the security system would prevent you from reformatting the hard drive (hopefully).

To address this problem, many systems administrators had two login accounts: one that gave them all permissions and one that gave them a reduced set of permissions so that it was not possible to "accidentally" do something bad. This solution was great for administrators, but many users had to be granted a greater set of permissions just to be able to run certain programs. Having a separate account for each set of permissions that you wanted to run was not a good overall solution. The managed environment under the CLR allows you to set up code permissions. All code is assigned evidence that gives information about the code, such as where it originated. It is possible to build a policy that greatly restricts code that originated from the Internet no matter who is running it. (In fact, this is one of the default policies.) Now .NET code can be safely downloaded from the Internet with the knowledge that the security system will not allow that code to do anything that the policy would deem "bad."

The CLR offers both a more traditional role-based security model and a code-based security model. Security was considered upfront in the design of the CLR—not as an afterthought or grafted in later. This security system requires a definition of a policy. Microsoft offers a great suite of tools to help in the administration of policy. Defining an appropriate policy is up to the user and the administrator of the system. Microsoft has gone to great lengths to define good default permission sets, but ultimately, to have a secure system, you need to fine-tune this policy. For purposes of this discussion on the benefits of managed code, it suffices to say that the hooks are there to build a secure operating environment.

The implementation of security in the CLR is complex. The CLR only adds to the underlying security of the OS. In many cases, the CLR offers wrappers around base-level security functions. It is possible to get at the Windows security tokens using the

WindowsPrincipal and **WindowsIdentity** classes. A class is also available that handles impersonation and the underlying security system. In this case, the CLR managed environment only adds to and does not remove any of the security features that are available with the underlying OS.

Support for Multiple Languages

A managed environment more easily allows for the support of multiple languages. More precisely stated, the Microsoft implementation of a managed environment allows for the support of many languages. It is theoretically possible to gather all of the compiler vendors and language designers and try to hammer out an agreement regarding data types, call structure, execution model, and so forth. That has not happened, however. Instead, Microsoft took the initiative and developed a standard that about 15 languages could support.

This is sort of a virtual machine of virtual machines. Virtual machines have been developed to support a particular language. For example, the Java Virtual Machine supports Java; it doesn't need to support ideas that are foreign to Java. One example that comes to mind is pointers. Java has no pointers, so the Java Virtual Machine (JVM) and the associated Java Byte Code do not have support for pointers. Lisp Virtual Machines support Lisp constructs, Pascal Virtual Machines supports Pascal, Prolog has its virtual machine, and so forth. You can generate code that mimics a particular language on a particular virtual machine. For example, Kawa takes the Scheme language and compiles it into Java Byte Code (`http://www.gnu.org/software/kawa/`).

These approaches usually fall short though; the IL and the virtual machine were not designed to be language independent. The idea behind the CLR or the Microsoft Virtual Machine is that it has support for the constructs of many different languages, and it was designed that way from the start.

Note

Although not specifically related to the CLR support of multiple languages, the interview (`http://msdn.microsoft.com/library/default.asp?url=/library/en-us/dndotnet/html/dotnetconvers.asp`) addresses some concerns about the possible "skewing" of functionality between different .NET Languages.

Anders Hejlsberg—Regarding C# versus Visual Basic, it really primarily comes down to what you already know and are comfortable with. It used to be that there was a large [performance] difference between Visual Basic and C++, but since C# and Visual Basic .NET use the same execution engine, you really should expect the same [performance]. C# may have a few more "power" features (such as unsafe code), and Visual Basic .NET may be skewed a bit more towards ease of use (e.g. late-bound methods calls), but the differences are very small compared to what they were in the past.

Q: Can you contrast C# with Visual Basic .NET? Questions usually come in the form of "I know you guys say Visual Basic .NET and C# let you do the same thing, but C# was designed for the CLR, so I don't believe you when you say Visual Basic .NET is just as good."

Anders Hejlsberg: Regarding C# versus Visual Basic .NET, the reality is that programmers typically have experience with either C++ or Visual Basic, and that makes either C# or Visual Basic .NET a natural choice for them. The already existing experience of a programmer far outweighs the small differences between the two languages.

Q: It has been said a few times that C# is the language designed for the CLR. Considering that all the languages that Microsoft will ship with Visual Studio .NET will be able to target all the features of the CLR, what makes C# more CLR "friendly" than the others?

Peter Golde: I don't think that C# is necessarily any more friendly to the CLR than other languages. The CLR has been designed to be accessible via multiple languages. However, you will probably find that C# is more strongly focused on the CLR than other languages like C++, which have a number of other facilities that are less oriented toward the CLR. By designing C# in conjunction with the CLR, we have the "luxury" of not having backward compatibility constraints.

Performance and Scalability

At first, performance and a managed environment seem to be contradictory. It does not seem possible to have high throughput *and* a managed environment. Sometimes performance considerations dictate the use of an unmanaged environment.

Note

Applications that require real-time control are one place where unmanaged code is the only solution, mainly because Microsoft cannot make strong guarantees as to garbage collection. That is only the current situation, however. Real-time friendly garbage collection algorithms are available for the CLR to implement, which will likely happen in the future.

Consider the following situation. As a software developer, you build an application that works wonderfully when compiled as a 32-bit application. You start to hear about the throughput that is possible on a 64-bit CPU and you have a decision to make. Do you port your existing code to take advantage of the new 64-bit architecture? Do you ship a 64-bit version and a 32-bit version?

With managed code, you can ship one version and have the CLR "port" your code for you. All of the code that you write is compiled to IL. If your customer is running a 64-bit processor, then the CLR on that machine takes advantage of its capabilities. When running on a 32-bit machine, the CLR JITs compile your code accordingly.

The CLR could have been used to alleviate a problem that existed when floating-point coprocessors were first introduced. For many years, CPUs shipped without a hardware means of evaluating floating point instructions, so the floating-point operations where handled in software. As floating-point coprocessors became more available, it was possible to have floating-point operations handled in hardware, which was much faster. Had the CLR been around back then, it could have made things easier. More recently, many advances have been made in the handling and generation of graphics. The capabilities of each graphics processor vary greatly. Using managed code is a good way to easily provide your customers with the maximum performance available on any given machine.

The previous paragraph discussed performance as a matter of convenience. A managed environment can perform equal to or better than an unmanaged environment in other ways as well. For example, an unmanaged application typically cannot adjust its operating parameters to account for the operation of other applications in the system to guarantee an overall level of performance. A managed application, or more specifically the CLR, can take advantage of a global view of the machine and allocate scarce processing resources based on that global view. The CLR can make decisions based on what is "best" for the overall throughput on a particular machine rather than how to achieve the best throughput for a single process.

Related to the idea of a global view is the scalability of the CLR. The CLR was designed to scale down to small handheld devices as well as scale up to large server farms. Your code is managed in much the same way on either end of the scale. You can print a string. You can also communicate the same string to and from the peer connection or simply build a Web page that displays the message. In addition, you can send a message to a compact device or cell phone, or you can build an XML Web service that returns a string. Another alternative is caching that value with ASP.NET so that many users can get the string at once. Finally, you could publish your Web service on a server farm so that if one machine is too busy sending out the message, it will automatically connect with another member of the server farm. The differences between the applications that support any one of these scenarios are small because of the CLR and the managed environment that it provides.

One of the reasons the managed environment that the CLR provides is so scalable is related to the type safety issue that was discussed earlier. Traditionally, when you wanted to perform a task, you started up a process that performed that task. Starting and stopping a process is an expensive operation, however. Starting a process requires assistance from the operating system and the hardware on which the operating system runs. When a process is started, one of the many tasks that occurs is the stack and frame pointers being set up on the hardware. Part of the reason that processes are so isolated is because the hardware dictates the addressing scheme. Because managed code that the CLR runs is type safe, the CLR can run what used to be two processes in parallel, separated by the software abstraction of an application domain. The CLR uses software to guarantee that two application domains do not interfere with each other. Now the CLR can host many application domains in a single process, many processes on a single machine, and many machines in a single domain. Because the overhead is so much less for application domains than for processes, the system now has greater performance.

Deployment

Using managed code provides some distinct benefits when it comes to deploying your code. Installation of applications used to involve some amount of doubt about whether the installation was going to make the system more or less stable. The larger the installation was, the greater the doubt. The managed runtime and the CLR go a long way toward resolving most of the issues involved with deploying an application.

Traditionally, code was identified solely by the name of the file that contained the code, which caused many problems that primarily came under the heading of DLL Hell. *DLL Hell* was when one application required a particular version of a shared DLL and another application required another version, and the versions of the shared DLL were mutually exclusive. Usually what would happen is that each application bundled the shared code with the installation of the application and simply replaced the shared DLL with the version that worked with that particular application. This frequently broke other applications that were depending on the functionality that was previously present in the shared component or DLL.

As part of the CLR, each shared component is uniquely identified; therefore, applications that depend on one version of the DLL can run side by side with applications that require another version because both physically exist in the system. The CLR also supports specific policy files that can be administratively changed to map one version of a shared component to another.

Part of deployment is related to security. Protecting against Trojan horse types of security infiltrations is becoming increasingly important. It should be impossible or at least

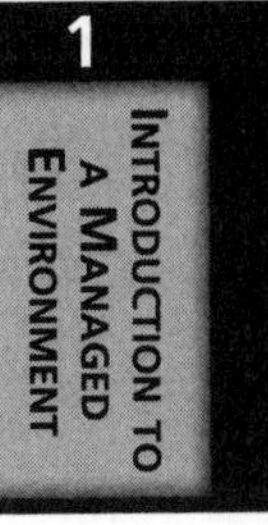

difficult for a third party to insert code as part of your application. When an assembly is given a strong name, the contents of the assembly and all the assemblies that are referenced are hashed. That way, if any portion of the application is modified, the hash will be different and the security violation will be detected.

Deployment issues are discussed in more detail in Chapter 6, "Publishing Applications."

Metadata and Self-Describing Code

To effectively manage code, you need to know as much about the code you are managing as possible. All of the information about code that is run in the .NET environment is maintained with the code as metadata. *Metadata*—data about data—is crucial to effectively manage code. With metadata, your program is no longer a set of obscure assembly opcodes; it now contains a powerful set of data that describes the code. Did metadata make it possible to manage code, or did managed code make metadata possible? With the CLR, these two ideas were developed in parallel.

To build XML Web Services, you need to describe the service that is being provided. It is inadequate and rather inefficient to use human terms such as *integer* to describe a return value or parameter type. To allow for a more automated discovery of the methods that are supported by a given interface, COM used IDL to describe the types and values that were part of the API. Because COM was designed as an implementation on a Microsoft platform, the IDL description allowed for types that were not available on other platforms (types such as VARIANT, SAFEARRAY, and BSTR). In addition, the information in the IDL description was not always completely transferred to the binary form (the type library)—some information was lost.

Metadata, in contrast, represents a rich set of data types and values. Rather than sticking with IDL, Microsoft built support for conversion to and from a standard data description language called Web Services Description Language, or WSDL (see `http://www.w3.org/TR/wsdl`). In the first version of .NET, metadata is a superset of WSDL. In other words, any data type that can be described with WSDL can also be described and implemented in metadata and .NET. The problem at least for the first version is that some metadata constructs cannot be represented in WSDL. Microsoft is proposing some additions to the standard that will make the conversion more one-to-one. The main idea is that it is possible to generate a WSDL description, which is universally accepted as standard, from the metadata within a .NET assembly. It is also conversely possible to generate a .NET assembly and the associated metadata from WSDL. Thus, support for XML Web Services is built into the core of the managed environment because of the presence of metadata.

Garbage Collection and Resource Management

One of the first things that comes to mind when talking about a managed environment is that now you don't have to worry about memory management anymore. This has long been recognized as an issue that many programmers have a hard time getting right. Numerous companies have been founded solely on the fact that programmers sometimes do not allocate and deallocate memory correctly. When a new managed environment is introduced to a room of programmers, you can feel the collective sigh of relief when it is revealed how the managed environment "automatically" handles memory allocation. The CLR is no different, but it also brings much more to the table.

The CLR enables a programmer to have a virtual garbage collection that allows him to release an object and later change his mind and reclaim it. This is done through a process of weak references. Also put into place is a distinct process for allocating and deallocating objects that are not necessarily related to memory, such as file handles, process handles, database connections, and so forth. The CLR allows a programmer to relinquish control for memory allocation, but puts hooks in place so that the programmer can acquire and release resources on demand.

COM Evolution

COM has become such a popular way of programming that all this talk about .NET has made many think that COM is dead. COM provided an interface that allowed programs written in many different languages to call and use. The interface became a sort of black box with which programs could interact. In addition, COM components had a distinct way of managing their own lifetime. As soon as it was detected that COM had no outstanding references, the COM component could simply delete itself. With respect to these two scenarios, the CLR is just COM improved, or COM+. (One of the original designations for the CLR was COM3.) The multiple language benefit has already been discussed at length. The CLR allows for more and better language interoperability than was possible with COM.

Everything that the CLR manages is an object, and as soon as no references exist for the object, the object is subject to garbage collection. This is the same process that the COM model uses, except you do not need to worry about explicitly calling `AddRef` and `Release` as you do in C/C++.

Because of the tremendous support for legacy COM and DLL APIs, the CLR enables you to interoperate with traditional COM servers and Win32 DLLs. Chapters 7, "Leveraging Existing Code—P/Invoke," 8, "Using COM/COM+ from Managed Code," and 9, "Using Managed Code as a COM/COM+ Component," are devoted to interoperation between COM and Win32 DLLs.

Threading

The CLR has abstracted physical threads into logical ones. This abstraction allows for instance threads, or threads that start on an instance of a particular class and can use that class to maintain state information.

Enhancements have been made that allow for thread pooling. Previously, each application had to do this.

The CLR strictly controls the physical threads that are started and stopped and allows threads to freely run between application domains. If the analogy is used between a lightweight process and an application domain, this obviously gives the programmer a new degree of freedom in communicating between what would be processes and what are now application domains.

Networking

Although the networking support within the .NET Framework is not strictly part of the CLR, it is so dependent on the services and low level enough that it could be considered part of the CLR. Much of the Web access, Web permissions, socket permissions, and serialization would not be possible without the services that the CLR offers. Chapter 12, "Networking," details some of the key features of networking within the .NET Framework.

Events

`Event`s are one of the base types; therefore, `event`s are available to all languages that support the .NET Framework. Now a consistent mechanism is available to handle callbacks in any .NET Language. The benefits of `event`s are also strongly tied with the issue of type safety that was discussed earlier. Managed code can check at runtime that the `event` that is being fired and the associated handler or handlers are of the correct type and have the correct signature to handle the event or callback. `Event`s and `delegate`s are discussed in greater detail in Chapter 14.

Consistent Error Handling

All errors within the .NET Framework are handled as exceptions. This not only is a better way of handling errors, but it also is another feature of a managed environment. A programmer marks specific regions of code as *protected*. In C#, the protected block is marked as a `try` block. If an error occurs, the CLR aborts the execution path that contains the protected instructions and starts the search for a handler for the error. Four different blocks of code could follow a protected block. You could have a typed exception handler, a filtered exception handler, a fault handler, or a finally handler. The CLR strictly prevents arbitrarily entering and leaving the protected blocks or any of the handler blocks of code. By managing the code execution path under error conditions, the CLR ensures consistent and secure error handling. Exceptions and error handling are covered in more detail in Chapter 15, "Using Managed Exceptions to Effectively Handle Errors."

Runtime Discovery of Type Information

Each assembly has a set of metadata that describes the assembly. When the CLR loads the assembly to run it, that information does not disappear. Rather, the .NET Framework gives the programmer a rich set of classes and APIs to access the type information at runtime through what is known as *reflection*. Reflection is covered in more detail in Chapter 17, "Reflection."

Globalization

One additional benefit of having an abstraction for physical threads is that additional data can be maintained in that thread. One piece of data that is stored in a thread is the culture information. This makes it possible to have an English thread, a Chinese thread, a Japanese thread, and so forth. This is certainly one way that an application can support multiple languages and cultures at the same time.

In addition, one piece of an assembly name is a cultural identifier. If an assembly is given a cultural identifier, it is different from the same assembly with a different cultural identifier. This is primarily used when building satellite assemblies that the CLR can load based on a culture assigned to a thread. The issues involved with globalization and localization are covered in Chapter 18, "Globalization/Localization."

Debugging and Profiling

When managed code performs virtually any task, it is with the knowledge of the CLR. This makes for a great environment in which to debug or profile. Not only is the CLR involved in most tasks, but a complete set of APIs have also been developed and documented to allow for the development of sophisticated debuggers and profilers. In addition, the CLR passes most of the information about its state on to the Performance Monitor. Now events such as JIT activity and garbage collection are easy to monitor and analyze. Debugging and profiling are covered in Chapters 19, "Debugging .NET Applications," and 20, "Profiling .NET Applications."

Summary

This chapter provided an overview of the benefits that are associated with running code in a managed environment—specifically in the CLR. You should now start to get a feel for how important the CLR is to the software development process. This new generation of software development should prove to be more productive and more efficient than before.

CHAPTER 2

The Common Language Runtime—The Language and the Type System

In This Chapter

One of the primary benefits of the .NET Framework is the interoperability among many different languages. The level at which languages can interoperate within the .NET Framework is achieved by the components of the Common Language Runtime (the CLR). A program written in one program can seamlessly access types, methods, and values that are implemented in another. A C# method can access a VB method, and a VB method can access a C# method. A class that is defined in C# can be accessed from VB in the same way that the VB program accesses classes that are defined in VB. Similar interoperability is available among any of the other supported languages. The number of languages that is supported is continually increasing. There are currently 15–20 languages that support the .NET Framework.

The CLR can be broken into three main categories:

- The type system (covered in this chapter)
- The execution system (covered in Chapter 3, "The Common Language Runtime—Overview of the Runtime Environment")
- The metadata system (covered in Chapter 4, "The Assembly")

Of course, all of these categories are interrelated. The execution system requires information from the metadata and the type system to effectively run a program. One portion of metadata describes a method signature, which the execution system can use to verify calling convention, parameter count, return type, and exception handling information. Therefore, sometimes it is hard to talk about one without mentioning the other. This chapter is primarily introductory in nature. Most of the topics and concepts that are introduced in this chapter are handled later in a section or in a completely different chapter later. The types are handled in this chapter. The implementation and the usages of those types are handled in subsequent chapters.

Common Type System

The .NET Framework has two kinds of objects: reference types and value types. Figure 2.1 illustrates the type hierarchy within the .NET Framework.

From this chart, you can see that all objects derive from either a value type or a reference type. This is a specification of how the object is to be passed around and how it is to be allocated. Value types are copied whenever an object needs to be moved. Value types are allocated from the local stack. Reference types are allocated from a global heap, and only a pointer or reference to the object is passed if the object needs to be used in another method. Another difference between value types and reference types is when two objects are compared. A value type is compared bit for bit. For example, comparing two variables that both have a value of 1 would result in an equal comparison. Comparing two reference objects simply compares the address or the reference of the objects. If two reference objects both contain the value of 1, then they are not equal because they are different objects. A reference type sometimes acts like a value type and is said to have *value semantics*. A prime example is a **string** in C#. Technically, a **string** is a reference type because it is passed by reference when given as an argument to a method and it does not derive from **System.ValueType**. However, copying a string copies the entire string and not just the reference. In addition, comparing two **string**s does not just compare the references; it compares the actual **string** values, as you would expect.

FIGURE 2.1
Type classification.

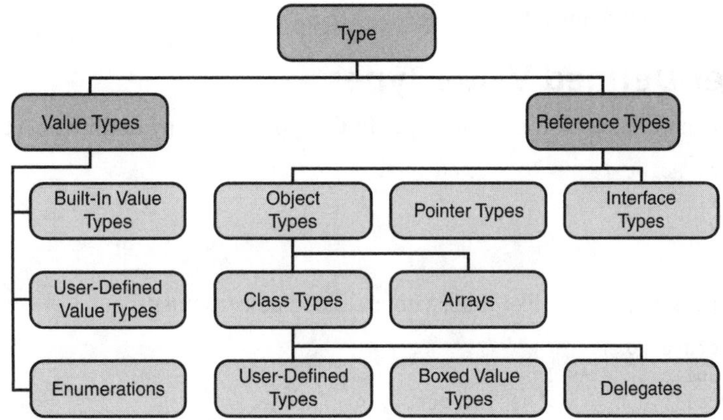

The following sections discuss the properties and characteristics of the value types and reference types within the Common Type System.

Value Types

As has been noted, value types are small; therefore, any memory that is required for instantiation is on the runtime-stack. Values are of three types: built-in value types, user-defined value types, and enumerations. Details of each of these types are included in the following sections.

Built-In Value Types

Examples of built-in values are the primitives such as **int** (**System.Int32**) and **double** (**System.Double**).

To efficiently handle some of the most used value types, the compiler recognizes certain types and generates specific instructions for built-in types. The list of built-in types is as follows:

- Bool.
- Char (16-bit Unicode).
- Integers, both signed and unsigned (8-, 16-, 32-, and 64-bit). Byte is an unsigned 8-bit integer.
- Floating point numbers (32- and 64-bit).
- Machine-dependent integers, both signed and unsigned. (Chapter 3 explains some of the uses for machine-dependent integers.)
- Machine-dependent floating point. (Chapter 3 explains the runtime handling of floating point values.)

User-Defined Value Types

You can define a custom value type. In C#, you do this by defining a **struct**:

```
struct Point {
int x;
int y;
}
```

In VB, it would look like this (with an added constructor):

```
Structure Point
   Public x, y As Integer
   Public Sub New(x As Integer, y As Integer)
      Me.x = x
      Me.y = y
   End Sub
End Structure
```

The resulting value type derives from **System.ValueType**. Because value types are passed by value and allocated on the stack, user-defined value types should be rather small (not more than 16 bytes). Keeping the user-defined value types small allows values to be transferred relatively quickly and reduces the stack size required to hold the object.

User-defined value types can have constructors that take arguments, but they cannot override the default constructor (no arguments). User-defined value types are inherently **sealed**. A sealed class cannot be inherited. In addition, although user-defined value types can inherit multiple interfaces, they cannot be a base class for another reference or value type. User-defined value types can have the following elements:

- Methods
- Fields
- Properties
- Events

Events are covered in more detail in Chapter 14, "Delegates and Events." The syntax of the other elements in C# can be found in Appendix A, "C# Basics." Listing 2.1 shows an example of a user-defined value type that has all four of these elements. The complete source for this example is in the ValuePoint directory in a file called ValuePoint.cs.

LISTING 2.1 Example of a User-Defined Value Type

```
public struct Point
{
    // An event that clients can use to be notified whenever the
    // elements of the list change:
    public event EventHandler Changed;
    private int _x;
    private int _y;
    // Invoke the Changed event; called whenever point changes:
    private void OnChanged(PointEventArgs e)
    {
        if (Changed != null)
            Changed(this, e);
    }
    public Point(int x, int y)
    {
        _x = x;
        _y = y;
        Changed = null;
    }
    public int X
    {
        get
        {
            return _x;
        }
        set
        {
            _x = value;
            PointEventArgs e = new PointEventArgs(_x, _y);
            OnChanged(e);
        }
    }
    public int Y
    {
        get
        {
            return _y;
        }
        set
        {
            _y = value;
            PointEventArgs e = new PointEventArgs(_x, _y);
```

LISTING 2.1 Continued

```
            OnChanged(e);
        }
    }
    public Point Coordinate
    {
        get
        {
            return this;
        }
        set
        {
            _x = value._x;
            _y = value._y;
            PointEventArgs e = new PointEventArgs(_x, _y);
            OnChanged(e);
        }
    }
}
```

This user-defined value type has three properties: X, Y, and Coordinate. This type also has an event called `Changed` and a private method called `OnChanged`. Listing 2.2 shows code that could be used to test this user-defined type.

LISTING 2.2 Testing a User-Defined Value Type

```
private static void Changed(object sender, EventArgs e)
{
    PointEventArgs pe = (PointEventArgs)e;
    Console.WriteLine("Point has changed. ({0}, {1})", pe.Point.X, pe.Point.Y);
}
. . .
Point p = new Point();
p.Changed += new EventHandler(Changed);
p.Coordinate = new Point(1, 2);
```

A handler is defined to handle the event when a point is changed. In this example, the event handler is called `Changed`. In the main body of the code, a point is created and the event handler is registered with the point instance. The point value is changed through one of the point properties. When the point is changed, it should trigger a call to the event handler. This is an ideal candidate for a value type. It is small (on a 32-bit machine it takes up just 8 bytes), yet despite the restrictions on creating a user-defined value type, the type has quite a bit of functionality.

Enumeration Types

A special value type known as an enumeration type, or **enum**, is an alternative name for the underlying type that defaults to **int**. Enumeration types have the following characteristics:

- An enumeration type has one instance field that defines the underlying type of the **enum**. This instance field is generally hidden from the user.
- An enumeration type derives from **System.Enum**.
- An enumeration type does not have methods, interfaces, properties, or events of its own. Methods are associated with **System.Enum**, but an enumeration type cannot define methods.
- An enumeration type does not have static fields unless they are literal.

Reference Types

A reference type is much like a pointer. A reference type is a combination of a location and the value or content of the reference type.

The location is like the address of an object, the location in memory where the content of the type is stored. The location gives the reference type its characteristic passing mechanism. When an object is passed "by reference," the location of the object is passed—not the value that the object contains.

Assume that you have a traditional C++ class that encapsulates a two-dimensional point much like the Point value type that was described in the previous section. To allocate and instantiate such an object, you would use the following code:

```
Point *p = new Point(1,2);
```

You can copy the pointer to any number of different variables like this:

```
Point *p1 = p;
```

Using p1 or p, you can change the contents of the object Point. You can pass the variable to a function and the function can use the pointer to modify the object. You have only one object, but you can change the object using p1 or a function because only the location is copied or passed, not the data at the location. Reference types are like an address. The main difference is that the address of a reference type is part of a heap that can be garbage collected, so the address can change. Because the address can change, a programmer cannot retrieve the address of a reference type.

Because the address is fluid and not easily obtainable, it is better to think of the address of a .NET object as its location. In addition, the .NET Framework has a specific definition of location. A location is typed, and it specifies not only the address of where an object is stored, but a description of valid usage of the object. The semantics are almost identical to a value type. Assume that you have a reference type `RefPoint`. (Source for a `RefPoint` class is in the `ReferencePoint` directory in the `ReferencePoint.cs` file.) This is similar to the `Point` object described in the previous section on value types. The object is allocated as follows:

```
RefPoint rp = new RefPoint(1, 2);
```

Now you can assign the reference to other variables just as with an address:

```
RefPoint rp1 = rp;
```

As with an address, you can use either `rp1` or `rp` to modify and examine the object because they both refer to the same object. If you were to compare the two reference types, they would be equal because they both point to the same object. The following change creates a new object:

```
rp1 = new RefPoint(1,2);
```

Now although `rp1` and `rp` both contain the same value, they refer to different objects and are not equal.

From Figure 2.1, you can see that there are three kinds of reference types:

- Object types
- Interface types
- Pointer types

A couple of built-in reference types should be discussed. The built-in reference types are discussed in a section after the object types. A typed reference is actually a fourth type that is not CLS compliant, but it is discussed briefly after the section on pointer types.

Object Types

An object type is also referred to as a *self-describing type*. Notice in Figure 2.1 that all object types are reference types, but the converse is not true. Not all reference types are object types. An object type is self describing in that the object class from which all object types are derived has several methods that each object type inherits that “describe” the object:

- **Equals**—The default implementation simply compares the identity of the current object with that of the object that is passed as an argument. It returns true if the two objects are equal. You override this method to provide an equality comparison. Overriding this method causes the compiler to generate a warning CS0659, which indicates that if **Equals** is overridden, then **GetHashCode** should be overridden as well. Listing 2.3 shows a possible override for **Equals** in `RefPoint`.

LISTING 2.3 Overridden **Equals** Method

```
public override bool Equals(object o)
{
    RefPoint target = o as RefPoint;
    if(target != null)
    {
        return (_x == target._x &&
              _y == target._y);
    }
    return false;
}
```

- **GetHashCode**—This returns the hash code for an object. The default implementation uses a hash function from the base class library that hashes based on an index that could be reused. In addition, different objects that contain the same value(s) result in different hash codes. These properties do not make the default hash function suitable for most applications. Listing 2.4 shows a possible override for **GetHashCode**. This override takes into account both of the values, generating a unique hash code for each combination of object values.

LISTING 2.4 Overridden **GetHashCode** Method

```
public override int GetHashCode()
{
    return _x ^ _y;
}
```

- **GetType**—This returns the **Type** for the object. Using the **Type** class that was returned by this method permits access to the metadata for the object. You don't need to override this method in a user-defined implementation.
- **ToString**—This returns a string representation of the object. The default implementation returns the full name (namespace and class name) of the object. Listing 2.5 shows a possible override of this function.

LISTING 2.5 Overridden **ToString** Method

```
public override string ToString()
{
    return  string.Format("{0},{1}", _x, _y);
}
```

- **MemberwiseClone (protected)**—This returns a shallow copy of the object. A shallow copy creates an instance of the same type as the instance and copies bit for bit the non-static fields for the object. If your object only contains value types, then the default **MemberwiseClone** implementation works fine. If you do not want a shallow copy, then you should implement the **ICloneable** interface, which contains a single **Clone** method that you can override to provide a clone of your object. This method cannot be overridden.
- **Finalize (protected)**—The garbage collector invokes this before an object's memory is reclaimed. In C# and C++, the syntax for this function is the same as a destructor, namely `~Object()`, where `Object` is the name of your class. You don't want to implement a **Finalize** method for the reasons that are detailed in Chapter 10, "Memory/Resource Management."

The **object** type has a static method called **ReferenceEquals**. This method takes two **object**s as arguments and returns a **bool** indicating whether the two **object**s refer to the same object. With this method, equality might be starting to get a bit fuzzy. For that reason, the different notions of equivalence within the .NET Framework will be reiterated.

The first notion is identity. This operator indicates whether two objects are identical. Three rules should be identified:

- If the types of the objects are different, then they are not identical.
- If the type is a value type and the values are the same, then the two objects are identical.
- If the type is a reference type and the locations and the values are the same, then the two objects are identical.

These identity rules are the rules that the **ReferenceEquals** method uses to determine whether an object is "equal" to another.

The second notion is the .NET Framework notion of equality. This operator indicates whether two objects are equal. This operator is based on the following rules:

- Equality must be reflexive (a op a always returns true), symmetric (if a op b is true, then b op a is true), and transitive (if a op b is true and b op c is true, then a op c is also true).

- If two objects are identical based on the identity rules, then they are equal.
- If either (or both) of the objects being compared are boxed types, then the objects that are boxed should be unboxed before comparison based on the identity rules proceeds.

The rules for equality are followed for the default implementation of the **Equals** method in the **object** class. Notice that it is similar to identity with the added exception for boxed value types. You can see this exception with the following code:

```
float a = 1.0F;
float b = 1.0F;
object ao = a;
object bo = b;
Console.WriteLine("Boxed Object comparison: {0}", ao.Equals(bo));
```

Here, two objects exist: ao and bo. According to the normal rules of identity, they should not be equal, yet the Equals method returns true to indicate that they are equal. Clearly, because these items are boxed (turned into a reference type), the exception for equality is applied.

The last equality concept is user defined. Because the **Equals** method in the object class can be overridden, you can override it and use whatever criteria that you consider best to determine equality. One notable exception to the rules outlined for equality is the **string** class. Technically, based on the rules for equality, if two different instances of a **string** class exist, then they should always be not equal even if they contain the same value. This is not the case here, because even though a **string** is a reference type, the comparison is always based solely on the value without regard to the identity of the objects that are being compared. This means that the following prints out true as expected:

```
string a = "This is a test";
string b = "This is a test";
Console.WriteLine("{0}", a.Equals(b));
```

Even the following, which uses **ReferenceEquals**, prints true even when the two objects are not the same:

```
Console.WriteLine("{0}", Object.ReferenceEquals(a, b));
```

If you override the **Equals** method in C#, then you probably also want to provide an override to the == operator. By default, the C# compiler translates == into a **ceq** IL instruction, which does the equivalent of an identity equality test. This means that for boxed values, although the **Equals** method correctly reports two boxed values as equal, if you compare the two objects using the binary == operator, they are reported as unequal because they are different objects. Because you do not have the source for the **object** class, you cannot do much about this, other than be aware of it. However, in your user-defined classes, you can provide a == and a != operator that will return the same results as the **Equals** method. If you provide an override to ==, then you receive a warning that you should also provide a != operator. The end result would be the set of methods shown in Listing 2.6.

LISTING 2.6 A == Operator, a != Operator, and a Modified **Equals** Method

```
public override bool Equals(object o)
{
    bool ret = true;
    try
    {
        RefPoint target = (RefPoint)o;
        ret = (_x == target._x &&
               _y == target._y);
    }
    catch(Exception)
    {
        // Expecting invalid cast if Equals is called
        // with the wrong argument.
        // Note that if I use the as operator and compare
        // the result for null, I end up in a recursive
        // situation because I have chosen to reuse this
        // method in the != and == operators.
        ret = false;
    }
    return ret;
}
public static bool operator == (RefPoint a, RefPoint b)
{
    return a.Equals(b);
}
public static bool operator != (RefPoint a, RefPoint b)
{
    return !a.Equals(b);
}
```

Now when you compare two of these `RefPoint` objects with the == operator or the **Equals** method, you get the same result.

Built-In Reference Types

The two built-in reference types are string and object. Just as with the built-in value types, the compiler recognizes these two types as special and has instructions to specifically handle them. For example, rather than just loading a literal string as an object onto the runtime stack (see Chapter 3 on the evaluation stack), a special instruction, **ldstr**, loads the literal string from the string heap. The compiler also recognizes an **object** as special and has instructions to efficiently handle it. For example, **ldfld** takes an object reference and loads a field of that object onto the stack.

Pointer Types

An unmanaged pointer type is not compliant with the Common Language Specification. It is a reference type, as shown in Figure 2.1, but the value of a pointer is not an object. You can't determine the type of the value from just the value; therefore, it is not an object. Generally, pointer types are abstracted away from the programmer and are not generally available. Some languages, such as C++ and C#, allow access and creation of pointer types.

A pointer type is desired in some cases for performance reasons. In C#, if you want to use a pointer type, you need to add the `/unsafe` option to the compilation of your assembly. This is available as an option in the Visual Studio IDE under the Configuration/Build property, Allow Unsafe Code Blocks. After the unsafe flag is set to true, you can include the following type of code in your C# program:

```
unsafe static void StringAddress(string s)
{
    fixed(char *p = s)
    {
        Console.WriteLine("0x{0:X8}", (uint)p);
    }
}
```

This simple code fragment prints the address of a string. You can find a more practical example of using pointers in Appendix A under the `ImageProcessing` directory.

Other types of pointers, such as a function pointer and a managed pointer, are accessible through C++.

In general, pointer types should be avoided because they essentially circumvent the management of the code and data in the .NET Framework. For example, using a pointer in C# causes the point in memory to be pinned, which requires extra work for the garbage collector. The collector must now go around the pinned object during a garbage collection operation (see Chapter 10).

Typed References

A typed reference is a combination of a runtime representation of type and a managed pointer to a location. A typed reference is used primarily to support C++ style variable argument lists (varargs). This value type is not CLS compliant. A class, **TypeReference**, is in the base class library that encapsulates many of the features of a type reference.

Interface Types

An interface type is a partial specification of a type. It is essentially a way of grouping a set of methods that should be implemented by the type that is derived from the interface. Because an interface is a partial specification of a type, it can never be instantiated; therefore, instance methods or fields don't exist. In other words, an interface is implicitly abstract. All methods that are defined as part of an interface are implicitly virtual. In addition to virtual methods, an interface can define properties and events because properties and events reduce to a set of methods. Although it is not considered "compliant," an interface can define a static method.

As far as accessibility is concerned, it is assumed that all methods that are defined as part of an interface are public. It is generally not possible to specify accessibility on an interface method. If a type declares that it supports an interface (through derivation), then the type declaration can make an interface less accessible than the type if desired. In addition, security attributes cannot be applied to a member of the interface or to the interface type.

Type Members

Both reference types and value types can have a substructure. In the simple example in Listing 2.1, both the `Point` and `RefPoint` types had members `_x` and `_y` that were of type `int`. In addition, each type had operations that were allowable. The `Point` value type (refer to Listing 2.1) had various properties that were essentially shorthand for methods, along with a private helper method `OnChanged`. The operations that are defined for the type are known as *methods* (`OnChanged` is a method). The values of the type are known as *fields* (`_x` and `_y` are fields). If you were to have an array of `Point` types, the array would be a reference type. Each member of a type that is accessible via an indexer is referred to as an *array element*. Each field can be declared as a different type; in contrast, every array element must have the same type.

Methods

Each method has a signature associated with it that specifies the number and types of arguments that can be supplied to the method along with the type of return (if any) that the method will have. If a method is not associated with an instance of the type, but rather is associated with the type itself, then it is known as a *static method*. If the method is associated with an instance of a type, then it is either an instance method or a virtual method. When either of these methods is invoked or called, an implicit reference to the instance is passed along with each of the arguments to the method. This instance reference is known as the **`this`** pointer, or simply as **`this`**.

The difference between an instance method and a virtual method is that a virtual method is typically invoked using a virtual call IL instruction (**callvirt**). This call allows for the type of the object that is passed on the stack to determine which method is invoked. When the method invoked is different from the base class method and the base class method is marked as virtual, the method is overridden.

Arrays

An array type is specified with the type of each element, the rank (the number of dimensions), and the bounds for each of the dimensions in the array. The bounds and the indices for the array are signed integers. Every element in an array is an object; therefore, to have an array of value types, the value types are boxed. The array is a reference type. Every array in the .NET Framework is based on the abstract class **System.Array**, but only compilers and the system can derive from this class.

If the lower bound of an array is zero and the array is a single dimension, then the runtime treats it specially and it is known as a *vector*. Vectors are created using the IL instruction **newarr**, whereas arrays that either do not have a lower bound of zero or that have a rank of greater than 1 are created with the IL instruction **newobj**.

Not all features of an array are available in all languages. For example, it is not possible to specify a lower bound for an array in C#. In C#, all arrays are zero based.

Boxed Value Types

Every value type has a defined and corresponding reference type that is known as the *boxed value type*. Not every reference type has a corresponding value type.

Boxing and unboxing are operations that are ultimately the result of the **box** and **unbox** IL instructions respectively. Because of this boxing and unboxing as most other operations is not dependent on a particular language. In addition, a specific language construct rarely explicitly invokes a **box** operation. Also keep in mind that boxing and unboxing are not free. The end result is that your code might have implicit calls to **box** and **unbox** where you did not intend and particularly where a performance penalty might result from having these calls there. Be aware of when and where a **box** or **unbox** instruction might be inserted.

- Objects cause boxing operations. If the left hand of an operation is an object and the right hand is a value type, then you can be assured that **box** is being called.
- As a corollary to the previous point, arrays are always arrays of objects. If, for example, you create an array of integers, it is an array of boxed integers, and a box operation is occurring for each element of the array. If the array of value types is large or frequently accessed, then the overhead of boxing and unboxing could become quite significant.

Eric Gunnerson provided a possible optimization to an array that is required to box and unbox continually at `http://msdn.microsoft.com/library/default.asp?url=/library/en-us/dncscol/html/csharp03152001.asp`. His solution involved creating a wrapper class around the value rather than having boxing and unboxing provide it for you. The advantage is that you can take the value out of the array as a reference (no unboxing), modify it using the methods it defined for your value type, and put it back into the array. (It is still a reference type, so boxing is not involved). Gunnerson made a valid comment that the simplification of code that boxing provides is valuable, and this kind of optimization should be considered only when performance is critical.

delegates

`delegates` are discussed in detail in Chapter 14, but for now, a **`delegate`** is the object-oriented equivalent of a function pointer. A **`delegate`** is created by deriving from **`System.Delegate`**. A **`delegate`** is an object type that the system tightly controls. It appears as another type, but the CLR, not user code, provides the implementations of the methods for a **`delegate`**. In general, a **`delegate`** type has one method, Invoke, which is called to forward calls to the appropriate method. The CLR supports the optional methods **`BeginInvoke`** and **`EndInvoke`** for asynchronous method callbacks.

Features of the Common Language Specification

Whereas CTS specifies the types that are available to be used by programs and applications in the .NET Framework, the Common Language Specification specifies how those types are to be used in a consistent manner to ensure compatibility with other languages. This section discusses the features that are available to all languages that support the Common Language Specification.

Naming

Because it is impractical to program using just numbers, names are given to types, values, instances, and so forth to identify and distinguish them. If the names become obscure and can no longer be relied upon to correctly and uniquely identify a programming element, then it might be better to program with just a sequence of numbers. To avoid this confusion, the CLS has set up some naming guidelines to eliminate name conflict and confusion if the CLS consumer (the programmer) and the CLS provider (the compiler, system tools, and so forth) adheres to them. The following sections discuss valid characters within a name, the scope of a name, and some general guidelines for naming.

Valid Characters

Identifiers within an assembly follow Annex 7 of Technical Report 15 of the Unicode Standard 3.0 (ISBN 0-201-61633-5) found at `http://www.unicode.org/unicode/reports/tr15/tr15-18.html`. Because symbol comparisons are done on a bit-by-bit basis, the identifier must be normalized so that the identifier cannot be represented in multiple different ways all having the same appearance on a display. Specifically, identifiers support normalization form C. In addition, it is not CLS compliant to have two identifiers differ by just case.

Name Scope

Names are collected into groups called *scopes*. For a name to be unique or to uniquely identify an element, it has to be qualified and have a name and a scope. Assemblies provide a scope for types, and types provide a scope for names. The following code provides an example of two names that are the same but in a different scope:

```
public struct A
{
    public int a;
    public int b;
}
public struct B
{
    public int a;
    public int b;
}
```

The field names `a` and `b` in each type are unique because they are qualified by the type. That is to say, field `a` in type `B` is different from field `a` in type `A`. If these types were part of a different assembly, then the types would be different because the assembly would qualify the types.

The CLS requires that each CLS-compliant language provide a mechanism that allows the use of reserved keywords as identifiers. For C#, this mechanism is with the @ prefix. Using this identifier, you can do the following:

```
int @int = 4;
Console.WriteLine("Int: {0}", @int);
```

This allows the use of a keyword as an identifier.

Important Naming Guidelines

Although the CLS supports a broad range of names as identifiers, not all languages support all of the names that are possible as dictated by the CLS. In addition, certain guidelines increase the readability of your code. Some important naming guidelines are as follows:

- Use one of the following capitalization styles:

  Pascal Case—The first letter and each subsequent concatenated word is capitalized.

  Camel Case—The first letter is lowercase and each subsequent concatenated word is capitalized.

  Uppercase—The whole identifier is capitalized. Table 2.1 provides some recommendations as to when to use each of these capitalization styles.

TABLE 2.1 Capitalization Styles

Identifier	*Capitalization Style*
Class	Pascal
Enum Type	Pascal
Enum Value	Pascal
Event	Pascal
Read-Only Static Field	Pascal
Interface	Pascal (prefix with an "I")
Method	Pascal
Namespace	Pascal
Parameter	Camel
Property	Pascal
Protected Instance Field	Camel
Public Instance Field	Pascal

- Avoid case sensitivity. Some languages that are not case sensitive cannot distinguish between two identifiers that differ only in case. Therefore, avoid relying on case to differentiate types and values. Avoid case sensitivity in namespaces:

```
namespace CLRUnleashed;
namespace clrUnleashed;
```

- Avoid case sensitivity with parameter names:

```
void MyMethod(string aa, string AA)
```

- Avoid case sensitivity with type names:

```
CLRUnleashed.Complex c;
CLRUnleashed.COMPLEX c;
```

- Avoid case sensitivity with property names:

```
int Property { get, set};
int PROPERTY { get, set};
```

- Avoid method names that differ only by case:

```
void Compute();
void compute();
```

- It is not CLS compliant to have the same name for a method and a field in a type.
- Don't use abbreviations or contractions as part of an identifier. For example, use GetDirectory rather than GetDir.
- Avoid using abbreviations that are not generally accepted in the computing field or in the field where the symbols will be exposed. Wherever possible, use these abbreviations to replace lengthy phrases. For example, use UI to replace User Interface and SQL to replace Structured Query Language.
- Use Pascal or Camel casing as appropriate for abbreviations that are longer than two characters. For identifiers that are two characters or less, capitalize all characters.
- Avoid using words that conflict with commonly used .NET Framework class library names and language keywords.
- Don't use names that describe a type. Use this:

```
void Write(double value)
```

  rather than this:

```
void Write(double doubleValue)
```

- Use namespaces with the following format:

```
Company.Technology[.Feature][.Design]
```

- Use a noun or noun phrase to name a class.
- Do not use a type prefix such as CFileStream. Use FileStream instead.
- Do not use an underscore character.
- Where appropriate, if you are deriving from a class, use the name of the base class as the last word in the class name. For example, **`ApplicationException`** is derived from **`Exception`**. Use **`CustomAttribute`** for a custom class that is derived from **`Attribute`**.
- Don't use **`Enum`** as part of the name of an **`Enum`** type.

- Use a singular name for most **Enum** types. Use plural for **Enum** types that are bit fields (**FlagsAttribute** attached to the **Enum** definition).
- Use the EventHandler suffix for the name of all **event** handlers.
- Use the EventArgs suffix for the name of all **event** argument classes.
- Two parameters should be passed to an **event** handler. The first should be named sender (the **object** that sent the **event**), and the second should be named e (the XXXEventArg that is associated with the **event**).
- **Event**s that can be canceled or occur "before" and "after" should be named as complementing pairs. The "before" should indicate the **event** is occurring but not complete (as in Closing). The "after" should indicate that the **event** action is complete (as in Closed). Avoid using BeforeXXX and AfterXXX.

Member Access

You can modify the code snippet from the "Name Scope" section to include access to type A:

```
public struct A
{
    public int a;
    public int b;
}
public struct B
{
    public int a;
    public int b;
    void AccessA()
    {
        A At = new A();
        At.a = 0;
    }
}
```

Because type A only has instance fields, you need to create an instance of A. You can create an instance of A because this type is visible. You can access a because that field has been made accessible to all through the use of the **public** keyword. In general, member access is determined by three criteria:

- Type visibility
- Member accessibility
- Security constraints

Type Visibility

A type falls into one of three categories with respect to visibility:

- Exported—A type declares that it is allowed to be exported. The configuration of the assembly determines whether the type is actually visible. With C#, a type can be not public (default), which means it is not visible outside the enclosing scope; internal, which means that it is visible only to the assembly; public, which means it is visible outside of the assembly; or it is exported or exporting is allowed.
- Not exported—Here, exporting is explicitly disallowed.
- Nested—The enclosing type determines the visibility of a type that is nested. A nested type is part of the enclosing type, so it has access to all of the enclosing type's members.

Member Accessibility

You can control the accessibility of each member of a type through the following supported levels:

- Compiler-controlled—This level of accessibility allows access only via a compiler. Members who have this level of accessibility usually support a particular language feature.
- Private—Private members are not accessible outside of the enclosing type. C# has a **private** keyword to denote this level of accessibility.
- Family—Family members are accessible to the enclosing type and types that are inherit from it. In C#, this level of accessibility is obtained with the **protected** keyword.
- Assembly—Assembly access means that access is granted only to referents in the same assembly that contains the implementation of the type. In C#, this level of accessibility is obtained with the **internal** keyword.
- Family-and-Assembly—This level of accessibility means that the member is accessible only to referents that qualify for both Family and Assembly access.
- Family-or-Assembly—This level of accessibility means that the member is accessible only to referents that qualify for either Family or Assembly access. In C#, this level of accessibility can be specified by using **protected internal**.
- Public—This is accessible to all referents. C# has a **public** keyword to denote this level of accessibility.

In general, the preceding accessibility levels have two restrictions:

- Members of an interface are public.
- If a type overrides a virtual member, then it can make the accessibility of a member greater; it cannot, however, further restrict accessibility. For example, the

implementation of an interface method cannot be made private. Because the interface method is public, the implementation cannot be more restrictive.

Security Constraints

Access to members can also be controlled through explicit security attributes or programmatic security permissions. Security demands are not part of a type, but they are attached to a type; therefore, they are not inherited. Accessibility security demands fall into two categories:

- Inheritance demand—This security attribute can be attached to either a type or a non-final virtual method. If it is attached to a type, then any type that attempts to inherit from it must have the requested security permissions. If it is attached to a non-final virtual method, then any attempt to override the method must first pass the security check. You can attach the inheritance demand security permission as follows:

  ```
  [CustomPermissionAttribute(SecurityAction.InheritanceDemand)]
  public class MyClass
  {
      public MyClass()
      {
      }
      public virtual void Message()
      {
          Console.WriteLine("This is a message from MyClass");
      }
  }
  ```

  This attaches a custom permission (implementation not included) to the class.
- Reference demand—When a reference demand is placed on an item, the requested security permissions must be in place to resolve the item.

You will learn more about security in Chapter 16, ".NET Security."

Type Members

Different languages access members of a type in different ways. What is common to all languages is some sort of access control and support for inheritance.

A derived type inherits all of the non-static fields of the base type. Static fields are not inherited.

A derived type inherits all of the instance methods and virtual methods of the base class. As with fields, the static methods are not inherited. A derived class can hide an instance or virtual method by using the **new** keyword. This causes the derived method to be invoked instead of the base class method. However, if the derived class is cast to the base class, the base class version of the hidden method is called. Therefore, it is hidden, not overridden.

If a method is marked in the base class as virtual and the derived class uses the **override** keyword, then the derived class method replaces the base class method and is not available. Listing 2.7 shows how to override a method in C#. The complete source for this listing is available in the `MethodHideOverrideCS` directory.

LISTING 2.7 Overriding and Hiding a Method in C#

```
class A
{
    public virtual void Message()
    {
        Console.WriteLine("This is a message from A");
    }
}
sealed class B: A
{
    public override void Message()
    {
        Console.WriteLine("This is a message from B");
    }
}
class C: A
{
    // methodhideoverride.cs(21,15): warning CS0114:
    // 'CLRUnleashed.C.Message()' hides inherited member
    // 'CLRUnleashed.A.Message()'. To make the current
    // member override that implementation, add the
    // override keyword. Otherwise, add the new keyword.
    // public void Message()
    public new void Message()
    {
        Console.WriteLine("This is a message from C");
    }
}
. . .
 Console.WriteLine("---- A method");
A a = new A();
a.Message();
Console.WriteLine("---- B method");
B b = new B();
b.Message();
Console.WriteLine("---- Cast B to A method");
((A)b).Message();

// Hide a method
```

LISTING 2.7 Continued

```
Console.WriteLine("---- C method");
C c = new C();
c.Message();
Console.WriteLine("---- Cast C to A method");
((A)c).Message();
```

A method can be marked as **final**, which prevents a derived class from overriding it. It is also possible, as noted under the "Security Constraints" section, to restrict the ability of overriding a method by demanding a security permission. With C#, you can mark an entire class as sealed. C# does not support a **final** keyword or the equivalent functionality, but JScript does. Listing 2.8 shows an example of using **final** and **hide** keywords to control how to override a method. The complete source for this sample is in the `MethodOverrideJS` directory.

LISTING 2.8 Using **final** in JScript

```
class A
{
   function Message() { print("This is a message from A") };
}

class B extends A
{
   final override function Message() { print("This is a message from B") };
}

class C extends A
{
   hide function Message() { print("This is a message from C") };
}
class D extends B
{
   // MethodHideOverrideJS.jsc(17,4) : error JS1174: Method matches a
   // non-overridable method in a base class. Specify 'hide' to suppress
   // this message
   // override function Message() { print("This is a message from D") };
   hide function Message() { print("This is a message from D") };
}

var AInstance : A = new A
var BInstance : B = new B
var BAInstance : A = new B
var CInstance : C = new C
var CAInstance : A = new C
var DInstance : D = new D
var DBInstance : B = new D

print("---- A");
AInstance.Message();
```

LISTING 2.8 Continued

```
print("---- B");
BInstance.Message();
print("---- B -> A");
BAInstance.Message();
print("---- C");
CInstance.Message();
print("---- C -> A");
CAInstance.Message();
print("---- D");
DInstance.Message();
print("---- D -> B");
DBInstance.Message();
```

VB provides this functionality as well with **Overrides** and **NotOverridable**. You can find a complete source for an example using these keywords in the `MethodOverrideVB` directory. From that source is a function that looks like Listing 2.9.

LISTING 2.9 Using **NotOverridable** in VB

```
Class B
    Inherits A
    Public NotOverridable Overrides Sub Message()
        Console.WriteLine("This is a message from B")
    End Sub
End Class
```

Now you can compile this program and look at the output with `ILDasm`. You will see the output reproduced in Listing 2.10.

LISTING 2.10 `ILDasm` Listing of **NotOverridable** VB Method

```
.method public final virtual instance void
        Message() cil managed
{
  // Code size       14 (0xe)
  .maxstack  8
  IL_0000:  nop
  IL_0001:  ldstr      "This is a message from B"
  IL_0006:  call       void [mscorlib]System.Console::WriteLine(string)
  IL_000b:  nop
  IL_000c:  nop
  IL_000d:  ret
} // end of method B::Message
```

Notice on the first line that one of the attributes of this Message method in the B class is that it is **final**. Therefore, **NotOverridable** in VB translates directly to the IL **final** attribute.

VC++ with managed extensions mimics the functionality of C# with regard to overriding methods. The managed extensions for VC++ don't have a final keyword, but like C#, a **__sealed** keyword can prevent an entire class from being inherited.

Properties

Properties provide a means to access private state in an object without exposing the state directly. If you are tempted to expose a field as public, consider using a property instead. Properties are collections of methods—usually a read method and a write method (get and set). You don't have to provide both. If you want to have a read-only property, then just supply the get portion of the property. Properties give you the flexibility of a method with the syntactical sugar that makes direct access to a field so tempting. Like all of the other features discussed in this section, properties are a feature of the Common Language Specification. Therefore, they are available in most languages that support the CLS. Listing 2.11 shows one possible implementation of properties. The complete source for this listing is in the `PropertiesCS` directory.

LISTING 2.11 Properties in C#

```
public struct Point
{
    private int x;
    private int y;
    public Point(int x, int y)
    {
        this.x = x;
        this.y = y;
    }
    public int X
    {
        get
        {
            return x;
        }
        set
        {
            x = value;
        }
    }
    public int Y
    {
        get
        {
            return y;
        }
        set
```

LISTING 2.11 Continued

```
        {
            y = value;
        }
    }
    public Point Coordinate
    {
        get
        {
            return this;
        }
        set
        {
            x = value.x;
            y = value.y;
        }
    }
}
. . .
Point p = new Point(1, 2);
Console.WriteLine("X: {0} Y: {1}", p.X, p.Y);
```

As you can see, three properties exist: one for the X coordinate, one for the Y coordinate, and one returning the complete structure. Each of the properties has a get and a set method, so each is readable and writeable. Listing 2.12 shows how to implement properties in VB. The complete source for this listing is in the `PropertiesVB` directory.

LISTING 2.12 Properties in VB

```
Class Point
    Private xcoordinate As Integer
    Private ycoordinate As Integer
    Sub New(ByVal x As Integer, ByVal y As Integer)
        xcoordinate = x
        ycoordinate = y
    End Sub
    Public Property X() As Integer
        Get
            Return xcoordinate
        End Get
        Set(ByVal Value As Integer)
            xcoordinate = Value
        End Set
    End Property
    Public Property Y() As Integer
        Get
            Return ycoordinate
        End Get
```

LISTING 2.12 Continued

```
        Set(ByVal Value As Integer)
            ycoordinate = Value
        End Set
    End Property
End Class
Sub Main()
    Dim p As Point = New Point(1, 2)
    Console.WriteLine("---- Point " & p.X & "," & p.Y)
End Sub
```

Listing 2.13 shows how to implement properties in JScript. The source for this listing is in the `PropertiesJS` directory.

LISTING 2.13 Properties in JScript

```
class Point
{
   // These variables are not accessible from outside the class.
   private var x: int;
   private var y: int;

   // Set the initial favorite color with the constructor.
   function Point(inputX : int, inputY : int)
   {
      x = inputX;
      y = inputY;
   }

   // Define an accessor to get the X coordinate
   function get X() : int {
      return x;
   }
   // Define an accessor to set the X coordinate
   function set X(inputX : int) {
      x= inputX;
   }
   // Define an accessor to get the Y coordinate
   function get Y() : int {
      return y;
   }
   // Define an accessor to set the X coordinate
   function set Y(inputY : int) {
      y = inputY;
   }

}

var here : Point = new Point(1, 2);
print("Here is " + here.X + "," + here.Y)
```

Looking at the compiled JScript assembly with ILDasm, you can see how properties are not a feature of any particular language; rather, they are components of the .NET Framework and the CLS. Listing 2.14 shows one of the properties that is exposed in the JScript assembly.

LISTING 2.14 ILDasm Listing of the X Coordinate Property from the JScript Assembly

```
.property int32 X()
{
  .get instance int32 Point::get_X()
  .set instance void Point::set_X(int32)
} // end of property Point::X
```

Listing 2.14 reveals that properties are simply a collection and mapping of methods. The implementation for the X property is in the `get_X` and the `set_X` methods. The compiler prevents direct access to `get_X` and `set_X`.

Events

`event`s are a way of safely specifying a callback function.

> **Note**
>
> **`event`**s and **`delegate`**s are covered in more detail in Chapter 14.

Listing 2.15 shows how to implement **`event`**s in VB. This sample adds **`event`**s to the property source of Listing 2.12. The complete source for this program is in the `EventsVB` directory.

LISTING 2.15 Implementing and Using Events with VB

```
Public Event PointChanged(ByVal x As Integer, ByVal y As Integer)
Sub New(ByVal x As Integer, ByVal y As Integer)
    xcoordinate = x
    ycoordinate = y
End Sub
Public Property X() As Integer
    Get
        Return xcoordinate
    End Get
    Set(ByVal Value As Integer)
        xcoordinate = Value
```

LISTING 2.15 Continued

```
        RaiseEvent PointChanged(xcoordinate, ycoordinate)
    End Set
End Property
. . .
Sub EventHandler(ByVal x As Integer, ByVal y As Integer)
    MessageBox.Show("Point changed " & CStr(x) & "," & CStr(y))
End Sub
Sub Main()
    Dim p As New Point(1, 2)
    AddHandler p.PointChanged, AddressOf EventHandler
    p.X = 5
End Sub
```

The **event** handler signature is provided by the following:

```
Public Event PointChanged(ByVal x As Integer, ByVal y As Integer)
```

The handler is the `EventHandler` function. (Notice that it has the same signature as the **Event** declaration.) The handler is registered with the following:

```
AddHandler p.PointChanged, AddressOf EventHandler
```

When a `Point` is changed, an **event** is raised:

```
RaiseEvent PointChanged(xcoordinate, ycoordinate)
```

When the **event** is raised, a `MessageBox` is displayed showing the new coordinates. That is triggered with the p.X = 5 statement.

Arrays

Most languages that support the CLS support arrays; however, with C#, JScript, and VB, arrays are always zero based and the lower bound is always zero. The following code shows how to initialize a vector and a two-dimensional array with C#.

```
int [] avec = new int[5] {1, 2, 3, 4, 5};
int [,] aarray = new int[2,2] {{1,2},{3,4}};
```

Again, based on the base class library class **System.Array**, VB also supports vectors and arrays. The following is a small set of code to initialize a one- and a two-dimensional array in VB:

```
Dim vec() As Integer = New Integer() {1, 2, 3, 4, 5}
Dim array(,) As Integer = New Integer(,) {{0, 1}, {2, 3}}
```

The following initializes two arrays using JScript.

```
var vec : int[] = [1,2,3,4,5];
var arr : int[][] = [ [0, 1], [2, 3] ];
```

Enumerations

C# directly supports the types that are derived from **System.Enum** as follows:

```
enum MathOperations
{
    Add,
    Subtract,
    Multiply,
    Divide
}
. . .
MathOperations mo = MathOperations.Add;
Console.WriteLine("MathOperation: {0}", mo);
```

VB also supports types that are derived from System.Enum:

```
Public Enum MathOperations
    Add
    Subtract
    Multiply
    Divide
    Invalid = -1
End Enum
```

The closest that JScript has to enumerators is what is termed as an *object literal*. An object literal allows a programmer to give a name to a number similar to an **enum**, but it is not derived from **System.Enum** and the type does not have the methods associated with **System.Enum**. An example of an object literal is as follows:

```
var MathOperations = { Add:1, Subtract:2, Multiply:3, Divide:4 };
```

Exceptions

Exceptions are the error-handling mechanism within the .NET Framework. Exceptions are covered in more detail in Chapter 15, "Using Managed Exceptions to Effectively Handle Errors." Listing 2.16 shows how to catch an exception with C#. The complete source for this sample is in the `ExceptionsCS` directory.

LISTING 2.16 Throwing and Catching an Exception with C#

```
try
{
    int a = 1;
    int b = 0;
    int c = a/b;
    Console.WriteLine("Result: {0}", c);
}
catch(Exception e)
{
    Console.WriteLine(e);
}
```

The C# code in Listing 2.16 catches a divide by zero exception thrown by the runtime. Listing 2.17 shows an example of using exceptions with VB. The complete source for this sample is in the `ExceptionVB` directory.

LISTING 2.17 Throwing and Catching an Exception with VB

```
Function TestError()
    Err.Raise(vbObjectError, "TestWidth", _
              "This is a test error message.")
End Function

Sub Main()
    Dim a As Integer
    Dim b As Integer
    Dim c As Integer
    a = 1
    b = 0
    Try
        ' Use integer division
        c = a \ b
    Catch ex As Exception
        Console.WriteLine(ex.Message)
    End Try
    Try
        TestError()
    Catch ex As Exception
        Console.WriteLine(ex.Message)
    End Try
End Sub
```

Notice that with this code, you have to specifically use integer division to generate a divide by zero error. In addition, this sample shows how to "throw" an exception using the VB `Err` object. If you examine the compiled code of Listing 2.17 with a tool such as ILDasm, you can see that a VB `Exception` translates directly into **`System.Exception`**. Listing 2.18 shows an example of the exception-handling mechanism in JScript. The complete source for this sample is in the `ExceptionJS` directory.

LISTING 2.18 Throwing and Catching an Exception with JScript

```
try {
    var A : int = 1, B = 0, C;
    C = A/B;
    print("C = " + C);
    throw "This is an error";
} catch(e) {
    print("Catch caught " + e);
```

LISTING 2.18 Continued

```
} finally {
    print("Finally is running...");
}
```

You would expect that this attempt at divide by zero would fail with an exception. Instead, the print statement in Listing 2.18 simply prints "Infinity". You don't actually get an exception until you specifically throw the exception with a string message. When this JScript code is examined with ILDasm, you can see that the exception being caught (and thrown) is directly connected with **System.Exception**. In addition, the exception framework is directly connected with `try/catch/finally`, which is part of the CLS.

Custom Attributes

Attributes are part of the metadata that is associated with any code that is run in the .NET Framework. Metadata is covered in more detail in Chapter 4, and attributes are covered more specifically in Chapter 17, "Reflection." Listing 2.19 shows how to define a custom attribute with VB. The complete source for this listing is in the `AttributesVB` directory.

LISTING 2.19 User Defined Custom Attributes with VB

```
<AttributeUsage(AttributeTargets.Class)> _
Class CustomAttribute
    Inherits System.Attribute

    'Declare two private fields to store the property values.
    Private msg As String

    'The Sub New constructor is the only way to set the properties.
    Public Sub New(ByVal _message As String)
        msg = _message
    End Sub
    Public Overridable ReadOnly Property Message() As String
        Get
            Return msg
        End Get
    End Property
End Class

' Apply the custom attribute to this class.
<Custom("Hello World!")> _
Class MessageClass
    ' Message
    Private msg As String
    Sub New()
```

LISTING 2.19 Continued

```
        Dim Attr As Attribute
        Dim CustAttr As CustomAttribute
        Attr = GetCustomAttribute(GetType(MessageClass), _
                                  GetType(CustomAttribute), False)
        CustAttr = CType(Attr, CustomAttribute)
        If CustAttr Is Nothing Then
            msg = "The attribute was not found."
        Else
            'Get the label and value from the custom attribute.
            msg = "The attribute label is: " & CustAttr.Message
        End If
    End Sub
    Sub Message()
        Console.WriteLine(msg)
    End Sub
End Class

Sub Main()
    Dim m As New MessageClass()
    m.Message()
End Sub
```

The code in Listing 2.19 shows how to define a class that derives from **`System.Attribute`** and defines a custom attribute that can be attached to any class. The only property of this simple attribute class is a message that the class can discover at runtime. Here, the string that is associated with the message is simply cached and written out to the console with a call to the `Message` method.

Summary

This chapter briefly described the Common Type System that allows programs that are written in many different languages to seamlessly communicate everything from simple types to more complex types and values. The CTS is a core part of the Common Language Runtime. This chapter also provided guidelines for naming your types and values so that your code is portable and easily maintained.

The Common Language Runtime—Overview of the Runtime Environment

IN THIS CHAPTER

At a high level, the CLR is simply an engine that takes in IL instructions, translates them into machine instructions, and executes them. This does not mean that the CLR is interpreting the instructions. This is just to say that the CLR forms an environment in which IL code can be executed. For this to work efficiently and portably, the execution engine must form a runtime environment that is both efficient and portable. Efficiency is key; if the code does not run quickly enough, all of the other features of the system become moot.

Portability is important because of the number of processors and devices on which the CLR is slated to run. For a long time, Microsoft and Intel seemed to be close partners. Microsoft more or less picked the Intel line of processors to run the software that the company produced. This allowed Microsoft to build and develop software without worrying about supporting multiple CPU architectures and instructions. The company didn't have to worry about shipping a Motorola 68XXX version of the software because it was not supported. Limiting the scope of processor support became a problem as Win16 gave way to Win32. (No APIs were called Win16, but this is the name I will give the APIs that existed before Win32.) Building software that took advantage of the features of a 32-bit CPU remained somewhat backward compatible with older Win16 APIs and proved to be a major undertaking. With Win64 on the horizon, Microsoft must realize that it cannot continue to "port" all of its software with each new CPU that is released if it wants to stay alive as a company. Microsoft is trying to penetrate the mobile phone, hand-held, and tablet markets that are powered by a myriad of different processors and architectures. Too much software is produced at Microsoft for it to continue to produce a CPU-bound version.

The answer to the problem of base address and data size (Win32 versus Win64) and to the problem of providing general portability to other processors came in the form of the runtime environment, or the Common Language Runtime. Without going into the details of the specific instructions that the CLR supports (this is done in Chapter 5, "Intermediate Language Basics"), this chapter details the architecture of the runtime that goes into making a managed application run.

Introduction to the Runtime

Before .NET, an executable (usually a file with an .exe suffix), was the application. In other words, the application was contained within one file. To make the overall system run more efficiently, the application would elect to use code that was shared (usually a file with a .dll suffix). If the program elected to use shared code, you could either use an import library (a file that points function references to the DLL that is associated with the import library), or you could load the DLL explicitly at runtime (using `LoadLibrary`,

LoadLibraryEx, and GetProcAddress). With .NET, the unit of execution and deployment is the assembly. Execution usually begins with an assembly that has an .exe suffix. The application can use shared code by importing the assembly that contains the shared code with an explicit reference. (You can add the reference via the "Add References" node in Visual Studio .NET or include it via a command-line switch /r). The application can also explicitly load an assembly with **Assembly.Load** or **Assembly.LoadFrom**.

Note

Before going further, you need to learn definitions of some of the terms:

- **Assembly**—The *assembly* is the primary unit of deployment within the .NET Framework. Within the base class libraries is a class that encapsulates a physical assembly appropriately named **Assembly**. When this book refers to the class or an instance of the class, it will be denoted as **Assembly**. This class exists in the **System** namespace. An assembly can contain references to other assemblies and modules. Chapter 4, "The Assembly," contains more detailed information about assemblies.
- **Module**—A *module* is a single file that contains executable content. An assembly can encapsulate one or more modules; a module does not stand alone without an assembly referring to it. Similar to assembly, a class exists in the base class library that encapsulates most of the features of a module called **Module**. When this book refers to **Module**, it is referring to the class in the base class library. This class exists in the **System** namespace.
- **AppDomain**—An application domain has been referred to as a lightweight process. Before .NET, isolation was achieved through separate processes through assistance from the OS and the supporting hardware. If one process ran amok, then it would not bring down the whole system, just that process. Because types are so tightly controlled with the .NET Framework, it is possible to have a mechanism whereby this same level of isolation can occur within a process. This mechanism is called the *application domain*, or *AppDomain*. As with modules and assemblies, a class in the base class library encapsulates many of the features and functionality of an application domain called **AppDomain**. This class exists in the **System** namespace. When this book refers to the class, it will be called **AppDomain**.
- IL or MSIL—IL stands for Intermediate Language, and MSIL stands for Microsoft Intermediate Language. IL is the language in which assemblies are written. It is a set of instructions that represent the code of the application. It is intermediate because it is not turned in to native code until needed. When the code that describes a method is required to run, it is compiled into native code with the JIT compiler. Chapter 5 contains information about individual IL instructions.

- JIT—JIT stands for Just-In-Time. This term refers to the compiler that is run against IL code on an as-needed basis.

After the code is "loaded," execution of the code can begin. This is where the old (pre-.NET) and the new (.NET) start to diverge significantly. In the case of unmanaged code, the compiler and linker have already turned the source into native instructions, so those instructions can begin to execute immediately. Of course, this means that you will have to compile a separate version of the code for every different native environment. In some cases, because it is undesirable to ship and maintain a separate version for every possible native environment, only a compatible version is compiled and shipped. This leads to a lowest common denominator approach as companies want to ship software that can be run on as wide a range of environments as possible. Currently, few companies ship programs that target environments that have an accelerated graphics engine. Not only would the manufacturer need to ship a different program for each graphics accelerator card, but a different program also would need to be developed for those cases where a graphics accelerator was lacking. Other examples of hardware environments in which specific optimizations could be taken advantage of would be disk cache, memory cache, high-speed networks, multiple CPUs, specialized hardware for processing images, accelerated math functions, and so forth. In numerous other examples, compiling a program ahead of time either results in a highly optimized yet very specific program, or an unoptimized and general program.

One of the first steps that the CLR takes in running a program is checking the method that is about to be run to see whether it has been turned into native code. If the method has not been turned into native code, then the code in the method is Just-In-Time compiled (JITd). Delaying the compilation of a method yields two immediate benefits. First, it is possible for a company to ship one version of the software and have the CLR on the CPU where the program is installed take care of the specific optimizations that are appropriate for the hardware environment. Second, it is possible for the JIT compiler to take advantage of specific optimizations that allow the program to run more quickly than a general-purpose, unmanaged version of the program. Systems built with a 64-bit processor will have a "compatibility" mode that allows 32-bit programs to run unmodified on the 64-bit CPU. This compatibility mode will not result in the most efficient or fastest possible throughput, however. If an application is compiled into IL, it can take advantage of the 64-bit processing as long as a JIT engine can target the new 64-bit processor.

The process of loading a method and compiling it if necessary is repeated until either all of the methods in the application have been compiled or the application terminates. The rest of this chapter explores the environment in which the CLR encloses each class method.

Starting a Method

The CLR requires the following information about each method. All of this data is available to the CLR through metadata in each assembly.

- Instructions—The CLR requires a list of MSIL instructions. As you will see in the next chapter, each method has a pointer to the instruction set as part of metadata that is associated with it.
- Signature—Each method has a signature, and the CLR requires that a signature be available for each method. The signature describes the calling convention, return type, parameter count, and parameter types.
- Exception Handling Array—No specific IL instructions handle with exceptions. There are directives, but no IL instructions. Instead of exception-handling instructions, the assembly encloses a list of exceptions. The exceptions list contains the type of the exception, an offset address to the first instruction after the exception try block, and the length of the try block. It also includes the offset to the handler code, the length of the handler code, and a token describing the class that is used to encapsulate the exception.
- The size of the evaluation stack—This data is available through the metadata of the assembly, and you will typically see it as `.maxstack x` in ILDASM listings, where x is the size of the evaluation stack. This logical size of the stack as x represents the maximum number of items that will need to be pushed onto the stack. The physical size of the items and the stack is left up to the CLR to determine at runtime when the method is JITd.
- A description of the locals array—Every method needs to declare up front the number of items of local storage that the method requires. Like the evaluation stack, this is a logical array of items, although each item's type is also declared in the array. In addition, a flag is stored in the metadata to indicate whether the local variables should be initialized to zero at the beginning of the method call.

With this information, the CLR is able to form an abstraction of what normally would be the native stack frame. Typically, each CPU or machine forms a stack frame that contains the arguments (parameters) or references to arguments to the method. Similarly, the return variables are placed on the stack frame based on calling conventions that are specific to a particular CPU or machine. The order of both the input and output parameters, as well as the way that the number of parameters is specified, is specific to a particular machine. Because all of the required information is available for each method, the CLR can make the determination at runtime of what the stack frame should look like.

The call to the method is made in such a way as to allow the CLR to have marginal control of the execution of the method and its state. When the CLR calls or invokes a method, the method and its state are put under the control of the CLR in what is known as the Thread of Control.

IL Supported Types

At the IL level, a simple set of types is supported. These types can be directly manipulated with IL instructions:

- int8—8-bit 2's complement signed value.
- unsigned int8 (byte)—8-bit unsigned binary value.
- int16 (short)—16-bit 2's complement signed value.
- unsigned int16 (ushort)—16-bit unsigned binary value.
- int32 (int)—32-bit 2's complement signed value.
- unsigned int32 (uint)—32-bit unsigned binary value.
- int64 (long)—64-bit 2's complement signed value.
- unsigned (ulong)—64-bit unsigned binary value.
- float32 (float)—32-bit IEC 60559:1989 floating point value.
- float64 (double)—64-bit IEC 60559:1989 floating point value.
- native int—Native size 2's complement signed value.
- native unsigned int—Native size unsigned binary value.
- F—Native size floating point variable. This variable is internal to the CLR and is not visible by the user.
- O—Native size object reference to managed memory.
- &—Native size managed pointer.

These are the types that can be represented in memory, but some restrictions exist in processing these data items. As discussed in the next section, the CLR processes these items on an evaluation stack that is part of the state data for each method. The evaluation stack can represent an item of any size, but the only operations that are allowed on user-defined value types are copying to and from memory and computing the addresses of user-defined value types. All operations that involve floating point values use an internal representation of the floating point value that is implementation specific (an `F` value).

The other data types (other than the floating point value just discussed) that have a native size are `native int`, `native unsigned int`, native size object reference (`O`), and native size managed pointer (`&`). These data types are a mechanism for the CLR to defer the choice of the value size. For example, this mechanism allows for a `native int` to be 64-bits on an IA64 processor and 32-bits on a Pentium processor.

Two of these native size types might seem similar, the `O` (native size object reference and the `&` (native size managed pointer). An `O` typed variable points to a managed object, but its use is restricted to instructions that explicitly indicate an operation on a managed type or to instructions whose metadata indicates that managed object references are allowed. The `O` type is said to point "outside" the object or to the object as a whole. The `&` type is also a reference to a managed object, but it can be used to refer to a field of an object or an element of an array. Both `O` and `&` types are tracked by the CLR and can change based on the results of a garbage collection.

One particular use of the native size type is for unmanaged pointers. Although unmanaged pointers can be strongly typed with metadata, they are represented as `native unsigned int` in the IL code. This gives the CLR the flexibility to assign an unmanaged pointer to a larger address space on a processor that supports it without unnecessarily tying up memory in storing these values on processors that do not have the capability to address such a large address space.

Some IL instructions require that an address be on the stack, such as the following:

- **`calli`** -..., arg1, arg2 … argn, **ftn** → … retVal
- **`cpblk`** - …, **destaddr**, **srcaddr**, size → …
- **`initblk`** …, **addr**, **value**, **size** → …
- **`ldind.*`** - …, **addr** → …, value
- **`stind.*`** - …, **addr**, val → …

Using a native type guarantees that the operations that involve that type are portable. If the address is specified as a 64-bit integer, then it can be portable if appropriate steps are taken to ensure that the value is converted appropriately to an address. If an address is specified as 32-bits or smaller, the code is never portable even though it might work for most 32-bit machines. For most cases, this is an IL generator or compiler issue and you should not need to worry about it. You should, however, be aware that you can make code non-portable by improperly using these instructions.

Short numeric values (those values less than 4 bytes) are widened to 4 bytes when loaded (copied from memory to the stack) and narrowed when stored (copied from stack to memory). Any operation that involves a short numeric value is really handled as a 4-byte operation. Specific IL instructions deal with short numeric types:

- Load and store operations to/from memory—**ldelem**, **ldind**, **stind**, and **stelem**
- Data conversion—**conv**, **conv.ovf**
- Array creation—**newarr**

Strictly speaking, IL only supports signed operations. The difference between signed and unsigned operations is how the value is interpreted. For operations in which it would matter how the value is interpreted, the operation has both a signed and an unsigned version. For example, a **cgt** instruction and a **cgt.un** operation compare two values for the greater value.

Homes for Values

To track objects, the CLR introduces the concept of a home for an object. An object's home is where the value of the object is stored. The home of an object must have a mechanism in place for the JIT engine to determine the type of the object. When an object is passed by reference, it must have a home because the address of the home is passed as a reference. Two types of data are "homeless" and cannot be passed by reference: constants and intermediate values on the evaluation stack from IL instructions or return values from methods. The CLR supports the following homes for objects:

- Incoming argument—**ldarg** and **ldarga** instructions determine the address of an argument home. The method signature determines the type.
- Local variable—**ldloca** or **ldloc** IL instructions determine the address of a local variable. The local evaluation stack determines the type of local variable as part of the metadata.
- Field (instance or static)—The use of **ldflda** for an instance field and **ldsflda** for a static field determine the address of a field. The metadata that is associated with the class interface or module determines the type of the field.
- Array element—The use of **ldelema** determines the address of an array element. The element array type determines the type of the element.

The Runtime Thread of Control

The CLR Thread of Control does not necessarily correspond with the native OS threads. The base class library class **System.Threading.Thread** provides the logical encapsulation of a thread of control.

> **Note**
>
> For more information on threading, see Chapter 11, "Threading."

Each time a method is called, the normal procedure of checking whether the method has been JITd must take place. Figure 3.1 shows a loose representation of what the CLR state looks like. This is loose in that it shows a simple link from one method to the other. This representation does not correctly portray situations that involve control flow that is exceptional, such as with jump instructions, exceptions, and tail calls.

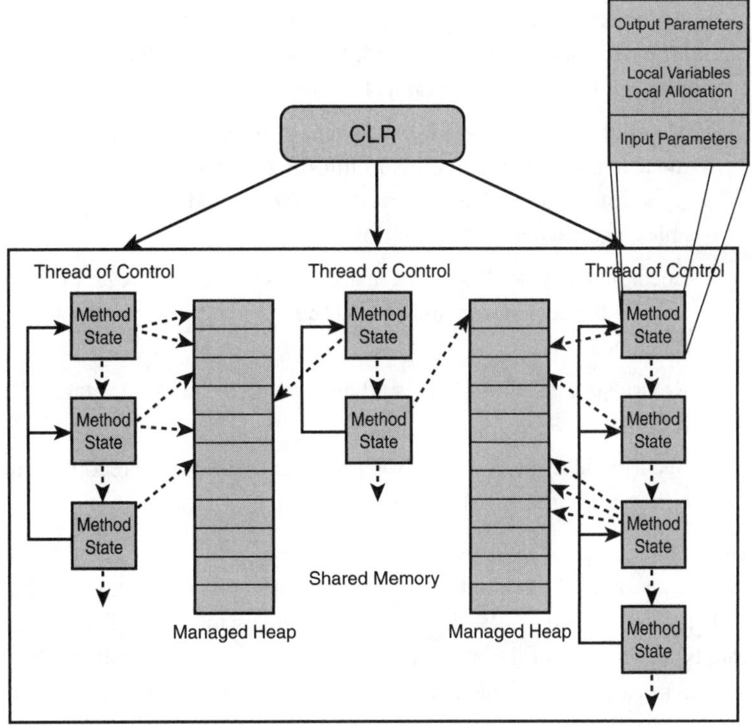

FIGURE 3.1
Machine state under the CLR.

The managed heap referenced in this diagram refers to the memory that the CLR manages. Details about the managed heaps and specifically garbage collection can be found in Chapter 10, "Memory/Resource Management." Each time a method is invoked, a method state is created. The method state includes the following:

- Instruction pointer—This points to the next IL instruction that the current method is to execute.
- Evaluation stack—This is the stack that the **`.maxstack`** directive specifies. The compiler determines at compile time how many slots are required on the stack.

- Local variable array—This is the same array that is declared and perhaps initialized in the metadata. Every time these variables are accessed from the IL, they are accessed as an index to this array. In the IL code, you see references to this array via instructions like the following: **`ldloc.0`** ("loading" or pushing local array variable 0 on to the stack) or **`stloc.1`** ("stores" the value on the stack in the local variable 1).
- Argument array—This is an array of arguments that is passed to the method. The arguments are manipulated with IL instructions such as **`ldarg.0`** ("loads" argument zero onto the stack) or **`starg.1`** ("stores" the value on the stack to argument 1).
- MethodInfo handle—This composite of information is available in the assembly metadata. This handle points to information about the signature of the method (types of arguments, numbers of arguments, and return types), types of local variables, and exception information.
- Local memory pool—IL has instructions that can allocate memory that is addressable by the current method (**`localloc`**). When the method returns, the memory is reclaimed.
- Return state handle—This is a handle used to return the state after the method returns.
- Security descriptor—The CLR uses this descriptor to record security overrides either programmatically or with custom attributes.

The evaluation stack does not directly equate to a physical representation. The physical representation of the evaluation stack is left up to the CLR and the CPU for which the CLR is targeted. Logically, the evaluation stack is made up of slots that can hold any data type. The size of the evaluation stack cannot be indeterminate. For example, code that causes a variable to be pushed onto the stack an infinite or indeterminate number of times is disallowed.

Instructions that involve operations on the evaluation stack are not typed. For example, an **`add`** instruction adds two numbers, and a **`mul`** instruction multiplies two numbers. The CLR tracks data types and uses them when the method is JITd.

Method Flow Control

The CLR provides support for a rich set of flow control instructions:

- Conditional or unconditional branch—Control can be transferred anywhere within a method as long as the transfer does not cross a protected region boundary. A *protected region* is defined in the metadata as a region that is associated with an exception handler. In C#, this region is known as a **`try`** block, and the associated

catch block is known as a *handler*. The CLR supports the execution of many different kinds of exception handlers to be detailed later. The important point here is that a conditional or unconditional branch cannot specify a destination that crosses an exception boundary. In the case of C#, you cannot branch into or out of a **try** or a **catch** block. This is not a limitation of the C# language; rather, it is a restriction of the IL code for which C# acts as a code generator.

- Method call—Several instructions allow methods to call other methods, thus creating other method states, as explained earlier.
- Tail call—This is a special prefix that immediately precedes a method call. It instructs the calling method to discard its stack frame before calling the method. This causes the called method to return to the point at which the calling method would have returned.
- Return—This is a simple return from a method.
- Method jump—This is an optimization of the tail call that transfers the arguments and control of a method to another method with the same signature, essentially "deleting" the current method. The following snippet shows a simple jump:

```
// Function A
.method static public void A()
{
// Output from A
    ret
}
// Function B
.method static public void B()
{
    jmp void A()
// Output from B
    ret
}
```

  The instructions represented by the comment `Output from B` will never be executed because the return from B is replaced by a return from A.

- Exception—This includes a set of instructions that generates an exception and transfers control out of a protected region.

The CLR enforces several rules when control is transferred within a method. First, control cannot be transferred to within an exception handler (catch, finally, and so on) except as the result of an exception. This restriction reinforces the rule that the destination of a branch cannot cross a protected region. Second, after you are in a handler for a protected region, it is illegal to transfer out of that handler by any other means other than the restricted set of exception instructions (**leave**, **end.finally**, **end.filter**, **end.catch**). Again, you will notice that if you try to **return** from a method from within a **finally** block in C#, the compiler generates an error. This is not a C# limitation, but a restriction that is placed on the IL code. Third, each slot in the evaluation stack must maintain its type throughout the lifetime of the evaluation stack (hence the lifetime of the method). In other words, you cannot change the type of a slot (variable) on the evaluation stack. This is typically not a problem because the evaluation stack is not accessible to the user anyway. Finally, control is not allowed to simply "fall through." All paths of execution must terminate in either a return (**`ret`**), a method jump (**`jmp`**) or tail call (**`tail.*`**), or a thrown exception (**`throw`**).

Method Call

The CLR can call methods in three different ways. Each of these call methods only differs in the way that the call site descriptor is specified. A call site descriptor gives the CLR and the JIT engine enough information about the method call so that a native method call can be generated, the appropriate arguments can be made accessible to the method, and provision can be made for the return if one exists.

The **`calli`** instruction is the simplest of the method calls. This instruction is used when the destination address is computed at runtime. The instruction takes an additional function pointer argument that is known to exist on the call site as an argument. This function pointer is computed with either the **`ldftn`** or **`ldvirftn`** instructions. The call site is specified in the `StandAloneSig` table of the metadata (see Chapter 4).

The **`call`** instruction is used when the address of the function is known at compile time, such as with a static method. The call site descriptor is derived from the `MethodDef` or `MethodRef` token that is part of the instruction. (See Chapter 4 for a description of these two tables.)

The **`callvirt`** instruction calls a method on a particular instance of an object. The instruction includes a `MethodDef` or `MethodRef` token like with the call instruction, but the **`callvirt`** instruction takes an additional argument, which refers to a particular instance on which this method is to be called.

Method Calling Convention

The CLR uses a single calling convention throughout all IL code. If the method being called is a method on an instance, a reference to the object instance is pushed on the stack first, followed by each of the arguments to the method in left-to-right order. The result is that the **`this`** pointer is popped off of the stack first by the called method, followed by each of the arguments starting with argument zero and proceeding to argument n. If the method call is to a static method, then no associated instance pointer exists and the stack contains only the arguments. For the **`calli`** instruction, the arguments are pushed on the stack in a left-to-right order followed by the function pointer that is pushed on the stack last. The CLR and the JIT must translate this to the most efficient native calling convention.

Method Parameter Passing

The CLR supports three types of parameter-passing mechanisms:

- By value—The value of the object is placed on the stack. For built-in types such as integers, floats, and so on, this simply means that the value is pushed onto the stack. For objects, a `O` type reference to the object is placed on the stack. For managed and unmanaged pointers, the address is placed on the stack. For user-defined value types, you can place a value on the evaluation stack that precedes a method call in two ways. First, the value can be directly put on the stack with **`ldarg`**, **`ldloc`**, **`ldfld`**, or **`ldsfld`**. Second, the address of the value can be computed and the value can be loaded onto the stack with the **`ldobj`** instruction.
- By reference—Using this convention, the address of the parameter is passed to the method rather than the value. This allows a method to potentially modify such a parameter. Only values that have homes can be passed by reference because it is the address of the home that is passed. For code to be verifiable (type safety that can be verified), parameters that are passed by reference should only be passed and referenced via the **`ldind.*`** and **`stind.*`** instructions respectively.
- Typed reference—A typed reference is similar to a "normal" by reference parameter with the addition of a static data type that is passed along with the data reference. This allows IL to support languages such as VB that can have methods that are not statically restricted to the types of data that they can accept, yet require an unboxed, by reference value. To call such a method, one would either copy an existing type reference or use the **`mkrefany`** instruction to create a data reference type. Using this reference type, the address is computed using the **`refanyval`** instruction. A typed reference parameter must refer to data that has a home.

Exception Handling

The CLR supports exceptional conditions or error handling by using exception objects and protected blocks of code. A C# **`try`** block is an example of a protected block of code. The CLR supports four different kinds of exception handlers:

- Finally—This block will be executed when the method exits no matter how the method exits, whether by normal control (either implicitly or by an explicit **`ret`**) or by unhandled exception.
- Fault—This block will be executed if an exception occurs, but not if the method normally exits.

- Type-filtered—This block of code will be executed when a match is detected between the type of the exception for this block and the exception that is thrown. This corresponds the C# **`catch`** block.
- User-filtered—The determination whether this block should handle the exception is made as the result of a set of IL instructions that can specify that the exception should be ignored, that this handler should handle the exception, or that the exception should be handled by the next exception handler. For the reader who is familiar with Structured Exception Handling (SEH), this is much like the `__except` handler.

Not every language that generates compliant IL code necessarily supports all of the types of exception handling. For instance, C# does not support user-filtered exception handlers, whereas VB does.

When an exception occurs, the CLR searches the exception handling array that is part of the metadata with each method. This array defines a protected region and a block of code that is to handle a specific exception. The exception-handling array specifies an offset from the beginning of the method and a size of the block of code. Each row in the exception-handling array specifies a protected region (offset and size), the type of handler (from the four types of exception handlers listed in the previous paragraph), and the handler block (offset and size). In addition, a type-filtered exception handler row contains information regarding the exception type for which this handler is targeted. The user-filtered exception handler contains a label that starts a block of code to be executed to determine at runtime whether the handler block should be executed in addition to the specification of the handler region. Listing 3.1 shows some C# pseudo-code for handling an exception.

LISTING 3.1 C# Exception-Handling Pseudo-Code

```
try
{
    // Protect block
    . . .
}
catch(ExceptionOne e)
{
    // Type-filtered handler
    . . .
}
finally
{
    // Finally handler
    . . .
}
```

For the code in Listing 3.1, you would see two rows in the exception handler array: one for the type-filtered handler and one for the **finally** block. Both rows would refer to the same protected block of code—namely, the code in the **try** block.

Listing 3.2 shows one more example of an exception-handling scheme, this time in Visual Basic.

LISTING 3.2 VB Exception-Handling Pseudo-Code

```
Try
    'Protected region of code
    . . .
Catch e As ExceptionOne When i = 0
    'User filtered exception handler
    . . .
Catch e As ExceptionTwo
    'Type filtered exception handler
    . . .
Finally
    'Finally handler
    . . .
End Try
```


The pseudo-code in Listing 3.2 would result in three rows in the exception-handling array. The first **Catch** is a user-filtered exception handler, which would be turned into the first row in the exception-handling array. The second **Catch** block is a type-exception handler, which is the same as the typed-exception handler in the C# case. The third and last row in the exception-handling array would be the **Finally** handler.

When an exception is generated, the CLR looks for the first match in the exception-handling array. A match would mean that the exception was thrown while the managed code was in the protected block that was specified by the particular row. In addition, for a match to exist, the particular handler must "want" to handle the exception (the user filter is true; the type matches the exception type thrown; the code is leaving the method, as in **finally**; and so forth). The first row in the exception-handing array that the CLR matches becomes the exception handler to be executed. If an appropriate handler is not found for the current method, then the current method's caller is examined. This continues until either an acceptable handler is found, or the top of the stack is reached and the exception is declared unhandled.

Exception Control Flow

Several rules govern the flow of control within protected regions and the associated handlers. These rules are enforced either by the compiler (the IL code generator) or by the CLR because the method is JITd. Remember that a protected region and the associated handler are overlaid on top of an existing block of IL code. You cannot determine the structure of an exception framework from the IL code that is specified in the metadata. The CLR enforces a set of rules when transferring control to or from exception control blocks. These rules are as follows:

- Control can only pass into an exception handler block through the exception mechanism.
- There are two ways in which control can pass to a protected region (the **`try`** block). First, control can simply branch or fall into the first instruction of a protected region. Second, from within a type-filtered handler a **`leave`** instruction can specify the offset to any instruction within a protected region (not necessarily the first instruction).
- The evaluation stack on entering a protected region must be empty. This would mean that one cannot push values on to the evaluation stack prior to entering a protected region.
- Once in a protected region any of the associated handler blocks exiting such a block is strictly controlled.

  One can exit any of the exception blocks by throwing another exception.

  From within a protected region or in a handler block (not `finally` or `fault`) a `leave` instruction may be executed which is similar to an unconditional branch but has the side effect of emptying the evaluation stack and the destination of a leave instruction can be any instruction in a protected region.

  A user-filtered handler block must be terminated by an **`endfilter`** instruction. This instruction takes a single argument from the evaluation stack to determine how exception handling should proceed.

  A `finally` or `fault` block is terminated with an **`endfinally`** instruction. This instruction empties the evaluation stack and returns from the enclosing method.

  Control can pass outside of a type-filtered handler block by rethrowing the exception. This is just a specialized case for throwing an exception in which the exception thrown is simply the exception that is currently being handled.
- None of the handler blocks or protected regions can execute a **`ret`** instruction to return from the enclosing method.
- No local allocation can be done from within any of the exception handler blocks. Specifically, the **`localloc`** instruction is not allowed from any handler.

Exception Types

The documentation indicates the exceptions that an individual instruction can generate, but in general, the CLR can generate the following exceptions as a result of executing specific IL instructions:

- `ArithmeticException`
- `DivideByZeroException`
- `ExecutionEngineException`
- `InvalidAddressException`
- `OverflowException`
- `SecurityException`
- `StackOverflowException`

In addition, the following exceptions are generated as a result of object model inconsistencies and errors:

- `TypeLoadException`
- `IndexOutOfRangeException`
- `InvalidAddressException`
- `InvalidCastException`
- `MissingFieldException`
- `MissingMethodException`
- `NullReferenceException`
- `OutOfMemoryException`
- `SecurityException`
- `StackOverflowException`

The `ExecutionEngineException` can be thrown by any instruction, and it indicates that the CLR has detected an unexpected inconsistency. If the code has been verified, this exception will never be thrown.

Many exceptions are thrown because of a failed resolution. That is, a method was not found, or the method was found but it had the wrong signature, and so forth. The following is a list of exceptions that are considered to be resolution exceptions:

- `BadImageFormatException`
- `EntryPointNotFoundException`
- `MissingFieldException`

- `MissingMemberException`
- `MissingMethodException`
- `NotSupportedException`
- `TypeLoadException`
- `TypeUnloadedException`

A few of the exceptions might be thrown early, before the code that caused the exception is actually run. This is usually because an error was detected during the conversion of the IL code to native code (JIT compile time). The following exceptions might be thrown early:

- `MissingFieldException`
- `MissingMethodException`
- `SecurityException`
- `TypeLoadException`

Exceptions are covered in more detail in Chapter 15, "Using Managed Exceptions to Effectively Handle Errors."

Remote Execution

If it is determined that an object's identity cannot be shared then a remoting boundary is put in place. A remoting boundary is implemented by the CLR using proxies. A proxy represents an object on one side of the remoting boundary and all instance field and method references are forwarded to the other side of the remoting boundary. A proxy is automatically created for objects that derive from **`System.MarshalByRefObject`**.

> **Note**
>
> Remoting is covered in more detail in Chapter 13, "Building Distributed Applications with .NET Remoting."

The CLR has a mechanism that allows applications running from within the same operating system process to be isolated from one another. This mechanism is known as the *application domain*. A class in the base class library encapsulates the features of an application domain known as **`AppDomain`**. A remoting boundary is required to effectively communicate between two isolated objects. Because each application domain is isolated from another application domain, a remoting boundary is required to communicate between application domains.

Memory Access

All memory access from within the runtime environment must be properly aligned. This means that access to `int16` or `unsigned int16` (**`short`** or **`ushort`**; 2-byte values) values must occur on even boundaries. Access to `int32`, `unsigned int32`, and `float32` (**`int`**, **`uint`**, and **`float`**; 4-byte values) must occur at an address that is evenly divisible by 4. Access to `int64`, `unsigned int64`, and `float64` (**`long`**, **`ulong`**, and **`double`**; 8-byte values) must occur at an address that is evenly divisible by 4 or 8 depending on the architecture. Access to any of the native types (`native int`, `native unsigned int`, `&`) must occur on an address that is evenly divisible by 4 or 8, depending on that native environment.

A side effect of properly aligned data is that read and write access to it that is no larger than the size of a `native int` is guaranteed to be atomic. That is, the read or write operation is guaranteed to be indivisible.

Volatile Memory Access

Certain memory access IL instructions can be prefixed with the **`volatile`** prefix. By marking memory access as `volatile` it does not necessarily guarantee atomicity but it does guarantee that prior to any read access to the memory the variable will be read from memory. A `volatile` write simply means that a write to memory is guaranteed to happen before any other access is given to the variable in memory.

The **`volatile`** prefix is meant to simulate a hardware CPU register. If this is kept in mind, **`volatile`** is easier to understand.

CLR Threads and Locks

The CLR provides support for many different mechanisms to guarantee synchronized access to data. Thread synchronization is covered in more detail in Chapter 11. Some of the locks that are part of the CLR execution model are as follows:

- Synchronized methods—Synchronized method locks that the CLR provides either lock on a particular instance (locks on the **`this`** pointer) or in the case of static locks, the lock is made on the type to which the method is defined. Once held, a method lock allows access any number of times from the same thread (recursion, other method calls, and so forth); access to the lock from another thread will block until the lock is released.
- Explicit locks—These locks are provided by the base class library.

- Volatile reads and writes—As stated previously, marking access to a variable volatile does not guarantee atomicity except in the case where the size of the value is less than or equal to that of a `native int` and it is properly aligned.
- Atomic operations—The base class library provides for a number of atomic operations through the use of the **`System.Threading.Interlocked`** class.

Summary

This chapter provided a brief overview of the framework under which managed code runs. If you keep in mind that at the lowest level, the CLR is an engine that allows the execution of IL instructions, you will have an easier time understanding both IL and how your code runs with the CLR.

This chapter detailed the rules for loading an assembly and starting execution of a method. It also supplied detailed information about control flow from within a method call. It explored in depth the built-in mechanisms for handling errors and exceptions from within this runtime environment. In addition, it discussed the runtime support for remoting that is built into the CLR. Finally, it revealed how the code that is running under the CLR accesses memory and synchronizes access to methods when multiple threads could potentially have access to the memory store.

Components of the CLR

PART II

IN THIS PART

CHAPTER 4

The Assembly

IN THIS CHAPTER

In manufacturing, you need to keep track of all the nuts, bolts, pieces, and parts. Every time a widget is manufactured as a unit, the company needs to keep track of the inventory of items that went into its construction. When the end piece is more complicated, such as a car or an airplane, a portion of the overall product might be tracked in and of itself. For example, one area or site might manufacture the dashboard. When the dashboard is shipped to the appropriate area to be incorporated into the car, the parts are tracked with a bill-of-materials and the dashboard becomes an assembly. The car then becomes a composite of assemblies. For example, there might be one dashboard assembly, two front seat assemblies (bucket seats), a right door assembly, a left door assembly, and so forth. In manufacturing, the bill-of-materials or the description of the pieces that make up the assembly is separate from the assembly. The bolt or nut cannot describe itself in human terms as to its size and makeup.

Note

An assembly is a list of the software components that make up an application just as a traditional assembly (from manufacturing) describes what makes up a part or finished piece.

This chapter is about the central unit of versioning and deployment within the .NET Framework: the .NET assembly. After understanding the information and metadata that is in a .NET assembly, you will wonder why it wasn't always like this? For software, it is a fairly revolutionary idea that requires you to think about the way it was to fully appreciate its merits.

Note

You might wonder about COM. Much of what you read about COM indicates that COM components are self-describing components much like in a .NET assembly. COM uses the type library to describe the interfaces and methods that the component implements.

COM's implementation of the self-describing component has several problems. First, the type library does not always have to be with the component. It is possible for a type library to be embedded in with the code that implements the COM interfaces (.exe or .dll), but it is not always the case. You have to guess where the type library is.

Second, the type library is severely limited in its ability to describe a method or interface. Much of the information about a type is lost in translation to a type library. Any time a method or interface uses types that are outside of the standard automation types, you start to push the limits of what the type library can describe.

Third, it is difficult (if not impossible) to glean dependency information from the type library. You cannot tell that one type library requires another to run or fully describe the interface.

Fourth, only the exposed interfaces and methods that are in the IDL are described in the type library. You have a black box view of the interface; you cannot drill into the interface and methods to find out implementation details. In other words, the type library is an assembly with a selected view. A type library is like a Hollywood movie set where you see only the façade.

This chapter covers what is in the assembly and why it is important. It also discusses two ways in which you can extract this information about the .NET assembly. A third method, reflection, can be used to extract the information that is contained in an assembly. *Reflection* enables a programmer or user to extract and write assembly information at runtime. Chapter 17, "Reflection," covers this topic in more detail.

Overview of the .NET Assembly

The .NET assembly is much like the term used in manufacturing. Within the .NET assembly is a detailed description of the pieces and parts that went into and are required by the assembly. The .NET assembly is self describing. The information about the assembly (as opposed to the executable code) is known as *metadata*. The following is a general list of the metadata that is typically associated with an assembly:

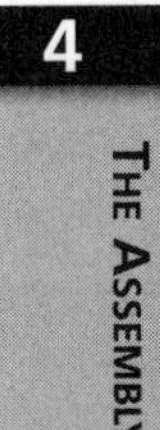

- Name—An assembly contains the name of the assembly as metadata. At first, you might wonder why this is required or even necessary. With traditional DLLs, simply renaming the DLL would cause an application to break. With assemblies, the name is embedded in the file that contains the assembly. An assembly that is referenced by another assembly, is referenced by the assembly name in the metadata, not by filename.

  Actually, the human readable name of the assembly is only part of an assembly name. An assembly is uniquely identified by the name, version, culture, and strong name.

It is possible, with some of the facilities discussed in depth in Chapter 6, "Publishing Applications," to redirect a reference to an assembly to another file that has a different version in it.

Many of the facilities with which one builds an internationalized application rely on the fact that culture is part of the assembly name. Culture is discussed in more detail in Chapter 18, "Globalization/Localization."

By associating an assembly with a strong name (the public key of a public/private key pair), you can be reasonably assured that this assembly is the assembly that you thought it was. With a strong name, it is extremely difficult to insert an assembly masquerading as your assembly, otherwise known as a Trojan horse. Again, Chapter 6 covers strong naming in more detail.

- Type—The assembly contains information about the types that are defined and referenced in the assembly. The type might be a simple value type (such as int, float, or char) or one of the built-in reference types (such as Array, string, or object). The type can be defined within the assembly or simply referenced by the assembly. All of this information is part of the metadata.
- Method—The assembly contains complete information about each method that is used and defined. If the method is simply used and defined elsewhere, then the assembly contains information about where the complete description of the method can be found (the implementing assembly). The return type, parameter count, parameter types, and pointer to the IL code that implements the method are all included in the assembly.
- Assembly—The assembly has metadata describing itself, such as number of methods, constants, enumerators, strings, and so on. An assembly can reference other assemblies. If many assemblies constitute an assembly, then one (and only one) of the assemblies is designated as the *main assembly*. This assembly holds what is known as the *manifest*, which describes not only the assembly in which the manifest is located, but also all the other assemblies in the chain. Thus, an assembly can be thought of as a logical .exe or .dll. Even though the main assembly that contains the manifest is contained in one physical file, it might reference many other assemblies, forming a network of interconnected assemblies.

Using the manufacturing analogy again, a car consists of many assemblies (the dashboard, steering wheel, engine, and so on), yet the car is the top-level assembly that incorporates all of the other assemblies. A top-level .NET assembly is the application that you build. Where this breaks down is that a .NET assembly can reference assemblies that do not reside on the computer on which they are run. An assembly can reference another assembly or module (a *module* is an assembly without a manifest) that is on the network. When a method from the module or assembly is called, the module or assembly is automatically downloaded. This would be like the steering wheel appearing when you need it.

Why metadata? For two processes to communicate with each other, they have to share the same notion of the types of data that are to be transferred between them. It is not so much that any particular format of data is better than another, but there must be an agreement. If you know that most of the processes with which you want to communicate are written in C, then the data can be packaged in a way that is easy for C to handle. The following sections discuss some of the benefits that metadata can bring to a programming environment.

Metadata Allows for Language Independence

In putting together COM, Microsoft decided early on that the specification of the data and the arguments needed to be described in a separate language so that no bias was shown toward any one language. IDL has other variants, and Microsoft did not "invent" IDL; however, Microsoft did decide on an IDL that is used to describe COM interfaces and libraries. The description of the interfaces and methods associated with a COM object using IDL was run through the MIDL compiler and a type library was produced. As a result, when one process wanted to talk to another, the contract between them was IDL, or more specifically, the type library that resulted from compiling IDL. A VB program could then easily talk via COM to a VC++ program because each program compiled with the types specified in the type library. This is just what was needed.

COM allows objects that are created in different languages to communicate with one another. In contrast, the .NET CLR integrates all languages and allows objects created in one language to be treated as equal citizens by code written in a completely different language. The CLR makes this possible due to its standard set of types, self-describing type information (metadata), and common execution environment.

With any application more complicated than `Hello World`, you quickly run into problems. First, the MIDL compiler is notoriously finicky. It changes the case of methods so that you are not always sure which method to call (spelling wise), error messages are often misleading, there is much confusion about what can and cannot be included in the library section of the IDL, and so on. Second, some of the ideas in any given programming language do not transfer well into IDL. Third, IDL often becomes a least common denominator in its attempt to embrace multiple languages. At best, it is another language that a programmer needs to know and understand to maintain and debug a COM interface.

Metadata, along with the Common Type System (CTS), frees you from all of these problems. You only need to worry about the syntax of a .NET compatible language and compiler and the rest is taken care of for you. The compiler automatically generates the metadata description of your types, methods, and values, allowing you to communicate with any other .NET-compatible language. COM indeed allows different languages to communicate with one another. With the .NET Framework, all languages are integrated. A VB assembly becomes a .NET assembly, a C# assembly becomes a .NET assembly, a J# assembly becomes a .NET assembly, and so forth.

Another benefit of metadata is that language-specific mechanisms for dealing with external components no longer exist. For example, if you call an external function with C or C++, you get the #include file and link with the import library that is associated with the DLL. With VB, you have a `Declare` statement and guess at the parameters. All of this goes away when you are calling a method that is compiled with a language that is supported in the .NET Framework.

Metadata Forms the Basis for Side-by-Side Deployment and Versioning

Because each assembly has its identity embedded in the file as part of the metadata, it is possible to run one application with one version of an assembly and another application on another version—at the same time. Metadata provides a solution to the DLL Hell that has plagued programmers for so long. Chapter 6 covers deployment and versioning in detail.

Metadata Allows for a Fine-Grained Security

You can describe the intended use of your code, and that information becomes part of the assembly metadata. The CLR honors this specification, thus making your program more secure because you know that it will not step outside the bounds that you have set. In addition, the CLR knows about your methods and types through the metadata, so it can ensure that the program does not stray outside the bounds that are set by the particular type or method. With C and most unmanaged code, it is possible to declare a character and read in an integer. At that point, the code oversteps the bounds of the character type; the results are unpredictable at best and could cause a crash at worst.

The identity of an assembly can be precisely controlled by giving it a strong name. The assembly then has a public key along with its other characteristics to identify it. At that point, it is virtually impossible to insert forged code into the list of assemblies in an application.

Metadata Makes You More Productive

All the data about your types as well as the types that you are using is available in the metadata. This enables tools to be developed to ensure that you are calling the method with the correct parameters. Often, this checking can occur on-the-fly as you are writing the code without the need for a compiler warning or error.

Metadata Allows for a Smooth Interaction with Unmanaged APIs

Metadata is crucial for .NET components to interoperate with unmanaged code, such as through P/Invoke with Win32 and with COM through class wrappers. For example, P/Invoke calls from C# turn a **`string`** instance into `LPSTR` or `LPWSTR`, arrays are correctly marshaled, references are turned into pointers, and so forth. With COM, exceptions are turned into failed `HRESULT`s, calls to events are turned into connection point calls, and so on. For this interoperation to work correctly, the runtime must have a correct view of the data that is being transferred. This is achieved with metadata.

Metadata Makes Remoting Possible

The current features of remoting are impossible without metadata. You can build an application that passes data to a remote endpoint without having to worry about how the data is converted from its in-memory version to a serialized version that will be correctly interpreted at the destination. Serialization relies heavily on the internal metadata to correctly transfer types and values in a distributed application. A popular demonstration of the power of remoting is adding an attribute to a method and seeing it become a Web service. This is impossible without metadata.

Metadata Makes Building Internationalized Applications Easier

Because the metadata of an assembly contains as part of its identifier a culture specification, it is easy to build and deploy applications that must run in multiple cultural environments. You can easily have a Japanese version, an English version, and a German version. Of course, the difficult task of translating and adjusting for cultural norms has not been done for you, but the idea of an international application is part of the very core of the assembly.

The Cost of Metadata

Metadata does not come free. For small programs, the code might take up little more than 2% of the file, with the rest of the file dedicated to information that is required to load and run the code or the metadata. The ratio of code to metadata is never large, but the overhead is well worth it when you consider factors such as programmer productivity, maintainability, readability, and interface management. A programmer who is using your assembly as a library has information available about the types and methods that are in the assembly. He doesn't have to search for the appropriate header file or files as with C and C++.

Using an assembly makes your application more maintainable. It supplies the information that is required to debug your application in case a problem arises. Although the structure of an assembly is somewhat intertwined, tools are available that make the information contained therein accessible.

Interfaces are no longer registered, as with COM interfaces. The assembly is either shared in the Global Assembly Cache (GAC), or it is a private assembly that is located in your application installation directory. Managing these interfaces becomes a simple matter of looking in the GAC or the application installation directory. If a version changes, code that depends on the "old" version continues to work, whereas new code that references the "new" version can run at the same time, with all of the enhancements of the new version.

> **Note**
>
> A simple C program that prints a string ("Hello World!") compiles to an executable image of about 32K. The same program in C++ compiles to an executable image of more than 173K. Functionally, the same program done in C# compiles to an executable of about 3K. Admittedly, the C# does not include as much code as the C or C++ program.

General Assembly Structure

You might take it for granted that the assemblies produced by the .NET Framework exist side by side with executables and DLLs that are produced by unmanaged tools (such as VC++ 6.0). When you think about the metadata that is contained in an assembly as well as the whole .NET Managed Runtime, you might wonder how this is accomplished. You don't have to run a .NET executable assembly with something such as `clr hello.exe`. You can just run the executable and magic happens. The executable automatically starts up in a managed environment. How is this accomplished?

The reason that unmanaged code can seamlessly coexist with managed code or .NET assemblies is because of the flexibility that is built into the Portable Executable (PE) file format. All .NET assemblies are PE files. You can prove this to yourself and see somewhat how this is done by dumping out the assembly as a PE file.

A listing of a PE file can be presented in two ways. The first way is to use a utility that has been around for a number of years now called **dumpbin**. With VC7, **dumpbin** is in `\Program Files\Microsoft Visual Studio .Net\vc7\bin`. You will need to set up your environment to run **dumpbin** by executing `\Program Files\Microsoft Visual Studio .Net\Common7\Tools\VSVARS32.bat`. The main reason for this extra bit of setup is that **dumpbin** requires a **link** to be in your path. **dumpbin** is a handy tool, and it has been updated to extract some of the CLR-specific information with VC7.

The second way of listing the contents of a PE file in a human-readable fashion is with a utility called `PEDump`. Matt Pietrek first wrote PEDump to accompany his article in the March 1993 issue of MSJ (`http://www.microsoft.com/msj/backissues96.asp`). Then in the February 2002 issue of MSDN, he updated `PEDump` (`http://msdn.microsoft.com/msdnmag/issues/02/02/PE/PE.asp`). This utility and the accompanying article provide insight into the internals of a PE file.

To begin the exploration of the format of a .NET assembly, start with a simple `Hello World` program shown in Listing 4.1. This program can be compiled with `csc helloworld.cs`.

LISTING 4.1 Code to Test PE File Format

```
using System;
class Hello
{
    public static void Main()
    {
        System.Console.WriteLine("Hello world!");
    }
}
```

After the code in Listing 4.1 is compiled into `HelloWorld.exe`, run the PEDump utility against the resulting assembly. You should get output similar to that shown in Listing 4.2.

LISTING 4.2 *PEDump* Output of `HelloWorld.exe`

```
Dump of file HELLOWORLD\HELLOWORLD.EXE

File Header
  Machine:                      014C (I386)
  Number of Sections:           0003
  TimeDateStamp:                3C3EBB88 -> Fri Jan 11 04:16:40 2002
  PointerToSymbolTable:         00000000
  NumberOfSymbols:              00000000
  SizeOfOptionalHeader:         00E0
  Characteristics:              010E
    EXECUTABLE_IMAGE
    LINE_NUMS_STRIPPED
    LOCAL_SYMS_STRIPPED
    32BIT_MACHINE

Optional Header
  Magic                         010B
  linker version                6.00
  size of code                  400
  size of initialized data      600
  size of uninitialized data    0
  entrypoint RVA                22DE
  base of code                  2000
  base of data                  4000
  image base                    400000
  section align                 2000
  file align                    200
  required OS version           4.00
  image version                 0.00
  subsystem version             4.00
  Win32 Version                 0
  size of image                 8000
  size of headers               200
  checksum                      0
  Subsystem                     0003 (Windows character)
  DLL flags                     0000
  stack reserve size            100000
  stack commit size             1000
  heap reserve size             100000
  heap commit size              1000
  RVAs & sizes                  10

Data Directory
  EXPORT           rva: 00000000  size: 00000000
  IMPORT           rva: 00002290  size: 0000004B
  RESOURCE         rva: 00004000  size: 00000340
  EXCEPTION        rva: 00000000  size: 00000000
  SECURITY         rva: 00000000  size: 00000000
  BASERELOC        rva: 00006000  size: 0000000C
```

LISTING 4.2 Continued

```
  DEBUG            rva: 00000000  size: 00000000
  ARCHITECTURE     rva: 00000000  size: 00000000
  GLOBALPTR        rva: 00000000  size: 00000000
  TLS              rva: 00000000  size: 00000000
  LOAD_CONFIG      rva: 00000000  size: 00000000
  BOUND_IMPORT     rva: 00000000  size: 00000000
  IAT              rva: 00002000  size: 00000008
  DELAY_IMPORT     rva: 00000000  size: 00000000
  COM_DESCRPTR     rva: 00002008  size: 00000048
  unused           rva: 00000000  size: 00000000

Section Table
  01 .text     VirtSize: 000002E4  VirtAddr:  00002000
    raw data offs:   00000200  raw data size: 00000400
    relocation offs: 00000000  relocations:   00000000
    line # offs:     00000000  line #'s:      00000000
    characteristics: 60000020
      CODE  EXECUTE  READ  ALIGN_DEFAULT(16)

  02 .rsrc     VirtSize: 00000340  VirtAddr:  00004000
    raw data offs:   00000600  raw data size: 00000400
    relocation offs: 00000000  relocations:   00000000
    line # offs:     00000000  line #'s:      00000000
    characteristics: 40000040
      INITIALIZED_DATA  READ  ALIGN_DEFAULT(16)

  03 .reloc    VirtSize: 0000000C  VirtAddr:  00006000
    raw data offs:   00000A00  raw data size: 00000200
    relocation offs: 00000000  relocations:   00000000
    line # offs:     00000000  line #'s:      00000000
    characteristics: 42000040
      INITIALIZED_DATA  DISCARDABLE  READ  ALIGN_DEFAULT(16)


Resources (RVA: 4000)
ResDir (0) Entries:01 (Named:00, ID:01) TimeDate:00000000
    -------------------------------------------------------------
    ResDir (VERSION) Entries:01 (Named:00, ID:01) TimeDate:00000000
        ResDir (1) Entries:01 (Named:00, ID:01) TimeDate:00000000
            ID: 00000000  DataEntryOffs: 00000048
            DataRVA: 04058  DataSize: 002E4  CodePage: 0

Imports Table:
  mscoree.dll
  Import Lookup Table RVA:  000022B8
  TimeDateStamp:            00000000
  ForwarderChain:           00000000
  DLL Name RVA:             000022CE
  Import Address Table RVA: 00002000
```

LISTING 4.2 Continued

```
  Ordn  Name
     0  _CorExeMain


.NET Runtime Header:
  Size:       72
  Version:    2.0
  Flags:      1
    ILONLY
  MetaData          rva: 0000207C  size: 00000214
  Resources         rva: 00000000  size: 00000000
  StrongNameSig     rva: 00000000  size: 00000000
  CodeManagerTable  rva: 00000000  size: 00000000
  VTableFixups      rva: 00000000  size: 00000000
  ExprtAddrTblJmps  rva: 00000000  size: 00000000
  ManagedNativeHdr  rva: 00000000  size: 00000000
```

The utility seemed to find all the pertinent PE file format information. Where is the assembly in all of this? To begin to answer this question, it is instructive to enumerate the steps that are involved in loading and running an assembly, or any PE file for that matter.

What happens when the assembly is executed? Answering this question is a good introduction to the format and architecture of the assembly file.

When an assembly is executed, one of the first tasks performed is that the import address table is queried to find what additional modules are required for this image to run. The import address table is found from the data directory. In Listing 4.2, see the line that looks like this:

```
IMPORT       rva: 00002290  size: 0000004B
```

RVA stands for relative virtual address. An RVA points to an area in one of the sections of the file. To decode where an RVA points, you first find in which section the RVA is (.text, .rsrc, .reloc, and so forth). Each section has a start address (virtual address) and a size. If the RVA is greater than the start address and less than the start address plus the size, then the RVA is pointing to an address in that section. Subtract the start address of the section from the RVA, and that forms an offset into the section. This import address points to an address in the file that looks like the output shown in Listing 4.3.

LISTING 4.3 Input Address Table for Managed Code

```
000290:  B8 22 00 00 00 00 00 00  00 00 00 00 CE 22 00 00 .".........."..
0002A0:  00 20 00 00 00 00 00 00  00 00 00 00 00 00 00 00 . ..............
0002B0:  00 00 00 00 00 00 00 00  C0 22 00 00 00 00 00 00 ........."......
0002C0:  00 00 5F 43 6F 72 45 78  65 4D 61 69 6E 00 6D 73 .._CorExeMain.ms
0002D0:  63 6F 72 65 65 2E 64 6C  6C 00 00 00 00 00 FF 25 coree.dll......%
```

This essentially tells the loading process to load the DLL, `mscoree.dll`, into the process. This DLL is the Microsoft .NET Execution Engine. Now the DLL on which all managed code depends is loaded.

The next step is to start things running. For any PE executable, execution starts at the entry point RVA in the optional PE header. For managed code, it is no different. For this simple program, the entry point looks like this:

```
entrypoint RVA                22DE
```

The entry point address contains the following bytes:

```
0002D0:  63 6F 72 65 65 2E 64 6C  6C 00 00 00 00 00 FF 25 coree.dll......%
0002E0:  00 20 40 00 00 00 00 00  00 00 00 00 00 00 00 00 . @.............
```

The bytes, 0xFF25, represent the assembly instruction for jump indirect. The next 4 bytes indicate the address that contains the address of the first executable instruction. This instruction causes execution to start in the execution engine. After the execution engine loads the CLR (the workstation version `mscorwks.dll`), the assembly manager (`fusion.dll`), the CLR class library (`mscorlib.dll`), the strong name support (`mscorsn.dll`), and the JIT compiler (`mscorjit.dll`), the assembly that is being run is queried for where managed execution should begin.

To discover where managed execution should begin, the CLR looks at a special table in the assembly called the CIL header table. In the CIL header table is an entry called the Entry Point Token. You will see the start address of the CIL header table in the data directory as the fourteenth entry.

Note

In later versions of code and in Listing 4.2, the CIL header table is known as the COM_DESRPTR table. In 1993, when Matt Pietrek first wrote this utility, it was simply an unused entry in the data directory.

The address can be seen in Listing 4.2 as follows:

```
  COM_DESCRPTR      rva: 00002008  size: 00000048
```

The actual data in this table looks like this:

```
000000:  C0 22 00 00 00 00 00 00  48 00 00 00 02 00 00 00 ."......H.......
000010:  7C 20 00 00 14 02 00 00  01 00 00 00 01 00 00 06 | ..............
000020:  00 00 00 00 00 00 00 00  00 00 00 00 00 00 00 00 ................
000030:  00 00 00 00 00 00 00 00  00 00 00 00 00 00 00 00 ................
000040:  00 00 00 00 00 00 00 00  00 00 00 00 00 00 00 00 ................
```

The details of the format of the CIL header table are discussed later. Within this table the entry point token is 0x60000001. You will run into tokens often when working with assembly images. A token contains a coded value that indicates which table it is referencing. Here, 0x6 indicates the method table. The rest of the token (the other 3 bytes) is an index into the particular table, in this case 1. The index will never be zero because the first entry of every assembly table is zero. Therefore, this index is one-based, not zero-based. Index 1 of the method table refers to the C# entry Main. As part of the method table, one entry refers to the address of the IL code that makes up this method. The address points to the following bytes in the assembly:

```
000050:  13 30 01 00 0B 00 00 00  00 00 00 00 72 01 00 00 .0.........r...
000060:  70 28 02 00 00 0A 2A 00  13 30 01 00 07 00 00 00 p(....*..0......
```

After setting up the header for the method, these bytes translate into the following IL instructions:

```
ldstr 0x70000001
call 0xA0000002
ret
```

The **ldstr** instruction loads a string token (0x7 indicates the user string table, and index 1 of the table refers to the string "Hello World!"). The call instruction makes a call into a referenced method (0xA refers to the member ref table, and index 2 indicates it is the **WriteLine** method). The last instruction is a return that finishes this method. The JIT compiles these instructions into native code, at which point they are executed and the program terminates.

From this simple program, you can see that when the C# compiler (or any compiler that supports the .NET Framework) generates an assembly, it generates a valid PE file. On the outside, these files look like any other managed executable or DLL. The differences between a PE file that is generated for managed execution and a PE file that is generated for unmanaged execution are as follows:

- .NET assembly PE files contain only a few bytes of x86 code. For the most part, it is simply a hook into the CLR via an x86 jump instruction. Most of the executable code in these files is intermediate language (IL, or more specifically MSIL).
- .NET assembly PE files contain metadata about the assembly and the types and methods used there. Metadata allows the CLR to load and run class types, lay out instances of the classes (and values) in memory, resolve method calls, enforce security, resolve and load other assemblies, and so forth. In essence, all of the features of the CLR depend on various portions of the metadata in the assembly.

Detailed Assembly Structure

This section will discuss one tool and one set of APIs that help you manipulate and view the assembly structure. This tool is shipped with the SDK in `\Program Files\Microsoft Visual Studio .NET\FrameworkSDK\bin`. The tool is called `ILDasm`, and it is extremely useful. `ILDasm` has online help available under the Help menu. Documentation about the advanced features of `ILDasm` can be found in `\Program Files\Microsoft Visual Studio .NET\FrameworkSDK\Tool Developers Guide\docs`.

To drill down into the structure of the assembly, you need to invoke `ILDasm` with the advanced option. Still looking at the simple `HelloWorld.exe` assembly, from a command prompt window, start up `ILDasm` as follows:

```
ILDasm /adv helloworld.exe
```

It's important to show and verify the structure of the assembly. To see the PE file format and the assembly format, select the View, COR header menu item. (If you did not invoke `ILDasm` with the `/adv` option, you will not see these menu items.) You will be presented with a window that looks like Figure 4.1.

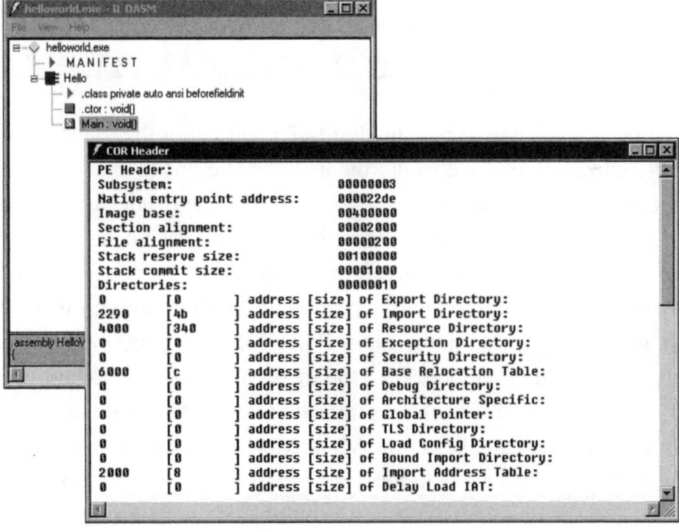

FIGURE 4.1
PE header for `HelloWorld.exe`.

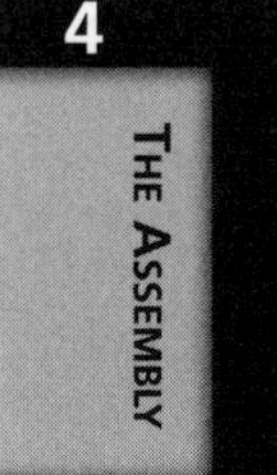

`ILDasm` presents the PE header for informational purposes only. This PE header is part of any PE file, not just .NET assemblies. From this figure, you can see the Import Address Table (`ILDasm` calls it the Import Directory) and the entry point (`ILDasm` calls it the

Native Entry Point Address). Remember from the previous discussion that the *entry point* is the simple managed hook into managed code. The Import Address Table (IAT) directs the loader of the PE file to load the execution engine. Notice also that 16 directories exist, but `ILDasm` shows only 15 because the last entry is reserved at this point and not used with .NET assemblies.

If you scroll down a little, you will see a human-readable version of the IAT, as shown in Figure 4.2.

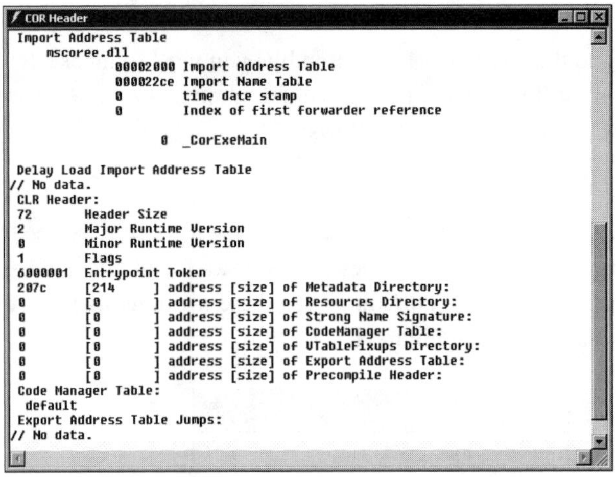

FIGURE 4.2
IAT and CLR header for `HelloWorld.exe`.

```
COR Header
 Import Address Table
     mscoree.dll
              00002000 Import Address Table
              000022ce Import Name Table
              0        time date stamp
              0        Index of first forwarder reference

                     0  _CorExeMain

 Delay Load Import Address Table
// No data.
 CLR Header:
 72        Header Size
 2         Major Runtime Version
 0         Minor Runtime Version
 1         Flags
 6000001   Entrypoint Token
 207c      [214      ] address [size] of Metadata Directory:
 0         [0        ] address [size] of Resources Directory:
 0         [0        ] address [size] of Strong Name Signature:
 0         [0        ] address [size] of CodeManager Table:
 0         [0        ] address [size] of VTableFixups Directory:
 0         [0        ] address [size] of Export Address Table:
 0         [0        ] address [size] of Precompile Header:
 Code Manager Table:
  default
 Export Address Table Jumps:
// No data.
```

From Figure 4.2, you can verify that the IAT is directing the loader to load `mscoree.dll`. From this figure, you can see where the metadata begins (Metadata directory). To follow the previous discussion, the most important part of the header is the Entry Point Token. For this simple assembly, a strong name has not been assigned, and no resources are associated with this assembly. Therefore, the directory entries for these items are zero. The only piece of information that is needed to run this program is the entry point of the program, which is encoded in the Entry Point Token as 0x60000001. As indicated earlier, this token is a reference to index 1 of the method table. The method table is part of the metadata, which starts at the address indicated by the Metadata directory entry. To view an outline of the metadata, select the View, Metainfo, Header menu item. Doing so puts a check mark on the Header menu item indicating what you want to view. To view the table, press Ctrl+M or select the View, Metainfo, Show menu item. A new window appears that looks like Figure 4.3.

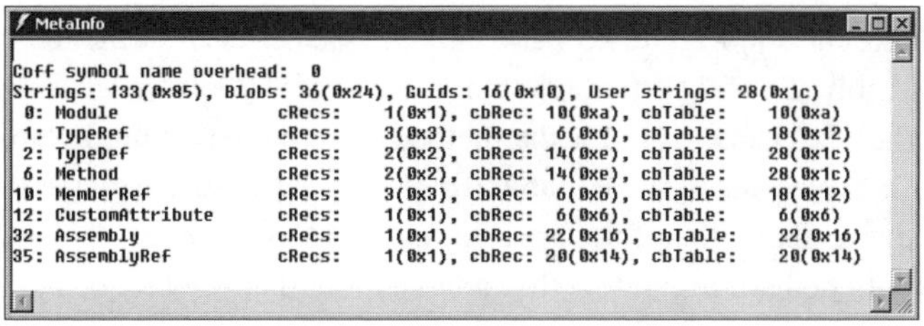

FIGURE 4.3
Metadata info.

```
MetaInfo
Coff symbol name overhead:  0
Strings: 133(0x85), Blobs: 36(0x24), Guids: 16(0x10), User strings: 28(0x1c)
 0: Module              cRecs:    1(0x1), cbRec: 10(0xa), cbTable:    10(0xa)
 1: TypeRef             cRecs:    3(0x3), cbRec:  6(0x6), cbTable:    18(0x12)
 2: TypeDef             cRecs:    2(0x2), cbRec: 14(0xe), cbTable:    28(0x1c)
 6: Method              cRecs:    2(0x2), cbRec: 14(0xe), cbTable:    28(0x1c)
10: MemberRef           cRecs:    3(0x3), cbRec:  6(0x6), cbTable:    18(0x12)
12: CustomAttribute     cRecs:    1(0x1), cbRec:  6(0x6), cbTable:     6(0x6)
32: Assembly            cRecs:    1(0x1), cbRec: 22(0x16), cbTable:    22(0x16)
35: AssemblyRef         cRecs:    1(0x1), cbRec: 20(0x14), cbTable:    20(0x14)
```

The first line in Figure 4.3 shows the main set of tables that make up the metadata. These are known as *heaps*, *stream heaps*, or just *streams*. `ILDasm` shows four heaps. A fifth heap exists that is a table of tables. This heap contains all the tables that are valid for the assembly at hand. This special stream is known as the #~ stream. Table 4.1 gives an explanation of each of the streams in the metadata.

TABLE 4.1 Streams in .NET Metadata

Stream	*Description*
#~	#~ contains the physical representation of the logical metadata streams.
#Strings	This is a physical representation of the logical strings table. It contains names that are used by other portions of the metadata for identifiers such as Main or WriteLine so that a human-readable name can be associated with a type, value, method, or field. This heap is a byte array; therefore, indexes into this heap are offsets.
#Blob	The blob heap contains most of the metadata information that is encoded in one form or another. For example, the blob heap contains signature metadata on each of the methods, type metadata about each type, parameter metadata, and so forth. This heap is a byte array; therefore, indexes into this heap are offsets.
#US	This heap contains a list of the user-defined strings in an assembly. For example, with `helloworld.exe`, a call was made as follows: `Console.WriteLine("Hello World!");` The string "Hello World!" is part of the user-defined string heap in the `hello.exe` assembly. This heap is a byte array; therefore, indexes into this heap are offsets.
#GUID	This heap contains a 16-byte representation of the GUIDs that this assembly uses. For most cases, this heap has only one 16-byte entry, which is the GUID for the assembly. Indexes into this table are numbered starting with 1 for the first GUID, 2 for the next, and so on.

The remaining lines in Figure 4.3 list characteristics of each of the tables that are valid for this assembly. The first column is the identifier for the table. Here you can see where the table ID of 0x6 came from for the method table. Other common tables are the Module table (0X0), the TypeDef table (0x2), and the Assembly table (0x20). The last table identifier is 0x29; therefore, approximately 41 tables exist. (Not all identifiers are used.) It would be hard to put together an assembly that used all of the tables. The simple Hello World program has eight tables. Table 4.2 provides a list of the possible tables in the metadata.

TABLE 4.2 Metadata Tables

Code	*Table Name*	*Columns*	*Description*
0x00	Module	5	This table contains one and only one row, which describes the module, its name, and the GUID that is assigned to it.
0x01	TypeRef	3	This table contains the necessary information that is required to resolve this type (index into Module, ModuleDef, AssemblyRef, or TypeRef tables) and the name of the type (name and namespace).
0x02	TypeDef	6	This table contains one row for each type that is defined in the module. Columns describe the name of the type and namespace (index into the #Strings heap), the type from which this type is derived, the fields that are contained by this type (FieldDef), and the methods that are owned by this type (MethodDef).
0x04	Field	3	This table defines the attributes of a field (accessibility, static, and so on), its name, and its signature.
0x06	Method	6	This table has an entry for each method that is defined in the module. A column describes how to get to the code associated with the method, the name of the method (index into #String stream), flags describing the methods (accessibility, static, final, and so on), the signature of the method (return type, number and type of parameters, and so on), and a pointer to the beginning of the parameters that is associated with this method.

TABLE 4.2 Continued

Code	Table Name	Columns	Description
0x08	Param	3	This table has one entry for each parameter that is used within the module. A column describes the name, and flags indicate whether it is an [in] parameter or an [out] parameter, whether it has a default value, and whether it is optional.
0x09	InterfaceImpl	2	This table describes each of the interfaces that is described by this module. The table has columns that describe the class with which this interface is implemented and the type of the interface.
0x0A	MemberRef	3	This table contains one entry for either a field or a method that is part of a class. Each row has a column that describes the signature of the member, the name of the member, and the type of the member.
0x0B	Constant	3	This table stores constants for this module. Each row describes a different constant, parent, value, and type.
0x0C	CustomAttribute	3	This table contains one entry for each custom attribute that is utilized in the module. Each row contains enough information to allow instantiation of the class object that is specified by the CustomAttribute. Each row contains an index into its parent table, an index into the type table, and the value of the constant.
0x0D	FieldMarshal	2	This table is used by managed code that interfaces with unmanaged code. This table links an existing row in the Field or Param table to information in the Blob heap that defines how that field or parameter should be marshaled when calling to or from unmanaged code via PInvoke.
0x0E	DeclSecurity	3	This table associates a security action with a permission set for a method or type.

TABLE 4.2 Continued

Code	*Table Name*	*Columns*	*Description*
0x0F	ClassLayout	3	This table specifies a layout for a particular class. One row exists for each specialized layout. The Class Layout table specifies the packing size, class size, and parent (the class).
0x10	FieldLayout	2	This table specifies how an individual field is positioned in a class. One row exists for each special kind of field layout.
0x11	StandAloneSig	1	This table is most often used to specify initialization for local variables in method calls. It also is used to specify a signature for IL calli instructions.
0x12	EventMap	2	This table provides a mapping between a list of events and a particular class that handles the events.
0x14	Event	3	This table provides a way to associate a group of methods with a single class. For events, you will typically see add and remove methods to add or remove a delegate from a chain, respectively. The Event table combines these two methods into a single class.
0x15	PropertyMap	2	This table maps a set of properties to a particular class.
0x17	Property	3	This table, like the Event table, gathers together methods and associates them with a single class.
0x18	MethodSemantics	3	This table specifies special semantics for dealing with events and properties.
0x19	MethodImpl	3	This table has a row for each interface that is implemented. The columns specify in which class it is implemented as well as the method body and the method declaration.

TABLE 4.2 Continued

Code	*Table Name*	*Columns*	*Description*
0x1A	ModuleRef	1	This table has a single column that is the name of the module. The name of the module must correspond to an entry in the file table so that the module can be resolved.
0x1B	TypeSpec	1	This table specifies a type via the single index into the blob heap.
0x1C	ImplMap	4	This table holds information about unmanaged code that can be reached with managed code with P/Invoke.
0x1D	FieldRVA	2	This table keeps track of each interface that a class implements.
0x20	Assembly	6	This table records the full definition of the current assembly. Columns exist for the name of the assembly, the version, the culture, the hash algorithm, and the public key of the public/private key pair used to give this module a strong name. A column also exists for flags that has settable options for specifying a full public key or side-by-side compatibility mode.
0x21	AssemblyProcessor	1	This table should be ignored by the CLI and treated as if it were zero. It should not be part of a PE file.
0x22	AssemblyOS	3	This table contains platform OS information such as processor and version. The CLI should ignore this table and treat it as if it were zero. It should not be part of a PE file.
0x23	AssemblyRef	6	This table contains references to other assemblies. The columns for this table are in a different order, but are similar to the columns in the Assembly table.
0x24	AssemblyRefProcessor	1	This table should be ignored by the CLI and treated as if it were zero. It should not be part of a PE file. It contains the processor and an index into the AssemblyRef table.

TABLE 4.2 Continued

Code	Table Name	Columns	Description
0x25	AssemblyRefOS	4	This table contains platform OS information such as processor and version for a referenced assembly. This table should be ignored by the CLI and treated as if it were zero. It should not be part of a PE file.
0x26	File	3	Assemblies can reference other files, such as documentation and other configuration files. An assembly references another file through the `.file` declaration in the assembly. This table contains all of the `.file` entries for a given assembly or module.
0x27	ExportedType	5	Each row in the Exported Type table is generated as a result of the `.class` extern directive in the IL code from which this assembly was built. The `.class` extern directive is required to export a type from a module that is not the main manifest assembly. This is to save space; each type's metadata is already available for export from the TypeDef table.
0x28	ManifestResource	4	The rows in this table result from the `.mresource` directive in the assembly. This directive associates a name with some data outside of the assembly. If the resource is not part of a standalone file, then the table contains a reference to the offset into one of the modules stream heaps.
0x29	NestedClass	2	This table records which type definitions are declared inside of other type definitions. It contains references to the nested type and the enclosing type for all nesting situations.

From Figure 4.3, you can see that not all of the tables have been defined. Each row in Figure 4.3—after the initial header showing the heaps—describes a table in the assembly.

The first column is the ID of the table (possible values indicated in Table 4.2). Following the first column is the name of the table. Next, the `cbRecs` item indicates how many rows are in this table. The `cbRec` column shows how large each row is. Finally, the `cbTable` column indicates how many bytes are in the given table.

If you toggle the header menu item in the View→Metainfo→Header and then either select the View→Metainfo→Show Menu item or press Ctrl+M, you will see ILDasm's view of the contents of each of the tables that are valid for this assembly. A portion of the contents is shown in Figure 4.4.

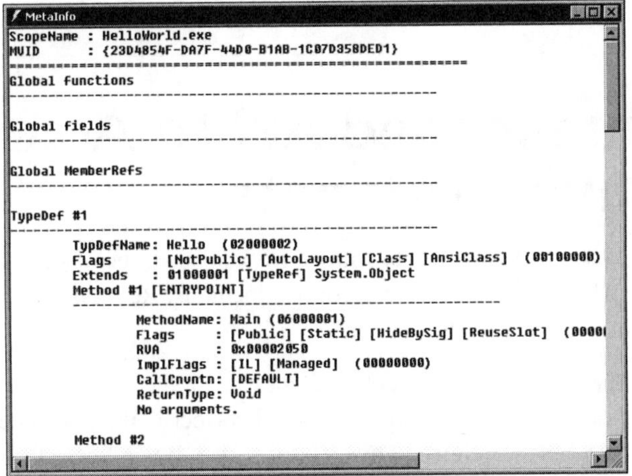

FIGURE 4.4
Metadata table dump.

This is a long listing, so you might want to invoke `ILDasm` on this assembly to view the complete output. `ILDasm` takes some liberties as to what it displays. It does not display a separate module table or a separate method table. `ILDasm` incorporates the data in these tables into the output listing. You probably do not want to use this output to understand the physical representation of the tables. Rather, this output gives you a view of the tables that is easier to understand than with a strict table view.

To round off this presentation of the assembly as viewed by ILDasm, Figure 4.5 shows the statistics on this file. This option is under the View, Statistics menu of `ILDasm`.

As mentioned earlier, the managed code is only a small fraction of the overall file size. Most of the file is taken up with either the PE information or the metadata. For real applications, the ratio of file size to IL code increases as each type is reused throughout the code. This statistics page gives you a rough guess at the disk overhead that is associated with a given assembly.

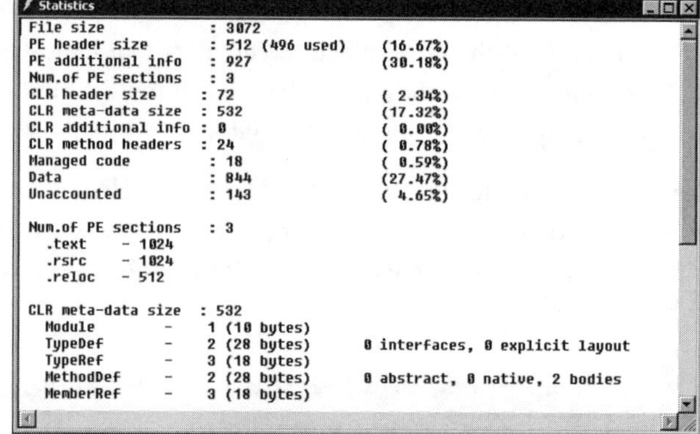

FIGURE 4.5
Metadata statistics.

An Unmanaged API to Access Assembly Metadata

Two methods to access the metadata with an assembly will be discussed. A third method, the Reflection API, is built on top of these two methods. Reflection will be covered in further detail in Chapter 17, "Reflection."

Both of the APIs covered in this chapter do not require the .NET CLR. The first method only requires that the `mscorwks.dll` be installed correctly on your system. It is an unmanaged COM API, which is relatively easy to use. It is a lower level than the Reflection API, but after you understand the basics of how an assembly is laid out, the unmanaged API is not that hard to use.

Jim Miller of Microsoft termed the second method "heroic." This method takes the assembly specification as submitted to ECMA and deciphers it byte by byte. Of course, this method requires some facility to read in the binary assembly. This requires more intimate knowledge of the physical layout of the assembly. This method is covered in the next section.

An interface in the unmanaged API is the gateway for all other interfaces. It is appropriately named `IMetaDataDispenser`, or `IMetaDataDispenserEx`. As the name implies, this interface literally dispenses all of the other interfaces. `IMetaDataDispenser` and `IMetaDataDispenserEx` are pretty similar, so either interface is fine. The `Ex` version simply adds a few methods that change the way an assembly is searched or allows you to view where the Framework was installed (the system directory path). Both of these interfaces are COM interfaces, so it's important to have some familiarity with COM to effectively use these interfaces. This example uses C++ to access the COM interfaces. If ATL had been used, the implementation would have been marginally simpler. A VB implementation should be even simpler still. The full source for this application is in the `AssemblyCOM` directory. Listing 4.4 shows how to obtain a pointer to the `IMetaDataDispenserEx` interface.

LISTING 4.4 Getting an Instance of the `IMetaDataDispenserEx` Interface

```
#include <cor.h>
. . .
HRESULT hr = CoCreateInstance(CLSID_CorMetaDataDispenser,
                              NULL,
                              CLSCTX_INPROC_SERVER,
                              IID_IMetaDataDispenserEx,
                              (void **) &m_pDisp);
```

Next, you will need to associate an assembly file with the set of metadata APIs. You do this with the `OpenScope` method of the `IMetaDataDispenser` interface. Listing 4.5 shows how to call `OpenScope`.

LISTING 4.5 `OpenScope` in `IMetaDataDispenser` Interface

```
#include <cor.h>
. . .
WCHAR szScope[1024];
wcscpy(szScope, L"file:");
wcscat(szScope, lpszPathName);

// Attempt to open scope on given file
HRESULT hr = m_pDisp->OpenScope(szScope,
                                0,
                                IID_IMetaDataImport,
                               (IUnknown**)&m_pImport);
```

The `IMetaDataImport` interface provides most of the functionality that is typically required. You might want to query the `IMetaDataImport` interface for the `IMetaDataAssemblyImport` interface, but you will find that most of the metadata information is available from methods on the `IMetaDataImport` interface.

Table 4.2 listed the tables that can be defined. How do you get at those tables? Table 4.3 shows the association between a method call on `IMetaDataImport` and the tables that are listed in Table 4.2.

TABLE 4.3 Metadata Tables

Code	*Table Name*	*Token*	*Method*
0x0C	CustomAttribute	**mdCustomValue**	EnumCustomAttributes
0x14	Event	**mdEvent**	EnumEvents
0x04	Field	**mdFieldDef**	EnumFields
0x09	InterfaceImpl	**mdInterfaceImpl**	EnumInterfaceImpls
0x0A	MemberRef	**mdMemberRef**	EnumMemberRefs
		mdToken	EnumMembers
0x06	Method	**mdMethodDef**	EnumMethods
0x1A	ModuleRef	**mdModuleRef**	EnumModuleRefs
0x08	Param	**mdParamDef**	EnumParams
0x0E	DeclSecurity	**mdPermission**	EnumPermissionSets
0x17	Property	**mdProperty**	EnumProperties
0x02	TypeDef	**mdTypeDef**	EnumTypeDefs
0x01	TypeRef	**mdTypeRef**	EnumTypeRefs
		mdString	EnumUserStrings

In addition to these method calls, a general table interface called `IMetaDataTables` has methods for enumerating through the tables, row by row. To illustrate how to use the unmanaged APIs, a project has been created that allows you to explore the metadata of an assembly. The full source for the application is in the `AssemblyCOM` subdirectory. When this application is run using the `hello.exe` assembly that was explored in the previous section, the tool looks like Figure 4.6.

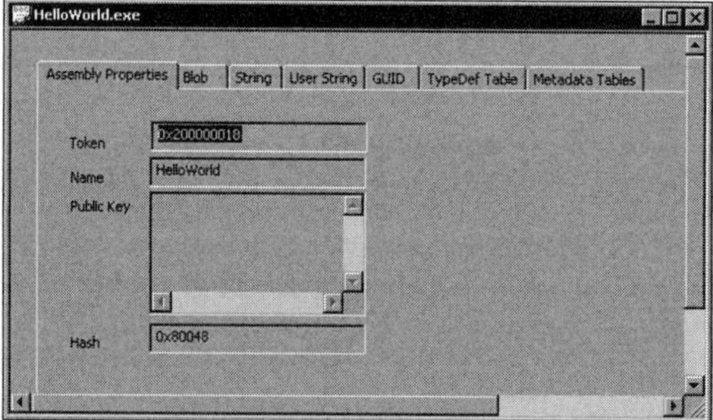

FIGURE 4.6
`AssemblyCOM` *application.*

This application uses many unmanaged APIs. A separate property page was built for different views into the assembly metadata. To understand how to use the unmanaged APIs, look at the property page labeled `TypeDef`. This property page looks at fields, methods, and parameters that are defined as a type. Listing 4.6 shows how the process is started.

LISTING 4.6 Enumerating Types

```
void DisplayTypeDefs(IMetaDataImport* pImport, CTreeCtrl& treeCtrl)
{
    HCORENUM typeDefEnum = NULL;
    mdTypeDef typeDefs[ENUM_BUFFER_SIZE];
    ULONG count, totalCount = 1;
    HRESULT hr;
    WCHAR lBuffer[256];
    HTREEITEM typedefItem;

    while (SUCCEEDED(hr = pImport->EnumTypeDefs(&typeDefEnum,
                                                typeDefs,
                                                NumItems(typeDefs),
                                                &count)) &&
            count > 0)
    {
        for (ULONG i = 0; i < count; i++, totalCount++)
        {
            wsprintf(lBuffer, _T("TypeDef #%d"), totalCount);
            typedefItem = treeCtrl.InsertItem(lBuffer);
            DisplayTypeDefInfo(pImport, typeDefs[i], treeCtrl, typedefItem);
        }
    }
    pImport->CloseEnum( typeDefEnum);
}
```

An `IMetaDataImport` interface was already obtained, as described earlier. Now you can step through each of the types that is defined in this module using `HelloWorld.exe`. `EnumTypeDefs` is called to enumerate all the types. To see how interconnected all these tables are, you could have just as easily started at the `TypeDef` table and iterated through each row in the table. For each of the types defined, `DisplayTypeDefInfo` is called to list the contents of a single type. A type can be a method, a property, an event, an interface, a permission class, or custom attributes. One of the more interesting subtrees in the `TypeDef` tree is the branch that deals with methods. The format of the enumeration is much the same as Listing 4.6. You can start the enumeration and then explicitly close it. Listing 4.7 shows an example of calling the `EnumMethods`.

LISTING 4.7 Enumerating the Methods That Are Defined for a Type

```
void DisplayMethods(IMetaDataImport* pImport,
                    mdTypeDef inTypeDef,
                    CTreeCtrl& treeCtrl,
```

LISTING 4.7 Continued

```
                    HTREEITEM treeItem)
{
    HCORENUM methodEnum = NULL;
    mdToken methods[ENUM_BUFFER_SIZE];
    DWORD flags;
    ULONG count, totalCount = 1;
    HRESULT hr;
    WCHAR lBuffer[512];
    HTREEITEM subTreeItem;
    while (SUCCEEDED(hr = pImport->EnumMethods( &methodEnum,
                                                 inTypeDef,
                                                 methods,
                                                 NumItems(methods),
                                                 &count)) &&
            count > 0)
    {
        for (ULONG i = 0; i < count; i++, totalCount++)
        {
            wsprintf(lBuffer, _T("Method #%d %ls"),
                                 totalCount,
                                 (methods[i] == g_tkEntryPoint) ?
                                 L"[ENTRYPOINT]" : L"");
            subTreeItem = treeCtrl.InsertItem(lBuffer, treeItem);
            DisplayMethodInfo(pImport, methods[i],
➥&flags, treeCtrl, subTreeItem);
            DisplayParams(pImport, methods[i], treeCtrl, subTreeItem);
            //DisplayCustomAttributes(methods[i], "\t\t");
            //DisplayPermissions(methods[i], "\t");
            //DisplayMemberRefs(methods[i], "\t");
            //// P-invoke data if present.
            //if (IsMdPinvokeImpl(flags))
            //    DisplayPinvokeInfo(methods[i]);
        }
    }
    pImport->CloseEnum(methodEnum);
}
```

You should see some thread of commonality between Listing 4.7 and Listing 4.6. The enumeration is started and a HCORENUM handle is passed back. When you are finished with the enumeration, call `CloseEnum` to close off the enumeration. Various EnumXXX methods have different inputs and outputs, but they all take a token as described in Table 4.3. The upper byte of this token describes the table that is being referenced. The remaining bytes specify an index into that table. For example, when you first start up the `AssemblyCOM` application and select the `TypeDef` property page for the `HelloWorld.exe` assembly, one of the tokens that you see in the debugger is 0x02000002. This is index 2 into table number 2, which is the `TypeDef` table. Index 2 refers to the

CLRUnleashed.Hello class of which Main is the only member. The indexes that are part of a token are 1-based. Zero is an indication that the feature or table entry is not present. This application is not finished, but it is far enough along to provide a good starting point for learning the unmanaged APIs.

From within the loop enumerating the TypeDefs are several other EnumXXX method calls. One of those loops is the EnumMethods method shown in Listing 4.7. Each of the EnumXXX methods is usually followed by a call to GetXXXProps. The pattern is to open the enumeration, get the detail, and close the enumeration. The "get the details" portion of the pattern is supported by the managed API call to GetXXXProps. In the sample code, the call to EnumMethods is succeeded by a call to GetMethodProps; however, because of the level of detail, it has been split out to an internal helper call to DisplayMethodInfo. If there is a particular OUT parameter in which you are not interested, you can simply pass NULL instead of a valid address to a variable. For some of the GetXXXProps, this can save productivity because you don't have to worry about setting up a variable that doesn't interest you. If you look at the call to GetTypeDefProps from within the internal TypeDefName function, you see that only the arguments to retrieve the name of the last three arguments are supplied with NULL. In a function like TypeDefName, these parameters are not important.

The one road block that you might run into in trying to crack the assembly metadata is with signatures. Signatures are necessarily complex because they have to generically describe a method, a field, and so on. Signatures need to describe the return type and each of the arguments (parameters) to the function or method. The signature data cannot be cracked easily. However, if your method signature is simple, then the corresponding metadata is relatively simple. The general format for a signature is as follows:

```
<calling convention>
<parameter count>
<return type>
<parameter #1 description>
. . .
<parameter #n description>
```

Where this gets complicated is the parameter count. The parameter count is not a simple number, but a compressed value that needs to be decompressed for correct interpretation. The return type is coded to describe returning a reference value, not returning a value (void), or returning a complex type. Each of the parameters can be simple or complex. If it is just a simple value, then a simple switch statement allows you to decode the signature values. If the parameter is more complex, then you might end up with recursion. Because of these complexities, the application, AssemblyCOM, was not built to crack the signature. That's an exercise for you. AssemblyCOM simply displays the hex bytes that represent the signature description in the metadata.

Physical Layout of the Assembly

This section relies heavily on the documentation of the assembly format that is contained in `\Program Files\Microsoft Visual Studio .NET\FrameworkSDK\Tool Developers Guide\docs\Partition II Metadata.doc`. This document provides detailed information about the architecture and layout of a .NET assembly.

As an introduction, run the "other" PE dump utility, `dumpbin`, on the `HelloWorld` assembly that was the focus of the previous section, with the /all option. Part of the resulting output shows the raw data in the assembly, as shown in Listing 4.8.

LISTING 4.8 Raw Dump of Section #1 Data

```
RAW DATA #1
  0402000: D0 22 00 00 00 00 00 00 48 00 00 00 02 00 00 00  _"......H.......
  0402010: 7C 20 00 00 20 02 00 00 01 00 00 00 01 00 00 06  | .. ...........
  0402020: 00 00 00 00 00 00 00 00 00 00 00 00 00 00 00 00  ................
  0402030: 00 00 00 00 00 00 00 00 00 00 00 00 00 00 00 00  ................
  0402040: 00 00 00 00 00 00 00 00 00 00 00 00 00 00 00 00  ................
  0402050: 13 30 01 00 0B 00 00 00 00 00 00 00 72 01 00 00  .0..........r...
  0402060: 70 28 02 00 00 0A 2A 00 13 30 01 00 07 00 00 00  p(....*..0......
  0402070: 00 00 00 00 02 28 03 00 00 0A 2A 00 42 53 4A 42  .....(....*.BSJB
  0402080: 01 00 01 00 00 00 00 00 0C 00 00 00 76 31 2E 30  ............v1.0
  0402090: 2E 33 37 30 35 00 00 00 00 00 05 00 6C 00 00 00  .3705.......l...
  04020A0: D0 00 00 00 23 7E 00 00 3C 01 00 00 94 00 00 00  _...#~..<.......
  04020B0: 23 53 74 72 69 6E 67 73 00 00 00 00 D0 01 00 00  #Strings...._...
  04020C0: 1C 00 00 00 23 55 53 00 EC 01 00 00 10 00 00 00  ....#US.ì.......
  04020D0: 23 47 55 49 44 00 00 00 FC 01 00 00 24 00 00 00  #GUID...ü...$...
  04020E0: 23 42 6C 6F 62 00 00 00 00 00 00 00 01 00 00 01  #Blob...........
  04020F0: 47 14 00 00 09 00 00 00 00 FA 01 33 00 02 00 00  G........ú.3....
  0402100: 01 00 00 00 03 00 00 00 02 00 00 00 02 00 00 00  ................
  0402110: 03 00 00 00 01 00 00 00 01 00 00 00 01 00 00 00  ................
  0402120: 00 00 0A 00 01 00 00 00 00 00 06 00 29 00 22 00  ............).".
  0402130: 06 00 61 00 4E 00 06 00 80 00 22 00 00 00 00 00  ..a.N.....".....
  0402140: 01 00 00 00 00 00 01 00 01 00 00 00 10 00 30 00  ..............0.
  0402150: 36 00 05 00 01 00 01 00 50 20 00 00 00 00 96 00  6.......P ......
  0402160: 43 00 0A 00 01 00 68 20 00 00 00 00 86 18 48 00  C.....h ......H.
  0402170: 0E 00 01 00 11 00 48 00 12 00 19 00 88 00 18 00  ......H.........
  0402180: 09 00 48 00 0E 00 2E 00 0B 00 1D 00 04 80 00 00  ..H.............
  0402190: 00 00 00 00 00 00 00 00 00 00 00 00 00 00 75 00  ..............u.
  04021A0: 00 00 01 00 00 00 E4 0C 00 00 00 00 00 00 01 00  ......ä.........
  04021B0: 19 00 00 00 00 00 00 00 00 3C 4D 6F 64 75 6C 65  .........<Module
  04021C0: 3E 00 48 65 6C 6C 6F 57 6F 72 6C 64 2E 65 78 65  >.HelloWorld.exe
  04021D0: 00 6D 73 63 6F 72 6C 69 62 00 53 79 73 74 65 6D  .mscorlib.System
  04021E0: 00 4F 62 6A 65 63 74 00 48 65 6C 6C 6F 00 43 4C  .Object.Hello.CL
  04021F0: 52 55 6E 6C 65 61 73 68 65 64 00 4D 61 69 6E 00  RUnleashed.Main.
  0402200: 2E 63 74 6F 72 00 53 79 73 74 65 6D 2E 44 69 61  .ctor.System.Dia
  0402210: 67 6E 6F 73 74 69 63 73 00 44 65 62 75 67 67 61  gnostics.Debugga
```

LISTING 4.8 Continued

```
0402220: 62 6C 65 41 74 74 72 69 62 75 74 65 00 48 65 6C  bleAttribute.Hel
0402230: 6C 6F 57 6F 72 6C 64 00 43 6F 6E 73 6F 6C 65 00  loWorld.Console.
0402240: 57 72 69 74 65 4C 69 6E 65 00 00 00 00 19 48 00  WriteLine.....H.
0402250: 65 00 6C 00 6C 00 6F 00 20 00 77 00 6F 00 72 00  e.l.l.o. .w.o.r.
0402260: 6C 00 64 00 21 00 00 00 58 C8 84 0E 16 51 41 45  l.d.!...XÈ...QAE
0402270: AB 94 A9 86 DE 62 B1 7E 00 08 B7 7A 5C 56 19 34  «.©._b±~..·z\V.4
0402280: E0 89 03 00 00 01 03 20 00 01 05 20 02 01 02 02  à...... ... ....
0402290: 04 00 01 01 0E 06 01 00 00 01 00 00 C4 22 00 00  ...........Ä"..
04022A0: 00 00 00 00 00 00 00 00 DE 22 00 00 00 20 00 00  ........_"... ..
04022B0: 00 00 00 00 00 00 00 00 00 00 00 00 00 00 00 00  ................
04022C0: 00 00 00 00 D0 22 00 00 00 00 00 00 00 00 00 00  ...._"..........
04022D0: 00 00 5F 43 6F 72 45 78 65 4D 61 69 6E 00 6D 73  .._CorExeMain.ms
04022E0: 63 6F 72 65 65 2E 64 6C 6C 00 00 00 00 00 FF 25  coree.dll.....ÿ%
04022F0: 00 20 40 00                                      . @.
```

One of the entries in the CIL header table shown in Figure 4.2 is the beginning address (RVA) of the metadata directory. The beginning RVA of the metadata is 207C and its size is 214 hex, or 532 bytes long. Thus, the metadata for this assembly starts at 207C and runs to 2290. From Listing 4.8, the following forms the beginning of the metadata:

```
0402070: 00 00 00 00 02 28 03 00 00 0A 2A 00 42 53 4A 42  .....(....*.BSJB
0402080: 01 00 01 00 00 00 00 00 0C 00 00 00 76 31 2E 30  ............v1.0
0402090: 2E 33 37 30 35 00 00 00 00 00 05 00 6C 00 00 00  .3705.......l...
```

Other than the CIL header table indicating that the metadata starts at 207C, the other indication of the start of the metadata is the signature, "BJSB," followed by a version string that indicates the version of the CLR against which this assembly was compiled. You will see the magic number, hex, 42534A42, as the documented beginning of the metadata. This hex number translates into the four letters that represent the last name of four of the developers who worked on the CLR. After more data, you run into the string "v1.0.3705." This is the version string that indicates which version of the CLR this assembly was compiled against. Following the version string in Listing 4.8 are the following lines:

```
04020A0: D0 00 00 00 23 7E 00 00 3C 01 00 00 94 00 00 00  _...#~..<.......
04020B0: 23 53 74 72 69 6E 67 73 00 00 00 00 D0 01 00 00  #Strings...._...
04020C0: 1C 00 00 00 23 55 53 00 EC 01 00 00 10 00 00 00  ....#US.ì.......
04020D0: 23 47 55 49 44 00 00 00 FC 01 00 00 24 00 00 00  #GUID...ü...$...
```

Table 4.1 already gave a description of each of the streams; therefore, a detailed description is not required for each stream. However, you can see the names of the streams from the output and maybe even deduce where each of the streams start.

You can gain much information from a simple hex dump of the file. The following paragraphs contain a more formal presentation of the physical layout of an assembly.

In `CorHdr.h` or `WinNT.h`, the CLR header structure is specified as shown in Listing 4.9.

LISTING 4.9 CLR Header Structure

```
// CLR 2.0 header structure.
typedef struct IMAGE_COR20_HEADER
{
    // Header versioning
    ULONG                   cb;
    USHORT                  MajorRuntimeVersion;
    USHORT                  MinorRuntimeVersion;

    // Symbol table and startup information
    IMAGE_DATA_DIRECTORY    MetaData;
    ULONG                   Flags;
    ULONG                   EntryPointToken;

    // Binding information
    IMAGE_DATA_DIRECTORY    Resources;
    IMAGE_DATA_DIRECTORY    StrongNameSignature;

    // Regular fixup and binding information
    IMAGE_DATA_DIRECTORY    CodeManagerTable;
    IMAGE_DATA_DIRECTORY    VTableFixups;
    IMAGE_DATA_DIRECTORY    ExportAddressTableJumps;

    // Precompiled image info (internal use only - set to zero)
    IMAGE_DATA_DIRECTORY    ManagedNativeHeader;

} IMAGE_COR20_HEADER;
```

The most interesting piece of information that can be gathered from the CIL (CLR) header is the address of the metadata. IMAGE_DATA_DIRECTORY is another structure that contains two entries: a 4-byte value for the RVA and a 4-byte value for the size. Using this information, it is possible to find the location of the metadata. The metadata begins with a magic number followed by a description of each of the streams that is defined for the assembly. Each stream has the following format:

```
typedef struct _META_STREAM_HEADER
{
    DWORD Offset;
    DWORD Size;
    char Name[1];
} META_STREAM_HEADER, *PMETA_STREAM_HEADER;
```

The `Offset` member is the offset from the beginning of the metadata table, the `Size` member is the size of the stream, and the `Name` is a variable length name of the stream. (The standard names are `#~`, `#Strings`, `#US`, `#GUID`, and `#Blob`.) As an example from

Listing 4.8, you can see the string `#Strings`. Four bytes before the string is the size of the `#Strings` stream. Four bytes before that is the offset to the beginning of the stream, which is 013C. The beginning of the metadata is at 207C; therefore, the beginning of the `#String` stream is 21B8. You can similarly calculate the beginning addresses of the other streams.

One of the more important streams is the `#~` stream because it contains the metadata associated with each type and value in the assembly. From Listing 4.8, you can see that the offset to the beginning of the `#~` stream is hex, 6C. This would place the beginning of the `#~` at 20E8. The `#~` stream has the following header:

```
typedef struct _META_COMPOSITE_HEADER
{
    DWORD Reserved;
    BYTE MajorVersion;
    BYTE MinorVersion;
    BYTE HeapSizes;
    BYTE Padding;
    ULONGLONG Valid;
    ULONGLONG Sorted;
} META_COMPOSITE_HEADER, *PMETA_COMPOSITE_HEADER;
```

The most important members of this structure are the `HeapSizes` and `Valid` members.

The `HeapSizes` member indicates the size of the index that is required for the `#Strings`, `#GUID`, and `#Blob` streams. If bit 0 (0x01) is set, then more than 65,536 (2^{16}) strings are in the `#Strings` stream and all indexes into this stream require 4 bytes. If the bit is not set, then all indexes to the `#Strings` stream will use a 2-byte index. Similarly, if bit 1 (0x02) is set, then `#GUID` indexes are all 4 bytes rather than 2. And if bit 3 (0x04) is set, then the indexes for the `#Blob` stream are required to be 4 bytes.

Notice that the `#US` stream is absent from this list. This is because all access to this stream comes from the code (IL). The `ldstr` IL instruction references this stream exclusively. The `ldstr` instruction takes a single 4-byte argument with the upper byte set to 0x70, and the remaining bytes are the index into the table. Inherently, all indexes into the `#US` stream use 3 bytes.

The `Valid` member of the `#~` stream header is a 64-bit (ULONGLONG) number that has a bit set for each table that is present in the assembly. For the `Hello World` application, this field is 0x0000000900001447. This number has bits 0, 1, 2, 6, 10, 12, 32, and 35 set, so the corresponding tables are valid and present in the assembly.

Immediately following the `#~` stream header is an array of 4-byte values that indicate the number of rows in the specified valid table. Again, in the `Hello World` application, the first 4-byte value indicates the number of rows that are in table 0. The next 4-byte value indicates the number of rows that are in table 1, the next for table 2, then table 6, table 10, and so forth. Because 8 bits are set in the `Valid` field, 8 4-byte values should follow the header.

Immediately following the table row size array is the data for each of the tables. Table 4.2 summarizes the information that is contained in each of the possible tables. The following sections detail the information that is contained in each of the tables for this `Hello World` application.

The Module Table (0x00)

This table has five columns, and it is an error for an assembly to have more than one row in this table. The first column is a 2-byte entry that is labeled in the documentation as `Generation`. This is essentially a reserved column that is always zero. The next column is an index into the `#Strings` stream that must be non-zero, and the index must refer to a non-null string that is the name of the module. This index can either be 2 bytes long or 4 bytes long depending on how large the `#Strings` stream is. The exact size of the index is determined from the `HeapSizes` member of the `#~` stream header (META_COMPOSITE_HEADER). Your code should have a check similar to the following:

```
if(t.HeapSizes & 0x01)
{
    wcscpy(lBuffer, pView->StringTableEntry(*((ULONG *)row)).c_str());
    row += 4;
}
else
{
    wcscpy(lBuffer, pView->StringTableEntry(*((USHORT *)row)).c_str());
    row += 2;
}
```

Listing 4.10 shows how to retrieve a string from the `#Strings` stream given an index (offset).

LISTING 4.10 Returning a String Given an Index into the `#Strings` Stream

```
std::wstring CAssemblyView::StringTableEntry(DWORD index) const
{
    if(index > stringsTableSize)
        return L"";
    PBYTE str = stringsTable + index;

    std::wstring ret;
    int nchars = MultiByteToWideChar(CP_UTF8, 0,
                                     (const char *)str,
                                     -1, NULL, 0);
```

LISTING 4.10 Continued

```
    wchar_t* buffer = (wchar_t *)_alloca(nchars);
    int err = MultiByteToWideChar(CP_UTF8, 0,
                                  (const char *)str,
                                  -1, buffer, nchars);
    if(err == 0)
    {
        ATLTRACE(L"Conversion error\n");
        return L"";
    }
    ret = buffer;
    return ret;
}
```

The routine shown in Listing 4.10 depends on two pieces of information that have been cached: the address of the `#Strings` stream (`stringsTable`) and the size of the `#Strings` stream (`stringsTableSize`). Both of these variables can be initialized from the metadata table (see Listing 4.9 and the associated discussion, especially the META_STREAM_HEADER structure). Each entry in the `#Strings` stream is a UTF-8 encoded string. Each index into the `#Strings` stream is assumed to be an offset from the beginning of the stream. The code in Listing 4.10 first calls `MultiByteToWideChar` to find out how many characters are required to convert this string to its wide character equivalent. Next, a buffer is allocated to hold the converted string, and the string is converted from UTF-8 to wide character (Unicode). Finally, the converted string is assumed to be '\0' terminated; therefore, the buffer is assigned to an STL `wstring` and the string is returned. For the `Hello World` application, the name of the module is simply `HelloWorld.exe`.

The next column in the Module table is an index into the `#GUID` stream that is identified as the Mvid, or the Module Version Identifier. This Globally Unique Identifier (GUID) is a 16-byte number that uniquely identifies a particular module. The CLR does not use this information, but compilers that are generating an assembly should add this identifier to support debuggers and other tools that might need to differentiate a module from a previous version of the same module. This column is a simple one-base index into the `#GUID` stream. Listing 4.11 shows how to retrieve a string representation of the GUID from the `#GUID` stream.

LISTING 4.11 Returning a String Representation of a GUID from the `#GUID` Stream

```
std::wstring CAssemblyView::GUIDTableEntry(DWORD index) const
{
    if(index*sizeof(GUID) > guidTableSize)
        return L"";
    if(index == 0)
```

LISTING 4.11 Continued

```
        return L"";
    // From Section 21
    // "The Guid heap is an array of GUIDs, each 16 bytes wide.
    //  Its first element is numbered 1, its second 2, and so on."
    GUID *pguid = (GUID*)(guidTable + (index - 1) * 16);
    WCHAR lBuffer[64];
    StringFromGUID2(*pguid, lBuffer, sizeof(lBuffer));
    return lBuffer;
}
```

The code in this listing also depends on the address of the `#GUID` stream and the size of the `#GUID` stream to have been previously cached. In the sample, this was done when the metadata table was parsed. For the `Hello World` application, this routine returns a string such as the following:

```
{23D4854F-DA7F-44D0-B1AB-1C07D358DED1}
```

The remaining two columns in the table are also indexes into the `#GUID` stream, but they are marked as reserved and always zero.

The `TypeRef` Table (0x01)

The `TypeRef` table contains three columns for each row. A row exists for each type that is referenced in the assembly. This table also has a pointer to where this type can be resolved—where it is defined. The pointer to the place where the type can be resolved is labeled as the `ResolutionScope` and is the first column in the `TypeRef` table.

`ResolutionScope` is a coded index into one of four different tables: `Module`, `ModuleRef`, `AssemblyRef`, and `TypeRef`. In a coded index, the least significant bits indicate the table to which the index points. Four tables exist, so it takes 2 bits to encode the table information.

> **Note**
>
> The released documentation incorrectly indicates that 3 bits are required to encode the table information. The Partition II Specification that can be downloaded from `http://msdn.micorosft.com/net/ecma/` correctly indicates 2 bits to encode the table information.

Table 4.4 shows how the 2 bits are used to encode the table information.

TABLE 4.4 `ResolutionScope` Encoded Index

ResolutionScope Table	*Tag*
Module	0
ModuleRef	1
AssemblyRef	2
TypeRef	3

You must determine how many bytes are required for the index. If the maximum number of rows in any one of these tables multiplied by 4 (2^2 because of the 2 bits to represent the encoding) exceeds 65,536 (the maximum value of a 2-byte integer), then the index has to be 4 bytes rather than just 2 bytes. Listing 4.12 shows one way of accomplishing this task of determining the size of the index.

LISTING 4.12 Calculating the Size of a `ResolutionScope` Index

```
maxRows = 0;
// Module
it = tables.find(Module);
if(it != tables.end() &&
   it->second.Rows > maxRows)
{
    maxRows = it->second.Rows;
}
// ModuleRef
it = tables.find(ModuleRef);
if(it != tables.end() &&
   it->second.Rows > maxRows)
{
    maxRows = it->second.Rows;
}
// AssemblyRef
it = tables.find(AssemblyRef);
if(it != tables.end() &&
   it->second.Rows > maxRows)
{
    maxRows = it->second.Rows;
}
// TypeRef
it = tables.find(TypeRef);
if(it != tables.end() &&
   it->second.Rows > maxRows)
{
    maxRows = it->second.Rows;
}
    it = tables.find(tableID);
```

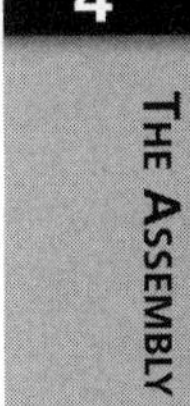

LISTING 4.12 Continued

```
if((maxRows << 2) > 0xffff)
{
    bytes = 4;
    it->second.IndexSizes |=  0x01;
}
else
{
    bytes = 2;
    it->second.IndexSizes &= ~0x01;
}
```

Listing 4.12 finds the number of rows in each of the tables that could be specified in a `ResolutionScope` coded index and computes the maximum number of rows contained in any one of these tables. The maximum number of rows is multiplied by four (shifted to the left by two bits) and compared with the maximum value that can be represented by a 2-byte value. If the comparison shows that 4 bytes are required, then a bit is set and this calculation does not need to be performed multiple times. If the comparison is false, then an index of 2 bytes is sufficient.

The remainder of the coded index is the index. Using this index and the table information that was encoded in the first 2 bits, you can find out how to resolve this type.

The next two columns are indexes into the `#Strings` stream for the name and namespace, respectively. The same process that was illustrated in Listing 4.10 (along with the associated discussion) can be applied to retrieving the names and namespaces of the referenced types. For the `Hello World` application, three rows correspond to **`System.Object`**, **`System.Diagnostics.DebuggableAttribute`**, and **`System.Console`**. Each of these references is resolved in the `mscorlib` assembly.

The `TypeDef` Table (0x02)

This table contains a definition for all the types that the assembly defines. Each row contains a definition for a different type, and each row contains six columns.

The first column is a 4-byte mask containing attributes that are enumerated by the `CorTypeAttr` enumeration in `CorHdr.h`. These attributes detail the accessibility of the type—whether the type is an interface or class; whether the class is abstract, sealed, or special; and how this class treats strings (Unicode, ANSI, or auto).

The next two columns in the `TypeDef` table are indexes into the `#Strings` stream and indicate the name and namespace, respectively. Use code similar to Listing 4.10 to retrieve the string from the `#Strings` stream.

The next column is a coded index that is similar to the `ResolutionScope` coded index that was encountered in the previous section. The coded index indicates the base class for this type and is given the name `Extends`. This coded index also requires 2 bits to encode the tables, but the tables that can be selected are the `TypeDef`, `TypeRef`, or `TypeSpec` tables. Table 4.5 shows how the particular table is encoded into this variable.

TABLE 4.5 `Extends` Encoded Index

Extends Table	*Tag*
TypeDef	0
TypeRef	1
TypeSpec	2

The row that the index specifies along with the table that the tag encodes will give you the class from which the type is derived. The `Hello World` application has two rows in the `TypeDef` table: one for "<Module>", which does not extend a class, and one for `CLRUnleashed.Hello`, which extends **`System.Object`**.

The next column is an index into the `Field` table. Actually, it is a starting index for a field list. Listing 4.13 shows how to get a list of fields for a type given the starting index.

LISTING 4.13 Listing a Field list

```
// FieldList
if(t.IndexSizes & 0x08)
{
    fields = *((DWORD *)row);
    if(index < t.Rows - 1)
        endFields = *((DWORD *)(row + t.RowSize));
    else
        endFields = 0;
    row += 4;
}
else
{
    fields = *((USHORT *)row);
    if(index < t.Rows - 1)
        endFields = *((USHORT *)(row + t.RowSize));
    else
        endFields = 0;
    row += 2;
}
. . .
// Only need to get a field table pointer if at the
// end of the list to see if this type has fields or not.
```

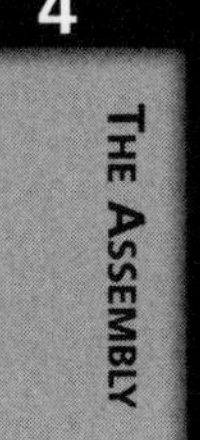

LISTING 4.13 Continued

```
if(index >= t.Rows - 1 ||
   fields < endFields)
{
    MetaDataConstantIterator it = pView->MetaDataFind((TableType)FieldDef);
    if(it != pView->MetaDataEnd())
    {
        // The start has to be within the allowed
        // parameter list values.
        if(fields < t.Rows)
        {
            // If at the end of the method list,
            // make sure that the end
            // of the parameter list is set.
            if(index >= t.Rows - 1)
                endFields = it->second.Rows + 1;
            while(fields < endFields)
            {
                HandleSingleFieldDef(fields - 1, it->second, pView, fieldsItem);
                fields++;
            }
        }
    }
}
```

The first section of code checks for the size of the Field table to ensure that the correctly sized index is retrieved. If the row in the `TypeDef` table is not the last row, then the ending index for the field is that referenced by the field list column in the next row of the `TypeDef` table. If the row is the last in the `TypeDef` table, then the last field for this class will be the last row in the fields table. If this class has no fields, then the field list index will either be zero or the same as the field list index in the next row of the `TypeDef` table.

The last column of the table is an index into the `MethodDef` table. Like the field list of the previous paragraph, this index is the starting point for a list of methods that are part of this class. Retrieving the methods that are associated with a given type is similar to the technique used in Listing 4.13. For the `Hello World` application, two methods are part of the `Hello` class: the constructor (**`.ctor`**) and **`Main`**.

The `MethodDef` Table (0x06)

This table contains a row for every method that is defined in this assembly. Each row contains six columns, as described next.

The `MethodDef` Table RVA

The first column in the `MethodDef` table is a 4-byte RVA for the IL instructions that make up this method. At the beginning of every instruction block is a header that indicates the type of instruction block that follows. The two kinds of instruction blocks are tiny and fat. The least significant 3 bits of the first byte of the instruction block indicates whether the instruction block is tiny or fat. If the 3 bits are 0x2, then the instructions are in a tiny format. If the 3 bits are 0x3, then the instructions are in a fat format.

For a method to have its IL instructions formatted in a tiny format, the following must be true:

- No local variables exist.
- No exceptions exist.
- No extra data sections exist.
- The operand stack cannot be longer than eight entries.
- The method is less than 64 bytes.

If these conditions are true, then a method can be coded tiny. The other 6 bits of the first byte contain the size of the method. IL instructions start with the next byte. Chapter 5, "Intermediate Language Basics," contains a detailed explanation of IL opcodes. That chapter should give you a good idea of how to go about translating the binary opcodes to IL instructions.

If any of the conditions specified for a tiny format are not true, then the method uses a fat format. The fat format header has the following structure:

```
typedef struct IMAGE_COR_ILMETHOD_FAT
{
    unsigned Flags    : 12;
    unsigned Size     :  4;
    unsigned MaxStack : 16;
    DWORD   CodeSize;
    mdSignature   LocalVarSigTok;
} IMAGE_COR_ILMETHOD_FAT;
```

Other than indicating that this is a fat format, two additional flags exist: one flag indicates that the local variables should be initialized, and another indicates that additional sections of code follow the instruction block.

All CLS-compliant code initializes local variables to a known state. One instance in which local variables are not initialized is in C# when the method has been marked as **`unsafe`**. In such a method, initialization of the local variables does not take place.

As of the first version of the .NET Framework, the only section that follows an instruction block is exception information. Thus, the "more sections" flag being set is equivalent to indicating that exception information follows the instruction block.

The `Size` field of the fat header indicates the size of the header in `DWORD`s. Currently, the `Size` is always 3 because the header is 12 bytes long, or 3 `DWORD`s.

The `CodeSize` field of the fat header indicates the size of the instruction block following the header in bytes.

The `LocalVarSigTok` field of the fat header describes the layout of the local variables on the stack. This token is either zero, which indicates that no local variables exist, or it is a token that indexes the `StandAloneSig` table. Each row in the `StandAloneSig` table has only one column that indexes the `#Blob` stream. The `LocalVarSigTok` is essentially an index into the `#Blob` stream. Listing 4.14 shows the basic code that is required to crack the local variable signature blob.

LISTING 4.14 Decoding a Local Signature Blob

```
DWORD localVariables = *((DWORD*)&instructions[8]);
if(localVariables == 0)
. . .
else
{
    BYTE localTable = (BYTE)(localVariables >> 24);
. . .
    MetaDataConstantIterator it = pView->MetaDataFind((TableType)localTable);
    if(it != pView->MetaDataEnd())
    {
        PBYTE standAloneSigRow;
        standAloneSigRow = it->second.Address + it->second.RowSize *
➥((localVariables & 0x00FFFFFF) - 1);
        DWORD signatureBlobIndex;
        if(it->second.HeapSizes & 0x04)
        {
            signatureBlobIndex = *((DWORD *)standAloneSigRow);
            standAloneSigRow += 4;
        }
        else
        {
            signatureBlobIndex = *((USHORT *)standAloneSigRow);
            standAloneSigRow += 2;
        }
        DWORD signatureBlobSize = 0;
        PBYTE signatureBlob = pView->BlobTableEntry(signatureBlobIndex,
➥&signatureBlobSize);
        ASSERT(*signatureBlob == IMAGE_CEE_CS_CALLCONV_LOCAL_SIG);
        signatureBlob += 1;
        DWORD index = 0;
        DWORD localVariableCount;
        index += CorSigUncompressData(&signatureBlob[index],
➥&localVariableCount);
        signatureBlob += index;
. . .
        for(USHORT variableIndex = 0; variableIndex < localVariableCount;
➥variableIndex++)
```

LISTING 4.14 Continued

```
        {
. . .
            // Constraint
            while(*signatureBlob == ELEMENT_TYPE_PINNED)
            {
. . .
                signatureBlob += 1;
            }
            if(*signatureBlob == ELEMENT_TYPE_BYREF)
            {
. . .
                signatureBlob += 1;
            }
            index = 0;
            TypeSig(signatureBlob, index);
. . .
            signatureBlob += index;
        }
    }
}
```

The first step is to get the local signature token. The most significant byte of any token contains the table to which the index applies. In this case, it must be the `StandAloneSigTok` table. If the token is zero, then no local variables exist. A reference is retrieved to the `StandAloneSigTok` table, and the only column in that table is used as an index into the `#Blob` stream. Using the index, a pointer is obtained to the blob that describes the local variables.

The blob that describes the local variables is prefixed by a single byte, which is 0x07 (IMAGE_CEE_CS_CALLCONV_LOCAL_SIG). Following the header byte is a compressed integer that contains the count (from 1 to 0xFFFE) of local variables for the method. A compressed integer can be represented by 1 to 4 bytes, depending on the upper 2 bits of the first byte. If the most significant bit is 0, then the integer is wholly contained in a single byte (thus, values from 0 to 0x7F are compressed to a single byte). If the most significant bit is set, then the integer is represented by 2 bytes; if the most significant 2 bits are set, then the integer is represented by 4 bytes (no compression). Luckily, a routine is available (`CorSigUncompressData`) to perform this decompression as part of the SDK.

The last part of the blob that describes the local variables is an array of types and possible modifiers for each of the local variables. The modifiers take the form of either a constraint or a `ByRef` modifier. The types that are available for local variables can be any of the types that the CLR supports.

Note

Currently, the only constraint is whether the local variable is pinned. A pinned local variable cannot have its address changed. This typically occurs with unsafe code blocks. A more detailed discussion of pinning and its performance implications can be found in Chapter 10, "Memory/Resource Management."

Because the `Hello World` application (`HelloWorld.cs`) has no routines that require local variables, try building `HelloWorld1.cs` to test the assembly for local variables.

The final section of this instruction block is the exception information. If the Flags portion of the fat header indicates that "MoreSects" exist, then exception information follows the instructions on the first 4-byte boundary.

Two types of exception information exist: fat and small. Listing 4.15 shows one way to decode the exception information.

LISTING 4.15 Decoding Exception Information

```
do
{
    exceptionKind = (*exceptionPointer & CorILMethod_Sect_KindMask);
    if(exceptionKind & CorILMethod_Sect_FatFormat)
    {
        IMAGE_COR_ILMETHOD_SECT_FAT *pExceptionHeader =
           (IMAGE_COR_ILMETHOD_SECT_FAT *)exceptionPointer;
. . .
        exceptionPointer += sizeof(IMAGE_COR_ILMETHOD_SECT_FAT);
        int clauses = (pExceptionHeader->DataSize -
                          sizeof(IMAGE_COR_ILMETHOD_SECT_FAT)) /
                          sizeof(IMAGE_COR_ILMETHOD_SECT_EH_CLAUSE_FAT);
        IMAGE_COR_ILMETHOD_SECT_EH_CLAUSE_FAT *pExceptionClause =
            (IMAGE_COR_ILMETHOD_SECT_EH_CLAUSE_FAT *)exceptionPointer;
        for(int i = 0; i < clauses; i++)
        {
. . .
            pExceptionClause++;
        }
        exceptionPointer += sizeof(IMAGE_COR_ILMETHOD_SECT_EH_CLAUSE_FAT) *
                             clauses;
    }
    else
    {
        IMAGE_COR_ILMETHOD_SECT_SMALL *pExceptionHeader =
           (IMAGE_COR_ILMETHOD_SECT_SMALL *)exceptionPointer;
. . .
```

LISTING 4.15 Continued

```
        exceptionPointer += sizeof(IMAGE_COR_ILMETHOD_SECT_SMALL);
        // Reserved word
        exceptionPointer += 2;
        int clauses = (pExceptionHeader->DataSize -
                           (sizeof(IMAGE_COR_ILMETHOD_SECT_SMALL) + 2)) /
                            sizeof(IMAGE_COR_ILMETHOD_SECT_EH_CLAUSE_SMALL);
        IMAGE_COR_ILMETHOD_SECT_EH_CLAUSE_SMALL *pExceptionClause =
           (IMAGE_COR_ILMETHOD_SECT_EH_CLAUSE_SMALL *)exceptionPointer;
        std::wstring tokenString;
        for(int i = 0; i < clauses; i++)
        {
            pView->MetaDataTokenToString(pExceptionClause->ClassToken,
                                         tokenString);
. . .
            pExceptionClause++;
        }
        exceptionPointer += sizeof(IMAGE_COR_ILMETHOD_SECT_EH_CLAUSE_SMALL) *
                                clauses;
    }
} while(exceptionKind & CorILMethod_Sect_MoreSects);
```

The code in Listing 4.15 loops until it is determined that no more sections are available. The code checks the first byte to determine the type of exception information and then processes the exception appropriately. Whether in a small format or in a fat format, each entry in the exception array includes the type of handler, the beginning address of the protected region, the byte count of the protected region, the beginning address of the handler, and the byte count for the handler. It is possible and common for the same protected region to be referenced by more than one handler.

The original `HelloWorld.cs` code does not contain exception handling. If you compile `HelloWorld2.cs`, exception handling will be put in the assembly on which you can test your code.

The `MethodDef` Table Flags

This section describes two columns. The first column of the `MethodDef` table is a 2-byte value that contains information in the form of flags about the implementation of this method. These flags indicate whether the method is managed or unmanaged, whether the code is in IL or native instructions, and various bits describing interop options.

The next column is a 2-byte value that contains information in the form of flags about the accessibility and other attributes of this method. These flags contain information about the method's accessibility, its scope, and its inheritance and inheritability status.

The `MethodDef` Table Name

The next column of the `MethodDef` table is an index into the `#Strings` stream that contains the name of the method. You can use this index to retrieve a string from the `#Strings` stream with code similar to Listing 4.10.

The `MethodDef` Table Signature

The next column in the `MethodDef` table is an index into the `#Blob` stream containing a description of the signature of the method. This includes the return type and the types and count of the parameters. A signature blob is one of the more complex data types in the assembly. It consists of the following parts:

- Instance flag—This flag, called the HASTHIS flag, indicates that the method is a part of class.
- The parameter count—This is a compressed integer that indicates the number of parameters that the method takes.
- Return type—This is a byte or sequence of bytes that describes the return type.
- List of parameters and the associated type—This is an array of sequences of bytes that describes each parameter and its associated type.

The `MethodDef` Table Parameter List

The last column in the `MethodDef` table gives a starting index into the `ParamDef` table. The resulting list gives you the name of parameters that the method uses.

Because `HelloWorld.cs` does not contain a method that has parameters, you might want to build `HelloWorld1.cs` to test an assembly that has this extra information about parameters.

The `MemberRef` Table (0x0A)

This table contains information about each member that the assembly references. Each row in the table contains three columns. The first column is a coded index into one of the `TypeRef`, `ModuleRef`, `MethodDef`, `TypeSpec`, or `TypeDef` tables. This coded index provides information about the class that contains the referenced method. The next column is an index into the `#Strings` stream, giving a name to the method that is referenced. The last column is an index into the `#Blob` stream, supplying a signature for the method in about the same format as that provided by the blob reference for a signature in the `MethodDef` table.

For the `Hello World` application, three rows exist: one for the constructor for the **`DebuggableAttribute`**, one for the constructor for Object, and one describing the **`WriteLine`** method of the **`System.Console`** class.

The `CustomAttribute` Table (0x0C)

This table contains a row for each custom attribute that is applied to any portion of the assembly. Custom attributes are not just the attributes that you define. Custom attributes refer to any of the attributes that could be assigned to your code. Each row in the `CustomAttribute` table has three columns. The first column is a coded index into virtually any table that could exist in the assembly. This coded index describes the parent of the attribute. For example, if an attribute is applied to an assembly, then the parent of the attribute is the assembly. If an attribute is applied to a class, then the parent of the attribute is the class. The next column is a coded index into the `MethodDef` or `MethodRef` tables, providing information about the constructor for the attribute. The final column is an index into the `#Blob` stream, describing the value or values given to each parameter in the attribute.

The `Hello World` application has only one row in this table that corresponds to the **`DebuggableAttribute`** that is automatically assigned to the assembly.

The `Assembly` Table (0x20)

This table is like the `Module` table in that it can contain one row at the most. The row in the `Assembly` table contains nine columns. The first column is a 4-byte constant indicating the hashing algorithm that this assembly uses. Currently, the only available hash algorithm options are None or SHA1. The next four columns contain major, minor, build, and revision version numbers. For example, an assembly that is assigned a version of 1.2.3.4 would have a column in this table with the major number set to 1, the minor number set to 2, the build number set to 3, and the revision number set to 4. The next 4-byte column contains flags that describe the assembly. Except for a flag that indicates the presence or absence of a public key, the remaining flags are reserved. The next column in this table contains an index into the `#Blob` stream, providing a public key for the assembly. The next column is an index into the `#Strings` stream to provide a name for the assembly. The last column in the `Assembly` table is an index into the `#Strings` stream, providing a culture identifier. Cultural identifiers are discussed in Chapter 18.

The `Hello World` application has one row in the `Assembly` table. This application specifies the SHA1 hashing algorithm, a version of 0.0.0.0, flags set to zero, the name of the assembly as `HelloWorld`, the public key set to zero, and no culture assigned to the assembly.

The `AssemblyRef` Table (0x23)

This table contains a row for each assembly that the assembly references. Each row has nine columns that have much the same meaning as in the `Assembly` table, but the order is changed. The first four columns contain the version information (major, minor, build, and revision) for the referenced assembly. The next column is a 4-byte value that contains the flags for the referenced assembly. The next column is an index into the `#Blob` stream that indicates a token or the public key that identifies the author of the referenced assembly. The next column contains an index into the `#Strings` stream, providing a name for the referenced assembly. The next column is also an index into the `#Strings` stream, indicating the culture that is to be assigned to the assembly. The final column is an index into the `#Blob` stream, providing a hash value for the referenced assembly.

The `Hello World` application has one row for the `AssemblyRef` table. This row references the `mscorlib` assembly, which provides much of the .NET Framework base class library functionality.

`MetaViewer` is an application that was built to provide a jump start in analyzing the architecture of an assembly. The complete source for this application is provided in the `MetaViewer` directory. Figure 4.7 shows what this application looks like when it is run.

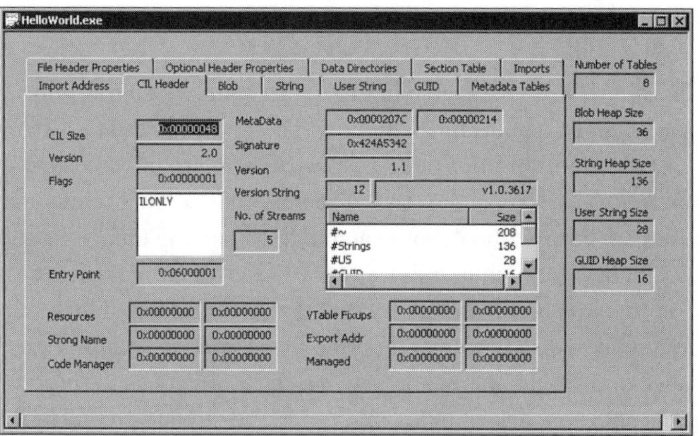

FIGURE 4.7
MetaViewer application.

To load an assembly into this application, use the File, Open menu item, which brings up a File dialog box so that you can browse for the assembly that you want to load into the application. The Metadata Tables tab contains a tree view of all the tables within the `#~` stream. If a node can be expanded, then double-clicking the node expands it.

The `MetaViewer` application does not provide the pretty view of methods that other tools such as `ILDasm` do, but it does provide a solid framework from which to explore the internals of an assembly.

Summary

This chapter showed the importance of the assembly and the metadata within it. Metadata allows for many features within a programming environment that would not be possible without it. To use metadata, you must be able to access it. This chapter showed two methods to look at the metadata. The first method uses a set of unmanaged COM APIs that should be suitable for most applications. These COM APIs contain sufficient detail to crack most assembly metadata. If you require a more detailed description of the metadata or you cannot depend on a COM component in your program, then you might want to crack the physical layout of the assembly to get at the metadata information.

CHAPTER

Intermediate Language Basics

In This Chapter

As the saying goes, "All roads lead to Rome." With the .NET Framework, all languages lead to Intermediate Language (IL). Specifically, for Microsoft platforms, it is MSIL. This chapter is about developing a sort of IL literacy so that you are able to at least read and understand basic IL instructions. You might be tempted to skip this chapter because you might feel like learning IL is like learning x86 assembly code. You program at a high level in C, C++, or VB, and you never have to worry about the assembly instructions that are generated. To a certain extent, you are right. It is certainly possible to go a long time programming in C# without having to know IL. However, knowing IL will be another tool in your tool chest that allows you to better understand the inner workings of your code and other third-party code.

ILDASM becomes a valuable debugging tool when you are relying on tools such as `SoapSuds` (see Chapter 13, "Building Distributed Applications with .NET Remoting") or tlbimp (see Chapter 8, "Using COM/COM+ from Managed Code"), or if you just want to see a version of an assembly for use with deployment. This chapter tries to remove any fear that you might feel with IL. Although you might not be ready to do all of your development in IL after reading this chapter, you will at least feel comfortable looking at IL and knowing what is going on. Before explaining the basics about IL, this chapter offers a brief tutorial on ILDSAM, which will become the main gateway into IL code.

Where Does IL Fit into the Development Scheme?

As the name implies, IL sits in the middle of a development scheme. A programmer works in one of the supported languages generating code. To run the code, this high-level language is compiled. Normally when a language is compiled, the output of the compiler is a program that can be directly run. With a managed code system, the compiler produces IL code that is turned into instructions that are specific to the machine on which the IL code is loaded by the Just-In-Time (JIT) compiler. This process is illustrated in Figure 5.1.

Rather than turn all of the IL code into machine instructions, only those methods that are used are turned into machine code. If the JIT compiler has already compiled the code, then the code is just executed. If the JIT compiler has not yet seen the code, then the code is compiled and then executed. This process goes on until either all of the IL code has been JIT compiled or the application ends.

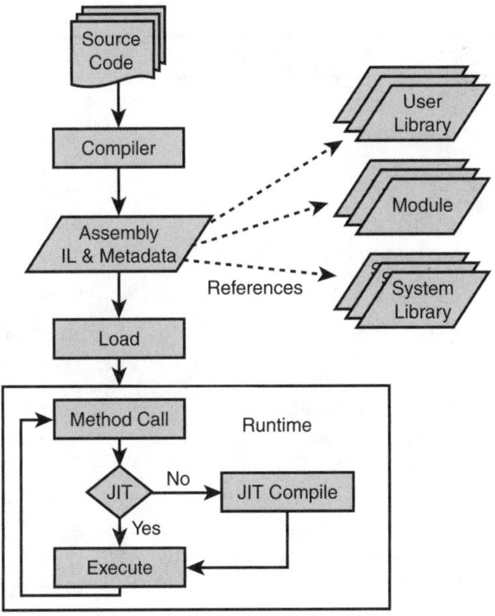

FIGURE 5.1
Basic runtime structure.

ILDASM Tutorial

The `ILDasm` tool (MSIL Disassembler) is an indispensable tool for most developers. This tool allows the developer to parse any .NET Framework Assembly and generate a human-readable format. It ships with the .Net Framework SDK and it is well worth your time to learn how to use it. To present the information in as compact a form as possible, `ILDasm` encodes key information about a type or section of the assembly with about 13 different symbols. After you become familiar with these symbols, you will have a much easier time understanding the UI output of `ILDasm`. Table 5.1 shows a list of the symbols and their meanings along with a small code snippet from C# and IL to illustrate how the data that is represented by the symbol can appear in your code.

TABLE 5.1 ILDASM Symbols

Icon	*Description*	*C#*	*IL*
	More Info		
	Namespace	`namespace CLRUnleashed.IL`	`.namespace CLRUnleashed.IL`
	Class	`class MathOperations`	`.class ... MathOperations`

TABLE 5.1 Continued

Icon	Description	C#	IL
	Interface	`interface IBasicArithmetic`	`.class interface ... IBasicOperations`
	Struct	`struct Complex {. . .}`	`.class ... Complex extends ValueType`
	Enum	`enum OperationType {. . .}`	`.class ... OperationType extends Enum`
	Method	`int Add(int a, int b) {. . .}`	`.method ... int32 Add(int32 a, int32 b)`
	Static Method	`static void Main(string[] args)`	`.method ... static void Main(string[] args)`
	Field	`int addCount;`	`.field ... int32 addCount`
	Static Field	`static int constructionCount = 0;`	`.field ... static int32 constructionCount`
	Event	`event OperationHandler Operation;`	`.event ... OperationHandler Operation`
	Property	`int Count { get {...} }`	`.property int32 Count()`
	Manifest		

A simple sample program has been put together that really doesn't have functionality except to illustrate each of the symbols of ILDasm. Many of the details of these data types are explored in later chapters, but for now, just focus on the source to IL mapping. ILSampler is in the `ILSampler` subdirectory. Compile this sample and use `ILDasm` to look at the code that is generated.

Note

As a reminder, the MSIL Disassemblier (`ILDasm`) is shipped with the .NET Framework SDK and is in `\Program Files\Microsoft Visual Studio .NET\FrameworkSDK\bin` as ILDasm.exe.

Basic IL

The CLR is what causes your code to execute. The CLR is like a virtual CPU. Just like your x86 CPU pulls in an instruction at a time (with pre-fetch, cache, and so forth, it might not be as simple as that, but logically, this is what is happening), you can think of the CLR as pushing and pulling variables from the stack and executing instructions. That doesn't happen in real life, but the model forms a basis for understanding IL. Because IL is "intermediate," it cannot depend on a CPU execution model. It cannot assume that registers will be available, even though most modern CPUs have registers; the number and types of registers vary greatly between CPUs. IL does not even have the concept of registers. IL is completely stack based. Instruction arguments are pushed on the stack and operations pull the variables off of the stack. In IL-speak, the process of pushing a variable onto the stack or copying from memory to the stack is called *loading*, and the process of writing to a variable on the stack from memory is called *storing*.

Consider the C# code in Listing 5.1.

LISTING 5.1 C# Code to Illustrate the Virtual Stack

```
public int LocalTest(int i, int j, int k)
{
    int a;
    int b;
    int c;
    int d;
    a = i;
    b = a + j;
    c = b + k;
    d = c + i;
    return i + j + k;
}
```

When the compiler compiles the C# code in Listing 5.1, a signature for the function is generated that looks like Listing 5.2.

LISTING 5.2 IL Function Declaration

```
.method public hidebysig instance int32  LocalTest(int32 i,
                                                   int32 j,
                                                   int32 k) cil managed
{
```

Following the signature, the compiler computes slots that the execution engine requires. The amount of stack that is allocated for the method appears right after the signature declaration. Following the stack declaration, the compiler initializes (if needed) and declares each of the local variables that is required to evaluate this method. The resulting IL looks something like the snippet of IL code shown in Listing 5.3.

LISTING 5.3 IL Virtual Stack Allocation

```
// Code size       28 (0x1c)
.maxstack  2
.locals init ([0] int32 a,
         [1] int32 b,
         [2] int32 c,
         [3] int32 d,
         [4] int32 CS$00000003$00000000)
```

Notice that this routine requires two stack slots to execute. One of the functions performed by the compiler (to IL) is to determine how large the stack needs to be. For this example, it has been determined that no more than two stack slots will ever be required.

Arguments are referenced with ldarg.1 (one-based except for the Argument Zero, which is discussed later). Local variables are referenced by ldloc.0 (zero-based). Listing 5.4 shows an example of the IL code that is used to push an argument (argument 1) onto the stack and store it in a variable (location zero).

LISTING 5.4 IL Storing a Number

```
IL_0000:  ldarg.1
IL_0001:  stloc.0
```

This puts argument number one on the stack (the variable i) and stores what is on the stack to location 0 (the variable a).

Listing 5.5 shows what the IL code would look like to add two numbers.

LISTING 5.5 IL Adding Two Numbers

```
IL_0002:  ldloc.0
IL_0003:  ldarg.2
IL_0004:  add
IL_0005:  stloc.1
```

This loads what is at location 0 (the variable a), loads argument number two, and adds them. This result is stored at location 1 (which is the variable b).

Every instance method is passed the address of the object's memory. This argument is called Argument Zero and is never explicitly shown in the method's signature. Therefore, even though the `.ctor` method looks like it receives zero arguments, it actually receives one argument. Listing 5.6 shows the source for a constructor.

LISTING 5.6 `MathOperations` Constructor

```
public MathOperations()
{
    constructionCount++;
}
```

Listing 5.7 shows the IL code that the compiler generates, as shown by `ILDasm`.

LISTING 5.7 `MathOperations` Constructor

```
IL_0000:  ldarg.0
IL_0001:  ldc.i4.0
IL_0002:  stfld       int32 CLRUnleashed.IL.MathOperations::addCount
IL_0007:  ldarg.0
IL_0008:  ldc.i4.0
IL_0009:  stfld       int32 CLRUnleashed.IL.MathOperations::subtractCount
IL_000e:  ldarg.0
IL_000f:  ldc.i4.0
IL_0010:  stfld       int32 CLRUnleashed.IL.MathOperations::multiplyCount
IL_0015:  ldarg.0
IL_0016:  ldc.i4.0
IL_0017:  stfld       int32 CLRUnleashed.IL.MathOperations::divideCount
IL_001c:  ldarg.0
IL_001d:  call        instance void [mscorlib]System.Object::.ctor()
IL_0022:  ldsfld      int32 CLRUnleashed.IL.MathOperations::constructionCount
IL_0027:  ldc.i4.1
IL_0028:  add
IL_0029:  stsfld      int32 CLRUnleashed.IL.MathOperations::constructionCount
IL_002e:  ret
```

It is obvious that the compiler has added some code. The compiler is initializing the four count variables to zero automatically. This code illustrates the Argument Zero being loaded repeatedly (ldarg.0) and used along with a constant zero (ldc.i4.0) to initialize one of the four count variables (stfld int32 CLRUnleased.IL.MathOperations::addCount,…).

It is necessary to present one more example from ILSampler before proceeding with a little more methodical description of IL instructions. For this discussion, refer to Listing 5.8 that shows creating a `MathOperations` object.

LISTING 5.8 C# to Create and Use a `MathOperations` Object

```
MathOperations c = new MathOperations();
. . .
int result = ib.Add(1, 2);
```

The IL code that corresponds to Listing 5.8 is shown in Listing 5.9.

LISTING 5.9 Creating a `MathOperations` Object and Calling a Method

```
.maxstack  4
  .locals init ([0] class CLRUnleashed.IL.MathOperations c,
           [1] int32 result)
  IL_0000:  newobj     instance void CLRUnleashed.IL.MathOperations::.ctor()
  IL_0005:  stloc.0
. . .
  IL_0018:  ldloc.0
  IL_0019:  ldc.i4.1
  IL_001a:  ldc.i4.2
  IL_001b:  callvirt   instance int32 CLRUnleashed.IL.MathOperations::Add(int32,
                                                                          int32)
  IL_0020:  stloc.1
```

A new instruction, the **`.maxstack`** instruction, has been introduced. It allocates space on the virtual stack. In Listing 5.9, the compiler has determined that it needs four slots in the virtual stack. The beginning of the executable instructions for Listing 5.9 shows how a new object is constructed with the **`newobj`** instruction (IL_0000) and how the result is stored at location 0 in the stack (the variable c). The value at location 0 (the variable c) is pushed onto the stack along with two constants, 1 and 2. These three arguments call the method on the `MathOperations` object `Add` using `callvirt`. The result of this method call is stored at location 1 (result) on the stack. Listing 5.10 shows the same code as Listing 5.9, but this time the code has been compiled in release mode. The default for the C# compiler is to compile in optimized mode so that the compiler picks the variable names. If the code is compiled in debug mode (csc /debug+ …), then the variable names that you chose are preserved.

LISTING 5.10 Creating a `MathOperations` Object and Calling a Method in Release Mode

```
.maxstack  4
  .locals init (class CLRUnleashed.IL.MathOperations V_0)
  IL_0000:  newobj     instance void CLRUnleashed.IL.MathOperations::.ctor()
  IL_0005:  stloc.0
. . .
  IL_0018:  ldloc.0
```

LISTING 5.10 Continued

```
  IL_0019:  ldc.i4.1
  IL_001a:  ldc.i4.2
  IL_001b:  callvirt   instance int32 CLRUnleashed.IL.MathOperations::Add(int32,
                                                                   int32)
  IL_0020:  pop
  IL_0021:  ret
```

Notice that the variable names are replaced with compiler-generated names. The variable `c` is replaced with `V_0`, and as an optimization. The variable `result` was not used; it was discarded entirely.

From these few simple examples, you can determine a lot about the IL code. It is really pretty easy to read.

Commonly Used IL Instructions

Most likely, you will see instructions with `ILDasm`, but you might instead want to build your own IL code.

> **Note**
>
> The counterpart to `ILDasm` is `ILasm`. `ILasm` takes in IL code instructions and generates an assembly. It is possible to take the output of `ILDasm` and feed it into `ILasm`.

These instructions can be grouped into loading, storing, branching or flow control, operations, and object model. They are covered in detail in the following subsections.

IL Instructions for Loading

Following is a list of instructions that are used for loading values onto the evaluation stack.

- **`ldc`**—This loads a numeric constant onto the stack. You will see this instruction whenever you have a hard-coded constant that you need to operate on or with. The general form for this instruction is `ldc.size[.num]`. The `size` portion of this instruction is i4 (4 byte integer), i8 (8 byte integer), r4 (4 byte float), or r8 (8 byte float).

  If the constant is less than 9 and greater than –1, then this instruction has a special form:

```
ldc.i4.m1   // loads a constant -1
ldc.i4.0    // loads a constant 0
ldc.i4.1    // loads a constant 1
ldc.i4.2    // loads a constant 2
ldc.i4.3    // loads a constant 3
ldc.i4.4    // loads a constant 4
ldc.i4.5    // loads a constant 5
ldc.i4.6    // loads a constant 6
ldc.i4.7    // loads a constant 7
ldc.i4.8    // loads a constant 8
```

Note

"Special" refers to a specific single byte opcode that is reserved for this instruction.

The previous code only illustrates the special form for i4. This is intentional. The preceding constants only have a special instruction if the instruction is loading a 4-byte integer. All other cases require the more general form.

If the constant is an integer and it is not between –1 and 8 inclusive, then the next candidate for the **ldc** instruction is the short form. This form requires that the constant be an integer less than or equal to 127 and greater than or equal to –128. Examples of this form are as follows:

```
ldc.i4.s   126
ldc.i4.s   127
ldc.i4.s   -127
```

The general case fits for all of the numeric types as follows:

```
ldc.r8     0.0             // Loads 0.0
ldc.r4     2.              // Loads 2.0
ldc.r4     (A4 70 9D 3F) // Loads 1.23F
ldc.r8     1.23            // Loads 1.23
ldc.i4     0x80            // Loads 128
ldc.i4     0x1f4           // Loads 500
```

- **ldarg**—This loads an argument from the stack. Similar to **ldc**, this instruction has several special forms. The special forms are for when the argument being loaded is less than or equal to 3. Examples of this special form follow:

```
ldarg.0
ldarg.1
ldarg.2
ldarg.3
```

Of these special arguments, one of them is extra special, and that is **ldarg.0**. The instruction **ldarg.0** is reserved for loading the equivalent of this pointer. Whenever an object needs to be referenced, it is referenced by a pointer to a specific instance. This pointer is what is loaded with **ldarg.0**. The remaining **ldarg** instructions reference an index to the argument list. The index starts at 1 and increases by 1 for each argument to function from left to right.

```
ldarg.s fourth
ldarg.s fifth
ldarg.s sixth
ldarg.s seventh
```

Here, the symbols such as fourth and fifth refer to the fourth and fifth arguments that are passed to the function respectively. You can reference the first 254 arguments with **ldarg.s**. If you have more than 254 arguments to your function, then you need to use **ldarg**.

This instruction has a cousin, **ldarga**, which returns the address of the argument on the stack. You would typically see this as a result of C# code (or other languages where a ByRef argument is to be passed) that is using **ref** or **out**.

- **ldloc**—This loads a local variable. This instruction has a "special" form just as **ldarg** does. If the variable is in slots 0 through 3, then the variable can be referenced with **ldloc.0**, **ldloc.1**, **ldloc.2**, and **ldloc.3**. If more than four variables exist, then the variable is referenced as `ldloc.s` *name*, where *name* is the name of the variable in debug mode and a compiler-generated name in release mode. The slots that are referenced are slots that are allocated with the **.locals** declaration. This looks like the following:

  ```
  .locals init ([0] float64 x,
  [1] float32 y,
  [2] float32 z,
  [3] float64 w,
  ```

  If more than 254 local variables exist, then all variables that are located in slots numbered 255 or greater must be loaded with the **ldloc** instruction (not **ldloc.s**). Similar to **ldarg**, there is a cousin to **ldloc** called **ldloca**, which returns the address of a local variable.

- **ldfld**—This loads a field from an object. This instruction takes a reference to the object from the stack and replaces it with the value of the field specified. For example:

  ```
  ldloc.0
  ldfld      int32 CLRUnleashed.IL.TestObject::testObjectFielda
  ```

In this example, the first stack location contains a reference to the object. The **ldfld** instruction loads the value of the field `testObjectFielda` in the instance that is specified by stack slot location 0 onto the stack. A cousin to this instruction is **ldflda**, which loads the address of the field onto the stack.

Also related to this instruction are the **ldsfld** and **ldsflda** instructions, which load the value of a static field and the address of a static field onto the stack respectively. These instructions refer to static members of the object. An instance reference to the object is not required to be on the stack.

- **ldelem**—This loads an element of an array. This instruction takes two arguments on the stack—a reference to an array and an index—and puts the value of the array at that index onto the stack. One possible scenario in which you would see this instruction is in the case of an array of strings. You might see this pattern:

  ```
  ldloc.2
  ldc.i4.1
  ldelem.ref
  ```

  In this sample, the stack slot location 2 contains a reference to an array of strings. The code loads the string in the array at index 1 (zero-based). The following is an example of referencing an item in an integer array at index 0. The array is referenced by the local variable at slot 1.

  ```
  ldloc.1
  ldc.i4.0
  ldelem.i4
  ```

  The possible types that can be loaded with **ldelem** are as follows:

  ```
  ldelem.i1    // Loads int8 value as int32
  ldelem.i2    // Loads int16 value as int32
  ldelem.i4    // Loads int32 value
  ldelem.i8    // Loads int64 value
  ldelem.u1    // Loads unsigned int8 as int32
  ldelem.u2    // Loads unsigned int16 as int32
  ldelem.u4    // Loads unsigned int32 as int32
  ldelem.u8    // Loads unsigned int64 as int64
  ldelem.r4    // Loads float32 as a float
  ldelem.r8    // Loads float64 as a float
  ldelem.i     // Loads native integer as native int
  ldelem.ref   // Loads object
  ```

  As you would expect, a cousin to this instruction loads the address of the element in the array. This instruction is called **ldelema**.

- **ldlen**—This instruction takes the array reference off of the stack and returns its length. An example of this instruction is as follows:

  ```
  ldloc.2
  ldlen
  ```

The second slot in the local variable stack is a reference to the array. The **ldlen** instruction returns the length of this array on the stack.

- **ldstr**—This loads a literal string. This instruction takes a literal string and pushes it onto the stack. This instruction is as simple as the following:

```
ldstr      "Hello"
```

- **ldnull**—This loads a null value on the stack. It provides a size agnostic null value, as opposed to **ldc.i4.0** or **ldc.i8.0**, which loads a specific size of zero on the stack.
- **ldind**—This replaces the address on the stack by the value at that address. All of the same types as ldelem can be used with **ldind**. For example, **ldind.i1**, **ldind.i2**, and **ldind.ref** are all valid instructions.

IL Instructions for Storing

- **starg**—This instruction takes a value off of the stack and stores that value in the argument array:

```
ldc.i4.s   10
starg.s    i
```

This set of instructions takes the value 10 and stores it in the argument stack location that is specified by the variable `i`. The short version, as shown in the preceding example, can be used to store to an argument with an index less than 255. If there are more arguments than 255, then they need to be referenced by the long version, something like, `starg i`.

- **stelem**—This stores an element of an array. It takes three elements off the stack: the array, the index, and the value.

```
ldloc.2
ldc.i4.1
ldstr      "is not"
stelem.ref
```

The array is located in the local stack slot 2. The index being used is 1, and the value that is to be stored in that location of the array is the string, "is not". An equivalent version of this for storing a value in an integer array would be as follows:

```
ldloc.1
ldc.i4.1
ldc.i4.s 10
stelem.i4
```

This sample shows an array at the local stack slot 1. The index for this operation is 1. The value to be stored at the specified index in the array is 10. The instruction **stelem** performs the operation. Other types that can be stored in an array are as follows:

```
stelem.i1   // Stores to an int8 array
stelem.i2   // Stores to an int16 array
stelem.i4   // Stores to an int32 array
stelem.i8   // Stores to an int64 array
stelem.r4   // Stores to a float32 array
stelem.r8   // Stores to a float64 array
stelem.i    // Stores to a native integer array
stelem.ref  // Stores to an object array
```

- **stfld**—This stores to a field of an object. It takes the object and the value off the stack and stores that value in the field of the object.

```
ldloc.0
ldc.i4.s    10
stfld       int32 CLRUnleashed.IL.TestObject::testObjectFielda
```

For this sample, the object is pushed onto the stack, the value is specified as a constant 10, and this value is stored in the field `testObjectFielda` of the given object.

IL Instructions for Flow Control

Following is a list of instructions that alter the execution path:

- **call**—This calls a method. Listings 5.11 and 5.12 illustrate a case in which the **call** instruction is used.

LISTING 5.11 A Complex Add Method in C#

```
public Complex Add(Complex a, Complex b)
{
    return new Complex(a.Real + b.Real, a.Imaginary + b.Imaginary);
}
```

When the C# code in Listing 5.11 is compiled, the resulting IL code should look like Listing 5.12.

LISTING 5.12 Calling Methods in IL

```
// Code size       40 (0x28)
.maxstack  4
.locals init ([0] valuetype CLRUnleashed.IL.Complex CS$00000003$00000000)
IL_0000:  ldarga.s   a
IL_0002:  call       instance float32 CLRUnleashed.IL.Complex::get_Real()
```

LISTING 5.12 Continued

```
IL_0007:  ldarga.s   b
IL_0009:  call       instance float32 CLRUnleashed.IL.Complex::get_Real()
IL_000e:  add
IL_000f:  ldarga.s   a
IL_0011:  call       instance float32 CLRUnleashed.IL.Complex::get_Imaginary()
IL_0016:  ldarga.s   b
IL_0018:  call       instance float32 CLRUnleashed.IL.Complex::get_Imaginary()
IL_001d:  add
IL_001e:  newobj     instance void CLRUnleashed.IL.Complex::.ctor(float32,
                                                                  float32)
IL_0023:  stloc.0
```

Listing 5.12 shows how two complex numbers are added together. At `IL_0000`, the address of the first argument is loaded on the stack. A call is made to the get_Real method of that instance. At `IL_0007`, the same thing occurs, this time for the second argument. This function has no arguments, so you only need to supply the address of the instance of the object on which the method is defined.

- **`callvirt`**—This calls a method that is associated at runtime with an object. It pops the values off the stack and calls the specified method on the function. The following example calls the Add method with two arguments, 1 and 2, on the `MathOperations` object.

  ```
  ldloc.0
  ldc.i4.1
  ldc.i4.2
  callvirt   instance int32
  CLRUnleased.IL.MathOperations::Add(int32,int32)
  ```

  This instruction makes sure that the appropriate Argument Zero is in place and calls the method with the given arguments. This is basically a late-bound call to a method on an object. The method supplied as an argument to the instruction is specified as a metadata token that describes the method, arguments, return values, accessibility, and so on.

  Because the metadata that is supplied to this function contains such extensive information, it is possible for this function to be replaced by the more general **`call`** instruction.

- **`ceq`**—This compares if equal. It compares two values on the stack for equality. If the two values are equal, then a 1 is pushed on the stack. If they are not equal, a 0 is pushed onto the stack.

- **`cgt`**—This compares if greater than. It compares two values on the stack to see if one is greater than the other. If the first value is greater than the second, then a 1 is pushed onto the stack; otherwise, a 0 is pushed on to the stack.

- **clt**—This compares if less than. It compares two values on the stack to see if one is less than the other. If the first value is less than the second, then a 1 is pushed on the stack; otherwise, a 0 is pushed on to the stack.
- **br**—This is unconditional branch. It is the equivalent of the `goto` in C or C++. The instruction looks like this:

  ```
  br.s        IL_0024
  ```

  If the instruction that is being branched to is more than 127 bytes away (int8), then it is not possible to use **br.s**. In that case, you must use **br**, which allows for a branch of up to 2,147,483,647 bytes away (int32).
- **brtrue**—This is branch on true. If the value on the stack is true (equal to one), then branch; otherwise, don't branch. The instruction **brinst** is an alias for this instruction. Like the **br** instruction, this instruction has a short version if the branch is no longer than 127 bytes away.
- **brfalse**—This is branch on false. If the value on the stack is false (equal to zero), then branch; otherwise, don't branch. The instructions **brzero** and **brnull** provide aliases for the **brfalse** instruction. Like the **br** instruction, this instruction has a short version if the branch is no longer than 127 bytes away.
- **beq**, **bgt**, **ble**, **blt**, **bne**—This is branch on the specified condition. All the rest of these branch instructions are identical to the equivalent compare instruction followed by a **brtrue** instruction. For example, **beq** is the same as **ceq** followed by **brtrue**.

Note

Most of the preceding instructions that involve comparison can perform an unsigned comparison by supplying a **.un** suffix to the comparison instruction. For instance, if two values are to be compared for equality without regard to sign, the instruction **ceq.un** would be used.

Before leaving these branching instructions, you should know some of the rules involved with comparing values. Of course, two values that have the same type can be easily compared. When the two values that are being compared are of different types, it becomes tricky. Table 5.2 summarizes the rules for comparison.

TABLE 5.2 Evaluation Stack Comparison Rules

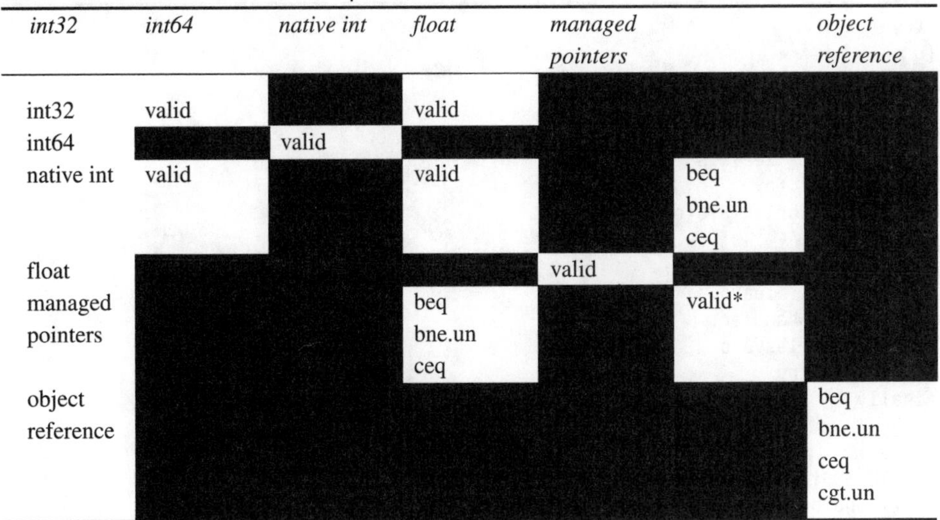

	int32	*int64*	*native int*	*float*	*managed pointers*	*object reference*
int32	valid		valid			
int64		valid				
native int	valid		valid		beq bne.un ceq	
float				valid		
managed pointers			beq bne.un ceq		valid*	
object reference						beq bne.un ceq cgt.un

The blacked out values indicate that the comparison is not valid. The boxes that have an asterisk associated with them indicate that this comparison is not verifiable. The boxes that have instructions in them indicate that the comparison is only valid for the given instructions.

The following presents a brief sample of what a **try/finally** block looks like. The C# source looks like Listing 5.13.

LISTING 5.13 C# Exceptions

```
try
{
. . .
}
catch(Exception e)
{
. . .
}
finally
{
. . .
}
```

The compiler takes this code and turns it into the IL shown in Listing 5.14.

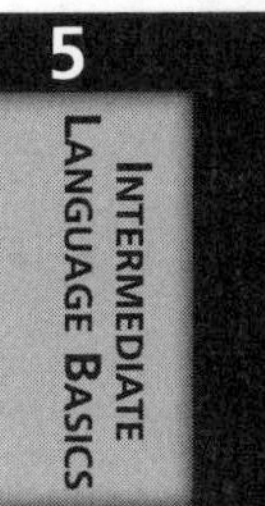

LISTING 5.14 IL Exceptions

```
.try
{
  .try
  {
. . .
    IL_0035:  leave.s    IL_0045
  }  // end .try
  catch [mscorlib]System.Exception
  {
. . .
    IL_0043:  leave.s    IL_0045
  }  // end handler
  IL_0045:  leave.s    IL_0052
}  // end .try
finally
{
. . .
    IL_0051:  endfinally
}  // end handler
IL_0052:  ret
```

The compiler turned the **try/catch/finally** block into a **try/catch** nested in a **try/catch**. This is the only way to get the functionality of `finally` in IL.

The next items of note are the numerous **leave** instructions, the **endfinally** instruction, and the **throw** instruction.

- **leave**—This exits a protected region of code. On the outset, the **leave** instruction looks like a **br** instruction. Both have a short version (**.s**), and both unconditionally jump to a label. The most important difference is that a **br** instruction cannot be used to transfer control outside a **try**, **filter**, or **catch** block. The branch instructions can only transfer control to portions of the code within these respective blocks. The **leave** instruction is an exception in that it is allowed to transfer control outside of a **try**, **filter**, or **catch** block; it cleans up the evaluation stack and ensures that any enclosing **finally** blocks are executed. Perhaps a **finally** block encloses where the **leave** instruction is located. If that is the case, before the **leave** instruction transfers control to the target address, it makes sure that the **finally** block has executed. It is not legal to execute a **leave** instruction from within a **finally** block.
- **endfinally**—This ends the **finally** clause of an exception block.
- **throw**—This throws an exception. The following is a brief sample of throwing an exception in IL:

```
newobj     instance void
```

```
[mscorlib]System.InvalidCastException::.ctor(string)
throw
```

The exception class is constructed and then the exception is thrown, much the same as it would be with C#.

IL Operation Instructions

Following is a list of instructions used to perform operations on the arguments on the evaluation stack.

- **conv**—This converts from one type to another. The types of conversions are listed next:

  ```
  conv.i1    // Convert to int8 pushing int32 on the stack
  conv.i2    // Convert to int16 pushing int32 on the stack
  conv.i4    // Convert to int32 pushing int32 on the stack
  conv.i8    // Convert to int64 pushing int64 on the stack
  conv.r4    // Convert to float32 pushing float on the stack
  conv.r8    // Convert to float64 pushing float on the stack
  conv.u1    // Convert to unsigned int8 pushing int32
  conv.u2    // Convert to unsigned int16 pushing int32
  conv.u4    // Convert to unsigned int32 pushing int32
  conv.u8    // Convert to unsigned int64 pushing int64
  conv.i     // Convert to native int pushing native int
  conv.u     // Convert to unsigned native int pushing native int
  conv.r.un  // Convert unsigned int to float32 pushing float
  ```

  conv.ovf is a companion to the **conv** instruction. The only difference is that if the conversion results in an overflow, then an exception is thrown.

- **add**—This takes two arguments from the stack, adds them, and puts the result back on the stack. The companion to this function, **add.ovf**, causes an exception to be thrown if an overflow condition exists.
- **sub**—This takes two arguments from the stack, subtracts them, and puts the result back on the stack. The companion to this function, **sub.ovf**, causes an exception to be thrown if an overflow condition exists.
- **mul**—This takes two arguments from the stack, multiplies them, and puts the result back on the stack. The companion to this function, **mul.ovf**, causes an exception to be thrown if an overflow condition exists.
- **div**—This takes two arguments from the stack, divides them, and puts the result back on the stack. The companion to this function, **div.un**, divides two values without respect to sign. Floating-point values never cause an exception to be generated. However, for integral values, you can get a **DivideByZeroException** if the divisor is zero. For Microsoft implementations, you can get an **OverflowException** when working with values near the minimum integer value –1.

- **rem**—This computes the remainder of two values. Its companion, **rem.un**, performs the same operation without respect to sign.
- **and**, **or**, **xor**—These are binary logical operations.
- **not**—This is a bitwise complement of the value on the stack.
- **neg**—This negates the value on the stack. If the value is an integer, then the standard twos complement is performed. If the value is a floating point value, then the value is negated.

IL Object Model Instructions

Following is a list of instructions that directly relate to the .NET object model.

- **box**, **unbox**—This converts a value type to a reference type (**box**) and a reference type to a value type (**unbox**). Following is a simple example of the boxing and unboxing operation:

```
ldarg.2
box         [mscorlib]System.Int32
stloc.s     o
. . .
ldloc.s     o
unbox       [mscorlib]System.Int32
ldind.i4
```

  This sequence of instructions takes the argument from the argument list (the second argument) and uses **box** to convert the value to an object. Specifically, **box** is being called to **box** an integer value. The object is then pushed on the stack and **unbox** is called to convert it back to an integer value.

- **castclass**—This casts one class to another. It takes the object from the stack and casts it to the specified class. If the object cannot be cast to the specified class, then an exception is thrown (**InvalidCastException**). The following are important to note about casting:
  1. Arrays inherit from System.Array.
  2. If Foo can be cast to Bar, then `Foo[]` can be cast to `Bar[]`.
- **isinst**—This tests to see if the object on the stack is an instance of the class that is supplied to the **isinst** instruction. Unlike **castclass**, this instruction will not throw an **InvalidCastException**. If the object on the stack is not an instance of the class, then a null value will be pushed on the stack. Following is a sample that implements this:

```
ldarg.0
isinst      CLRUnleased.IL.IComplexArithmetic
```

The first argument is pushed on the stack and tested to see if it is an instance of `IComplexArithmethic`. In this case, the instructions are in a static method, so an Argument Zero doesn't contain the 'this' pointer.

- **`ldtoken`**—This loads the runtime interpretation of the metadata. If, for example, you have the following C# code:

```
Type t = typeof(IBasicArithmetic);
```

it translates into the following IL code:

```
ldtoken    CLRUnleashed.IL.IBasicArithmetic
call       class [mscorlib]System.Type
[mscorlib]System.Type::GetTypeFromHandle(valuetype
[mscorlib]System.RuntimeTypeHandle)
```

The **`ldtoken`** instruction gets the handle associated with the type and then a **`Type`** class is constructed from that.

- **`newarr`**—This creates a new single-dimension array with a capacity that is defined by the value on the stack. For example:

```
ldc.i4.5
newarr     [mscorlib]System.Int32
```

This sample creates an array with five elements.

- **`newobj`**—This creates a new object and calls the object's constructor (if available).

```
newobj     instance void
CLRUnleashed.IL.Complex::.ctor(float32,float32)
```

This creates a `Complex` object and calls the constructor that takes two `float32` arguments.

Summary

Event though you might never build a large-scale application using only IL, it is important that you are at least literate in IL and can read and understand most IL patterns. As you can see from this chapter, IL is relatively easy to understand. All IL code assumes a simple stack-based model of execution. After you understand that, the rest is just learning the syntax and calling conventions for each of the instructions. Most of the instructions have a one-to-one correspondence with C#; when they deviate, it is usually because that feature presents the user with unsafe or unverifiable code. This chapter presented most of the instructions that you are likely to run into.

> **Tip**
>
> You can find complete documentation on IL instructions in the Partition III CIL.doc file in the `Tool Developers Guide` directory in the same location that the .NET Framework was installed.

CHAPTER 6

Publishing Applications

IN THIS CHAPTER

A developer spends substantial time developing and debugging an application within the confines of his development environment. Then, when the application seems to perform as desired and has the requisite features, it is turned over to manufacturing to be distributed to customers. At that point, the developer gets a call from an irate customer who indicates that the application either fails or seems to have caused the failure of other seemingly unrelated applications. If it can be assumed that the developer has sufficiently debugged the application, the problem can be more than likely blamed on what is known as *DLL Hell*. Either the customer installed another application that changed one or more of the system DLLs, or manufacturing built an installation script that overwrote some system DLLs for your application to function properly, but that causes other applications on the customer's machine to fail. DLL Hell is almost impossible to resolve satisfying all parties. One of the design criteria for the .NET Framework was to solve this problem. This chapter shows what can be done to make sure that your application works as well in the field as it does on your desktop. In addition, it covers some of the deployment-related security issues with which you should be concerned.

Windows Client Installation Problems

DLL Hell is manifest when you install your application that relies on certain system DLLs to provide specific functionality. After your system is installed and running, someone else installs his software and updates the DLLs on which your system relies. In the worst-case scenario, your application no longer functions as it did. The APIs in the replaced DLLs no longer function as your software expects them to, and your code breaks. You could take a Draconian stance that no modifications should be made to the software on a given system, but this is your customer's computer—you really cannot dictate what happens.

When you upgrade to a new version of a DLL, the old version is removed by necessity. If the new version does not work, it is not easy to go back to the old version.

Often, fragments of applications are left behind when an application or a version of an application is removed. Unused registry entries, old configuration files, sample programs, and so on might still exist.

In addition to the problem with system DLLs and DLL Hell, the old system of DLLs was insecure, and security is of great importance today. Chapter 16, ".NET Security," is devoted completely to security issues, but this chapter explores the insecurities of the old system of DLLs that are being left behind.

A simple application is included that relies on a DLL to generate an appropriate greeting. The main portion of this file is illustrated in Listing 6.1.

LISTING 6.1 Calling a Function in a DLL

```
#include "stdafx.h"
#include <iostream>
#include "GoodDll\GoodDll.h"

int _tmain(int argc, _TCHAR* argv[])
{
    LPCTSTR message = Greeting();
    std::cout << message << std::endl;
    return 0;
}
```

The function in the DLL simply returns a string. The Greeting method looks like Listing 6.2.

LISTING 6.2 The DLL Greeting Function

```
GOODDLL_API LPCTSTR Greeting(void)
{
    return _T("Hello from the good DLL.");
}
```

When the program runs, you get the following output:

```
Hello from the good DLL.
```

The output is satisfactory, so you can declare the application as ready to ship. The application is shipped, but at the customer's site, someone replaces the good DLL with a bad one simply by copying over the shipped file. As long as the export method signature is the same, no errors will occur. This bad DLL has a greeting that looks like Listing 6.3.

LISTING 6.3 A Bad DLL Greeting Function

```
BADDLL_API LPCTSTR Greeting(void)
{
    return _T("I am a bad DLL. You don't want to interact with me");
}
```

Now when the application runs, you get this:

```
I am a bad DLL. You don't want to interact with me.
```

You can imagine this bad DLL doing something much worse than changing the message around, but you can see that it is easy to cause a program to do things that were not part of its original design. You can prevent such spoofing or tampering in numerous ways (such as file access permissions, encrypting file system, physical access restrictions, and so on), but the default allows for some large holes. The .NET Framework addresses this problem.

Deploying and Publishing a .NET Application

One of the first tasks in building a deployment scheme is identifying shared and unshared code. If you determine that your application is not distributed in any way and no portion of it is shared, then your deployment task is simple. However, your options for versioning and side-by-side operation become more complex. In fact, if you decide that your code is not shared, then versioning and side-by-side operation is left to you. If your code is not shared, then you can take full advantage of the xcopy deployment scheme that is advertised so widely. On the other hand, if you choose to share portions of your code—even if it's only with other components of your application—then your deployment is not quite so simple, but your options for versioning, side-by-side, delay load, and so on increase. It is a tradeoff, and you need to make a decision as to what is best for your application.

Identifying Code with Strong Names

Code must be uniquely identified to be shared. The Global Assembly Cache (GAC) does not support an assembly that does not have a strong name. You should seriously consider giving even your private assemblies a strong name that uniquely identifies your code. A strong name provides a unique identifier to a set of code that is statistically impossible to be duplicated. In other words, a strong name is a means of uniquely identifying this code as yours. A strong name is part of an **`AssemblyName`** that consists of four parts:

- Name—Visual Studio assigns a name to an assembly that is the name of the output DLL, minus the DLL suffix. This name can be any name that you choose.
- Publisher Key—The actual public key stored in the assembly is about 160 bits. When the full name of the assembly is referenced, you see a key token. Because the full public key takes so many bytes to represent, Microsoft hashes the public

key and takes the last eight bytes of the hashed value to form what is known as a *key token*. This eight-byte string is unique.

- Version—This four-part string identifies the version of the assembly. It refers to three logical parts: the assembly version, build number, and revision number. Physically, the assembly version consists of a major and a minor version number. Assuming that it is a policy for a company to build an assembly every day, the build number should increment with every build. If it is necessary for two builds to occur in a day, then the revision should be incremented. If a version attribute is specified with a wildcard such as `[assembly: AssemblyVersion("1.2.*")]`, then Visual Studio takes care of incrementing the build and revision number for you.
- Culture—This is a string of the form xx-yy, where xx is the language and yy is the country. Specifying only xx is known as language neutral, and not specifying anything or specifying a blank culture string is known as a neutral culture. Chapter 18, "Globalization/Localization," goes into more detail about culture. An assembly's culture can be assigned at link time using the al.exe utility (al /c[ulture]:<xx-yy>) or with an assembly attribute such as `[assembly: AssemblyCulture("xx-yy")]`. Assemblies lacking MSIL code that have just resource information are known as *satellite assemblies*. These satellite assemblies are important in building international applications.

If the assembly is missing the public key or the public key token, then it does not have strong name. Figure 6.1 summarizes the important information that is contained in an **AssemblyName**.

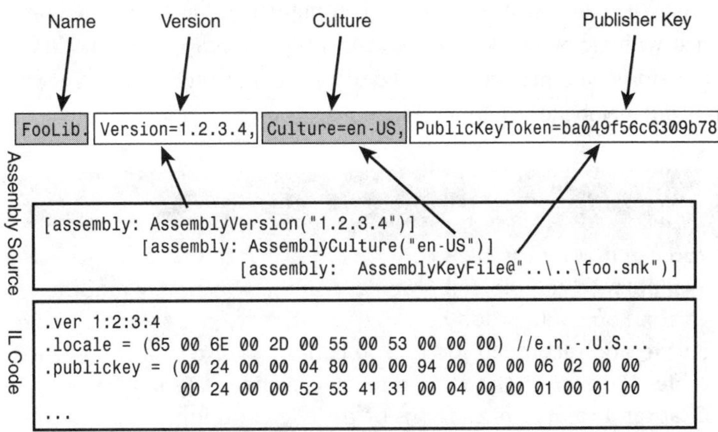

FIGURE 6.1
Decoding an assembly name.

When any portion of the **AssemblyName** is different, the runtime considers it a different assembly. Most commonly, you see differences in the version (to reflect bug fixes, updates, and so on) and culture (to reflect support for different cultures). After an assembly is uniquely identified with a strong name, the strong name can be further used to enforce runtime version checks, enforce binding policy, provide security evidence, and prevent spoofing or tampering. These topics are covered later in this chapter.

Figure 6.2 shows the process of linking the main assembly with a referenced assembly.

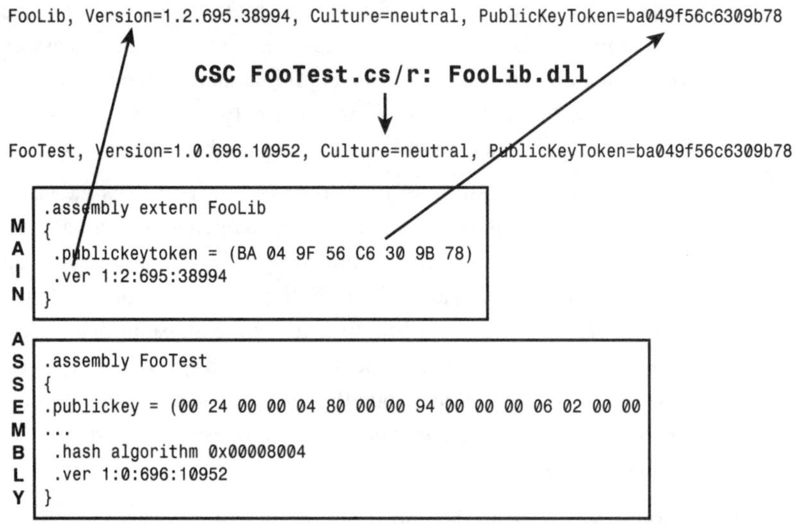

```
FooLib, Version=1.2.695.38994, Culture=neutral, PublicKeyToken=ba049f56c6309b78

CSC FooTest.cs/r: FooLib.dll

FooTest, Version=1.0.696.10952, Culture=neutral, PublicKeyToken=ba049f56c6309b78

MAIN ASSEMBLY

.assembly extern FooLib
{
 .publickeytoken = (BA 04 9F 56 C6 30 9B 78)
 .ver 1:2:695:38994
}

.assembly FooTest
{
.publickey = (00 24 00 00 04 80 00 00 94 00 00 00 06 02 00 00
...
 .hash algorithm 0x00008004
 .ver 1:0:696:10952
}
```

FIGURE 6.2
Referencing a strongly named assembly.

Particularly notice that the main assembly has the version and a key token for the referenced assembly. The first benefit that this gives you is security against spoofing or tampering. When an assembly is given a strong name, the entire contents of the file are hashed with the private key. To replace a file or even slightly modify it successfully, the perpetrator would need to know the private key to successfully generate a hash for the file and the embedded public key.

Note

You can modify the file's contents to prove to yourself that adequate security is available. To complete this demo, the file was simply modified with a binary editor. You could modify the file in other ways. You could convert the file to IL, edit it, and recompile the IL. You could also use reflection to modify the string table. Another method could be to use the set of unmanaged APIs detailed in Chapter 4 to modify portions of the file containing the assembly. You could also memory map the filewith write permission and modify it that way. The way you decide to prove that a hash is indeed being generated is your choice. You could even try all of these suggestions to see if you are able to thwart the hash security.

If you try to modify only one character of the assembly, tools such as `PEVerify` and `ILDasm` work fine. After the assembly has been generated, use `ILDasm` to look at the edited version. Listing 6.4 illustrates the modified IL.

LISTING 6.4 Using `ILDasm` to Illustrate Assembly Tampering

```
.method public hidebysig specialname rtspecialname
        instance void  .ctor() cil managed
{
  // Code size       17 (0x11)
  .maxstack  1
  IL_0000:  ldarg.0
  IL_0001:  call       instance void [mscorlib]System.Object::.ctor()
  IL_0006:  ldstr      "I am the neutraf version of Foo."
  IL_000b:  call       void [mscorlib]System.Console::WriteLine(string)
  IL_0010:  ret
} // end of method Foo::.ctor
```

Notice the misspelling of *neutral*. Nothing so drastic has been done to make the file unreadable. However, the assembly fails to load with an exception:

```
Unhandled Exception: System.IO.FileLoadException: Strong name
➥validation failed for assembly 'FooLib'.
```

Now when a hash is computed, it is different because of the single character change that was made to the file. If you edit this DLL and change the letter back, the assembly loads without error. Giving an assembly a strong name has more benefits than just being able to share the assembly. It is recommended that all assemblies be given a strong name. Specifically, the following presents some additional considerations for strongly naming an assembly:

- After an assembly is signed, it can be shared and redistributed.
- Runtime version checking is possible after an assembly has a strong name.
- Runtime policy checking is possible with strong-named assemblies.
- If the strong-named assembly is shared, you can take full advantage of side-by-side deployment.

You have learned the benefits of giving an assembly a strong name. You will now learn a step-by-step approach to developing and deploying an assembly with a strong name:

1. Generate a public/private key pair using the `sn` (Strong Name) utility. To do so, enter the following at a command prompt:

   ```
   sn -k secret.snk
   ```

This generates a public/private key pair and exports them to a file called `secret.snk`. This file should be guarded and not exposed to anyone but a select group of lead developers. After the public/private key pair is generated, then a public key needs to be generated that can be distributed to all developers with the following command:

```
sn -p secret.snk public.snk
```

This command generates a file called `public.snk` that contains the public key to be used for a project or projects. This file can be freely distributed, and its use in signing files is encouraged.

2. Mark each assembly with an attribute that identifies the assembly key file for signing the assembly. Actually, for the assembly to compile successfully, an assembly needs two attributes, as follows:

```
[assembly: AssemblyDelaySign(true)]
[assembly: AssemblyKeyFile(@"..\..\pubfoo.snk")]
```

The **`AssemblyDelaySignAttribute`** indicates that the assembly is in development and does not need to be signed now. If the **`AssemblyDelaySignAttribute`** is not present and is not set to **`true`**, then you get a compile error:

```
Cryptographic failure while signing assembly 'FooLib.dll'
➥-- 'Key file '..\..\pubfoo.snk' is missing the
➥private key needed for signing'
```

The **`AssemblyKeyFileAttribute`** identifies the public key file that was generated in the first step. An assembly that is specified by these two attributes is known as *partially signed* because the private key was not available to fully sign the assembly.

3. Now when you try to use this assembly, you get the following exception:

```
Unhandled Exception: System.IO.FileLoadException: Strong name
validation failed for assembly 'FooLib'.
```

To prevent this error, you need to again use the `sn` utility to register for strong name verification to be turned off. Registering an assembly for verification skip requires administrative privileges.

```
sn -Vr foolib.dll
```

Registering an assembly using `sn` adds the following key to the registry:

```
HKEY_LOCAL_MACHINE\SOFTWARE\Microsoft\StrongName\Verification\
➥FooLib,BA049F56C6309B78
```

When the CLR verifies an assembly, it first checks this registry to see if an appropriate entry exists. If it does, then the verification is skipped. When the development phase is finished, the developer can unregister the assembly as follows:

```
sn -Vu foolib.dll
```

Alternatively, you can unregister the verification skips like this:

```
sn -Vx
```

It is possible to register all assemblies of a given public key:

```
sn -Vr *,BA049F56C6309B78
```

or register all assemblies to be skipped:

```
sn -Vr *
```

It is also possible to skip verification for a comma-separated list of users:

```
sn -Vr foolib.dll machine\me,machine\you
```

Caution

All options for the Strong Name Utility are case sensitive.

4. After the strong-named assembly is registered, the developer can develop software as before. The assembly can be removed and rebuilt. The registry entry is causing the verification skip.
5. When development is completed for that particular assembly, its entry can be removed from the registry, either with the `-Vx` or the `-Vu <assembly>` flag.
6. As part of the build process for shipping a product, each assembly needs to be signed. This is done with the sn utility again as follows:

   ```
   sn -R foolib.dll secret.snk
   ```

   To fully sign the assembly, the private key is required, and that is contained in the secret.snk file. Again, access to the secret.snk file should be tightly controlled. After signing an assembly with the private key, it is fully signed.

Deploying a Private Assembly

Private deployment results in an isolated application where the application is a directory tree. Everything that you need to run your application is self contained and a part of the directory structure that is designed into the application.

This is the simplest case. If possible, this is how you should deploy your application. With a private assembly, you simply copy the files to a unique directory and run the code from there. When the software needs to be upgraded, you create another directory and copy the new files to the new directory and run. The added overhead of the disk storage space for the two versions of your software is undoubtedly minimal, and your customer can easily switch between the two versions if the latest is not all it was supposed to be.

After you are sure you don't need the old version, you can remove it by simply deleting the directory where the old application resided. You don't need to unregister portions of your application because you did not register them in the first place. What are the advantages and disadvantages of private assemblies? The advantages of a private assembly are as follows:

- The installation procedure is simpler to perform and simpler to understand. After all, you are just copying files.
- All files both with and without strong names (signed and unsigned) are simply copied to an installation folder. You could have a directory structure like this:

  My Company
    Application
      1.0
      1.1
      1.2
- All code is private to your application. You don't have to worry about interactions with other software. It is harder for others to easily use and abuse your software. This is a security through obscurity approach.
- Other applications cannot early-bind to your assemblies. This is related to the previous bullet; you prevent others from using your software.

The disadvantages of a private assembly are as follows:

- Because a global area to look for an assembly is unavailable, and no registration process exists, assemblies are located by filename alone. This requires that all of the files be located so that they can be found. For a simple application, this might be easy; however, for a complex distributed application, it is sometimes difficult.
- If you need the equivalent of side-by-side applications, then you will have to do it yourself. You will probably have to design some type of version directory tree.
- It might be hard to locate and debug a problem assembly.
- You must verify the strong name every time the assembly is loaded. This can make the startup time of your application longer. If an assembly is loaded in the GAC, then the strong name is verified once when the assembly is entered into the GAC rather than every time the assembly is used.
- Because none of your code is shared, your application might have a larger working set than it would if all or part of it were shared.

Installing Shared Code

To demonstrate the installation and development processes, a simple application has been created that calls a method in an assembly. The main portion of this code is shown in Listing 6.5.

LISTING 6.5 FooTest an Application to Test a Class Foo That Resides in FooLib

```
[STAThread]
static void Main(string[] args)
{
    FooLib.Foo f = new FooLib.Foo();
    Console.WriteLine("Foo: {0}", f.Version);
}
```

This application references an assembly also in the project that implements the Version property, as shown in Listing 6.6.

LISTING 6.6 Implementation of FooLib

```
[assembly: AssemblyDelaySign(true)]
[assembly: AssemblyKeyFile(@"..\..\pubfoo.snk")]
[assembly: AssemblyVersion("1.2.*")]
. . .
public class Foo
{
    public Foo()
    {
    }
    public string Version
    {
        get
        {
            Assembly a = Assembly.GetAssembly(GetType());
            return a.GetName().Version.ToString();
        }
    }
}
```

The code in Listings 6.5 and 6.6 will be used to illustrate how to fully sign the `FooLib` assembly and install it into the GAC. At that point, the version of the `FooLib` assembly will be changed and the new version of the `FooLib` assembly will be installed, demonstrating side-by-side installation and use of assemblies.

You can install code to the Global Assembly Cache with a few simple steps:

- `sn -R foolib.dll foo.snk`—Here you are re-signing with the private key. This is not the public key file that was generated with `sn -p`. This is the original file that contains both the public and private key pair. Because this file is sensitive, you should perform this step in a guarded environment where it is unlikely that the file containing the public and private key pair would be compromised.
- `gacutil -i foolib.dll`—You perform this step at install time to install the assembly into the GAC.
- `sn -Vx`—This is an optional step that you can do on the development platform so that the development site does not have a security hole. This essentially turns on all strong name verification. As illustrated previously, you can unregister an assembly from the "skip verification" list in numerous ways.
- `gacutil -l FooLib`—This verifies that the assembly is really in the GAC. After you install the assembly, you get the following output:

  ```
  The Global Assembly Cache contains the following assemblies:
   foolib, Version=1.2.697.17891, Culture=neutral,
  ➥PublicKeyToken=ba049f56c6309b78, Custom=null
  ```

When you install the assembly into the GAC and run the test program, you get this:

```
Foo: 1.2.697.17891
```

Now that the code is released, the developer is free to work on the next version. The developer continues to work with the public key file that was given to him. When the next version is ready to ship, you repeat the process of re-signing the assembly (with the new version), installing it in the GAC (at a customer's site), and unregistering the assembly from the skip verification list. Now when you list the contents of the GAC, you get the following output:

```
The Global Assembly Cache contains the following assemblies:
        FooLib, Version=1.2.697.17891, Culture=neutral,
➥PublicKeyToken=ba049f56c6309b78, Custom=null
        FooLib, Version=1.3.697.17959, Culture=neutral,
➥PublicKeyToken=ba049f56c6309b78, Custom=null
```

Now two different versions of the assembly are in the GAC. If you want to reproduce this scenario on your computer, you need to ensure that you have one version of FooTest.exe that is built against version 1.2 of FooLib and one version that is built against version 1.3. To simulate this situation, you need to build FooTest.exe first with version 1.2 and copy it to a 1.2 directory. From there, modify the FooLib assembly version number to be 1.3 and rebuild FooTest.exe. Now that you have version 1.3 of

FooTest.exe, you need to copy it to a 1.3 directory. Copies have been made of the applications that called each of these assemblies in two separate directories, 1.2 and 1.3. When you run the version from the 1.2 directory, you get this:

```
Foo: 1.2.697.17891
```

When you run the version from the 1.3 directory, you get this:

```
Foo: 1.3.697.17959
```

Each application runs side-by-side in that each is retrieving a different version of the assembly. Both versions of the assembly are installed.

Now you can use the browser to look at the assemblies that are installed in the GAC. If you point your Explorer to `%SystemRoot%\Assembly`, you see a list of assemblies that are in the GAC. Your screen should look something like Figure 6.3.

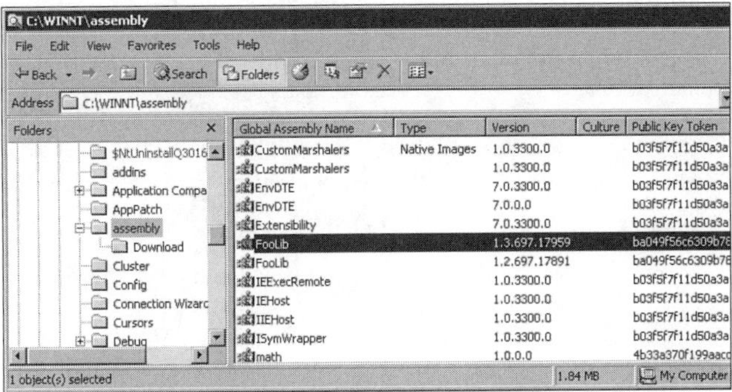

FIGURE 6.3
Explorer GAC assembly listing.

Selecting the properties by right-clicking on FooLib yields a Properties dialog box that looks like Figure 6.4.

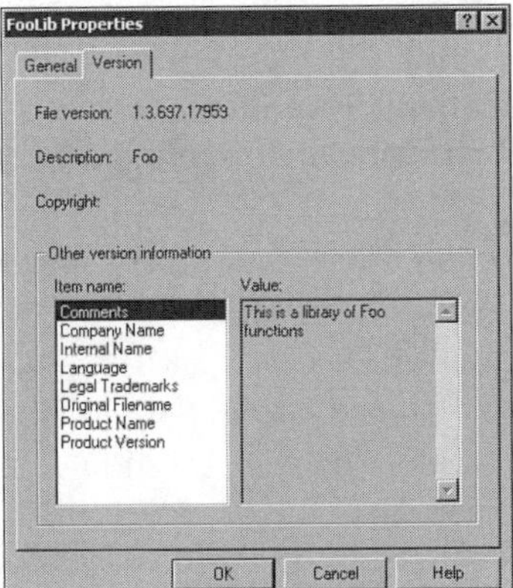

FIGURE 6.4
FooLib assembly properties.

From this figure, you are able to see not only general properties (on the General properties tab), but you also can see specific properties of your assembly. Figure 6.4 shows the Comments version information that is set using the assembly attribute, like this:

```
[assembly: AssemblyDescription("This is a library of Foo functions")]
```

From the version property page, you can see a number of other version-related properties. Table 6.1 shows the mapping between assembly attributes and these version properties. The IDE sets most of these attributes to "", so you should take the time to fill in the appropriate values so that this information is available at runtime.

TABLE 6.1 Assembly Attribute to Version Property Mapping

Assembly Attribute	*Version Property*
`AssemblyCompany`	Company Name
`AssemblyCopyright`	Copyright
`AssemblyCulture`	Language
`AssemblyDescription`	Comments
`AssemblyProduct`	Product Name
`AssemblyTitle`	Description
`AssemblyTrademark`	Legal Trademarks
`AssemblyVersion`	Assembly Version
n/a	The name of the DLL
`AssemblyVersion`	File Version (same as Assembly Version)
`AssemblyInformationalVersion`	Product Version (defaults to `AssemblyVersion`)

Note

Both private assemblies and shared assemblies share some commonalties:

- If the assembly has a strong name, it is verified and version checked. A strong name prevents most tampering and spoofing attempts from succeeding.
- Publisher and machine policy files affect both private and shared assemblies.
- For most cases, it is not required that a user have system administrative rights to deploy an application. This applies to both private and shared assemblies. To access configuration files, the user should have access to the system directory (`%SystemRoot%`).

Locating Assemblies

To successfully deploy an application, you need to understand the process by which the CLR locates an assembly. By default, an application specifies an assembly with the same full name that was used when the application was built. You can see what assembly the application is looking for in the manifest of the application assembly. It might look like Listing 6.7.

LISTING 6.7 External References to Dependent Assemblies

```
.assembly extern mscorlib
{
  .publickeytoken = (B7 7A 5C 56 19 34 E0 89 )
  .ver 1:0:3300:0
}
.assembly extern FooLib
{
  .publickeytoken = (BA 04 9F 56 C6 30 9B 78 )
  .ver 1:2:697:15012
}
```

Listing 6.7 shows that this application looks for two assemblies: version 1.0.3300 of mscorlib and version 1.2.697.15012 of FooLib.

> **Note**
>
> If an assembly load fails, an entry is made in a log file. You can use `fuslogvw` (Assembly Binding Log Viewer) to see the possible causes of an assembly load failure.

The CLR uses the information that is recorded in the manifest to try to locate each assembly that is listed in the manifest. For assemblies that do not have strong names, version information is ignored. The first step in trying to locate an assembly is to examine applicable policy files. The following section enumerates the different policy files that are a part of the .NET Framework; it also moves step-by-step through the assembly load process.

Examining Policy Files

The first step that the runtime takes to locate a particular assembly is to examine the contents of three different policy files: the machine policy, the publisher policy, and the application policy. These files modify the way that the runtime locates a particular assembly. These files all have the same syntax, but they have different priorities when the same information is contained in each. The lowest in priority is the application policy file. The next priority is the publisher policy file, which can override all application policy files. Of highest priority is the machine policy file, which overrides all configurations on the machine.

Each file is an XML configuration file that consists of the following tags:

- `<assemblyBinding>`—This tag is a subtag of `<runtime>` and sits in the hierarchy of tags in the configuration file as follows:

  ```
  <configuration>
      <runtime>
          <assemblyBinding>
  ```

  This tag has a required namespace attribute, so the actual tag looks like this:

  ```
  <assemblyBinding xmlns="urn:schemas-microsoft-com:asm.v1">
      . . .
  </assemblyBinding>
  ```

  It can have the following subtags:

  ```
  <dependentAssembly>
  <probing>
  <publisherPolicy>
  ```

- `<dependentAssembly>`—This tag is a subtag of `<assemblyBinding>`, and one of these tags will be included for each assembly that is described by the policy. The contents of this tag describe the assembly that the policy is about and how the assembly should be handled. It sits in the hierarchy of the configuration as follows:

  ```
  <configuration>
      <runtime>
          <assemblyBinding>
              <dependentAssembly>
  ```

  It has the following subtags:

  ```
  <assemblyIdentity>
  <codeBase>
  <bindingRedirect>
  <publisherPolicy>
  ```

- `<bindingRedirect>`—This tag instructs the runtime to redirect one assembly version for another. It sits in the hierarchy of the configuration as follows:

  ```
  <configuration>
      <runtime>
          <assemblyBinding>
              <dependentAssembly>
                  <bindingRedirect>
  ```

This tag does not have subtags. It has only two required attributes, so this tag looks like this:

```
<bindingRedirect oldVersion="a.b.c.d"
                 newVersion="w.x.y.z" />
```

The `oldVersion` attribute can also be a range of version numbers.

- `<codeBase>`—This tag is where the runtime can find this assembly if it is not on this machine. It sits in the hierarchy of the configuration as follows:

```
<configuration>
    <runtime>
        <assemblyBinding>
            <dependentAssembly>
                <codeBase>
```

This tag does not have subtags, but it has two required attributes. The format of the tag looks like this:

```
<codebase version="a.b.c.d"
          href="url of assembly" />
```

See Listing 6.8 for an example of most of these tags.

Application Policy Files

The runtime checks for an application policy file. An application policy file for client executables resides in the same directory as the executable and has a name that is the same name as the executable application with a `.config` suffix appended to it. For example, if the application were `foo.exe`, then the application configuration file would be `foo.exe.config`.

Publisher Policy Files

The publisher policy file starts out as a file that looks identical to the application policy file. However, to be a publisher policy file, it must be wrapped by an assembly and put in the GAC. When it is wrapped, the file takes on a name of `policy.major.minor.assembly.dll`. The first part, "policy", is fixed and must be the word "policy". The next two parts are the major and minor numbers that correspond to the version of the assembly to which this policy is to apply. The assembly portion is the name of the assembly.

A publisher policy file overrides an application policy file that refers to the same assembly. Normally, a publisher policy is installed as part of an upgrade. If anything goes wrong with the upgrade, then the user can be returned to the last known good configuration with **`<publisherPolicy apply="yes|no"/>`** that would be part of an application configuration file. This is known as *safe mode*. Safe mode can be applied to just one assembly or to all of the assemblies in an application.

Machine Policy Files

Administers use a machine policy file to specify overriding binding policy for the machine.

> **Note**
>
> Machine and application policy files can be directly edited with the .NET Framework Configuration tool. It makes editing these configuration files much easier. Whenever you can, use the .NET Framework Configuration tool instead of hand editing the raw XML files.

Checking to See if the File Has Been Previously Referenced

After examining the policy files, the runtime checks whether the assembly has been loaded. If the assembly has been previously referenced, a cached valued is returned instead of reloading the assembly.

Checking the GAC

The third step that the runtime takes in loading an assembly is examining the GAC. If the assembly has not been previously found, the binding policy files are merged to form a full assembly name that is looked up in the GAC. If a matching assembly is found in the GAC, then it is returned.

Probing for the Assembly

If an assembly still has not been found, then it is not in the GAC. If the assembly is not in the GAC, the runtime probes the path specified in the `<codebase>` token in the application configuration file.

In the absence of `<codebase>`, the application directory is probed for the following directories:

```
[application directory] / [assembly name].dll
[application directory] / [assembly name] / [assembly name].dll
```

If a culture is specified, the following paths are probed instead:

```
[application directory] / [culture] / [assembly name].dll
[application directory] / [culture] / [assembly name] / [assembly name].dll
```

Finally, if a private path is specified via the `<probing>` element, then each semi-colon separated path is probed, replacing the application directory with the path.

If this fails, then the search for the assembly fails and a **`System.IO.FileNotFoundException`** is thrown to indicate the failure.

Administering Policy

Binding is the mapping of an assembly reference to a physical assembly. A physical assembly is usually a DLL. A binding policy is a statement of the rules on how the binding should take place. Most likely you will use policy to upgrade an assembly from one version to another. Although you can also use it to specify the source for a file in case a portion of the assembly needs to be downloaded. A binding policy can be modified in three ways: through an application policy file, through a publisher policy file, and through a machine policy file. Administering each of these policy files is discussed next.

Default Binding Policy

As shown earlier, applications have the identity of referenced assemblies that are stored at compile time. The default binding policy is to bind to the version of assembly with which the application was built. Specific policy files need to be in place for this default policy to be overridden.

Changing the Binding Policy with an Application Policy File

To illustrate building, application policy, use the snap-in from `%SystemRoot%\Microsoft.NET\Framework\<version>\mscorcfg.msc` to edit the `<application>.exe.config` file in the directory where the application is installed. The easiest way of invoking this tool is to simply create a shortcut on your desktop to the snap-in. After the shortcut is created, you should have an icon on your desktop like Figure 6.5.

FIGURE 6.5
Shortcut to .NET Framework configuration snap-in.

Now if you double-click the shortcut, you bring up the .NET Framework Configuration tool. To demonstrate one aspect of application policy that is specifically related to assemblies, a policy will be formed that redirects all references to old assemblies to new assemblies for this application only. In the section "Installing Shared Code," you learned to install two different versions of the same FooLib.dll assembly. Assume that the new version is safe and that all references to the old version should use the new version instead. The following steps illustrate the procedure that is required to build an application policy file that redirects an old version to a new version:

1. Click on the entry titled "Applications" that can be found on the left side of the .NET Framework Configuration tool.
2. Click on the hyperlink that displays "Add an Application to Configure" on the right side of the page. This brings up a dialog box that prompts you for the application that you want to configure.
3. Check Other if the `FooTest` application is on the list, and then browse for the `FooTest` application that was placed in the 1.2 directory. This was the version of `FooTest` that specifically referenced the 1.2 version of the `FooLib` assembly. If the `FooTest` is in the initial list, then make sure that it is the correct one. Its location should be in the 1.2 subdirectory.
4. Click on the hyperlink "Managed Configured Assemblies" that is displayed after the application is selected. This brings up another page.
5. Select the "Configure an Assembly" hyperlink. This hyperlink brings you to a page that provides several options for locating the assembly you are trying to configure.
6. Select the option `Choose an Assembly from the List of Assemblies This Application Uses` to limit the number of choices that need to be made. This is a simple application, so it does not depend on many assemblies. The assembly for which you want to create a policy is FooLib.
7. Select FooLib with your mouse. Your screen should look something like Figure 6.6.

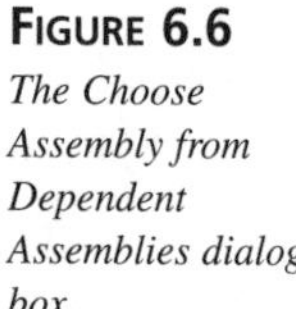

FIGURE 6.6
The Choose Assembly from Dependent Assemblies dialog box.

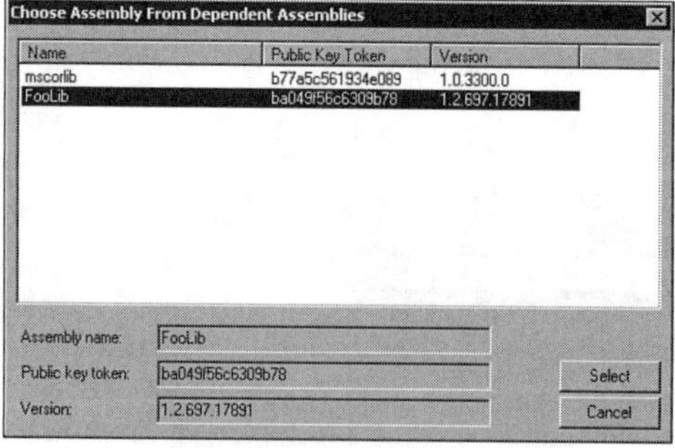

8. Click the Select button and then click the Finish button on the dialog box to which you fall back. You are presented with a set of property pages.
9. Select the Binding Policy tab to create a binding policy. A page appears that prompts you to fill in the old version and the new version.
10. Fill in the version numbers, and your property page should look like Figure 6.7.

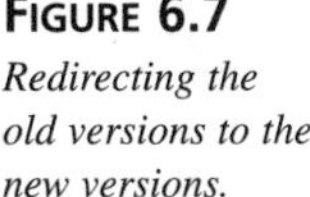

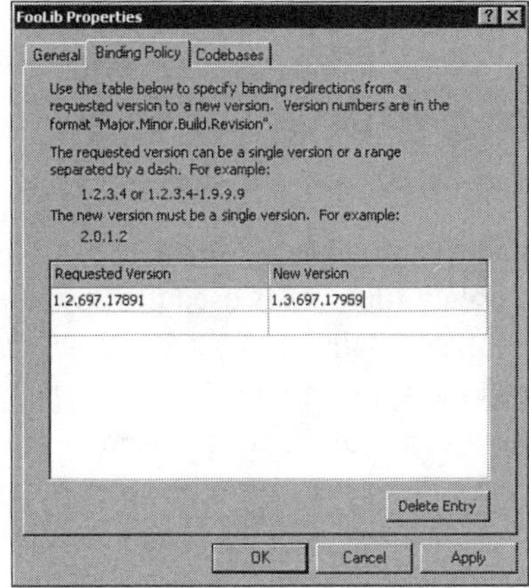

FIGURE 6.7
Redirecting the old versions to the new versions.

11. Click the Apply button followed by the OK button.
12. Exit the .NET Framework Configuration tool.

Now when you run the 1.2 version of the FooTest.exe application (FooTest.exe was created previously in the section illustrating side-by-side installation. It is assumed that the FooTest.exe that you are using is bound to the 1.2 version of FooLib in the 1.2 directory), you get the following:

```
Foo: 1.3.697.17959
```

Notice that a new file has been created in the directory of the application, titled FooTest.exe.config. The contents of this file illustrate that the .NET Framework Configuration tool has just been a convenient editor. Listing 6.8 shows the essential contents of the file.

LISTING 6.8 Redirection of FooLib Version Numbers

```
<?xml version="1.0" encoding="UTF-8"?>
<configuration>
<runtime>
  <assemblyBinding xmlns="urn:schemas-microsoft-com:asm.v1">
    <dependentAssembly>
```

LISTING 6.8 Continued

```
      <assemblyIdentity name="FooLib" publicKeyToken="ba049f56c6309b78" />
      <bindingRedirect oldVersion="1.2.697.17891"
➥newVersion="1.3.697.17959" />
    </dependentAssembly>
  </assemblyBinding>
</runtime>
</configuration>
```

Changing the Binding Policy with a Publisher Policy File

As an alternative to an application policy, a publisher can create a publisher policy file. This policy overrides all application policy files and is used to allow a publisher to make a statement about compatibility. A publisher policy file is an assembly that wraps an XML file that is of the same format as the application policy file. The publisher policy file is applied to the correct assembly because of the unique naming convention that is used in specifying a publisher policy file. Three steps are involved in creating a publisher policy file. The last step is placing the publisher policy file into the GAC, which should be done on a customer's machine. The other two steps prepare a file for distribution. To perform the same function that was done previously (mapping the old assembly version to the new assembly version), you can create a publisher policy file as follows:

1. Edit or otherwise create a file that is identical to Listing 6.8. Call it FooLib.Config.
2. Create an assembly that wraps the configuration file with `al`:

   ```
   al /link:FooLib.Config /out:policy.1.2.FooLib.dll /keyfile:foo.snk
   ```

   The name of the policy file must begin with *policy* and end with *dll*. You need to include the major and minor number of the *assembly version* in the name. You are applying this against version 1.2 of the assembly, so the publisher policy reflects this in the name. The last part of the policy filename before the suffix must be the name of the main assembly. The publisher policy must be signed with the same key that was used to sign the original assembly.

   Just as for the application policy case, the version has been redirected.

Changing the Binding Policy with a Machine Policy File

Using the shortcut that you created in the section on application policy, double-click the shortcut to bring up the .NET Framework Configuration tool. To demonstrate one aspect of machine policy that is specifically related to assemblies, a policy will be formed to redirect all references to old assemblies to new assemblies. This is the same policy that was built in the section on application policy, but now a machine-wide policy will be created for all applications that reference a given assembly. The steps to create or modify a machine policy file are as follows:

1. Click the entry titled "Configured Assemblies" that is on the left side of the .NET Framework Configuration tool.
2. Click the hyperlink that displays "Configure an Assembly" on the right pane. You are presented with a form offering you two different choices to find the assembly that you want to configure.
3. Either choose the assembly from among the assemblies in the cache, or enter the assembly information manually (assembly name and public key token). Because it's easy to recognize your assembly, choose Choose an Assembly from the Assembly Cache and click the Choose Assembly button. You are presented with a list box of all of the assemblies in the GAC.
4. Scroll down to FooLib and select the old version (it might be 1.2.697.17891). Your screen should now look like Figure 6.8.

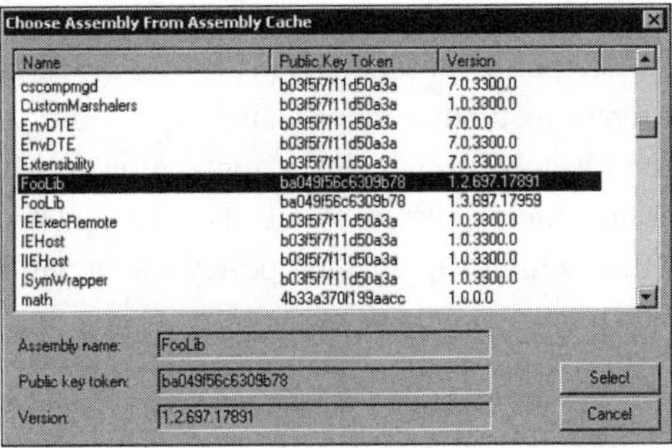

FIGURE 6.8
The Choose Assembly from Assembly Cache dialog box.

5. Click the Select button and then click Finish on the Configure an Assembly dialog box. You are presented with a Properties dialog box for the FooLib assembly.
6. Select the Binding Policy tab and enter the old version in the requested version column and the new version in the new version column. Your screen should look something like Figure 6.7, which was introduced in the "Application Policy" section.
7. Click the Apply button if everything looks good. Then click OK, and you can close out the .NET Framework Configuration tool.

Now when you run the 1.2 version of the application (FooTest.exe was created previously in the section illustrating side-by-side installation. It is assumed that the

FooTest.exe that you are using is bound to the 1.2 version of FooLib in the 1.2 directory), you get this:

```
Foo: 1.3.697.17959
```

The references to the old version of the assembly have been redirected to the new version. The tool merely acted as an editor. If you want to effect the change without the tool, then add the equivalent information to the machine.config file in `%SystemRoot%\Microsoft.NET\Framework\<version>\Config`. This file contains a lot of information, but if you search the file for `FooLib`, you will see an entry that looks like Listing 6.8. It is identical to the XML that was entered for the application policy.

Summary

This chapter focused on deploying applications and some of the tools available to make that task easier and more reliable. It illustrated the problems that are faced by those who are trying to install Windows applications today. The chapter then looked at how .NET addresses and solves many of these problems. It discussed the two types of installations, private and shared, and the advantages and disadvantages of both. You learned how to sign an assembly and place it in the Global Assembly Cache where it can be shared. You also discovered how the GAC supports multiple versions of an assembly running simultaneously. You saw three different methods for upgrading or changing the normal binding policy, which is to bind to the assembly to which the application was built. Finally, you explored a common scenario in which an assembly needs to be updated with a different version, and how that is handled with an application policy file, a publisher policy file, and a machine policy file.

Runtime Services Provided by the CLR

PART III

IN THIS PART

CHAPTER 7

Leveraging Existing Code—P/Invoke

IN THIS CHAPTER

A quote by Albert Einstein is a good way to start this chapter: “Keep it simple, but not too simple.” In other words, the material should be simple but sufficiently complete to answer the problem. In recent software history, major languages acknowledge their dependency on “legacy” software (“legacy” would refer to the way software was developed before a particular language was introduced) through some method of interoperation. With C++, you called on ‘C’ functions by specifying the function as `extern "C"`. Java used `JNI`. Even most flavors of ‘C’ allowed for `__asm` constructs so that a programmer could drop down to assembly if he felt so compelled.

With the .NET Framework, a method is available by which you can call legacy C/C++ code, unmanaged code. The first of these methods is known as *platform invocation,* or *P/Invoke*. This chapter explains how to call methods and functions that were written before the .NET Framework existed. This chapter shows how the .NET Framework makes working with simple calls into legacy C/C++ code easy and complex calls into legacy C/C++ code doable. Einstein would approve. It is simple for simple cases and can be about as complex as you need it to be.

Platform Invoke Overview

A large investment has been made in ensuring that unmanaged code is a full participant. For most cases, it is simple to seamlessly interoperate with legacy code. Listings 7.1 through 7.4 show how to interoperate with `MessageBox` in some of the languages that are supported under the .NET Framework.

Listing 7.1 shows how to set up a call to the legacy code in the user32.dll from C#.

LISTING 7.1 Message Box Interaction from C#

```
using System;
using System.Runtime.InteropServices;

public class Win32 {
   [DllImport("user32.dll", CharSet=CharSet.Auto)]
   public static extern int MessageBox(int hWnd, String text,
                  String caption, uint type);
}

public class HelloWorld {
        public static void Main() {
      Win32.MessageBox(0, "Hello World", "Platform Invoke Sample", 0);
        }
}
```

Listing 7.2 shows how to set up a call to the legacy code in the user32.dll from Visual Basic.

LISTING 7.2 Message Box Interaction from VB

```
Imports System.Runtime.InteropServices

Public Class Win32
    <DllImport("USER32.DLL", CharSet:=CharSet.Unicode)> _
    Public Shared Function _
    MessageBox(ByVal hWnd As Integer,
               ByVal txt As String,
               ByVal caption As String,
               ByVal Type As Integer) As Integer
    End Function
End Class

Public Class HelloWorld
   Public Shared Sub Main()
      Win32.MessageBox(0, "Hello World", "Platform Invoke Sample", 0)
   End Sub
End Class
```

Listing 7.3 shows how to set up a call to the legacy code in the user32.dll from C++.

LISTING 7.3 Message Box Interaction from C++

```
using namespace System::Runtime::InteropServices;

typedef void* HWND;
[DllImport("user32", CharSet=CharSet::Auto)]
extern "C" int MessageBox(HWND hWnd,
                          String* pText,
                          String* pCaption,
                          unsigned int uType);
void main(void) {
     String* pText = L"Hello World!";
     String* pCaption = L"Platform Invoke Sample";
     MessageBox(0, pText, pCaption, 0);
}
```

Listing 7.4 shows how to set up a call to the legacy code in the user32.dll from J#.

LISTING 7.4 Message Box Interaction from J#

```
public class HelloWorld
{
    /** @attribute DllImportAttribute("USER32") */
    private static native int MessageBox(int hWnd, System.String  text,
                                         System.String  caption, int type);

    public static void main(String[] args)
```

LISTING 7.4 Continued

```
    {
        MessageBox(0, "Hello World from J#!", "Platform Invoke Sample", 0);
    }
}
```

You can see that P/Invoke is a feature of the .NET Framework and not a feature of any particular language. You can see how you could start a new project with C# experts and still not have to throw away or port all of the existing code in which you have invested. The following section lists some of the reasons that you would want to interoperate with old code.

Why Platform Invoke Interop?

First, you need to preserve your investment. It is a little hard to see in the simple examples in Listings 7.1–7.4, but many companies invest considerable time and money into software. It would be impractical to suggest to management that you want to spend X amount of time porting existing software to a new platform that will have no new features that a customer can see. In some cases, the functionality of the existing software might be so involved and complex that porting it to another language would be the equivalent of rewriting it. The "bean counters" see this as an investment of time and money that has at best no return on investment, and at worst, a negative return. For the most part, the bean counters are right. Being on the latest platform does not count much for the bottom line. However, being able to reuse software is appealing to engineers and accountants alike.

Second, the new platform might offer significant advantages (.NET Framework clearly does), so you would like to begin to take advantage of these features as soon as possible. In the end, you would like to have all of your code under one roof, but for now, you just want to use the old code. In this case, interop gives you the option of phasing in the pieces of your application one at a time. While your new app is generating revenue, your engineers can be working on porting pieces of the old code to the new platform. This might have the added benefit of compartmentalizing your software, making it easier to upgrade and maintain in the long run.

Third, some things do not change. It might be a black box that you cannot change because it is from a third party, you don't have the source any more, the tools are not available that are needed to compile it, and so on.

> **Note**
>
> I was on a project such as this where the company inherited a large body of code, a portion of which required a tool to generate files to parse input. The tool is no longer available, which means that it is not practically possible to do anything with the code that requires any new parsing constructs. You might find yourself in a similar situation.

With interop, you can still use the existing code in a new environment that was not available when the original software was written.

Some Other Interop Methods

Looking at the samples in Listings 7.1 to 7.4, you might notice the similarities between this method of interoperation and Visual Basic 6.0's `Declare` statement. You can achieve much of the same functionality as P/Invoke with the following VB 6 `Declare` statement:

```
Declare Function MessageBox Lib "user32" Alias "MessageBoxW"( hWnd As Long,
     txt As String, caption As String, Typ As Long) As Long
```

In fact, using `Declare` is still supported as a viable means to use old code with Visual Basic .NET. The old `Declare` and the new `Declare` still have issues that center around type safety; regardless, you can use `Declare` to interop with code that was not written in VB .NET.

Another means of interoperating with legacy code is to use the `LoadLibrary` API followed by a call to `GetProcAddress`. These two functions give a C/C++ program a means of loading a DLL and calling into the functions implemented in the DLL. These routines were originally developed to provide for binary interoperability. These routines are inherently type unsafe. Because they return what effectively is an address pointer, they cannot be used alone in a safe managed environment.

> **Note**
>
> A tool called *depends* was designed to show DLL dependency information about an executable or DLL. `Depends` is found in `\Program Files\Microsoft Visual Studio .NET\Common7\Tools\Bin`. This tool has a feature called *profiling* that tracks how DLLs are loaded into a process as it is running. If you run this tool on the executable that is generated from Listing 7.1 (calling an unmanaged MessageBox API), you get the following output:

```
LoadLibraryExW("f:\user32.dll", 0x00000000, LOAD_WITH_ALTERED_SEARCH_PATH)
➥called from "MSCORWKS.DLL" at address 0x791BDE66.
LoadLibraryExW("f:\user32.dll", 0x00000000, LOAD_WITH_ALTERED_SEARCH_PATH)
➥returned NULL. Error: The specified module could not be found (126).
LoadLibraryExW("user32.dll", 0x00000000, 0x00000000) called from
➥"MSCORWKS.DLL" at address 0x791BDE66.
LoadLibraryExW("user32.dll", 0x00000000, 0x00000000) returned 0x77D40000.
GetProcAddress(0x77D40000 [USER32.DLL], "MessageBox") called from
➥"MSCORWKS.DLL" at address 0x791F2ECB and returned NULL.
➥Error: The specified procedure could not be found (127).
GetProcAddress(0x77D40000 [USER32.DLL], "MessageBoxW") called from
➥"MSCORWKS.DLL" at address 0x791F2F49 and returned 0x77D78839.
```

From this output, you can see that the CLR is essentially calling `LoadLibrary` and `GetProcAddress` as you do P/Invoke call.

Details of Platform Invoke

To fully use P/Invoke services, you need to understand the concepts of marshaling and callbacks. This section explores each of these topics. Pay particular attention to marshaling because COM Interop uses the same underlying marshaling service as P/Invoke. COM Interop is covered in Chapters 8, "Using COM/COM+ in Managed Code," and 9, "Using Managed Code as a COM/COM+ Component."

> **Note**
>
> It would not be practical to show examples from every language throughout this chapter, so the focus has been narrowed to C#. The same features that are shown are available in most languages supported in the .NET Framework.

Declaring the Function: `DllImport` Attribute

All P/Invoke calls are declared through **`DllImportAttribute`**. In its simplest form, **`DllImportAttribute`** declares the name of the DLL in which the function containing the unmanaged code lives. This attribute is applied to an external static function that, by default, has the same name as the unmanaged function. After this function is declared, managed code can call the function by name to initiate a managed to unmanaged transition and call the function in the DLL specified as unmanaged code. You have already seen a couple of examples using the **`DllImport`** attribute.

To use the **`DllImportAttribute`**, you need to know what functions are defined in the DLL. One place that you can look is the documentation. Often, the documentation states which DLL implements the function. Many of the functions that Microsoft (and others) document include some indication in to which DLL the function is implemented in. If you don't have this documentation or it is incomplete, then you can use `dumpbin -exports foo.dll` or `link -dump -exports foo.dll`. You need to have both dumpbin.exe and link.exe in your PATH environment variable or these calls will fail. Currently, both of these programs are in `\Program Files\Microsoft Visual Studio .NET\Vc7\bin`). Executing this function on kernel32.dll yields Listing 7.5.

LISTING 7.5 DumpBin Output for Kernel.dll

```
Microsoft (R) COFF/PE Dumper Version 7.00.9372.1
Copyright (C) Microsoft Corporation.  All rights reserved.


Dump of file kernel32.dll

File Type: DLL

  Section contains the following exports for KERNEL32.dll

    00000000 characteristics
    3A1B5EB6 time date stamp Tue Nov 21 23:50:46 2000
        0.00 version
           1 ordinal base
         823 number of functions
         823 number of names

    ordinal hint RVA      name

          1    0 0000CC71 AddAtomA
          2    1 0000CC61 AddAtomW
          3    2 00044521 AddConsoleAliasA
          4    3 000444EA AddConsoleAliasW
          5    4 000452D8 AllocConsole
          6    5 0003308F AllocateUserPhysicalPages
          7    6 00007828 AreFileApisANSI
          8    7 00043C78 AssignProcessToJobObject
          9    8 00028DE8 BackupRead
         10    9 00029044 BackupSeek
. . .
        708  2C3 00006779 Sleep
         709 2C4 00006787 SleepEx
. . .
```

If you wanted to P/Invoke the `Sleep` function, you now know that it is in kernel32.dll. To learn what the arguments are to this function, you need to consult the documentation for this function. You can use `dumpbin` to similarly examine other DLL files. All you need to call the function with P/Invoke are the DLL in which the function is implemented, the name of the function, and the arguments it takes.

Take the following call declaration:

```
[DllImport("unmanaged.dll")]
public static extern void Foo();
```

Listing 7.5 shows a declaration of a function that is implemented in the DLL `"unmanaged.dll"`. The name of the function defaults to the name given to the managed function. Listing 7.5 shows that the managed function does not return anything, and no arguments exist. The CLR looks for a function in `"unmanaged.dll"` that has the same signature as specified by the managed function. In the DLL `"unmanaged.dll"`, a function should exist called `Foo` that takes no arguments and does not return anything. If the CLR does not find the function as specified, you get an **`EntryPointNotFoundException`** when you try to call the function. From C, the function should be declared like the following:

```
extern "C" _declspec(dllexport) void Foo();
```

`DllImportAttribute` has several options that can be used to change the behavior of the interop:

- **`CallingConvention`**—This changes the calling convention that is used to call the unmanaged function. Following are the possible values for the **`CallingConvention`** enum:

  `Cdecl`—The caller cleans the stack.

  `FastCall`—This is not supported in this version of the CLR.

  `StdCall`—The callee cleans the stack. This is the default.

  `ThisCall`—The first argument passed is the `this` pointer.

  `Winapi`—`StdCall` on Windows, **`Cdecl`** on Windows CE.

  ```
  [DllImport("unmanaged.dll", CallingConvention=
  CallingConvention.StdCall)]
  ```

  This declaration indicates that the runtime should use **`StdCall`** as a calling convention (this is the default). Practically speaking, you should take the default and just be aware that other options are available. Using **`StdCall`** covers a vast majority of the cases where interop is useful.

- **`CharSet`**—This controls the name mangling (with macros) and the way that string arguments are passed to the unmanaged function. The following are possible values for the **`CharSet`** enum:

Ansi—Marshal strings as 1 byte strings. If the parameter **ExactSpelling** is false or not specified, setting the **CharSet** to **Ansi** also has the effect of having the runtime look for the function with an 'A' appended to the end of the name, in addition to the name of the function.

Auto—The character set is set to **Unicode** for Windows NT and **Ansi** for Windows 95.

Unicode—Marshal strings as Unicode 2-byte characters. As with **Ansi**, if **ExactSpelling** is false or is not specified, setting **CharSet** to Unicode results in the runtime looking for the function with a 'W' appended to the name in addition to searching for the name of the function.

```
[DllImport("unmanaged.dll", CharSet=CharSet.Unicode)]
```

- **EntryPoint**—This specifies the name or ordinal of the DLL. This function allows the programmer to override the default of taking the name of the function that is declared in the managed code:

```
[DllImport("unmanaged.dll", EntryPoint="Foo")]
public static extern void FooBar();
```

Now the managed code references this function as `FooBar`, but the runtime looks for the signature `Foo` in the DLL. The signature still needs to match that defined in the DLL.

- **ExactSpelling**—This specifies whether the name of the function should be appended with 'A' or 'W' for accessing ANSI or Unicode respectively. This parameter in the **DllImportAttribute** is a Boolean:

```
[DllImport("unmanaged.dll", ExactSpelling=false)]
public static extern void FooBar();
```

With this declaration, the runtime looks for `FooBarA` and `FooBar`. If **CharSet** is set to Unicode, it would look for `FooBarW` and `FooBar`.

- **PreserveSig**—Typically, all COM functions return an `HRESULT` value that indicates whether the function succeeded. ATL and VB transform a COM function that returns `HRESULT` to a function that returns the parameter marked with `[out, retval]` in the IDL. If the wrapper function call for ATL or VB finds that the "raw" COM call returned an error, then the wrapper function throws an exception to indicate the error. This parameter of **DllImportAttribute** indicates whether you want this kind of function transformation to occur. You would rarely want this transformation for P/Invoke, so the default of false is proper.

- **SetLastError**—This is another Boolean parameter. If it is true, it causes a call to the Win32 function `SetLastError` before returning from the method. If you need to retrieve the error set by this unmanaged code, you can call the static method **Marshal.GetLastWin32Error**. The error code that was returned by the last managed method called will be returned. Listing 7.6 shows an example of using this option to call the LogonUser Win32 API.

LISTING 7.6 DllImport Specification for a Group of Functions That Support LogonUser

```
struct NativeMethods
{
    [DllImport("advapi32.dll", SetLastError=true)]
    public static extern bool LogonUser(string lpszUsername,
                                        string lpszDomain,
                                        string lpszPassword,
                                        int dwLogonType,
                                        int dwLogonProvider,
                                        out IntPtr phToken);
    [DllImport("Kernel32.dll")]
    public static extern uint FormatMessage(
        uint dwFlags,          // source and processing options
        IntPtr lpSource,      // message source
        uint dwMessageId,      // message identifier
        uint dwLanguageId,      // language identifier
        StringBuilder lpBuffer,     // message buffer
        uint nSize,           // maximum size of message buffer
        IntPtr arguments      // array of message inserts
        );
    [DllImport("Kernel32.dll")]
    public static extern int CloseHandle(IntPtr token);
}
```

Using the specifications in Listing 7.6, you can call `LogonUser`. If it returns false (indicating that the logon was unsuccessful), you can call **`Marshal.GetLastWin32Error`** to find out why. (You probably did not supply the correct password.) You can also pass the value returned from **`Marshal.GetLastWin32Error`** to `FormatMessage` (another P/Invoke call to unmanaged code to get a human-readable string explaining what the error was). By specifying **`SetLastError`**, you are assured that the error code returned will be applicable to the method that you tried to call.

Marshaling

Marshaling in the classical sense is the process of packing one or more items into a data buffer for transport over a communication channel (serial, network, and so on). Its companion process, demarshaling, takes that data stream and converts it back into its constituent parts. .NET interop does not use a traditional communication channel; rather, a layer is inserted between your managed code and your unmanaged code that translates your arguments and return values to the correct format. Look at the following declaration:

```
[DllImport("unmanaged.dll")]
public static extern int AddInteger(int a, int b);
```

You can call as follows:

```
int retInt = Native.AddInteger(1, 2);
Console.WriteLine("AddInteger after: {0}", retInt);
```

The preceding snippet is part of a project built to exercise some of the P/Invoke marshaling in the `Marshal` directory.

To interop, you do not need to have the source available, but it is available in this case. If you check the debug option to allow stepping into unmanaged code, you can step into the DLL code. The `AddInteger` function looks like this:

```
UNMANAGED_API int AddInteger(int a, int b)
{
    return a + b;
}
```


This is a simple example because `int` in unmanaged code is similar to `int` in managed code. Little if any true marshaling is taking place. It is possible to interop with many functions with this kind of ease.

Marshaling Simple Value Types

For simple value types, interop is easy. Table 7.1 shows how to specify a function or marshal simple value types.

TABLE 7.1 Simple Value Marshaling Translation

Unmanaged Type	*Managed Type*
unsigned char	byte
short	short
unsigned short	ushort
int	int
unsigned int	uint
long	int
unsigned long	uint
DWORD	uint
char	char
float	float
double	double

If the arguments of the unmanaged function are of the type in the first column, then you declare the managed function to have the type of the second column. Notice that with

C#, a long is 64 bits. If you were to specify a long when the argument for the unmanaged function was a long, the result would be too many bytes on the unmanaged end.

If you need to pass the address of a simple value type so that it can be filled in by the unmanaged function, add the keyword **out** to the declaration as follows:

```
[DllImport("unmanaged.dll")]
public static extern void FloatOutFunc(float a, out float o);
```

This function passes the address to a float to the unmanaged function. If you need to pass information in both directions, use the keyword **ref**.

Marshaling Strings

The next sample (still from the `Marshal` directory) requires you to marshal a string between managed and unmanaged code. The .NET Framework "knows" about strings, so the declaration is simple and straightforward:

```
[DllImport("unmanaged.dll")]
public static extern int StringLength(string str);
```

Calling and using the function is equally as simple:

```
string str = "This is a test";
int retLength = Native.StringLength(str);
Console.WriteLine("String after: {0}", retLength);
```

This unmanaged function takes in a string and returns the length of the string. You know that a string in C# is a 16-bit per character Unicode sequence. The default for marshaling strings is to marshal all strings as 8-bit per character null-terminated `char` arrays (`char *`). By default, the runtime is converting **string** to a `char *` array. The signature of the unmanaged code is as follows:

```
UNMANAGED_API int StringFunction(LPCSTR str);
```

If the unmanaged code that you were trying to call took a Unicode sequence (or at least a `wchar_t *` array), then the declaration of the function would look like this:

```
[DllImport("unmanaged.dll")]
public static extern int UnicodeStringLength(
     [MarshalAs(UnmanagedType.LPWStr)] string str);
```

or this:

```
[DllImport("unmanaged.dll", CharSet=CharSet.Unicode)]
public static extern int UnicodeStringLength(string str);
```

You call the function just as you called the ANSI string length function. The signature of the unmanaged function looks like this:

```
UNMANAGED_API int UnicodeStringLength(wchar_t * str);
```

Table 7.2 summarizes marshaling for string arguments.

TABLE 7.2 String Marshaling Translation

Marshal Description	*Unmanaged String Type*	*Managed String Type*
Return value	char *	String
Value	char *	String
Reference	char *	StringBuilder

You have seen examples of passing a string by value. The other two marshaling contexts require some explanation.

The declaration for returning a string looks familiar:

```
[DllImport("unmanaged.dll")]
public static extern string ConcatString(string a, string b);
```

Using the function is the same as you would expect; however, the implementation of the unmanaged function might require some modification. Because the .NET runtime assumes that memory allocation is done with `CoTaskMemAlloc`, it calls `CoTaskMemFree` after the string has been copied to the result **`string`**. The implementation needs to look like Listing 7.7.

LISTING 7.7 Implementation of an Unmanaged Function That Allocates Memory

```
UNMANAGED_API char* ConcatString(char* a, char* b)
{
    size_t size = strlen(a) + strlen(b) + 1;

    // CoTaskMemAlloc must be used instead of the new operator
    // because code on the managed side will call Marshal.FreeCoTaskMem
    // to free this memory.

    char* buffer = (char*)CoTaskMemAlloc( size * sizeof(char) );

    strcpy(buffer, a);
    strcat(buffer, b);

    return buffer;
}
```

If you want to use P/Invoke to interop with a function that uses `new` or `malloc`, a clean solution doesn't really exist. If you have access to the source of the DLL, you could write a small DLL that wraps your function. The code for this function would look something like Listing 7.8.

LISTING 7.8 Implementation of a Wrapper Around an Unmanaged Function That Allocates Memory

```
UNMANAGED_API char* WrapperConcatString(char* a, char* b)
{
    size_t size = strlen(a) + strlen(b) + 1;

    // This is assuming that the source to ConcatString is unavailable
    // The function allocates enough memory to hold the concatenation of
    // a and b. This is a stub function that the managed code calls instead
    // of directly calling ConcatString because we need to return memory
    // that is allocated with CoTaskMemAlloc.

    char* buffer = (char*)CoTaskMemAlloc( size * sizeof(char) );

    char* temp = ConcatString(a, b);

    strcpy(buffer, temp);
    delete [] temp;

    return buffer;
}
```

This wrapper function assumes that the `ConcatString` function allocates memory with `new []`. When the string is returned from `ConcatString`, it is copied to a buffer that is allocated with `CoTaskMemFree`. The intermediary buffer is deleted, and the pointer to the buffer is returned. The pointer is then freed with `CoTaskMemFree` after the contents are copied to the result **`string`**.

Another instance of marshaling strings listed in Table 7.2 that requires some explanation is when the string is passed by reference to unmanaged code. This implies that the unmanaged code is to fill in the string with some value. You need to use the **`StringBuilder`** class to pre-allocate a memory buffer large enough to hold the string that is expected from the function. The declaration would look like the following:

```
[DllImport("unmanaged.dll")]
public static extern void ConcatOutString(string a, string b, StringBuilder o);
```

To call the function, you would use code like the following:

```
StringBuilder sbr = new StringBuilder(128);
Native.ConcatOutString(a, b, sbr);
Console.WriteLine("After String Out Concat: {0}", sbr);
```

To call an unmanaged function that passes back a string in one of the arguments, you need to allocate space to hold the string. The preceding snippet of code allocates space for 128 bytes. This buffer is then passed to the unmanaged code. The runtime converts the **`StringBuilder`** instance to a string pointer into which memory can be copied. The implementation for this type of function would look something like this:

```
UNMANAGED_API void ConcatOutString(char* a, char* b, char * o)
{
    size_t size = strlen(a) + strlen(b) + 1;
    strcpy(o, a);
    strcat(o, b);
}
```

Notice that the last argument (`char *o`) is large enough to contain the result of the concatenation of both strings. In addition, if Unicode characters are used in the unmanaged function, then the declaration requires that each string be decorated with the **`[MarshalAs(UnmanagedType.LPWStr)]`**, or that the character set of the function be declared as **`CharSet.Unicode`**.

Marshaling Structures

A specific structure is often either passed to the unmanaged code or passed back from the unmanaged code. Of course, a structure in unmanaged code is different from a structure in managed code; therefore, a structure needs to be marshaled when passed to or from unmanaged code. Little needs to be done to declare a function that writes to or reads from managed structures. Most of the work is declaring the structure in such a way in managed code that it mimics the layout in unmanaged code. By default, managed code makes no guarantees as to the layout of the data in a structure. In fact, it is more likely that the final position of a field in a structure is more determined by its size than how it is specified in the declaration and definition. In unmanaged code, particularly 'C' code, the declaration and definition almost exclusively determine the layout of a structure. For example, look at the structure in Listing 7.9.

LISTING 7.9 Simple Raw Structure

```
public struct TestStruct
{
    public byte a;
    public short b;
    public int c;
    public byte d;
    public short e;
    public int f;
}
```

It is more likely that the layout of this structure in memory will cluster fields `a` and `d`, `b` and `e`, and `c` and `f` together. You would not want to pass this to unmanaged code. For this reason, an attribute is available that can specify the layout of a structure. Listing 7.10 shows the same structure now specifying the layout.

LISTING 7.10 Structure with a Specific Layout

```
[StructLayout(LayoutKind.Sequential)]
public struct TestStruct
{
    public byte a;
    public short b;
    public int c;
    public byte d;
    public short e;
    public int f;
}
```

Now the runtime will not move the fields around and the order will be `a`, `b`, `c`, `d`, `e`, and `f`, as expected for an unmanaged structure. When passing structures to and from unmanaged code, you should always specify the **`StructLayoutAttribute`**; otherwise, the memory layout will be unpredictable. For structures that are marshaled with P/Invoke, this marshaling seems to be automatic **`LayoutKind.Sequential`**. (You shouldn't count on this fact, however. For classes in which a layout attribute is not attached to the class, an exception is thrown: **`System.Runtime.InteropServices.MarshalDirectiveException`**. Additional information: Cannot marshal parameter #1: The type definition of this type has no layout information).

After you have the marshaling characteristics specified, you can call the unmanaged code and pass in a managed structure, as shown in Listing 7.11.

LISTING 7.11 Calling an Unmanaged Function with a Structure Argument

```
Native.TestStruct s = new Native.TestStruct();
s.a = 0x11;
s.b = 0x22;
s.c = 0x33;
s.d = 0x44;
s.e = 0x55;
s.f = 0x66;
Native.TestStructFunction(ref s);
```

In this sample, the structure is being passed by reference so that the called function can modify the structure and pass it back. If the structure is passed by value, then all modifications in the called function are ignored.

As a slightly more complicated example, the following declares a function that takes two complex numbers, adds them together, and returns the result as a return value. The structure looks like Listing 7.12.

LISTING 7.12 A Complex Number to Be Passed to Unmanaged Code

```
[StructLayout(LayoutKind.Sequential)]
public struct Complex
{
    public Complex(float re, float im)
    {
        this.re = re;
        this.im = im;
    }
    float re;
    float im;
}
```

The declaration of the function looks like this:

```
[DllImport("unmanaged.dll")]
public static extern Complex ComplexAdd(Complex a, Complex b);
```

Again, with little code, you can pass instances of structures that are defined in managed code to unmanaged code.

Not only can the layout be controlled with an attribute attached to the structure, but the marshaling of individual fields of the structure can also be controlled with attributes. For example, you could have a string as a field in a structure. That field could be controlled with marshaling attributes. For example, you could have a function that takes the following structure:

```
typedef struct _StructStringRef
{
    wchar_t *a;
    char *b;
}
```

This structure is particularly tricky because it contains both an ANSI string and a Unicode string. You cannot simply specify a **CharSet** that would be used to marshal the whole class. You must specify how each **string** in managed space will be marshaled. You end up with the structure declaration in managed space that is shown in Listing 7.13.

LISTING 7.13 A Structure with ANSI and Unicode Strings

```
[StructLayout(LayoutKind.Sequential)]
public struct StructStringRef
{
    public StructStringRef (string a, string b)
    {
        this.a = a;
        this.b = b;
    }
```

LISTING 7.13 Continued

```
    [MarshalAs( UnmanagedType.ByValTStr)]
    public string a;
    [MarshalAs( UnmanagedType.ByValTStr)]
    public string b;
}
```

Now you can call an unmanaged function that takes this structure as follows:

```
Native.StructStringRef sr = new Native.StructStringRef("Testing.",
                                                      "One, Two, Three.");
Native.TestStructStringRef(sr);
```

This sample shows an example of specifying a marshaling type to a specific field. You can specify any one of the marshaling types to individual fields as appropriate.

Marshaling Arrays

It is possible to marshal arrays of all of the simple value types that have been discussed so far, as well as arrays of strings. You can call a function that takes an array of integers with the following declaration:

```
[DllImport("unmanaged.dll")]
public static extern int IntArrayFunction(int [] ia, int length);
```

Now you can call this function with the following code:

```
int[] ia = {1, 2, 3, 4};
Console.WriteLine("Int array before: {0}", ia.Length);
retInt = Native.IntArrayFunction(ia, ia.Length);
Console.WriteLine("Int array after: {0}", retInt);
```

The signature for the unmanaged implementation of this function looks like this:

```
UNMANAGED_API int IntArrayFunction(int *pia, int length);
```

All of the value types listed in Table 7.1 can be easily marshaled in the same way that has been shown for `int`. Even string arrays can be passed to an unmanaged function:

```
[DllImport("unmanaged.dll")]
public static extern int StringArrayFunction(string [] sa, int length);
```

The arrays are not restricted to one dimension. Listing 7.14 shows the declaration for a function that takes two two-dimensional matrices in and outputs an array that is the result of multiplying the two input matrices.

LISTING 7.14 Declaring a Function That Multiplies Two Matrices

```
[DllImport("unmanaged.dll")]
public static extern void MatrixMultiplyFunction(int [,] a,
                                                  int [,] b,
            [Out] int [,] c,
            int x, int y, int z);
```

It is easy to call unmanaged code using this signature. You simply allocate the arrays as would seem appropriate to the language. Listing 7.15 shows one possible call to the multiplication routine shown in Listing 7.14.

LISTING 7.15 Calling an Unmanaged Array Multiplication Function

```
int [,] am = new int [2,2] {{1,-2},{3,4}};
int [,] bm = new int [2,3] {{5,4,-2},{-3,0,1}};
int [,] cm = new int [2,3];
Native.MatrixMultiplyFunction(am, bm, cm, 2, 2, 3);
```

You can see that this can easily be extended to higher order dimensions.

It is also possible to marshal arrays of structures. To illustrate this, you can create an unmanaged function that takes an array of complex numbers, averages them, and returns the result. The declaration would look like this:

```
[DllImport("unmanaged.dll")]
public static extern Complex ComplexAverage(Complex [] a, int length);
```

Calling this function would look something like what is shown in Listing 7.16.

LISTING 7.16 Returning the Average of an Array of Complex Numbers

```
Native.Complex [] ca = new Native.Complex [] {new Native.Complex(1,2),
                                              new Native.Complex(3,4),
                                              new Native.Complex(5,6),
                                              new Native.Complex(7,8)};
Native.Complex cr = Native.ComplexAverage(ca, ca.Length);
Console.WriteLine("Complex average: {0} {1}", cr.Real, cr.Imaginary);
```

Callbacks

You can pass a delegate from managed code to unmanaged code. The marshaled delegate will be treated by the unmanaged code as if it were a function pointer. This effectively allows unmanaged code to callback into managed code. Unfortunately, as of the first version of the .NET Framework, it is not possible to do the reverse (pass a function pointer back from unmanaged code that managed code could callback into unmanaged code). Perhaps this functionality will be available in the next version.

Note

The programs for this section are available in the `Callback` directory as a single solution called Callback.

For the first simple case, an array of integers will be passed to unmanaged code. In addition, a delegate will be called from unmanaged code for each member of the array. The input arguments to the callback will be the index of the array and the value that was at that index. The declarations that are required for this callback to work are shown in Listing 7.17.

LISTING 7.17 Declarations That Are Required for Unmanaged Code to Callback into Managed Code

```
public delegate void IntegerEchoCallback(int index, int integerValue);
[DllImport("unmanaged.dll")]
. . .
public static extern void IntegerCallback(int [] intArray,
                                          int nints,
                                          IntegerEchoCallback callback);
```

Calling the function requires the construction of the delegate and simply calling the function as shown in Listing 7.18.

LISTING 7.18 Illustrating a Callback That Echoes the Members of an Integer Array

```
static void IntegerEcho(int index, int integerValue)
{
    Console.WriteLine("{0} - {1}", index, integerValue);
}
. . .
int [] ia = new int [] {1, 2, 3, 4, 5};
IntegerEchoCallback integerCallback = new IntegerEchoCallback(IntegerEcho);
Native.IntegerCallback(ia, ia.Length, integerCallback);
```

This is a simple example. It is possible to put directives on the callback to control the marshaling behavior. One example would be doing what is shown in Listings 7.17 and 7.18, but with strings. Listing 7.19 shows the declarations to use for a string callback.

LISTING 7.19 Declarations for a Callback Involving Strings

```
public delegate void StringEchoCallback(int index,
                                        [MarshalAs(UnmanagedType.LPWStr)]
                                        string str);
. . .
```

LISTING 7.19 Continued

```
[DllImport("unmanaged.dll", CharSet=CharSet.Unicode)]
public static extern void StringCallback(string [] stringArray,
                                         int nstrings,
                                         StringEchoCallback callback);
```

Notice that the delegate has a specific marshaling attribute attached to one of its arguments. Now when the unmanaged code calls back, the argument will be marshaled in reverse. (Here, it's converted from a pointer to a Unicode string to a **string** class.)

With these declarations in place, you can call the unmanaged function, specifying the callback address as shown in Listing 7.20.

LISTING 7.20 Calling an Unmanaged Function with a Callback That Echoes Strings

```
static void StringEcho(int index, string str)
{
    Console.WriteLine("{0} - {1}", index, str);
}
. . .
string [] sa = new string [] {"This", "is", "a", "test"};
StringEchoCallback stringCallback = new StringEchoCallback(StringEcho);
Native.StringCallback(sa, sa.Length, stringCallback);
```

Using VC++ Managed Extensions

This chapter originally indicated that it would only show samples in C#, but VC++ has two different models that can be used for interop. The first uses the VC++ version of **DllImport**. You will see some samples using VC++ just for completeness, but except for the syntax differences, VC++ is much like C#. The other model is IJW (It-Just-Works). This model does not require **DllImport**, and the legacy DLL is linked into the application much like you have always linked in DLLs in the past. IJW has many advantages and disadvantages that will become clear as you read the following sections.

Using VC++ DllImport

Listing 7.21 shows some lines from the `VCMarshal` solution to give you an idea of the flavor of the VC++ implementation of **DllImport**.

LISTING 7.21 Using **DllImport** with VC++

```
namespace Native
{
    [DllImport("unmanaged")]
    extern "C" int AddInteger(int a, int b);
```

LISTING 7.21 Continued

```
    [DllImport("unmanaged")]
    extern "C" int StringLength(String* str);
    [DllImport("unmanaged", CharSet=CharSet::Unicode)]
    extern "C" int UnicodeStringLength(String* str);

    [DllImport("unmanaged.dll")]
    extern "C" unsigned char ByteFunc(unsigned char a);
    [DllImport("unmanaged.dll")]
    extern "C" short ShortFunc(short a);
    [DllImport("unmanaged.dll")]
    extern "C" unsigned short WordFunc(short a);
    [DllImport("unmanaged.dll")]
    extern "C" unsigned int UintFunc(unsigned int a);
    [DllImport("unmanaged.dll")]
    extern "C" int LongFunc(int a);
    [DllImport("unmanaged.dll")]
    extern "C" unsigned int UnsignedLongFunc(unsigned int a);
    [DllImport("unmanaged.dll")]
    extern "C" char CharFunc(char a);
    [DllImport("unmanaged.dll")]
    extern "C" float FloatFunc(float a);
    [DllImport("unmanaged.dll")]
    extern "C" double DoubleFunc(double a);

. . .
}

int _tmain(void)
{
    Console::WriteLine(S"Hello World");
    int retInt = Native::AddInteger(1, 2);
    Console::WriteLine(S"AddInteger after: {0}", __box(retInt));

    String *str = S"This is a test";
    int retLength = Native::StringLength(str);
    Console::WriteLine(S"String length: {0}", __box(retLength));

    retLength = Native::UnicodeStringLength(str);
    Console::WriteLine(S"Unicode string length: {0}", __box(retLength));

    unsigned char byteRet = Native::ByteFunc(10);
    short shortRet = Native::ShortFunc(10);
    unsigned short ushortRet = Native::WordFunc(10);
    unsigned int uintRet = Native::UintFunc(10);
    int longRet = Native::LongFunc(10);
    unsigned int ulongRet = Native::UnsignedLongFunc(10);
    char charRet = Native::CharFunc((char)10);
    float floatRet = Native::FloatFunc(10);
    double doubleRet = Native::DoubleFunc(10);
```

Notice that, unlike C#, `char` and `long` are compatible (size-wise) with their unmanaged counterparts. In addition, most of what used to be objects are now pointers to objects (**`string`** `a` becomes **`String`** `*a`). The values supplied as arguments to **`Console::WriteLine`** need to be **`__box`**'d to compile and display correctly. For the most part, all of these modifications are related to syntax and are not much different from using **`DllImport`** and `P/Invoke` with C#.

Using VC++ IJW

Traditionally, VC++ applications could link in DLLs using an export library that contained enough information about the DLL to allow it to be loaded and the required function called. Information about the signature of the function to be called was contained in a header file that described each of the functions in the DLL. This method of importing DLLs still works, but now, the C++ code that is doing the importing can be managed.

It's unnecessary to use **`DllImport`** when using IJW. One simple include that describes the signatures of the functions that you want to call is all that is required. The header file might be part of an existing project if you have the source, or it might be a system file that describes the function, such as for `MessageBox` (which is declared in WinUser.h). You will need to find the header file that is appropriate for the function that you want to call. If you know the signature for the function that you want to call, it might be possible to omit a header describing the function. (Many of these headers describe more than you want to know about everything you don't care about, and mixed in there is the description of the function that you want to call. If you can neatly describe your function without the associated header file, then do so.) For the sample, just include this:

```
#include "unmanaged.h"
```

If your function only contains simple value types with a one-to-one mapping between the type in managed code and the type in unmanaged code, it is probably a blittable type and little marshaling is taking place. *Blittable* types can be copied from one location to the other with no translation or transformation required. Listing 7.22 shows a call to a function where the arguments and the return are simple blittable types.

LISTING 7.22 Using IJW in VC++ with Simple Types

```
int retInt = AddInteger(1, 2);
Console::WriteLine(S"AddInteger after: {0}", __box(retInt));
```

Notice that the arguments 1 and 2 are passed to the function and the addition of the two are returned, which is also an integer. No marshaling is required. You want to do the same thing with a string (add two strings together). Listing 7.23 shows how to do this with IJW.

LISTING 7.23 Using IJW in VC++ with a String

```
String *str = S"This is a test";
IntPtr sPtr = Marshal::StringToHGlobalAnsi(str);
int retLength = StringLength((char*)sPtr.ToPointer());
Console::WriteLine(S"String length: {0}", __box(retLength));
Marshal::FreeHGlobal(sPtr);
```

The code that is involved to do a simple operation like this can be overwhelming. This is one of the drawbacks of using this method of interop. The code is substantial, and it's highly possible to make a mistake that will cause a leak or a crash of your application. At the same time, because you are doing all of this work explicitly, you have more control and are able to see the exact cost of marshaling. Other languages and methods of interoperation hide this level of detail.

First, you create and initialize the **String**. This is mandatory because the marshaling requires a **String** input to properly marshal. Notice that the **String** does not directly participate in the marshaling process; the data is simply copied from the **String** and then it is left alone. Next, you marshal the data and allocate memory to handle the marshaled data. The **Marshal** class has several methods that handle the marshaling. Now that the **String** has been marshaled, you can pass it to the unmanaged function. It is necessary to pull a pointer from the marshaled data (void *) and cast it to (char *) for the unmanaged function. Finally, you print the results of the function call and free the allocated memory. Requiring unmanaged code to explicitly free allocated memory is counter to the idea of managed code, but that is the way things are done for interop using IJW. If you do not free the memory, your program will leak memory.

Just for variety, a simple sample of a function that returns a **String** that is the result of the concatenation of two input **String**s is included next. Listing 7.24 shows the essential parts of calling this function.

LISTING 7.24 Using IJW in VC++ to Concatenate Two Strings

```
IntPtr aPtr = Marshal::StringToHGlobalUni(a);
IntPtr bPtr = Marshal::StringToHGlobalUni(b);
String *result = ConcatUnicodeString((wchar_t*)aPtr.ToPointer(),
                                     (wchar_t*)bPtr.ToPointer());
Console::WriteLine(S"After Unicode String Concat: {0}", result);
Marshal::FreeHGlobal(aPtr);
Marshal::FreeHGlobal(bPtr);
```

To show that it's possible to marshal different types of strings, this sample marshals the **String**s to Unicode rather than ANSI. Notice that you still allocate memory and marshal as before, and you still have to free the memory afterward, but you don't allocate or explicitly do any marshaling with the return value, which is a **String**.

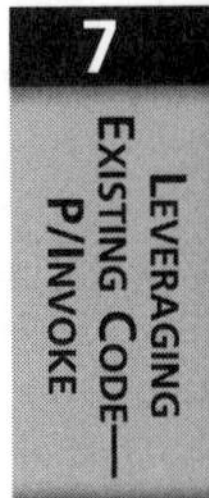

The following are the advantages of IJW:

- `DllImport` is not needed. You do not need to duplicate the signature of the unmanaged function that you want to call. Just use the existing header file and link the import library.
- Using IJW is slightly faster. With `DllImport`, every call requires a check to see if pinning the data is required or if the data needs to be copied. Because all of this work is done explicitly by the developer in IJW, these checks are not required.
- Because nothing is hidden from the developer, it is possible to see exactly where performance is being hurt and possibly come up with solutions.
- For some calls, it might be possible to marshal the data once and use it many times. This is a clear win in favor of IJW. It is not possible for `DllImport` to "cache" the marshaled data for subsequent calls or to know that the same data is to be passed to another function. The work to marshal the data can be saved for that call in IJW.

IJW also has some disadvantages:

- Doing the marshaling for every argument in most function calls is tedious and prone to error. It also significantly muddies up the code so that it is sometimes hard to understand the flow of the program.
- An extra call to `ToPointer()` is required to maintain portability between 32-bit and 64-bit operating systems.

Performance Considerations with P/Invoke

As you probably already guessed, all of the nice things that the runtime does for you as you call unmanaged code don't come for free. However, the picture is not bleak enough for you to consider dumping interop with unmanaged code for a full port or other options.

It is estimated that each P/Invoke call requires between 10 and 30 x86 assembly instructions. This means that the overhead is small. Perhaps you have a 1Ghz Pentium and each of those 30 instructions takes one clock cycle to complete. That would mean that the overhead for a P/Invoke call is approximately 0.03 microseconds. Even if each instruction took two clock cycles to complete, that would still only be 0.06 microseconds. Clearly, the overhead is small. In addition to that is the cost of marshaling each argument. It is hard to estimate what this overhead is, but if it concerns you, do some measurements to see how much overhead that marshaling your data is costing. Remember:

If the arguments that you are passing and the return result are blittable types, then marshaling overhead is zero (or close to it). If you are consistently passing long strings to be translated from Unicode to ANSI, then the marshaling overhead can be significantly more. All in all, the overhead for P/Invoke is small. It takes a contrived set of code to make a case that the overhead for P/Invoke is too high.

Always consider the alternatives. You could port your unmanaged code to managed code so that no overhead is present in calling unmanaged code functions. You could invent other methods that are not portable and might be tied to specific implementations of the CLR. This would be a maintenance nightmare. Clearly, if you need to interop with legacy DLLs, P/Invoke is the best method.

Summary

This chapter focused on the methods and techniques available to interoperate with legacy C/C++ unmanaged code that is implemented in DLLs. You learned how to specify the type of marshaling that is required to move your data in the managed world to the unmanaged world using the **`DllImport`** attribute. Although many of the samples that were provided were in C#, you saw that it is possible to use these same techniques in many different languages. You learned that with VC++ and the managed extensions it provides, It Just Works (IJW) is an alternative to P/Invoke. Using IJW, you can call unmanaged code without the **`DllImport`** attribute. The most significant drawback to using IJW is that you have to explicitly do the marshaling yourself. You learned about the performance hit that P/Invoke requires. P/Invoke doesn't require much overhead, but it does require some, and that could be important to your application. Measure!

The services of P/Invoke are simple and easy to use, but when you need a complex function call, P/Invoke can also handle those needs.

CHAPTER

Using COM/COM+ from Managed Code

In This Chapter

COM has become the standard for allowing binary interoperability. It has provided a means for most languages to instantiate and use methods defined on a COM server. VB, Perl, C++, Java, JavaScript, VBScript, and other languages instantiate objects and call methods on COM components. This level of interoperability has greatly contributed to the popularity of this technology. Reusing components in environments that were not anticipated when the component was developed has become the norm. Many people have benefited from the COM's features.

However, as good as COM is, it still can be improved. The .NET Framework makes many of these improvements and evolves COM to a new level. The .NET Framework is easier to use, it does more, and it has transformed the way software is developed; however, the world is still heavily invested in the older technology. Kraig Brockschmidt paved the way for COM with books on OLE (*Inside OLE* and *Inside OLE 2*) in 1994. After it was realized that other applications existed for COM besides Object Linking and Embedding (OLE), programmers started to develop COM-based applications en masse. Looking at Microsoft's own estimates (`http://www.microsoft.com/com/about.asp`), COM has had an enormous impact on software development. Microsoft claims that COM is in use in more than 150 million systems worldwide, with the market for third-party COM applications growing to more than $3 billion in 2001. The .NET Framework goes to great lengths to ensure that all of the existing COM code that has been developed and is relied upon will be able to play in the managed world of .NET.

That is what this chapter is about. COM is fully supported in the managed world of .NET, and .NET applications can easily and powerfully access and use existing COM components. Of course, using COM interop is no substitute for fully porting code to the .NET Framework, but COM interop does provide the best possible means to continue to use COM components in newly developed .NET applications. The interop layer is easy to use, overhead has been kept to a minimum so that in most cases no "penalty" is associated with using the .NET interop facilities, and the general programming model for .NET has been maintained.

The Runtime Callable Wrapper

As has already been shown in earlier chapters, information about methods and properties, metadata, is stored in assemblies. With COM, the type library provides information to the caller about interfaces, properties, and methods. To call a COM method from .NET, a bridge needs to be formed to translate between the information contained in the type library and the metadata information required in a .NET application. This bridge in the case of .NET calling a COM component is the Runtime Callable Wrapper (RCW for short). Figure 8.1 shows how a .NET application interacts with a COM component through the RCW. For reference, this figure also shows how a "traditional" unmanaged application calls into a COM component.

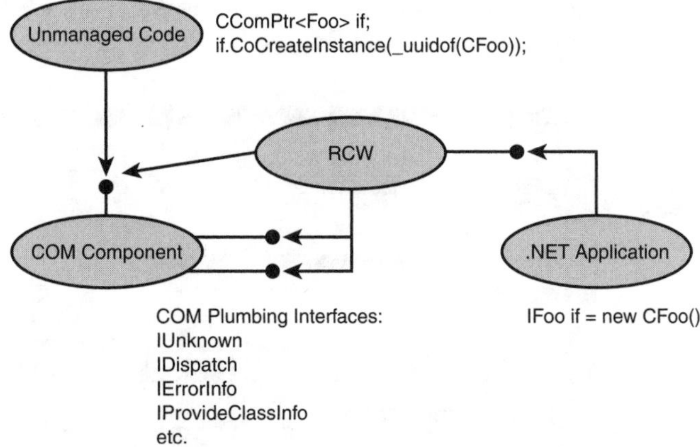

FIGURE 8.1
.NET and an RCW.

The RCW is key to the .NET Framework successfully interacting with a COM component. The RCW is the required bridge between the .NET Framework (managed code) and COM (unmanaged code). By using the RCW, a COM component appears to the programmer as any other .NET object.

When the RCW is wrapped in an assembly, it is called an interop assembly. When an interop assembly is signed or given a strong name, it is a primary interop assembly (PIA). A utility called Type Library Importer (tlbimp) ships with the .NET SDK. tlbimp takes a COM type library and turns it into an interop assembly or a primary interop assembly. At the simplest level, you would call tlbimp as follows to generate an interop assembly:

```
tlbimp mycom.dll /out:interop.mycom.dll
```

To create a PIA, you need to supply a /primary argument as well as the public key, key file, or key container for the public/private key pair that you want to associate with your primary interop assembly. It is recommended that you not get into the habit of using only an interop assembly; use a PIA for all interactions with your COM components. This chapter focuses solely on the interop assembly for simplicity purposes and because it is the default (and only) option to build interop assemblies within Visual Studio.

Tip

Do as I say, not as I do. A PIA is simply an interop assembly that has a strong name.

It is possible within Visual Studio to essentially have tlbimp called for you. By adding a reference to your existing project that refers to your COM component, you form an interop assembly almost transparently. If you select the menu item Add Reference that is available by right-clicking on the References node of the Solutions Explorer tree, you are presented with a dialog box that looks like Figure 8.2.

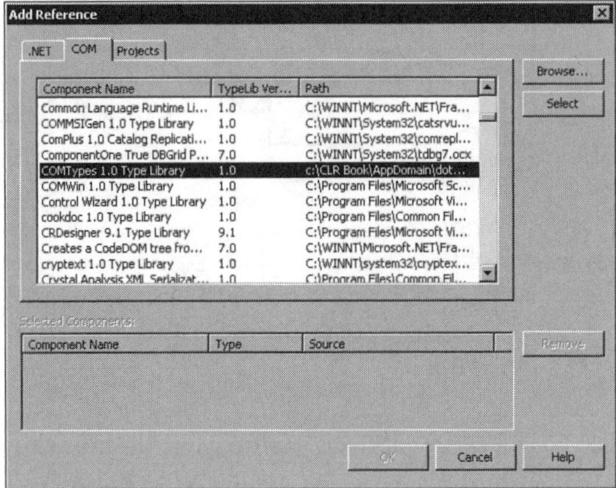

FIGURE 8.2
Building an interop assembly with Visual Studio.

By selecting the COM tab, you see a list of all of the COM components that are registered on your computer. By selecting one or more of these components, you essentially build interop assemblies for each component selected. Your project will be augmented to link to each of these new formed assemblies. You can see the result of this type library conversion by looking in the destination folder for your project for one or more new DLL files that have the prefix "interop". These files are your interop assemblies for the RCW associated with each of your COM components. Figure 8.3 shows a sample of the directory listing showing an interop assembly.

```
Command Prompt
11/05/2001  09:36a      <DIR>          .
11/05/2001  09:36a      <DIR>          ..
11/05/2001  09:28a              12,800 Interop.COMTypes.dll
11/05/2001  09:28a              36,864 TypeTester.exe
11/05/2001  09:28a              30,208 TypeTester.pdb
               3 File(s)         79,872 bytes
               2 Dir(s)  10,577,231,872 bytes free
```

FIGURE 8.3
Directory listing showing an interop assembly.

The interop assembly provides three basic functions:

- Model consistency—When you are accessing a COM component from managed code, you would not expect to use `CoCreateInstance` or other Win32 calls to create and manage the COM component. The COM object is expected to behave as all other objects in the .NET Framework. When you are handling errors from the .NET Framework, you typically would expect an exception to be thrown rather than an error code returned. The interop assembly detects a failed `HRESULT` from a COM method or property and translates that into an exception. Many other examples could be presented of how an interop assembly provides model consistency, but the idea is that a COM object should behave and have features similar to any other .NET object.

- Marshaling of types—This is probably the interop assembly's most important job. Most of the COM automation data types have an equivalent managed type. When marshaling a managed type, a check is made to see if a corresponding COM automation type exists; if there is, the managed type is marshaled as the COM automation type. A managed **`object`** is turned into a `VARIANT`, a **`string`** type is turned into a `BSTR`, and **`DateTime`** is turned into `DATE`. All of the .NET value types are turned into appropriate unmanaged types (**`uint`** to `unsigned integer`, **`int`** to `int`, **`byte`** to `unsigned char`, **`ushort`** to `unsigned short`, **`short`** to `short`, and so on). **`IEnumerator`** is turned into `IEnumVARIANT`, **`System.Array`** is turned into a `VARIANT` that wraps a `SAFEARRAY` of the appropriate type, and **`System.Drawing.Color`** is turned into a `VARIANT` that wraps `IDispatch`, which resolves to the appropriate `OLE_COLOR`.
- Lifetime management—The interop assembly creates the RCW associated with a COM object. The RCW is an object just as any other .NET object, and it is subject to the same rules for garbage collection. A programmer should be aware of this, but he doesn't need to explicitly call `AddRef` and `Release` to control the lifetime of an object. These methods are handled for you, and they are not even exposed.

A Sample Application That Illustrates an RCW at Work

An application has been put together that illustrates some of the major features of an RCW. The solution builds a COM component, although in reality, you would probably just be supplied with the type library and the DLL implementing the COM interfaces. This solution also builds a user interface that allows a user to send data back and forth across the managed/unmanaged boundary through the RCW. The source for this solution is in the `Marshal` directory. When the application starts up, it looks like Figure 8.4.

All of the date types that are illustrated are marshaled to the COM component, which caches the data sent to it and immediately fires a callback with the information passed to it as its only argument. You will notice a small text box in the upper-right corner that is continually incrementing. It illustrates a background thread in the instance of the COM object that fires a callback (connection-point) every second, incrementing the count with each invocation.

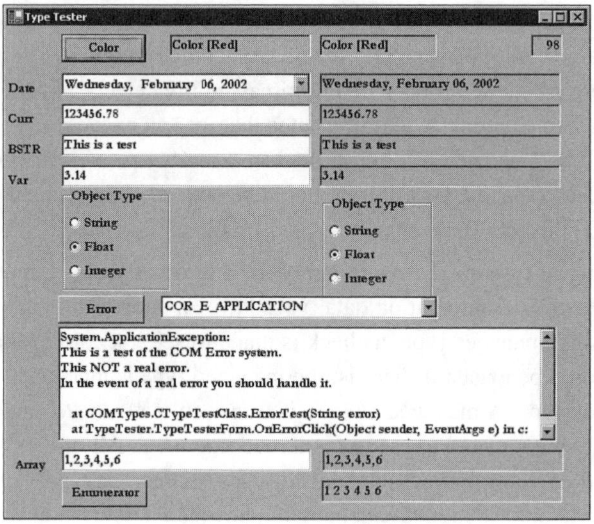

FIGURE 8.4
COM interop test application.

Clicking on the Color button starts up a Color Picker dialog box. After you select a color, a string representation for the color is placed in the left text box, and the right text box is filled in by the callback for color.

Clicking on the drop-down arrow on the `Date` line brings up a calendar. Selecting a date on the calendar causes a `DateTime` object to be marshaled to the instance of the COM object. The COM object fires a connection-point with a `DATE` argument, which is displayed in the right text box.

On the `Curr` line, it is expected that a **`decimal`** value will be entered. After the **`decimal`** value is entered and focus is taken away from the input text box, a **`decimal`** is marshaled to the COM object. The COM object immediately fires a connection-point with an equivalent `CURRENCY` value, which is displayed in the right text box.

On the `BSTR` line, an arbitrary **`string`** is entered. When focus is taken from this text box, the **`string`** is marshaled to the COM object. The COM object immediately fires a connection point with an equivalent `BSTR` argument, which is displayed in the right text box.

The `Var` line is a little backward. You select the type of object that is to be transferred to the COM object by selecting the type in the radio group box on the left of the application. After selecting the type, you enter the value into the text box just to the right of the `Var` label. When focus is taken from the input text box, the **`string`** is marshaled to the COM object; alternatively, the value of either an **`int`** or **`float`** is boxed in an **`object`** and marshaled to the COM object. This call immediately fires a connection-point with a single argument of the object passed in, which is displayed in the text box on the right side along with the type of the object.

To generate an error, select the type of error that you want to generate using the combo box and then click the `Error` button. This causes the COM object to return the selected error `HRESULT`, which, in turn, causes the RCW to throw an appropriate exception.

On the `Array` line, you can enter an array of integers, floats, or strings. None of the values can contain a comma because that character is used to delimit each entry in the array. You can simply split the string in the text box into an array using a comma as a delimiter. Then, try to convert each item into an integer (from the string). If that fails, try float. If you still fail, assume that the array is an array of strings. When focus is removed from the input text box, the array is marshaled to the COM object and a callback is immediately fired with the same data as was passed. On receipt of the callback, you not only display the array on the right text box, but you also enable the `Enumerator` button so that you can enumerate through the array passed.

The `Enumerator` line passes back an `IEnumVARIANT` interface from the COM object. Take the marshaled **`IEnumerator`** interface and enumerate through the items passed. Because you are enumerating through the array that is passed in the array, the data should be the same.

Now you know what the application is supposed to do. It's time to look at the code that implements this functionality. With most projects that require some sort of interop, you might end up looking at the interop assembly with ILDASM just to see what code has been generated. Figure 8.5 shows the ILDASM output for the interop assembly that is associated with the `COMTypes` COM object.

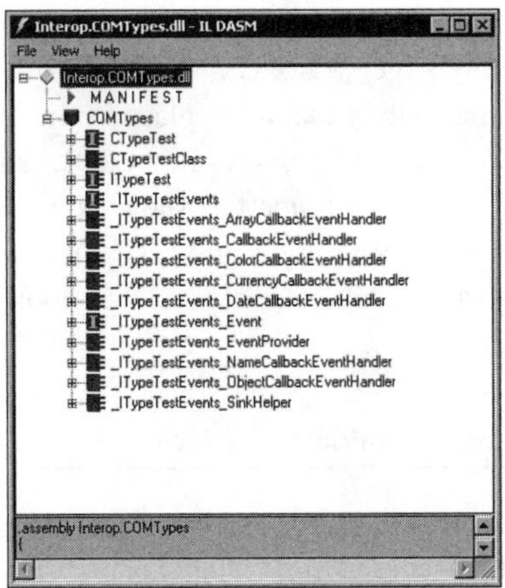

FIGURE 8.5
ILDASM's view of an interop assembly.

Compare the output of Figure 8.5 with the IDL for the COM object that is shown in compacted form in Listing 8.1.

LISTING 8.1 IDL for COMType's Main Interface

```
[
    object,
    uuid(57101F2B-8A4F-44FB-AE5F-8011CD13D564),
    dual,
    helpstring("ITypeTest Interface"),
    pointer_default(unique)
]
interface ITypeTest : IDispatch {
    [propget, id(1), …] HRESULT Name([out, retval] BSTR* pVal);
    [propput, id(1), …] HRESULT Name([in] BSTR newVal);
    [propget, id(2), …] HRESULT Date([out, retval] DATE* pVal);
    [propput, id(2), …] HRESULT Date([in] DATE newVal);
    [propget, id(3), …] HRESULT Color([out, retval] VARIANT* pVal);
    [propput, id(3), …] HRESULT Color([in] VARIANT newVal);
    [propget, id(4), …] HRESULT Currency([out, retval] CY* pVal);
    [propput, id(4), …] HRESULT Currency([in] CY newVal);
    [propget, id(5), …] HRESULT Object([out, retval] VARIANT* pVal);
    [propput, id(5), …] HRESULT Object([in] VARIANT newVal);
    [propget, id(6), …] HRESULT Array([out, retval] VARIANT* pVal);
    [propput, id(6), …] HRESULT Array([in] VARIANT newVal);
    [id(7), …] HRESULT ErrorTest([in] BSTR error);
    [propget, id(8), …] HRESULT Enumerator([out, retval] IEnumVARIANT** pVal);
};
```

If you expand the `ITypeTest` interface, you will see that each of these properties (with the red triangle) implements by methods (get_XXX and set_XXX, indicated by purple squares). Here, you start to see the marshaling that takes place in the interop assembly. For example, look at the argument for the `Name` property in the IDL (`BSTR`). In the interop assembly, the argument is a **`string`**. The other properties show similar translations. Because this is the only interface that the .NET application sees (it does not see the IDL), you can start to see that this looks just like any other object. Now look at the connection point interface shown in Listing 8.2.

LISTING 8.2 IDL for COMType's Connection-Point Interface

```
[
    uuid(9FA87D5F-F726-421F-869B-A84AF2A9B22A),
    helpstring("_ITypeTestEvents Interface")
]
dispinterface _ITypeTestEvents {
methods:
```

LISTING 8.2 Continued

```
    [id(1),…] HRESULT  Callback([in] LONG count);
    [id(2),…] HRESULT  NameCallback([in]BSTR objectName);
    [id(3),…] HRESULT  DateCallback([in]DATE objectDate);
    [id(4),…] HRESULT  ColorCallback([in]VARIANT objectColor);
    [id(5),…] HRESULT  CurrencyCallback([in]CY objectCurrency);
    [id(6),…] HRESULT  ObjectCallback([in]VARIANT objectVariant);
    [id(7),…] HRESULT  ArrayCallback([in]VARIANT objectArray);
};
```

This interface has been named `_ITypeTestEvents`, so you will also find in the interop assembly an `_ITypeTestEvents` interface. If you expand that interface, you will see all of the same methods shown in Listing 8.2. You can also see the same type of marshaling that must occur because of the mismatch between the arguments in the IDL and the interop assembly. Look also at the class that implements these two interfaces as described by the IDL, shown in Listing 8.3.

LISTING 8.3 IDL for `COMTypes` `CoClass`

```
[
    version(1.0),
    uuid(57DE8B2D-2A18-447B-917C-17AD18849A8C),
    helpstring("TypeTest Class")
]
coclass CTypeTest {
    interface ITypeTest;
    [default, source] interface _ITypeTestEvents;
};
```


With the interop assembly in place defining the `CTypeTest` class, all you need to do to create a `CTypeTest` object is the C# code:

```
CTypeTest ctt = new CTypeTest();
```

This gives you a reference to the RCW, which, in turn, points to the COM object. It does not get much easier than this. This is consistent with how objects are created within the .NET Framework.

Next, you need to get an interface pointer to the interface that you will be using. This is equally easy; all you have to do is cast from the class to the interface:

```
ITypeTest tt = ctt;
```

This is equivalent to `QueryInterface` in the managed world. Again, everything has been adjusted so that the model does not change; the implementation changes so that the model can be maintained. Now set up some asynchronous callbacks. This is a little more involved, especially because a key piece to understanding hasn't been introduced yet. In the end, the model is maintained, and handling asynchronous events from a COM component is no different from handling a mouse event.

From Listing 8.3, you can see that the `CTypeTest` implements two interfaces: `ITypeTest` and `_ITypeTestEvents`. These interfaces are described in Listings 8.1 and 8.2. Expanding the node in the ILDASM listing for `CTypeTest`, you can see that `CTypeTest` implements the two interfaces `ITypeTest` and `_ITypeTestEvents_Event`. `CTypeTestClass` technically serves the same role as the `coclass` because it is a class that implements the `CTypeTest` interface as well as the other two interfaces (`ITypeTest` and `_ITypeTestEvents_Event`). It is important to explore the callbacks further so that setting them up makes sense. (To gain a full understanding of callbacks, refer to Chapter 14, "`Delegates` and `Events`." For now, just think of an event as a helper for a delegate and a delegate as a function pointer.)

If you expand the `_ITypeTestEvents_Event` interface in ILDASM, you see all of the events that have been defined. These events are described by the lines that have an upside down green triangle icon on the left side. Each of these events takes a single argument that is a description of the function or callback. For example, `ArrayCallback` has the `_ITypeTestEvents_ArrayCallbackEventHandler`, and `NameCallback` has the `_ITypeTestEvents_NameCallbackEventHandler`. Descriptions for each of the event handlers take up most of the space in the ILDASM listing for the COM interop assembly. To add an event handler, you need to construct one of these classes passing in a pointer to a method that matches the description, and add this to the event list. Listing 8.4 shows how this is done for this sample COM object.

LISTING 8.4 Hooking into COM Connection Points

```
ctt.ArrayCallback += new
_ITypeTestEvents_ArrayCallbackEventHandler(ArrayCallback);
ctt.CurrencyCallback += new
 _ITypeTestEvents_CurrencyCallbackEventHandler(CurrencyCallback);
ctt.DateCallback += new
_ITypeTestEvents_DateCallbackEventHandler(DateCallback);
ctt.NameCallback += new
_ITypeTestEvents_NameCallbackEventHandler(NameCallback);
ctt.ObjectCallback += new
_ITypeTestEvents_ObjectCallbackEventHandler(ObjectCallback);
ctt.ColorCallback += new
_ITypeTestEvents_ColorCallbackEventHandler(ColorCallback);
ctt.Callback += new
_ITypeTestEvents_CallbackEventHandler(COMCallback);
```

The interfaces and the new concepts of events and delegates might be confusing to you. However, they are easier to understand and more consistent than dealing with connection-points, such as Advise and Unadvise.

That is about all there is to setting up the COM component. Now you can call methods on the instance of the COM component that you created. To exchange **System.Drawing.Color** with an unmanaged component, you just need to do the following:

```
colorDialog.ShowDialog();
tt.Color = colorDialog.Color;
```

The following is the code required to marshal a string:

```
tt.Name = name.Text;
```

Marshaling from a managed **DateTime** object to an unmanaged DATE object requires the following lines of code:

```
DateTimePicker dtp = sender as DateTimePicker;
tt.Date = dtp.Value;
```

Marshaling from a managed **decimal** value to an unmanaged CURRENCY type requires the following line:

```
tt.Currency = Convert.ToDecimal(currency.Text);
```

Marshaling from a managed **object** to an unmanaged VARIANT type is done with the following code:

```
tt.Object = Convert.ToInt32(variant.Text);
```

Marshaling from a managed array **object []** to the unmanaged SAFEARRAY(VARIANT) requires the following lines of code:

```
object [] oa = new object [sa.Length];
tt.Array = oa;
```

Marshaling an IEnumVARIANT to **IEnumerator** is accomplished with code that looks like this:

```
StringBuilder sb = new StringBuilder();
IEnumerator en = tt.Enumerator;
while(en.MoveNext())
{
    sb.Append(en.Current.ToString());
    sb.Append(" ");
}
```

Finally, COM components usually return error codes in the form of HRESULT. The interop assembly takes error code returned from the COM component and generates a corresponding exception. It also takes the rich information about the error from `IErrorInfo` and adds it to the exception. Using this error information is as simple as the following code:

```
try
{
    tt.ErrorTest(errorType.Text);
}
catch(Exception exception)
{
    errorText.Text = exception.ToString();
}
```

It is easy to use the interop facilities built into the .NET Framework. More importantly, the whole .NET Framework object model is maintained as you work with COM objects, so you can almost forget that you are using a COM object and not a managed object type. It's true that the setup with `tlbimp` and even with Visual Studio requires some thought to get everything done correctly. After setup is complete, however, working with the RCW and interop assembly is a breeze.

Programmatically Generating an Interop Assembly

The same functionality that is provided with the tlbimp utility is exposed in the **`TypeLibConverter`** class. To use this class, load a type library description. Listing 8.5 shows the most straightforward method to load a type library. The full source to this sample is available in the `TypeLibraryConversion` directory.

LISTING 8.5 Loading a Type Library

```
private enum RegKind
{
    RegKind_Default = 0,
    RegKind_Register = 1,
    RegKind_None = 2
}

[ DllImport( "oleaut32.dll", CharSet = CharSet.Unicode, PreserveSig = false )]
private static extern void LoadTypeLibEx(String strTypeLibName,
                                         RegKind regKind,
                                         [MarshalAs(UnmanagedType.Interface)]
                                         out Object typeLib);
```

LISTING 8.5 Continued

```
[STAThread]
static void Main(string[] args)
{
    Object typeLib;
    LoadTypeLibEx( "COMTypes.dll", RegKind.RegKind_None, out typeLib );

    if( typeLib == null )
    {
        Console.WriteLine( "LoadTypeLibEx failed." );
        return;
    }
```

No easy way exists to retrieve the type library—or more specifically the `ITypeLib` interface—from a file. You can use **`DllImport`** and the P/Invoke services (covered in Chapter 7, "Leveraging Existing Code—P/Invoke") to call `LoadTypeLibEx`. `LoadTypeLibEx`, a Win32 function, is exactly applicable to this situation. `LoadTypeLibEx` reads in the file from the path specified. If it is a `TLB` file (a stand-alone type library), then it is loaded directly. If it is a `DLL` or `EXE` file, it locates the first resource that has a type of `ITypeLib`, loads the type library information, and returns an `ITypeLib` interface to that loaded type library information. If your DLL or EXE has multiple type libraries, you might need to append an integer to the path to indicate which type library you want to load (see the Win32 documentation on `LoadTypeLib`). Notice that in Listing 8.6, this function is called with an argument of `RegKind.RegKind_None`, indicating that the type library will not be registered, just loaded. If this function succeeds, then you have an `ITypeLib` interface.

With an `ITypeLib` interface, you can proceed with the conversion, as shown in Listing 8.6. The source that corresponds to this listing is in the `TypeLibraryConversion` directory.

LISTING 8.6 Converting a Type Library

```
        TypeLibConverter c = new TypeLibConverter();
        ConversionEventHandler eventHandler = new ConversionEventHandler();
        AssemblyBuilder asm = c.ConvertTypeLibToAssembly( typeLib,
➥"Interop.COMTypes.dll", 0, eventHandler,
➥null, null, null, new Version("1.0.0.0") );
        asm.Save( "Interop.COMTypes.dll" );
    }
}
public class ConversionEventHandler : ITypeLibImporterNotifySink
{
    public void ReportEvent( ImporterEventKind eventKind,
                             int eventCode,
                             string eventMsg )
```

LISTING 8.6 Continued

```
    {
        // Simply report that this method was called.
        // This mimics the /verbose option of the tlbimp utility.
        Console.WriteLine("ReportEvent {0}: {1}", eventKind, eventMsg);
    }

    public Assembly ResolveRef( object typeLib )
    {
        // Resolve reference here and return a correct assembly...
        Console.WriteLine("ResolveRef");
        return null;
    }
}
```

The **ConvertTypeLibToAssembly** method of the **TypeLibConverter** class performs most of the work in converting a type library to an assembly. A couple of things are worth noting about this code snippet—in particular, this method call. Notice that the path has been hard coded to the destination of the interop assembly. Naturally, in a really useful application, you would make this a variable or have a heuristic to generate an output filename. Notice, too, that no flags have been passed as the third argument to **ConvertTypeLibToAssembly**. The available flags are as follows:

- **PrimaryInteropAssembly**—This mimics the `tlbimp /primary` option flag in creating a primary interop assembly (PIA).
- **SafeArrayAsSystemArray**—This is like the `tlbimp /sysarray` option flag. It allows for marshaling `SAFEARRAY` arguments as **System.Array**. The default behavior is to wrap a `SAFEARRAY` argument as a `VARIANT` containing `SAFEARRAY`.
- **UnsafeInterfaces**—This is like the `tlbimp /unsafe` option flag. It removes the CLR stack crawl for permission to run unmanaged code. This results in some performance benefit at the expense of opening a rather egregious security hole.

The next argument is a reference to an implementation of the **ITypeLibImporterNotifySink** interface. The user can be notified of events that are called as the conversion process proceeds. This is much like the `tlbimp /verbose` option flag. The next two arguments deal primarily with the creation of a primary interop assembly. The first of these security arguments is a byte array containing the public key for the interop assembly. The next of these security arguments is **StrongNameKeyPair**, which contains the public and private keys to be associated with the interop assembly. These arguments roughly correspond to the `tlbimp /publickey`, `/keyfile`, and `/keycontainer` option flags. In this sample code, **null** has been passed to each of these security arguments so that the created assembly will not be a PIA. The next argument is a namespace for the assembly. This is similar to the `tlbimp /namespace` option flag. Again, **`null`** has been passed to indicate that no namespace should be associated with this interop assembly. Finally, the last argument is the version of the interop assembly to be created. This is similar to the `tlbimp /asmversion` option flag. An instance of **`Version`** has been passed for this argument, which will create an interop assembly with a version of 1.0.0.0.

When the **`ConvertTypeLibToAssembly`** succeeds, it creates an **`Assembly`** (specifically an **`AssemblyBuilder`**) object. The only thing left to do is write the Assembly out to a file on disk, which is done with the Save method on the **`AssemblyBuilder`** class. This code is woefully lacking in error handling, but it illustrates a programmatic way of accomplishing the same functionality that tlbimp provides.

Late-Binding to a COM Component

It is possible to avoid using tlbimp if you are willing to give up some performance and use late binding. To use late binding, your component must implement `IDispatch` and preferably `IProvideClassInfo` to provide type information about your COM methods and properties. Listing 8.7 shows a simple example of using late binding. The full source to this sample is available in the `LateBinding` directory.

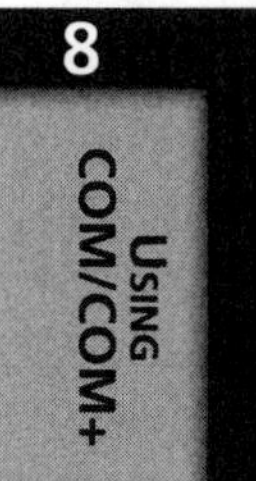

LISTING 8.7 Late Binding to a COM Component

```
String progId = "COMTypes.TypeTest";
Type t = Type.GetTypeFromProgID(progId);
Object o = Activator.CreateInstance(t);

t.InvokeMember("Name",
        BindingFlags.SetProperty |
        BindingFlags.Public |
        BindingFlags.Instance,
        null, o, new Object[] {"Testing"}, null, null, null);
Object result = t.InvokeMember("Name",
        BindingFlags.GetProperty |
        BindingFlags.Public |
        BindingFlags.Instance,
        null, o, null, null, null, null);
Console.WriteLine("Name: {0}", result);

t.InvokeMember("Date",
        BindingFlags.SetProperty |
        BindingFlags.Public |
        BindingFlags.Instance,
        null, o, new Object[] {DateTime.Now}, null, null, null);
```

LISTING 8.7 Continued

```
result = t.InvokeMember("Date",
        BindingFlags.GetProperty |
        BindingFlags.Public |
        BindingFlags.Instance,
        null, o, null, null, null, null);
Console.WriteLine("Date: {0}", result);
```

This simple example shows the creation of a **Type** based on a version-independent prog-id. After the **Type** is created and an **object** is created from the **Type**, it is possible to call methods on that COM object. The `COMTypes` sample is used, implementing the prog-id for the `COMTypes`. Naturally, this COM object needs to be built and registered before this sample will work. As you'll recall, the COM object has two properties on the `COMTypes`: `Name` and `Date`. The sample in Listing 8.7 writes to each property and reads back what was written by specifying **SetProperty** and **GetProperty** flags appropriately when calling **InvokeMember**.

Interop with ActiveX Controls

An ActiveX control relies on COM to be activated, modified, have its properties invoked, and so on. Using tlbimp on an ActiveX control doesn't work well. The aximp utility calls tlbimp and creates an appropriate interop assembly; in addition, it creates a second interop assembly that specifically deals with the properties of the ActiveX component.

After you have the interop assemblies, you can reference them in the build and create classes that implement the desired interfaces. For an ActiveX component, you can set the properties and add them to the controls for the form. You can do all of this by hand, but it's not necessary.

This sample used an ActiveX control that was developed by Brent Rector as part of the book he co-authored with Chris Sells, *ATL Internals*. The control has been slightly modified so that it can be used as part of a VS7 solution. For details on the development of an ActiveX control, refer to Rector's discussion in *ATL Internals* (ISBN 0-201-69589-8). Two projects are associated with this sample: `BullsEyeCtl` and `BullsEyeApp`. `BullsEyeCtl` is the project that builds the ActiveX control. `BullsEyeApp` builds a Window Forms application that uses the `BullsEyeCtl` ActiveX control.

The first thing that you should do is build the ActiveX control. You can build the ActiveX control by loading the `BullsEyeCtl` project and selecting the "Rebuild Solution" option under the Build menu. This should build the control with no problem; however, if you have another instance of Visual Studio open and it is referencing the control, the control might fail because the "old" control could not be deleted.

Next, build the application that uses the `BullsEyeCtl` ActiveX control. This is the `BullsEyeApp` project. It might be a little tricky because the control has been added as part of the components available for the project. The tricky part is that you probably have installed the application and the control in a different directory. The easiest solution is to remove the control from the form and everywhere in the C# source. (It is called `axBullsEye`.) It will be easier if you just comment out the lines that look like this:

```
axBullsEye.OnRingHit += new AxBullsEyeLib._IBullsEyeEvents_
➥OnRingHitEventHandler(OnRingHit);
axBullsEye.OnScoreChanged += new AxBullsEyeLib._IBullsEyeEvents_
➥OnScoreChangedEventHandler(OnScoreChanged);
```

If you comment out those lines in the source, it will be easier to add them back later.

Then, build the application. It should build without errors because the ActiveX control is not referenced any more. Next, you want to add the `BullsEyeCtl` to the toolbox (and the project). To do this, you need to select Customize Toolbox. This option is available if you are viewing the application in Design mode and you right-click on the Components section of the toolbox. You should see something like Figure 8.6.

FIGURE 8.6
Customizing the toolbox.

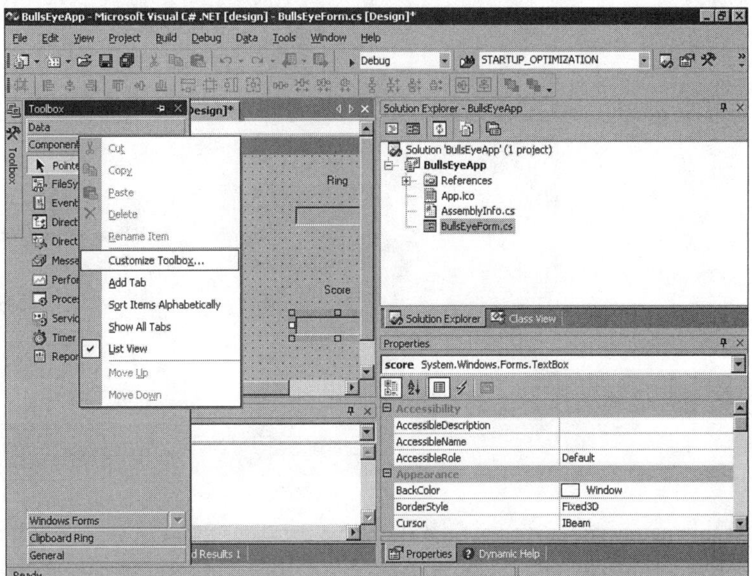

With Customize Toolbox selected, you will be presented with a list of controls that can be added to the toolbox. Select the `BullsEye` Class. Your selection should look like Figure 8.7.

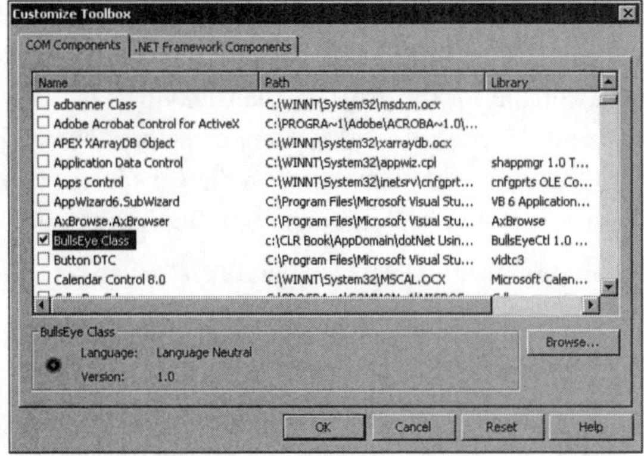

FIGURE 8.7
Adding `BullsEyeCtl` *to the toolbox.*

Now your toolbox should look like Figure 8.8.

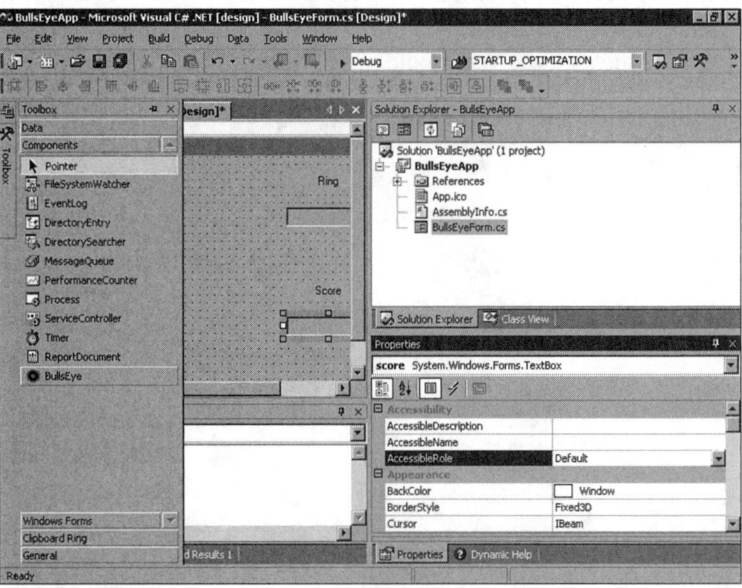

FIGURE 8.8
`BullsEyeCtl` *successfully added to toolbox.*

At this point, you can select the BullsEye from the toolbox and place it on the Windows Forms just as any other control. After you adjust its position, change the `RingCount` property to 9, and rename the control to `axBullsEye`, the design looks like Figure 8.9.

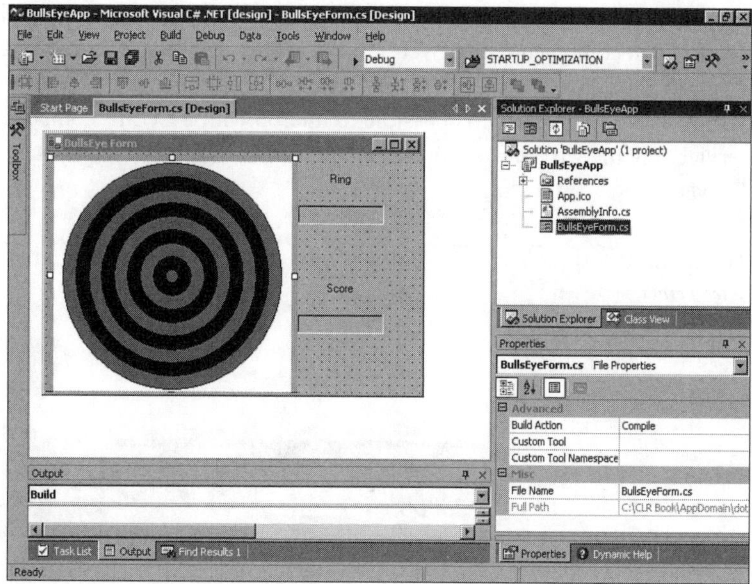

FIGURE 8.9
`BullsEyeCtl` *added to the application form.*

Notice in the references section for the project that two new references have been added: `AxBullsEyeLib` and `BullsEyeLib`. You should be able to return to the code view, uncomment the lines that were commented out previously, and rebuild the application. Now when the application is run, you should see a bulls-eye with nine rings. Every time you click on one of the rings, you get two callbacks that indicate the ring you hit and a score associated with the hit.

After the control is successfully added to your toolbox in the project and you have fixed the location of the control, you can add the control easily to any other part of this or any other form in the project.

You learned how to insert an ActiveX control into a .NET project. You can see, however, that Visual Studio is building the interop assemblies for you when you add the control to your project from the toolbox. You can see the actual assemblies because they are placed in the same output directory as is used to place the application. (If you are doing a debug build, it would probably be in `bin\debug`). In addition, you can change the properties from within Visual Studio to persist between project loads. Most of the features of an integrated control are available to a legacy ActiveX control.

Interop with SOAP

SOAP stands for Simple Object Access Protocol. SOAP is a protocol and a standard for interoperating using XML. Currently, the primary transport that is used for SOAP communications is HTTP, although the specification does not demand that HTTP be used. When combined with a Web server such as IIS, SOAP forms the basis for Web services. With COM+ 1.5 (which is only available on Windows XP platforms and Windows.NET servers), it is possible to interop with a COM+ component through a Web service. Figure 8.10 shows a block diagram of how the interaction is possible with COM+ 1.5.

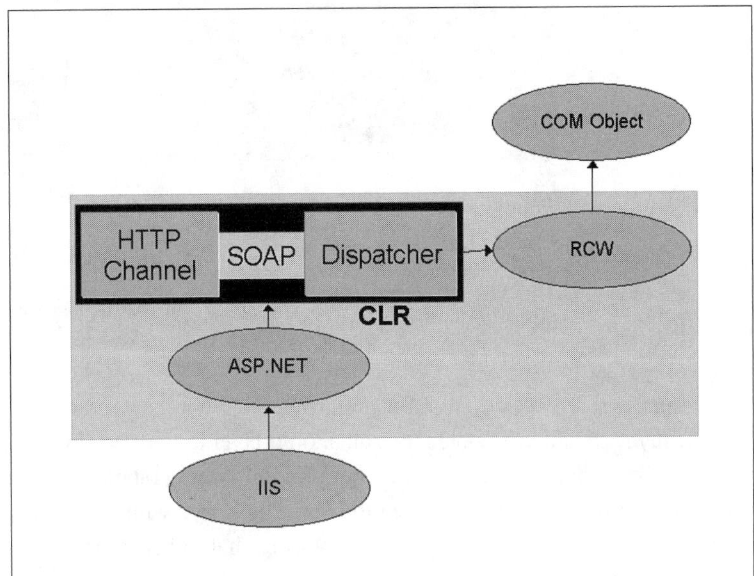

FIGURE 8.10 *Interoperating with SOAP.*

If you are unfamiliar with how to place a COM object under the control of the COM+ services, read on for a step-by-step overview. For more detail on COM+ services, refer to *Transactional COM+: Building Scalable Applications* by Tim Ewald (ISBN 0-201-61594-0, Addison-Wesley) or *COM and .NET Component Services* by Juval Lowy (ISBN 0-596-00103-7, O'Reilly).

- First, click Control Panel, Administrative Tools, Component Services.
- Second, drill down into My Computer in the Component Services portion of the tree until you reach the COM+ Applications node.
- Third, select the COM+ Applications node. Then right-click to select the menu item New, Application. The wizard guides you through creating a new COM+ application. In the wizard, select `Create an Empty Application` and give it any name that is appropriate. The Arithmetic COM component has been named Arithmetic.

- Fourth, select the application you have just created. On the right pane, right-click on the Components folder and select New, Component. Again, a wizard guides you through adding a new component to your application. Select Install New Component(s), which brings up a File dialog box that you can use to point to your DLL that implements your COM object. If you are going through these steps to install the Arithmetic COM object, look for the Arithmetic DLL. After you have selected your DLL, a dialog box appears where you can add more components. Just click on the Next button and Finish to complete this session with the wizard.
- Fifth, you should see your component in the Components folder. Go back to select your application and right-click to select the Properties menu. This brings up a dialog box with many property pages. Select the Activation tab.
- Sixth, in the SOAP group box is a Uses SOAP check box. Check the Uses SOAP check box and fill in the name for the IIS virtual directory in the SOAP VRoot text box. This is the virtual IIS directory by which you can access your component. For example, you need to go through these steps for the Arithmetic component and a reasonable name for this application would be Arithmetic. With this name, you can access your component through SOAP with the URL `http://localhost/Arithmetic`.
- Seventh, type the URL for your component in Internet Explorer (using localhost as the address portion of the URL). You should see the name of your application as a header followed by a hyperlink to the WSDL description for your COM component. Again, if you were using the Arithmetic component, it would look like this: `Arithmetic.BinaryOperations.1.soap?WSDL`.
- Finally, to access your COM object through .NET, you can use the wsdl tool to generate code for you. From a command prompt, enter something like:

```
wsdl http://localhost/Arithmethic/Arithmetic.BinaryOperations.1.soap?WSDL
➥/out:Arithmetic.cs
```

These steps have used the Arithmetic COM object as an example. You need to perform these steps to install the Arithmetic sample that is supplied in the `Arithmetic` directory. You would naturally change the appropriate arguments to point to your COM object.

After completing these steps, you are ready to build a .NET application that uses these new Web services. I have included a sample application that uses the Arithmetic COM component in the SOAP directory. As part of this project, the code that was generated from the wsdl tool (`Arithmetic.cs`) has been included. The code that actually calls the methods on this component is shown in Listing 8.8.

LISTING 8.8 Calling a COM Component Methods Using SOAP

```
CBinaryOperationsClassBinding math = new CBinaryOperationsClassBinding();
Console.WriteLine("Add: {0}", math.Add(1.0F, 2.0F));
Console.WriteLine("Subtract: {0}", math.Subtract(6.0F, 3.0F));
Console.WriteLine("Multiply: {0}", math.Multiply(2.0F, 1.5F));
Console.WriteLine("Divide: {0}", math.Divide(6.0F, 2.0F));
```

Listing 8.8 shows how you can interop with an existing COM component using SOAP and .NET; with this method, however, any application that understands SOAP can interoperate with your COM component. You do not have to know anything about SOAP to use this technology and you do not need to reprogram your COM component. It just works!

Summary

This chapter explored the various ways that are available through the .NET Framework to continue to use COM components that have already been built, tested, and relied on for many years. The .NET Framework can interop with COM components and still maintain the programming model that makes it such a great platform on which to develop. COM interop is key to the .NET Framework. It is possible to interop with COM components using a late binding approach, as would be required with scripting types of applications. COM interop is integrated nicely with Visual Studio, but tools are available to perform the same functions, such as `tlbimp` and `aximp`. You learned that the APIs exist, so you can write your own tlbimp by using the **`TypeLibConverter`** class. You also saw how the .NET Framework and indeed Visual Studio work nicely with ActiveX controls with the associated UI and properties. Finally, you explored a powerful feature of Windows XP and Windows .NET Server that allow the functionality of a COM component to be exposed as a Web service with no extra programming.

CHAPTER 9

Using Managed Code as a COM/COM+ Component

IN THIS CHAPTER

The previous two chapters focused on how the .NET Framework can use and leverage existing code. They discussed how the .NET Framework can use either existing DLLs or existing COM components while still maintaining the .NET programming model. Maintaining model consistency seems to be a high priority goal when designing interoperation layers. This is particularly true for interop with legacy COM components.

This chapter switches gears a little and focuses on how existing components and programs are able to interoperate with .NET components. It is not possible to do the equivalent of P/Invoke in the opposite direction; that is, unmanaged code cannot directly call managed code. However, it is possible for unmanaged code to call a .NET component as if it were a COM component. This chapter focuses on how a .NET component can be built to mimic a legacy COM component.

Why Build a .NET Component to Look Like a COM Component?

The previous two chapters showed why .NET should and does interoperate with existing COM components and DLLs. The reasons why existing COM components and DLLs should be able to interoperate with .NET are similar yet different. You want to have access to existing COM components and DLLs so that any development does not need to involve a full port of the functionality that has already been developed. Interop in the other direction (from legacy code to .NET) allows development to be done with the tools and facilities of the .NET Framework and still have the code accessible from legacy code (unmanaged code). In addition, consider the following as you consider your next project:

- Many significant unmanaged clients and hosts still exist and are not likely to be changed soon. ASP.NET is primarily focused on building server-side components. Internet Explorer still relies on calling unmanaged COM components on the client side. It will be necessary for your application to build components that Internet Explorer can call as unmanaged COM components. Office XP has extensive hooks available that allow Excel, Word, PowerPoint, and the other Office XP applications to be extended with COM components. You will later see a simple example of interoperation with an Office XP application. The Windows shell currently does not have specific knowledge about managed code. Scripts in particular can interoperate only with a COM interface. If your development cycle includes Visual Basic 6.0, then your component needs to have a COM interface.

- Consider ease of development. Developing a COM component within the .NET Framework is much simpler than that required for an unmanaged COM component. Managed code is the simplest way to build COM objects. For example, the CLR handles the lifetime management of the component. With the interop layer that is available, you have little reason to develop new components with unmanaged code.

Unmanaged to Managed Interop Basics

Every unmanaged object is potentially a COM object. When managed code needs to access unmanaged code in the form of a COM component, the type library needs to be converted to assembly metadata information. This assembly metadata is used to form a Runtime Callable Wrapper (RCW) that handles marshaling, error conversion, and lifetime management. For unmanaged code to access a managed COM component, the assembly metadata needs to be converted into type library information. In addition, the registry needs to be modified appropriately to support the .NET component. All of this sets up the framework for building another wrapper component known as a COM Callable Wrapper (CCW). The CCW is illustrated in Figure 9.1.

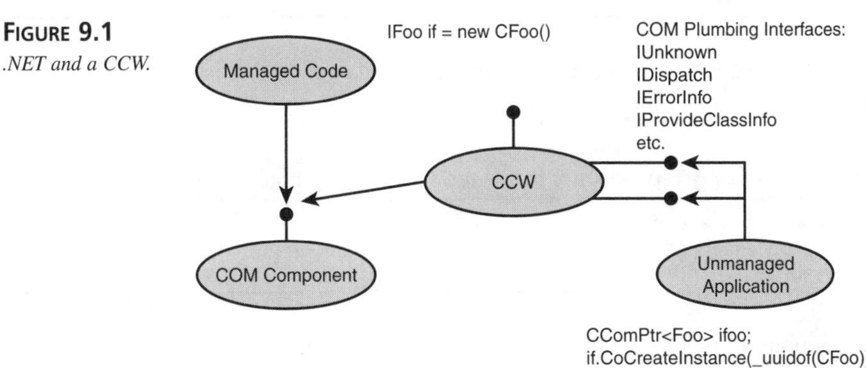

FIGURE 9.1
.NET and a CCW.

The assembly is converted into type library information with a utility called `tlbexp`. Listing 9.1 shows the usage information for `tlbexp` when it is invoked with `/help` or when no arguments are supplied.

LISTING 9.1 tlbExp Options

```
Syntax: TlbExp AssemblyName [Options]
Options:
    /out:FileName              File name of type library to be produced
    /nologo                    Prevents TlbExp from displaying logo
    /silent                    Prevents TlbExp from displaying success message
    /verbose                   Displays extra information
    /names:FileName            A file in which each line specifies the
                               captialization of a name in the type library.
    /? or /help                Display this usage message
```

For most cases, it is possible to simply export the metadata to a type library and begin using the component as a COM component. You need to be aware of some details when exporting assembly metadata to a type library.

Exporting Metadata to a Type Library

This is a simple utility to use for most cases. It can be invoked with the single argument as the path to the assembly to be exported. Listing 9.2 shows the default output.

LISTING 9.2 Exporting Type Library Information from an Assembly

```
> tlbexp Arithmetic.dll
Assembly exported to Arithmetic.tlb
```

If you specify `/verbose`, you can see each interface and coclass that is exported. Listing 9.3 shows an example of using the `/verbose` option.

LISTING 9.3 Exporting Type Library Information Using `/verbose`

```
Type IBasicOperations exported.
Type Arithmetic exported.
Assembly exported to Arithmetic.tlb
```

The other options allow you to change the name of the output type library file and make the output less verbose, which is useful when this utility is used in an installation script.

Note that `tlbexp` creates a type library, but it does not register the type library or the component. If you need to create and register a type library, you should use the `regasm` tool. In addition, this utility cannot be used to export a type library from an assembly that is generated by the `tlbimp` tool. The metadata of an assembly is much richer than the type library information; therefore, information will be lost when metadata is exported. Because of this difference, it's important to cover in some detail how the assembly metadata is exported.

Listing 9.4 illustrates an ILDasm output for a simple assembly. It will be used to illustrate the export process. ILDasm has an option to dump an assembly to IL. This is the option that is used to generate Listing 9.4.

LISTING 9.4 Assembly Header Information

```
.assembly extern mscorlib
{
  .publickeytoken = (B7 7A 5C 56 19 34 E0 89
  .ver 1:0:3300:0
}
.assembly Arithmetic
{
. . .
.custom instance void [mscorlib]System.Reflection.
➥AssemblyDescriptionAttribute::.ctor(string) =
➥( 01 00 12 41 72 69 74 68 6D 65 74 69 63 20 6C 69
➥   // ...Arithmetic li
62 72 61 72 79 00 00 )
➥  // brary..
. . .
  .hash algorithm 0x00008004
  .ver 1:0:677:42941
  .locale = (65 00 6E 00 2D 00 75 00 73 00 00 00 )
➥              // e.n.-.u.s...
}
.module Arithmetic.dll
// MVID: {135A81AF-B1D9-4322-862D-45D63DC8C151}
.imagebase 0x11000000
.subsystem 0x00000003
.file alignment 512
.corflags 0x00000001
// Image base: 0x02e50000
```

This is converted into the following type library information that is shown in Listing 9.5. The OLE/COM Object Viewer generates this output, as the first comment line explains. The OLE/COM Object Viewer is a tool that can be invoked from the Tools menu of the Visual Studio .NET IDE or directly from `\Program Files\Microsoft Visual Studio .NET\Common7\Tools\` as oleview.exe.

LISTING 9.5 Type Library Exported from an Assembly

```
// Generated .IDL file (by the OLE/COM Object Viewer)
//
// typelib filename: Arithmetic.tlb

[
```

LISTING 9.5 Continued

```
  uuid(4B1FAA13-E1A1-3319-BE37-DB70BCC525C7),
  version(1.0),
  helpstring("Arithmetic library"),
  custom(90883F05-3D28-11D2-8F17-00A0C9A6186D, Arithmetic,
➥Version=1.0.686.32110, Culture=en-us, PublicKeyToken=null)
]
library Arithmetic
{
    // TLib : Common Language Runtime Library :
➥{BED7F4EA-1A96-11D2-8F08-00A0C9A6186D}
    importlib("mscorlib.tlb");
    // TLib : OLE Automation : {00020430-0000-0000-C000-000000000046}
    importlib("stdole2.tlb");

. . .

    [
      uuid(ED26581E-3557-3D7C-82EE-F480C55EBC9E),
      version(1.0),
      custom(0F21F359-AB84-41E8-9A78-36D110E6D2F9,
➥ProfilingSamples.Arithmetic)
    ]
    coclass Arithmetic {
        interface _Object;
        [default] interface IBasicOperations;
    };
};
```

Listings 9.4 and 9.5 illustrate some important aspects about the export process. An assembly is identified by the signature of the originator (not shown), the locale ID (also not shown), and the version. A type library, in contrast, is identified by the library ID (TLBID), the version, and the locale. The TLBID is generated from an originator key and the name of the assembly. A type library is generated from each uniquely identified assembly. It is possible to override this automatic generation of the TLBID by specifying a **GuidAttribute** to the assembly. A type library only recognizes a two-part version number, whereas an assembly has a four-part version number. Exporting an assembly to a type library causes the last two parts of the assembly version to be truncated. A locale identifier string (“us-en”, “de-de”, and so on) is converted to an LCID that is stored as part of the type library. Notice that this locale identifier string is specified by the **AssemblyCultureAttribute** as follows:

```
[assembly: AssemblyCulture("en-us")]
```

A couple of miscellaneous notes about this part of the conversion process are worth making. Assemblies often contain periods as part of the assembly name. All of the periods in the assembly name are converted to underscores. This conversion process is not illustrated in Listings 9.4 and 9.5. If an assembly has an **AssemblyDescriptionAttribute** applied to it, it is transferred to a type library **helpstring**. Module information is discarded during the export process.

If you have your class nested in a hierarchy of namespaces such as the following:

```
namespace CLRUnleashed
{
    namespace COMInteropSamples
    {
```

then the assembly looks like Listing 9.6.

LISTING 9.6 Nested Namespaces in an Assembly

```
.namespace CLRUnleashed.COMInteropSamples
{
  .class interface public abstract auto ansi IBasicOperations
  {
  } // end of class IBasicOperations

  .class public auto ansi beforefieldinit Arithmetic
         extends [mscorlib]System.Object
         implements CLRUnleashed.COMInteropSamples.IBasicOperations
  {
  } // end of class Arithmetic

} // end of namespace CLRUnleashed.COMInteropSamples
```

You would expect that the names of the interfaces would change dramatically on export, but all that changes in the type library is this:

```
custom(0F21F359-AB84-41E8-9A78-36D110E6D2F9,
CLRUnleashed.COMInteropSamples.IBasicOperations)
```

The rest of the type library remains the same. The only time that significant changes will appear in the names of the interfaces due to namespace nesting is if the export procedure detects a naming conflict. If a class or interface is exported that has the same name in different namespaces, then the class or interface name is prefaced with the appropriate namespace (with periods replaced by underscores). For example, if you have a hierarchy that looks like Listing 9.7:

LISTING 9.7 Naming Conflict Within C# Namespace

```
namespace A {
   namespace B {
      public class LinkedList : IList {…}
      public interface IList {…}
   }
}
   namespace C {
      public interface IList {…}
}
```

then a potential conflict exists with the interface name IList. If you add the preceding structure, you get an assembly that looks like Listing 9.8.

LISTING 9.8 Naming Conflict Within an Assembly

```
.namespace CLRUnleashed.A
{
  .class interface public abstract auto ansi IList
  {
  } // end of class IList
} // end of namespace CLRUnleashed.A
.namespace CLRUnleashed.A.B
{
  .class interface public abstract auto ansi IList
  {
  } // end of class IList
  .class public auto ansi beforefieldinit LinkedList
         extends [mscorlib]System.Object
         implements CLRUnleashed.A.B.IList
  {
  } // end of class LinkedList
} // end of namespace CLRUnleashed.A.B
.namespace CLRUnleashed.C
{
  .class interface public abstract auto ansi IList
  {
  } // end of class IList
} // end of namespace CLRUnleashed.C
. . .
  } // end of class Arithmetic
} // end of namespace CLRUnleashed.COMInteropSamples
```

The type library looks like Listing 9.9. Notice that the name of the interface has changed only where a conflict exists.

LISTING 9.9 Naming Conflict Resolved in the Exported Type Library

```
library Arithmetic
{
. . .
    // Forward declare all types defined in this typelib
    interface CLRUnleashed_A_IList;
    interface CLRUnleashed_A_B_IList;
    interface CLRUnleashed_C_IList;
    interface IBasicOperations;
    interface _LinkedList;
. . .
```

Each of the IList interfaces is in a different namespace; therefore, the interfaces are given different names. From the previous examples, you should note that the namespace hierarchy has been flattened. Type libraries do not support any kind of hierarchy.

It's important to look at the various options that are available for classes. The simplest case can be shown in Listing 9.10, where the class directly implements a set of methods.

LISTING 9.10 Class Implementation

```
public class Arithmetic
{
    public int Add(int a, int b)
    {
        return a + b;
    }
    public int Subtract(int a, int b)
    {
        return a - b;
    }
    public int Multiply(int a, int b)
    {
        return a * b;
    }
    public int Divide(int a, int b)
    {
        if(b != 0)
            return a / b;
        else
            return 0;
    }
}
```

This is turned into the IL structure shown in Listing 9.11.

LISTING 9.11 Class IL Structure

```
.namespace COMInteropSamples
{
  .class public auto ansi beforefieldinit Arithmetic
         extends [mscorlib]System.Object
  {
  } // end of class Arithmetic

} // end of namespace COMInteropSamples
```

This is exported to the type library that looks like Listing 9.12. All but the most pertinent parts of the listing have been omitted.

LISTING 9.12 Class Exported Type Library

```
library Arithmetic
{
. . .
    // Forward declare all types defined in this typelib
    interface _Arithmetic;

. . .
    coclass Arithmetic {
        [default] interface _Arithmetic;
        interface _Object;
    };
. . .
    [
      odl,
      uuid(5BCABC37-3545-355C-B7A9-B7E07986B7F2),
      hidden,
      dual,
      oleautomation,
      custom(0F21F359-AB84-41E8-9A78-36D110E6D2F9, COMInteropSamples.Arithmetic)
    ]
    interface _Arithmetic : IDispatch {
    };
};
```

Notice that an `_Arithmetic` interface has been created. This interface is dual (supports both late binding and early binding). The problem is that all of the methods have disappeared, which, in essence, makes this interface accessible only via late binding. A better approach if this class is to be designed for interoperability is to define an interface and have the class implement it. COM follows this model; it is no wonder that this makes interop much easier. Change the interface shown in Listing 9.10 to look like Listing 9.13.

LISTING 9.13 Class That Implements an Interface

```
public interface IBasicOperations
{
    int Add(int a, int b);
    int Subtract(int a, int b);
    int Multiply(int a, int b);
    int Divide(int a, int b);
}
public class Arithmetic : IBasicOperations
. . .
```

Now when you export the class, you get a type library that looks like Listing 9.14.

LISTING 9.14 Type Library Exported from a Class That Implements an Interface

```
. . .
library Arithmetic
{
. . .
    // Forward declare all types defined in this typelib
    interface IBasicOperations;
    interface _Arithmetic;

    [
      odl,
      uuid(0E9DAAEF-47F7-3F0D-AE3D-B412A7C853D6),
      version(1.0),
      dual,
      oleautomation,
      custom(0F21F359-AB84-41E8-9A78-36D110E6D2F9,
➥COMInteropSamples.IBasicOperations)

    ]
    interface IBasicOperations : IDispatch {
        [id(0x60020000)]
        HRESULT Add(
                        [in] long a,
                        [in] long b,
                        [out, retval] long* pRetVal);
        [id(0x60020001)]
        HRESULT Subtract(
                        [in] long a,
                        [in] long b,
                        [out, retval] long* pRetVal);
        [id(0x60020002)]
        HRESULT Multiply(
                        [in] long a,
                        [in] long b,
                        [out, retval] long* pRetVal);
```

LISTING 9.14 Continued

```
        [id(0x60020003)]
        HRESULT Divide(
                        [in] long a,
                        [in] long b,
                        [out, retval] long* pRetVal);
    };

. . .
    coclass Arithmetic {
        [default] interface _Arithmetic;
        interface _Object;
        interface IBasicOperations;
    };

. . .
    interface _Arithmetic : IDispatch {
    };
```

Now you have the methods and the interface, so you are ready to query the object for the interface that you want and call each of the methods. One problem is that you still have the class interface `_Arithmetic`, and the real interface in which you are interested is not the default interface. This could be a problem if you used this component with VB or scripting clients. The default behavior for a class is to generate a class interface, specifically to generate an **`AutoDispatch`** interface. You can see this in Listing 9.14. The class interface, `_Arithmetic`, is derived from `IDispatch`. Now you can augment the class with a **`ClassInterfaceAttribute`** specifying that the class interface should be **`AutoDual`**. This modification is shown in Listing 9.15.

LISTING 9.15 Specifying an AutoDual Class Interface

```
[ClassInterface(ClassInterfaceType.AutoDual)]
public class Arithmetic : IBasicOperations
```

The class interface portion of the type library now looks like Listing 9.16.

LISTING 9.16 Exporting an AutoDual Class Interface

```
. . .
[
   odl,
   uuid(C96F1753-AD3A-3AD7-920F-4F5902302FEF),
   hidden,
   dual,
   nonextensible,
```

LISTING 9.16 Continued

```
   oleautomation,
   custom(0F21F359-AB84-41E8-9A78-36D110E6D2F9, COMInteropSamples.Arithmetic)
]
interface _Arithmetic : IDispatch {
. . .
```

This sample illustrates the option, but the documentation strongly discourages its use. Even the default **AutoDispatch** option is discouraged. The recommended **ClassInterfaceAttribute** is **None**, as shown in Listing 9.17.

LISTING 9.17 Eliminating a Class Interface

```
[ClassInterface(ClassInterfaceType.None)]
public class Arithmetic : IBasicOperations
```

Look at the resulting exported type library in Listing 9.18.

LISTING 9.18 An Exported Type Library Without a Class Interface

```
. . .
library Arithmetic
{
. . .
    // Forward declare all types defined in this typelib
    interface IBasicOperations;
. . .
    interface IBasicOperations : IDispatch {
        [id(0x60020000)]
        HRESULT Add(
                        [in] long a,
                        [in] long b,
                        [out, retval] long* pRetVal);
        [id(0x60020001)]
        HRESULT Subtract(
                        [in] long a,
                        [in] long b,
                        [out, retval] long* pRetVal);
        [id(0x60020002)]
        HRESULT Multiply(
                        [in] long a,
                        [in] long b,
                        [out, retval] long* pRetVal);
        [id(0x60020003)]
        HRESULT Divide(
                        [in] long a,
                        [in] long b,
                        [out, retval] long* pRetVal);
    };
```

LISTING 9.18 Continued

```
    [
      uuid(79149B17-6D8E-30E1-8B57-09DC7FD44F94),
      version(1.0),
      custom(0F21F359-AB84-41E8-9A78-36D110E6D2F9, COMInteropSamples.Arithmetic)
    ]
    coclass Arithmetic {
        interface _Object;
        [default] interface IBasicOperations;
    };
};
```

The exported type library is much closer to what you would expect a COM type library to look like. The class interface has been eliminated, and the default interface is `IBasicOperations`. This is what you want. For most interop projects, **`ClassInterfaceAttribute`** should be applied to all exported classes with **`ClassInterfaceType.None`**.

If you require that the DISPIDs of the methods on your interface be fixed, you might need to add another attribute specifying the DISPID that you require. Notice in Listing 9.18 that the exported method has a type library attribute of the form `id(0x60020000)`. This is the DISPID of the method. The export utility automatically generates these DISPIDs for each of the methods in a dispatch interface. Rather than have the export utility automatically pick DISPID values, you might need to specify these values. You can pre-assign the DISPIDs, as illustrated in Listing 9.19.

LISTING 9.19 Attributes to Specify DISPIDs

```
public interface IBasicOperations
{
    [DispId(1)]
    int Add(int a, int b);
    [DispId(2)]
    int Subtract(int a, int b);
    [DispId(3)]
    int Multiply(int a, int b);
    [DispId(4)]
    int Divide(int a, int b);
}
```

Now the DISPID will be known ahead of time for each of the methods.

Of course, if you wanted this interface to derive from IUnknown, you would not need to worry about DISPIDs. Listing 9.20 shows an example of specifying an IUnknown interface.

LISTING 9.20 Attributes to Specify an Interface Derived from IUnknown

```
[InterfaceTypeAttribute(ComInterfaceType.InterfaceIsIUnknown)]
public interface IBasicOperations
{
    int Add(int a, int b);
    int Subtract(int a, int b);
    int Multiply(int a, int b);
    int Divide(int a, int b);
}
```

Now, when you look at the exported type library, you don't see `DISPID`s, and the interface is derived from `IUnknown` rather than `IDispatch`. This is illustrated in Listing 9.21.

LISTING 9.21 An Exported Interface Derived from IUnknown

```
interface IBasicOperations : IUnknown {
    HRESULT _stdcall Add(
                    [in] long a,
                    [in] long b,
                    [out, retval] long* pRetVal);
    HRESULT _stdcall Subtract(
                    [in] long a,
                    [in] long b,
                    [out, retval] long* pRetVal);
    HRESULT _stdcall Multiply(
                    [in] long a,
                    [in] long b,
                    [out, retval] long* pRetVal);
    HRESULT _stdcall Divide(
                    [in] long a,
                    [in] long b,
                    [out, retval] long* pRetVal);
};
```

The default **`ComInterfaceType`** for an **`InterfaceTypeAttribute`** is **`InterfaceIsDual`**, which causes a dual interface to be exported. Other options for **`InterfaceTypeAttribute`** are **`InterfaceIsIUnknown`** (illustrated in Listing 9.20) and **`InterfaceIsIDispatch`**.

Now you can add two complex numbers. In the Arithmetic class, you can define a complex structure to hold the complex number. You then add a convenience function to convert the complex number to polar form. Listing 9.22 shows the resulting type along with a method to add two complex numbers.

LISTING 9.22 Adding a User-Defined Type to an Assembly

```
[StructLayout(LayoutKind.Sequential)]
public struct Complex
{
    public double real;
    public double imaginary;
    public void Polar(out double r, out double t)
    {
        r = Math.Sqrt(real*real + imaginary * imaginary);
        t = Math.Atan2(imaginary, real);
    }
}
. . .
[InterfaceTypeAttribute(ComInterfaceType.InterfaceIsIUnknown)]
public interface IBasicOperations
{
    int Add(int a, int b);
    int Subtract(int a, int b);
    int Multiply(int a, int b);
    int Divide(int a, int b);
    Complex Add(Complex a, Complex b);
}

[ClassInterface(ClassInterfaceType.None)]
public class Arithmetic : IBasicOperations
{
    public Complex Add(Complex a, Complex b)
    {
        Complex c;
        c.real = a.real + b.real;
        c.imaginary = a.imaginary + b.imaginary;
        return c;
    }
. . .
```

Now, using the OLE/COM Object Viewer, you can see how the exported type library represents the new type and your new interface method. Listing 9.23 shows the resulting type library changes.

LISTING 9.23 Exporting a User-Defined Type

```
. . .
typedef
[
 uuid(FDF28CC4-27DE-3F78-AB04-21FE30661629),
 version(1.0),
 custom(0F21F359-AB84-41E8-9A78-36D110E6D2F9, COMInteropSamples.Complex)
]
struct tagComplex
```

LISTING 9.23 Continued

```
{
    double real;
    double imaginary;
} Complex;
. . .
interface IBasicOperations : IUnknown {
    HRESULT _stdcall Add(
                    [in] long a,
                    [in] long b,
                    [out, retval] long* pRetVal);
    HRESULT _stdcall Subtract(
                    [in] long a,
                    [in] long b,
                    [out, retval] long* pRetVal);
    HRESULT _stdcall Multiply(
                    [in] long a,
                    [in] long b,
                    [out, retval] long* pRetVal);
    HRESULT _stdcall Divide(
                    [in] long a,
                    [in] long b,
                    [out, retval] long* pRetVal);
    custom(0F21F359-AB84-41E8-9A78-36D110E6D2F9, Add)
    HRESULT _stdcall Add_2(
                    [in] Complex a,
                    [in] Complex b,
                    [out, retval] Complex* pRetVal);
    };
. . .
```

Notice that a new user-defined type has been added to the type library corresponding to the type that was added to the assembly metadata; however, the convenience function that you added has disappeared. A user-defined type cannot contain methods, so the export process silently removes the methods from the type library. The method to add two complex numbers has been added to the interface, but it is not the same name that you gave it in the assembly. Again, this is a limitation of type libraries that do not support overloaded methods. The additional overloaded method for adding two complex numbers is given a new name to avoid a naming conflict. If this is not the behavior you desire, then you should modify your assembly so that it does not require overloading. In this case, you would need to rename `Add` to something like `AddComplex`.

Now you can add some constants to your class to aide in error processing. Listing 9.24 shows some errors that you can define.

Listing 9.24 Defining an Enumerated Type

```
public enum ArithmeticErrors
{
    DivideByZero = 0,
    Overflow,
    Underflow
}
```

To see how this will appear when exported, see Listing 9.25, which shows the exported enumerated type.

Listing 9.25 Type Library Representation of an Enumerated Type

```
typedef
[
 uuid(A5419667-F77A-33FA-AB03-002120E8B203),
 version(1.0),
 custom(0F21F359-AB84-41E8-9A78-36D110E6D2F9,
        COMInteropSamples.ArithmeticErrors)
]
enum
{
    ArithmeticErrors_DivideByZero = 0,
    ArithmeticErrors_Overflow = 1,
    ArithmeticErrors_Underflow = 2
} ArithmeticErrors;
```

To ensure uniqueness, the exported version of the enumeration has each enumerated value prefaced by the name of the enumeration (in this case, `ArithmeticErrors_`). If you define an enumeration and do not use it in any part of the assembly, it is silently ignored when exported to a type library.

One of the most significant aspects of exporting metadata to a type library is the marshaling and method signature transformation. In the previous examples, you saw methods like this:

```
public int Add(int a, int b)
```

turn into the following in the type library:

```
HRESULT _stdcall Add(
                [in] long a,
                [in] long b,
                [out, retval] long* pRetVal);
```

For most cases, this is exactly what you want. In fact, this will be what you want 99% of the time. However, an attribute allows you to preserve the signature of the method so that it does not return an HRESULT and create an automatic [out,retval]. If you change the assembly to look like this:

```
[PreserveSig]
public int Add(int a, int b)
```

the type library looks like this:

```
long _stdcall Add(
                [in] long a,
                [in] long b);
```

The signature of the method has been preserved, and the result is returned rather than an HRESULT. Using this option breaks the COM convention of returning an HRESULT.

Properties are supported during export. You can define the following property on the interface:

```
ArithmeticErrors LastError
{
    get;
}
```

and this turns into the following in the type library:

```
[propget]
HRESULT _stdcall LastError([out, retval] ArithmeticErrors* pRetVal);
```

You could define this property to be read/write by defining a **get** and a **set** portion of the property. The type library would have an additional [propput] method if you did this, instead of the singular [propget] that you see in the previous example.

Following are some of the restrictions on exporting types:

- Only public types are exposed.
- Only public members are exposed.
- Shared/static members are not accessible.
- Creatable classes require a public default constructor. Remember a default constructor is a constructor that does not take any arguments.

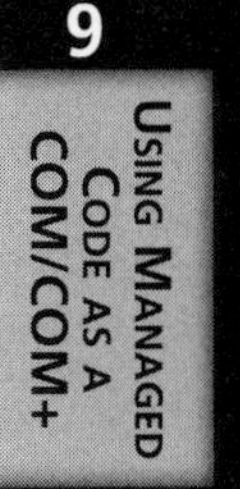

This chapter covers some of the more complex aspects of exporting to a type library later, but this section sets forth the basics to get you started.

Registering Type Library Information

Although exporting to a type library is important and it forms the key link in interop with a .NET component as a COM component, one more step needs to happen: The type library needs to be registered. This step is performed by the regasm tool. This tool performs both the export and the registration. Listing 9.26 shows some of the options available on the `regasm` tool.

LISTING 9.26 `regasm` Options

```
Syntax: RegAsm AssemblyPath [Options]
Options:
    /unregister            Unregister types
    /tlb[:FileName]        Export the assembly to the specified type library
                           and register it
    /regfile[:FileName]    Generate a reg file with the specified name
                           instead of registering the types. This option
                           cannot be used with the /u or /tlb options
    /codebase              Set the code base in the registry
    /registered            Only refer to already registered type libraries
    /nologo                Prevents RegAsm from displaying logo
    /silent                Silent mode. Prevents displaying of success messages
    /verbose               Displays extra information
    /? or /help            Display this usage message
```

Many of these options are similar to the options for `tlbexp`. Some of the additions include `/unregister`, `/registered`, and `/regfile`. The `/tlb` option performs the same function as the `/out` option of `tlbexp`. Notice that `regasm` does not support `/names`. Using this tool is much the same as using `tlbexp`. The following command line exports to the specified type library, registers it, and ensures that `codebase` is part of the registry information. Specifying `codebase` ensures that the assembly can be found if it is not installed into the local machine's global assembly cache (GAC).

```
> regasm Arithmetic.dll /codebase /tlb:Arithmetic.tlb /verbose
RegAsm warning: Registering an unsigned assembly with /codebase can cause your
assembly to interfere with other applications that may be installed on the
same computer. The /codebase switch is intended to be used only with signed
assemblies. Please give your assembly a strong name and re-register it.
Types registered successfully
Type Complex exported.
Type ArithmeticErrors exported.
Type IBasicOperations exported.
Type Arithmetic exported.
Assembly exported to 'arithmetic.tlb', and the type library was
➥registered successfully
```

The warning about the `/codebase` switch should concern you. If used improperly, the codebase switch could circumvent all the work that has gone into preventing DLL hell, as discussed in Chapter 6, "Publishing Applications." Also discussed in Chapter 6, an assembly is given a strong name by generating a key pair for the assembly with the `sn` utility as follows:

```
sn -k Arithmetic.snk
```

Then in the AssemblyInfo.cs file, make sure you have the following line:

```
[assembly: AssemblyKeyFile("Arithmetic.snk")]
```

Now you will not get the warning because the assembly has a strong name that will uniquely identify it.

After you have successfully registered the exported type library, you can look at what was done with either a registry editor or the OLE/COM Object Viewer.

The Visual Studio IDE simplifies the process even further by allowing you to check a box indicating that this class should be exported. Figure 9.2 shows the COM interop check box.

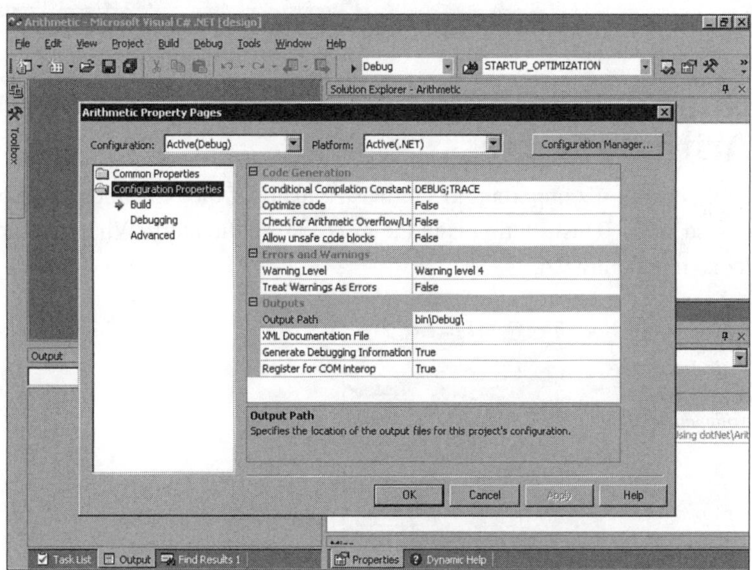

FIGURE 9.2
Using the IDE to generate and register an exported type library.

If you set the `Register for COM Interop` to true and do not have a strong name associated with your assembly, you will not get a warning as you do when you register the assembly manually. An option entitled `Wrapper Assembly Key File` is available to associate a key file with an assembly.

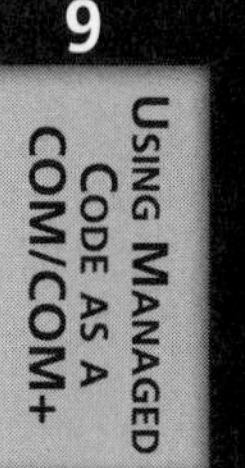

Figure 9.3 shows what a sample registry entry looks like after it has been successfully registered.

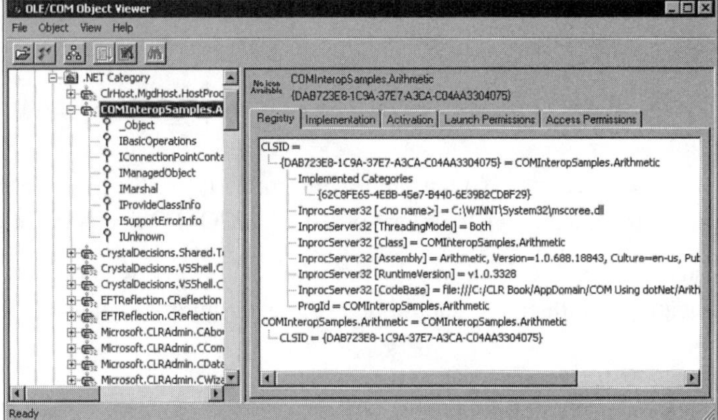

FIGURE 9.3
Registry after successfully registering the Arithmetic class.

Demonstration of Basic COM Interop with an Arithmetic Class

At this point, it's important to summarize many of the principles that have been discussed so far. This solution is in the `Arithmetic` directory. When the sample is run, it looks like Figure 9.4.

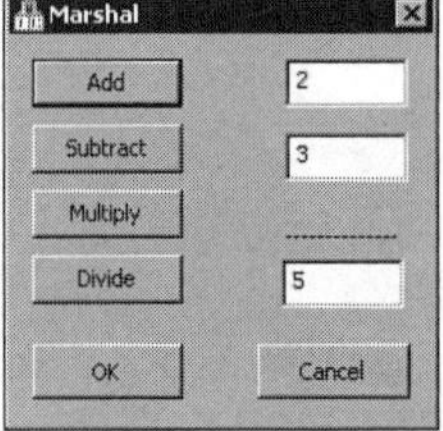

FIGURE 9.4
Basic demonstration for the Arithmetic class.

To use this application, you simply enter numbers on the right and select the operation to be performed on the left. Select the OK or Cancel button when you want to quit.

The source for many of the listings shown earlier is part of this sample. You might want to look at the sample, run it through the debugger, and see how easy it is to build a COM component by using interop.

Demonstration of Basic COM Interop with Excel

Another sample has been put together that illustrates how representing a .NET managed component as a COM component can be useful. This application takes a range of values specified by a named range in Excel and performs matrix operations on those values.

Note

The source for this Excel application is included in the file Matrix.xls in the `bin\Debug` directory, in the solution Matrix, in the `Matrix` directory. This ensures that the interop assembly is correctly found. If you have trouble running this Excel spreadsheet, you might need to adjust your permissions to allow macros to be executed. In addition, if this is the first time that you have used this project, you will need to rebuild the solution. Then, in the Visual Basic Editor (Alt+F11 or Tools, Macro, Visual Basic Editor), select the References menu (Tools, References). Add the Matrix reference to the project (make sure that this Matrix refers to the Matrix class that you are expecting). Adding this reference should look something like Figure 9.5.

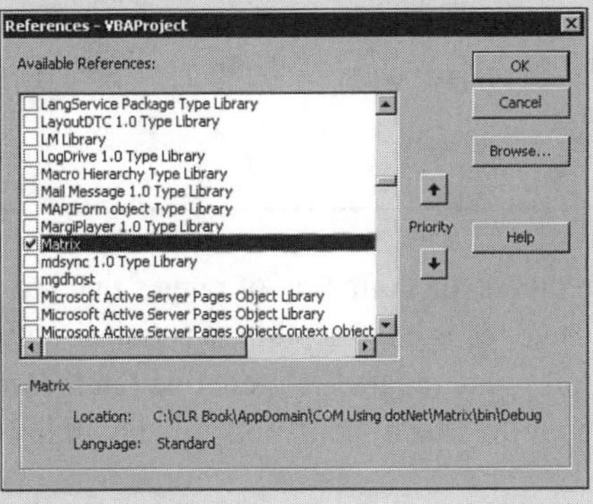

FIGURE 9.5
Adding a reference to the Matrix class.

For example, to multiply one matrix to another, use the VBA code shown in Listing 9.27.

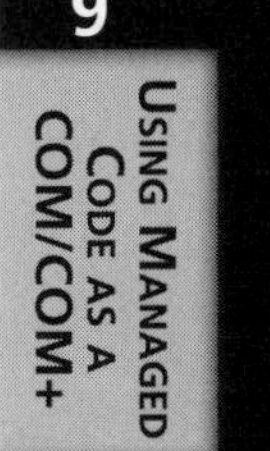

LISTING 9.27 VBA Code to Add Two Matrices Together

```
Dim Matrix As New Matrix.MatrixOperations
Dim Operations As IMatrix
Public Sub Multiply()
    On Error GoTo ErrorHandler

    Dim m1 As Name
    Dim m2 As Name
    Dim m3 As Name
    Dim r1 As Range
    Dim r2 As Range
    Dim r3 As Range

    Set m1 = Names.Item("A")
    Set m2 = Names.Item("B")
```

LISTING 9.27 Continued

```
    Set m3 = Names.Item("Result")
    Set r1 = m1.RefersToRange
    Set r2 = m2.RefersToRange
    Set r3 = m3.RefersToRange

    r3.Clear
    ReDim Result(1 To r3.Rows.Count, 1 To r3.Columns.Count) As Variant

    Set Operations = Matrix
    Operations.Multiply r1.value, r2.value, Result

    r3.value = Result

    Exit Sub

ErrorHandler:
    MsgBox "Failed. " + Err.Description + " " + Err.Source + " " +
➥Hex(Err.Number)

End Sub
```

As you can see, each macro requires the definition of ranges that are defined by the names `A`, `B`, and `Result`. The macro `Inverse` is an exception; it requires only `A` and `Result`. A couple of matrices and the appropriate ranges are predefined in the matrix.xls file. If you just want to see it work, bring up the Macro dialog box as shown in Figure 9.6.

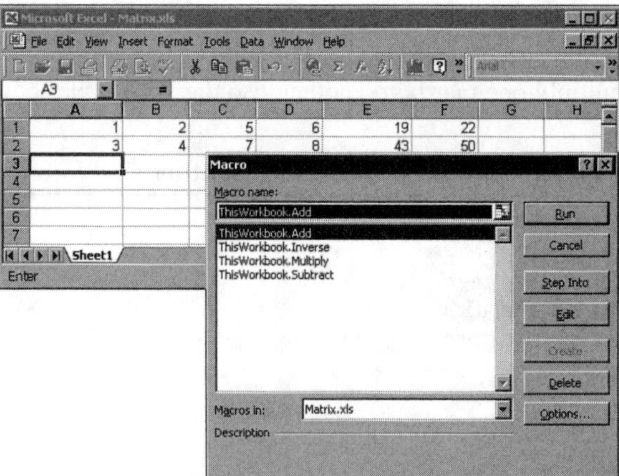

FIGURE 9.6
Calling an Excel macro.

As you can see from Figure 9.6, you are presented with a list of options that allow you to Add, Subtract, Multiply, or take the Inverse of the matrices defined with the ranges named by `A`, `B`, and `Result`. Using the default matrices, if you select Multiply, the Excel spreadsheet updates to look like Figure 9.7.

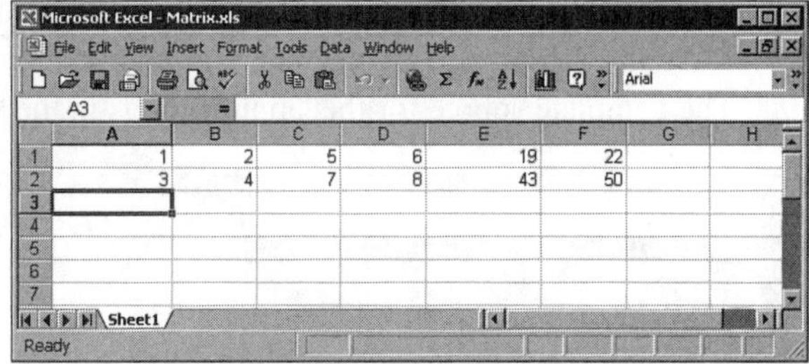

FIGURE 9.7
Results of multiplying two matrices.

The point of this exercise is not to add this matrix processing functionality to Excel (Excel already has MMULT and MINVERSE, among others), but to show that you can call a .NET component from Excel using interop. This call happens in the macro where a method is being called on the Operation interface. In Listing 9.27, this call is Operation.Multiply. This call calls the .NET component to do the work. In fact, if you want to debug your call, you can set the driver program from the Matrix solution to point to the Excel executable. These options are part of the Configuration Properties of your project—specifically the Debugging Configuration properties. Set your debug mode to Program and the path should point to the Excel executable in this case. Now, you can set breakpoints in your code to be executed when Excel calls into your function. A debug path has been set in the solution that you will probably have to modify to debug the matrix solution so that the debug path points to where you have installed Excel.

> **Note**
>
> VBA's and Excel's notion of an array has already been compensated for. However, if you try to access the array that is passed from Excel and you are thinking that it is a zero-based array, you might get an **`IndexOutOfRangeException`**. In marshaling the arrays from VBA, no compensation has been made to the array to account for the difference in array indexing between a .NET component and VBA.

More Advanced Features of COM Interop

The most important and compelling feature of interop with a .NET component as a COM object is that it provides for model consistency both on the COM side and on the managed side. The CCW transforms .NET exceptions to `HRESULT`s. The description information associated with a .NET exception is passed to an IErrorInfo object. **`String`**s are marshaled to `BSTR`s, **`decimal`** as `DECIMAL`, **`object`** as `VARIANT`, **`System.Drawing.Color`** as `OLE_COLOR`, **`IEnumerator`** as `IEnumVARIANT`, and Callback events to `IConnectionPoints`.

An application has been created that illustrates how to use the marshaling and translation that occurs in the Com Callable Wrapper (CCW). When this application first starts up, it looks like Figure 9.8. The complete source for this application is in the `Marshal` directory.

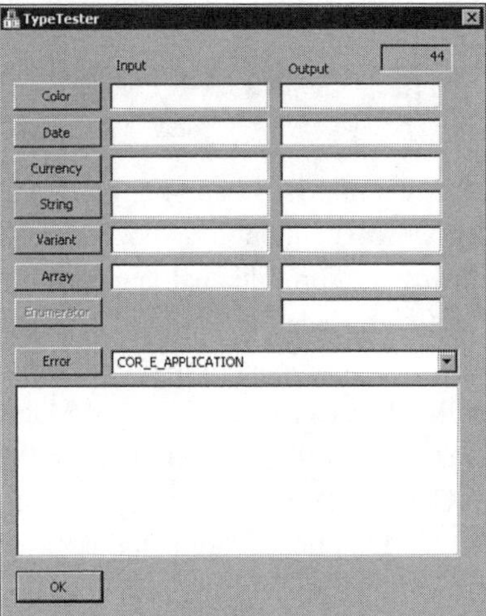

FIGURE 9.8
COM interop type tester.

To use this utility, you enter the data in the Input column and select the button that corresponds to the row where you entered the data. Selecting this button initiates a transfer of the data you entered to the .NET component (it looks like a COM component). After the .NET component receives the data, an event is fired that echoes the original data entered. This model is not followed in the application in three areas. The first is the counter in the upper-right corner of the application. This counter is asynchronously updated every second with a new value of counter from the .NET component. The second exception is in the enumerator row of the application. The enumerator button is only enabled when an array has been successfully transferred to the .NET component. After an array exists, you can click this button to retrieve an IEnumVARIANT interface pointer, which you can use to enumerate the items in the array. The final exception is in the error processing. Selecting the error button transfers a string to the .NET component. The .NET component uses this string to select an error exception to throw. The testing side does not have an exception handling `try/catch` block because the CCW catches the exception and turns the exception into an `HRESULT`, which is displayed in the text box that is directly underneath the error button. Small portions of the code can be found in Listings 9.28–9.33. The full source for this sample is in the `Marshal` directory.

Because the callback mechanism is used for almost all of the tests, it will be discussed first. Listings 9.28–9.30 illustrate what is involved in setting up the asynchronous callback on the .NET component. Listing 9.28 shows how to declare the delegates used for callbacks.

LISTING 9.28 Declaring Delegate Callbacks

```
[ComVisible(false)]
public delegate void ColorHandler(Color o);
[ComVisible(false)]
public delegate void DateHandler(DateTime dt);
[ComVisible(false)]
public delegate void NameHandler(string s);
[ComVisible(false)]
public delegate void DecimalHandler(decimal d);
[ComVisible(false)]
public delegate void VariantHandler(object o);
[ComVisible(false)]
public delegate void ArrayHandler(object [] o);
[ComVisible(false)]
public delegate void CounterHandler(int c);
```

Think of a delegate as a type-safe function pointer. See Chapter 14, "`Delegates` and `Events`," for more detail on this topic. A **`ComVisibleAttribute`** has been applied to each of these declarations to prevent `tlbexp` from placing type library information on each of these declarations. These methods can only be used within the context of the callback event, so having the declaration in the type library just confuses anyone trying to read the exported types. In Listing 9.29, the event interface is declared.

LISTING 9.29 Declaring the Connection-Point Interface

```
[InterfaceType(ComInterfaceType.InterfaceIsIDispatch)]
public interface _IComTypesEvents
{
    [DispId(1)]
    void ColorChanged(Color o);
    [DispId(2)]
    void DateChanged(DateTime d);
    [DispId(3)]
    void NameChanged(string s);
    [DispId(4)]
    void DecimalChanged(decimal d);
    [DispId(5)]
    void VariantChanged(object o);
    [DispId(6)]
    void ArrayChanged(object [] o);
    [DispId(7)]
    void Counter(int c);
}
```

Here it is declared that the connection point interface that is supported is an `IDispatch` type of interface. Each of the methods on the interface is given a `DISPID` instead of a `tlbexp` to generate `DISPID`s. Listing 9.30 takes this interface and declares it as a source interface for connection-point events.

LISTING 9.30 Declaring the COM CoClass and the Background Thread

```
[ClassInterface(ClassInterfaceType.None)]
[ComSourceInterfaces("InteropSample._IComTypesEvents, dotNETCOMTypes")]
public class CComTypes : IComTypes
{
    public event ColorHandler ColorChanged;
    public event DateHandler DateChanged;
    public event NameHandler NameChanged;
    public event DecimalHandler DecimalChanged;
    public event VariantHandler VariantChanged;
    public event ArrayHandler ArrayChanged;
    public event CounterHandler Counter;
    Hashtable errorExceptions;
    void CounterEntry()
    {
       try
       {
            while(true)
            {
                Thread.Sleep(1000);
                if(Counter != null)
                    Counter(counter++);
            }
        }
        finally
        {
            Debug.WriteLine("Exiting counter thread!");
        }
    }
    public CComTypes()
    {
        counter = 0;
        counterThread = new Thread(new ThreadStart(CounterEntry));
        counterThread.Start();
. . .
```

With the **`ComSourceInterfaceAttribute`**, it is declared that the `_IComTypesEvents` interface is the default source of events for this component and that these events come from the `dotNETCOMTypes` library. From this listing, you can also see events declared for each of the possible methods that could be called on the connection-point interface. When a client to this component wants to register its interest in one of the events on the

_IComTypesEvents interface, it issues a DispAdvise call, which is translated into a registration on one of these events. When one or more clients have registered, the event is non-null. A check is done for a null event handler just in case no one has registered interest in these events. The Counter event is particularly simple in that a **Thread** is started up at CounterEntry. This **Thread** simply falls into a loop that goes to sleep for one second, wakes up to fire an event, and goes back to sleep. Unfortunately, threading has not yet been covered. For details, skip ahead to Chapter 11, "Threading."

The error code is simple. It looks up in a map the exception that should be thrown for a given string and then throws the exception. Listing 9.31 shows how a map is built up for each possible error code.

LISTING 9.31 Throwing an Exception in the .NET Component

```
errorExceptions = new Hashtable();
errorExceptions.Add("COR_E_APPLICATION",
                    new ApplicationException("This is a test"));
errorExceptions.Add("COR_E_ARGUMENT",
                    new ArgumentException("This is a test"));
errorExceptions.Add("E_INVALIDARG",
                    new ArgumentException("This is a test"));
errorExceptions.Add("COR_E_ARGUMENTOUTOFRANGE",
                    new ArgumentOutOfRangeException("This is a test"));
errorExceptions.Add("COR_E_ARITHMETIC",
                    new ArithmeticException("This is a test"));
errorExceptions.Add("ERROR_ARITHMETIC_OVERFLOW",
                    new ArithmeticException("This is a test"));

. . .
public void ErrorTest(string error)
{
    throw (Exception)errorExceptions[error];
}
```


As you can see from the code snippet illustrated in Listing 9.31, a lookup table is built on construction for each type of exception to be handled. When an error call is received, the string is matched with what is in the table and the appropriate exception is thrown.

The rest of the code shows examples of marshaling different data types. Listing 9.32 shows the methods that are associated with the main interface.

LISTING 9.32 Data Marshaling Interface

```
public interface IComTypes
{
    Color ColorValue
```

LISTING 9.32 Continued

```
    {
        get;
        set;
    }
    DateTime Date
    {
        get;
        set;
    }
    string Name
    {
        get;
        set;
    }
    decimal Decimal
    {
        get;
        set;
    }
    object Variant
    {
        get;
        set;
    }
    object [] Array
    {
        get;
        set;
    }
    IEnumerator Enumerator
    {
        get;
    }
    void ErrorTest(string error);
}
```

`Tlbexp` or `regasm` takes the type information in the assembly and generates a type library that is partially shown in Listing 9.33.

LISTING 9.33 Type Library for Marshaling Test Interface

```
interface IComTypes : IDispatch {
    [id(0x60020000), propget]
    HRESULT ColorValue([out, retval] OLE_COLOR* pRetVal);
    [id(0x60020000), propput]
    HRESULT ColorValue([in] OLE_COLOR pRetVal);
```

LISTING 9.33 Continued

```
    [id(0x60020002), propget]
    HRESULT Date([out, retval] DATE* pRetVal);
    [id(0x60020002), propput]
    HRESULT Date([in] DATE pRetVal);
    [id(0x60020004), propget]
    HRESULT Name([out, retval] BSTR* pRetVal);
    [id(0x60020004), propput]
    HRESULT Name([in] BSTR pRetVal);
    [id(0x60020006), propget]
    HRESULT Decimal([out, retval] wchar_t* pRetVal);
    [id(0x60020006), propput]
    HRESULT Decimal([in] wchar_t pRetVal);
    [id(0x60020008), propget]
    HRESULT Variant([out, retval] VARIANT* pRetVal);
    [id(0x60020008), propputref]
    HRESULT Variant([in] VARIANT pRetVal);
    [id(0x6002000a), propget]
    HRESULT Array([out, retval] SAFEARRAY(VARIANT)* pRetVal);
    [id(0x6002000a), propput]
    HRESULT Array([in] SAFEARRAY(VARIANT) pRetVal);
    [id(0x6002000c), propget]
    HRESULT Enumerator([out, retval] IEnumVARIANT** pRetVal);
    [id(0x6002000d)]
    HRESULT ErrorTest([in] BSTR error);
};

[
  uuid(0072A76F-9720-323A-A3B7-EE77ECFEA053),
  version(1.0),
  custom(0F21F359-AB84-41E8-9A78-36D110E6D2F9, InteropSample.CComTypes)
]
coclass CComTypes {
    interface _Object;
    [default] interface IComTypes;
    [default, source] dispinterface _IComTypesEvents;
};
```

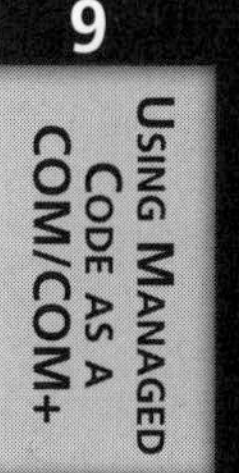

Comparing Listings 9.33 and 9.32, you can see that all of the types are automatically marshaled. COM has its vision of the world that is maintained with OLE_COLOR, VARIANT, BSTR, and so on. .NET has its vision of the world that is also maintained with Color, object, and string, among others. Both models of operation are maintained. To unmanaged code, the component looks like any other COM component. From the managed side, the interfaces and methods are built just like any other managed method and interface.

Summary

This has been a quick tour of how to develop a COM component using the .NET Framework. This chapter covered how and why to develop a COM component by using the .NET Framework. It explored some of the options available to you, the developer, in building a COM component using the .NET Framework. It provided examples to illustrate that a COM component developed with the .NET Framework can be used virtually anywhere a "normal" COM component can be used. In conclusion, the following guidelines might be useful in developing COM components with .NET:

- Design for interoperability—Particularly if you expect to use this component as a COM component, expose only those properties and methods that can easily be implemented via the marshaling layer and the CCW. The CCW is not meant to replace the need for a port of your software to .NET. Some functionality will be missing when using the CCW that only can be replaced by a full port.
- Don't use class interfaces—Factor your code so that the functionality can be expressed using abstract interfaces that are used as a base for an implementation class. Whenever possible, use `[ClassInterface(ClassInterfaceType.None)]` so that class interfaces are not generated.
- Become familiar with ILDASM and the OLE/COM Object Viewer—When dealing with interop, each of these tools can be valuable in diagnosing problems.

CHAPTER 10

Memory/Resource Management

In This Chapter

Much of the reason that managed code is called managed is because resources—and in particular, memory that is allocated by managed code—is managed. Responsibility for the deallocation of the memory does not rest with the programmer. With unmanaged code, all memory that is allocated requires the programmer to deallocate it. The CLR has a good scheme for managing the memory allocation and deallocation for an application. The CLR gives the programmer a world-class general-purpose garbage collector that frees the programmer from undue concern about memory allocation and deallocation. The strict type system in the .NET Framework ensures that code does not stray into memory in which it was not meant to be. One of the central focuses for this chapter is the general architecture for memory management within the .NET Framework.

Sometimes a programmer needs to take a proactive role in managing memory and resources. This chapter shows you how to gain more control over the garbage collector when it is too automatic. It is important to know what role the garbage collector plays and how you can efficiently manage resources other than memory within the .NET Framework. (Non-memory resources include file handles, database connections, Windows handles, and so on.)

Overview of Resource Management in the .NET Framework

As you are probably aware, the CLR takes an active role in managing the lifetime of objects that your application allocates. Actively managing objects is based on the premise that every object requires memory. It is the CLR's job to manage the allocation and deallocation of memory in an efficient and timely manner. In addition, every object requires that the memory associated with it be initialized. The programmer must properly initialize the object; the CLR cannot and should not interfere with this process. The .NET Framework requires that all objects be allocated from a managed heap. Each language expresses this allocation and initialization differently, but the concept is the same. For C#, an object is allocated and initialized as follows:

```
class Foo
{
    public Foo()
    {
        Console.WriteLine("Constructing Foo");
    }
}
. . .
```

```
Foo f = new Foo();
```

This statement allocates memory for the object and initializes it using the default constructor for the class Foo. Managed C++ performs this function with the following:

```
__gc class Foo
{
public:
    Foo()
    {
        Console::WriteLine(S"Constructing Foo");
    }
};
. . .
Foo *f = new Foo();
```

In Visual Basic, it looks like this:

```
Public Class Foo
    Public Sub New()
        MyBase.New()
        Console.WriteLine("Constructing Foo")
    End Sub
End Class
. . .
Dim f As New Foo()
```

Each language has syntax for constructing an object, but in the end, each language generates code that is remarkably the same IL. What follows is the IL for the Foo constructor from the C# code, but the code is much the same for each of the three languages listed earlier.

```
IL_0000:  ldarg.0
IL_0001:  call       instance void [mscorlib]System.Object::.ctor()
IL_0006:  ldstr      "Constructing Foo"
IL_000b:  call       void [mscorlib]System.Console::WriteLine(string)
IL_0010:  ret
```

Note

For all languages that support the Common Language Specification (CLS), the base **Object** constructor is called by default. In the .NET Framework, when you construct an object, you are also constructing the base class **Object** from which all objects are implicitly derived.

Before any of this code can execute, it needs some space in which to execute. C++ had syntax that would allow a programmer to explicitly separate the allocation and the initialization (construction) of an object using the new placement syntax. The new placement looks something like this:

```
Foo *p = new (address) Foo();
```

You need to look at constructing objects in the .NET Framework as two steps: allocation and initialization. *Allocation* is the allotment of memory, whereas *initialization* is the filling in of default values for the object. The .NET Framework does not support separating the two steps explicitly as C++. A clear division of labor exists; the CLR handles the memory, and your application handles the rest.

Just before the construction or initialization of your object, the .NET Framework allocates enough memory to hold your object. This allocation process is depicted in Figure 10.1.

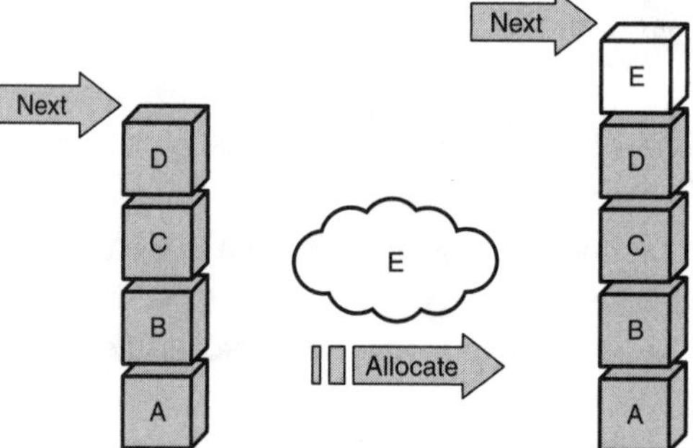

FIGURE 10.1
.NET allocation.

All that is necessary to allocate an object is to examine the type information (pictured as a cloud) and bump up the `Next` pointer to make room for the new object. This process is extremely fast. In basic terms, it just involves calculating the size and incrementing a pointer appropriately. This is somewhat idealized, however. What happens when the height of the stack is limited, as shown in Figure 10.2?

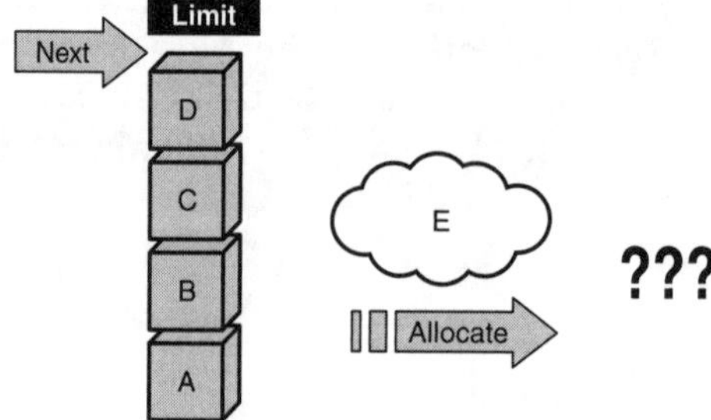

FIGURE 10.2
.NET allocation with a limit.

An error might occur because of the lack of room. To make room, you could remove one or more of the old objects to make room for the new object. This is where a process known as garbage collection comes into play.

When the CLR determines that it has no more room, it initiates a garbage collection cycle. Initially, the assumption is that all objects are garbage. The garbage collector then proceeds to examine all roots to see if the program can reach the object. A *root* is virtually any storage location to which the running program has access. For example, a processor's CPU registers can act as roots, global and static variables can act as roots, and local variables can be roots. A simple rule is that if the object is reachable by the program, then it has a root referring to it somewhere. You might have the following code:

```
Foo f = new Foo();
. . .
// Use object . . .
. . .
f = null;
```

A local variable, `f`, refers to the object `Foo`. After you set the local variable that references the object `Foo` to **`null`**, you have effectively disconnected the local variable from the object. By doing this, you have not destroyed the object. You have merely removed a root reference to the object. Figure 10.3 shows the roots referring to two of the objects. Because the other two objects have no reference, they are considered garbage and can be collected.

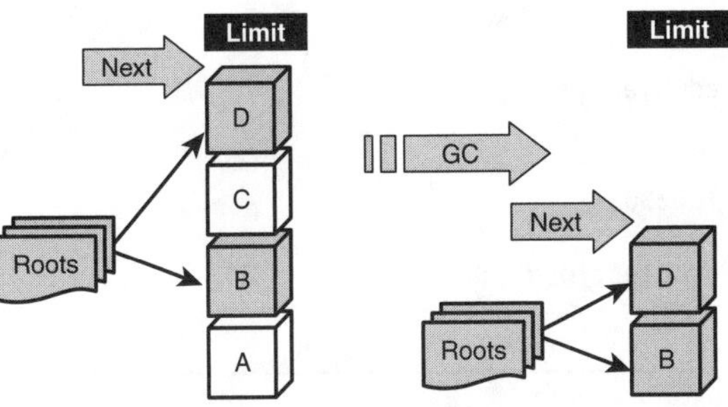

FIGURE 10.3
Simple garbage collection.

When a collection cycle is complete, the garbage objects are removed, the pointers adjusted, and the heap coalesced. As you can imagine, the garbage collection cycle is expensive. It requires the CLR to find all of the unused objects, find all of the roots and other objects that refer to these unused objects, and adjust the references to null as these objects are removed. If the heap needs to be coalesced, then all of the references to the objects to be moved need to be adjusted so they still refer to the same object. Luckily, a garbage collection cycle occurs only when it is either explicitly started (using the **`GC.Collect()`** method) or when the heap is full (no room exists for a new object).

As a further illustration of the principles behind garbage collection, consider the code in Listing 10.1 that builds a linked list.

LISTING 10.1 C# Code to Build a Linked List of Objects

```
public class LinkedObject
{
    private LinkedObject link;
    public LinkedObject()
    {
    }
    public LinkedObject(LinkedObject node)
    {
        link = node;
    }
    public LinkedObject Link
    {
        get
        {
            return link;
        }
        set
        {
            link = value;
        }
    }
}
. . .
if(head == null)
{
    head = new LinkedObject();
}
LinkedObject node;
for(int i = 0; i < 100000; i++)
{
    node = new LinkedObject(head);
    head = node;
}
```

The first part of the listing shows the definition of the `LinkedObject` class. This class simply contains a link to other linked objects, and as such, it is only an illustrative example. In a real application, this class would contain pertinent data. The next section of the listing illustrates how to use this class to build a linked list of 100,000 objects. The list starts out with just a `head` node. After the first node is added to the list, the instance of the object that was referred to by `head` becomes the tail of the list, and the `head` reference is adjusted to refer to the new beginning of the list. If you want to remove every item in the linked list, all you have to do is set the `head` reference to **`null`**:

```
head = null;
```

The only root that references the list is the `head` variable. As a result, after this reference is removed, the program no longer has access to any portion of the list. The entire list is considered garbage and is collected during the next garbage collection cycle. Of course, this does not work if you try something like the following:

```
myhead = head;
. . .
head = null;
```

Now the beginning of the list has another reference in `myhead`. Setting `head` to `null` only removes one of the root references to the linked list; the other (`myhead`) keeps the list from being collected.

Comparison of .NET Framework Allocation and C-Runtime Allocation

Before going further in this discussion on .NET Framework garbage collection and memory allocation, you need to compare this allocation to what it is replacing: the traditional C-Runtime heap allocation. Two of the main problems with the C-runtime heap are that it fragments memory and it is not efficient.

The C-Runtime heap (Win32 heap works much the same) consists of a list of free blocks. Each block is a fixed size. If the size of memory that you are trying to allocate is not the same size as the block and it is not some even multiple of the block size, then extra bytes or holes will be in the memory. If the size of the block is 1024 bytes and you try to allocate 1000 bytes, then 24 bytes will be left over. If you again try to allocate 1000 bytes, then you will be allocating from the next free block. If you have many of these holes, it can add up to a significant loss of memory. Fragmented memory is the result of the cumulative effect of each of these leftover pieces of memory.

The other drawback of the C-Runtime heap is efficiency. For each allocation, the allocator needs to walk the list of free blocks in search of a block of memory that is large enough to hold the requested allocation. This can be time consuming, so many schemes have been developed to work around the inefficiency of the C-Runtime heap. A simple program has been put together that allocates 100,000 items in a linked list at a time. The application displays the time for the allocation and the deallocation. This program is in the `HeapAllocation` subdirectory, but the essential parts of the program are shown in Listing 10.2.

LISTING 10.2 Building a Linked List of Objects from the C-Runtime Heap

```
class LinkedList
{
public:
    LinkedList *link;
    LinkedList(void)
    {
        link = NULL;
    }
    LinkedList(LinkedList* node)
    {
        link = node;
    }
    ~LinkedList(void)
    {
    }
};
. . .
if(head == NULL)
{
    head = new LinkedList();
}
__int64 start, stop, freq;
LinkedList *node = NULL;
for(int i = 0;i < 100000;i++)
{
    node = new LinkedList(head);
    head = node;
}
```

This code looks similar to Listing 10.1. The functionality was mimicked as much as possible to allow comparison between the different allocation schemes. The complete source that is associated with Listing 10.1 is in the `LinkedList` subdirectory. Figure 10.4 shows a typical screenshot after an allocation and deallocation have occurred.

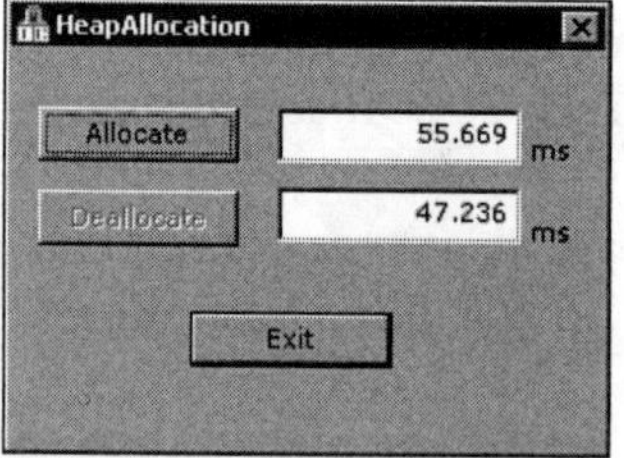

FIGURE 10.4 *Timing C-Runtime allocation.*

This figure shows the timing for one particular machine. See how the allocation and deallocation performs on your machine. Do not run this timing in debug mode because the hooks that have been placed in the debug memory allocation scheme cause the allocation and deallocation to be extremely slow. LinkedList is an application that can be used to compare the management allocation and deallocation of memory. Figure 10.5 shows a typical screenshot after allocating 100,000 items and placing them in a linked list. The essential code was already shown in Listing 10.1. The complete application is in the `LinkedList` subdirectory. Reminder: The Collect button initiates a garbage collection cycle; therefore, it will be the only one to deallocate memory in this sample.

FIGURE 10.5
Timing garbage collection.

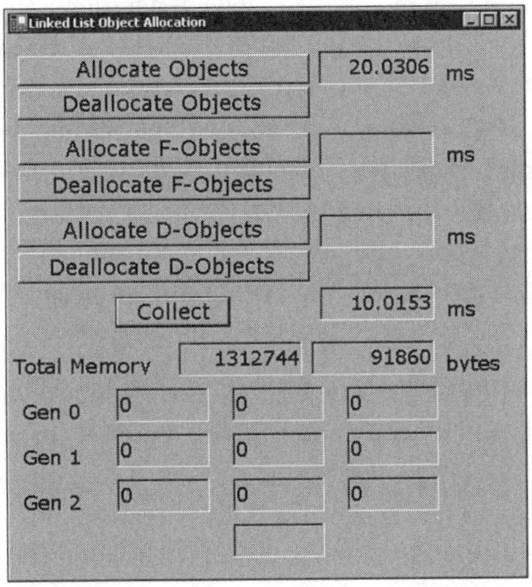

The allocation times can be compared directly. It is best to compare the deallocation times for the C-Runtime heap deallocation with the times for a collection cycle. Even then, because a destructor doesn't exist in managed code, the comparison between the C-Runtime and managed deallocation is not entirely an apples to apples comparison, but it is close. You can see that, as predicted, the allocation from managed code is fast. These two figures show that the managed code allocation is about four times as fast. Suffice it to say, it is significantly faster to allocate from a managed heap than from the C-Runtime heap. For this case, you see that even an expensive operation such as garbage collection is about five times faster than cleaning up a linked list using the C-Runtime heap.

Optimizing Garbage Collection with Generations

One significant observation that has been made is that objects seem to fall into two categories: objects that are short lived and objects that are long lived. One of the drawbacks of using the C-Runtime heap is that only one heap exists. With a managed heap, most objects have three parts that correspond to the age of the objects, known as `generation`

0, generation 1, and generation 2. Initially, allocations occur at generation 0. If an object survives a collection (it is not destroyed or it is space reclaimed), then the object is moved to generation 1. If an object survives a collection of generation 1, then it is moved to generation 2. The CLR garbage collector currently does not support a generation higher than generation 2; therefore, subsequent collections will not cause the object to move to another generation.

The LinkedList application shown in Figure 10.5 shows the progression from one generation to the next. To show an object moving from one generation to the next, click the Allocate Objects button. You will see the left column labeled with Gen0, Gen1, and Gen2. After allocating the list of objects, you will see a count of the number of objects in each of the three generations. By forcing a collection without freeing up the list, you will see the objects moving from one generation to the next. When all of the objects are in generation 2, forcing a collection does not move the objects further. The number of allocated bytes does not change significantly until you deallocate the objects and then force a collection, at which time the memory that is occupied by each object is reclaimed.

The obvious performance benefit from having multiple generations is that the garbage collector need not examine the entire heap to reclaim the required space. Remember that generation 0 objects represent objects that are the newest. Based on studies, these generation 0 objects are likely to be the shortest lived; therefore, it is likely that enough space will be reclaimed from generation 0 to satisfy an allocation request. If enough space is available after collecting objects in generation 0, then it is not necessary to examine generation 1 or generation 2 objects. Not examining these objects saves a good deal of processing.

If a new object in generation 0 is a root to an object that is in an older generation, then the garbage collector can choose to ignore this item when forming a graph of all reachable objects. This allows the garbage collector to form a reachable graph much faster than if that graph had to contain all objects reachable through generation 0 objects.

With C-Runtime heap, allocation memory is obtained from wherever room is available. It is quite possible that two consecutive allocations be separated by many megabytes of address space. Because the garbage collector is constantly collecting and coalescing space on the managed heap, it is more likely that consecutive objects are allocated consecutive space. Empirically in terms of memory, objects tend to interact and access other objects that are related or are nearby. On a practical level, this allows objects to quickly access objects that are close, possibly near enough for the access to be in cache.

Finalization

When C++ programmers look at the garbage collection scheme, their first reaction is typically that it's impossible to tell when an object is destroyed. In other words, managed code has no destructors. C# offers a syntax that is similar to C++ destructors. An example destructor is shown in Listing 10.3.

LISTING 10.3 A Class with a Destructor

```
class Foo
{
    public Foo()
    {
        Console.WriteLine("Constructing Foo");
    }
    ~Foo()
    {
        Console.WriteLine("In destructor");
    }
}
```

When the compiler sees this syntax, it turns it into the pseudo code shown in Listing 10.4.

LISTING 10.4 Pseudo Code for a C# Destructor

```
class Foo
{
    public Foo()
    {
        Console.WriteLine("Constructing Foo");
    }
    protected override void Finalize()
    {
        try
        {
            Console.WriteLine("In destructor");
        }
        finally
        {
            base.Finalize();
        }
    }
}
```

To further confuse the issue, if you try to implement the pseudo code in Listing 10.4, you get two errors from the C# compiler. The first error forces you to supply a destructor:

```
Class1.cs(11): Do not override object.Finalize.
➥Instead, provide a destructor.
```

This is confusing because even though `~Foo()` is syntactically identical to the C++ destructor, they are different in many ways—enough that you could say that a destructor does not exist in managed code. The second error is a result of calling the base class **Finalize**:

```
Class1.cs(14): Do not directly call your base class Finalize method.
➥It is called automatically from your destructor.
```

However, the IL code for this destructor is exactly the C# code that is shown. The IL code that is generated for the C# destructor in Listing 10.3 is shown in Listing 10.5.

LISTING 10.5 IL Code for a C# Destructor

```
.method family hidebysig virtual instance void
        Finalize() cil managed
{
  // Code size       20 (0x14)
  .maxstack  1
  .try
  {
    IL_0000:  ldstr      "In destructor"
    IL_0005:  call       void [mscorlib]System.Console::WriteLine(string)
    IL_000a:  leave.s    IL_0013
  }  // end .try
  finally
  {
    IL_000c:  ldarg.0
    IL_000d:  call       instance void [mscorlib]System.Object::Finalize()
    IL_0012:  endfinally
  }  // end handler
  IL_0013:  ret
} // end of method Foo::Finalize
```

Don't let the syntax fool you. Although Listing 10.5 looks like it has a destructor, it is not a destructor in the same sense as a C++ destructor. Many of the properties of a destructor that C++ programmers have come to know and love are missing from finalization.

You can get some of the same effects from a Finalize method that you can with a destructor. For example, using the class that is illustrated in Listing 10.3, you are notified when an object is destroyed. Listing 10.6 shows an example.

LISTING 10.6 Being Notified When an Object Is Destroyed

```
Foo f = new Foo();
. . .
f = null;
GC.Collect(0);
```

Forcing a collection as in Listing 10.6 ensures that the Finalize (destructor) method is called. The output from the code in Listing 10.6 looks like the following:

```
Constructing Foo
In destructor
```

That is about where the similarities end. Finalization is syntactically similar in C# and functionally similar in simplistic allocation schemes. What are the differences?

First, you cannot specifically destroy a single object using finalization. Managed code has no equivalent to a C++ `delete` or a C `free`. Because at best, you can force a collection, the order in which the **`Finalize`** methods are called is indeterminate. A destructor along with some means of identifying each of the objects was added to the `LinkedObject` class illustrated in Listing 10.1. In the destructor, the ID was printed of the object that was being destroyed. Listing 10.7 shows a portion of the result.

LISTING 10.7 Out of Order Finalization

```
Destroying: 5
Destroying: 4
Destroying: 3
Destroying: 2
Destroying: 1
Destroying: 0
Destroying: 4819
Destroying: 4818
Destroying: 4817
Destroying: 4816
Destroying: 4815
Destroying: 4814
Destroying: 4813
Destroying: 15058
Destroying: 4812
Destroying: 4811
Destroying: 4810
. . .
```

It is easy to prove that the **`Finalize`** method is not called in any particular order. Besides, even if it turned out that this simple example showed that the objects were in fact destroyed in order, Microsoft explicitly states in the documentation not to make assumptions on the order of the **Finalize** calls. This could cause a problem if your object contains other objects. It is possible that the inner object could be finalized before the outer object; therefore, when the outer object's **Finalize** method is called and it tries to access the inner object, the outcome might be unpredictable. If you implement a **Finalize** method, don't access contained members.

If your **Finalize** method is put off to near the end of the application, it might appear that the **Finalize** method is never called because it was simply in the queue when the application quit.

Adding a **Finalize** method to a class can cause allocations of that class to take significantly longer. When the C# compiler detects that your object has a **Finalize** method, it needs to take extra steps to make sure that your **Finalize** method is called. The application shown in Figure 10.6 illustrates the allocation performance degradation of a class due to an added **Finalize** method.

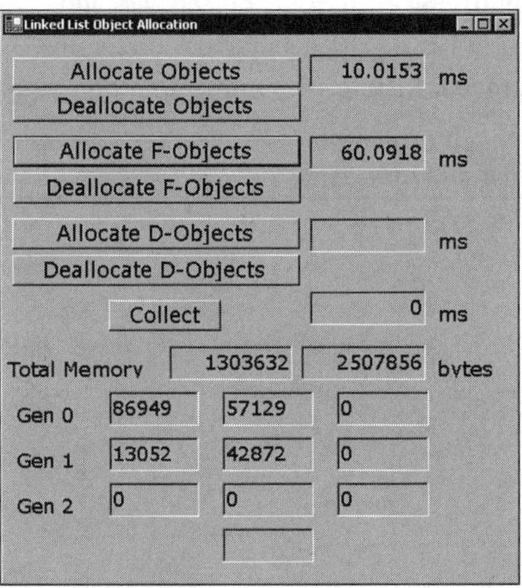

FIGURE 10.6
Timing allocation for a class with a **Finalize** *method.*

This figure shows that allocating 100,000 objects with a **Finalize** method takes about twice as long as doing the same operation on objects without a **Finalize** method. Sometimes allocations take five to six times as long just because the class has a **Finalize** method. This application is the same as that pictured in Figure 10.5; the complete source is in the `LinkedList` subdirectory.

Another drawback of objects with a **Finalize** method is that those objects hang around longer, increasing the memory pressure on the system. During a collection, the garbage collector recognizes that an object has a **Finalize** method and calls it. The garbage collector cannot free an object (reclaim its memory) until the **Finalize** method has returned, but the garbage collector cannot wait for each **Finalize** method to return. Therefore, the garbage collector simply starts up a thread that calls the **Finalize** method and moves on to the next object. This leaves the actual destruction of the object and reclamation of the memory to the next collection cycle. Thus, although the object is not reachable and essentially is destroyed, it is still taking up memory until it is finally reclaimed on the next collection cycle. Figure 10.7 illustrates this problem.

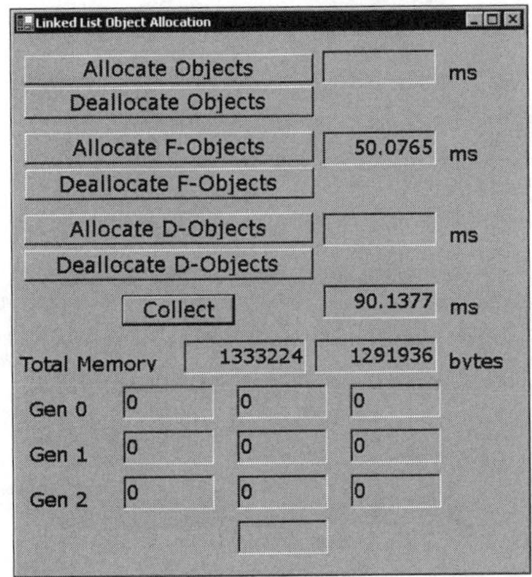

FIGURE 10.7
Deallocation of an object with a **Finalize** *method.*

In Figure 10.7, the objects have been allocated with a **Finalize** method by clicking on the Allocate F-Objects button. Then the objects were deallocated by clicking on the Deallocate F-Objects button. Finally, to arrive at the point illustrated in Figure 10.7, the Collect button was clicked to force a collection. Notice that collecting objects with a **Finalize** method takes longer (sometimes up to four times longer). The important point is that the number of bytes allocated is still virtually the same as before the collection. In other words, the collection resulted in no memory being reclaimed. You must force another collection to see something like Figure 10.8.

The total memory that was allocated before the collection was about 1.3MB, and after the collection, it was only about 95KB. This is where the memory allocated to the linked list is finally released. By watching this same process with the Performance Monitor, you can gather further evidence that the **Finalize** method call delays the reclamation of memory. This is shown in Figure 10.9.

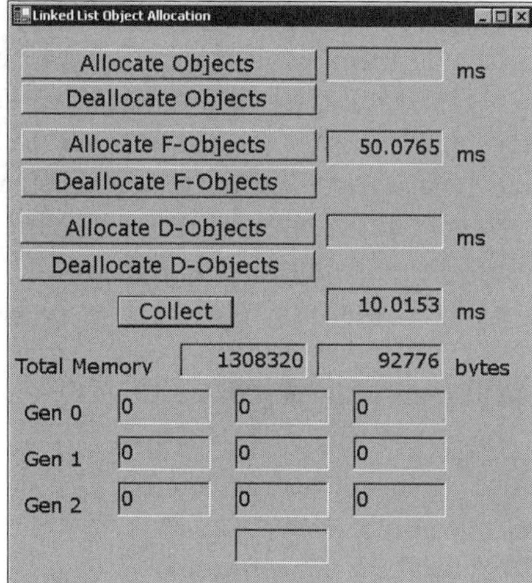

FIGURE 10.8
A second collection is required to reclaim memory with finalized objects.

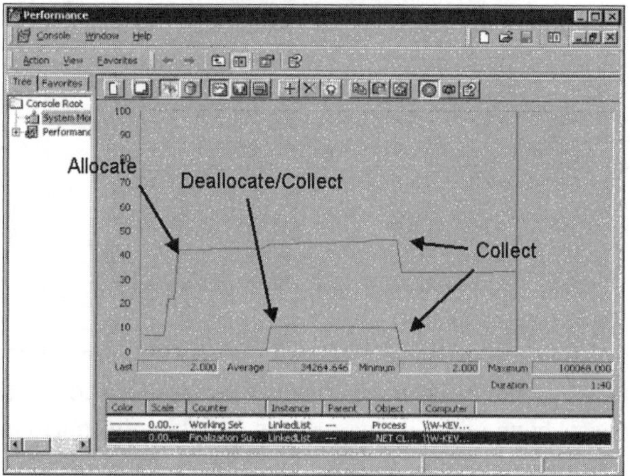

FIGURE 10.9
Watching the deallocation of a list of finalized objects.

This figure introduces `Finalization Survivors`. This is a term used by the Performance Monitor counters. When an object that has a **`Finalize`** method is collected, the actual object is put aside and the **`Finalize`** method is called. All of the objects that have a **`Finalize`** method are put on the `Finalization Survivor` list until the next collection, at which time they are destroyed and the memory they occupied reclaimed. You can see from Figure 10.9 that the memory is actually being reclaimed. At the same time that the number of `Finalization Survivors` goes to 0, the working set for the application also falls by an amount equivalent to the size of the 100,000 objects that were allocated.

If certain objects still do not have their **Finalize** methods called when it comes time for the application to shut down, their **Finalize** methods are ignored. This allows an application to shut down quickly and not be held up by **Finalize** methods. This could present a problem if your object becomes unreachable and a collection does not occur before the application shuts down. A similar scenario can occur if objects are created during an application shutdown, when an **AppDomain** is unloading, or if background threads are using the objects. In essence, it is not guaranteed that the **Finalize** method will be called because of these types of scenarios.

Inner Workings of the Finalization Process

If an object has a **Finalize** method, then the CLR puts a reference to that object on a finalization queue when the object is created. This is partly why objects with a **Finalize** method take longer to create. When the object is not reachable and is considered garbage, the garbage collector scans the finalization queue for objects that require a call to a **Finalize** method. If the object has a reference to it on the `finalization` queue, then that reference is moved to another queue called the `f-reachable` queue. When items are on the `f-reachable` queue, a special runtime thread wakes up and calls the **Finalize** method that corresponds to that object. That is why you cannot assume anything about the thread that calls the **Finalize** method associated with your object.

When the **Finalize** method returns, the reference to the object is taken off the `f-reachable` queue and the `f-reachable` thread moves on to the next item in the queue. Therefore, it is important that your object's **Finalize** method is relatively short and does not block; otherwise, it could hold up the other pending calls to **Finalize** methods. The references to the object in the `f-reachable` queue are like root references. As long as a reference to the object exists, it is not considered garbage even though it is only reachable through an internal `f-reachable` queue. After the **Finalize** method returns and the reference to the object is removed from the `f-reachable` queue, then no references to the object exist and it is truly not reachable. That means it is free to be collected as any other object and have its memory reclaimed. This explains why it takes two collection cycles for an object with a **Finalize** method to have its memory reclaimed.

Managing Resources with a Disposable Object

With all of the drawbacks of having an object implement a **Finalize** method, why consider it at all? When you have a file handle, socket connection, database connection, or other resource that is non-memory related, the runtime garbage collector does not know how to tear it down. You must implement a method to deterministically finalize the resource. Building an object that implements a **Finalize** method is one means to this end, but it is not the best overall solution. A **Finalize** method is meant to be part of a scheme to support deterministic finalization, not as a solution on its own. The scheme involves implementing an **IDisposable** interface and uses **Finalize** as a backup in case the object is not explicitly finalized as expected. The complete template for code that implements **IDisposable** and **Finalize** is shown in Listing 10.8.

LISTING 10.8 Building a Deterministically Finalizable Object

```
public class DisposeObject : IDisposable
{
    private bool disposed = false;
    public DisposeObject()
    {
        disposed = false;
    }
    public void Close()
    {
        Dispose();
    }
    public void Dispose()
    {
        // Dispose managed and unmanaged resources.
        Dispose(true);
        GC.SuppressFinalize(this);
    }
    protected virtual void Dispose(bool disposing)
    {
        // Check to see if Dispose has already been called.
        if(!this.disposed)
        {
            // If disposing equals true, dispose all managed
            // and unmanaged resources.
            if(disposing)
            {
                // Dispose managed resources.
            }
            // Release unmanaged resources. If disposing is false,
            // only the following code is executed.
        }
       // Make sure that resources are not disposed
       // more than once
        disposed = true;
    }
    ~DisposeObject()
    {
        Dispose(false);
    }
}
```

Listing 10.9 shows the same pattern being implemented in Visual Basic.

LISTING 10.9 A Design Pattern for **IDisposable** Objects in Visual Basic

```
Public Class DisposeObject
    Implements IDisposable
    ' Track whether Dispose has been called.
    Private disposed As Boolean = False

    ' Constructor for the DisposeObject Object.
    Public Sub New()
        ' Insert appropriate constructor code here.
    End Sub

    Overloads Public Sub Dispose()Implements IDisposable.Dispose
        Dispose(true)
        GC.SuppressFinalize(Me)
    End Sub

    Overloads Protected Overridable Sub Dispose(disposing As Boolean)
        If Not (Me.disposed) Then
            If (disposing) Then
                ' Dispose managed resources.
            End If
        ' Release unmanaged resources
        End If
        Me.disposed = true
    End Sub
    Overrides Protected Sub Finalize()
        Dispose(false)
    End Sub
End Class
```

Listings 10.8 and 10.9 provide a template for the same pattern. Each implementation as shown does not perform functions other than creating and disposing of an object. In a real application, these template functions would be filled in with code that is pertinent to the application. For readability, comments were limited. To clarify some of the more important concepts regarding this pattern, each part of this pattern will be briefly discussed.

To make an **IDisposable** object, you need to derive from the **IDisposable**. This ensures that you implement the proper methods and provides a means of discovering whether this object supports the deterministic finalization model by querying the object for the **IDisposable** interface.

With C#, it is possible to use an object that implements an **IDisposable** interface and be assured that the Dispose method is called on that object when execution passes beyond the scope that is defined by the **using** keyword. This syntax looks like this:

```
using(f)
{
    // Use the object
}
```

This is roughly equivalent to something like this:

```
IDisposable d = (IDisposable)f
try
{
    // Use the object
}
finally
{
    d.Dispose();
}
```

If the object that is specified does not implement **IDisposable**, then the compiler generates an error like the following:

```
LinkedList.cs(525): Cannot implicitly convert type
➥'LinkedList.LinkedObject' to 'System.IDisposable'
```

Therefore, the cast will always succeed at runtime. In addition, users of your object might not know that you implement **IDisposable**, so they might want to execute the following code to test:

```
if(node is IDisposable)
{
    // Now that it is known that the
    // object implements IDisposable,
    // the object can be disposed.
    . . .
}
```

Therefore, although it is possible to implement your own finalization scheme, using the **IDisposable** interface makes your object integrate better with the rest of the .NET Framework.

Cache the state of this object to ensure that the object is finalized only once. It is up to the designer of the object to protect the object from users who call **Close** or **Dispose** multiple times.

Only the default constructor is implemented in Listing 10.8. In a real application, the resource that is encapsulated by this object could be constructed as part of the default constructor. Another constructor might be dedicated to creating the resource, or an explicit "open" method could exist for constructing the resource. It would be up to the designer of the class to decide how the encapsulated resource or resources are allocated and initialized.

The method that disposes of the object has been called `Close` because that method name is familiar to most programmers. This method is primarily in place to make it easier for the user of this class to remember how to clean up an allocated object. A user could always call **`Dispose`** directly, but that method name might not be as familiar as `Close`. This would be the primary method that an object should expose to allow for deterministic finalization. The pattern would be that the object is "opened" via **`new`** and a constructor (or an explicit "open" call) and then explicitly closed with this method.

`Dispose` is the only method to implement in the **`IDisposable`** interface. Do not make it virtual. A derived class should not be able to override **`Dispose`**. The derived class overrides the **`Dispose(bool)`** method, and this method ends up calling that overridden method through polymorphism. As part of the pattern, make sure that **`Dispose(true)`** is called to indicate that the object is being disposed directly as a result of a user's call. In addition, ensure that the object is taken off the `finalization` queue so that the object is removed promptly rather than waiting for **`Finalize`** to complete. To guarantee that finalization is done properly, do not make **`Dispose(bool)`** virtual.

Take this object off the finalization queue to prevent finalization code for this object from executing a second time. Because the object is caching its state with the `disposed` variable, the call to the **`Finalize`** method would be a no operation (NOP) anyway. The key is that if this object is not taken off the finalization queue, it is retained in memory while the `freachable` queue is being emptied. By removing the object from the finalization queue, you are ensuring that the memory that the object occupies is reclaimed immediately.

`Dispose(bool disposing)` executes in two distinct scenarios. If `disposing` equals **`true`**, the method has been called directly or indirectly by a user's code. Managed and unmanaged resources can be disposed. If `disposing` equals **`false`**, the method has been called by the runtime from inside the **`Finalize`** method and you should not reference other objects. Only unmanaged resources can be disposed in such a situation; this is because objects that have **`Finalize`** methods can be finalized in any order. It is likely that the managed objects that are encapsulated by this object could have already been finalized. Consequently, it is best to have a blanket rule that states that access to managed objects from inside the **`Finalize`** method is forbidden. Calling **`Dispose(false)`** means that you are being called from inside a **`Finalize`** method.

Thread synchronization code that would make disposing this object thread safe was not added intentionally. This code is not thread safe. Another thread could start disposing the object after the managed resources are disposed but before the disposed flag is set to true. If synchronization code is placed here to make this thread safe, it needs to be written to guarantee not to block for a long time. Otherwise, this code might be called from the destructor, and hence, from the `freachable` queue thread.

This destructor runs only if the **Dispose** method is not called. If **Dispose** is called, then **GC.SupressFinalize()** is called, which ensures that the destructor for this object is not called. It gives your base class the opportunity to finalize. Providing a **Finalize** method allows a safeguard if the user of this class did not properly call **Close** or **Dispose**. Do not provide destructors in types that are derived from this class. Calling **Dispose(false)** signals that only unmanaged resources are to be cleaned up.

Figure 10.10 shows the allocation of the same linked list. This time, each node implements the **IDisposable** interface.

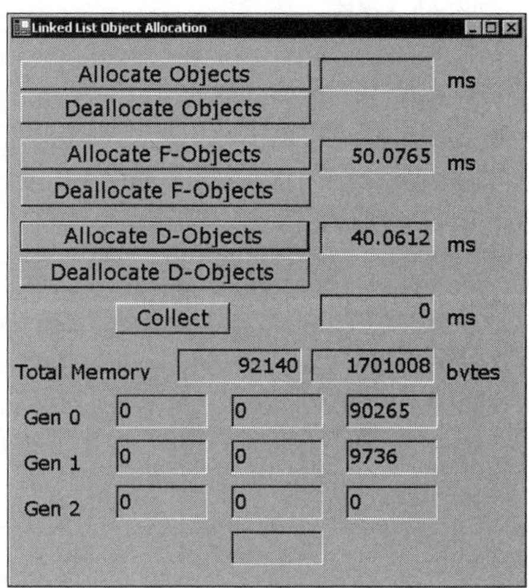

FIGURE 10.10
Allocation of a disposable object list.

The allocation takes roughly the same time as a class that just implements a **Finalize** method. This is probably because part of the disposable object pattern is the implementation of a **Finalize** method as a safeguard in case **Dispose** or **Close** is not called. If your design requires more performance than safety, you could take the **Finalize** safeguard out by removing the **Finalize** (destructor) from the class. Doing so will allow the object to allocate more quickly, but **Close** or **Dispose** must be called or the encapsulated resource will not be properly cleaned up. Deallocation of the list involves explicitly calling **Close** on every object, so deallocation is rather slow. Of course, that is the purpose of implementing an algorithm to allow deterministic finalization. If you do not need deterministic finalization, then the disposable pattern is more overhead than you need. The bright spot is the deallocation. Because each object is explicitly closed, and part of the call to **Close** is the removal of this object from the finalization queue, the object is destroyed immediately. It does not take two collection cycles to reclaim an object as it did when only a **Finalize** method was implemented.

Large Objects

You need to be aware of one more optimization. If an object is larger than 20,000 bytes, then it is allocated from the large object heap. The heap looks identical programmatically to the managed heap for smaller objects. An object in the large object heap ages through three generations, just like an object in the managed heap for small objects. The same rules apply for finalization of large objects as for small objects. The CLR makes one distinction in handling objects in the large object heap versus the managed heap for small objects: After objects in the large object heap are freed, the CLR does not try to compact the objects in the heap.

Two samples have been built in the `LargeObject` and `LOC` subdirectories that allocate a large object and then free it. The sample in the `LargeObject` subdirectory is a Windows application. The sample in the `LOC` subdirectory is a Console application. The `LOC` sample simply tries to eliminate the confusion about what memory is allocated for Windows and what is allocated as part of the large object. Figure 10.11 shows a running `LargeObject` application.

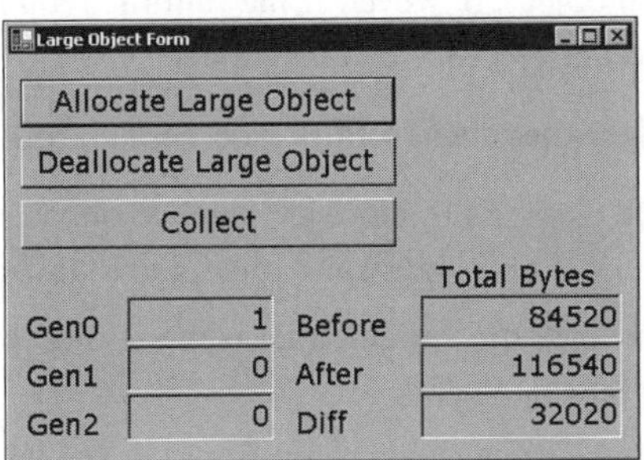

FIGURE 10.11
Allocation and deallocation of a large object.

Figure 10.11 shows the correct byte allocation (32,000 bytes), but on deallocation, the large object seems to be mixed up with other allocations that are happening due to the various Windows controls. Therefore, the deallocation is not what you would expect. Using the Console application from the `LOC` subdirectory yields the output of Listing 10.10.

LISTING 10.10 Using a Console Application to Allocate and Deallocate a Large Object

```
Total bytes before allocation: 20736
Total bytes after allocation: 56852
Object is at generation 0
Collect
Total bytes after collection: 60052
```

LISTING 10.10 Continued

```
Object is at generation 1
Deallocating object
Collect
Total bytes after collection: 28044
Collect
Total bytes after collection: 28044
```

The correct number of bytes is allocated and also deallocated, as you can see from the differences in the numbers before and after allocation and deallocation.

WeakReference or Racing with the Garbage Collector

As long as an application root references an object, it is said to have a *strong reference* to it. As long as an object has a *strong reference*, the garbage collector cannot collect it. The .NET Framework also has the concept of a *weak reference*. A weak reference allows the programmer to retain access to an object; however, if the runtime requires memory, the object that is referenced by the *weak reference* can be collected.

It is all about timing. To use the **`WeakReference`** class, you need to follow the next steps:

1. Allocate memory to be used as a buffer, an object, and so on. The variable that references the allocated memory is now the strong reference to this object.
2. Construct a **`WeakReference`** from the variable that is the strong reference to the memory. This is done as follows:

   ```
   WeakReference wr = new WeakReference(sr);
   ```
3. Remove the strong reference to the memory. This can be as simple as the following:

   ```
   sr = null;
   ```

   Your memory is now subject to collection by the garbage collector.
4. Convert the weak reference into a strong reference if you want to use the object again (without re-creating it). This is done through the **`Target`** property of the **`WeakReference`** class.

   ```
   sr = (YourObject)wr.Target;
   ```

   If the strong reference returned from the **`Target`** property of the **`WeakReference`** class is null, then the garbage collector has beaten you to the object and you will need to re-create this object. If it is not null, then you can use the object as normal.

You now have a strong reference to the object. Eventually, you need to relinquish this strong reference because the garbage collector will not collect an object that has a strong reference to it.

To illustrate the use of the `WeakReference` class, the `WeakReference` sample has been built that reads into memory all of the documents in a specific `docs` directory that have the suffix of .txt. These documents were retrieved primarily from the Project Gutenberg (`http://www.gutenberg.net`) to make this sample a little more real. One screenshot of the running program is shown in Figure 10.12. The source for this application is in the `WeakReference` subdirectory.

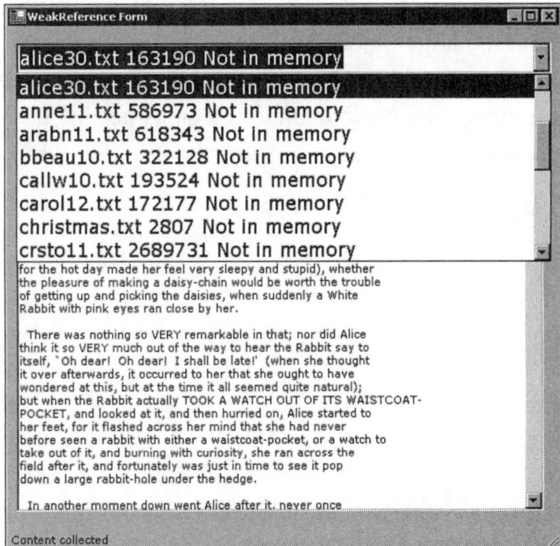

FIGURE 10.12
Using `WeakReferences` *to hold several documents in memory.*

The program attempts to read into memory all of the documents in the `docs` directory that have a suffix of .txt. Each time a document is read into memory, a **`WeakReference`** is made to that memory and the strong reference is removed, thereby making that memory available for collection. The program automatically adapts to the RAM that is installed on your computer. If you have little RAM, then only a few documents will be able to be read into memory without causing a garbage collection cycle. In contrast, if you have more RAM, more documents will be able to fit into RAM without triggering a garbage collection cycle. Running this under the debugger, you can tell when a document has been retained in memory from the message `Target in memory` that will appear in the output window of the IDE.

Summary

This chapter explored the general architecture of CLR memory management. It discussed what the CLR does to efficiently manage your memory allocations so that you do not have to. This chapter also showed that, in many cases, a garbage collection scheme outperforms what is traditionally used for memory allocation and memory management with unmanaged code. It uncovered the details of what looks like a C++ destructor and explained that managed code has no destructors. You discovered an alternative to destructors, using the **`IDisposable`** interface, that allows your code to deterministically finalize your object in an efficient manor with safeguards built in for misuse of your object. You also learned about some optimizations that the runtime garbage collector employs, such as generations, and about the large object heap that bring numerous performance gains to your application. Finally, you found out how to set up a reference to memory that allows your application to hold many objects in memory on an as-needed basis, using the **`WeakReference`** class.

CHAPTER

Threading

In This Chapter

Threads grew out of the need to do, or appear to do, many things at the same time. Before threads, the finest granularity at which the OS could schedule was at the process level. Programmers worried about spawning processes and tweaking the priority of processes. Starting up a process incurred much overhead, it was heavy, and communicating between processes was inefficient.

On the Unix platform, `fork()` and `exec()` allowed the programmer to split the execution path of a program into two pieces without much of the overhead of starting a new process. Probably most importantly, `fork()` and `exec()` allowed a programmer to easily share data between two different paths of execution. The problem became one of synchronization. With the ease of splitting a process came the responsibility of knowing how and when the operating system would schedule each path of execution.

For many reasons, most all modern operating systems adopted the idea of preemptive scheduling. With preemptive scheduling, an operating system does not allow one process or path of execution to dominate the system. Rather, it preempts or interrupts each process or path of execution for a small time-slice so that other processes have a chance to use the CPU. This was a good thing, because the machine locked up less frequently because a misbehaving process could not take over the CPU. However, sharing data truly became an issue. A method needed to be devised to allow the programmer to communicate to the operating system when it was safe to access shared data. What started out with the simple synchronization primitives of *P()* and *V()* (proposed by Dijkstra) grew into synchronization algorithms that became events, mutexes, semaphores, read/write locks, and critical sections.

Using `fork()` and `exec()` became unwieldy when trying to do much more than two or three things at one time. In addition, these APIs were not natively supported for the Windows programmer. Out of this, the concept of threads was born. Threads did not carry as much overhead (lighter weight) as a process. Threads had access to all of the same address space as the parent process. The idea of a thread was easier to grasp than a forked process, and threads were natively supported by the operating system. Threads provided the operating system with a scheduling unit, and they provided the programmer a hook into the operating system to control the flow of a program.

With the advent of multiprocessor machines, instead of just appearing to run in parallel, threads allowed the programmer to actually do two things at one time. Suddenly, a multithreaded application was inherently better than a single-threaded application largely because it was seen as more scalable than a single-threaded application.

Threads Overview

Threads can bring many benefits to a program or application, but threading is difficult to get right. This chapter could show many simple samples of threading that work flawlessly and are relatively easy to understand and implement, but real-world applications aren't so flawless and neat. As spinning a thread becomes easier, it becomes more necessary to design an application so that threading is either not necessary or that each thread is understood completely in all possible contexts in which it can run. It is well understood in software engineering circles that developing a real-time application is at least twice as hard as developing a normal application. Whether the application is meant to have real-time characteristics or not, when threads are thrown into the mix of an application life cycle, it is like developing a real-time application.

Threads in a managed environment are much easier to start and maintain than threads created with `_beginthreadex()` or `CreateThread()`. Thread state can be managed in a much more intuitive fashion. Although the primitives provided to synchronize threads have a notable omission, the classes provided to synchronize threads are easy to understand and implement. In short, managed threads are a great improvement over unmanaged threads. The next section will explore what is available.

Creating and Starting a Thread

The pseudo-code in Listing 11.1 shows just how easy it is to start a thread. This pattern is repeated throughout this chapter, so understanding it is important.

LISTING 11.1 Starting a Thread

```
void ThreadEntry()
{
// Do the work of the thread
. . .
}
. . .
Thread t = new Thread(new ThreadStart(ThreadEntry));
t.Start();
```

A thread is encapsulated in a **`Thread`** class; therefore, it is constructed just as any other class with **`new`**. The argument to the constructor is a **`delegate`**. **`Delegates`** are treated in more detail in Chapter 14, "`Delegates and Events`," but you need to know that **`delegates`** provide an entry point at which the **`Thread`** can begin execution. The particular **`delegate`** that is expected in constructing a **Thread** is a **ThreadStart delegate**. A **ThreadStart** delegate specifies a signature for the routine that is to act as the starting point or entry point for the thread. The **ThreadStart delegate** looks like this:

```
public delegate void ThreadStart();
```

That entry point for a **Thread** cannot take arguments and does not return anything. How do you pass information to a thread? At least with `_beginthread()` and `_beginthreadex()`, an argument can be passed to the started thread. This seems like a regression. This chapter will cover that later, but first you need to get through the basics.

The **Thread** does not begin running when it is created. Before the **Thread** is actually started, you can set a couple of properties on it. First, you can give the **Thread** a name with the **Name** property. Giving a **Thread** a name can aide in debugging because it is easier to track a name than a **Thread** hash code. Use the following example to give a Thread a name:

```
Thread t = new Thread(new ThreadStart(ThreadEntry));
t.Name = "Thread1";
```

When the thread exits and it is in a debugging environment, you will see something like the following on the output window:

```
The thread 'Thread1' (0x8ac) has exited with code 0 (0x0).
```

If you do not give a name to the thread, then the output will look like this:

```
The thread '<No Name>' (0x878) has exited with code 0 (0x0).
```

Another property that can be set before a thread actually starts is Priority. Using the Priority property, a Thread can be assigned one of the priorities in Table 11.1.

TABLE 11.1 `ThreadPriority` Enumeration Values

Member Name	*Description*
Highest	The Thread has the highest priority.
AboveNormal	The Thread has the higher priority.
Normal	The Thread has the average priority.
BelowNormal	The Thread has the lower priority.
Lowest	The Thread has the lowest priority.

A **Thread**'s priority can greatly affect how it is scheduled. This is a relative priority because the OS can adjust the absolute priority of a thread up and down based on context. If a **Thread** is not explicitly given a priority, it is assigned a priority of **Normal**.

After the **Thread** is created and optional properties assigned it can be started with the **Start** method. This will start execution of the thread at the entry specified by the **delegate**.

Hello World

Just to make sure that these concepts are clear, I present a Hello World application for threads shown in Listing 11.2. The source for this sample is available as part of the `ThreadHelloWorld` solution in the `ThreadHelloWorld\HelloWorld` directory.

LISTING 11.2 Threading Hello World

```
using System;
using System.Threading;

namespace ThreadHelloWorld
{
    class ThreadHelloWorldTest
    {
        static void ThreadEntry()
        {
            Console.WriteLine("Hello Threading World!");
        }
        static void Main(string[] args)
        {
            Thread t = new Thread(new ThreadStart(ThreadEntry));
            t.Name = "Hello World Thread";
            t.Priority = ThreadPriority.AboveNormal;
            t.Start();
            t.Join();
        }
    }
}
```

Remember that setting the **Name** and **Priority** properties is optional; it is shown here only as an illustration. You might notice an extra call to a **Join** method after the thread is started. Calling **Join** causes the calling thread to wait until the given **Thread** returns. It was included in Listing 11.2 so that the program would not exit until the **Thread** was completed.

Multicast Thread Delegate

No restrictions are placed on the **delegate** passed to the **Thread** constructor. You might have heard about a multicast **delegate**. The Thread entry point does not have to be a single routine. The **delegate** can be built separately, and numerous routines can be part of a **delegate**. The Thread will simply call each of the routines in turn until each member of the **delegate** chain has been called. Again **delegate**s will be covered in more detail in Chapter 14, but Listing 11.3 shows how a **Thread** can be set up to have multiple entry points. The source for this sample is available as part of the ThreadHelloWorld solution in the ThreadHelloWorld\MulticastThread directory.

LISTING 11.3 Multicast Thread

```
using System;
using System.Threading;

namespace ThreadHelloWorld
{
    class MulticastThreadTest
    {
        static ManualResetEvent stopEvent;
        static void ThreadEntry1()
        {
            Thread currentThread = Thread.CurrentThread;
            Console.WriteLine("Hello World from ThreadEntry1 {0} {1}!",
                              currentThread.GetHashCode(),
                              Environment.TickCount);
            stopEvent.WaitOne();
        }
        static void ThreadEntry2()
        {
            Thread currentThread = Thread.CurrentThread;
            Console.WriteLine("Hello World from ThreadEntry2 {0} {1}!",
                               currentThread.GetHashCode(),
                               Environment.TickCount);
        }
        static void Main(string[] args)
        {
            stopEvent = new ManualResetEvent(false);
            ThreadStart tsd = new ThreadStart(ThreadEntry1);
            tsd += new ThreadStart(ThreadEntry2);
            Thread t = new Thread(tsd);
            t.Start();
            Thread.Sleep(1000);
            stopEvent.Set();
            t.Join();
        }
    }
}
```

The output of Listing 11.3 is shown in Figure 11.1.

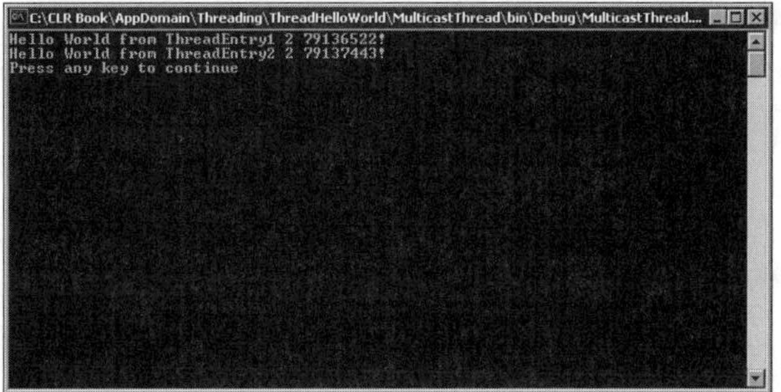

FIGURE 11.1
Thread multicast delegate.

Each method in the **delegate** chain is called in turn, and the methods are not multicast in the same sense as a multicast network. The methods are not executed in parallel. This simple sample builds a **ManualResetEvent** that the first method in the **delegate** chain waits on using the **WaitOne()** method. After the thread is started, the main thread goes to sleep for one second and then signals the **ManualResetEvent**. This causes the **Thread** to continue to fall through and exit. After this method has completed, the next method in the **delegate** chain is called. This time, a message is printed, but nothing can stop its execution. From the output, you can see that each method is executed within the same **Thread**. You can also see from the time stamp that the second method follows the first by about one second (1000 milliseconds). As a test, what would be the output if the order of the methods in the **delegate** were reversed? Try it out.

Passing Information to a Thread

The first rather unspectacular means of passing information to a **Thread** is through global variables. Any static member of the class in which the **delegate** is implemented can be accessed from a running **Thread**. Of course, this information is shared, and access to it needs to be synchronized with methods that will be covered later in the chapter. You have already seen an example of accessing global static data with the multicast sample (the **ManualResetEvent** was static and global to **Main**) but Listing 11.4 presents a more explicit example. The source for this sample is available as part of the `ThreadHelloWorld` solution in the `ThreadHelloWorld\StaticThreadInformation` directory.

LISTING 11.4 Thread Accessing Static Data

```
using System;
using System.Threading;

namespace ThreadHelloWorld
{
    class StaticThreadInformation
```

LISTING 11.4 Continued

```
    {
        static string message;
        static void ThreadEntry()
        {
            Console.WriteLine(message);
        }
        static void Main(string[] args)
        {
            Thread t = new Thread(new ThreadStart(ThreadEntry));
            message = "Hello World!";
            t.Start();
            t.Join();
        }
    }
}
```

This is a simple example, but you can see that the **Thread** is constructed, the message **string** is assigned a value, the **Thread** is started, and the **Thread** prints the contents of the message.

The second way that a **Thread** gets information is much more interesting because it deviates from how threads were handled in the past. It also adds considerably to the flexibility that a programmer has in dealing with **Thread**s in a managed environment. In the past, a thread had to have a static entry point that did not know about a particular instance of a class. With `_beginthread()` and `_beginthreadex()`, an argument was made available that could be passed to the thread entry point. One trick that programmers used was to pass `this` as an argument to the entry point. After the thread entry point was called, the thread had information about the instance with which the thread had to deal. Information could be passed back and forth from the instance of the class to the running thread. With **Thread**s in a managed environment, that changes. An argument is no longer available to pass to the **Thread** entry point. This is because it is no longer needed. The **delegate** that is passed to the **Thread** constructor does not have to be a static function in a managed environment. If the **delegate** is non-static, then the `this` pointer is implicitly part of the information that the **delegate** maintains and the entry point will be in a running instance of a class. Listing 11.5 shows an example of a non-static **delegate** being passed to the **Thread** constructor. The source for this sample is available as part of the `ThreadHelloWorld` solution in the `ThreadHelloWorld\DynamicThreadInformation` directory.

LISTING 11.5 Thread Accessing Instance Data

```
using System;
using System.Threading;

namespace ThreadHelloWorld
{
    class HelloWorld
    {
        private string message;
        public string Message
        {
            get
            {
                return message;
            }
            set
            {
                message = value;
            }
        }
        public void ThreadEntry()
        {
            Console.WriteLine(message);
        }
    }
    class DynamicThreadInformation
    {
        static void Main(string[] args)
        {
            HelloWorld first = new HelloWorld();
            first.Message = "Hello World from the first instance!";
            HelloWorld second = new HelloWorld();
            second.Message = "Hello World from the second instance!";
            ThreadStart tsd = new ThreadStart(first.ThreadEntry);
            tsd += new ThreadStart(second.ThreadEntry);
            Thread t = new Thread(tsd);
            t.Start();
            t.Join();
        }
    }
}
```

Listing 11.5 built two instances of the `HelloWorld` class. As part of each class, an entry point is present that is designed to be an entry point for a **`Thread`**. A multicast delegate is built where the first method in the chain points to an entry point in the first instance and the second method points to an entry in the second instance. The output shown in Figure 11.2 shows that the entry point is being called on the instance of the class.

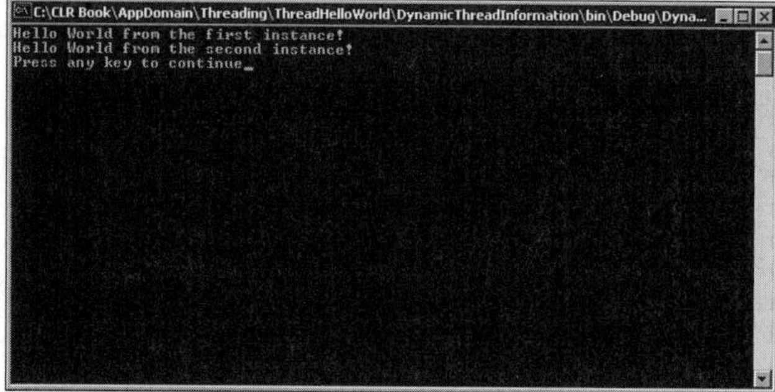

FIGURE 11.2
Thread instance delegate.

A third method exists for passing information to a **`Thread`**. This is not really passing information as much as it is giving a **`Thread`** a means to maintain state, or allowing a thread to pass information and store information that is not available to other threads. The third method is traditionally called thread local storage (TLS). In the managed world, they are called data slots or named data slots. This is actually an example of how to prevent information from passing from one **`Thread`** to another. Listing 11.6 shows an example of using an unnamed data slot. The source for this sample is available as part of the `ThreadHelloWorld` solution in the `ThreadHelloWorld\ThreadLocalStorage` directory.

LISTING 11.6 Thread Local Storage

```
using System;
using System.Threading;

namespace ThreadHelloWorld
{
    class ThreadLocalStorage
    {
        static LocalDataStoreSlot slot;
        static void ThreadEntry()
        {
            Console.WriteLine("The data in the slot for {0} is: {1}",
➥Thread.CurrentThread.GetHashCode(), (string)Thread.GetData(slot));
        }
        static void Main(string[] args)
        {
            string message = "Hello World!";
            slot = Thread.AllocateDataSlot();
            Thread.SetData(slot, message);
            Thread t = new Thread(new ThreadStart(ThreadEntry));
            t.Start();
            t.Join();
```

LISTING 11.6 Continued

```
            Console.WriteLine("The data in the slot for {0} is: {1}",
➥Thread.CurrentThread.GetHashCode(), (string)Thread.GetData(slot));
        }
    }
}
```

When this program is run, the "Hello World!" message is stored in the **`Main Thread`**. Even though the same slot is used as was allocated in **`Main`**, the **`Thread`** cannot locate it. The data is available to **`Main`** because that is the **`Thread`** that put the data there. This just demonstrates that the data is truly **`Thread`** local. One unnamed data slot can be allocated for all threads as well as any number of named data slots that can be allocated for all threads. The named data slots must be deallocated. Typically, the slots will be allocated (and deallocated if necessary) in the **`Main Thread`**, which provides the storage for all **`Thread`**s allocated after the data slots have been allocated.

What Else Can Be Done to a Thread?

You can interrupt a thread, suspend a thread, resume a thread, and abort a thread. Figure 11.3 shows an application running whereby all these operations are interacting. The full source to this application is available in the `ThreadAbort` directory.

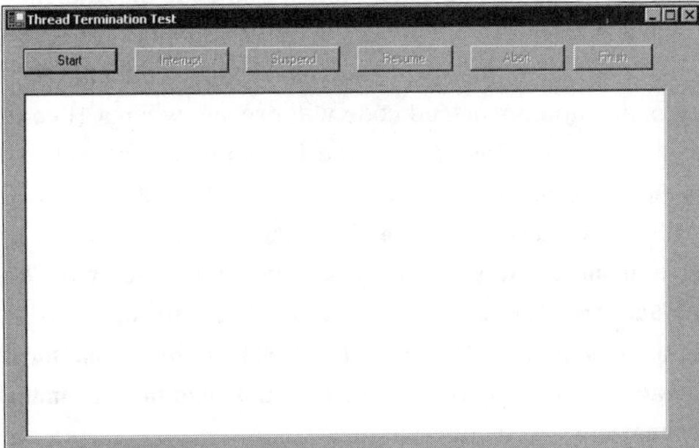

FIGURE 11.3
Thread manipulation.

Only one button is enabled at startup: the Start button. By pressing this button, a **`Thread`** is started. When the **`Thread`** is started, it waits for the **`ManualResetEvent`** to be signaled. One of the first things that you might try is to start it again. Notice that the `Start` button is not disabled after a **Thread** has started. If the **Thread** is **Start**ed after it has already been **Start**ed, then an exception will be thrown similar to that shown in Figure 11.4.

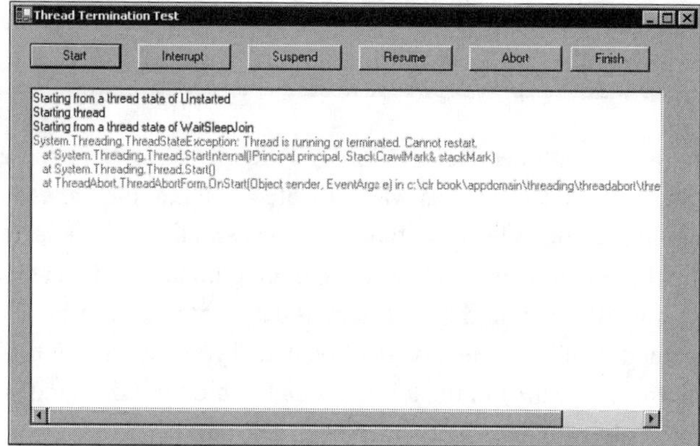

FIGURE 11.4
Restarting a running thread.

The **Suspend** and **Resume** methods can also suspend and resume a **Thread**. When a **Thread** is first created, it is in a state of **Unstarted**. Starting a **Thread** puts the Thread in a **Running** state. When a Thread suspends itself because of a wait (**WaitOne**, **WaitAll**, and so on), **Sleep**, or **Join**, the **Thread** will be in a **WaitSleepJoin** state. If the **Thread** is in a wait state (which most likely is the case here), it is actually in unmanaged code (probably `CoWaitForMultipleObjects`, `MsgWaitForMultipleObjects`, `MsgWaitForMultipleObjectsEx`, `WaitForMultpleObjects`, or `WaitForMultipleObjectsEx`). The exact unmanaged code that the **Thread** is in depends on the OS and the apartment model under which the **Thread** is executing. When a **Suspend** is issued to a Thread that is in a **WaitSleepJoin** state, the only guarantees that the CLR makes is that no unmanaged code will execute when a **Thread** is **Suspend**ed. Until the code exits the unmanaged code, the Thread is waiting to be suspended and its state is **SuspendRequested**. (It is also in a **WaitSleepJoin** state. Remember that the **ThreadState** values are flags, so a **Thread** can theoretically have any combination of the flags.) To reverse the **Suspend**, you can can call **Resume**, which will "unfreeze" the **Thread**. Calling **Suspend** any number of times has the same effect as calling it once. Calling **Resume** on a **Suspend**ed **Thread** puts the **Thread** in a **Running** state. If **Resume** is called on a **Thread** that is in any other state than **Suspend** or **SuspendRequested**, a **ThreadStateException** will be thrown.

A **Thread** can be interrupted with the **Interrupt** method call. This method causes the **Thread** to throw a **ThreadInterruptedException**. It is up to the application to decide what to do after an interrupt occurs. For this simple demonstration, the Thread was simply put back into the processing loop. Listing 11.7 shows a small code snippet from the application that shows one way that an interrupt could be handled. Basically, a message is printed and the **Thread** goes back to waiting.

LISTING 11.7 Thread Interrupt

```
catch(ThreadInterruptedException e)
{
    string msg = "ThreadInterruptedException occured\r\n" + e.ToString();
    BeginInvoke(messageDelegate, new object[] {msg, MessageType.Error});
    // Yeah, I know about "GOTO considered harmful, Edsger W. Dijkstra" at
    // http://www.net.org/html/history/detail/1968-goto.html, but I saw no
    // other choice here.
    goto start;
}
```

The last operation that can be performed on a **Thread** is to stop it with **Abort**. This might take some re-education for those who grew up with the managed threads. The API `TerminateThread` has been available for some time, but its use was discouraged for all but the most extreme circumstances. Its use was discouraged because it caused a thread to terminate with no chance to do any cleanup. Because of this, a programmer typically would have a special event that was signaled when the thread was supposed to exit. With managed threads, **Abort** is the preferred method for terminating a **Thread**.

Like **Interrupt**, **Abort** causes an exception to be thrown. This exception is a special exception called the **ThreadAbortException**. Listing 11.8 shows an example of how to handle this exception.

LISTING 11.8 Thread Abort

```
catch(ThreadAbortException e)
{
    string msg = "ThreadAbortException occured\r\n" + e.ToString();
    BeginInvoke(messageDelegate, new object[] {msg, MessageType.Error});
    // Notice that this is ignored.
    goto start;
}
```

Abort is a special exception because although it can be caught, any code that causes the exception to be ignored is silently ignored. Notice in Listing 11.8 that it was attempted to handle **Abort** just like the Interrupt. The **goto** `start` statement is silently ignored, and processing proceeds to the finally block. If **Abort** is called on a **Suspend**ed **Thread**, it puts the **Thread** (and the application) in deadlock. (You can try this by commenting out the code that disables the **Abort** button when the `Suspend` button is pressed.) If you have the correct permission set, you can essentially ignore the **Abort** by issuing a

Thread.ResetAbort call just before the **goto** statement. After calling **Thread.ResetAbort**, you can handle the exception just like **ThreadInterruptException**. Be aware that using this function can defeat **AppDomain.Unload**, the host's attempt to defeat denial-of-service attacks, prevent **HttpResponse.End** from working correctly, as well as other things. Using **Thread.ResetAbort** is not a nice thing to do, and in general, it should be disallowed. To use this function, the code has to have **ControlThread** permission, so it probably would be a good idea to deny this permission by default.

AppDomain

Now you have a brief understanding about what a **Thread** is. At this point, you will learn about the environment in which every **Thread** runs, and that is the **AppDomain**. In the unmanaged world, a system had multiple processes, and each process had one or more threads. In the managed world, the system still has many processes, but it now has an additional boundary called the **AppDomain**. An **AppDomain** has been described as a lightweight process. Although this is mostly correct conceptually in that **AppDomain**s provide isolation like a process for security, faults, and errors, when it comes to **Thread**s, the **AppDomain** no longer seems like a process. **Thread**s can easily weave in and out of an **AppDomain**, which is very much unlike a process.

An **AppDomain** supports and encapsulates a substantial amount of security information, but that will not be discussed here. The **AppDomain** class encapsulates the **AppDomain**, so a good place to start reading about **AppDomain**s would be in the SDK documentation on the **AppDomain** class. For instance, you can find out about all of the assemblies that are loaded on behalf of the **AppDomain**. Listing 11.9 shows how to get at some of the properties available from the **AppDomain** class. The source for this sample is available as part of the AppDomain solution in the `AppDomain\AssemblyList` directory.

LISTING 11.9 AppDomain Properties

```
using System;
using System.Reflection;

namespace AppDomainTest
{
    class AssemblyList
    {
        static void Main(string[] args)
        {
            AppDomain ad = AppDomain.CurrentDomain;
            Assembly [] assemblyList = ad.GetAssemblies();
            Console.WriteLine("There are {0} assemblies loaded in this
➥AppDomain", assemblyList.Length);
```

LISTING 11.9 Continued

```
            foreach(Assembly a in assemblyList)
            {
                Console.WriteLine(a.FullName);
            }
            Console.WriteLine("Base directory: {0}", ad.BaseDirectory);
        }
    }
}
```

You can access much of the information about the **AppDomain** in which you are running. Although this is interesting and important, what you really want to do is create your own **AppDomain**.

When I created my first **AppDomain** and made calls into the loaded **AppDomain**, it seemed a lot like inproc COM, or for that matter COM in general. I don't know what I was expecting, but the interface to the "other" **AppDomain** seemed so seamless that I immediately wanted to find a tool that told me that I was indeed talking to an **AppDomain** that I created. Listings 11.10 and 11.11 are in essence the "Hello World!" for creating **AppDomain**s. Listing 11.10 shows how to create, load, and communicate with an **AppDomain**. The source for this sample is available as part of the **AppDomain** solution in the `AppDomain\CreateAppDomain` directory.

LISTING 11.10 AppDomain Creation

```
using System;
using System.Threading;
using System.Reflection;
using System.Runtime.Remoting;
using InterAppDomain;

namespace AppDomainTest
{
    class InterAppDomain
    {
        static void Main(string[] args)
        {
            // Set ApplicationBase to the current directory
            AppDomainSetup info = new AppDomainSetup();
            info.ApplicationBase = "file:\\\\" +
System.Environment.CurrentDirectory;

            // Create an application domain with null evidence
            AppDomain dom = AppDomain.CreateDomain("RemoteDomain", null, info);

            // Load the assembly HelloWorld and instantiate the type
            // HelloWorld
```

LISTING 11.10 Continued

```
            BindingFlags flags = (BindingFlags.Public | BindingFlags.Instance |
➥BindingFlags.CreateInstance);
            ObjectHandle objh = dom.CreateInstance("HelloWorld",
➥"InterAppDomain.HelloWorld", false, flags, null, null, null, null, null);
            if (objh == null)
            {
                Console.WriteLine("CreateInstance failed");
                return;
            }

            // Unwrap the object
            Object obj = objh.Unwrap();

            // Cast to the actual type
            HelloWorld h = (HelloWorld)obj;

            Console.WriteLine("In the application domain: {0} thread {1}",
➥Thread.GetDomain().FriendlyName, Thread.CurrentThread.GetHashCode());
            // Invoke the method
            h.SayHello("Hello World!");

            // Clean up by unloading the application domain
            AppDomain.Unload(dom);
        }
    }
}
```

First, notice that you need a reference to the **Assembly** that you will be loading. Second, you create the **AppDomainSetup** class. You could set many properties on this class, but for now, you are only interested in the directory path at which your **Assembly** can be found. Here it is the same directory as the working directory of the application. Third, you actually create an **AppDomain**. The first argument is the name of the **AppDomain**. Like giving a name to a Thread can help debugging run a little more smoothly, giving a name to an **AppDomain** is not required, but it makes life easier for whomever needs to debug this application. The next argument to **CreateDomain** is an instance of an **Evidence** class. This is where you would prove that this assembly is okay. You set it to `null`. The final argument is the **AppDomainSetup** that was created earlier.

After the **AppDomain** has been created, you create an instance of the object with which you want to communicate using **CreateInstance**. **CreateInstance** has many arguments, most of which you set to `null`. The first argument is the name of the **Assembly** followed by the name of the type within the **Assembly** in which you are interested. The third argument flags whether you are interested in case. The fourth argument is a set of flags indicating how the **Assembly** is to search for your type.

```
using InterAppDomain;
```

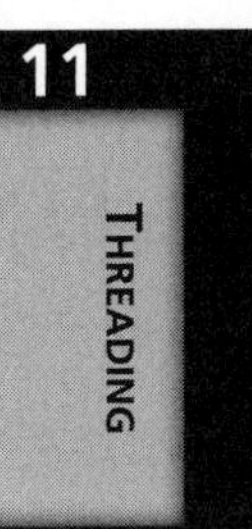

This at first seems like cheating. How are you to know that you are really talking to a remote **Assembly** and not the copy of the DLL that is loaded right here? You need it because the object, or at least a handle to the object, will be instantiated on this side, so you need to know the signatures of the methods that you can call. Essentially, you need type-library information.

Listing 11.11 shows the Assembly that you are loading. The source for this sample is available as part of the AppDomain solution in the `AppDomain\CreateAppDomain\HelloWorld` directory.

LISTING 11.11 AppDomain Assembly

```
using System;
using System.Threading;
namespace InterAppDomain
{
    public class HelloWorld : MarshalByRefObject
    {
        public void SayHello(String greeting)
        {
            if (greeting == null)
            {
                throw new ArgumentNullException("Null greeting!");
            }
            Console.WriteLine("In the application domain: {0} thread {1}",
➥Thread.GetDomain().FriendlyName, Thread.CurrentThread.GetHashCode());
            Console.WriteLine(greeting);
        }
    }
}
```

Not much is involved in the process. You just print out the name of the **AppDomain** and the **Thread** ID so that you can compare them to the printout before the **AppDomain** was entered.

Synchronization

Starting and manipulating a **Thread** is the easy part, made easier with the classes and facilities that the CLR provides. The hard part is synchronizing access to and manipulation of shared data.

When you are accessing or manipulating shared data, critical sections of code often have to happen atomically or not at all. In Listing 11.12, the critical section is the loop in the **Thread** entry point. You want all of the data generated in the loop to occur at the same time, uninterrupted. This could just as easily have been links in a linked list or shared variables being swapped. It is easier to show the interruption with a simple loop. To make sure that the OS will preempt the **Thread**, a Fibonacci number will be computed to simulate some work. (Making the program compute a larger Fibonacci number involves more work, and the **Thread** is more likely to be interrupted.) The source for this sample is available as part of the `ThreadSynchronization` solution in the `Synchronization\Unsynchronized` directory.

LISTING 11.12 Unsynchronized Threads

```
using System;
using System.Threading;

namespace MultithreadedQueue
{
    class Worker
    {
        private int Fib(int x)
        {
            return ((x<=1)?1:(Fib(x-1)+Fib(x-2)));
        }
        public void DoWork()
        {
            string item = Convert.ToString(Thread.CurrentThread.Name) + " ";
            for(int i = 0; i < 10; i++)
            {
                Console.WriteLine("Thread {0} {1} {2}", item, i, Fib(30));
            }
        }
    }

    class UnsynchronizedTest
    {
        static void Main(string[] args)
        {
            Worker wq = new Worker();
            Thread a = new Thread(new ThreadStart(wq.DoWork));
            a.Name = "a";
            Thread b = new Thread(new ThreadStart(wq.DoWork));
            b.Name = "b";
            Thread c = new Thread(new ThreadStart(wq.DoWork));
            c.Name = "c";
            Thread d = new Thread(new ThreadStart(wq.DoWork));
            d.Name = "d";
            Thread e = new Thread(new ThreadStart(wq.DoWork));
            e.Name = "e";

            // Start the threads
            a.Start();
            b.Start();
```

LISTING 11.12 Continued

```
            c.Start();
            d.Start();
            e.Start();
        }
    }
}
```

The output of this program looks like Figure 11.5.

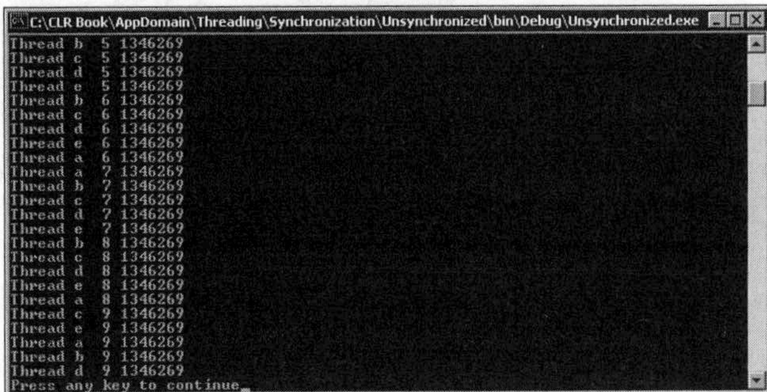

FIGURE 11.5
Unsynchronized threads.

This is obviously not what you want. Remember that the whole loop must be completed before another thread gets access to the critical section. One way to perform this synchronization is with the **Monitor** class.

Monitor and Lock

Listing 11.13 shows the changed routine DoWork that now uses **Monitor** to synchronize access to the object Worker. The full source for this sample is available as part of the ThreadSynchronization solution in the Synchronization\Synchronized directory.

LISTING 11.13 Synchronized Threads Using Monitor

```
public void DoWork()
{
    Monitor.Enter(this);
    string item = Convert.ToString(Thread.CurrentThread.Name) + " ";
    for(int i = 0; i < 10; i++)
    {
        Console.WriteLine("Thread {0} {1} {2}", item, i, Fib(30));
    }
    Monitor.Exit(this);
}
```

Now the output looks more orderly (see Figure 11.6).

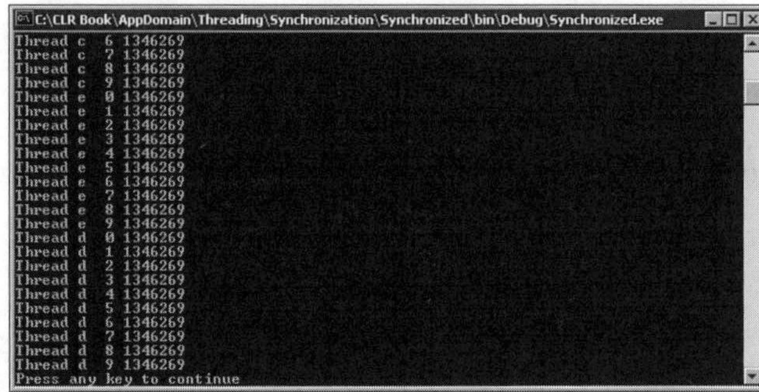

FIGURE 11.6
Synchronized threads with monitor.

At this level, this class acts very much like the Win32 calls `EnterCriticalSection` and `LeaveCriticalSection`, except this class does not require an initialization (`InitializeCriticalSection`) or explicit destruction (`DeleteCriticalSection`). The Monitor class has a few other methods that are useful. I just can't go into them here.

You have not built a robust routine. If any of the code executes after **`Monitor.Enter`** throws an exception, the lock will be held and it might be difficult to release it. You could enclose the **`Monitor.Enter`** in a **`try`** block and the **`Monitor.Exit`** in a **`finally`** block to guarantee that the lock will be released on exit, even in the case of an error. This happens frequently enough that C# has a helper function `lock()`.

```
lock(this)
{
. . .
}
```

translates to

```
try

    System.Threading.Monitor.Enter(this);
}
finally
{
    System.Threading.Monitor.Exit(this);
}
```

Modifying the original code to use lock instead of Monitor directly looks like Listing 11.14. The source for this sample is available as part of the `ThreadSynchronization` solution in the `Synchronization\SynchronizedLock` directory.

LISTING 11.14 Synchronized Threads Using Monitor

```
public void DoWork()
{
     lock(this)
     {
        string item = Convert.ToString(Thread.CurrentThread.Name) + " ";
        for(int i = 0; i < 10; i++)
        {
             Console.WriteLine("Thread {0} {1} {2}", item, i, Fib(30));
         }
     }
}
```

Again, the output is orderly and exactly how you want it to be.

Synchronized Collections

The collection classes that are available in **System.Collections** are not thread safe. In other words, certain sections of code could be interrupted by another thread, causing the collection to be in an invalid state. If multiple threads are accessing a particular collection at one time, the **Synchronized** version of the collection should be used. For the **ArrayList** class, getting the Synchronized version looks like this:

```
ArrayList arr = ArrayList.Synchronized(new ArrayList());
```

The other collection classes also have a **Synchronized** method that will return an instance of the class that is thread safe.

Thread Synchronization Classes

The **System.Threading** namespace offers a number of **Thread** synchronization primitive classes. You have already seen a few examples of **ManualResetEvent**, and the others are listed in Table 11.2.

TABLE 11.2 Thread Synchronization Classes

Class	*Description*
AutoResetEvent	This class remains in an unsignaled state until it is explicitly signaled using Set. Upon Set, one Thread that is waiting on the event is allowed to pass. All other threads waiting on this event remain unaffected.
Interlocked	This class provides uninterrupted Increment, Decrement, Exchange, and CompareExchange for int and long types.

TABLE 11.2 Continued

Class	*Description*
ManualResetEvent	This class provides an event that must be manually Set and Reset to enter a signaled and unsignaled state, respectively.
Monitor	This class provides a low-level locking mechanism for locking access to an object.
Mutex	Because this synchronization class accepts a name, it is possible to use this class to lock resources outside of the current process boundary.
ReaderWriterLock	This class provides a lock that supports multiple readers and a single writer.

Waiting with `WaitHandle`

The classes **`AutoResetEvent`**, **`ManualResetEvent`**, and **`Mutex`** are derived from **`WaitHandle`**. Using these classes, you can form an array of objects for which to wait. With the array, you can wait for *all* of the **`WaitHandle`**s to become signaled (**`WaitAll`**), or you can wait for *any* of the **`WaitHandle`**s to become signaled (**`WaitAny`**). For example

```
WaitHandle[] waits = new WaitHandle[2];
waits[0] = (instance of AutoResetEvent, ManualResetEvent, or Mutex);
waits[1] = (instance of AutoResetEvent, ManualResetEvent, or Mutex);
WaitHandle.WaitAll(waits);
```

Duplicates in the array passed to **`WaitAll`** or **`WaitAny`** will cause the wait to fail. Calling **`WaitAll`** or **`WaitAny`** with an array that contains more than 64 elements can cause a **`NotSupported`** exception to be thrown.

Interlocked Class

It is poor and dangerous form for a multithreaded application to increment a shared variable like this:

```
variable++;
```

The thread safe way to do this is as follows:

```
Interlocked.Increment(ref variable);
```

`Decrement()`, **`Exchange()`**, and **`CompareExchange()`** are guaranteed by the runtime to be uninterruptible.

Volatile Keyword

If the overhead for a `lock()` is too high, you might want to consider declaring a variable volatile. This keyword ensures that the current value is read at the time it is requested, even if a previous instruction already read the variable. Also, writing a volatile variable occurs immediately on assignment and prevents the reordering of instructions.

Thread Join Methods

When execution cannot continue until a **`Thread`** completes, use Join. Without arguments, **`Join`** waits forever for a **`Thread`** to exit. Two other forms allow a time limit to be placed on the **`Join`** so that either the **`Thread`** exits or a time out will occur. **`Join`** is a member of the **`Thread`** class, so the **`Thread`** calling the **`Join`** method will cause the caller to block until the **`Thread`** exits. This is the only way that currently exists to wait for a **`Thread`** to complete. In addition, no facilities exist for waiting for multiple **`Thread`**s like you could with `WaitForMultipleObjects` in the unmanaged Win32 world. Ideally, a method would be available to return some sort of **`WaitHandle`** associated with the **`Thread`**; at that point, you could use **`WaitAll`** and **`WaitAny`**. However, this is not available in the current version. You have already seen a number of examples showing how to use **`Join`**.

Invoke, BeginInvoke/EndInvoke

Some objects do not support multithreaded access at all. Most of these types of objects are user interface controls. In most cases, these objects have a special Invoke method (and the BeginInvoke/EndInvoke asynchronous counterparts) that marshals the arguments passed to the **`delegate`** to the **`Thread`** that created the object. To use these methods, you must define and declare a delegate:

```
private delegate void ColorChangeDelegate(Color color);
private ColorChangeDelegate colorChangeDelegate;
```

Construct a specific instance of the delegate:

```
colorChangeDelegate = new ColorChangeDelegate(ColorChange);
```

Define the appropriate callback function that was passed as an argument to the **`delegate`** constructor:

```
private void ColorChange(Color color)
{
     this.BackColor = color;
     this.Refresh();
}
```

The call Invoke (or BeginInvoke):

```
BeginInvoke(colorChangeDelegate, new object[] {Color.Blue});
```

This example defines a **delegate** that takes a single **Color** argument. You need not be restricted to just one argument. Because you are defining the **delegate** signature, you can virtually define the **delegate** to have any number and type of argument. The arguments declared in the **delegate** and the array passed as the second argument to **Invoke** (or **BeginInvoke**) must match.

Synchronization Sample 1—The Dining Philosophers

The dining philosopher's problem was originally stated and solved by Dijkstra (Dijkstra, E., *Cooperating Sequential Processes in Programming Languages*, F. Genuys (ed.), New York: Academic Press, New York (1968), p. 43–112) in 1965. Since then, it has been considered a classic synchronization problem. Most any textbook on operating systems contains a discussion of this problem and its solution.

The problem is as follows. A number of philosophers (Dijkstra originally proposed 5) sit down at a table to eat and think. One bowl of rice is available for each of the philosophers. However, each of the philosophers has only one chopstick. When the philosopher is not eating, he is thinking. He might get hungry while he is thinking, but to eat, he must share his chopstick with his neighbor. After a philosopher has two chopsticks, he can eat. When a philosopher is finished eating, he releases his chopsticks, and his neighbor then has a chance to eat. If the solution is incorrect, it could illustrate two problems that commonly occur with multithreaded applications: *deadlock* and *starvation*.

The deadlock situation occurs if each of the philosophers grabs the chopstick on his left and then waits for the chopstick on his right to begin eating. Because the chopstick on his right is already held, the philosopher will wait forever for the second chopstick. This has often been referred to as the "selfish dining philosopher."

The starvation situation occurs if one philosopher puts down his chopsticks and immediately picks them back up again, preventing his neighbors from eating. Starvation can also occur if a cycle is established. Philosopher A picks up the chopsticks, eats, and puts down his chopsticks. Philosopher B then picks up the chopsticks and eats. Instead of going in a round robin scheme, Philosopher A again picks up the chopsticks. With this cycle, if more than five philosophers are at the table, then Philosophers C, D, and E might starve from never getting to eat.

A visual implementation of the Dining Philosophers problem is located in the `DiningPhilosophers` directory. I have color coded the output to provide visual feedback as to the state of each philosopher seated at the table. If the philosopher is green, then he is eating. If the philosopher is blue, then the philosopher is thinking. If the philosopher is red, then he is very hungry. Any other color is meant to show the philosopher getting increasingly hungry. When the program is running, it looks somewhat like Figure 11.7.

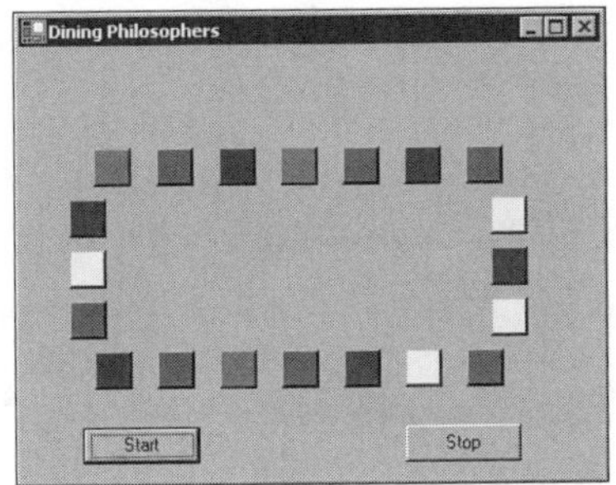

FIGURE 11.7
Dining philosophers.

For completeness, a TableForm5.cs file has been included, which solves the problem for 5 philosophers instead of 20. If this file is used to overwrite the supplied TableForm.cs and the project is rebuilt, then you will see a solution to just 5 philosophers seated around a table like Dijstra originally proposed.

Synchronization Sample 2—A Bucket of Colored Balls

The idea for this sample came from Jeffrey Richter's book *Advanced Windows* (pages 398–401). His original "Bucket of Balls" sample application has been modified and moved to the managed world.

The idea behind this sample is that multiple readers and multiple writers are trying to access a shared resource. In this case, 5 readers and 5 writers exist. The readers just read what is in the bucket of balls and report their findings to the display. The writers add a ball to the bucket. Each of the readers and writers runs in a separate thread, and each does his work at a random time interval.

The main purpose of this sample is to demonstrate the use of the `ReaderWriterLock` class. This class follows a simple set of rules:

- Multiple readers can access the resource at the same time.
- A writer cannot write to a resource that is locked by a reader.
- A reader cannot read from a resource that is locked by a writer.

This class has many other features that make it suitable for large-scale demanding applications. You are encouraged to read the online documentation for this class.

On startup, five reader threads and five writer threads are started up. When a reader thread becomes active, it reads the bucket of balls and reports the number of balls that it read to the UI portion of the application. You will notice Suspend and Resume buttons. When you press the Suspend button, all **Thread**s are suspended and the results are sorted based on the last read time stamp (0 being the oldest and 4 being the newest). If a write has occurred after the reported read, then the sorted value appears in red. With this information, you should be able to determine if everything is okay. Pressing Resume starts things back up again.

The source for this application is in the Buckets directory for this chapter. Figure 11.8 shows how this application appears.

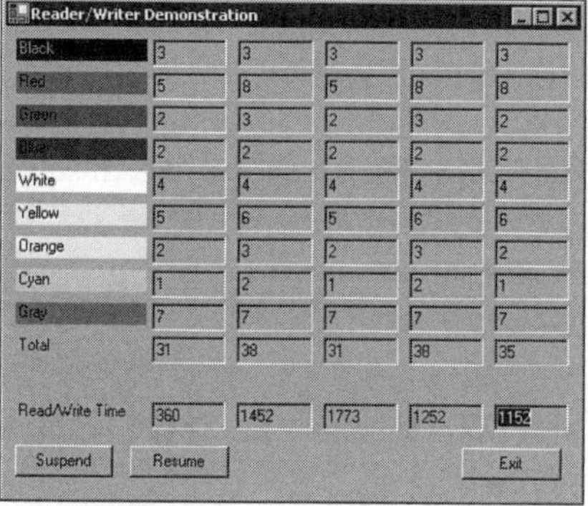

FIGURE 11.8
Bucket of colored balls.

Thread Pool

Now you have **AppDomain**s that have been described as lightweight processes, and **Thread**s that are contained in **AppDomain**s. It is time to introduce a lighter still **Thread** that is spawned from the **ThreadPool** class. Starting up a **Thread** takes little overhead, but even a little overhead is some overhead. Starting a `Thread` from a pool of **Thread**s removes much of the startup costs associated with starting a **Thread** from scratch. The **Thread** is queued, and the system (the CLR) determines when and with what resources it should be run.

QueueUserWorkItem

The **Thread** that is queued by **QueueUserWorkItem** is part of a pool and it can be assigned to some other work immediately after completing the work that you assigned it to do. Therefore, you are not notified when the **Thread** completes its assignment, or more precisely, when the work that has been queued up has completed. Listing 11.15 shows the relevant code for using **QueueUserWorkItem**. The full source to this sample is available as part of the `ThreadPool` solution in `ThreadPool\QueueUserWorkItem`.

LISTING 11.15 ThreadPool.QueueUserWorkItem

```
private void OnStart(object sender, System.EventArgs e)
{
    fibonacciResultsDelegate = new FibonacciResultsDelegate(OnFibonacciResults);
    Fibonacci fib = new Fibonacci(0);
    try
    {
        fib.Start();
        ThreadPool.QueueUserWorkItem(new WaitCallback(fib.Compute), this);
    }
    catch (NotSupportedException)
    {
        Debug.WriteLine("NotSupportedException was caught because: ");
        Debug.WriteLine("\tSystem.ThreadPool.QueueUserWorkItem Not Supported on
➥this system.");
        Debug.WriteLine("\tMust be running on Win2K, or the extra Win32
➥Support");
    }
}
```

When the user presses the `Start` button, a delegate is created, the Fibonacci series is initialized to start at 0, and the work of computing the Fibonacci number is queued up using **`QueueUserWorkItem`**. When a **`Thread`** is assigned to the queued work from the **`ThreadPool`**, then the `Compute` method of the Fibonacci class is called. On entry to this function, the Fibonacci number is computed, the elapsed time calculated, the results are reported to the UI, and the next Fibonacci calculation is queued.

This sample looks like Figure 11.9 after it has been run.

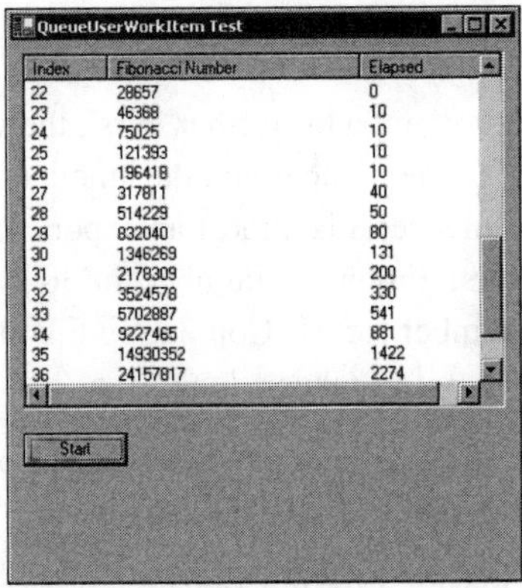

FIGURE 11.9
Testing `QueueUserWorkItem.`

How much lighter is the **`Thread`** started from the **`ThreadPool`** and a "normal" **`Thread`**? That is difficult to answer because you are not guaranteed to even get a **`Thread`** when invoking **`QueueUserWorkItem`**. As the name implies, the work is "queued," not necessarily started. I built an application that tries to quantify when it is best to use the **ThreadPool** and when it is best to start a Thread manually. At first, the numbers did not seem to be correct because I was expecting a Thread for each work item that was queued. I looked at the Task Manager and the Performance Monitor and noticed that if I queued up 100 work items, at no time did I get 100 **Thread**s to service these work items. What is up?

The **ThreadPool** works off a set pool of about 25 **Threads**. When no more **Thread**s are available, the work item is queued waiting for a **Thread** to become available to service the work. I came to the realization that the **ThreadPool** is a finite system-wide resource that should be used with care. If my application uses up all of the available **Thread**s in the pool for a long time, then the **ThreadPool**'s overall performance degrades significantly. The other issue that I learned in developing this benchmark application is that the savings over doing the same work in a Thread becomes smaller as the task or work to be performed takes longer. In other words, the **ThreadPool** should be used for performing short tasks. The benchmark program is available as part of the ThreadPool solution in ThreadPool\Benchmark. When the application is run, it looks like Figure 11.10.

FIGURE 11.10
Benchmark for QueueUserWorkItem.

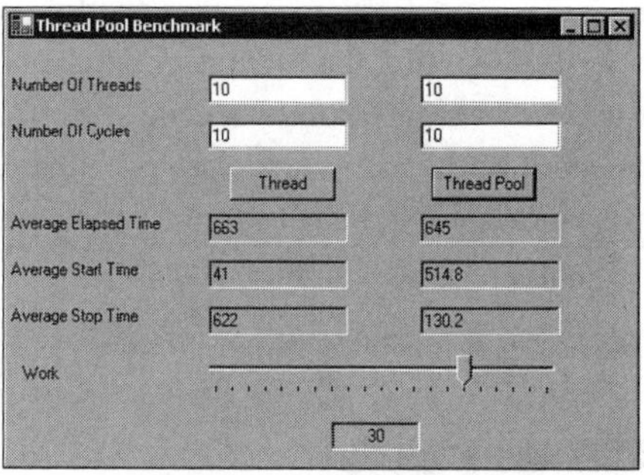

You need to understand the benchmark program a bit further. First, the work that is performed is computing a Fibonacci number. The number and the amount of work that is performed do not have a linear correspondence; it is almost an exponential relationship. For example, the work needed to compute a Fibonacci number for 30 is less than half the work required to compute a Fibonacci number for 31. Computing Fibonacci numbers for values greater than 40 (at least on my computer) takes a long time.

Second, it probably is not useful to increase the iterations too high. This input is merely provided to smooth over any spikes that might occur in the benchmark.

Third, the number of **Thread**s only has meaning for the **Thread** test case. What this really means is the number of times that the work will be performed. With a **ThreadPool**, there will not necessarily be a **Thread** per work item. This will definitely not be the case if the number of work items queued is larger than about 25.

Try running this benchmark with a fixed "thread count" of 10 and an iteration count of 10 for both of the tests. With both of these numbers fixed, slowly increase the work from about 10 to 35 or 40 (depending on your patience). The average elapsed time for the ThreadPool Test moves up closer to the average elapsed time for the Thread Test. This shows again that **QueueUserWorkItem** should be used for performing short tasks because its benefits become smaller as the length of the task increases.

RegisterWaitForSingleObject

The method **RegisterWaitForSingleObject** allows the programmer to perform the same operation that is available with **WaitHandle** functions such as **WaitOne**, but in an asynchronous fashion. The first argument to **RegisterWaitForSingleObject** is the object for which to wait. If the object becomes signaled before the timeout period specified, then the callback specified by the **WaitOrTimerCallback delegate** will be called with the second argument specifying that a timeout has not occurred. If a timeout occurs (the amount of time specified by the timeout argument to **RegisterWaitForSingleObject** has elapsed and the object passed as the first argument has not been signaled yet), then the callback is called with the second argument indicating that a timeout has occurred.

A sample has been put together that illustrates the usage of **ThreadPool.RegisterWaitForSingleObject**. Unlike the previous sample that arbitrarily limited the values for which a Fibonacci number was computed to 40, this sample computes values until computing the number takes longer than 5 seconds.

When this sample is run, it looks like Figure 11.11. The full source to this sample is available as part of the `ThreadPool` solution in `ThreadPool\RegisterWaitForSingleObject`.

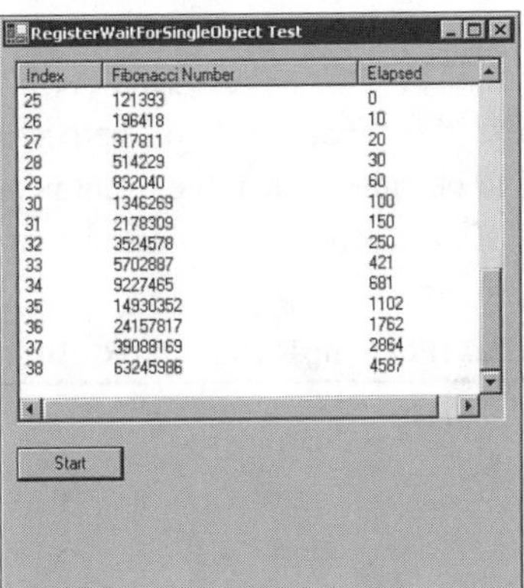

FIGURE 11.11
`RegisterWaitForSingleObject.`

The relevant code is shown in Listing 11.16 and in Listing 11.7.

LISTING 11.16 ThreadPool.RegisterWaitForSingleObject

```
private void OnStart(object sender, System.EventArgs e)
{
    fibonacciList.Items.Clear();
    fibonacciResultsDelegate = new FibonacciResultsDelegate(OnFibonacciResults);
    Fibonacci fib = new Fibonacci(0, 5000);
    WaitOrTimerCallback callback = new WaitOrTimerCallback(fib.Result);
    try
    {
        fib.Event.Reset();
        Thread t = new Thread(new ThreadStart(fib.Compute));
        t.Start();
        ThreadPool.RegisterWaitForSingleObject(fib.Event, callback, this,
➥fib.Timeout, true);
    }
    catch (NotSupportedException)
    {
        Debug.WriteLine("NotSupportedException was caught because: ");
        Debug.WriteLine("\tSystem.ThreadPool.RegisterWaitForSingleObject Not
➥Supported on this system.");
        Debug.WriteLine("\tMust be running on Win2K, or the extra Win32
➥Support");
    }
}
```

When the user presses the Start button, all the items in the results list are cleared, a delegate is created, and the `Fibonacci` class is constructed with a start value of 0 and a timeout value of 5000 milliseconds. The Fibonacci class also creates a `ManualResetEvent` that is used to signal that a result is ready. Next, a callback is constructed for **`RegisterWaitForSingleObject`**. This **`delegate`** must have a signature specified by **`WaitOrTimerCallback`**. Then the "all done" event is **`Reset`**. This event will be signaled by the **`Thread`** performing the work. Next, the `Thread` that will be performing the work is started. Finally, a callback is registered to be called when the event is signaled or when a timeout occurs. As shown in Listing 11.17, the process is repeated if no timeout occurs.

LISTING 11.17 ThreadPool.RegisterWaitForSingleObject (continued)

```
public void Compute()
{
    Start();
    result = fib(fibnumber);
    Stop();
    jobstart.Set();
}
```

LISTING 11.17 Continued

```
public void Result(Object o, bool timedout)
{
    if(!timedout)
    {
        RegisterWaitForSingleObjectForm form =
➥(RegisterWaitForSingleObjectForm)o;
        form.BeginInvoke(form.Results, new object[]{fibnumber, result,
➥Elapsed});
        fibnumber++;
        jobstart.Reset();
        Thread t = new Thread(new ThreadStart(Compute));
        t.Start();
        ThreadPool.RegisterWaitForSingleObject(jobstart, new
➥WaitOrTimerCallback(Result), o, timeout, true);
    }
}
```

Listing 11.17 also shows the entry point for the `Thread` that is performing the work.

Summary

This chapter has given you a flavor for the services that the CLR offers with regards to threading. This chapter has really been a showcase for the kinds of tasks that the CLR allows you to do. In closing, following are some tips and advice on multithreaded applications:

- Benchmark—Before starting any multithreaded application, make sure you are aware of the resources that are involved. Spinning many threads might actually degrade your application performance. Consider the **`ThreadPool`**. Many of the performance gains that come from using this class are because handing out **`Thread`**s to perform work is so miserable as compared to an application that starts up 100 or so **`Thread`**s, where each **`Thread`** must synchronize with the others and a context switch must occur just to make sure that all of the **`Thread`**s will be able to run.
- Understand—Understand that a multithreaded application requires time and effort to get it right. When it is wrong, it is either difficult to find out why, or it causes big problems with the rest of the applications that are running on your machine. It took a long time to develop the code samples in this chapter.
- Increase Responsiveness—If this is a requirement of your application, then using **`Thread`**s might be your answer. I remember doing a graphics application once. I found that if I could lock up the application for a brief period of time, the operation performed significantly faster. This argument did not win too many people over

because the users of the application required some sort of feedback that the operation was still occurring. Even though putting up a "Working…" message with some progress indication or putting up a hourglass made the operation complete as much as 50 to 70% slower, it became a requirement because users hate to be in the dark.

- Better Utilization of CPU—Another application that I developed involved transferring large (2048 × 2048 × 8) images. Most of these transfers were done directly from disk to memory or disk to network with little CPU involvement. These transfers were excellent candidates to be put into a background thread while the foreground actually used the CPU do other things. One of the challenges of using higher speed processors and even multiprocessor machines is to keep the CPU(s) busy. Making the CPU wait in an idle state while something else is being done is a waste of the CPU.
- Simplified Design—Being able to isolate specific functionality to that performed by a **`Thread`** goes a long way toward simplifying the overall design of the application. If it is known that this `Thread` only performs a specific function, then where do you go when that function goes bad? A properly designed multithreaded application seems to be naturally object oriented.

CHAPTER 12

Networking

In This Chapter

Networking has been around for a long time. The concept of building a distributed application is equally old. Using the term *client/server* to describe your application dates your application. If these concepts are so old, why do they still generate so much attention? One of the reasons is that to do "networking" correctly and to build a distributed application requires a lot of work. In addition, the tools available to debug and follow the flow of such an application have been limited. The success of Java—certainly in the server market—attests to the need for a new approach. In the .NET Framework, in only a few other areas can the power of a managed environment be used to provide such a wide array of services and functionality. At the core of the .NET Framework is Web Services. At the core of Web Services is **`System.Net`** or the .NET Framework classes for networking.

Because this chapter is a bit long, you might benefit from an overview of where this chapter is heading. First, this chapter explores the background of networking in general and what the networking classes need to replace and build on. Then the lowest level class, the **`Socket`**, is discussed, and from there, the chapter moves on to higher-level classes such as **`TcpClient`** and **`TcpListener`**. At that point, the discussion moves toward classes that were specifically built to address Internet access with **`WebRequest`** and **`WebResponse`** classes. Finally, some of the technology that Microsoft has provided to improve the security of an application is explored.

Brief History of the Distributed Application

Network programming started in the early 1980s. I can still remember the excitement that I experienced when I first started to build programs that talked to and controlled other machines. When I wrote data to a `socket` and it appeared on a completely different machine, I felt that that was the epitome of programming bliss. At the outset, everything seemed to work. I could write to a `socket` on a PC and the data would appear on a Unix platform. Much of the success of `sockets` in the early days is due to the model that was applied to networking.

The official model of networking lists seven layers:

- Application
- Presentation
- Session
- Transport
- Network

- Data Link
- Physical

In practicality, however, this model has been reduced to four layers:

- Application layer (telnet, ftp, http, rpc, and so on)
- Host-to-Host Transport layer (TCP and UDP)
- Internet layer (IP and routing)
- Network Access layer (Ethernet, ATM, and so on)

TCP (Transmission Control Protocol) has become the defacto protocol for transferring information throughout the world. Although the original RFC for this protocol was written in the early 1980s (see RFC 793 at `http://www.rfc-editor.org/rfc/rfc793.txt`), this protocol has stood the test of time for 20 years. In developing the .NET Networking classes, Microsoft built strong support for this standard.

As a close rival to TCP and the only choice in certain applications, User Datagram Protocol (UDP) has also stood the test of time. The original specification (see RFC 768 at `http://www.rfc-editor.org/rfc/rfc768.txt`) was first published in the early 1980s. UDP has been adopted by a wide range of applications.

IP (Internet Protocol) is a separate protocol used primarily for routing. Although it is not wrong to use TCP/IP, strictly speaking, you are only dealing with TCP (see RFC 791 at `http://www.rfc-editor.org/rfc/rfc791.txt`).

Traditional Sockets

Two types of `sockets` are in general use: TCP `sockets` and UDP `sockets` (`SOCK_STREAM` and `SOCK_DGRAM` respectively). A "raw" `socket` is also available that is used for specialized applications such as "ping" and "traceroute" (tracert).

In the beginning, the network programmer had to deal with the structures in Listing 12.1 just to establish a connection.

LISTING 12.1 `socket` Address Structures

```
struct sockaddr {
      unsigned short sa_family; // address family, AF_xxx
      char sa_data[14];       // 14 bytes of protocol address
};
struct sockaddr_in {
      short int sin_family;        // Address family
      unsigned short int sin_port; // Port number
```

LISTING 12.1 Continued

```
     struct in_addr sin_addr;      // Internet address
     unsigned char sin_zero[8];    // Same size as struct sockaddr
};

struct in_addr {
     unsigned long s_addr;
};
```

In addition, because this was a brave new world in which different machines using different processors were not communicating, you needed to remember Network Byte Order. Remember the following?

- `htons()`—"Host to Network Short"
- `htonl()`—"Host to Network Long"
- `ntohs()`—"Network to Host Short"
- `ntohl()`—"Network to Host Long"

If that was not enough, the pattern that was established for client/server applications was to use `fork` when a client connection was accepted on the server. In addition, when asynchronous operation was desired, the common approach was to use `select`. The problem that Windows programmers faced was that Windows did not have the Unix APIs of `fork` or select for client/server applications, so it was hard for a Windows programmer to enter the world of network programming. As an answer to this problem, Microsoft developed WinSock.

WinSock

Later versions of NT and Windows 2000 had strong support for threading and multiprocessing. WinSock 2 took full advantage of this support and created a set of APIs that were distinctly Windows and did not require `fork` and `select`. Windows developed a model based on non-blocking `sockets`, overlapped I/O, and I/O completion ports. In large measure, Windows programmers were now able to perform the same functions as were becoming common in the Berkley `sockets` world. As a good introduction to WinSock, see the Winsock programmers FAQ at `http://www.cyberport.com/~tangent/programming/winsock/`. Many of the concepts and solutions that existed for WinSock programmers had been carried forward to the .NET Framework and fully integrated into the CLR.

Why not just stop there and "fix" WinSock? The main problem was that programmers still had none of the benefits of programming in a managed environment. In addition to developing in a truly productive environment, there was a strong dependency on MFC wrappers, which carried too much overhead for some. Finally, it still seemed overly complex.

.NET Networking Classes

The .NET Framework classes for networking in the **System.Net** namespace greatly improve on the networking interfaces built in the past without imposing proprietary formats or APIs. Programming with these classes provides a consistent programming model that the programmer can access at many different levels. These classes come in a form that assumes a client/server relationship.

Productive Network Development

With the classes in the **System.Net** namespace, the programmer can quickly bring an application online using high-level classes. If it is required, the application can be easily modified to use lower-level functionality while adhering to the same application-specified protocol. Details that the programmer need not deal with are handled "correctly." In other words, most properties have "reasonable" defaults that are not explicitly set.

Layered Networking Stack

It is possible to work from the lowest level to a high level. You can program down at the lowest **Socket** level where you have a great deal of freedom to modify the application functionality. You can also work at a high level such as with a **WebClient** that is easy to use and provides a great deal of functionality but is targeted at a specific function.

Target Client and Server-Side Scenarios

TcpClient, **TcpListener**, **WebRequest**, and **WebResponse** target a client/server scenario. The standard APIs that start a server listening and a client connecting have been encapsulated into these classes with little overhead.

Extensible

Classes can be overridden. All of the classes can be used as a base class so that a user can override/replace certain functionality. For example, what if the user must get at the underlying **Socket** in the **TcpClient** class? To do this, you need to build a class that uses **TopClient** as a base class and simply return the "internal" **Socket** from a new method. It would look like this:

```
class MyTcpClient : TcpClient
{
    Socket GetSocket()
    {
        return Client;
    }
}
```

Standards Based

Little in System.Net is proprietary to Microsoft. Almost all of the classes support established standards such as TCP, UDP, HTTP, and SOAP. Using these standards allows your .NET application to communicate with any other program as long as it also supports the same standard. Specific examples of where a standard is not being used would be something like NT LanMan (NTLM) authentication or using the binary formatter for serialization. These exceptions are few and can be either avoided or segregated out so that the entire application does not become dependent on something that is not an established standard. Communicating by using a standard is becoming a requirement.

.NET Socket

The lowest level of network interface is the `socket`. If you are familiar with standard Berkley `sockets`, most of these interfaces and APIs should be familiar. The .Net `socket` class (hereafter referred to as just `socket`) is a thin layer around the `socket` interface. The `socket` gives the user maximum control over the interface. Although it is possible to create many different kinds of `sockets`, the most prevalent are the `sockets` that deal with the Defense Advanced Research Projects Agency (DARPA) Internet addresses; hence, they are called Internet `sockets`.

Internet `sockets` come in two types: Datagram `sockets` and Stream `sockets`. From this point forward, Datagram `sockets` will be referred to as Universal Datagram Protocol (UDP) `sockets`, and Stream `sockets` will be referred to as Transmission Control Protocol (TCP) `sockets`.

You can create a third type of `socket`, called a "raw" `socket`. A "raw" `socket` can only be used under special circumstances to debug or profile a network connection. Generally, this type of `socket` requires a special permission to create (usually Administrator), and its functionality can only be exploited from Windows 2000 or NT. From here, this chapter will briefly cover one type of application using a "raw" `socket` and discuss at length two specific `socket` types: UDP `sockets` and TCP `sockets`.

UDP Socket

A UDP **Socket** is also known as a "connectionless" **Socket** because unlike the "connection oriented" TCP **Socket**, it does not have to maintain an open connection for communication to occur. Every packet or block of data that is sent or received using a UDP **Socket** is given header information regarding its destination or source, so no connection is maintained. Each packet is completely autonomous. You can send a packet of information using a UDP **Socket** to "Server A" and "Server B" without having to worry about maintaining a connection to either machine. Why would you want to use any other kind of **Socket**?

UDP **Socket**s also have the distinction of being unreliable. Because there is no connection maintained, you can send two packets of data. After the first packet is sent, something could happen causing the second packet to be lost. The receiving end will never know that the second packet is lost because no notification indicated that it was sent. In addition, it is entirely possible and permissible for the second packet to arrive before the first. The UDP protocol does not specify that any time-dependent order must be maintained. One more drawback of the UDP **Socket** is its size. If you need to send large blocks of data, it is best to use TCP. Certainly for Windows, any packet that is larger than 8192 bytes will certainly cause trouble. In general, the Berkley `socket` implementation for UDP has similar size limitations. On the positive side, if a packet has been received with no errors, you can rely on the integrity of the data within that packet.

Given these restrictions, why would you choose UDP? In some applications, the reliability of the packet delivery is second to the overhead associated with maintaining a connection. Often, such applications build protocols on top of UDP to detect packet loss. One possible scheme would be to require that an acknowledgement packet be sent for each packet received. The sender waits for a certain period, and if this "ACK" packet is not received within the timeout period, the packet is resent.

UDP Server

Given that brief overview of the characteristics of a UDP **Socket**, it's time to look at an application using UDP **Socket**s to communicate. The UDP client/server application beginning with Listing 12.2 starts a server "listening" for information from a client. When the message is received from the client, the server prints the message on the **Console** and then listens for another message. The server exits if the message quits. The code for the server (dubbed the "listener") starts with Listing 12.2. The source associated with this listing (Listings 12.2–12.8) is in `UdpP2P\UdpP2PSocket\UdpListener\socketlistener.cs`.

LISTING 12.2 UDP **Socket** Server

```
using System;
using System.Net;
using System.Text;
using System.Net.Sockets;

class Listener
{
        public static void Main()
        {
        Console.WriteLine("Ready to process requests...");
        ProcessRequests();
    }
```

This is not surprising so far—just the required namespace declarations and the **Main** entry point. The next sections discuss the `ProcessRequests` method shown in Listing 12.2.

Creating a Socket

Listing 12.3 illustrates the beginning of the `ProcessRequests()` method. It is a continuation of the code listing for `SocketListener.cs` that was begun in Listing 12.2.

LISTING 12.3 Creating a UDP **Socket**

```
public static void ProcessRequests()
{
    Socket listener = new Socket(AddressFamily.InterNetwork,
                                 SocketType.Dgram,
                                 ProtocolType.Udp);
```

The **Socket** is created. Notice that because there are three arguments to the constructor of the **Socket** (and each has more than one value), it is certainly possible to create more than two or three types of **Socket**s. For the first argument, Table 12.1 (from the documentation **AddressFamily** Enumeration `ms-help://MS.VSCC/MS.MSDNVS/cpref/html/frlrfSystemNetSocketsAddressFamilyClassTopic.htm`) lists the possibilities.

TABLE 12.1 **AddressFamily** Enumeration Values

Member Name	*Description*
AppleTalk	AppleTalk address
Atm	Native ATM services address
Banyan	Banyan address

TABLE 12.1 Continued

Member Name	*Description*
Ccitt	Addresses for CCITT protocols, such as X.25
Chaos	Address for MIT CHAOS protocols
Cluster	Address for Microsoft cluster products
DataKit	Address for Datakit protocols
DataLink	Direct data-link interface address
DecNet	DECnet address
Ecma	European Computer Manufacturers Association (ECMA) address
FireFox	FireFox address
HyperChannel	NSC Hyperchannel address
Ieee12844	IEEE 1284.4 workgroup address
ImpLink	ARPANET IMP address
InterNetwork	Address for IP version 4
InterNetworkV6	Address for IP version 6
Ipx	IPX or SPX address
Irda	IrDA address
Iso	Address for ISO protocols
Lat	LAT address
Max	MAX address
NetBios	NetBios address
NetworkDesigners	Address for Network Designers OSI gateway-enabled protocols
NS	Address for Xerox NS protocols
Osi	Address for ISO protocols
Pup	Address for PUP protocols
Sna	IBM SNA address
Unix	Unix local to host address
Unknown	Unknown address family
Unspecified	Unspecified address family
VoiceView	VoiceView address

This chapter will only cover the `InterNetwork` type. This is the address family that is used for Internet Protocol (IP) and is the most prevalent type of address. It is possible that `InterNetworkV6` will become increasingly important as the world runs out of IP addresses and moves on to the next-generation Internet. You should realize that explicitly specifying **InterNetwork** in this sample limits this code to just IPv4. A much better approach would be to get the address that you want to listen on and then get the address family from the address. This approach is used in the TCP **Socket** samples.

The next argument (the **SocketType**) has six possible enumeration values. This chapter will cover primarily the **Dgram** type and the **Stream** type, although the **Raw** type is covered briefly. These three types of **Socket**s make up the vast majority of **Socket** types.

The last argument (the **ProtocolType**) has 15 possible values. The protocol type **Udp** goes with the **SocketType** of **Dgram**. Similarly, the protocol type **Tcp** goes with the **SocketType** of **Stream**. This chapter will show an application that makes use of the protocol type of **IP** and **SocketType.Raw** in the NetSniff sample. This sample is discussed in the upcoming section, "**IOControl**."

> **Note**
>
> Of the permutations and combinations available (36 **AddressFamily**, 6 **SocketType**, and 15 **ProtocolType** translate into 3,240 possibilities), this chapter will focus on two, with minor treatment of a third type of **Socket**. I am not sure what other combinations of these arguments do and have not been able to test them. If you have interest in any of these, probe the RFC associated with the particular address family or protocol. Reading about the Berkley **Socket** implementation in a good **Socket** programming book (*Unix Network Programming*, W. Richard Stevens, Volumes 1 and 2, Prentice Hall, Inc., 1990) would be a good start.

Creating an IPEndPoint and Binding to it

The server needs to be made aware of the address that it will be serving. Listing 12.4 is a continuation from Listing 12.3. Listing 12.4 illustrates the construction of an endpoint that encapsulates an address and port number pair. (Technically, a third member is the type of address, but that is virtually fixed.)

LISTING 12.4 UDP **Socket** Server (continued)

```
        IPEndPoint localEP = new IPEndPoint(IPAddress.Any, 5001);
    listener.Bind(localEP);
```

Listing 12.4 shows your first introduction to the **IPEndPoint** class. The **IPEndPoint** class contains the host IP address and port information needed by an application to connect to a service on a host.

This class encapsulates the `struct sockaddr_in`. This encapsulation is helpful. Regardless of the time I spent working with `sockets`, I always got mixed up with `struct in_addr`, `struct sockaddr_in`, and the `sin_port`, `sin_family`, and `sin_addr` members. In addition, macros "helped" the user get to the right members of the `struct in_addr`, appropriately named `s_addr`, `s_host`, `s_net`, and so on. Confused? In addition, it was necessary to remember the host-to-network and network-to-host conversion utilities (`htonl`, `htons`, `ntohl`, and `ntohs`) so that the port number and address were properly converted to network-byte-order. I always had to look at a printed version of each of these structures before I got it right.

With the **`IPEndPoint`** class, you simply need to remember that it contains an address family, a host address, and a port number. The address family is the same address family that is passed to the constructor for the **`Socket`** class. For most cases, this will be **`AddressFamily.InterNetwork`**. In fact, this is a read-only property of the **`IPEndPoint`** class, so you don't have the option to set it to any other value. The host address is encapsulated with an **`IPAddress`** class. Typically, the user will have a string formatted as dotted-decimal (dotted-quad), such as 192.45.67.10. To convert it to an **`IPAddress`** class, you call the static **`IPAddress.Parse`** (address), which returns an instance of the **`IPAddress`** class appropriate to the string or throws an exception indicating that the address was improperly formatted.

If you really must deal with network-byte-order, then this is the class where you will find the .NET equivalent for the series of functions `htonl`, `htons`, `ntohl`, and `ntohs`. These are static methods called (more descriptively) **`HostToNetworkOrder`** and **`NetworkToHostOrder`**.

In this example, the address is not obtained by any of the methods mentioned previously; the address is specifically given as **`IPAddress.Any`**. This is essentially a network address of 0.0.0.0, indicating that a client can connect to this server at any address. My computer has only a loopback adapter and the address that is associated with the NIC in the computer. By specifying **`IPAddress.Any`**, a client can connect to this server from localhost (which is essentially the loopback adapter address) or from the server's machine address. If this machine supported several addresses (had several NIC cards), then **`IPAddress.Any`** would allow a client to connect from any one of the interface addresses that it supported. Other special addresses are **`IPAddress.Broadcast`**, **`IPAddress.Loopback`**, and **`IPAddress.None`**.

The final argument to build an **`IPEndPoint`** is the port number. Ports from 1–5,000 are reserved (1–1,023 are reserved, and 1,024–5,000 are reserved for the system). Static methods to **`IPEndPoint`** specify a minimum and maximum port number that can be assigned to a given **`IPEndPoint`** (properties **`Min`** and **`Max`** respectively). If the port number is assigned dynamically in your application, then you might want to limit the range of ports that can be assigned in this manner.

After an instance of the **IPEndPoint** is constructed, it can be passed to **Bind**. The **Socket**'s class method of **Bind** is functionally equivalent to the traditional `bind` done with Berkley **Sockets**. It tells the system "This is my address, and any messages received for this address are to be given to me."

Listening for Incoming Messages and Conncections

Continuing the code listing, you are now to the point that you can announce to the world your intentions to listen on this **Socket**. Listing 12.5 continues the code from Listing 12.4.

LISTING 12.5 Start the UDP **Socket** Server Listening

```
bool continueProcessing = true;
while(continueProcessing)
{
    // negative timeout implies blocking operation
    // basically block until data is available and then read it.
    listener.Poll(-1, SelectMode.SelectRead);
```

You enter a loop. The only exit point for the loop is if the server receives the string "quit."

The first function that is called is **listener.Poll()**. The first argument passed to this function is the timeout value. If no data is ready by the specified timeout (in microseconds), then the function will return `false`. Specifying –1 as the first argument to **Poll** implies (as the comment indicates) that a timeout does not exist. The second argument indicates that you are interested in read events. Table 12.2 indicates the possible values for **SelectMode** and the return values.

TABLE 12.2 **SelectMode** Enumeration Values

Mode	*Return Value*
SelectRead	`true` if Listen has been called and a connection is pending, Accept will succeed -or- `true` if data is available for reading -or- `true` if connection has been closed, reset, or terminated; otherwise, returns `false`.
SelectWrite	`true` if processing a non-blocking Connect, and connection has succeeded -or- `true` if data can be sent; otherwise, returns `false`.

TABLE 12.2 Continued

Mode	*Return Value*
`SelectError`	`true` if processing a non-blocking Connect, and connection has failed -or- `true` if OutOfBandInline is not set and out-of-band data is available; otherwise, returns `false`.

Receiving Data from a Client

Continuing from Listing 12.5, Listing 12.6 shows how the property **`Available`** is filled in after the **`Poll`** returns `true`.

LISTING 12.6 UDP **`Socket`** Server (continued)

```
// receive as much data as is available
// to read from the client socket
int available = listener.Available;
byte[] buffer = new byte[available];
```

After the **`Poll`** successfully completes, the number of bytes read from the network and available to be read is retrieved from the **`Available`** property. (You might argue that it is better to just shut down the server here because the only possible `false` return is an error.)

Caution

If the number of bytes expected is more than 8192, you might expect trouble with a UDP arrangement. In one failure mode, the **`Available`** property returns 8192. The buffer is allocated for 8192 and then in the **`ReceiveFrom`** method, an exception is thrown indicating that the buffer is too small. If the number of bytes returned from **`Available`** is ignored and a "large enough" buffer is constructed, then **`ReceiveFrom`** succeeds.

Continuing the code listing in Listing 12.7, you can see how the server reads data from a client.

LISTING 12.7 UDP **`Socket`** Server Reading Data From a Client

```
IPEndPoint tempRemoteEP = new IPEndPoint(IPAddress.Any, 5002);
EndPoint trEP = (EndPoint)tempRemoteEP;

int bytesRead = listener.ReceiveFrom(buffer, ref trEP);
```

The server constructs an address from which to receive data. You have already seen the **IPEndPoint** class. Other than the fact that this endpoint uses a different port, the construction is the same.

> **Note**
>
> The **ReceiveFrom** method requires an **EndPoint** reference. **EndPoint** is an abstract base class for **IPEndPoint** so that it is easy to convert. I cannot understand why **ReceiveFrom** should be passed by reference. A plausible explanation would be that passing an **IPEndPoint** or **EndPoint** by value is unacceptably slow, and passing by reference speeds up the overall throughput.

Listing 12.8 concludes the listing of this code and continues where Listing 12.7 left off.

LISTING 12.8 UDP **Socket** Server Decoding the Message from a Client

```
                string message = Encoding.ASCII.GetString(buffer, 0, bytesRead);
                if(message == "quit")
                {
                    continueProcessing = false;
                    break;
                }
                else
                {
                    Console.WriteLine("The message received was " + message);
                }
            }
        }
        listener.Close();
    }
}
```

Now you have the data in a buffer. Because you know that this data is text, you convert it to an appropriate format using the **Encoding** class. This is the **Encoding** class, not the **Encoder** class. The client and server both have to agree on the format of the data. If the client assumes **ASCII** and the server assumes **Unicode**, a crash would be imminent. The formats that the **Encoding** class supports are **ASCII**, **Unicode**, **UTF7**, and **UTF8**.

After the message is received and encoded into the proper form, all that is left to do on the server end is to echo the received string and print the message to the **Console**.

UDP Client

Listing 12.9 starts the listing for the client code that will form the peer to the UDP server in the previous section. The full source for the client shown in Listings 12.9 and 12.10 is available at `UdpP2P\UdpP2PSocket\UdpSender\socketsender.cs`.

LISTING 12.9 UDP **Socket** Client

```
using System;
using System.Net;
using System.Text;
using System.Net.Sockets;

class Sender
{

    public static void Main(string[] args)
    {
        string address = "localhost";
        if(args.Length == 1)
            address = args[0];

        bool continueSending = true;
        while(continueSending)
        {
            Console.WriteLine("Enter the message to send. Type 'quit' to
exit.");
            string message = Console.ReadLine();
            SendMessage(message, address);
            if(message == "quit")
            {
                SendMessage(message, address);
                continueSending = false;
            }
        }
    }
```

This is the main driver for the client program. A user would start the program as follows:

```
udpsender your-host
```

If the host name is not entered, it is assumed that the server is running on localhost.

As you can see from the code, the program accepts input from the user and sends that input to the server. When the word "quit" is entered, then the program sends the string to the server and exits successfully.

Listing 12.10 continues the listing begun in Listing 12.9. It completes the listing for the client portion of the application.

LISTING 12.10 Sending a Message from a UDP **Socket** Client

```
    public static void SendMessage(string message, string server)
    {
        try
        {
                        Socket client = new Socket(AddressFamily.InterNetwork,
                                                   SocketType.Dgram,
                                                   ProtocolType.Udp);
            IPEndPoint localEP = new IPEndPoint(IPAddress.Any, 5002);
            client.Bind(localEP);
            byte[] buffer = Encoding.ASCII.GetBytes(message);
            IPAddress address = Dns.Resolve(server).AddressList[0];
            IPEndPoint remoteEP = new IPEndPoint(address, 5001);
            client.SendTo(buffer, 0, buffer.Length, SocketFlags.None, remoteEP);
            client.Close();
        }
        catch(Exception ex)
        {
            Console.WriteLine(ex.ToString());
        }
    }
}
```

Compare the code shown in Listing 12.10 with the server code that is shown in Listings 12.3–12.7. Many similarities are worth noting. A **Socket** is created and bound to a local port, and the message is converted to a string. Next, the server name is **Resolve**d using the **Dns** class.

The **Resolve** method is a static method in the **Dns** class. This method takes a string, which can be a dotted-quad format (such as 192.168.1.2) or a name (such as `www.microsoft.com`). The result of this operation is an instance of **IPHostEntry**. **IPHostEntry** is a wrapper around the `struct hostent` structure that is returned by Win32 APIs `gethostbyname` or `WSAAsyncGetHostByName`. This is another class where the encapsulation is welcome. This class contains a host name, an array of aliases, and an array of addresses. The code shown in Listing 12.10 assumes that the first address in the list is the address with which to communicate, as is evidenced by the following line:

```
IPAddress address = Dns.Resolve(server).AddressList[0];
```

It would be better to loop through each address on the address list and either just handle the first address that you can without error or handle all addresses. In the code for TCP **Socket**s, the first address in the list that can be handled without error is the address that is used, rather than strictly the first address, as is done here.

In addition to the **Resolve** method, static methods are available for getting the host name of the computer, getting host information for a specific computer, getting host information for a specific address, and turning a long value representing the address into a dotted-quad string.

After the **IPEndPoint** is created, the client sends the data to the server and closes. The client then reads more input from the Console until `quit` is entered.

Figure 12.1 shows a typical client server arrangement.

```
Command Prompt
07/18/2001  03:03p      <DIR>          .
07/18/2001  03:03p      <DIR>          ..
06/23/2001  08:21a               2,426 AssemblyInfo.cs
07/18/2001  03:03p      <DIR>          bin
06/23/2001  08:22a               1,394 socklistener.cs
06/23/2001  08:22a               3,363 UdpListener.csproj
06/23/2001  08:22a               1,551 UdpListener.csproj.user
06/23/2001  08:21a                 918 UdpListener.sln
               5 File(s)          9,652 bytes
               3 Dir(s)  10,323,279,872 bytes free

C:\CLR Book\Attachments\Samples\Chapter12\UdpP2P\UdpP2PSocket\UdpListener>bin\de
bug\udplistener
Ready to process requests...
The message received was This is a test
The message received was This is another test
The message received was When I enter quit both the client and server will quit

C:\CLR Book\Attachments\Samples\Chapter12\UdpP2P\UdpP2PSocket\UdpListener>
```

```
Command Prompt
06/23/2001  08:22a                 914 UdpSender.sln
               5 File(s)          9,483 bytes
               3 Dir(s)  10,323,279,872 bytes free

C:\CLR Book\Attachments\Samples\Chapter12\UdpP2P\UdpP2PSocket\UdpSender>bin\debu
g\udpsender
Enter the message to send. Type 'quit' to exit.
This is a test
Enter the message to send. Type 'quit' to exit.
This is another test
Enter the message to send. Type 'quit' to exit.
When I enter quit both the client and server will quit
Enter the message to send. Type 'quit' to exit.
quit

C:\CLR Book\Attachments\Samples\Chapter12\UdpP2P\UdpP2PSocket\UdpSender>_
```

FIGURE 12.1
UDP client/server session on the same machine.

TCP Socket

TCP allows you to build a connection-oriented application. The code difference between a TCP **Socket** client/server application and the UDP client/server application presented in the previous section is minimal. However, the two applications are quite different in the way they function. Using UDP is inherently unreliable because a persistent connection is not maintained. It is impossible to know with certainty that a UDP message has been received on the other end. Hence, UDP is called a connectionless protocol. TCP, on the other hand, maintains a constant connection for all traffic between the client and the server. The sender of a message on a TCP connection can be assured that the message sent was received. UDP is good for communication of small lightweight packets. TCP has more overhead, but it can successfully and reliably transfer large blocks of information. The following sections illustrate how to construct a simple TCP client/server application.

TCP Server

Listing 12.11 introduces the code for the server. The full source for this sample shown in Listings 12.11–12.12 can be obtained from `TcpP2P\TcpP2PSocket\TcpListener\TcpListener.cs`.

LISTING 12.11 TCP **Socket** Server

```
using System;
using System.Text;
using System.Net;
using System.Net.Sockets;

class Listener
{
    public static void Main()
    {
        Console.WriteLine("Ready to process requests...");
        ProcessRequests();
    }

    public static Socket GetListenerSocket(string host, int port)
    {
        Socket s = null;
        IPHostEntry iphe = Dns.Resolve(host);
        foreach(IPAddress ipa in iphe.AddressList)
        {
            IPEndPoint lep = new IPEndPoint(ipa, port);
            Socket ts = new Socket(lep.AddressFamily,
                                   SocketType.Stream,
                                   ProtocolType.Tcp);
            try
            {
                ts.Bind(lep);
                ts.Listen(2);
                s = ts;
                break;
            }
            catch (ArgumentNullException ae)
            {
                Console.WriteLine("ArgumentNullException: " + ae.ToString());
            }
            catch (SocketException se)
            {
                Console.WriteLine("SocketException: " + se.ToString());
            }
            catch (Exception e)
            {
                Console.WriteLine("Connection failed: " + e.ToString());
            }
        }
        return s;
    }
    public static void ProcessRequests()
    {
        Socket server = GetListenerSocket(Dns.GetHostName(), 5000);
        Socket s = server.Accept();
```

The server is setting up to receive data. A TCP **Socket** is created by specifying **SocketType.Stream** and **ProtocolType.Tcp** for the arguments to the **Socket** constructor. An **IPEndPoint** is created, which designates the address(es) in which this server is interested. Unlike the UDP server, however, the TCP server calls **Socket.Listen**.

Two points must be emphasized on the code snippet of Listing 12.11. The first point is that, unlike the UDP server code, this listing is correctly looping through the available addresses in the list of addresses returned from **Dns.Resolve**, to determine which addresses can be handled without error. Doing this ensures that in the near future when IPv6 is more prevalent, your code will not break. It would be entirely possible for the list of addresses returned from **Dns.Resolve** to contain IPv4 and IPv6 addresses. If you simply went with the first address that was an IPv6 address, and your code did not support IPv6 addresses, your code would break because it would not move on to an address that was supported. The second point is that the **Socket** is created using the **AddressFamily** from the resolved address rather than explicitly specifying the enumerated type of **AddressFamily.InterNetwork**. Again, this is a defensive measure in your code that will not lock your code into a particular **AddressFamily**.

Listen is a thin wrapper around the traditional **Socket** `listen` function. Like `listen()`, **Listen** takes a single argument that is documented as "Maximum length of the queue of pending connections." This argument specifies how many connection requests can be queued by the system while it waits for the server to execute the **Accept** call. For example, if the backlog is 1, one client application can connect to the server and exchange data. While this is going on, another client application that tries to connect will think that it has actually connected to the server, but its first attempt to transmit data will block until the server calls **Accept**. If more clients try to connect, then each client above the queue limit will receive a **SocketException** indicating that "No connection could be made because the target machine actively refused it." There does not seem to be a limit imposed on this argument, but traditionally, `listen` quietly scales the argument to be within the range of 1 to 5. The `listen` function doesn't fail. **Listen** does the same thing.

Note that the last line of Listing 12.11 shows a single call to **Accept**. By calling **Accept**, the server blocks until a client connection is received. When a client connection is received and accepted, a new **Socket** is constructed that is a connection to its peer. Again, if a client that is within the backlog limit imposed by **Listen** connects, it is connected. If the server terminates, the client receives a **SocketException** such as the following: "An existing connection was forcibly closed by the remote host."

Continuing from Listing 12.11, Listing 12.12 illustrates the processing that occurs after the **Accept** call returns.

LISTING 12.12 TCP **Socket** Server Receiving and Decoding a Client Message

```
byte[] responseData = new byte[128];
bool continueProcessing = true;

while(continueProcessing)
{
    try
    {
        int bytesRead = s.Receive(responseData);
        // string message = Encoding.ASCII.GetString(responseData, 0,
bytesRead);
        string message = Encoding.Unicode.GetString(responseData, 0, bytesRead);
        if(message == "quit")
        {
            continueProcessing = false;
            break;
        }
        else
        {
            Console.WriteLine("The message received was " + message);
        }
    }
    catch(Exception ex)
    {
        Console.WriteLine(ex.ToString());
    }
}
s.Close();
server.Close();
```

The rest of the code is much the same as the UDP server. With a TCP server, the data is received by a call to **Receive** rather than **ReceiveFrom**. Like **ReceiveFrom**, **Receive** blocks until the client has sent "all of the data." What "all of the data" means is dependent on the buffering scheme in place, but in this case, it means that a line (delimited by a CR/LF) has been received from the client.

The next section discusses the code for the TCP client that is associated with this server.

TCP Client

This listing for the client code begins with Listing 12.13. The full source (Listings 12.13–12.14) for this code can be found at `TcpP2P\TcpP2PSocket\TcpSender\TcpSender.cs`.

LISTING 12.13 TCP **Socket** Client

```
public static void Main(string[] args)
{
    string address = "localhost";
    if(args.Length == 1)
        address = args[0];

    SendMessage(address);
}

public static Socket GetSocket(string host, int port)
{
    Socket s = null;
    IPHostEntry iphe = Dns.Resolve(host);
    // Loop through all addresses, not just
    // the first address.
    foreach(IPAddress ipa in iphe.AddressList)
    {
        IPEndPoint ipe = new IPEndPoint(ipa, port);

        // Use the AddressFamily that
        // is part of the endpoint.
        // AddressFamily.InterNetwork limits you to
        // just IPv4
        Socket ts = new Socket(ipe.AddressFamily,
                               SocketType.Stream,
                               ProtocolType.Tcp);
        try
        {
            // Return the first socket that
            // we can connect to.
            ts.Connect(ipe);
            s = ts;
            break;
        }
        catch (ArgumentNullException ae)
        {
            Console.WriteLine("ArgumentNullException: " + ae.ToString());
        }
        catch (SocketException se)
        {
            Console.WriteLine("SocketException: " + se.ToString());
        }
        catch (Exception e)
        {
            Console.WriteLine("Connection failed: " + e.ToString());
        }
    }
    return s;
}
```

LISTING 12.13 Continued

```
public static void SendMessage(string server)
{
    Socket s = GetSocket(server, 5000);
    if(s == null)
        return;
```

Like the TCP server code, this code does not assume anything about the connection. The first address to which you can connect is returned. The **AddressFamily** is based on the **AddressFamily** that is associated with the address rather than a hard-coded **AddressFamily.InterNetwork**. The first address that successfully connects to the specified server and port is used to create the **Socket** that is returned from GetSocket. You cannot specify the first address in the address list and hard-code the **AddressFamily** in the server. This code shows you how to prevent these same mistakes in the client.

Because this is a connection-oriented link, the client calls **Connect**, which specifies to which server endpoint to connect. The endpoint that is an argument to **Connect** is actually an **EndPoint**. Unlike the **EndPoint** required for the **ReceiveFrom** call in the UDP case, the **EndPoint** required by **Connect** is passed by value so that it can be implicitly converted.

Note

The documentation indicates that a **Bind** is required before **Connect** can be called. Traditionally, the bind is optional for the client. In fact, if a **Bind** is called for the client, the call will fail when the client and server are running on the same machine. You can then leave the call to **Bind** out.

Continuing from Listing 12.13, Listing 12.14 illustrates the main loop for the client.

LISTING 12.14 TCP **Socket** Client Sending a Message to the Server

```
        bool continueSending = true;
        while(continueSending)
        {
            Console.WriteLine("Enter the message to send. Type 'quit' to
➥exit.");
            string message = Console.ReadLine();
            // byte[] buffer = Encoding.ASCII.GetBytes(message);
            byte[] buffer = Encoding.Unicode.GetBytes(message);
            s.Send(buffer);
```

LISTING 12.14 Continued

```
            if(message == "quit")
            {
                continueSending = false;
            }
        }
        s.Close();
    }
}
```


The rest of the client code is virtually identical to the UDP client code. The exception is that with TCP, the connection remains for the entire session; a TCP client calls **Send** to transmit data to the server rather than **SendTo**, which requires an **EndPoint** with every call.

Figure 12.2 shows a typical client/server arrangement. It has been set up to be functionally the same as the UDP example. Except for the name changes, the output should look the same as the UDP example shown previously.

```
Command Prompt
07/18/2001  03:03p      <DIR>          .
07/18/2001  03:03p      <DIR>          ..
07/18/2001  03:03p      <DIR>          TcpP2PClass
07/19/2001  09:46a      <DIR>          TcpP2PSocket
               0 File(s)              0 bytes
               4 Dir(s)  10,326,728,704 bytes free

C:\CLR Book\Attachments\Samples\Chapter12\TcpP2P>cd TcpP2PSOcket

C:\CLR Book\Attachments\Samples\Chapter12\TcpP2P\TcpP2PSocket>cd TcpListener

C:\CLR Book\Attachments\Samples\Chapter12\TcpP2P\TcpP2PSocket\TcpListener>bin\de
bug\tcplistener
Ready to process requests...
The message received was This is a test.
The message received was This is another test
The message received was I about to enter 'quit'

C:\CLR Book\Attachments\Samples\Chapter12\TcpP2P\TcpP2PSocket\TcpListener>
```

```
Command Prompt
07/14/2001  01:10p                  41 test.js
               5 File(s)          6,681 bytes
               3 Dir(s)  10,326,728,704 bytes free

C:\CLR Book\Attachments\Samples\Chapter12\TcpP2P\TcpP2PSocket\TcpSender>bin\debu
g\tcpsender
Enter the message to send. Type 'quit' to exit.
This is a test.
Enter the message to send. Type 'quit' to exit.
This is another test
Enter the message to send. Type 'quit' to exit.
I about to enter 'quit'
Enter the message to send. Type 'quit' to exit.
quit

C:\CLR Book\Attachments\Samples\Chapter12\TcpP2P\TcpP2PSocket\TcpSender>
```

FIGURE 12.2
TCP client/server session on the same machine.

Socket Options

At this level, the interface again shows how thin it is. There is almost a one-to-one correspondence between the **Socket** options available on an unmanaged **Socket** and those available on the .NET managed **Socket**. The methods to get and set **Socket** options are **GetSocketOption** and **SetSocketOption** respectively. Compare these member functions with the WinSock `getsockopt` and `setsockopt` respectively.

```
int getsockopt(SOCKET s, int level, int optname,
➥char FAR *optval, int FAR *optlen );
int setsockopt(SOCKET s, int level, int optname,
➥const char FAR *optval, int optlen );
```

To get **Socket** option values, a **SocketOptionLevel** and a **SocketOptionName** must be supplied. The **SocketOptionLevel** is a simple enumeration that can take on the values listed in Table 12.3. The rough equivalent WinSock option names have been modified.

TABLE 12.3 SocketOptionLevel Enumeration Values

Member Name	*Description*	*WinSock Equivalent*
IP	**Socket** options apply to IP **Socket**s.	IPPROTO_IP
Socket	**Socket** options apply to the **Socket**.	SOL_SOCKET
Tcp	**Socket** options apply to TCP **Socket**s.	IPPROTO_TCP
Udp	**Socket** options apply to UDP **Socket**s.	IPPROTO_UDP

Similarly, **SocketOptionName** is an enumeration of values listed in Table 12.4.

TABLE 12.4 SocketOptionName Enumeration Values

Member Name	*Description*	*WinSock Equivalent*
AcceptConnection	Accept a connection.	SO_ACCEPTCONN
AddMembership	Add an IP group membership.	IP_ADD_MEMBERSHIP
AddSourceMembership	Join a source group.	
BlockSource	Block data from a source.	
Broadcast	Permit sending broadcast messages on the **Socket**.	SO_BROADCAST
BsdUrgent	Use urgent data as defined in RFC 1222. This option can be set only once. After it is set, it cannot be turned off.	TCP_BSDURGENT
ChecksumCoverage	Set or get UDP checksum coverage.	
Debug	Record debugging information.	SO_DEBUG
DontFragment	Refrain from fragmenting IP datagrams.	IP_DONTFRAGMENT
DontLinger	Close **Socket** gracefully without lingering.	SO_DONTLINGER
DontRoute	Do not route; send directly to interface addresses.	SO_DONTROUTE

TABLE 12.4 Continued

Member Name	*Description*	*WinSock Equivalent*
DropMembership	Drop an IP group membership.	IP_DROP_MEMBERSHIP
DropSourceMembership	Drop a source group.	
Error	Get error status and clear.	SO_ERROR
ExclusiveAddressUse	Bind a **Socket** for exclusive access.	SO_EXCLUSIVEADDRUSE
Expedited	Use expedited data as defined in RFC 1222. This option can be set only once, and after it is set, it cannot be turned off.	
HeaderIncluded	Indicate that the application is providing the IP header for outgoing datagrams.	
IPOptions	Specify IP options to be inserted into outgoing datagrams.	IP_OPTIONS
IpTimeToLive	Set the IP header time-to-live field.	IP_TTL
KeepAlive	Send keep-alives.	SO_KEEPALIVE
Linger	Linger on close if unsent data is present.	SO_LINGER
MaxConnections	Set the maximum queue length that can be specified by **Listen**.	
MulticastInterface	Set the interface for outgoing multicast packets.	IP_MULTICAST_IF
MulticastLoopback	Allow IP multicast loopback.	IP_MULTICAST_LOOP
MulticastTimeToLive	Enable IP multicast time to live.	IP_MULTICAST_TTL
NoChecksum	Send UDP datagrams with checksum set to zero.	
NoDelay	Disable the Nagle algorithm for send coalescing.	TCP_NODELAY
OutOfBandInline	Receive out-of-band data in the normal data stream.	SO_OOBINLINE
PacketInformation	Return information about received packets.	
ReceiveBuffer	Send low water mark.	SO_RCVBUF
ReceiveLowWater	Receive low water mark.	SO_RCVLOWAT
ReceiveTimeout	Receive time out.	SO_RCVTIMEO

TABLE 12.4 Continued

Member Name	*Description*	*WinSock Equivalent*
ReuseAddress	Allow the **Socket** to be bound to an address that is already in use.	SO_REUSEADDR
SendBuffer	Specify the total per-**Socket** buffer space reserved for sends. This is unrelated to the maximum message size or the size of a TCP window.	SO_SNDBUF
SendLowWater	Specify the total per-**Socket** buffer space reserved for receives. This is unrelated to the maximum message size or the size of a TCP window.	SO_SNDLOWAT
SendTimeout	Send timeout.	SO_SNDTIMEO
Type	Get **Socket** type.	SO_TYPE
TypeOfService	Change the IP header type of service field.	
UnblockSource	Unblock a previously blocked source.	
UseLoopback	Bypass hardware when possible.	SO_USELOOPBACK

To see the default options, I wrote a program to display some of the options for a TCP, UDP, and raw **Socket**. A partial listing of the code for this sample is shown in Listing 12.15. The full source can be obtained from `SocketOptions\SocketOptions.cs`.

LISTING 12.15 **Socket** Options Listing

```
using System;
using System.Net.Sockets;

namespace SocketOptions
{
    /// <summary>
    /// Summary description for Class1.
    /// </summary>
    class SocketOptionsTest
    {
        static void ListRawDefaultOptions(Socket s)
        {
            Object option;
            . . .
```

LISTING 12.15 Continued

```
            Console.WriteLine("Raw Type {0}",
                ((int)option == 1) ? "SOCK_STREAM" :
                ((int)option == 2) ? "SOCK_DGRAM" :
                ((int)option == 3) ? "SOCK_RAW" :
                ((int)option == 4) ? "SOCK_RDM" :
                ((int)option == 5) ? "SOCK_SEQPACKET" : "Unknown type");
            . . .
        }
        static void ListUDPDefaultOptions(Socket s)
        {
            Object option;
            . . .
            Console.WriteLine("UDP DontFragment {0}", option);
            option = s.GetSocketOption(SocketOptionLevel.Socket,
➥SocketOptionName.Error);
            Console.WriteLine("UDP Error {0}", option);
            option = s.GetSocketOption(SocketOptionLevel.IP,
                                       SocketOptionName.MulticastInterface);
            Console.WriteLine("UDP MulticastInterface {0}", option);
            . . .
        }
        static void ListTCPDefaultOptions(Socket s)
        {
            Object option;
            . . .
            option = s.GetSocketOption(SocketOptionLevel.Socket,
➥SocketOptionName.KeepAlive);
            Console.WriteLine("TCP KeepAlive {0}", option);
            option = s.GetSocketOption(SocketOptionLevel.Socket,
➥SocketOptionName.Linger);
            Console.WriteLine("TCP Linger {0} {1}",
                                   ((LingerOption)option).Enabled,
                                   ((LingerOption)option).LingerTime);
            option = s.GetSocketOption(SocketOptionLevel.Tcp,
➥SocketOptionName.NoDelay);
            Console.WriteLine("TCP NoDelay {0}", option);
            . . .
            option = s.GetSocketOption(SocketOptionLevel.Socket,
➥SocketOptionName.ReceiveBuffer);
            Console.WriteLine("TCP ReceiveBuffer {0}", option);
            option = s.GetSocketOption(SocketOptionLevel.Socket,
                                            SocketOptionName.ReceiveTimeout);
            Console.WriteLine("TCP ReceiveTimeout {0}", option);
            option = s.GetSocketOption(SocketOptionLevel.Socket,
➥SocketOptionName.ReuseAddress);
            Console.WriteLine("TCP ReuseAddress {0}", option);
            option = s.GetSocketOption(SocketOptionLevel.Socket,
➥SocketOptionName.SendBuffer);
            Console.WriteLine("TCP SendBuffer {0}", option);
```

LISTING 12.15 Continued

```
            option = s.GetSocketOption(SocketOptionLevel.Socket,
➥SocketOptionName.SendTimeout);
            Console.WriteLine("TCP SendTimeout {0}", option);
            . . .
        }
        static void Main(string[] args)
        {
            Console.WriteLine("TCP Socket");
            Socket s = new Socket(AddressFamily.InterNetwork,
                                 SocketType.Stream, ProtocolType.Tcp);
            ListTCPDefaultOptions(s);
            s.Close();
            Console.WriteLine("UDP Socket");
            s = new Socket(AddressFamily.InterNetwork,
                           SocketType.Dgram, ProtocolType.Udp);
            ListUDPDefaultOptions(s);
            s.Close();
            s = new Socket(AddressFamily.InterNetwork,
                           SocketType.Raw, ProtocolType.Raw);
            ListRawDefaultOptions(s);
            s.Close();
        }
    }
}
```

The output of this program is shown in Figure 12.3.

```
Command Prompt
C:\CLR Book\Attachments\Samples\Chapter12\SocketOptions>bin\debug\socketoptions
TCP Socket
TCP AcceptConnections 0
TCP BsdUrgent 0
TCP Debug 0
TCP DontLinger 1
TCP DontRoute 0
TCP Error 0
TCP ExclusiveAddressUse 0
TCP Expedited 0
TCP IpTimeToLive 32
TCP KeepAlive 0
TCP Linger False 0
TCP NoDelay 0
TCP OutOfBandInline 0
TCP ReceiveBuffer 8192
TCP ReceiveTimeout 0
TCP ReuseAddress 0
TCP SendBuffer 8192
TCP SendTimeout 0
TCP Type SOCK_STREAM
TCP TypeOfService 0
UDP Socket
UDP Broadcast 0
UDP Debug 0
UDP DontFragment 0
UDP Error 0
UDP MulticastInterface 0
UDP MulticastLoopback 1
UDP MulticastTimeToLive 1
UDP NoChecksum 0
UDP Type SOCK_DGRAM
UDP TypeOfService 0
Raw Debug 0
Raw Broadcast 0
Raw Error 0
Raw Type SOCK_RAW
Raw MulticastInterface 0
Raw MulticastLoopback 1
Raw MulticastTimeToLive 1

C:\CLR Book\Attachments\Samples\Chapter12\SocketOptions>_
```

FIGURE 12.3
Default values for various **Socket** *options.*

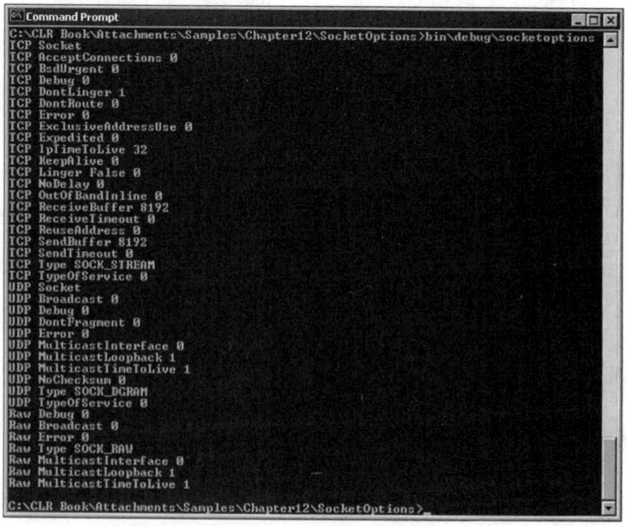

Many of these options are infrequently used. However, some are important, and the default values might not be sufficient. For example, setting **SocketOptionName.NoDelay** (TCP_NODELAY) to true disables the Nagel algorithm. The Nagel algorithm tries to stuff as many characters into a packet as possible by delaying the transmission of data until enough data is queued or until a sufficient time interval has passed from the system's receipt of the last character from the application before sending the packet. If data of a known size is being transferred back and forth in a peer-to-peer arrangement, and the minimal delay imposed by the Nagel algorithm causes the application to appear less "snappy," then you can disable the Nagel algorithm.

Some other options that might be useful are **SocketOptionName**, **ReceiveBuffer** (SO_RCVBUF), and **SocketOptionName.SendBuffer** (SO_SNDBUF). The send and receive buffer size might be too small or too large depending on the application. If the application tends to send large chunks of data at a time, the data needs to be split into chunks that fit into the buffer size specified. If the buffer size is too small, then there might be (as a percentage of the total packet size) substantial overhead to send multiple packets. If the application uses only small chunks of data at a time, then a lot of wasted space would exist in each packet sent.

The **SocketOptionName.ReuseAddress** (SO_REUSEADDR) might need to be used if the applications require repeated connections and disconnections. When a **Socket** is closed, it might not go completely away immediately; when an application tries to bind (**socket.Bind**()) to the port, the user might receive an "Address already in use" exception. Figure 12.4 shows this exception. **SocketOptionName.ReuseAddress** prevents that error by reusing the address even if it is being used.

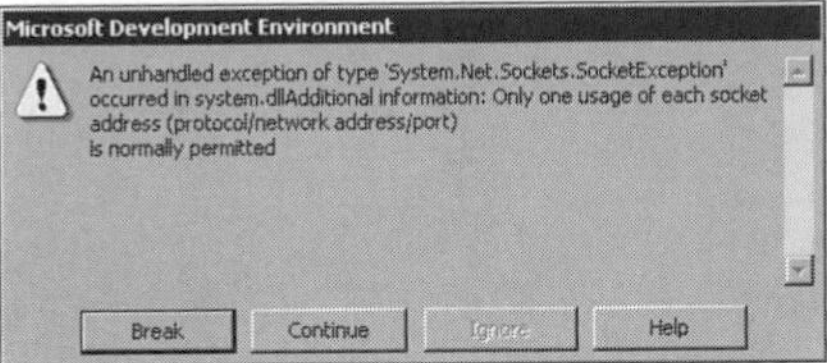

FIGURE 12.4
Reuse address exception.

Each of the **Socket** options has existed for quite some time, and new **Socket** options are being developed. It is good that the programmer has access to the low-level functionality of the **Socket**. Microsoft has made it easier to do network programming by providing reasonable defaults as well as providing access to the low-level details.

Using IOControl on a Socket

Another low-level operation that can be performed on **Socket**s is **IOControl**. For those who are familiar with programming traditional sockets, this is not new. All of the options cannot be explained in this book, but if you are interested, consult the documentation available for `WSAIoctl` or `ioctlsocket`.

One particularly interesting application of **`IOControl`** is to debug network traffic. A raw **`Socket`** is created and the **`IOControl`** method is used to enable `SIO_RCVALL`. Listing 12.16 illustrates the core functionality of the `NetSniff` sample.

LISTING 12.16 **`IOControl`** **in the** **`NetSniff`** **Sample**

```
listenerSocket = new Socket(AddressFamily.InterNetwork,
➥SocketType.Raw, ProtocolType.IP);
IPEndPoint localEP = new IPEndPoint(
➥Dns.GetHostByName(Dns.GetHostName()).AddressList[0], 80);
this.listenerSocket.Bind(localEP);
// SIO_RCVALL
int code = unchecked((int)(0x80000000 | 0x18000000 | 1));
byte[] inBuf = new byte[4];
inBuf[0] = 1;
byte[] outBuf = new byte[4];
listenerSocket.IOControl(code, inBuf, outBuf);
```

This allows sniffing of bytes going to and from a certain port. Figure 12.5 shows the application after a short session at `msdn.microsoft.com`.

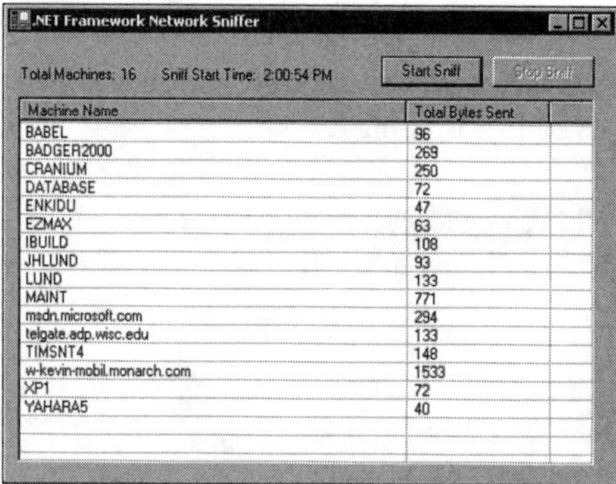

FIGURE 12.5
Network sniffer.

Full source for this application is in the `NetSniff` directory.

Asynchronous `Socket` Operation

A program often can't wait around for the results of a network operation. For example, perhaps a user wanted to download a large file. If the user were unable to perform any other function until the download completed, he would be unhappy. This would be a poor user interface design. The user at least wants the appearance that more than one operation is occurring at a time. In situations like this, the .NET Framework—and particularly the networking classes—provide asynchronous methods to perform certain operations.

Building an application that supports asynchronous operations is not a trivial task. Many programmers build asynchronous or multithread applications because they feel that it would be more efficient to do it that way. Speed or throughput should not be the only consideration when deciding to use the asynchronous methods. The application might not run faster because it is now asynchronous. In addition, the code takes some effort to get right and might be harder to maintain and debug.

Listing 12.17 shows a simple asynchronous client/server application. Strictly speaking, the server is asynchronous. The client sends some data to the server and the server echoes it back to the client (asynchronously). This code is rather lengthy, so it will be dissected into sections. Listing 12.17 introduces the server code with some standard namespace declarations and the definition of a class that will be used to hold state information. The full source for Listings 12.17–12.24 can be found at `AsyncP2P\AsyncSrv\AsyncSrv.cs`. A listing of the client code is not included here because it primarily mimics the standard synchronous network calls that have been illustrated earlier in this chapter. The full source for the client can be found at `AsyncP2P\AsyncClnt\AsyncClnt.cs`.

LISTING 12.17 Asynchronous TCP Server

```
using System;
using System.Net;
using System.Net.Sockets;
using System.Text;
using System.Threading;

public class AsyncData
{
    public Socket socket;
    public byte[] RecBytes = new byte[256];
}
```

This is the preliminary setup for the application. The namespaces that you will be using are declared, and a simple class is defined to hold the asynchronous data that is sent and received. As you will see in Listings 12.18–12.23, one of the arguments to the asynchronous network methods is an object that will be passed to the callback as state information. This is not the only way to pass state information. If the callback (delegate) is a non-static member of a class, it will callback on the instance of the class that was used to create the delegate. In other words, the class that implements the delegate function can hold state information. The following application does not use this fact. Other samples are included that hold state in the instance of the class that holds the callback.

Listing 12.18 continues the listing begun in Listing 12.17.

LISTING 12.18 Asynchronous TCP Server Synchronization Events

```
public class AsyncSrv
{
    private static ManualResetEvent AcceptEvent = new ManualResetEvent(false);
    private static ManualResetEvent ReceiveEvent = new ManualResetEvent(false);
    private static ManualResetEvent SendEvent = new ManualResetEvent(false);

    private static AsyncData ad = new AsyncData();
```

Every asynchronous operation needs to make sure that access to the data is "serialized" and controlled. Events are created to make sure that access to the **`Socket`** is synchronized. Synchronization would include ensuring that the data is completely sent out before waiting for data to come back; likewise, it would include making sure that all of the data is read before more data is sent out. That is the purpose of the **`ManualResetEvent`**'s, `AcceptEvent`, `ReceiveEvent`, and `SendEvent`.

> **Note**
>
> Synchronization and threading issues are discussed in more detail in Chapter 11, "Threading."

The single instance of `AsyncData` is created here. It is only passed for use by the receiving portion of the application.

Listing 12.19 continues the code from Listing 12.18. It shows the creation of the **`Socket`** and entering into the main processing loop.

LISTING 12.19 Asynchronous TCP Server **`Socket`** Creation and **`BeginAccept`**

```
public static Socket GetListenerSocket(string host, int port)
{
    Socket s = null;
    IPHostEntry iphe = Dns.Resolve(host);
    foreach(IPAddress ipa in iphe.AddressList)
    {
        IPEndPoint lep = new IPEndPoint(ipa, port);
        Socket ts = new Socket(lep.AddressFamily,
```

LISTING 12.19 Continued

```
                                SocketType.Stream,
                                ProtocolType.Tcp);
        try
        {
            ts.Bind(lep);
            ts.Listen(2);
            s = ts;
            break;
        }
        catch (ArgumentNullException ae)
        {
            Console.WriteLine("ArgumentNullException: " + ae.ToString());
        }
        catch (SocketException se)
        {
            Console.WriteLine("SocketException: " + se.ToString());
        }
        catch (Exception e)
        {
            Console.WriteLine("Connection failed: " + e.ToString());
        }
    }
    return s;
}
public static void Main()
{
    Socket srv = GetListenerSocket(Dns.GetHostName(), 5000);
    if(srv == null)
        return;

    Console.WriteLine("Now listening on port 5000\n");

    while (true)
    {
        AcceptEvent.Reset();
        ReceiveEvent.Reset();
        SendEvent.Reset();
        Console.WriteLine("calling BeginAccept");
        srv.BeginAccept(new AsyncCallback(AcceptCallback), srv);
        AcceptEvent.WaitOne();
    }
}
```

This code is merely an asynchronous sample of a TCP connection. Again, this code makes no assumptions about the address to which it is listening. All of this code is in the `GetListenerSocket` helper function. Creation of **`Socket`**, **`Bind`**, and **`Listen`** are identical to the calls needed to set up a synchronous TCP server; however, it is here that the application takes a different turn.

First, each of the **ManualReset** events is manually reset. **Reset** means the same as the Win32 ResetEvent in the unmanaged world. Resetting an event means the event is put in an unsignaled state. Any call to wait on that event blocks until the event is in a signaled state (a **ManualReset** event is put in a signaled state with a call to **Set**).

Next, the server calls **BeginAccept** with two arguments specifying an **AsyncCallback delegate** and the state data to be passed to the callback when the **Accept** occurs. The **AsyncCallback delegate** is constructed with a single argument that specifies the method to call, and then the callback is invoked. In this case, when the **Accept** occurs, the static method AcceptCallback is called. When **BeginAccept** is called, the call returns immediately with an object **IAsyncResult**. In general, with any of the asynchronous methods, the **IAsyncResult** object should be checked to ensure that the call did not complete synchronously. In this case, a call to **IAsyncResult.CompletedSynchronously** indicates how the call completed or if it completed at all.

The **AsyncCallback delegate** is constructed in such a way that the single argument to the construction (AcceptCallback) is called when the **Accept** occurs. **Delegate**s are handled in more detail in Chapter 14, "Delegates and Events."

Finally, the thread blocks on the AcceptEvent, waiting for a client **Accept** to occur with the **WaitOne** method. The **WaitOne** method is completely analogous to the Win32 WaitForSingleObject function in unmanaged code. What about a comparable function to WaitForMultipleObjects? A **WaitAll** is available that waits for an array of **WaitHandle**s to become signaled or a timeout to occur. **WaitAny** waits for anyone of the array of **WaitHandle**s to become signaled or a timeout to occur.

Listing 12.20 continues the code from Listing 12.19. This listing shows the first steps that the server performs after the callback is called, indicating that an **Accept** has occurred.

LISTING 12.20 Asynchronous TCP Server Accepting a Connection from a Client

```
private static void AcceptCallback(IAsyncResult result)
{
    Socket temp = (Socket) result.AsyncState;
    Socket a = temp.EndAccept(result);
```

When this function is entered, an **Accept** has occurred. The first operation is to retrieve the state information passed as an argument to **BeginAccept**, which in this case is the **Socket** that the server is using for the **Accept**. After the **Socket** is retrieved from the **AsyncState** property, this **Socket** is then used to retrieve the results of the **Accept** operation, which is always another **Socket** that is connected to the client.

Listing 12.21 is a continuation of Listing 12.20. This listing shows the server printing information about the client that has just connected and initiation of the receipt of data from the client.

LISTING 12.21 Asynchronous TCP Server Starting a Receive Operation

```
Console.WriteLine("EndAccept() Socket.EndPoint: " +
                  a.RemoteEndPoint.ToString());
ad.socket = a;

IAsyncResult recres = a.BeginReceive(ad.RecBytes,
                                      0,
                                      256,
                                      0,
                                      new AsyncCallback(ReceiveCallback),
                                      ad);

ReceiveEvent.WaitOne();
```


When a server accepts a client connection, the **Socket** that is returned as a result of the **Accept** call is a **Socket** that will be used to communicate with the client. Because this **Socket** is connected with a client, it will have a **RemoteEndPoint** property that will contain information about the endpoint associated with the client that has just connected. The client's endpoint information is printed out in Listing 12.21. Next, the server needs to initiate receiving data from the client.

In this application, a single AsyncData instance is used exclusively for **Receive**. The instance of this class is static; therefore, only one instance of this class will exist. The **Socket** that is returned from the **Accept** call is assigned to the **Socket** member of this class, as you can see in Listing 12.21. Next, the read is started with a call to **BeginReceive**.

The arguments to **BeginReceive** are similar to **Receive**. Only the last two arguments are different. The first of these (the fifth argument) is a **delegate** for a callback to occur when data is available. The second is the state information that you want to pass to the callback. These two arguments are functionally the same as the arguments passed to **BeginAccept**.

As is the case with **BeginAccept**, the thread blocks on **WaitOne** while waiting for the **Receive** to finish.

Listing 12.22 continues where Listing 12.21 left off. Remember: This is still in the AcceptCallback routine.

LISTING 12.22 Asynchronous TCP Server Sending an Asynchronous Message to the Client

```
        Byte[] byteSend = Encoding.ASCII.GetBytes(
➥"This is a test of the emergency broadcast system");

        IAsyncResult sendres = a.BeginSend(byteSend,
                                           0,
                                           byteSend.Length,
                                           0,
                                          new AsyncCallback(SendCallback),
                                          a);
        SendEvent.WaitOne();

        a.Close();
        AcceptEvent.Set();

        return;
    }
```

After the **WaitOne** call falls through because of the **Receive** completing, the next set of code sets up an asynchronous send. The arguments to **BeginSend** are identical to **BeginReceive**, with the callback set to the routine `SendCallback`.

Because the **BeginSend** completes immediately, the executing thread blocks on the **SendEvent.WaitOne**. After the send completes, and the `SendEvent` is signaled, and execution falls through to close the **Socket** and signal the `AcceptEvent` so that the server can issue another **Accept**.

Listing 12.23 continues the listing of the server code from Listing 12.22. This listing shows the callback that is called when data is received from the client.

LISTING 12.23 Asynchronous TCP Server `ReceiveCallback`

```
    private static void ReceiveCallback(IAsyncResult result)
    {
        int bytes = ad.socket.EndReceive(result);

        Console.WriteLine("[AsyncSrv] ReceiveCallback: bytes = " + bytes);

        if (bytes > 0)
        {
            string data = Encoding.ASCII.GetString(ad.RecBytes, 0, bytes);
            Console.WriteLine("Received: [" + data + "]\n");
        }

        ReceiveEvent.Set();
    }
```

The receive callback gets the results of the **Receive** by calling **EndReceive**. In this case, the "result" is the number of bytes received. Notice that this callback makes use of the fact that the instance of AsyncData is a static member value. This same AsyncData information is available from **result.AsyncState**.

Listing 12.24 is a continuation of the server code listing from Listing 12.23. This listing illustrates the first steps that are taken when the "send" callback is called.

LISTING 12.24 Asynchronous TCP Server SendCallback

```
    private static void SendCallback(IAsyncResult result)
    {
        Socket socket = (Socket) result.AsyncState;

        int bytes = socket.EndSend(result);
        Console.WriteLine("Sent: " + bytes + " bytes");

        SendEvent.Set();
    }
}
```


When this function is called, the **Send** has completed. The first thing that this function does is to call **result.AsyncState** to retrieve the state object that was passed as part of **BeginSend**. In this case, the state information is the **Socket** that is connected to the client. Calling **EndSend** retrieves the results of the **Send**, which is the number of bytes transferred. The event is then **Set**, causing it to signal any thread waiting on it that the **Send** has completed.

Because the server starts an **Accept** upon finishing with a request, a client can reconnect with the server multiple times. The output when both client and server are run on a single machine looks like Figure 12.6.

Another asynchronous sample that retrieves the contents of a Web page is included in the Samples directory for this chapter, and it is called SimpleAsync. This sample looks much the same as the AsyncClient sample illustrated in Listings 12.20–12.24, except that the connection is made to an HTTP server that serves up Web pages instead of the canned message. Look in the samples for SimpleAsync.

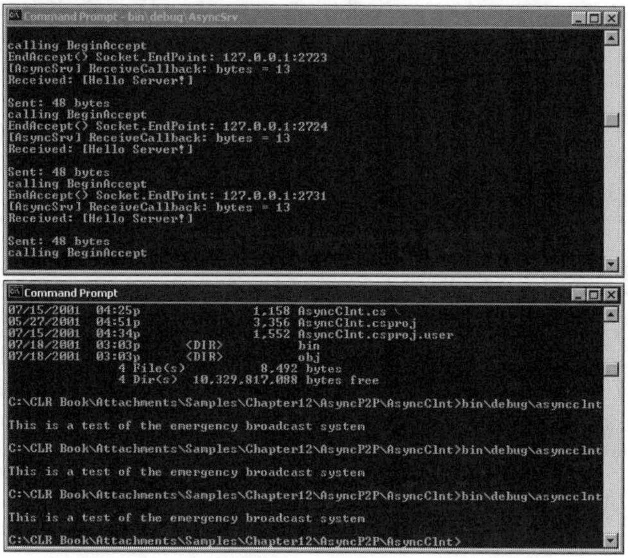

FIGURE 12.6
Asynchronous client/server.

```
calling BeginAccept
EndAccept() Socket.EndPoint: 127.0.0.1:2723
[AsyncSrv] ReceiveCallback: bytes = 13
Received: [Hello Server!]

Sent: 48 bytes
calling BeginAccept
EndAccept() Socket.EndPoint: 127.0.0.1:2724
[AsyncSrv] ReceiveCallback: bytes = 13
Received: [Hello Server!]

Sent: 48 bytes
calling BeginAccept
EndAccept() Socket.EndPoint: 127.0.0.1:2731
[AsyncSrv] ReceiveCallback: bytes = 13
Received: [Hello Server!]

Sent: 48 bytes
calling BeginAccept
```

```
07/15/2001  04:25p               1,158 AsyncClnt.cs
05/27/2001  04:51p               3,356 AsyncClnt.csproj
07/15/2001  04:34p               1,552 AsyncClnt.csproj.user
07/18/2001  03:03p      <DIR>          bin
07/18/2001  03:03p      <DIR>          obj
               4 File(s)          8,492 bytes
               4 Dir(s)  10,329,817,088 bytes free

C:\CLR Book\Attachments\Samples\Chapter12\AsyncP2P\AsyncClnt>bin\debug\asyncclnt

This is a test of the emergency broadcast system

C:\CLR Book\Attachments\Samples\Chapter12\AsyncP2P\AsyncClnt>bin\debug\asyncclnt

This is a test of the emergency broadcast system

C:\CLR Book\Attachments\Samples\Chapter12\AsyncP2P\AsyncClnt>bin\debug\asyncclnt

This is a test of the emergency broadcast system

C:\CLR Book\Attachments\Samples\Chapter12\AsyncP2P\AsyncClnt>
```

.NET Networking Transport Classes

Because TCP and UDP protocols are used so often, Microsoft built wrapper classes to handle most of the functionality required of a TCP or UDP client/server distributed application. These classes are **`TcpListener`**, **`TcpClient`**, and **`UdpClient`**. Because UDP is a connectionless protocol, the client and server can be handled with one class so there is not a `UdpListener` class.

Building a client/server application using these classes is similar to building an application using the **`Socket`** class. A higher level abstraction is involved, but the sequence of calls is essentially the same. For all but the specialized applications, you should use these classes.

UDP Class

A server using the **`UdpClient`** class is shown starting with Listing 12.25. The complete source for the code is in `UdpP2P\UdpP2Pclass\UdpListener\UDPListener.cs`. This source is illustrated in Listings 12.25–12.27.

LISTING 12.25 UDP Server Using the **UdpClient** Class

```
using System;
using System.Net;
using System.Text;
using System.Net.Sockets;

class Listener
{
    public static void Main()
    {
        Console.WriteLine("Ready to process requests...");
        ProcessRequests();
    }

    public static void ProcessRequests()
    {
        UdpClient listener = new UdpClient(5001);
        IPEndPoint remoteEp = new IPEndPoint(IPAddress.Any, 5001);
```

A **UdpClient** class is constructed with a single argument specifying with which port this class is to communicate. Alternatively, the constructor takes an **IPEndPoint** as an argument. To simplify this code, you could move the constructor for **UdpClient** below the constructor for **IPEndPoint** and pass the **IPEndPoint** instance to the constructor. You're not limited to using the **IPEndPoint** instance only once for **Receive**.

Listing 12.26 completes the listing for the server that was begun in Listing 12.25.

LISTING 12.26 UDP Server Receiving Data Using the **UdpClient** Class

```
        bool continueProcessing = true;
        while(continueProcessing)
        {
            byte[] buffer = listener.Receive(ref remoteEp);

            // string message = Encoding.ASCII.GetString(buffer,
➥0, buffer.Length);
            string message = Encoding.Unicode.GetString(buffer,
➥0, buffer.Length);
            if(message == "quit")
            {
                continueProcessing = false;
                break;
            }
            else
            {
                Console.WriteLine("The message received was " + message);
            }
```

LISTING 12.26 Continued

```
        }

        listener.Close();
    }
}
```

After the **Receive** completes, the message is decoded into a string. When the message quits, the server simply exits; otherwise, the message is printed on the **Console**. This is the same functionality as the sample using UDP **Sockets**. The user wouldn't be able to tell the difference just based on external functionality.

Listing 12.27 shows how a client might be implemented using **UdpClient**. The source that is associated with this listing is in the `UdpSender.cs` file.

LISTING 12.27 UDP Client Using **UdpClient** Class

```
using System;
using System.Net;
using System.Text;
using System.Net.Sockets;

class Sender
{

    public static void Main(string[] args)
    {
        string address = "localhost";
        if(args.Length == 1)
            address = args[0];
        bool continueSending = true;
        while(continueSending)
        {
            Console.WriteLine(
➥"Enter the message to send. Type 'quit' to exit.");
            string message = Console.ReadLine();
            SendMessage(message, address);
            if(message == "quit")
            {
                SendMessage(message, address);
                continueSending = false;
            }
        }
    }

    public static void SendMessage(string message, string server)
    {
```

LISTING 12.27 Continued

```
        try
        {
                UdpClient client = new UdpClient(5002);
                // byte[] buffer = Encoding.ASCII.GetBytes(message);
                byte[] buffer = Encoding.Unicode.GetBytes(message);
                client.Send(buffer, buffer.Length, server, 5001);
                client.Close();
        }
        catch(Exception ex)
        {
            Console.WriteLine(ex.ToString());
        }
    }
}
```


The code for **Main** is virtually identical to that used for a **Socket** implementation. The only code that has changed from using a **Socket** is that in `SendMessage`. Compare the code for `SendMessage` with the code for `SendMessage` in Listing 12.10. There is considerably less code here than with `SendMessage` using **Socket**. The **Bind** occurs in the constructor for the **UdpClient**. Converting the data using the **Encoding** class is the same. The **UdpClient** sends data using **Send** rather than the **Socket** class **SendTo**. Adding code to account for this is hidden so far, which is possible within the **UdpClient** class.

Because the output is so similar to the UDP **Socket** client/server, the output is not included here.

TCP Class

For a TCP client/server, Listing 12.28 illustrates a server that uses the **TcpListener** class. The complete source that is associated with this class is in the `TcpP2P\TcpP2PClass` directory.

LISTING 12.28 TCP Server Using **TcpListener**

```
using System;
using System.Text;
using System.Net;
using System.Net.Sockets;

class Listener
{

    public static void Main()
    {
        Console.WriteLine("Ready to process requests...");
        ProcessRequests();
```

LISTING 12.28 Continued

```
    }

    public static void ProcessRequests()
    {
        TcpListener client = new TcpListener(5000);
        client.Start();
        Socket s = client.AcceptSocket();
```

You construct the **TcpListener** using a single argument of the port on which this server is to listen. This causes the server to listen on the specified port and **IPAddress.Any**. If you want more control over the address to which the server is to listen, two other forms of the constructor take either an **IPEndPoint** or an **IPAddress** and port number.

Notice that no calls are to **Bind** or **Listen**. You can't specify the number of queued connections to be used by the **Listen** call. All of this is handled in the **Start** method. If you need this added control, consider dropping down to the **Socket** level and implementing the required functionality there. You could also use **TcpListener** as a base class and override **Start** to implement a custom **Start**.

The server blocks waiting for a client connection in the call to **AcceptSocket**. This is a wrapper around **Socket.Accept**.

Listing 12.29 shows how the server reads the data from the client using the **Socket** created from **AcceptSocket**. This listing is a continuation of Listing 12.28.

LISTING 12.29 TCP Server Reading a Message from a Client Using **TcpListener**

```
        byte[] responseData = new byte[128];
        bool continueProcessing = true;

        while(continueProcessing)
        {
            try
            {
                int bytesRead = s.Receive(responseData);
                // string message = Encoding.ASCII.GetString(responseData,
➥0, bytesRead);
                string message = Encoding.Unicode.GetString(responseData,
➥0, bytesRead);
                if(message == "quit")
                {
                    continueProcessing = false;
                    break;
                }
                else
                {
```

LISTING 12.29 Continued

```
                    Console.WriteLine("The message received was " + message);
                }
            }
            catch(Exception ex)
            {
                Console.WriteLine(ex.ToString());
            }
        }
        client.Stop();
    }
}
```

This is the receiving portion of the server that uses the **Socket** returned from **AcceptSocket**. The call to **s.Receive(responseData)** uses a form of the **Receive** function that assumes the size of the data from the size of the buffer. You can optionally use the other forms of this function that take an offset and size so that a buffer can be "appended" in chunks.

If you do not want to have a lowly **Socket**, then you can call **AcceptTcpClient**, which builds an instance of **TcpClient** from the **Socket** that is returned from **Accept**. If you use **AcceptTcpClient**, you need to replace the code shown in Listing 12.29 with that shown in Listing 12.30; **TcpClient** does not have a **Receive** method.

LISTING 12.30 TCP Server Using **TcpClient** Rather Than a **Socket**

```
// Socket s = client.AcceptSocket();
TcpClient s = client.AcceptTcpClient();
. . .
NetworkStream stream = s.GetStream();
. . .
while(continueProcessing)
{
    try
    {
        bytesRead = stream.Read(responseData, 0, responseData.Length);
        if(bytesRead == 0)
        {
            // The client disconnected
            continueProcessing = false;
            break;
        }
        else
        {
            message = Encoding.Unicode.GetString(responseData,
➥0, bytesRead);
```

LISTING 12.31 Continued

```
            if(message == "quit")
            {
                continueProcessing = false;
                break;
            }
            else
            {
                Console.WriteLine(
➥"The message received was " + message);
            }
        }
    }
    catch(Exception ex)
    {
        Console.WriteLine(ex.ToString());
    }
```

This code reads the data into a buffer from a stream. This implementation requires that the data that the user types fit into the 128-byte `responseData` buffer. By sending and receiving Unicode in this sample, you are limiting the text that the user can enter to 64 characters. If this is too severe a limitation, it is easy enough to modify the code to read in a chunk at a time, appending the data to a buffer as you go.

You have seen the two different ways that a server can receive an **`Accept`**ed **`Socket`** and read data from a client. Both have advantages, so the ultimate decision rests in the design of the application in which these classes are used.

The next set of listings shows a client implementation using the **`TcpClient`** class. The complete source for the code is in `TcpP2P\TcpP2PClass\TcpSender\TcpSender.cs` and illustrated in Listings 12.31–12.32.

LISTING 12.31 TCP Client Using **`TcpClient`**

```
using System;
using System.Text;
using System.IO;
using System.Net;
using System.Net.Sockets;

class Sender
{

    public static void Main(string[] args)
    {
        string address = "localhost";
        if(args.Length == 1)
```

LISTING 12.31 Continued

```
            address = args[0];

        SendMessage(address);
    }

    public static void SendMessage(string server)
    {
        TcpClient client = new TcpClient();
        client.Connect(server, 5000);
        NetworkStream stream = client.GetStream();
```


A **TcpClient** is constructed to communicate with the server. A default constructor is used, but alternatively, you could construct an **IPEndPoint** and pass that to the constructor and the **Connect** method. **Connect** takes the same types of arguments that the constructor supports, so it is reasonable to build an **IPEndPoint** or an **IPAddress** and port number. After the client is connected, the code retrieves a **NetworkStream** from the instance of the client. This stream will be used to write to the port.

Listing 12.32 is a continuation of Listing 12.31 and completes the listing for this client application.

LISTING 12.32 TCP Client Sending a Message to a Server Using **TcpClient**

```
        bool continueSending = true;
        while(continueSending)
        {
            Console.WriteLine(
➥"Enter the message to send. Type 'quit' to exit.");
            string message = Console.ReadLine();
            // byte[] buffer = Encoding.ASCII.GetBytes(message);
            byte[] buffer = Encoding.Unicode.GetBytes(message);
            stream.Write(buffer, 0, buffer.Length);
            if(message == "quit")
            {
                continueSending = false;
            }
        }

        client.Close();

    }
}
```

Just like the client/server applications described earlier, this code stays in a `while` loop until the user enters “quit”. Each message is written to the server using **stream.Write**.

Because the output is so similar to the TCP **Socket** client/server, the output is not included here.

What about using the network classes to send SOAP? Although doing so might sound difficult, it is surprisingly easy. What if the client and server illustrated previously talked in SOAP instead? Listing 12.33 illustrates a server communicating using SOAP.

Note

You can find a more detailed discussion of SOAP in Chapter 13, "Building Distributed Applications with .NET Remoting."

LISTING 12.33 TCP Server Communicating Via SOAP

```
using System;
using System.Net;
using System.Net.Sockets;
using System.Runtime.Serialization.Formatters.Soap;
using System.Runtime.Serialization.Formatters.Binary;

class Listener
{

    public static void Main()
    {
        Console.WriteLine("Ready to process requests...");
        ProcessRequests();
    }

    public static void ProcessRequests()
    {
        TcpListener client = new TcpListener(455);
        client.Start();
        bool continueProcessing = true;
        while(continueProcessing)
        {
            Socket s = client.AcceptSocket();
            NetworkStream ns = new NetworkStream(s);
            // BinaryFormatter channel = new BinaryFormatter();
            SoapFormatter channel = new SoapFormatter();
            string message = (string)channel.Deserialize(ns);
            if(message == "quit")
            {
                continueProcessing = false;
            }
            else
```

LISTING 12.33 Continued

```
            {
                Console.WriteLine("The message received was " + message);
            }
        }
        client.Stop();
    }
}
```

This server code is almost identical to the server code that is using a **TcpListener**, but this code creates an instance of a **NetworkStream** from the **Socket** returned from **AcceptSocket**. A **SoapFormatter** instance is also created.

> **Note**
>
> If the client and server agree on the format of the data being passed, the commented out code constructing a **BinaryFormatter** could be used instead of the **SoapFormatter**. This would have some significant performance benefits at the expense of limiting the type of client that can connect with this server. A binary formatted message might also be harder to understand.

The server is expecting a SOAP message. The **SoapFormatter** class does the work of deserializing the message from the client into the object that the client intended to send (in this case, it was a string). Serialization issues are covered in Chapter 13 and in Chapter 17, "Reflection."

The client code in Listing 12.34 shows how the string is serialized and transferred to the server.

LISTING 12.34 TCP Client Communicating Via SOAP

```
using System;
using System.IO;
using System.Net;
using System.Net.Sockets;
using System.Runtime.Serialization.Formatters.Soap;
using System.Runtime.Serialization.Formatters.Binary;

class Sender
{

    public static void Main(string[] args)
    {
```

LISTING 12.34 Continued

```
        string address = "localhost";
        if(args.Length == 1)
            address = args[0];

        bool continueSending = true;
        while(continueSending)
        {
            Console.WriteLine("Enter the message to send.");
            string message = Console.ReadLine();
            SendMessage(message, address);
            if(message == "quit")
            {
                continueSending = false;
            }
        }
    }

    public static void SendMessage(string message, string server)
    {
        TcpClient client = new TcpClient();
        client.Connect(server, 455);

        // BinaryFormatter channel = new BinaryFormatter();
        SoapFormatter channel = new SoapFormatter();

        channel.Serialize(client.GetStream(), message);
        client.Close();
    }
}
```

Again, the code is almost identical to the client code presented previously. The exception is that here you serialize the object (string) out on the network by using the **SoapFormatter** class.

Understanding the **SoapFormatter** and the **BinaryFormatter** becomes more important when you delve into remoting in the following chapter. After entering the string "Hello World!" on the client, you can see the serialized version of the string, using the **SoapFormatter**, as shown in Listing 12.35.

LISTING 12.35 SOAP Message for "Hello World!"

```
<SOAP-ENV:Envelope xmlns:xsi="http://www.w3.org/2001/XMLSchema-instance"
xmlns:xsd="http://www.w3.org/2001/XMLSchema" xmlns:SOAP-
ENC="http://schemas.xmlsoap.org/soap/encoding/" xmlns:SOAP-
ENV="http://schemas.xmlsoap.org/soap/envelope/" SOAP-
ENV:encodingStyle="http://schemas.xmlsoap.org/soap/encoding/">
```

LISTING 12.35 Continued

```
<SOAP-ENV:Body>
        <SOAP-ENC:string id="ref-1">Hello World!</SOAP-ENC:string>
</SOAP-ENV:Body>
</SOAP-ENV:Envelope>
```

To keep the SOAP message as well-formed XML, you might have to escape some of the characters. If you enter the string "<>[]&Testing", you will see the SOAP that is sent, as shown in Listing 12.36.

LISTING 12.36 SOAP Message for "<>[]&Testing"

```
<SOAP-ENV:Envelope xmlns:xsi="http://www.w3.org/2001/XMLSchema-instance"
xmlns:xsd="http://www.w3.org/2001/XMLSchema" xmlns:SOAP-
ENC="http://schemas.xmlsoap.org/soap/encoding/" xmlns:SOAP-
ENV="http://schemas.xmlsoap.org/soap/envelope/" SOAP-
ENV:encodingStyle="http://schemas.xmlsoap.org/soap/encoding/">
<SOAP-ENV:Body>
        <SOAP-ENC:string id="ref-1">&#60;&#62;[]&#38;Testing</SOAP-ENC:string>
</SOAP-ENV:Body>
</SOAP-ENV:Envelope>
```

Some of the characters have been turned into XML escaped characters to avoid the conflict with characters that XML uses. On deserialization, these characters are automatically and properly converted back into the characters that were typed.

Benchmark

Before moving on, I would like to introduce a tool that I have found useful in understanding the difference between network programming in an unmanaged world and network programming in a managed world. This tool allows me to compare implementations within the managed world. I can compare the low level **Socket** implementation versus the higher level classes for performance. I can also implement a managed version using asynchronous methods so I can compare the throughput.

In designing an application, you should certainly consider more than the throughput illustrated by this application. This application might not even adequately simulate your application, so the performance numbers might not apply.

I have found the Benchmark tool useful for two reasons:

- It has eased my concern considerably about the performance of a managed application. The numbers are so close that you could not reject the managed approach strictly on these performance figures.

- It further illustrates that throughput should not be the only reason to make an application multithreaded or asynchronous. You will not see much difference in throughput between the asynchronous and the synchronous versions.

How does Benchmark work? In all cases, I have tested only a client. Each test connects with a well-known "echo" service on a given machine. Following the connection, a "packet" is sent to the service of a specified size. The service takes this packet of information and echoes it back (hence the name of the service is "echo"). This process is repeated for the number of times specified in the dialog box.

A screenshot of this benchmark tool is shown in Figure 12.7.

I have purposely not included specific benchmark figures because these figures are highly dependent on the client and server hardware on which this test is run. You should build and run this tool on an environment that is of interest. All of the source can be found in the directory `Benchmark` with the other source. I hope that more tests can be developed. Please let me know if you experience problems, if you find this tool particularly useful, or if you are able to extend the test set. I can be reached at `Kevin.Burton@iNewsRoom.com`.

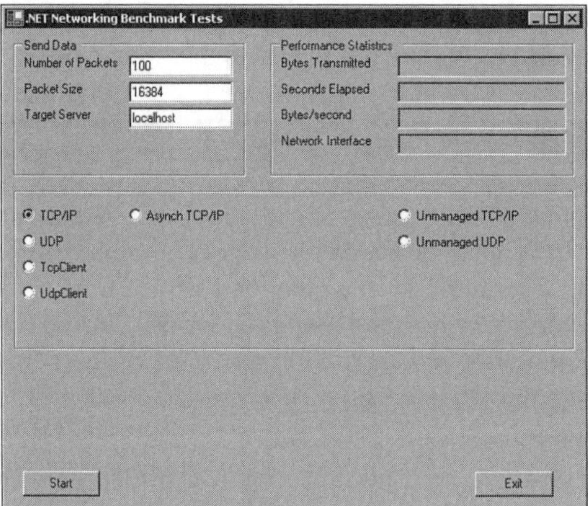

FIGURE 12.7
Benchmark tool.

.NET Protocol Classes

Some classes within the System.Net namespace make connecting to a Web site easy. These classes include **`WebRequest`**, **`WebResponse`**, **`HttpWebRequest`**, **`HttpWebResponse`**, **`FileWebRequest`**, **`FileWebResponse`**, and **`WebClient`**.

These classes provide the following features:

- Support for HTTP, HTTPS, FILE, and so on
- Asynchronous development
- Simple methods for uploading and downloading data

This list of classes might seem like too many classes to handle; however, with the exception of **`WebClient`**, the request classes derive from **`WebRequest`**, and the response classes derive from **`WebResponse`**.

Support for HTTP, HTTPS, and FILE

The request object is generated from the static **`WebRequest.Create`** method, and the **`WebResponse`** object is generated from the request object's (`WebRequest`) **`GetResponse`** method. The type of request that is generated (http or file) depends on the scheme that is passed as part of the URL. If you use `http://www.microsoft.com` as your URL, then an **`HttpWebRequest`** object is generated from **`WebRequest.Create`**. Using SSL/TSL with `https://` is handled automatically by the **`HttpWebRequest`** object. In contrast, if you are trying to access a file such as `file:///C:\temp\sample.txt`, then a **`FileWebRequest`** object is generated.

The **`WebClient`** client is similar to the `WebRequest` classes in that the protocol is handled automatically. If a URL such as `https://www.microsoft.com/net/` is given to the `WebClient`, then the SSL/TSL communication is handled automatically. Similarly, if you use a "file" URL, it is also transparently handled. Try using the following URL:

`file:///D:/Program%20Files/Microsoft.Net/FrameworkSDK/Samples/StartSamples.htm.`

The instance of the **`WebClient`** recognizes that the protocol to be used is file rather than going through IIS or a valid HTTP server.

One of the easiest ways to interact with a Web page is using the `WebClient` class. Listing 12.37 shows an example of using the `WebClient` class. The complete source for this sample is included with the other source in the directory `WebPage/WebBuffer`.

LISTING 12.37 Retrieving the Content of a Web Page Using `WebClient`

```
using System;
using System.Net;
using System.Text;
using System.IO;

public class WebBuffer
```

LISTING 12.37 Continued

```
{
    public static void Main(string[] args)
    {
        try
        {
            string address = "http://www.microsoft.com";
            if(args.Length == 1)
                address = args[0];

            WebClient wc = new WebClient();

            Stream stream = wc.OpenRead(address);

            StreamReader reader = new StreamReader(
➥wc.OpenRead(address), Encoding.ASCII);
            Console.WriteLine(reader.ReadToEnd());
        }
        catch(Exception ex)
        {
            Console.WriteLine(ex.ToString());
        }
    }
}
```

Even simpler, the three lines in Listing 12.37

```
Stream stream = wc.OpenRead(address);
StreamReader reader = new StreamReader(wc.OpenRead(address), Encoding.ASCII);
Console.WriteLine(reader.ReadToEnd());
```

can be replaced with a single line:

```
Console.WriteLine(Encoding.ASCII.GetString(wc.DownloadData(address)));
```

This achieves the same effect and is easy.

Alternatively, but just as easy, you can use the **WebRequest/WebResponse** classes. Listing 12.38 shows how to use the **WebRequest/WebResponse** classes to retrieve the contents of a Web page. The source for this listing is under the directory `WebPage/HttpBuffer`.

LISTING 12.38 Retrieving the Content of a Web Page Using **WebRequest/WebResponse** Classes

```
using System;
using System.Net;
using System.Text;
using System.IO;
```

LISTING 12.38 Continued

```
public class HttpBuffer
{
    public static void Main(string[] args)
    {
        try
        {
            string address = "http://www.microsoft.com";
            if(args.Length == 1)
                address = args[0];

            WebRequest request = WebRequest.Create(address);
            WebResponse response = request.GetResponse();
            StreamReader reader = new StreamReader(
➥response.GetResponseStream(), Encoding.ASCII);
            Console.WriteLine(reader.ReadToEnd());
            response.Close();
        }
        catch(Exception ex)
        {
            Console.WriteLine(ex.ToString());
        }
    }
}
```


You can choose from so many different options! Remember that because the code shown in Listings 12.37 and 12.38 uses either **`WebClient`** or **`WebRequest`**, you are not restricted to just `http://` schemes.

Asynchronous Development

The request object does not do anything until either **`GetResponse`** (or its asynchronous version **`BeginGetResponse`** discussed later) or **`GetRequestStream`** is called. By calling **`GetResponse`**, you are telling the request object to connect to the URL given and download the contents that the URL specifies when the request is generated (typically, this is HTML). If a **`Stream`** is retrieved via **`GetRequestStream`**, commands can be written directly to the server, and **`GetResponse`** is called to retrieve the results of those commands.

Because of this separation between the response and the request, you are able to easily build an asynchronous Web page content extractor. Listings 12.39–12.42 illustrate how to use the asynchronous methods to asynchronously obtain the contents of a Web page. The full source for this sample can be found in `WebPage\WebAsynch`. Listing 12.39 shows a declaration of the state classes that will be used in this sample.

LISTING 12.39 Retrieving the Content of a Web Page Using Asynchronous **WebRequest/WebResponse** Classes

```
using System;
using System.Net;
using System.Text;
using System.IO;
using System.Threading;

public class AsyncResponseData
{
    public AsyncResponseData (WebRequest webRequest)
    {
        this.webRequest = webRequest;
        this.responseDone = new ManualResetEvent(false);
    }
    public WebRequest Request
    {
        get
        {
            return webRequest;
        }
    }
    public ManualResetEvent ResponseEvent
    {
        get
        {
            return responseDone;
        }
    }
    private WebRequest webRequest;
    private ManualResetEvent responseDone;
}
public class AsyncReadData
{
    public AsyncReadData (Stream stream)
    {
        this.stream = stream;
        bytesRead = -1;
        readDone = new ManualResetEvent(false);
                page = new StringBuilder();
    }
    public Stream GetStream
    {
        get
        {
            return stream;
        }
    }
    public byte [] Buffer
    {
```

LISTING 12.39 Continued

```
        get
        {
            return buffer;
        }
        set
        {
            buffer = value;
        }
    }
    public int ReadCount
    {
        get
        {
            return bytesRead;
        }
        set
        {
            bytesRead = value;
        }
    }
    public StringBuilder Page
    {
        get
        {
            return page;
        }
        set
        {
            page = value;
        }
    }
    public ManualResetEvent ReadEvent
    {
        get
        {
            return readDone;
        }
    }
    private Stream stream;
    private byte[] buffer = new byte[4096];
    private int bytesRead = 0;
    private StringBuilder page;
    private ManualResetEvent readDone;
}
```

This first part declares the state classes for the response and the read of the data. Compare this to the `AsyncData` class in the `AsynchSrv` sample illustrated in Listings 12.17–12.24. These classes have considerably more code than in the `AsynchSrv` sample.

The only difference is that synchronization events have been encapsulated and accessors have been added for better programming practice. Continue this sample with Listing 12.40.

LISTING 12.40 Retrieving the Content of a Web Page Using Asynchronous **WebRequest/WebResponse** Classes (continued)

```
public class WebAsynch
{
    public static void Main(string[] args)
    {
        try
        {
            string address = "http://localhost/QuickStart/HowTo/";
            if(args.Length == 1)
                address = args[0];

            WebRequest request = WebRequest.Create(address);

            AsyncResponseData ad = new AsyncResponseData (request);
            IAsyncResult responseResult =
➥request.BeginGetResponse(new AsyncCallback(ResponseCallback),
                                     ad);
            ad.ResponseEvent.WaitOne();
        }
        catch(Exception ex)
        {
            Console.WriteLine(ex.ToString());
        }
    }
```

Here is the main entry point for the sample. First, a **WebRequest** object is constructed. Next, an AsyncResponseData object is constructed with a single argument of the **WebRequest** object. This constructor initializes its members and constructs a synchronization object. With the construction of these two objects, the process of getting the Web page is started with **BeginGetResponse**. The call to **BeginGetResponse** immediately returns in all cases. The case that has not been accounted for is if the asynchronous event completed synchronously—in other words, if it were such a short operation that the OS decided it was not worth it to call the callback specified. It has been assumed here that the callback will always occur.

This listing waits for the operation to complete by waiting for the ResponseEvent to be signaled. This event is signaled in the ResponseCallback routine, which is illustrated in Listing 12.41.

LISTING 12.41 Retrieving the Content of a Web Page Using Asynchronous `WebRequest/WebResponse` Classes (continued)

```
    private static void ResponseCallback(IAsyncResult result)
    {
        AsyncResponseData ar = (AsyncResponseData)result.AsyncState;
        WebRequest request = ar.Request;
        WebResponse response = request.EndGetResponse(result);
        Stream stream = response.GetResponseStream();
        AsyncReadData ad = new AsyncReadData(stream);
        IAsyncResult readResult = stream.BeginRead(ad.Buffer,
                                                   0,
                                                   ad.Buffer.Length,
                                                   new AsyncCallback(ReadCallback),
                                                   ad);
        ad.ReadEvent.WaitOne();
        ar.ResponseEvent.Set();
    }
```


Much of this code should be familiar to you by now. The state object that was passed (**`WebRequest`**) is retrieved with **`AsyncState`**. The **`WebRequest`** object is retrieved and **`EndGetResponse`** is called to retrieve the **`WebResponse`** object. Although the types might change, this sequence is repeated for just about every **`AsyncCallback`** delegate that is called. Now you are in position to read the data.

Caution

The stream that is associated with the **`WebResponse`** is retrieved using **`GetResponseStream()`**. When I first built this example, I was trying to keep it as simple as possible. I tried to read all of the data from the stream by building a **`StreamReader`** class and calling the **`ReadToEnd()`** as was done with the code illustrated in the synchronous version in Listing 12.38. Doing this caused the application to lock up, and the read never completed. Upon further investigation and after some advice, I concluded that mixing asynchronous code with synchronous code wasn't a good idea. After I made the read asynchronous as well, the read completed and the application worked just fine.

Don't mix synchronous code with asynchronous code. In particular, don't call synchronous methods on objects that were constructed asynchronously (in a callback for instance).

With that lesson learned, I called **`BeginRead`** to start an asynchronous read from the stream. Next, I waited for the read to complete. Listing 12.42 continues from Listing 12.41 illustrating the read callback. After the read has completed, you can set the

`ResponseEvent` so that the main thread can fall through and the application can terminate cleanly.

LISTING 12.42 Retrieving the Content of a Web Page Using Asynchronous **WebRequest/WebResponse** Classes (continued)

```
    private static void ReadCallback(IAsyncResult result)
    {
        AsyncReadData ad = (AsyncReadData)result.AsyncState;
        Stream stream = ad.GetStream;
        int bytesRead = stream.EndRead(result);
        if(bytesRead == 0)
        {
            // The end of the read
            Console.WriteLine(ad.Page.ToString());
            ad.ReadEvent.Set();
        }
        else
        {
            ad.Page.Append(Encoding.ASCII.GetString(ad.Buffer, 0, bytesRead));
            IAsyncResult readResult = stream.BeginRead(ad.Buffer,
                                                       0,
                                                       ad.Buffer.Length,
                                                       new AsyncCallback(ReadCallback),
                                                       ad);
        }
    }
}
```

This code retrieves the `AsyncReadData` object using the **`AsyncState`** method of the **`IAsyncResult`** interface. From there, the number of bytes read is returned. If the number of bytes is not zero, then another read request is queued up after the current read is appended to the contents of the page. If the number of bytes read is zero, then no more data is available to be read. When no more data is to be read, the page contents are written out to the **`Console`** and the `ReadEvent` is set to indicate that reading has finished. This process is a little more involved than synchronously reading the contents of a Web page, but it is nice to know that the option is available.

Simple Methods for Uploading and Downloading Data

The final key feature of the .NET Protocol classes is they provide simple and effective methods for uploading and downloading data.

Download to a Buffer

You have already seen many examples of downloading data from a Web page into a buffer. You have looked at methods of reading data from a Web page a chunk at a time, and you have seen methods that put the entire page into a buffer at one time. (Look at the discussion following Listing 12.37 on alternatives for the **DownloadData** method of **WebClient**.) You don't need to belabor this issue any further.

Download to a File

After data is in memory, a programmer can write code to write that data to a file with relative ease. Be aware, however, that a method of the **WebClient** class can do that for you. If you want the data to go directly to a file, then replace code like this:

```
byte[] buffer = wc.DownloadData(address);
Console.WriteLine(Encoding.ASCII.GetString(buffer));
```

with

```
wc.DownloadFile(address, "default.aspx");
```

The data will be downloaded to a file called `default.aspx`. Alternatively, you could supply a full path to the file, and the file would be created at the path that is specified.

Download with a Stream

If you need a little more control over the read process, you can replace the **DownloadFile** method in the previous section with the following code shown in Listing 12.43.

LISTING 12.43 Retrieving the Content of a Web Page Using a Stream

```
Stream stream = wc.OpenRead(address);

// Now read in s into a byte buffer.
byte[] bytes = new byte[1000];
int numBytesToRead = (int) bytes.Length;
int numBytesRead = 0;
while ((numBytesRead = stream.Read(bytes, 0, numBytesToRead)) >= 0)
{
    // Read may return anything from 0 to numBytesToRead.
    // You're at EOF
    if (numBytesRead == 0)
        break;
    Console.WriteLine(Encoding.ASCII.GetString(bytes, 0, numBytesRead));
}

stream.Close();
```

Uploading Data

The methods for uploading data to a server include **UploadFile**, **UploadData**, and **OpenStream**. These methods take similar arguments to the download functions. Before testing these functions, make sure that the server is prepared to handle the upload; otherwise, you will get an exception:

```
System.Net.WebException: The remote server returned an error:
➥(405) Method Not Allowed.
   at System.Net.HttpWebRequest.CheckFinalStatus()
   at System.Net.HttpWebRequest.EndGetResponse(IAsyncResult asyncResult)
   at System.Net.HttpWebRequest.GetResponse()
   at System.Net.WebClient.UploadData(String address,
➥String method, Byte[] data)
   at System.Net.WebClient.UploadData(String address, Byte[] data)
   at WebUpload.Main(String[] args) in webupload.cs:line 18
```

Windows Applications

Before concluding, this section will present two more samples. These samples show that all of the APIs and classes presented earlier in this chapter can be integrated easily into a Windows application.

The first sample gets the source for a Web page and displays some rudimentary properties of that connection. Most of this sample is code to display the result, so it will be discussed here. The sample is available as part of the source to this book. The core functionality boils down to the following few lines in Listing 12.44. The full source to this sample can be found in the directory `WebPage\HTMLViewer`. This listing comes from `HTMLViewer.cs`.

LISTING 12.44 Retrieving the Content of a Web Page

```
string strAddress = url.Text.Trim();
strAddress = strAddress.ToLower();
. . . .
// create the GetWebPageSource object
page = new HTMLPageGet(strAddress);
strSource = page.Source;
showSource();
```

The `HTMLPageGet` is a class that has been defined and will be shown next. This class is constructed with the URL that the user inputs into the text box. As part of the construction, the class retrieves the Web page associated with the URL given. The Web page is then passed back to the user via the `page.Source` property. Finally, `showSource()` is called to display the page.

Now look at the HTMLPageGet class, which does all of the work. Listing 12.45 shows the essential parts of the source. The full source can be found in WebPage\HTMLViewer. This listing comes from the file HTMLPageGet.cs.

LISTING 12.45 HTMLPageGet Class

```
        private WebRequest request;
        private WebResponse response;
        private StringBuilder strSource = new StringBuilder();
        public HTMLPageGet(string url)
        {
            try
            {
                request = WebRequest.Create(url);
                response = request.GetResponse();
                // get the stream of data
                StreamReader sr = new StreamReader(
➥response.GetResponseStream(), Encoding.ASCII);
                string strTemp;
                while ((strTemp = sr.ReadLine()) != null)
                {
                    strSource.Append(strTemp + "\r\n");
                }
                sr.Close();
            }
            catch (WebException ex)
            {
                strSource.Append(ex.Message);
            }
```


This code snippet shows the essential portions of the class: the request and response objects and a portion of the constructor. This shows how easy it is to communicate with a Web server. The request object is constructed with **WebRequest.Create**. This function returns either an **HttpWebRequest** (if the scheme is http:// or https://) or **FileWebRequest** (if the scheme is file://). Both of these classes are derived from **WebRequest**; therefore, an **HttpWebRequest** object or a **FileWebReqeust** object can be created from **WebRequest.Create**. If you really want to know what object has been returned, then you can run a test like this in C#:

```
if(request is HttpWebRequest)
{
. . . . .
}
```

After the request object has been constructed, a call is made to **GetResponse** to return the contents of the file or Web page. The contents are read back using an instance of the **StreamReader** class and **Append**ed a line at a time to a string.

The application starts out like Figure 12.8.

FIGURE 12.8
Initial Web application startup.

After the URL has been entered and the Source button has been activated, the application looks like Figure 12.9.

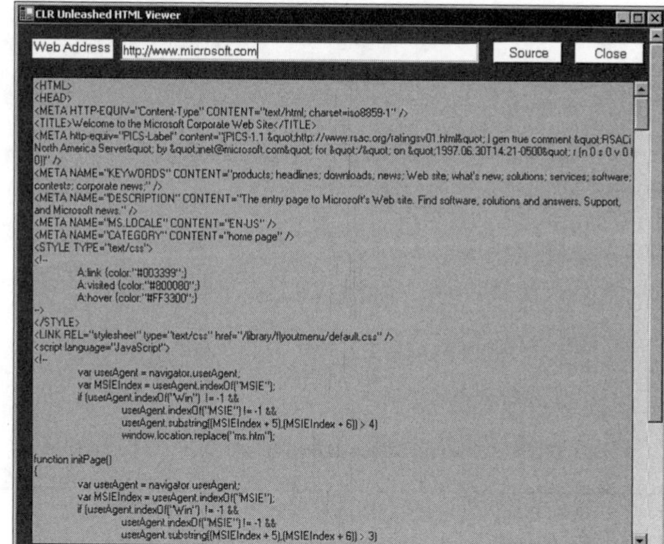

FIGURE 12.9
Web application after entering a URL.

This application demonstrates that a small amount of code can do a job that used to take substantially more custom code.

One common practice today is to pull information from a Web site by parsing the Web page and extracting the information desired. This is known as *screen-scraping*. It is far from an ideal solution because the producers of the Web page have no obligation to keep the format the same. Changing the font color or style or even changing the order of the rendered items could radically alter the format of the HTML that is presenting the information, causing the parse or the screen-scrape to fail. Using Web services or SOAP yields a much better way to present information to the user.

Now look at a simple application that pulls stock information from a Web site. The application pulls the interesting data from the page and caches it away so that it can be retrieved and displayed. Again, most of the code displays the UI, so that code will not be presented here. Figure 12.10 shows the initial appearance of the stock-quote application. The complete source for this application is in the `WebPage\StockInfo` directory.

FIGURE 12.10
Initial screen of stock quote application.

Figure 12.11 shows the raw HTML that forms the source of the stock quote information.

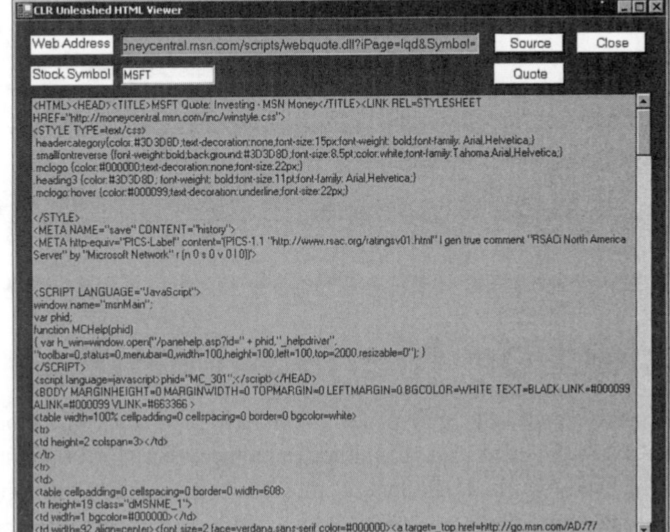

FIGURE 12.11
Source of the Web page supplying the stock quote information.

Figure 12.12 shows the stock quote information that has been successfully extracted from the Web page source.

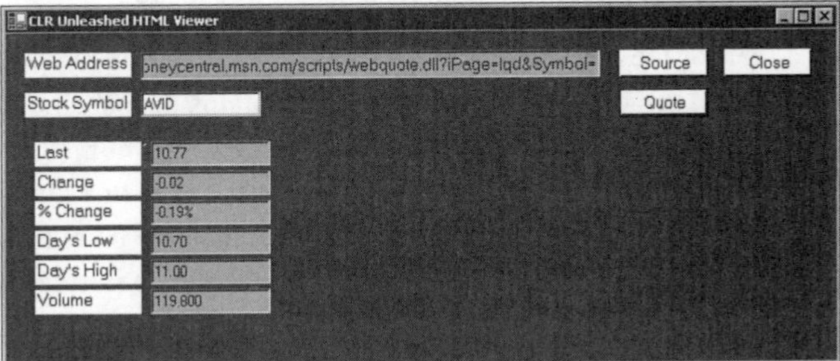

FIGURE 12.12
The quote information.

Figure 12.13 shows what the Web page looks like when viewed with Internet Explorer.

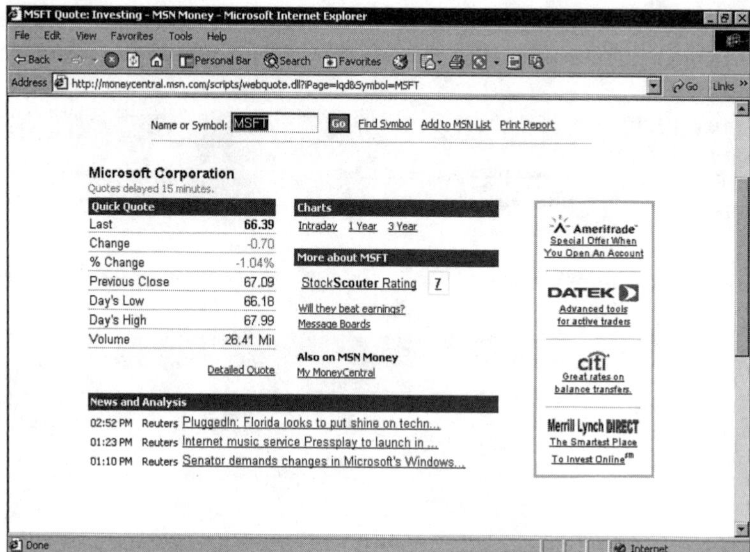

FIGURE 12.13
Viewing the Web page with Internet Explorer.

The complete source for this project is in the `WebPage\StockInfo` directory.

Connection Management

The CLR manages code at a "global" level. You have seen many of the benefits of managed code. One of the benefits is that although an individual thread might have lowered performance because of the additional overhead of "management," the application as a whole greatly benefits. This same philosophy is behind managing connections.

A **`ServicePoint`** provides an application with an endpoint to connect to Internet resources. More important, a **`ServicePoint`** class contains information that can aide in optimizing connections. Each **`ServicePoint`** is identified with a Uniform Resource Identifier (URI), or more specifically, an instance of **`Uri class`**.

You can get a feel for the type of information contained in a **`Uri`** by looking at the **`Uri`** class (or the **`UriBuilder`** class) documentation. It contains the scheme, the address, and path information. For the URL `https://www.microsoft.com/net/`, the scheme is `https`, the address is `www.microsoft.com`, and the path is `/net/`. The **`Uri`** class can determine if a query (after the ?), fragment (after the #), or any name/value pairs (&name=value) exist. Based on the scheme, the **`Uri`** class can determine which port should be used to communicate using the specified scheme. A **`Uri`** contains much information.

A **ServicePointManager** can use the information contained in the **Uri** of a **ServicePoint** to categorize each **ServicePoint**. For example, the two URLs `http://msdn.microsoft.com/library/default.asp?url=/library/en-us/cpref/html/frlrfsystemnetauthorizationclasstopic.asp` and `http://msdn.microsoft.com/library/default.asp?url=/library/en-us/cpref/html/frlrfsystemnetcookieclasstopic.asp` have the same scheme (`http`) and the same host (`www.microsoft.com`). Rather than performing two connections, a managed application should realize that one connection has already been established and use that connection to perform the specified action given by the rest of the URL. That is in part what the **ServicePointManager** does.

ServicePoint and ServicePointManager

The **ServicePointManager** creates a **ServicePoint** whenever an application requests a resource that does not already have a **ServicePoint** associated with it in a given category. In two cases, the **ServicePoint** is destroyed. If the **ServicePoint** has been around for too long (it exceeds the **MaxServicePointIdleTime** property of **ServicePointManager**; default value of 900,000 milliseconds, or 15 minutes), the **ServicePoint** is removed from the list of active connections. In addition, if there are too many **ServicePoint**s (it exceeds **MaxServicePoints**; default of 0, which means no limit), the **ServicePoint** that has the longest idle time is destroyed.

Perhaps the single most influential property of a **ServicePoint** is its **ConnectionLimit**. For an **HttpWebRequest**, the default **ConnectionLimit** is set to 2. This means that at most, two persistent connections will exist between a client and server for a given application. The **ConnectionLimit** can be set on a per-**ServicePoint** basis, or a default value for each new **ServicePoint** that the **ServicePointManager** creates can be set with **DefaultConnectionLimit**.

Connection Management and Performance

Listings 12.46–12.50 demonstrate the performance increase that is possible by modifying the **ConnectionLimit** on a **ServicePoint**. The source for this code can be found in the `ServicePoint` directory.

LISTING 12.46 **ServicePoint.ConnectionLimit** RequestState

```
using System;
using System.Net;
using System.Threading;
using System.Text;
using System.IO;
```

LISTING 12.46 Continued

```
namespace ServicePointDemo
{
    public class RequestState
    {
        private StringBuilder _RequestData;
        internal byte[] _bufferRead;
        public HttpWebRequest Request;
        public Stream ResponseStream;

        public RequestState()
        {
            _bufferRead = new byte[1024];
            _RequestData = new StringBuilder();
            Request = null;
            ResponseStream = null;
        }

        public StringBuilder RequestData
        {
            get
            {
                return _RequestData;
            }
            set
            {
                _RequestData = value;
            }
        }
    }
```

Listing 12.47 first shows the required namespace declarations. Next, it shows a definition of the state class that is used to collect data during the asynchronous read. The listing for the `ServicePoint` application continues with Listing 12.47.

LISTING 12.47 **`ServicePoint.ConnectionLimit`** Configuration Data

```
    class ServicePointTest
    {
        public static ManualResetEvent allDone = null;
        public static int NumRequests = 100;
        public static int GlobalCallbackCounter = 0;
        public static int NumConnections = 2;
```

Some global variables are defined. **`ManualResetEvent`** (`allDone`) signals that one cycle of the test has completed. The `NumRequests` variable is the number of times that a Web page, or more precisely a group of Web pages, is retrieved. The `GlobalCallbackCount` is an internal counter used to keep track of the number of Web page requests that are made. `NumConnections` is the controlling variable for the test that you are doing. This value is assigned to the **`ServicePoint.ConnectionLimit`** before the Web page requests are made. The code has been built so that this value can be modified from the command line. For example, entering the following:

```
ServicePoint 4
```

would assign a value of 4 to **`ServicePoint.ConnectionLimit`**.

The code continues with Listing 12.48.

LISTING 12.48 Declaring URLs for **`ServicePoint.ConnectionLimit`** Test

```
        static void Main(string[] args)
        {
            string [] addresses = {
"http://msdn.microsoft.com/library/default.asp?
➥url=/library/en-us/cpref/html/
➥frlrfsystemnetauthorizationclasstopic.asp",
"http://msdn.microsoft.com/library/default.asp?
➥url=/library/en-us/cpref/html/
➥frlrfsystemnetcookieclasstopic.asp",
"http://msdn.microsoft.com/library/default.asp?
➥url=/library/en-us/cpref/html/
➥frlrfsystemnetcookiecollectionclasstopic.asp",
"http://msdn.microsoft.com/library/default.asp?
➥url=/library/en-us/cpref/html/
➥frlrfsystemnetcookiecontainerclasstopic.asp",
"http://msdn.microsoft.com/library/default.asp?
➥url=/library/en-us/cpref/html/
➥frlrfsystemnetcookieexceptionclasstopic.asp",
"http://msdn.microsoft.com/library/default.asp?
➥url=/library/en-us/cpref/html/
➥frlrfsystemnetcredentialcacheclasstopic.asp",
"http://msdn.microsoft.com/library/default.asp?
➥url=/library/en-us/cpref/html/
➥frlrfsystemnetdnsclasstopic.asp",
"http://msdn.microsoft.com/library/default.asp?
➥url=/library/en-us/cpref/html/
➥frlrfsystemnetdnspermissionclasstopic.asp",
"http://msdn.microsoft.com/library/default.asp?
➥url=/library/en-us/cpref/html/
➥frlrfsystemnetdnspermissionattributeclasstopic.asp",
"http://msdn.microsoft.com/library/default.asp?
➥url=/library/en-us/cpref/html/
➥frlrfsystemnetendpointclasstopic.asp",
"http://msdn.microsoft.com/library/default.asp?
➥url=/library/en-us/cpref/html/
```

LISTING 12.48 Continued

```
➥frlrfsystemnetendpointpermissionclasstopic.asp",
"http://msdn.microsoft.com/library/default.asp?
➥url=/library/en-us/cpref/html/
➥frlrfsystemnetfilewebrequestclasstopic.asp",
"http://msdn.microsoft.com/library/default.asp?
➥url=/library/en-us/cpref/html/
➥frlrfsystemnetfilewebresponseclasstopic.asp"};
            if(args.Length == 1)
            {
                NumConnections = Convert.ToInt32(args[0]);
            }
```

Listing 12.48 shows the array of URLs that will be used for the test. They all have the same server and scheme, so this should provide the maximum possibility for optimization. Naturally, you will want to change these address to test URLs that interests you.

In addition, the `NumConnections` variable is set from the command line if it is supplied.

The code continues with Listing 12.49.

LISTING 12.49 Retrieving the Contents of the URLs for the **`ServicePoint.ConnectionLimit`** Test

```
    for (int j = 0;j < 5;j++)
    {
        int start = 0;
        int end = 0;
        int total = 0;
        GlobalCallbackCounter = 0;
        allDone = new ManualResetEvent(false);
        start = Environment.TickCount;

        try
        {
            GetPages(addresses);
        }
        catch(WebException webex)
        {
            Console.WriteLine(webex.ToString());
        }

        allDone.WaitOne();
        end = Environment.TickCount;
        total = end - start;

        Console.WriteLine(total);
    }
}
```

This code performs the test on the set of Web pages five times in this loop. Each time the loop completes, the elapsed time that it took to perform the test is printed on the console.

You could have put the following:

```
ServicePointManager.DefaultConnectionLimit = NumConnections;
```

at the beginning of the loop and avoided assigning the **ConnectionLimit** for each **ServicePoint**.

The code continues with Listing 12.50.

LISTING 12.50 GetPages and Setting **ServicePoint.ConnectionLimit**

```
public static void GetPages(string [] addresses)
{

    int i;
    for (i=0; i < NumRequests; i++)
    {
        foreach(string address in addresses)
        {
            HttpWebRequest Request =
➥(HttpWebRequest)WebRequest.Create(address);
            RequestState requestState = new RequestState();
            Request.ServicePoint.ConnectionLimit = NumConnections;
            Request.Pipelined = false;
            requestState.Request = Request;
            Request.BeginGetResponse(
➥new AsyncCallback(RespCallback), requestState);
        }
    }

    return;
}
```

Here you can see that NumRequests **HttpWebRequest**s are asynchronously started up for each address in the address group. For each request that is initiated, you get the **ServicePoint** for that **HttpWebRequest** and set the **ConnectionLimit** to NumConnections.

The remaining code is almost identical to code presented earlier when discussing asynchronous Web requests (compare Listing 12.39 to Listing 12.42), so the listing will not be shown here.

With this code, you can vary the **ConnectionLimit** property of a **ServicePoint** and see the resulting performance increase/decrease. Figure 12.14 shows a sample run.

FIGURE 12.14
Varying `ServicePoint.ConnectionLimit`.

```
C:\CLR Book\Attachments\Samples\Chapter12\ServicePoint>bin\Release\ServicePoint
2
4026
3775
3765
4307
4116

C:\CLR Book\Attachments\Samples\Chapter12\ServicePoint>bin\Release\ServicePoint
4
2233
2053
2063
2253
2413

C:\CLR Book\Attachments\Samples\Chapter12\ServicePoint>bin\Release\ServicePoint
6
1913
1472
1683
1612
1903

C:\CLR Book\Attachments\Samples\Chapter12\ServicePoint>
```

From the sample run shown in Figure 12.14, you can see an almost two-fold increase in throughput when increasing the connection limit from 2 to 4. Increasing the limit to 6 introduces a still significant, yet not as dramatic, performance boost of about 20%. The **`ConnectionLimit`** has little or no effect on connections made through the loopback adapter (localhost).

Network Security

As wonderful as the Internet is today, it does not take much more than a network sniffer to pull out sensitive information that is sent as plain text over the wire. See Figure 12.15 for an example, using the Network Monitor available on every Microsoft Server platform.

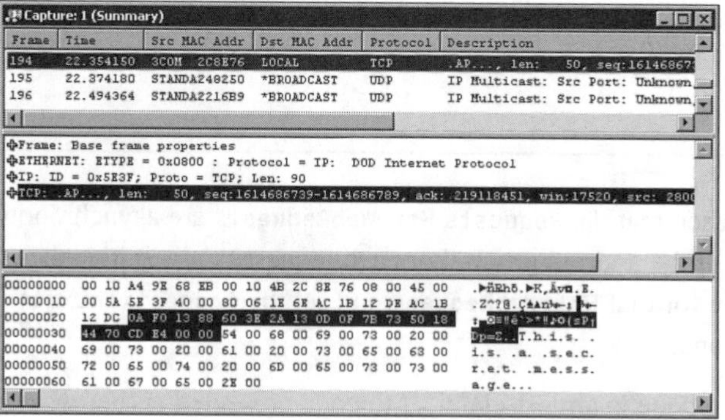

FIGURE 12.15
Using Network Monitor to spy.

Chapter 16, ".NET Security," is devoted to security in the .NET Framework and the CLR. Specific network security is covered only briefly. Even in this section on network security, not enough space is available to cover all of the aspects of security that are related to managed code.

Microsoft has added a considerable suite of tools to make security easier and better. One of the first tasks is to verify that the person connecting is who he says he is, or to provide sufficient proof that I am who I say I am. This is called *authentication*.

Authentication

Two types of authentication support are offered in the .NET Framework. The first type is using public/private key pairs (PKI) with Secure Sockets Layer (SSL) and the standard Internet methods of authentication: basic, digest, negotiate, NTLM, and Kerberos.

The first type of authentication happens automatically when a scheme of `https://` is specified in the URL. This triggers the SSL algorithm and doesn't involve extra programming. If you were to use the Web page extraction routines and supply `https://www.microsoft.com/net/`, the program would be the same.

The other authentication methods rely on a **`NetworkCredential`** class. For example, for you to get at the Web mail page to view e-mail from across the Web, the Web page requires an NT authentication. If you supplied `http://webmail.avstarnews.com` to the program in Listing 12.38, you would get an exception thrown that looks like Figure 12.16.

```
Command Prompt
 Directory of C:\CLR Book\Attachments\Samples\Chapter12\WebPage\WebAuth

07/24/2001  02:20p      <DIR>          .
07/24/2001  02:20p      <DIR>          ..
07/22/2001  01:57p               2,426 AssemblyInfo.cs
07/23/2001  03:56p      <DIR>          bin
07/23/2001  03:56p      <DIR>          obj
07/23/2001  03:57p                 541 WebAuth.cs
07/22/2001  02:01p               3,350 WebAuth.csproj
07/22/2001  02:09p               1,552 WebAuth.csproj.user
07/24/2001  02:20p               3,584 WebAuth.exe
07/22/2001  01:57p                 910 WebAuth.sln
               6 File(s)         12,363 bytes
               4 Dir(s)  10,336,403,456 bytes free

C:\CLR Book\Attachments\Samples\Chapter12\WebPage\WebAuth>WebAuth
System.Net.WebException: The remote server returned an error: (401) Unauthorized
.
   at System.Net.HttpWebRequest.CheckFinalStatus()
   at System.Net.HttpWebRequest.EndGetResponse(IAsyncResult asyncResult)
   at System.Net.HttpWebRequest.GetResponse()
   at System.Net.WebClient.DownloadData(String address)
   at WebAuth.Main(String[] args)

C:\CLR Book\Attachments\Samples\Chapter12\WebPage\WebAuth>
```

FIGURE 12.16
Unauthorized access.

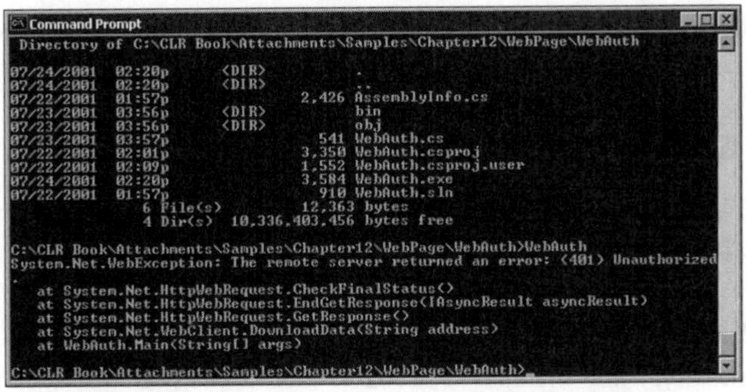

You know that to be able to connect with Exchange and be verified as a valid user, you must be authenticated. For now, NTLM is being used. If you modified the code in Listing 12.38 to add the following lines:

```
NetworkCredential nc = new NetworkCredential("username", "password", "domain");
wc.Credentials = nc;
```

you would get a page back prompting you to log on. (Of course, you would supply your real username, password, and domain.) You became authenticated with just two lines of code. The credentials required to authenticate a user on a given network or machine are stored in instances of the **`NetworkCredential`** class or in an instance of the

CredentialCache class. Whenever a credential is required, one of these two places is checked for the appropriate credential. The static **AuthenticationManager** class handles the actual authentication. By default, the authentication modules to perform authentication for basic, digest, negotiate, NTLM, and Kerberos are registered with the **AuthenticationManager** class. If you have a proprietary authentication scheme, you can extend the **AuthenticationManager** class by registering with the **AuthenticationManager** via the **Register** method. A custom authentication scheme also needs to implement the **IAuthenticationModule** interface.

Code Access Security

You should apply the standard code access security to an application so that the code you develop cannot be used for purposes for which you had not intended. General code access security is discussed in more detail in Chapter 16.

Some specific security configuration and coding can be done to protect your code in a networked environment. You might do well to skip ahead to Chapter 16 and read about code access security and then come back to this section. You can also just treat this as an early introduction to code access security.

The following sections show brief programmatic access to specific permission classes. Undoubtedly, in the real world, an application would use the security administration tool, caspol, to set up either a user, machine, or enterprise-wide security set.

HTTP Access

If you are using the HTTP protocol, you can use a special class to control Web access from your code. This is the **WebPermission** class.

Using WebPermission

Programmatically, using the **WebPermission** class looks like this:

```
string policy = Regex.Escape("http://www.microsoft.com/") + "*";
WebPermission sp = new WebPermission (PermissionState.None);
sp.AddPermission(NetworkAccess.Connect,
                 new Regex(policy));
```

After all of the permissions for the code have been built up, the permissions are applied to the code with **Assert**, **Demand**, **Deny**, and **PermitOnly**. If **PermitOnly** is applied to the preceding code snippet, the code will only be able to access http://www.microsoft.com/ and the pages that are children of the main page.

Socket Access

Just as with the higher level HTTP access control through **WebPermission**, an application can call and set lower level **SocketPermission**s.

SocketPermission

Programmatically, using the **SocketPermission** class looks like this:

```
SocketPermission sp = new SocketPermission(PermissionState.None);
sp.AddPermission(NetworkAccess.Connect,
                 TransportType.Tcp,
                 "enkidu",
                 5000);
sp.AddPermission(NetworkAccess.Accept,
                 TransportType.Tcp,
                 "0.0.0.0",
                 5000);
```

Just as with the **WebPermission** class, after the **SocketPermission**s have been built, they are applied to the code with **Assert**, **Demand**, **Deny**, and **PermitOnly**.

Enable/Disable Resolution of DNS Names

Like **WebPermission** and **SocketPermission**, a permission class is available that deals with code access permission and DNS. This class is called **DnsPermission**.

DnsPermission

Programmatically, using the **DnsPermission** class looks like this:

```
DnsPermission sp = new DnsPermission(PermissionState.None);
```

Just as with the **WebPermission** class, after the **DnsPermission**s have been built, they are applied to the code with **Assert**, **Demand**, **Deny**, and **PermitOnly**. The only difference with **DnsPermission** is that an **AddPermission** method does not exist; therefore, either the code has unrestricted access to DNS, or access to DNS is not allowed, all based on the constructor.

Summary

This chapter has been a showcase for the CLR. Little of the functionality provided by the classes in **System.Net** would exist without the CLR. You have started with the lowest level **Socket** and moved up to a **WebClient**. You have seen along the way how these classes encapsulate features that are based on long-standing standards. Most of the code illustrated in this chapter will interoperate with a peer running unmanaged code, running on an older version of Microsoft OS, or not running a Microsoft OS at all. This interoperation is made possible through the support for standards such as TCP, UDP, and SOAP.

This has been a long chapter, but hopefully you have gained some insight into using the .NET Framework for networking. The following are some recommendations for using the `System.Net` classes:

- Use `WebRequest` and `WebResponse` whenever possible instead of typecasting to `HttpWebRequest` or `FileWebRequest`. Applications that use `WebRequest` and `WebResponse` can take advantage of new Internet protocols without needing extensive code changes. Sometimes you might need to access the specific functionality of a particular class. Try to isolate the specific usage of a class.
- You can use the `System.Net` classes as code-behind to write ASP.NET applications that run on a server. It is often better from a performance standpoint to use the asynchronous methods for `GetResponse` and `GetResponseStream`. In any server arrangement, when it is possible to service many requests at a time, it is best to use the OS to keep the processing pipe full. This is done by relinquishing control to the OS with asynchronous methods.
- The number of connections opened to an Internet resource can have a significant impact on network performance and throughput. Setting the `ConnectionLimit` property in the `ServicePoint` instance for your application can increase the number of connections from the default of two. In the final application, you need to profile the code to see how many open connections result in the best performance. Making the limit arbitrarily large wastes system resources and could cause a degradation in performance. Making the limit too low could make an application spend too much time building up and tearing down connections.
- When writing `Socket`-level protocols, try to use `TcpClient` or `UdpClient` whenever possible, instead of writing directly to a `Socket`. This recommendation is largely the same as for using `WebRequest` and `WebResponse`, except the protocol is fixed. Using the higher level classes allows a programmer to leverage the work of the engineers at Microsoft presently and in the future.
- When accessing sites that require credentials, use the `CredentialCache` class to create a cache of credentials rather than supplying them with every request. This relieves you of the responsibility of creating and presenting credentials based on the URL. This class has not been discussed in detail, but it would be wise to read up on this class as an alternative to building up a `NetworkCredential` class each time a network resource is accessed.

CHAPTER 13

Building Distributed Applications with .NET Remoting

In This Chapter

Building distributed Windows applications did not start with .NET. The goal to build Windows applications that were composed of pieces of software executing on multiple platforms goes back to OLE and Kraig Brockschmidt's groundbreaking book, *Inside OLE* (first and second editions). The first edition of this book was published in 1993 with the second edition following in 1995. In the preface to the second edition, Brockschmidt draws an analogy between what he perceived as the current state of affairs and a book he had read titled *The Chalice and the Blade*, by Riane Eisler (San Francisco: Harper, 1987). He states the following:

> I see a similar crossroads in the state of the software industry today. Perhaps the choices we have in the software business are merely metaphorical aspects of humanity's overall cultural evolution. (Perhaps this is stage three of OLE nirvana.) Today we have a dominator mode—millions of computer users are limited by a few applications created by a few large companies. Component software, however, is a computing environment in which diverse objects created by varied groups and individuals work together, in partnership, to empower all users to solve problems themselves and to create their own software solutions. The software industry can choose either to perpetuate its excessively competitive ways or to build a market in which winning does not have to come at the expense of everything else. Our current ways seek a homogeneous end—one company's products dominating the market. Instead, we can seek an end for which diversity is the most important factor. In a component software environment, one's potential is enriched by the diversity of available components and the diversity of available tools. The greater the diversity, the greater our potential. This holds true whether we are discussing software or society. (*Inside OLE, Second Edition*, pp. xxi–xxii).

That statement was made almost seven years ago, but technology is in much the same situation today. OLE, COM, ActiveX, and DCOM have given us technology to aid in building software that puts a premium on interoperability. The .NET Framework carries this interoperability to a new level. Most of the interoperability is due to the remoting services that the .NET Framework offers.

This chapter is about .NET Remoting. After reading this chapter, you should have a good understanding of how the .NET Framework allows you to easily connect and distribute applications. You will see how to offer a level of interoperability to your application that has previously not been possible. Part of the reason why software has largely adopted a "dominator model" is because the alternative has been so difficult. Everyone working together on an equal basis, a "partnership model," required too much work. Now with emerging standards such as HTTP, SOAP, WSDL, and UDDI, it is easier to interoperate with other applications. More importantly, it is becoming *expected* that your application interoperate with other applications and conform to accepted standards. This chapter shows you how you can use the .NET Framework to fully embrace these standards in your application.

Distributed Applications

What does it mean to have a distributed application? When you think about it, you can understand why it has taken so long and will continue to take a long time before a distributed application is the norm. For an application to be truly distributed, it needs to be able to seamlessly communicate with each of its constituent parts. Communication between multiple server applications in a network involves the ability to incorporate the following characteristics into your application:

- Parts of the application might be physically running locally and parts might be considerably more distant.
- Parts of the application might require access to code or data that is behind a firewall erected to help ensure the integrity of the network behind the firewall.
- Parts of your application might share common protocols (SOAP, WSDL) but not a common platform. For example, you might be required to extract data from a platform running Linux, or you might need to have a Java application call methods in your application or access your application's data.
- Parts of your application might share common protocols and a common platform (such as .NET). You don't want a least-common-denominator type of solution. You want to be able to take advantage of the speed and functionality that is specific to your platform of choice.

Using .NET to Distribute an Application

The .NET Remoting Architecture splits support between two types of distributed applications. The first type is between a .NET application and a non-.NET application. The second type is between two .NET applications.

.NET Interop with Non-.NET Applications

Allowing broad interoperation with other non-.NET applications requires a common base or standard. You might not have the resources to understand all of the applications that fall under the broad term "non-.NET," so you need to adopt a standard by which you can communicate. The .NET Framework has fully adopted three key standard technologies used for the purpose of interoperating and distributing an application: HTTP, SOAP, and WSDL.

Hypertext Transfer Protocol as a Means for Interoperabililty

The first standard that .NET supports is Hypertext Transfer Protocol (HTTP). In RFC-2616 (`ftp://ftp.isi.edu/in-notes/rfc2616.txt`), HTTP is described as follows:

> ...[it] is an application-level protocol for distributed, collaborative, hypermedia information systems. It is a generic, stateless protocol which can be used for many tasks beyond its use for hypertext, such as name servers and distributed object management systems, through extension of its request methods, error codes, and headers.

Prior to HTTP 1.1 was HTTP 1.0. HTTP 1.0 is described in RFC-1945 (`ftp://ftp.isi.edu/in-notes/rfc1945.txt`), which claims that HTTP has been used since 1990. In its simplest form, it is a protocol that describes a command and a response:

```
Simple - Request = "GET" SP Request-URI CRLF
Simple - Response = [ Entity-Body ]
```

SP is a space, CRLF is a carriage-return line-feed character sequence, and the Request-URI is of two forms: an absolute URI and an absolute path:

```
Absolute URI = "http:" "//" [":" port ] [absolute path]
```

The absolute path is simply the absolute URI with the scheme, host, and port removed. As an example, the following is an absolute URI and the equivalent absolute path:

```
Absolute URI = http://www.w3.org/pub/WWW/TheProject.html
Absolute Path = /pub/WWW/TheProject.html
```

More complete specifications of URIs are given in RFC-1808 (`ftp://ftp.isi.edu/in-notes/rfc1808.txt`) and RFC-1630 (`ftp://ftp.isi.edu/in-notes/rfc1630.txt`).

Even though simple requests and the corresponding responses are easier to understand than *full-request* and *full-response* that are in the following discussion, their use is discouraged. It is more common and more acceptable to use full-request and full-response. The full-request has the following form:

```
Request-Line
(General-Header | Request-Header | Entity-Header)*
CRLF
[ Entity-Body ]
```

The request-line takes the following form:

```
Request-Line = Method SP Request-URI SP HTTP-Version CRLF
```

The method can be as follows:

```
"GET"
"HEAD"
"POST"
```

If you are using HTTP 1.1, the method might also include the following:

```
"OPTIONS"
"PUT"
"DELETE"
"TRACE"
"CONNECT"
```

SP is one or more space characters. Request-URI has already been described, HTTP-Version has the form of HTTP/1.0 or HTTP/1.1, and CRLF includes the linefeed characters described previously.

What follows next is one or more of a General-Header, Request-Header, or Entity-Header. An example of a General-Header can be as simple as the following:

```
Date: Mon, 3 Dec 2001 9:12:31 GMT
```

Other types that are part of HTTP/1.1 General-Header include the following:

```
Cache-Control
Connection
Pragma
Trailer
Transfer-Encoding
Upgrade
Via
Warning
```

HTTP/1.0 has five options for Request-Header:

```
Authorization
From
If-Modified-Since
Referer
User-Agent
```

HTTP/1.1 adds about 13 more options.

The Entity-Header for HTTP/1.0 contains the following:

```
Allow
Content-Encoding
Content-Length
Content-Type
Expires
Last-Modified
```

HTTP/1.1 adds these:

```
Content-Language
Content-Location
Content-MD5
Content-Range
```

After this header information, the request starts a new line with the Entity-Body, which is the payload of the message. This can be any 8-bit sequence of characters in which the Content-Length header determines the length of the Entity-Body.

That is the request. In response, a Full-Response is returned of the form:

```
Full-Response = Status-Line
                (General-Header | Response-Header | Entity-Header)*
                CRLF
                [ Entity-Body ]
```

The Status-Line has the form:

```
Status-Line = HTTP-Version SP Status-Code SP Reason-Phrase CRLF
```

The portions of this message that have not been discussed yet are the Status-Code and the Reason-Phrase. The Reason-Phrase is a field that contains a human-readable explanation of the response. The Status-Code is a three-digit code. The first digit defines the class of the response:

- 1xx—Informational
- 2xx—Success
- 3xx—Redirection
- 4xx—Client Error
- 5xx—Server Error

The Response Header consists of the following:

```
Location
Server
WWW-Authenticate
```

HTTP/1.1 adds six more Response Header types.

Most of the details that deal with the HTTP protocol are handled for you by the .NET Framework. Typically, all you need to specify is that you want to use the HTTP protocol. However, if you are concerned about performance or you want to perform some complex asynchronous function, then you need to be aware of HTTP and its origins.

HTTP was designed as a simple and lightweight command and response protocol. Because it is used on every desktop to display the "hypertext" portion of its name,

HTML, most companies allow HTTP traffic in and out of their facility. Because HTTP has been so widely adopted, numerous facilities are part of a firewall to analyze and detect potentially harmful HTTP requests and responses. In addition, HTTP traffic by default occurs on port 80 for browsing. An administrator can easily allow traffic only on port 80 and be reasonably certain that it will accommodate most of the user's needs. For these reasons, HTTP is termed *firewall friendly*. Typically, no new administration is needed as far as security to get into and out of a computing facility using HTTP.

The final field, Entity-Body, is the most interesting and the most broadly defined. The Entity-Body can be anything. Typically, a command would be to "GET" a Web page. The command would contain the address of the Web page to retrieve, and the Entity-Body would be empty. The response would be the contents of the Web page to be displayed in the browser. However, the Entity-Body is unspecified and can be anything. This is important to understand in the next section, which discusses SOAP.

A more real-world example would be to go to `www.msn.com` and start out with the request shown in Listing 13.1.

LISTING 13.1 Initial HTTP Request

```
GET /isapi/redir.dll?prd=ie&pver=6&ar=msnhome HTTP/1.1
Accept: */*
Accept-Language: en-us
Accept-Encoding: gzip, deflate
User-Agent: Mozilla/4.0 (compatible; MSIE 6.0;
➥Windows NT 5.1; Q312461; .NET CLR 1.0.3512)
Host: www.microsoft.com
Connection: Keep-Alive
Cookie: MC1=V=3&LV=200110&HASH=0707&GUID=AC110707DD6749E4A09EA16ED562CA40
```


You get the response shown in Listing 13.2.

LISTING 13.2 Initial HTTP Response

```
HTTP/1.1 302 Object.Moved
Location:.http://home.microsoft.com/

Server: Microsoft-IIS/5.0
Content-Type: text/html
Content-Length: 149
<head><title>Document.Moved</title></head>
<body><h1>Object Moved</h1>This document may be found
➥<a.HREF="http://home.microsoft.com/">here</a></body>
```

The browser notes that the document has moved and tries the location that is suggested. This address redirects you to another site. You get a site that provides some HTML. Listing 13.3 shows the final HTTP request required to display the home page.

LISTING 13.3 Final HTTP Reqest

```
GET / HTTP/1.1
Accept: */*
Accept-Language: en-us
Accept-Encoding: gzip, deflate
User-Agent:.Mozilla/4.0 (compatible; MSIE.6.0; Windows NT 5.1; Q312461;
.NET.CLR.1.0.3512)
Connection: Keep-Alive
Host: www.msn.com
Cookie:.STATE=1; MC1=V=2&GUID=6E487E199A6B4A7A9E4FA8B05D9DF5C7;
➥mh=MSFT; lang=en-us; Cn=1
```

Based on this request, you get the home page contents that are partially shown in Listing 13.4.

LISTING 13.4 Abbreviated Final HTTP Response

```
HTTP/1.1 200.OK
Server: Microsoft-IIS/5.0
Date: Mon, 03 Dec.2001 22:39:37 GMT
P3P: CP="4E BUS CUR CONo FIN IVDo.ONL OUR PHY SAMo TELo"
Set-Cookie: y=1; domain= msn.com; path=/
Cache-Control: private
Expires: Fri, 23 Nov.2001 22:39:38 GMT
Content-Type: text/html; charset=utf-8
Content-Length: 27842

<?xml version="1.0" encoding="UTF-8" ?>
<!DOCTYPE html PUBLIC "-//W3C//DTD.XHTML 1.0 Strict//EN"
➥"DTD/xhtml1-strict dtd">
<html xmlns="http://www.w3.org/1999/xhtml">
<head>
<title>Welcome to MSN com</title>
<meta.http-equiv="PICS-Label" content="(pics-1.1
. . .
</table></body></html>
```

Obviously, not all 27842 bytes are shown for space reasons, but you get the idea. The page is downloaded and the browser displays the contents.

As an example of a simple HTTP request in which the client makes a request of the server would be using POST to send a command to the HTTP server:

```
POST /foobar HTTP/1.1
Host: 209.110.197.12
Content-Type: text/plain
Content-Length: 12

Hello, World
```

It is up to the application that is at `/foobar` to determine what to do with this simple text string. Perhaps the application simply echoes the text back. The response might look like this:

```
200 OK
Content-Type: text/plain
Content-Length: 12

Hello, World
```

The Entity-Body of the last section in this case is the string "Hello, World" in the request and the response. This is the programming model for HTTP. Use GET to browse and retrieve Web pages, and use PUT to interact and command the server to perform some function.

Using Simple Object Access Protocol and HTTP to Communicate with a Non-.NET Application

The content and format of the Entity-Body portion of the HTTP request and response is up to the application that is handling the request. In particular, when using the POST HTTP method, the command that is required is up to the server to interpret. You might use the strict conventions of XML to form a "command" to the server to make it easier for the server to parse the data. You might have a server that accepts commands to purchase books. In this case, you might have a POST method that looks like this:

```
POST /cgi-bin/purchase-book.cgi HTTP/1.1
User-Agent: . . .
Content-Type: text/xml; charset="utf-8"
Content-Length: 58
Connection: Keep-Alive
Host: services.book.publishers

<PurchaseBook>
    <ISBN>0201379368</ISBN>
</PurchaseBook>
```

The server would look at this request and easily make the correct purchase. By using XML, the server does not have to work as hard to parse the command. Many parsers could recognize valid XML and parse it, one of which is SOAP. SOAP brings a format and structure to the XML data that is presented to the server. Every SOAP message contains a least an `Envelope` and a `Body` (and if an error exists, a `Fault` is also present). The exact details of what is contained in a valid SOAP message are documented at `http://www.w3.org/TR/SOAP`, but a simple example will be provided here of a SOAP message that is used to retrieve the temperature if given a zip code. A Web service is available that takes in a zip code and outputs the current temperature at that zip code (`http://www.xmethods.net/ve2/ViewListing.po;jsessionid=aYDqLZCq_VNlZvhN_pKmzS8r(QCcd0CRM)?serviceid=8`). Listings 13.5 and 13.6 show some sample SOAP messages. The SOAP request is shown in Listing 13.5, and the response is shown in Listing 13.6. Although it is possible to write a program that generates and accepts these messages (such samples occur later in this chapter), these listings are meant to be text samples of SOAP messages.

LISTING 13.5 SOAP Request to a Temperature Web Service

```
POST /soap/servlet/rpcrouter HTTP/1.1
User-Agent: Mozilla/4.0+(compatible; MSIE.6.0; Windows.5.1.2600.0;
➥MS .NET.Remoting; MS .NET CLR 1.0.3512.0)
Content-Type: text/xml; charset="utf-8"
SOAPAction: ""
Content-Length: 486
Expect: 100-continue
Connection:.Keep-Alive
Host: services.xmethods.net

<SOAP-ENV:Envelope xmlns:xsi="http://www.w3.org/1999/XMLSchema-instance"
xmlns:xsd="http://www.w3.org/1999/XMLSchema"
xmlns:SOAP-ENC="http://schemas.xmlsoap.org/soap/encoding/"
xmlns:SOAP-ENV="http://schemas.xmlsoap.org/soap/envelope/"
SOAP-ENV:encodingStyle="http://schemas.xmlsoap.org/soap/encoding/">
<SOAP-ENV:Body>
<i2:getTemp id="ref-1" xmlns:i2="urn:xmethods-Temperature">
<zipcode xsi:type="xsd:string">98052</zipcode>
</i2:getTemp>
</SOAP-ENV:Body>
</SOAP-ENV:Envelope>
```

The important part of all this data is in the Body of the SOAP message where you see the `getTemp` element. The server understands this to be a request for the temperature at a given location (specified by the zip code). The Web service response to the request shown in Listing 13.5 is shown in Listing 13.6.

LISTING 13.6 SOAP Response from a Temperature Web Service

```
HTTP/1.1.200 OK
Date: Mon, 03 Dec 2001 21:10:49 GMT
Status: 200
```

LISTING 13.6 Continued

```
Set-Cookie2: JSESSIONID=To67692mC292786195111038At;Version=1;
➥Discard;Path="/soap"
Servlet-Engine: Tomcat.Web.Server/3.1 (JSP.1.1;.Servlet.2.2;
➥Java.1.3.0; Linux.2.2.19-6.2.1.2RS.x86; java.vendor=IBM Corporation)
Set-Cookie: JSESSIONID=To67692mC292786195111038At;Path=/soap
Content-Type: text/xml; charset=utf-8
Content-Length: 465
Content-Language: en


<?xml version='1.0' encoding='UTF-8'?>
<SOAP-ENV:Envelope xmlns:SOAP-ENV="http://schemas.xmlsoap.org/soap/envelope/"
xmlns:xsi="http://www.w3.org/1999/XMLSchema-instance"
xmlns:xsd="http://www.w3.org/1999/XMLSchema">
<SOAP-ENV:Body>
<ns1:getTempResponse xmlns:ns1="urn:xmethods-Temperature"
SOAP-ENV:encodingStyle="http://schemas.xmlsoap.org/soap/encoding/">
<return xsi:type="xsd:float">45.0</return>
</ns1:getTempResponse>
</SOAP-ENV:Body>
</SOAP-ENV:Envelope>
```

At this particular time, it is 45 degrees at the location specified by the zip code (Redmond, Washington).

Using Web Service Description Language to Describe Types

In the previous example, it was understood that the `getTemp` element in the SOAP message meant that the server was to look up the temperature for the area specified by the zip code and return that temperature as a floating point number. The final "standard" that .NET has embraced is known as the *Web Service Description Language* (WSDL). WSDL is actually not quite a standard yet; version 1.1 is technically a draft (`http://www.w3.org/TR/wsdl`) and is subject to change and revision.

It is instructive to look at portions of the WSDL description for the `getTemp` method used earlier. The description of the `getTemp` method is illustrated in Listing 13.7. This listing can be generated by pointing your browser to `http://www.xmethods.net/sd/2001/TemperatureService.wsdl`.

LISTING 13.7 WSDL Description of `getTemp`

```
<portType name="TemperaturePortType">
  <operation name="getTemp">
       <input message="tns:getTempRequest" name="getTemp" />
       <output message="tns:getTempResponse" name="getTempResponse" />
  </operation>
</portType>
```

In the WSDL description, you see that what is known as the `getTemp` operation is part of a `portType` called `TemperaturePortType` and consists of an input, `tns:getTempRequest`, and an output, `tns:getTempResponse`. The input and output messages are further described in the WSDL shown in Listing 13.8.

LISTING 13.8 WSDL Description of the Arguments and Return Types for `getTemp`

```
<message name="getTempRequest">
  <part name="zipcode" type="xsd:string" />
</message>
<message name="getTempResponse">
  <part name="return" type="xsd:float" />
</message>
```

The input to this service is a string called the `zipcode`, and the output is a floating point number as the `return`. For this simple method, that is the key information that can be gleaned from the WSDL description of this Web service.

Two points about this simple Web service are noteworthy:

- This Web service is not implemented by another .NET application or component. As you can see from the HTTP header information, this Web service is implemented in Java on a Linux platform. Because this Web service also adheres to the SOAP and the WSDL 1.1 draft, the application that consumes this Web service neither knows nor cares about the language that implements the service or the platform on which it is implemented. See Listing 13.6 and particularly the HTTP header that indicates the implementation of the Web service.
- You do not need to know much about the details of WSDL to build a .NET application to consume this Web service. You can use a utility that ships with the .NET SDK called `soapsuds`. WSDL describes types, and `soapsuds` takes this description and turns it into types that are familiar to a .NET application. `soapsuds` directly generates an assembly, or it is possible to turn the WSDL description into C# code. Listing 13.9 shows the code that is generated for the temperature Web service. Listing 13.9 is generated with the following command:

  ```
  soapsuds -url: http://www.xmethods.net/sd/2001/TemperatureService.wsdl -gc
  ```

  This command generates a file called `InteropNS.cs`, which is based on the namespace that was assigned to this Web service.

LISTING 13.9 C# Code Generated By soapsuds from WSDL

```
using System;
using System.Runtime.Remoting.Messaging;
using System.Runtime.Remoting.Metadata;
using System.Runtime.Remoting.Metadata.W3cXsd2001;
namespace InteropNS {
    [SoapType(SoapOptions=SoapOption.Option1|SoapOption.AlwaysIncludeTypes|
                         SoapOption.XsdString|SoapOption.EmbedAll,
                         XmlElementName="Temperature",
                         XmlNamespace=
➥"http://www.xmethods.net/sd/TemperatureService.wsdl",
                         XmlTypeName="Temperature",
                         XmlTypeNamespace=
➥"http://www.xmethods.net/sd/TemperatureService.wsdl")]
    public class Temperature :
➥System.Runtime.Remoting.Services.RemotingClientProxy
    {
        // Constructor
        public Temperature()
        {
            base.ConfigureProxy(this.GetType(),
➥"http://services.xmethods.net:80/soap/servlet/rpcrouter");
        }

        public Object RemotingReference
        {
            get{return(_tp);}
        }

        [SoapMethod(SoapAction="",
         ResponseXmlElementName="getTemp",
         ReturnXmlElementName="return",
         XmlNamespace="urn:xmethods-Temperature",
         ResponseXmlNamespace="urn:xmethods-Temperature")]
        public Single getTemp(String zipcode)
        {
            return ((Temperature) _tp).getTemp(zipcode);
        }
    }
}
```

This is much easier to read than the WSDL. To generate the assembly, you simply reference the URL that contains the WSDL description of the Web service with a command line:

```
soapsuds -url:http://www.xmethods.net/sd/TemperatureService.wsdl
➥-gc -oa:Temperature.dll
```

When this command successfully returns, you have a remoting assembly for which you can construct the type and call a method on just as if the service were local:

```
temperatureService = new Temperature();
float temp = temperatureService.getTemp(zipcodes);
```

.NET and Other .NET Applications

Although it is compelling, it is not always practical to force all interaction between .NET Applications to adhere to standardized protocols and formats. When interacting with another .NET component or application, the .NET offers a rich binary serialization scheme. In fact, whenever any communication occurs between objects in different `AppDomain`s, a remoting framework is put in place and the data is serialized and deserialized using the .NET Framework proprietary binary serialization scheme. This offers the rich object fidelity of the .NET programming languages and it is fast. If part of your application resides behind a firewall, then it is possible to use HTTP with a binary serialization scheme for the maximum speed in this situation.

Remoting Architecture

Now that this chapter has established the two different logical styles of remoting that are available from the .NET Framework, it will move to a discussion of how remoting allows for such distinctly different modes of operation. Figure 13.1 shows a broad overview of the remoting architecture.

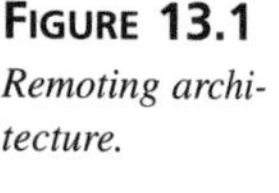

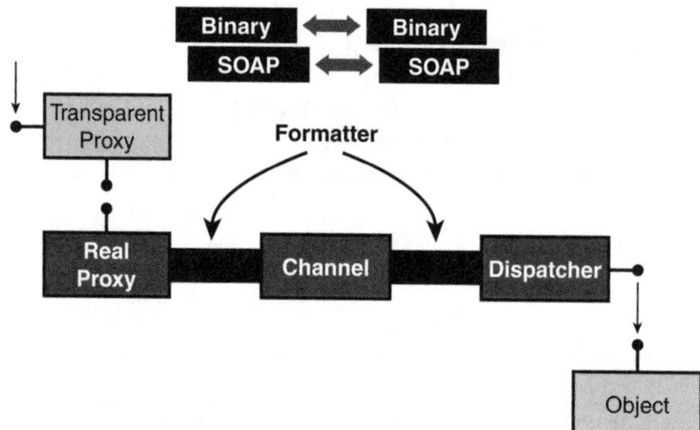

FIGURE 13.1
Remoting architecture.

Starting from the left side of the figure, the client is presented with a transparent proxy. The client cannot easily tell that it is working with a proxy rather than a real object because all of the methods and properties are exposed through the transparent proxy in the same manner as a real object. Because it is required that an assembly that represents the real object be present when building the client, it is possible that you might not really be talking to a remoted object. To remedy this, you can make a call to **IsTransparentProxy** to make sure that you are indeed connected to a remote object. This call would take on the following form:

```
if (true == RemotingServices.IsTransparentProxy(timeService))
{
    Debug.WriteLine("TimeObject activated on server");
    . . .
}
```

The transparent proxy calls a real proxy, which in turn turns the calling stack frame of your method call with its arguments into an **IMessage**. **IMessage** is then passed through a chain of channel sinks. The proxy contains a reference to the first **IMessageSink** object in the chain so that it can start the call cycle. The first channel sink must implement **IMessageSink**, but typically, the first channel sink implements either **IClientFormatterSink** or **IServerFormatterSink** and is known as a formatter sink because it turns a message into a series of bytes.

Currently, the .NET Framework implements two formatter sinks as **BinaryClientFormatterSink** and **SoapClientFormatterSink**. The formatter sink turns a message into a byte stream. The binary sink provides a high-speed method to transfer all .NET objects from one **AppDomain** to another. The SOAP sink turns a message into a stream of bytes that is SOAP 1.1 compliant.

Message sinks and channel sinks provide a mechanism whereby remoting can be extended. Message sinks can forward a message, log a message, transform a message, or generate a new message. By inserting a class that implements **IMessageSink**, **IClientChannelSink**, or **IServerChannelSink**, you can modify the message (which is the method call and its arguments) as it flows from one sink to another.

Each sink in the chain receives the message object, performs a specific operation, and calls the next sink in the chain. Each sink provides some kind of service such as security and synchronization.

Notice that two methods must be implemented for every **IMessageSink** object: **AsyncProcessMessage** and **SyncProcessMessage**. When an asynchronous call is made on a remoted object, each sink provides a reply sink to be called by the next sink when the reply is on its way back.

Figure 13.1 shows a single block that is labeled "channel." Logically, this is probably true, but there is much more to a channel than that. Look at Figure 13.2 for a more accurate picture of what a channel is composed of.

FIGURE 13.2
Channel sinks and remoting.

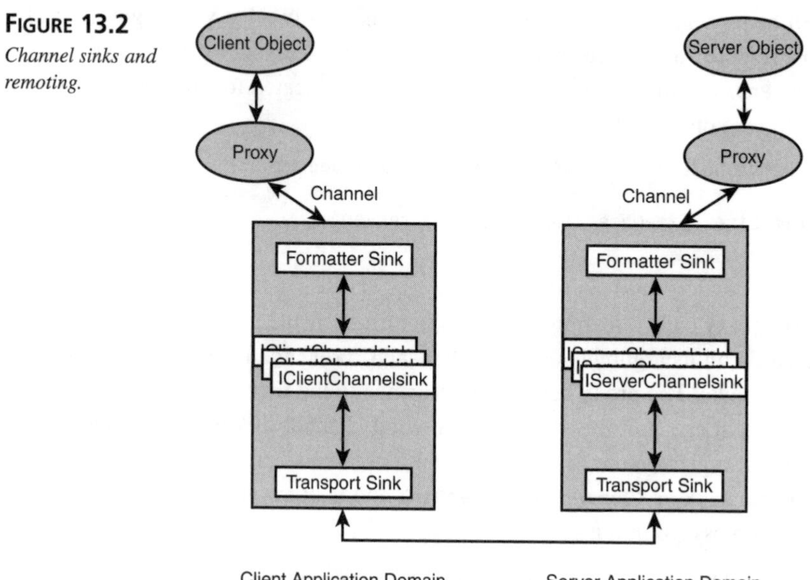

Logically, a channel's main task is to transport a byte stream from the client to the server or vice versa if it is carrying a reply message. Figure 13.2 shows that as only one component of the channel—the transport sink. A channel is composed of a chain of channel sinks, each one implementing at least an **`IClientChannelSink`** or an **`IServerChannelSink`** interface.

The .NET Framework includes two channels as part of the shipped product: an HTTP and a TCP channel. As you can guess, the HTTP channel implements the HTTP protocol and is good to use when it is necessary to cross firewalls and HTTP proxy servers. The TCP channel implements a high-speed socket that is good for a more direct peer-to-peer communication. Of course, it is possible to create your own channel. A `TimeLog` sample illustrates how to hook into the list of channel sinks to provide a log of the traffic that occurs within the channel. In addition, a `TimeFilter` sample shows how to implement some rudimentary security checks in a sink by rejecting calls from certain IP addresses.

On the server side, the remaining code to transfer a message to the server primarily does what the client side did in reverse. It reads in the message from the transport sink, runs the message through the server side chain of channel sinks, converts the serialized data to a message, constructs a call stack from the message, and invokes the appropriate method on the object.

Remoting Objects

With COM, the default and practically only means of transporting an object was by reference. It was not easy to create an object that was passed by value. In fact, doing so became a frequently discussed topic among COM programmers. With .NET, a remoted object can be either by value or by reference. The objects can include complex types such as arrays, structs, or datasets. The limiting factor in remoting an object is usually in the SOAP formatter because not all data types that can be represented in the .NET languages can be accurately represented with SOAP. For example, with SOAP 1.1, it is difficult to represent two or more dimensioned arrays or arrays of arrays.

If the class author decides that the object should be marshaled by reference, then the class extends or derives from **`MarshalByRefObject`**. If the object is to be marshaled by value, then the class must be serializable. To be serializable, the class should be marked with the **`SerializableAttribute`** and optionally implement the **`ISerializable`** interface if more explicit control is required during the marshaling process.

Every remoted object requires a host. The host listens for incoming requests and calls the appropriate methods on the remote object. You can create your own host (also known as a direct host), or you can rely on Internet Information Server (IIS) to act as a host for your object.

A user-defined or direct host requires a server and one or more clients. You can implement this in several ways, but the simplest to understand is for the user to create both client and server configuration files. The configuration file is read in and processed with **`RemotingConfiguration.Configure`**. The process of configuring a client allows a client to easily create or activate an object with **`new`**, as would be expected of any object. This is because the client is actually dealing with a transparent proxy, as discussed earlier. When the server calls **`RemotingConfiguration.Configure`**, it is primarily establishing the objects for which it is listening and determining how it will be listening (HTTP or TCP). After the server starts listening for an object and the client has been properly configured, the client can create the remoted object and call methods on that object. For both the client and the server, the convention is to name the configuration file with the name of the executable followed by a .config suffix. For example, if the client program was called `client.exe`, the configuration file would be called `client.exe.config`.

Two things are required for IIS to act as the host for a remoted object: the assembly that contains that implementation of the remoted object and a configuration file. This is done by creating a virtual directory with the Internet Information Services plug-in (available from the Administrative Tools portion of the Control Panel). The virtual directory will be given a name and will refer to a physical directory. The physical directory will embody a configuration file and a bin directory that contains the assembly that implements the remote object. By default, IIS looks for a `web.config` to be the configuration file. It is easier to just follow this convention.

An object can be either client activated or server activated. A server-activated object is known as a *well-known type* because the server registers its interest in serving the object. A well-known type can be further broken down into a `SingleCall` or a `Singleton`.

With `SingleCall`, each call that the client makes on the object causes the server to create a new instance of the object, call the method, and destroy the object. Because no state can be maintained in the object, this type of object is ideally suited for a server farm where the remote call can be satisfied from any number of physical CPUs.

A `Singleton` object is also instantiated on the server, but only one instance of the object is created. All clients that specify the same URI for a given type are connected to the same object instance on the server. The object is instantiated upon the first method call, as with a `SingleCall` object. The object is instantiated by the server using the default constructor. A server cannot instantiate a `Singleton` object using any constructor that requires arguments. However, the `Singleton` object is only instantiated once on the server; as such, it can maintain state between client method calls. The client can participate in the lifetime management of a `Singleton` object through **ILease** and **`ISponsor`**, just as with a `Client-Activated` object (which is discussed next). Because the lifetime management is so similar to client-activated objects, see the section "Extending and Controlling the Lifetime of a Remoted Object" for more detail.

A `Client-Activated` object, as its name implies, is activated on the client. The client creates the object with **`new`** or **`Activator.CreateInstance`** and can use any of the constructors with or without arguments that are available to the object. After the object is constructed, it is mirrored on the server and maintains state as long as the client holds reference to the transparent proxy for the object. When the client releases the proxy, the object is destroyed on the server. If the client does not release the object, the server waits for a configurable amount of time before attempting to destroy the object. When the object is about to be destroyed, its "lease" is expired and is destroyed if it has not registered a "sponsor." If a sponsor is registered, then the sponsor is called before the object is destroyed. The sponsor has the option of extending the lease on the object so that it is not destroyed right away. The lifetime issues that are involved with a `Client-Activated` object are discussed later in this chapter in the section "Extending and Controlling the Lifetime of a Remoted Object."

A Basic Time Server Using Remoting

A simple example has been put together that illustrates many of the principles that have been discussed. Another example shows client and server configuration files. The client instantiates the object and repeatedly calls two methods on that object to retrieve the date and time at the server. The solution is in the `Time` directory and consists of a client, a server, and a library that implements the remote time object. Listing 13.10 shows the relevant parts of the server implementation.

LISTING 13.10 `SingleCall` Time Server

```
[STAThread]
static void Main(string[] args)
{
    string configfile = "timeserver.exe.config";

    if(args.Length != 0)
        configfile = args[0];

    if(!Initialize(configfile))
        return;

    String keyState = "";
    Console.WriteLine("Press <cr> to exit");
    keyState = Console.ReadLine();
}
static bool Initialize(string configfile)
{
    if(!File.Exists(configfile))
    {
        configfile = @"..\..\" + configfile;
        if(!File.Exists(configfile))
            return false;
    }
    RemotingConfiguration.Configure(configfile);
    return true;
}
```

The server goes through some heuristics to find the configuration file, configures itself based on the configuration file, and then goes to sleep waiting for the user to terminate it by pressing the Enter key.

Listing 13.11 shows how to implement a client. Most of the code for the client is devoted to the UI, so the relevant parts of the code that pertain to remoting have been extracted.

LISTING 13.11 Time Client

```
if(!Initialize(configFilename))
    return;

timeService = new TimeObject();
if (true == RemotingServices.IsTransparentProxy(timeService))
{
    Debug.WriteLine("TimeObject activated on server");
    timer.Enabled = true;
}
. . .
private static bool Initialize(string configfile)
{
    if(!File.Exists(configfile))
    {
        configfile = @"..\..\" + configfile;
        if(!File.Exists(configfile))
            return false;
    }
    RemotingConfiguration.Configure(configfile);
    return true;
}
. . .
private void OnTick(object sender, System.EventArgs e)
{
    if(timeService != null)
    {
        try
        {
            time.Text = timeService.Time;
            date.Text = timeService.Date;
            dateCount.Text = Convert.ToString(timeService.DateCount);
            timeCount.Text = Convert.ToString(timeService.TimeCount);
        }
        catch(Exception exception)
        {
            Debug.WriteLine(exception);
            timeService = null;
            timer.Enabled = false;
        }
    }
}
```

On startup, the client initializes its UI components. Then you can call a method to initialize the remoting services using the client configuration file. This initialization is essentially the same as the server with the exception of the content of the configuration file. When the client has been properly configured, the client instantiates the `TimeObject` with a call to **new**. The reference returned from **new** should be a reference to a transparent proxy; if it is not, then an error has been made in the configuration file for the client, server, or both. Ensure that you are indeed connected to the server by checking whether the object is a transparent proxy with **RemotingServices.IsTransparentProxy**. The client then enables a timer that wakes up the client at a periodic rate at which time the client reads the current date and time from the server (via the transparent proxy). You can also retrieve the values for two properties that reflect the number of times that the date and time properties of the object have been accessed.

Listing 13.12 shows the implementation of the remoted object.

LISTING 13.12 Time Object

```
namespace CLRUnleashed.Remoting
{
    public class TimeObject : MarshalByRefObject
    {
        public TimeObject()
        {
            Console.WriteLine("TimeObject activated");
            dateCount = 0;
            timeCount = 0;
        }
        public string Time
        {
            get
            {
                timeCount++;
                return DateTime.Now.ToLongTimeString();
            }
        }
        public string Date
        {
            get
            {
                dateCount++;
                return DateTime.Now.ToLongDateString();
            }
        }
        public int DateCount
        {
            get
            {
                return dateCount;
            }
        }
        public int TimeCount
        {
            get
            {
                return timeCount;
            }
        }
```

LISTING 13.12 Continued

```
        private int dateCount;
        private int timeCount;
    }
}
```

The key feature of this class as it pertains to remoting is that it is derived from the **`MarshalByRefObject`** object. For an object to be used by the remoting services by reference, it must be derived from **`MarshalByRefObject`**. This simple object has a `Date` property that returns a string representing the current date and a `Time` property that returns a string representing the current time. With each access to the properties, the appropriate counter is incremented. These counters have been added to illustrate the different activation models. A print statement is also included that is issued each time the object is constructed.

Both the client and server need to be configured to function properly. A configuration file specifies the address of the server, the port to be used, the activation model, and so forth.

Client and Server Configuration Files

Figure 13.3 illustrates the client and server configuration files. These configuration files are part of the `Time` remoting application.

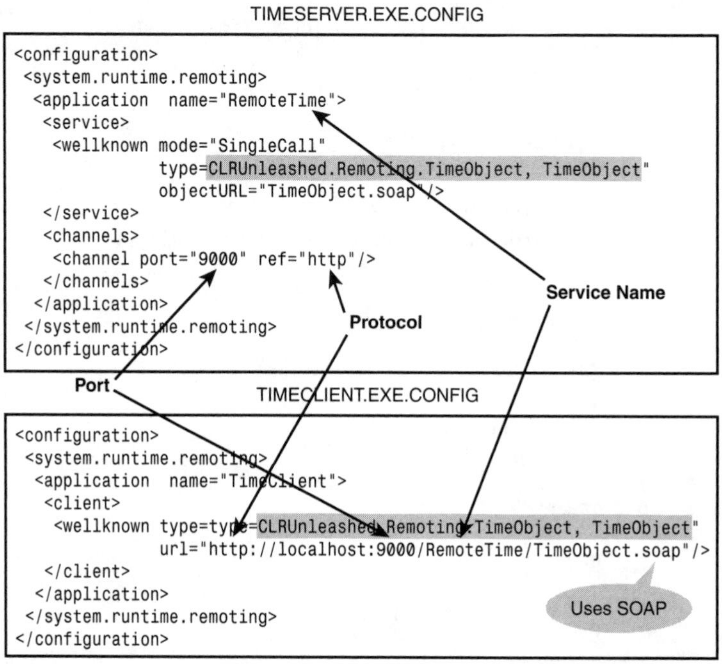

FIGURE 13.3
Direct client and server configuration files.

TIMESERVER.EXE.CONFIG

```
<configuration>
 <system.runtime.remoting>
  <application  name="RemoteTime">
   <service>
    <wellknown mode="SingleCall"
               type=CLRUnleashed.Remoting.TimeObject, TimeObject"
               objectURL="TimeObject.soap"/>
   </service>
   <channels>
    <channel port="9000" ref="http"/>
   </channels>
  </application>
 </system.runtime.remoting>
</configuration>
```

Service Name
Protocol
Port

TIMECLIENT.EXE.CONFIG

```
<configuration>
 <system.runtime.remoting>
  <application  name="TimeClient">
   <client>
    <wellknown type=type=CLRUnleashed.Remoting.TimeObject, TimeObject"
               url="http://localhost:9000/RemoteTime/TimeObject.soap"/>
   </client>
  </application>
 </system.runtime.remoting>
</configuration>
```

Uses SOAP

As you can see from the figure, the configuration files are well-formed XML files. These configuration files might contain other configuration information, but the portion that is specific to remoting is contained in the `<system.runtime.remoting>` tag.

The server declares its name with the `<application>` tag that has a single attribute: the name of the application. This name is important because the client uses this name to connect to a direct host implementation. The name attribute of the `<application>` tag has no meaning when IIS is a host and should be blank.

The server configuration file describes the object that it will be servicing with the `<wellknown>` tag. By using the `<wellknown>` tag, the configuration file indicates that a server-activated object will be served. The mode attribute indicates the activation type to be used for the object. The mode can be either the string `SingleCall`, as illustrated in the figure, or `Singleton`. The type is the specification of the object that is to be serviced. This attribute has two comma-separated values that specify the type that is being serviced followed by the assembly in which it is defined. Notice that this type identification string is identical to the type identification string in the client configuration file. They need to refer to the same object, so they should match. The last attribute to the `<wellknown>` tag is the `objectUri`. The `objectUri` specifies the name of the endpoint of the object's uniform resource identifier (URI). The `objectUri` attribute must end in .soap or .rem if IIS hosts the object so that the request can be properly routed.

The client configuration file shown in Figure 13.3 is about the same format as the server configuration file. Note that the type attribute of the `<wellknown>` tag is identical. Also note that the client specifies a `url` attribute that indicates where the server is to be found. The first part of the URL specifies that the protocol to be used is HTTP (compare the `<channel>` element in the server configuration file). The second part is a description of the address and port at which the server can be found. It is of the following form:

```
address:port
```

where address is either a name that your DNS server knows or an IP address followed by a colon and the port number that is to be used. Notice that the port number in this URL needs to match the port number that is assigned to the server in the server configuration file.

The URL then specifies the name of the server, which should be the same name as provided in the server configuration file as an attribute to `<application>`.

At that point, the URL specifies the endpoint that will be used to connect to the server. This URL also has encoded into the name the format of the data. For SOAP calls, the suffix is .soap; all other formats use the .rem suffix to the endpoint.

To start the application from a command prompt, move to the directory where the Time solution has been installed and then change to the `Timeserver` directory. From that directory, start up the server as follows:

```
Start bin\debug\TimeServer.exe
```

or

```
bin\debug\TimeServer.exe
```

Next start up the client, and you should see an application similar to Figure 13.4.

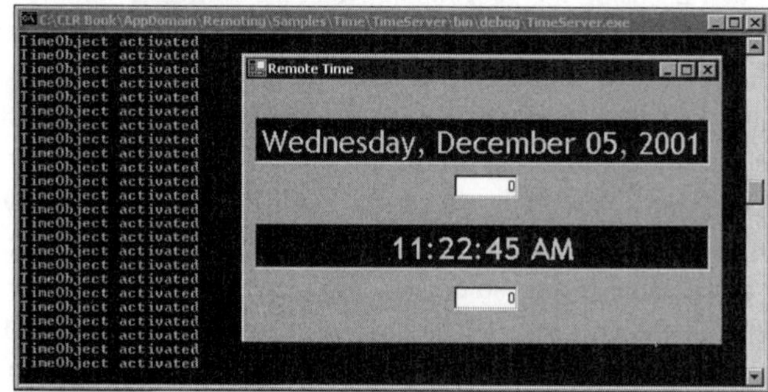

FIGURE 13.4
Directly hosted TimeClient.

You can see evidence that the server is serving a `SingleCall` type of object in two ways: from the window where the server is activated, and from the client display. First, notice in the window where the server was activated that a continuous stream of messages is similar to what follows:

```
TimeObject activated
TimeObject activated
. . .
TimeObject activated
TimeObject activated
TimeObject activated
```

These messages come from the constructor of the object. Because a new object is constructed with each method call, you should see about four of these messages every second. The timer fires an event every second, and you can make two method calls to `Date` and `Time`, followed by two method calls to `DateCount` and `TimeCount`.

In the second evidence of a SingleCall server, you can see that the small numbers underneath the date and time displays never increment. These values are incremented each time the `Date` or `Time` properties are accessed. They are zero because every call into the object results in a new instance of the object, including the call to `DateCount` and `TimeCount`. Therefore, these values are always zero.

Changing the mode attribute of the `<wellknown>` tag in the configuration file of the server to `Singleton` dramatically changes the characteristics of the `TimeServer`. The output screen of `TimeServer` looks like this:

```
Press <cr> to exit
TimeObject activated
```

Notice that the counters underneath the date and time displays are incrementing. In addition, only one activation takes place and it maintains state between client method calls. These are characteristic of a server-activated `Singleton`.

The Time Server Using IIS as a Host

Now you can take advantage of IIS by making it the host for this application. This solution is in the `TimeIIS` directory. This section illustrates what has changed from the previous direct host `Time` application.

Because IIS is the host, you don't need a server; IIS acts as the server. You need to create a virtual directory as part of IIS. For this demo, `TimeIIS` is the alias used to access the service. The physical directory that you will be using is where you installed the `TimeIIS` sample files (`...\Remoting\TimeIIS` is a possibility).

Construct a file called `web.config` and place it in the same physical directory to which you pointed the IIS virtual directory. Because you need to modify the client configuration file and essentially copy the server configuration file to `web.config` and modify it, the two configuration files are compared side-by-side in Figure 13.5.

WEB.CONFIG

```
<configuration>
 <system.runtime.remoting>
  <application>
   <service>
    <wellknown mode="SingleCall"
               type=CLRUnleashed.Remoting.TimeObject,TimeObject"
               objectURi="TimeObject.soap"/>
   </service>
  </application>
 </system.runtime.remoting>
</configuration>
```

Looks for TimeObject Assembly in bin directory

TIMECLIENT.EXE.CONFIG

```
<configuration>
 <system.runtime.remoting>
  <application  name="TimeClient">
   <client>
    <wellknown type=type="CLRUnleashed.Remoting.TimeObject, TimeObject"
               url="http://localhost/TimeIIS/TimeObject.Soap"/>
   </client>
  </application>
 </system.runtime.remoting>
</configuration>
```

IIS Virtual Directory

IIS Host Name

FIGURE 13.5
IIS hosted TimeClient configuration files.

Notice that the `web.config` is almost an exact copy of the server configuration file. The only exception is that a name attribute is no longer attached to the `<application>` tag. Because IIS is hosting the object, the name no longer makes sense. The rest of the file is identical to the configuration file that was used for a direct-hosted object.

The client configuration file has a small change that is required to locate the host. The host is IIS, so the port is defaulted to port 80 for HTTP. You still are using localhost, although in a real application, this would be the address of the machine that is running IIS. The next part of the URL specifies the alias name that was given to the IIS virtual directory. For this example, it is named `TimeIIS`. The endpoint has not changed. You still are interested in the `TimeObject`, and you still are interested in using SOAP.

That is all there is to using IIS for a host. Because IIS is no doubt already running, you don't have to worry about starting a separate server. If you start the client, you get the same output as described earlier and as illustrated in Figure 13.5. Because you do not have access to the console output for IIS, all of the print statements that were issued in the constructor essentially go into a bit bucket somewhere and are silently ignored. The only indication that you have now that this is a `SingleCall` or a `Singleton` is from the counters below the date and time displays. If you change the `web.config` `<wellknown>` tag to have a mode of `Singleton`, then the counters continuously increment once a second. Putting the mode back to `SingleCall` causes zeros to be displayed.

Instantiating a Remoted Object Using `Activator.GetObject`

Configuration files are easy to use and flexible. You can make changes to the configuration file without needing to recompile. Sometimes you might not want to use configuration files, however. The .NET Framework gives you several ways to connect to a remotely hosted object without a configuration file.

The first method that a client can use to avoid a configuration file is to instantiate an object with **`Activator.GetObject`**. Listing 13.13 shows how to use this method call. The full source for an application that uses **`Activator.GetObject`** is in the `TimeGO` subdirectory.

LISTING 13.13 **`Activator.GetObject`** on `TimeObject`

```
string url = "http://localhost:9000/RemoteTime/TimeObject.soap";
Type type = typeof(TimeObject);
timeService = (TimeObject)Activator.GetObject(type, url);
if (true == RemotingServices.IsTransparentProxy(timeService))
{
    Debug.WriteLine("TimeObject activated on server");
    timer.Enabled = true;
}
```

This project is basically the same as the solution in the `Time` subdirectory. No changes are required to the object, and no changes are required to the server. The client no longer calls **`RemotingConfiguration.Configure`**, so the configuration file is no longer required for the client. Instead of calling new to instantiate the object, you can call **`Activator.GetObject`**. No other changes exist. The client application for this sample looks identical to Figure 13.4.

Instantiating a Remoted Object Using `RemotingServices.Connect`

Another alternative to using configuration files on the client is to use a function **`RemotingServices.Connect`**. A sample on how to use this method is included in part in Listing 13.14. The full source for this application is included in the `TimeConnect` subdirectory.

LISTING 13.14 **`RemotingServices.Connect`** on `TimeObject`

```
Type type = typeof(TimeObject);
string url = "http://localhost:9000/RemoteTime/TimeObject.soap";

timeService = (TimeObject)RemotingServices.Connect(type, url);
if (true == RemotingServices.IsTransparentProxy(timeService))
{
    Debug.WriteLine("TimeObject activated on server");
    timer.Enabled = true;
}
```


Calling this method seems to be almost identical to calling **`Activator.GetObject`**. Which one to use is simply a matter of choice.

Instantiating a Remoted Object with `RegisterWellKnownClientType`

One final way that the client can instantiate and use a remoted object without the use of a configuration file is by registering a well-known type. A sample of how to do this is included in Listing 13.15. The full source for this application is in the `TimeRWKT` subdirectory.

LISTING 13.15 Registering a Well-Known Type

```
ChannelServices.RegisterChannel(new HttpChannel());
string url = "http://localhost:9000/RemoteTime/TimeObject.soap";
Type type = typeof(TimeObject);
RemotingConfiguration.RegisterWellKnownClientType(type, url);
timeService = new TimeObject();
```

All three of these applications that do not require a configuration file have the URI used to contact the server hard-coded. As it stands, changing the URI would require a recompile of the source. You could devise a scheme in which the URI is read in from a file, but then you would just be re-creating the configuration file and you might as well use it.

Using a `Client-Activated` Object

`Client-Activated` objects require a sizable change to an application that is currently using a server-activated or well-known type. You need to change the configuration files (if you are using `Client-Activated` objects, you no longer use `<wellknown>`), and you need to change the client slightly. The full source to this application is in the `TimeCA` subdirectory.

The server configuration file now looks like Listing 13.16.

LISTING 13.16 Server-Side Configuration File for a `Client-Activated` Object

```
<configuration>
  <system.runtime.remoting>
    <application name="RemoteTime">
      <service>
        <activated type="CLRUnleashed.Remoting.TimeObject, TimeObject"/>
      </service>
      <channels>
        <channel port="9000" ref="http" />
      </channels>
    </application>
  </system.runtime.remoting>
</configuration>
```

The only change to the server configuration file is that the `<wellknown>` tag has been replaced by the `<activated>` tag. The `<activated>` tag has a single attribute, type, that is the same type that was specified for `<wellknown>`, only now the server is made aware that the client is activating this type and not the server. On the client side is an `<activated>` tag that looks identical to the server side `<activated>` tag.

On the client side, you need to replace the `<client>` element and all its subelements with the following:

```
<client url="http://localhost:9000/RemoteTime">
  <activated type="CLRUnleashed.Remoting.TimeObject, TimeObject"/>
</client>
```

That is all that must be changed. The client reads in the configuration file, initializes the remoting services, instantiates the remote object, and calls methods on those objects. A slight change has been made to the client (and the object) to illustrate that the object can be constructed on the client with arguments. When you right-click on the form, you are presented with a list of culture strings. Selecting any one of these causes a new `TimeObject` to be constructed and the time on the server to be presented in a localized fashion. You pass a culture identification string to the constructor so that the time string being passed back will be localized to that culture. Figure 13.6 shows the screenshot of the `TimeClient` after a culture string has been passed to the `TimeObject`.

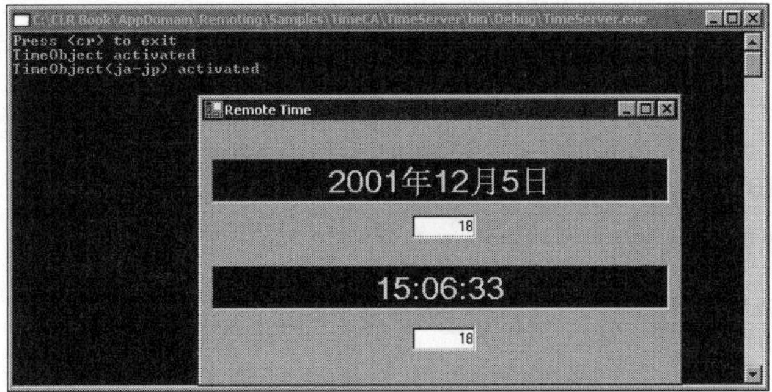

FIGURE 13.6
Client-Activated TimeClient.

Asynchronous Calls to a Remote Object

Now assume that the operation that is to perform on the server is time intensive. You don't want to have to tie up resources waiting for the operation to finish. The goal is to start up a request and have it notify you when it is done. You can do this using the asynchronous programming model that is discussed in Chapter 11, "Threading," and Chapter 14, "`Delegates` and `Events`." Asynchronously calling a method on a remote object requires no changes to the object being remoted or to the server. The changes are just to the client code. Listing 13.17 shows how the client code changes to initialize the delegates and the asynchronous callback. The complete source that is associated with Listing 13.17 is in the `TimeAsync` directory.

LISTING 13.17 Asynchronous Client Setup

```
public delegate string ReturnTimeDelegate();
public delegate string ReturnDateDelegate();
. . .
string configFilename = "timeclient.exe.config";
if(!Initialize(configFilename))
    return;

timeService = new TimeObject();
if (true == RemotingServices.IsTransparentProxy(timeService))
```

LISTING 13.17 Continued

```
{
    returnTimeDelegate = new ReturnTimeDelegate(timeService.Time);
    returnDateDelegate = new ReturnDateDelegate(timeService.Date);
    asyncDateCallback = new AsyncCallback(DateCallBack);
    asyncTimeCallback = new AsyncCallback(TimeCallBack);
    Debug.WriteLine("TimeObject activated on server");
    timer.Enabled = true;
}
```

Now that you have the delegates in place, you can asynchronously call the remoted objects methods, as shown in Listing 13.18.

LISTING 13.18 Asynchronously Calling Remote Methods

```
public void DateCallBack(IAsyncResult ar)
{
    ReturnDateDelegate d = (ReturnDateDelegate)((AsyncResult)ar).
➥AsyncDelegate;
    string rdate = d.EndInvoke(ar);
    date.Text = rdate;
    dateCount.Text = Convert.ToString(timeService.DateCount);
}

public void TimeCallBack(IAsyncResult ar)
{
    ReturnTimeDelegate d = (ReturnTimeDelegate)((AsyncResult)ar).
➥AsyncDelegate;
    string rtime = d.EndInvoke(ar);
    time.Text = rtime;
    timeCount.Text = Convert.ToString(timeService.TimeCount);
}
. . .
IAsyncResult ar;
ar = returnTimeDelegate.BeginInvoke(asyncTimeCallback, null);
ar = returnDateDelegate.BeginInvoke(asyncDateCallback, null);
```

This simple example shows that you don't have to wait around for the result from a remote method call.

Generating and Using a WSDL Description of a Remote Object

It is possible to give a remoting server that is running an HTTP channel a command such as the following:

```
GET /RemoteTime/TimeObject.soap?WSDL HTTP/1.1
Connection: Keep-Alive
Host: localhost
```

It returns the WSDL description of the object that it is servicing:

```
<?xml version="1.0" encoding="UTF-8" ?>
<definitions name="TimeObject"
➥targetNamespace="http://schemas.microsoft.com/clr/nsassem/
➥CLRUnleashed.Remoting/TimeObject%2C%20Version%3D1.0.700.27936%2C
➥%20Culture%3Dneutral%2C%20PublicKeyToken%3Dnull"
➥xmlns="http://schemas.xmlsoap.org/wsdl/"
. . .
```

Two tools can take advantage of this fact and create an assembly or C# code from the WSDL that is generated. These two tools are `soapsuds` and `wsdl`. Either of these two tools allows you to generate from the server an assembly that communicates with a server. The real power in these tools is in the ability to generate code from WSDL. Converting WSDL to C# code can be used to interop with non-.NET servers. This is done in the section "Consuming a Web Service Using Remoting." First, an understanding of how to generate proxy code and assemblies from .NET servers is required.

A sample project illustrates code that is generated from a remoting host. The complete project is in the `TimeWSDLDirect` subdirectory.

First, start up the host. This project is geared to work with the `TimeServer` in the `Time` subdirectory. If this project has not been built, then you will need to build it so that this remoting host is available. Next, start up the remoting host with a line like this:

```
TimeServer
```

or this:

```
start TimeServer
```

If you are not in the same directory as `TimeServer.exe`, then you will either need to move to that directory or move to the same directory as the application solution (.sln file) and supply a complete path to the executable.

After you have started the host, you can generate an assembly that describes the methods required for the proxy using the soapsuds tool. A `build.bat` file contains a specific command required to generate the assembly. The batch file executes a single command:

```
soapsuds -url:http://localhost:9001/RemoteTime/TimeObject.soap?WSDL
➥-oa:TimeObject.dll
```

This creates a proxy assembly that allows you to communicate with the host against which the soapsuds tool was run.

Now you can start up the solution in the `TimeWSDLDirect` subdirectory. The solution should have a reference to the local assembly created with the soapsuds tool. You will now be able to build the project and the `TimeClient`, which has been unmodified from the `TimeClient` in the `Time` subdirectory.

You can also perform a similar task if the host is IIS. The full source to this solution is in the `TimeWSDL` subdirectory. Using the same setup that you had in place for the `TimeIIS` solution, you can create a proxy by pointing the `soapsuds` tool at the URL that corresponds to the remote host. For this test, you can use the local host so that the `build.bat` file contains a single line:

```
soapsuds -url:http://localhost/TimeIIS/TimeObject.soap?WSDL
➥-oa:TimeObject.dll
```

Using the same `TimeClient` that was used for the `TimeWSDLDirect` project, you can produce the same UI.

You can use the `wsdl` tool in two different, yet virtually identical ways. The first method is to use Web References within Visual Studio 7. The second method is to call `wsdl` directly from the command line. Both methods generate the same code. The following example uses Visual Studio to illustrate the code that is generated from `wsdl`. Figure 13.7 shows Visual Studio in one part of adding a Web reference.

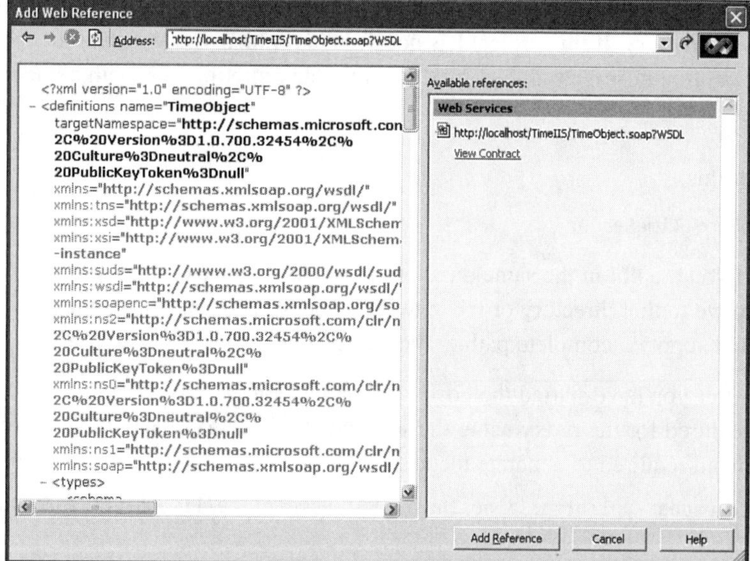

FIGURE 13.7
Adding a Web reference.

The code that is generated from adding a Web reference is significantly different from code that is generated from a tool such as `soapsuds`. For comparison purposes, the following will show the client code that changes from that which is required to use the code generated by soapsuds in the previous example. The changed client code is shown in Listing 13.19.

LISTING 13.19 Client Code to Use Proxy Code Generated from Visual Studio's Add Web Reference

```
. . .
using TimeClient.localhost;
. . .
timeService = new TimeObjectService();
timer.Enabled = true;
. . .
try
{
    time.Text = timeService.get_Time();
    date.Text = timeService.get_Date();
    dateCount.Text = Convert.ToString(timeService.get_DateCount());
    timeCount.Text = Convert.ToString(timeService.get_TimeCount());
}
catch(Exception exception)
{
    Debug.WriteLine(exception);
    timeService = null;
    timer.Enabled = false;
}
```


To avoid continual prefacing of each object with the namespace, a using statement is included. Then a proxy class wrapper that is generated from adding a Web reference is instantiated. Notice that `TimeObject` is not instantiated, as it was originally when generating the code for the server. When you construct an object, the URL that was used to generate the code is embedded in the generated code. The default constructor looks like this:

```
public TimeObjectService() {
   this.Url = "http://localhost:80/TimeIIS/TimeObject.soap";
}
```

If you want to access a different URL using this same proxy, you at least need to modify this URL. Listing 13.20 shows how the object methods are called on the remote object via the proxy.

LISTING 13.20 Calling Proxy-Generated Methods

```
private void OnTick(object sender, System.EventArgs e)
{
    if(timeService != null)
    {
        try
        {
            time.Text = timeService.get_Time();
            date.Text = timeService.get_Date();
            dateCount.Text = Convert.ToString(timeService.get_DateCount());
            timeCount.Text = Convert.ToString(timeService.get_TimeCount());
        }
        catch(Exception exception)
        {
            Debug.WriteLine(exception);
            timeService = null;
            timer.Enabled = false;
        }
    }
}
```

Now the code is complete and this sample can be compiled and run. The UI has not changed from Figure 13.4.

Adding a Web reference is the automated way to call the `wsdl` tool. You can generate proxy code as follows:

```
wsdl http://localhost/TimeIIS/TimeObject.soap?WSDL
```

In this case, the C# code file that is generated is `TimeObjectService.cs`. If you compile this file as follows:

```
csc /t:library TimeObjectService.cs
```

you will have an assembly that you can reference. If you remove the Web reference, remove the **`using TimeObject.local;`** statement, and add a reference to this file, the code compiles and runs just the same as with a Web reference.

Consuming a Web Service Using Remoting

The real power of tools such as soapsuds is that as long as a WSDL description of the service is provided by the SOAP server, soapsuds can automatically generate an assembly that contains the transparent proxy to the object. This works with .NET and non-.NET SOAP servers. You have seen how to use this tool with another .NET SOAP server. Now will see how to use this tool to connect to a non-.NET SOAP server.

This sample requires a little setup for it to work. The sample is in the `WebServiceClient` directory. You need to open a command-line window and change to where you installed the `WebServiceClient` sample. The proxy assemblies need to be built. A simple batch file runs the soapsuds tool against several Web services and generates the proxy assemblies for each of the services. The `build.bat` batch file consists of three lines:

```
soapsuds -url:http://www.vbws.com/services/weatherretriever.asmx?WSDL
➥-oa:Weather.dll
soapsuds -url:http://www.itfinity.net:8008/soap/Calculator/Calculator.wsdl
➥-oa:Calculator.dll
soapsuds -url:http://www.xmethods.net/sd/2001/TemperatureService.wsdl
➥-oa:Temp.dll
```

Now you can bring up Visual Studio and compile and run the project. You already have references to the assemblies built in the project. When you run the application, you can enter the zip code. Upon either leaving the zip code field or pressing the Enter key, the application initiates a call to two Web services that offer simple weather information. One service gives more detailed information on the weather at a particular location, and the other just returns the current temperature. The other Web service that is illustrated in this application is an algebraic expression evaluator. The Web service takes in an algebraic expression (such as (1+3)*5) and returns the result. Many more Web services are available, some of them with a price. Some are just demonstrations of Web services.

Using Remoting APIs to Consume a Web Service

Although the `soapsuds` tool provides an easy-to-use and powerful function, you might want to programmatically perform the same function. Within the **`System.Runtime.Remoting.MetadataServices`** name space is a class called **`MetaData`** that exposes several methods for converting WSDL to a type, converting WSDL to C# code, and converting C# code to assemblies. Some of the methods that are available are as follows:

- **`ConvertTypesToSchemaToStream`**—Converts the specified types to an XML schema and writes it to a stream
- **`RetrieveSchemaFromUrlToStream`**—Downloads an XML scheme from the specified URL and writes it to a stream
- **`ConvertSchemaStreamToCodeSourceStream`**—Converts the specified XML schema (in a stream) to a C# source code representing a proxy
- **`ConvertCodeSourceStreamToAssemblyFile`**—Compiles the specified source code stream into an assembly file

These APIs are the same ones that the soapsuds tool uses; therefore, all of the uses for the soapsuds tool also apply to these APIs. You just need to write a program to use them. A simple project, located in the WeatherProg subdirectory, illustrates the use of these APIs. This project takes a hardcoded URL, converts it to an assembly, loads the assembly, and calls methods on this assembly.

Making SOAP Calls from COM

For Windows XP and Windows.NET Server platforms, a moniker is available that allows remoting services to be called from COM. To use this moniker, perform the following steps:

- GetObject("soap:wsdl=http://url_to_wsdl"). This call causes the WSDL to be downloaded. The Remoting Metadata Proxy Generation engine turns the WSDL into a type library that is saved at a temporary location on disk. A remoting proxy is returned to the COM caller using the interop services. This proxy looks like a COM interface to the caller.
- Make calls on the proxy object that is passed back from GetObject. Calls on the interface that are passed back to the caller result in calls to the proxy, which, in turn, are translated to SOAP messages that are exchanged with the server.

In the ComPlusWebServices\SoapMoniker\VBScript directory, several scripts illustrate the usefulness of this moniker. The first script calls the Web service that was created earlier when discussing remoting using IIS as a host. It relies on the TimeIIS virtual directory still being intact and the assembly in the bin directory up to date. The script is shown in Listing 13.21.

LISTING 13.21 Calling the Time Service from VB Script

```
Set timeService = GetObject("soap:wsdl=http://localhost/TimeIIS/
➥TimeObject.soap?WSDL")
WScript.Echo "Made a SOAP call from VBS ... time " & timeService.Time
```

This simple script instantiates a proxy to the TimeServer (hosted by IIS) and calls a method on it to retrieve the time.

This also works for truly remote Web services. Listing 13.22 shows a script that queries the Barnes & Noble database for the price of a book. The book is identified by its ISBN number. This sample is in the same directory as the TimeServer.vbs script shown previously.

LISTING 13.22 Using Remoting to Query for a Book Price

```
Set bnQuoteService = GetObject(
➥"soap:wsdl=http://www.xmethods.net/sd/BNQuoteService.wsdl")

name="ASP.NET Unleashed"
isbn = "0672320681"
price = bnQuoteService.getPrice(isbn)
WScript.Echo "SOAP call from VBS ... isbn " & isbn & " " & name &
➥"  returned $" & price
name="C# Unleashed"
isbn = "067232122-X"
price = bnQuoteService.getPrice(isbn)
WScript.Echo "SOAP call from VBS ... isbn " & isbn & " " & name &
➥ "  returned $" & price
name=".NET and COM, The Complete COM Ineroperability Guide"
isbn = "067232170-X"
price = bnQuoteService.getPrice(isbn)
WScript.Echo "SOAP call from VBS ... isbn " & isbn & " " & name &
➥ "  returned $" & price
name=".NET Framework Security"
isbn = "067232184-X"
price = bnQuoteService.getPrice(isbn)
WScript.Echo "SOAP call from VBS ... isbn " & isbn & " " & name &
➥ "  returned $" & price
name = ".NET Common Language Runtime Unleashed"
isbn = "00672321246"
price = bnQuoteService.getPrice(isbn)
WScript.Echo "SOAP call from VBS ... isbn " & isbn & " " & name &
➥ "  returned $" & price
```


The transparent proxy to be built and a COM interface are returned. Then a remoting method is called to retrieve the price of the book. The output for this script is shown in Listing 13.23.

LISTING 13.23 Output for the Book Prices Query

```
SOAP ... isbn 0672320681 ASP.NET Unleashed  returned $54.99
SOAP ... isbn 067232122-X C# Unleashed  returned $49.95
SOAP  ... isbn 067232170-X .NET and COM, The Complete COM Interoperability
➥Guide returned $59.99
SOAP ... isbn 067232184-X .NET Framework Security  returned $54.99
```

In this same directory is a script that retrieves the current price of a stock.

The `ComPlusWebServices\SoapMoniker\DotNetClient` directory has two source files—one for VB and the other for C#. Both of these scripts use the .NET Framework Class libraries to retrieve a stock quote.

One last application for COM callable remote service is illustrated with an Excel spreadsheet. Three different worksheets are in the `ComPlusWebServices\SoapMoniker\ExcelClient` directory. One of the worksheets, `Temperature.xls`, displays an array of cities with the corresponding zip code. In the area where the contents of the cell are edited, you can see that the current cell calls a macro called `getTemp` to fill in the value for the cell. Figure 13.8 shows this worksheet.

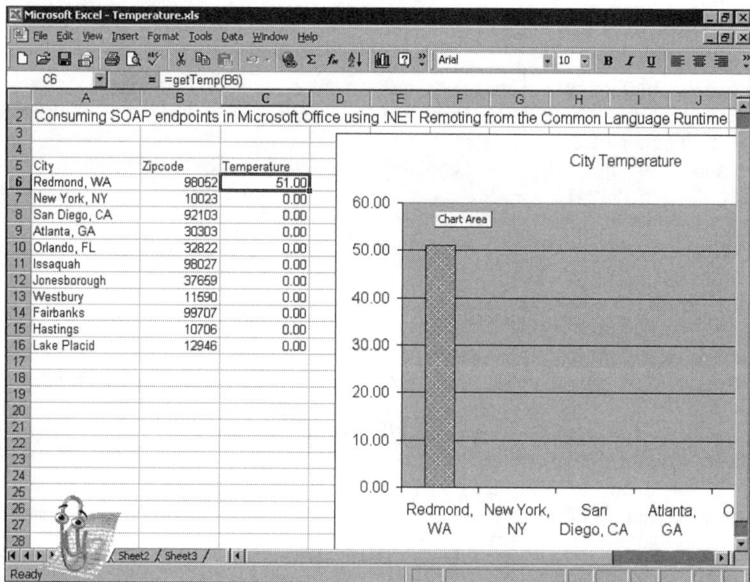

FIGURE 13.8
Remoting from an Excel spreadsheet.

The `getTemp` macro is defined as a VBA script. To see the functions that the script performs, bring up the Visual Basic Macro Editor, as shown in Figure 13.9.

As you can see from Figure 13.9, this macro contains a call to `GetObject`, which is responsible for returning a COM object based on the moniker that is passed to it. As explained earlier in this section, the COM object that is returned is wired to a remote proxy. Therefore, when you call a method on this COM object, that method (in this case `getTemp(zipcode)`) is translated into a remote call to the SOAP server that is specified in the moniker to `GetObject`.

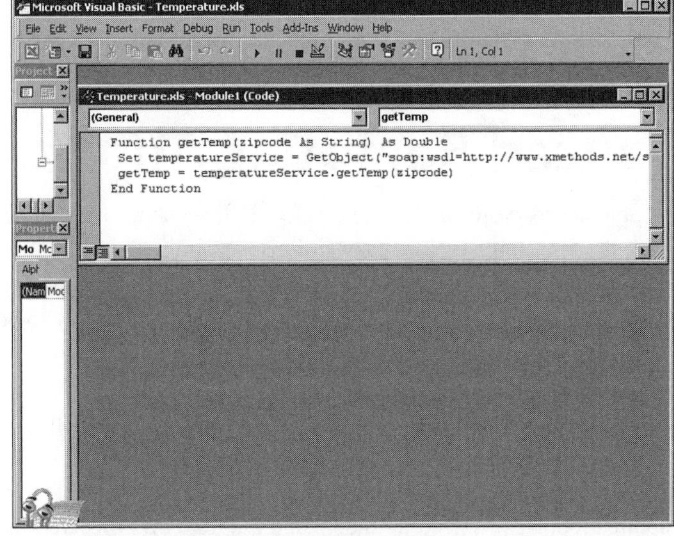

FIGURE 13.9
Definition for the `getTemp` *macro.*

> **Note**
>
> A few Web services have been illustrated in this chapter, but you can find many more at sites such as `http://www.xmethods.net/ilab/`.

Converting a COM+ Component to a Web Service by Using Remoting

In the final section of Chapter 8, "Using COM/COM+ from Managed Code," you learned how to turn a COM+ component into a Web service. That method uses both interop services and the remoting services that are available from the .NET Framework. Actually, this allows the COM+ services to act as a host for a remote object. Now a remote object has three possible hosts: direct, IIS, and COM+. This functionality is extremely powerful. As reinforcement, the following steps are involved in using this feature:

1. Click in the COM+ Admin tool.
2. Click the Application Activation tab.
3. Configure the COM components for .NET Remoting.
4. Create the IIS Virtual directory.
5. Generate web.config.
6. Generate metadata.

The important point is that all of this is made possible through the combination of the remoting services and COM/COM+ interop. The combination gives your "legacy" components new life.

Advanced Remoting Topics

For most applications, you can use the services that are available. Visual Studio .NET makes using the remoting services easy and gives you the flexibility to build powerful applications without having to know a lot about what is actually happening. One of the more powerful features of .NET Framework Remoting is its ability to be extended. Two samples are included that illustrate building an extension to remoting. The first extension is a custom channel sink that blocks incoming calls based on the IP address of the caller. The second is a logging sink that logs the traffic to and from the client and server. It is also possible to control the default lifetime management for `Singleton` and `Client-Activated` objects with **`ISponsor`** and **`ILease`**. You might need to tune the performance of your application, so you need to understand the tradeoffs involved in choosing a protocol and formatter combination.

Implementing a Custom Channel Sink to Block Certain IP Addresses

To enable you to understand what needs to change for your application to take advantage of the extensibility features of .NET Remoting, the necessary code was inserted into the `Time` application so that you can hook into the appropriate hooks. Compare this application with the original `Time` application and see that little has changed to dramatically affect the functionality of this application. Listing 13.24 shows the output from the server when a client is connected from an acceptable address (localhost) and when a client tries to connect from a disallowed address. The full source for this application is in the `TimeFilter` directory.

LISTING 13.24 Output of a Server That Filters IP Addresses

```
Listening...
Mode: Accept
Mask: 255.255.255.255  IP: 127.0.0.1
***** Press 0 to exit this service *****
127.0.0.1
Hello.
152.165.92.100
Reject.
```

When the client is rejected, an exception is thrown. This exception is shown in Listing 13.25.

LISTING 13.25 Exception That Is Generated When a Client Is Rejected

```
Unhandled Exception: System.Net.WebException:
➥The remote server returned an error: (403) Forbidden.

Server stack trace:
   at System.Runtime.Remoting.Channels.Http.HttpClientTransportSink.
➥ProcessResponseExceptin(WebException webException,
➥HttpWebResponse& response)
   at System.Runtime.Remoting.Channels.Http.HttpClientTransportSink.
➥ProcessMessage(IMessage msg, ITransportHeaders requestHeaders,
➥Stream requestStream, ITransportHeaders& responseHeaders,
➥Stream& responseStream)
   at System.Runtime.Remoting.Channels.SoapClientFormatterSink.
➥SyncProcessMessage(IMessage msg)

Exception rethrown at [0]:
   at System.Runtime.Remoting.Proxies.RealProxy.HandleReturnMessage(
➥IMessage reqMsg, IMessage retMsg)
   at System.Runtime.Remoting.Proxies.RealProxy.PrivateInvoke(
➥MessageData& msgData, Int32 type)
```


The server can reject a client based on his IP address. The specification for which IP addresses are valid and how that validation is carried out is in the configuration file for the client and server. Listing 13.26 illustrates the client configuration file.

LISTING 13.26 Client Configuration File Showing an Additional Channel Sink

```
<configuration>
  <system.runtime.remoting>

    <channelSinkProviders>
        <serverProviders>
            <provider id="ip filter" type=
➥"IPFilter.IPFilterChannelSinkProvider, IPFilterSink" />
        </serverProviders>
    </channelSinkProviders>

    <application name="TimeClient">
      <client>
        <wellknown type="CLRUnleashed.Remoting.TimeObject, TimeObject"
➥url="http://localhost:9000/RemoteTime/TimeObject.soap" />
      </client>
    </application>

  </system.runtime.remoting>
</configuration>
```

The only change to the "normal" configuration file is the addition of a section that specifies a channel sink on the server. An ID has been given to it, and the type is the same format as with any other "type" in the configuration, namely "*type, assembly name*". To resolve this type, the remoting services look in the assembly that is specified. The shortest version of the full assembly name is provided. You could also supply the version, culture, and public key token information to further specify an assembly. This would be particularly important if the assembly that you were referencing resided in the global assembly cache.

You need to modify the server configuration file. Listing 13.27 shows the configuration file after it has been modified.

LISTING 13.27 Server Configuration File Showing an Additional Channel Sink

```
<configuration>
  <system.runtime.remoting>

    <channelSinkProviders>
        <serverProviders>
            <provider id="ip filter" type=
➥"IPFilter.IPFilterChannelSinkProvider, IPFilterSink" />
        </serverProviders>
    </channelSinkProviders>

    <application name="RemoteTime">
      <service>
        <wellknown mode="SingleCall"
➥type="CLRUnleashed.Remoting.TimeObject, TimeObject"
➥objectUri="TimeObject.soap" />
      </service>
      <channels>
        <channel port="9000" ref="http">
            <serverProviders>
                <provider ref="ip filter" mode="accept">
                    <filter mask="255.255.255.255" ip="127.0.0.1" />
                </provider>
                <formatter ref="soap" />
            </serverProviders>
        </channel>
      </channels>
    </application>

  </system.runtime.remoting>
</configuration>
```

The first section that is inserted is the section that describes the channel sink. This section is enclosed in the `<channelSinkProviders>` tag. This section is identical to the description that is given in the client configuration file. Note that the order is important because you are describing a channel sink and giving it an ID. That ID is referenced later in the configuration file. If the ID were defined after it was referenced, then the configuration file would fail to load properly in the **RemotingConfiguration.Configure** call and an exception would be thrown.

The next section that is modified is the section that is enclosed in the `<channel>` tag. When a custom channel sink was not involved, this `<channel>` tag had no content. It only had two attributes that defined the port and the format. Now, it also has a section that is specific to the service provider, namely in the content for `<serviceProviders>`.

The `<provider>` tag must either have a `ref` attribute or must specify a type attribute that is the same format as the `<channelSinkProviders>` tag. Here, a `ref` attribute is specified, indicating that this `<provider>` tag has specific information that pertains to the provider that is specified by the ID. The mode attribute is a custom attribute that is specific to this provider. In this case, the mode will be either “accept” or “reject.” This means that the IP address enclosed is either a list of the addresses that will be accepted (all other addresses will be rejected) or a list of addresses that will be rejected (all other addresses will be accepted).

The `<filter>` element in this configuration file is a custom element that describes an IP address. For this sample, only one `<filter>` element that specifies `localhost` is specified. Because the `<provider>` attribute of mode was “accept,” the only address that will be accepted is from `localhost`. All other addresses will be rejected.

The code that implements the filter is in the `IPFilter` assembly, which has a separate project assigned to it. Listing 13.28 illustrates the beginning portion of the channel sink implementation.

LISTING 13.28 `IPFilter` Channel Sink Implementation

```
namespace IPFilter
{
    public class IPFilterChannelSinkProvider : IServerChannelSinkProvider
```

This is where the type name comes from. The namespace is `IPFilter` and the class name is `IPFilterChannelSinkProvider`. This class is derived from **IServerChannelSinkProvider**, so it must implement two methods (**CreateSink** and **GetChannelData**) and one property (**Next**).

When the server is starting up and the configuration file is being read, an instance of that channel sink is created using **Activator.CreateInstance**. This, in turn, calls the constructor shown in Listing 13.29.

LISTING 13.29 `IPFilter` Channel Sink Provider Construction

```
public IPFilterChannelSinkProvider(IDictionary properties,
➥ICollection providerData)
{
    String mode = (String)properties["mode"];
    if (String.Compare(mode, "accept", true) == 0)
        _acceptMode = true;
    else
    if (String.Compare(mode, "reject", true) == 0)
        _acceptMode = false;
    providerData = providerData;
}
```

From the dictionary of properties (the attributes supplied in the configuration file), you can read the "mode" and store it. The `providerData` represents the contents or subelements of the `<provider>`. In this case, one item represents the IP address that will be accepted. This collection is just cached. This provider needs to provide a sink when the configuration file is being processed. To provide a sink, the **`CreateSink`** method of the **`IServerChannelSink`** is called. The implementation of this method is shown in Listing 13.30.

LISTING 13.30 IPFilter Channel Sink Provider **`CreateSink`**

```
public IServerChannelSink CreateSink(IChannelReceiver channel)
{
    IServerChannelSink nextSink = null;
    if (_next != null)
        nextSink = _next.CreateSink(channel);

    IPFilterChannelSink sink = new IPFilterChannelSink(_acceptMode, nextSink);

    // add filters
    foreach (SinkProviderData data in _providerData)
    {
        String maskStr = (String)data.Properties["mask"];
        String ipStr = (String)data.Properties["ip"];
        String machineStr = (String)data.Properties["machine"];

        IPAddress mask = null;
        IPAddress ip = null;

        if (ipStr != null)
        {
            mask = IPAddress.Parse(maskStr);
            ip = IPAddress.Parse(ipStr);
        }
        else
```

LISTING 13.30 Continued

```
        {
            mask = IPAddress.Parse("255.255.255.255");
            ip = Dns.Resolve(machineStr).AddressList[0];
        }

        sink.AddFilter(mask, ip);
    }

    return sink;
}
```

The **CreateSink** method transfers the information that was supplied during the creation of an instance of this class and passes it to the actual channel sink. This sink is inserted before any of the existing sinks in the channel sink chain. The private member _next tells you if other sinks are in the chain. The call to **CreateSink** at the beginning builds up all of the other sinks in the chain before passing back the head of the chain. The filtering sink is constructed and becomes the new head of the list. After the channel sink is constructed, each of the accepted or rejected address or machine names is added to the channel sink. This channel sink is passed back as a return value from **CreateSink**. Now the channel sink chain is in place and ready to start accepting messages.

Each sink is given an opportunity to process the message that is sent from the client through the **ProcessMessage** method. This implementation of **ProcessMessage** is shown in Listing 13.31.

LISTING 13.31 IPFilter Channel Sink **ProcessMessage**

```
public ServerProcessing ProcessMessage(IServerChannelSinkStack sinkStack,
            IMessage requestMsg,
            ITransportHeaders requestHeaders, Stream requestStream,
            out IMessage responseMsg, out ITransportHeaders responseHeaders,
            out Stream responseStream)
{
    IPAddress ipAddress =
➥requestHeaders[CommonTransportKeys.IPAddress] as IPAddress;
    Console.WriteLine(ipAddress);

// Match the address
    bool accept = !MatchIPAddress(ipAddress) ^ _bAccept;
    if (accept)
    {
        return _nextSink.ProcessMessage(sinkStack, requestMsg,
                                        requestHeaders, requestStream,
                                        out responseMsg, out responseHeaders,
                                        out responseStream);
    }
```

LISTING 13.31 Continued

```
    else
    {
        responseHeaders = new TransportHeaders();
        responseHeaders["__HttpStatusCode"] = "403";
        responseHeaders["__HttpReasonPhrase"] = "Forbidden";
        Console.WriteLine("Reject.");

        responseMsg = null;
        responseStream = null;

        return ServerProcessing.Complete;
    }
} // ProcessMessage
```

The IP address of the caller (the client) is retrieved from the `requestHeaders`. If the address is acceptable, then the message is forwarded to the next sink in the chain. If the message is not from an acceptable IP address, then an error message is constructed in the response headers. The message and the stream are released and the method returns to indicate that the server has processed the message. This response is passed back to the client and eventually returned as an exception if the address is rejected.

Implementing a Logging Custom Channel Sink

One more example will demonstrate implementing a custom channel sink. This example implements a custom sink to log the messages as they are received on the client or the server. Every message is logged to a file, and a sample of the output is generated for a typical session, as shown in Listing 13.32. The full source for this sample is in `TimeLog` directory.

LISTING 13.32 Sample Logging Output

```
------------Request #1------------
Time: 12/9/2001 6:10:35 PM
------Headers-------
__ConnectionId: 1
__IPAddress: 127.0.0.1
__RequestUri: /RemoteTime/TimeObject.soap
Content-Type: text/xml; charset="utf-8"
__RequestVerb: POST
__HttpVersion: HTTP/1.1
User-Agent: Mozilla/4.0+(compatible; MSIE 6.0; Windows 5.1.2600.0;
➥MS .NET Remoting; MS .NET CLR 1.0.3512.0 )
SOAPAction: "http://schemas.microsoft.com/clr/nsassem/
➥CLRUnleashed.Remoting.TimeObject/TimeObject#get_Time"
Host: localhost
```

LISTING 13.32 Continued

```
---End of Headers---
<SOAP-ENV:Envelope xmlns:xsi="http://www.w3.org/2001/XMLSchema-instance"
➥xmlns:xsd="http://www.w3.org/2001/XMLSchema"
➥xmlns:SOAP-ENC="http://schemas.xmlsoap.org/soap/encoding/"
➥xmlns:SOAP-ENV="http://schemas.xmlsoap.org/soap/envelope/"
➥xmlns:clr="http://schemas.microsoft.com/soap/encoding/clr/1.0"
➥SOAP-ENV:encodingStyle="http://schemas.xmlsoap.org/soap/encoding/">
<SOAP-ENV:Body>
<i2:get_Time id="ref-1" xmlns:i2="http://schemas.microsoft.com/clr/nsassem/
➥CLRUnleashed.Remoting.TimeObject/TimeObject">
</i2:get_Time>
</SOAP-ENV:Body>
</SOAP-ENV:Envelope>
---------End of Request #1--------
------------Response #1-----------
Time: 12/9/2001 6:10:35 PM
------Headers-------
Content-Type: text/xml; charset="utf-8"
---End of Headers---
<SOAP-ENV:Envelope xmlns:xsi="http://www.w3.org/2001/XMLSchema-instance"
➥xmlns:xsd="http://www.w3.org/2001/XMLSchema"
➥xmlns:SOAP-ENC="http://schemas.xmlsoap.org/soap/encoding/"
➥xmlns:SOAP-ENV="http://schemas.xmlsoap.org/soap/envelope/"
➥xmlns:clr="http://schemas.microsoft.com/soap/encoding/clr/1.0"
➥SOAP-ENV:encodingStyle="http://schemas.xmlsoap.org/soap/encoding/">
<SOAP-ENV:Body>
<i2:get_TimeResponse id="ref-1"
➥xmlns:i2="http://schemas.microsoft.com/clr/nsassem/
➥CLRUnleashed.Remoting.TimeObject/TimeObject">
<return id="ref-3">6:10:35 PM</return>
</i2:get_TimeResponse>
</SOAP-ENV:Body>
</SOAP-ENV:Envelope>
---------End of Response #1--------
. . .
```

This type of information can be useful in trying to debug a remoting application. From Listing 13.32, you can see that most of the useful information about requests and responses to and from a remote server is logged as part of the output. You can see the SOAP request message that was transferred, the HTTP headers, and similar information for the response. As you will see later, this logging information can be turned on or off based on entries in the configuration files for the client or server. The sample that demonstrates this feature is in the `TimeLog` directory.

Listing 13.33 shows the configuration file for the client.

LISTING 13.33 Client Configuration File for a Logging Sink

```
<configuration>
  <system.runtime.remoting>

    <channelSinkProviders>
        <clientProviders>
            <provider id="logging" type=
➥"Logging.LoggingClientChannelSinkProvider, LoggingSinks" />
        </clientProviders>
    </channelSinkProviders>

    <application name="TimeClient">
      <client>
        <wellknown type="CLRUnleashed.Remoting.TimeObject, TimeObject"
➥url="http://localhost:9000/RemoteTime/TimeObject.soap" />
      </client>
      <channels>
        <channel ref="http">
            <clientProviders>
                <provider ref="logging" logfile="timeclient.log"/>
                <formatter ref="soap" />
            </clientProviders>
        </channel>
      </channels>
    </application>

  </system.runtime.remoting>
</configuration>
```

As with the `TimeFilter` sample, you can identify the sink provider by the type and the assembly in which you can find the type. You also give it an ID; in this case, you give the provider an ID of "logging." For the client configuration of the `TimeFilter` sample, no client-specific configuration information was available to input. For the `TimeLog` sample, the logging information is read in during the constructor for the client logging channel sink provider. The information that is contained in the `<provider>` element is passed to the constructor as an **`IDictionary`** interface for the attributes and an **`ICollection`** interface for the subelements or contents of the `<provider>` element. The configuration file shown in Listing 13.33 demonstrates how to specify the path to a log file.
Many options are available for the logging sink, which you can see in the `BaseLoggingChannelSinkProvider` class. The following options are available:

- binarylogging—Valid values of "true" or "false." Controls whether binary formatted channels should be logged.
- bytesperline—Number of bytes per line in a binary formatted log.

- exceptionsonly—Valid values of “true” or “false.” Controls whether only exceptions should be logged.
- headersonly—Valid values of “true” or “false.” Controls whether only the headers should be logged.
- httpliteralrequest—Valid values of “true” or “false.” Controls whether HTTP requests should be logged in a literal form.
- logfile—The path to a file to which logging output should be directed.
- synchronized—Valid values of “true” or “false.” Controls whether steps should be taken to synchronize the output.
- textlogging—Valid values of “true” or “false.” Controls whether text should be logged.
- timestamp—Valid values of “true” or “false.” Controls whether a timestamp should be included in the log.
- xmlprettyprint—Valid values of “true” or “false.” Controls whether XML data should be run through a pretty printer filter.

In addition to these configuration settings, you can redirect the logging output to virtually any stream, as shown in Listing 13.34.

LISTING 13.34 Client Programmatically Redirecting the Log Information

```
// get logging control object
IDictionary properties = ChannelServices.GetChannelSinkProperties(server);
ILoggingSink logging = (ILoggingSink)properties[typeof(LoggingSinkKey)];

// redirect logging to a file
logging.Out = new StreamWriter(File.OpenWrite("client.log"));
```

This listing shows redirecting the log information to another file, but this pattern could be used to set the output to go to any **`TextWriter`**-based class.

The server configuration file is much like the client configuration file. The server configuration file is shown in Listing 13.35.

LISTING 13.35 Server Configuration File for a Logging Sink

```
<configuration>
  <system.runtime.remoting>

    <channelSinkProviders>
        <serverProviders>
            <provider id="logging"
```

LISTING 13.35 Continued

```
➥type="Logging.LoggingServerChannelSinkProvider, LoggingSinks"/>
        </serverProviders>
    </channelSinkProviders>

    <application name="RemoteTime">
      <service>
        <wellknown mode="Singleton"
➥type="CLRUnleashed.Remoting.TimeObject, TimeObject"
➥objectUri="TimeObject.soap" />
      </service>
      <channels>
        <channel port="9000" ref="http">
            <serverProviders>
                <provider ref="logging" logfile="timeserver.log"/>
                <formatter ref="soap" />
            </serverProviders>
        </channel>
      </channels>
    </application>

  </system.runtime.remoting>
</configuration>
```

The configuration file in Listing 13.35 specifies a different log file for the server than was specified for the client in Listing 13.33. The two providers are completely separate. In fact, you could remove either one and still have the remaining channel sink provider provide a logging channel sink.

Just like the `TimeFilter` sample, the sink provider calls **`CreateSink`** during configuration file load time and a custom sink is added to the sink chain. When the sink's **`ProcessMessage`** is called, the only processing that is done is to log the data as specified in the configuration file. This is a little more complicated than with `TimeFilter` because no support is in place for asynchronous processing; therefore, the appropriate entries need to be made in the sink stack. Otherwise, **`ProcessMessage`** simply processes the message and logs the request and the response.

Extending and Controlling the Lifetime of a Remoted Object

For `Singleton` and `Client-Activated` objects, the server has control of the lifetime of the object. With `SingleCall` objects, the server also has control of the lifetime of the object, but it is known that the object will only live for the duration of the remote method call. With `Singleton` and `Client-Activated` objects, it is possible that the server will consider the object inactive and destroy it. In the meantime, the client might decide to attempt to access an object that the server has destroyed, which could be a problem. To alleviate this problem, a client can ask to be notified when the server is considering destroying an object. The client has the option of extending the lifetime of the object if needed. An application has been built in the `TimeLifetime` subdirectory to illustrate these principles.

Listing 13.36 shows a possible configuration file that specifies a lifetime for a `Singleton` object.

LISTING 13.36 Specifying Object Lifetime in the Server Configuration File

```
<configuration>
  <system.runtime.remoting>
    <application name="RemoteTime">
      <lifetime leaseTime="2S" renewOnCallTime="2S"
➥leaseManagerPollTime="1S" />
      <service>
        <wellknown mode="Singleton" type=
➥"CLRUnleashed.Remoting.TimeObject, TimeObject"
➥objectUri="TimeObject.soap" />
      </service>
      <channels>
        <channel port="9000" ref="http" />
      </channels>
    </application>
  </system.runtime.remoting>
</configuration>
```

A `<lifetime>` element has been added to the configuration file, which gives the server information about how long objects should live. Each of the attributes of the `<lifetime>` element specifies a time, and the units can be specified as days (D), hours (H), minutes (M), seconds (S), and milliseconds (MS). If no unit is given, it is assumed to be seconds (for example 10 is the same as 10S). It is possible to specify the following attributes for a `<lifetime>` element:

- `leaseTime`—This attribute specifies how long the object will be kept alive. The default is 5 minutes.
- `sponsorShipTimeout`—This attribute specifies how long the lease manager will wait for the sponsor to respond before destroying the object. The default is 2 minutes.
- `renewOnCallTime`—This attribute specifies how long the lease is extended with each method call. With each method call, the object is considered active. This attribute allows for the specification of how much time is added to the lease with each method call on the object. The default is 2 minutes.

- `leaseManagerPollTime`—This attribute specifies the amount of time that the lease manager sleeps between checking for expired leases. This attribute essentially supplies the granularity of the lease time. If your `leaseTime` is 2 seconds but the lease manager only wakes up every 10 seconds to check for expired leases, then an 8-second gap exists from when the lease expired to when the object can be destroyed.

If you add a `<lifetime>` element, as in Listing 13.36, and you lengthen the timer period to 3 seconds (one second over the lifetime of the object), you see the following output from the server:

```
TimeObject activated 12/8/2001 11:57:32 PM
TimeObject activated 12/8/2001 11:57:37 PM
TimeObject activated 12/8/2001 11:57:40 PM
TimeObject activated 12/8/2001 11:57:43 PM
TimeObject activated 12/8/2001 11:57:46 PM
TimeObject activated 12/8/2001 11:57:49 PM
```

With every firing of the timer method, calls are made on the remote object. Remember that this is a `Singleton` object, so you should not see the object activated this many times. The reason for the numerous activations is that the object has actually expired and each new method call causes a reactivation of the object (much like `SingleCall`). If you shorten the timer period to under the 2-second lifetime of the object, you see the following:

```
TimeObject activated 12/9/2001 12:07:04 AM
```

For a `Singleton` object, this is more like what you expect. Now the method calls come at a rate that is faster than the expiration of the object. Each method call renews the lease so that object never gets destroyed. You can add the following override to the remoted object:

```
public override object InitializeLifetimeService()
{
    return null;
}
```

Now you can lengthen the timer to something greater than 2 seconds and you only see one activation for the `Singleton` object. This is because returning a null causes the object to have an unlimited lifetime.

Choosing the Best Channel and Formatter Combination

Many factors go into choosing which channel protocol and formatter that an application that relies on remoting services should use. If you are trying to reach a wide audience or you require interoperability with non-.NET applications, then you will probably lean toward using HTTP with SOAP. If your application only talks to other .NET applications and some of your application resides behind a firewall, then the HTTP and binary combination seems to be the best. If you need a performance boost and your non-.NET clients can work with sockets, then you probably can use TCP and SOAP. If you just want raw speed and you are working only with .NET components, then you will want to use TCP and the binary formatter.

An application has been put together that illustrates the performance differences between each of these choices. This takes the same time remoting object that was used throughout the chapter and calls it enough times to form a conclusion as to how fast calls can be made using a given protocol and format combination. Figure 13.10 shows what this application looks like when it is running.

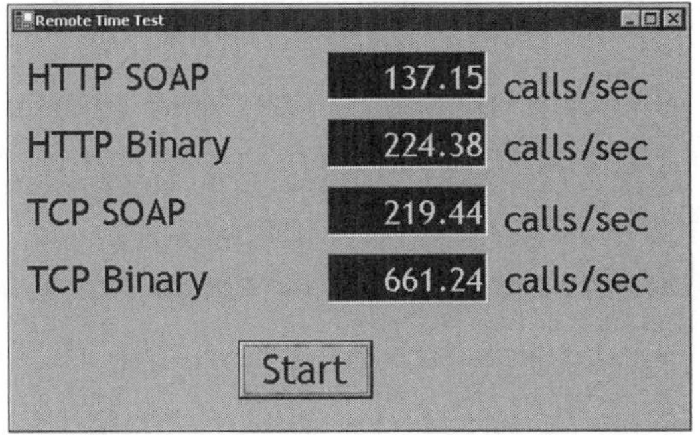

FIGURE 13.10
Timing format and protocol combinations.

As you would expect, the slowest of the group is the combination of HTTP and SOAP. HTTP used with the binary formatter is almost twice as fast as HTTP using the SOAP formatter. Switching protocols to TCP with a SOAP payload is not quite as fast as HTTP using a binary formatter, but it is almost as fast. With all of the header information that HTTP must generate and parse, it exacts a toll on the overall throughput of the transaction. Listing 13.37 shows a typical TCP message that is using SOAP encoding.

LISTING 13.37 TCP Header Information

```
0x000000   2E 4E 45 54 01 00 00 00 00 00 33 02 00 00 04 00    .NET......3.....
0x000010   01 01 2F 00 00 00 74 63 70 3A 2F 2F 6C 6F 63 61    ../...tcp://loca
0x000020   6C 68 6F 73 74 3A 38 30 30 31 2F 52 65 6D 6F 74    lhost:8001/Remot
0x000030   65 54 69 6D 65 2F 54 69 6D 65 4F 62 6A 65 63 74    eTime/TimeObject
0x000040   2E 73 6F 61 70 06 00 01 01 19 00 00 00 74 65 78    .soap........tex
0x000050   74 2F 78 6D 6C 3B 20 63 68 61 72 73 65 74 3D 22    t/xml; charset="
0x000060   75 74 66 2D 38 22 01 00 01 0A 00 00 00 53 4F 41    utf-8".......SOA
0x000070   50 41 63 74 69 6F 6E 01 5F 00 00 00 22 68 74 74    PAction._..."htt
0x000080   70 3A 2F 2F 73 63 68 65 6D 61 73 2E 6D 69 63 72    p://schemas.micr
```

LISTING 13.37 Continued

```
0x000090   6F 73 6F 66 74 2E 63 6F 6D 2F 63 6C 72 2F 6E 73    osoft.com/clr/ns
0x0000A0   61 73 73 65 6D 2F 43 4C 52 55 6E 6C 65 61 73 68    assem/CLRUnleash
0x0000B0   65 64 2E 52 65 6D 6F 74 69 6E 67 2E 54 69 6D 65    ed.Remoting.Time
0x0000C0   4F 62 6A 65 63 74 2F 54 69 6D 65 4F 62 6A 65 63    Object/TimeObjec
0x0000D0   74 23 67 65 74 5F 54 69 6D 65 22 00 00 3C 53 4F    t#get_Time"..<SO
0x0000E0   41 50 2D 45 4E 56 3A 45 6E 76 65 6C 6F 70 65 20    AP-ENV:Envelope
0x0000F0   78 6D 6C 6E 73 3A 78 73 69 3D 22 68 74 74 70 3A    xmlns:xsi="http:
0x000100   2F 2F 77 77 77 2E 77 33 2E 6F 72 67 2F 32 30 30    //www.w3.org/200
. . .
```

Compare that with the overhead of the header information in an HTTP request message. Listing 13.38 shows a typical request using HTTP and the SOAP formatter.

LISTING 13.38 HTTP Header Information

```
0x000000   50 4F 53 54 20 2F 52 65 6D 6F 74 65 54 69 6D 65    POST /RemoteTime
0x000010   2F 54 69 6D 65 4F 62 6A 65 63 74 2E 73 6F 61 70    /TimeObject.soap
0x000020   20 48 54 54 50 2F 31 2E 31 0D 0A 55 73 65 72 2D     HTTP/1.1..User-
0x000030   41 67 65 6E 74 3A 20 4D 6F 7A 69 6C 6C 61 2F 34    Agent: Mozilla/4
0x000040   2E 30 2B 28 63 6F 6D 70 61 74 69 62 6C 65 3B 20    .0+(compatible;
0x000050   4D 53 49 45 20 36 2E 30 3B 20 57 69 6E 64 6F 77    MSIE 6.0; Window
0x000060   73 20 35 2E 31 2E 32 36 30 30 2E 30 3B 20 4D 53    s 5.1.2600.0; MS
0x000070   20 2E 4E 45 54 20 52 65 6D 6F 74 69 6E 67 3B 20     .NET Remoting;
0x000080   4D 53 20 2E 4E 45 54 20 43 4C 52 20 31 2E 30 2E    MS .NET CLR 1.0.
0x000090   33 35 31 32 2E 30 20 29 0D 0A 43 6F 6E 74 65 6E    3512.0 )..Conten
0x0000A0   74 2D 54 79 70 65 3A 20 74 65 78 74 2F 78 6D 6C    t-Type: text/xml
0x0000B0   3B 20 63 68 61 72 73 65 74 3D 22 75 74 66 2D 38    ; charset="utf-8
0x0000C0   22 0D 0A 53 4F 41 50 41 63 74 69 6F 6E 3A 20 22    "..SOAPAction: "
0x0000D0   68 74 74 70 3A 2F 2F 73 63 68 65 6D 61 73 2E 6D    http://schemas.m
0x0000E0   69 63 72 6F 73 6F 66 74 2E 63 6F 6D 2F 63 6C 72    icrosoft.com/clr
0x0000F0   2F 6E 73 61 73 73 65 6D 2F 43 4C 52 55 6E 6C 65    /nsassem/CLRUnle
0x000100   61 73 68 65 64 2E 52 65 6D 6F 74 69 6E 67 2E 54    ashed.Remoting.T
0x000110   69 6D 65 4F 62 6A 65 63 74 2F 54 69 6D 65 4F 62    imeObject/TimeOb
0x000120   6A 65 63 74 23 67 65 74 5F 54 69 6D 65 22 0D 0A    ject#get_Time"..
0x000130   43 6F 6E 74 65 6E 74 2D 4C 65 6E 67 74 68 3A 20    Content-Length:
0x000140   35 36 33 0D 0A 45 78 70 65 63 74 3A 20 31 30 30    563..Expect: 100
0x000150   2D 63 6F 6E 74 69 6E 75 65 0D 0A 43 6F 6E 6E 65    -continue..Conne
0x000160   63 74 69 6F 6E 3A 20 4B 65 65 70 2D 41 6C 69 76    ction: Keep-Aliv
0x000170   65 0D 0A 48 6F 73 74 3A 20 6C 6F 63 61 6C 68 6F    e..Host: localho
0x000180   73 74 0D 0A 0D 0A 3C 53 4F 41 50 2D 45 4E 56 3A    st....<SOAP-ENV:
0x000190   45 6E 76 65 6C 6F 70 65 20 78 6D 6C 6E 73 3A 78    Envelope xmlns:x
0x0001A0   73 69 3D 22 68 74 74 70 3A 2F 2F 77 77 77 2E 77    si="http://www.w
0x0001B0   33 2E 6F 72 67 2F 32 30 30 31 2F 58 4D 4C 53 63    3.org/2001/XMLSc
. . .
```

Using TCP with the binary formatter is close to 5 times as fast as HTTP using SOAP. What are the reasons for such a performance gain? Most of it is due to the difference in the number of bytes that are transferred over the wire. Look at Listing 13.39, which shows a typical transaction using TCP and the binary formatter.

LISTING 13.39 TCP Binary Request Message

```
0x000000   2E 4E 45 54 01 00 00 00 00 00 8C 00 00 00 04 00   .NET............
0x000010   01 01 2F 00 00 00 74 63 70 3A 2F 2F 6C 6F 63 61   ../...tcp://loca
0x000020   6C 68 6F 73 74 3A 38 30 30 31 2F 52 65 6D 6F 74   lhost:8001/Remot
0x000030   65 54 69 6D 65 2F 54 69 6D 65 4F 62 6A 65 63 74   eTime/TimeObject
0x000040   2E 73 6F 61 70 06 00 01 01 18 00 00 00 61 70 70   .soap........app
0x000050   6C 69 63 61 74 69 6F 6E 2F 6F 63 74 65 74 2D 73   lication/octet-s
0x000060   74 72 65 61 6D 00 00 00 00 00 00 00 00 00 00 00   tream...........
0x000070   01 00 00 00 00 00 00 00 15 11 00 00 00 12 08 67   ...............g
0x000080   65 74 5F 54 69 6D 65 12 69 43 4C 52 55 6E 6C 65   et_Time.iCLRUnle
0x000090   61 73 68 65 64 2E 52 65 6D 6F 74 69 6E 67 2E 54   ashed.Remoting.T
0x0000A0   69 6D 65 4F 62 6A 65 63 74 2C 20 54 69 6D 65 4F   imeObject, TimeO
0x0000B0   62 6A 65 63 74 2C 20 56 65 72 73 69 6F 6E 3D 31   bject, Version=1
0x0000C0   2E 30 2E 37 30 37 2E 31 37 33 36 30 2C 20 43 75   .0.707.17360, Cu
0x0000D0   6C 74 75 72 65 3D 6E 65 75 74 72 61 6C 2C 20 50   lture=neutral, P
0x0000E0   75 62 6C 69 63 4B 65 79 54 6F 6B 65 6E 3D 6E 75   ublicKeyToken=nu
0x0000F0   6C 6C 0B 2E 4E 45 54 01 00 00 00 00 00 8C 00 00   ll..NET.........
```

Listing 13.39 shows the header information, but the listing also shows the entire request message. The whole message is roughly the same size as just the header information with TCP using the SOAP formatter. The response is even more terse. Listing 13.40 shows a typical response message using TCP binary.

LISTING 13.40 TCP Binary Response Message

```
0x000000   2E 4E 45 54 01 00 02 00 00 00 23 00 00 00 00 00   .NET......#.....
0x000010   00 00 00 00 00 00 00 00 00 01 00 00 00 00 00 00   ................
0x000020   00 16 11 08 00 00 12 0A 39 3A 33 39 3A 32 38 20   ........9:39:28
0x000030   41 4D 0B 2E 4E 45 54 01 00 02 00 00 00 23 00 00   AM..NET......#..
```

The entire response is about 50 bytes in length.

You can see that if overall throughput and message overhead were the only determining factors, using TCP with a binary formatter is a clear choice. However, as mentioned earlier, other factors influence the choice of one combination over another. With four possible choices, it is likely that one of the combinations will be a good fit for your application.

Debugging Remote Applications

In most cases, the hard part about debugging remote applications is that you don't know for sure what messages are being passed between remote locations. It would be nice if you could determine that a message was received and it was the proper format or that it was sent in a format that was expected. For this level of debugging, you need a tool that is inserted into the message stream. Microsoft provides a tool called `MSSoapT`, or the Microsoft SOAP trace utility, that does just that. This tool is available as part of the Microsoft SOAP Toolkit. `MSSoapT` can be inserted into part of the message stream, and it automatically forwards the messages that it receives. For example, assume that your application connects to a remote port 8000 on a machine called `foo`. Under normal circumstances, you would connect to this service using a URL like this:

```
http://foo:8000/FooService/foo.soap
```

To use the SOAP trace utility, you need to configure your client to connect to a different port, perhaps 8001. While you are debugging, your client would use the following URL:

```
http://foo:8001/FooService/foo.soap
```

The SOAP trace utility would be configured to listen to port 8001 on the server machine (assuming that is where you suspect a problem and that is where you are focusing your debug efforts) so that all incoming requests to port 8001 are satisfied by the trace utility. The other part of the trace utility is where the traffic should be forwarded. If you are on the server, specify localhost and port 8000. In essence, the trace utility routes messages from port 8001 to port 8000. In addition, it logs all traffic that passes between the client and the server. You can select a formatted display that shows both the request and response SOAP messages. The other option is to select the unformatted display. With the unformatted display, you can see the HTTP headers as well as the SOAP messages; it just does not look as "pretty" as the formatted display. Figure 13.11 shows a typical formatted display for this trace utility. With this utility, it is possible to see the exact message that is being transmitted and the response, which can greatly aid in tracking down a problem with your remote application.

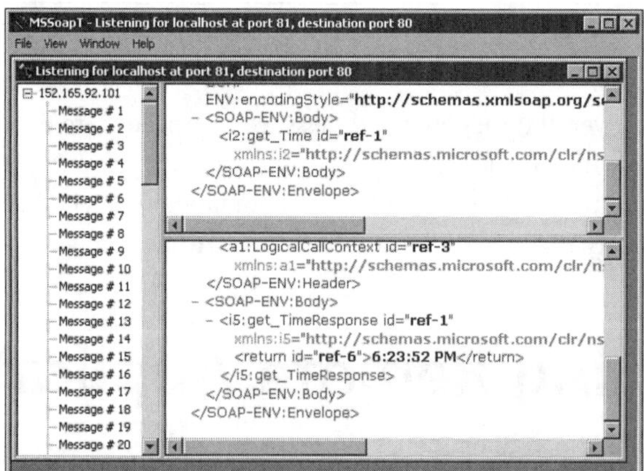

FIGURE 13.11
MSSoapT tool in action.

Summary

This has been a rather long chapter, but you should have gleaned from this chapter the following points:

- Remote objects are easy to build and easy to use.
- Remoting provides a consistent programming model.
- Binary format can transfer any .NET object.
- SOAP allows for interoperability between .NET and non-.NET platforms.
- `SingleCall`, `Singleton`, and `Client-Activated` models allow for much flexibility in designing your remoting service.
- Synchronous and asynchronous calls allow for a responsive application that scales easily.
- Remoting allows the programmer to extend the channel and formatters. It is possible to hook into the remoting services at almost any level. You have seen two examples of how to hook into **`IServerChannelSink`** and **`IClientChannelSink`**. You can hook into the remoting services at other points by inserting your custom processing into other parts of the sink chain.

Note

The SDK has additional samples that show how to hook into the transport layer so that you can transport data via another medium such as a named pipe. The SDK also has samples on how to create your own proxy and how to dynamically modify the proxy.

- Remoting allows the user to use IIS as a host or server. A direct host can be run as a service or from the command line, or you can allow IIS to be a host for a remoting service that you want to provide.

CHAPTER 14

Delegates and Events

In This Chapter

A **delegate** is a type safe function pointer. Although the idea of a **delegate** is not difficult to grasp, how it is implemented, what additional functionality has been added, and just how universally it is applied and used are all topics that deserve much more discussion.

The Windows APIs are becoming more asynchronous in nature. For example, when a user clicks on a button in your application, notification of this event is undoubtedly happening asynchronous to your application. Much of the APIs dealing with I/O can be greatly streamlined by utilizing an asynchronous model. Chapters 12, "Networking," and 13, "Remoting," have already utilized **event**s and **delegate**s to simplify and enhance the overall usability of distributed applications. Before the CLR, it was cumbersome and error prone to define callback functions required as part of an **event**-driven model. Somehow you need to give the software that is providing a service for you a definition of how and where you would like to be notified when the service is complete. This chapter discusses what is new and different about **delegate**s as opposed to more traditional forms of notification specification. It also covers **event**s, which are used extensively not only in the framework, but also add a good deal of functionality to **delegate**s.

Why delegates?

In the past, you could pass a function pointer, cast as an `int`, and it was up to the function being called to know what type of function pointer was passed. This improved somewhat with later versions of C where the return type of function, number of arguments, and argument type could all be specified. The problem is that it was not type-safe. One example that is used frequently is `qsort`. This function was passed a `void` pointer to what was to be sorted, the number of elements to be sorted, the size of the elements, and a comparison function. The call to `qsort` when you are sorting an array of int might look like this:

```
int a[100]
// Initialize array a
. . .
qsort((void *)a, 100, sizeof(int), compare);
```

The comparison routine would look like this:

```
int compare(const void *a, const void *b)
{
    int ta = *(int *)a;
    int tb = *(int *)b;
    if(ta == tb) return 0;
    else if(ta < tb) return -1;
    else return 1;
}
```

If some unlucky person happened to see this comparison routine declared, he might be tempted to call it with an array of `float`, an array of `char`, or an array of structures for that matter. All would result in an incorrect sort at best and a program crash at worst. A method is needed to tell the compiler about a function that does not exist yet! With templates, C++ solved the problem elegantly. Templates turned the function pointer into a class. These types of classes were called *function objects*.

With the advent of templates, the following type of declaration became important:

```
template <class T>
int compare (const T& a, const T& b)
{
     if(a < b) return -1;
     else if(a == b) return 0;
     else return 1;
}
```

As long as the class that was passed as an argument to the compare function had a < operator and an == operator, this function would work just fine. The problem was that passing this type of function as an argument to another function (such as `qsort`) was problematic. The function that was to use this compare routine needed to specify what kinds of functions it accepted. The equivalent `qsort` had to be defined for each type that was sorted. The next step was to create a class or structure that wrapped the functionality of the function. The following code snippet shows how this is done:

```
template <class T> struct compare
{
public:
  int operator () (T a, T b)
   {
     if(a < b) return -1;
     else if(a == b) return 0;
     else return 1;
   }
};
```

With Standard Template Library (STL) (as part of the C++ ANSI Standard, you can now call the sort function like this:

```
compare<int> mycompare;

std::vector<int> v;
v.push_back(1);
v.push_back(2);
std::sort(v.begin(), v.end(), mycompare);
```

This is essentially what **`delegate`**s do to function pointers. **`Delegate`**s wrap a class around the function. By wrapping the function pointer, the code that calls or uses the

delegate can be written in a generic fashion. This code also has the added benefit of being type-safe. Another benefit of **delegate**s is that they are part of the language. You can achieve the functionality of **delegate**s with function objects, but that is limited to C++. **Delegate**s that are a part of the .NET Framework are available to any language that is supported by the .NET Framework.

The next section spells out some of the characteristics of this **delegate** class.

delegate Basics

A **delegate** is similar to a COM (or a C# **interface** for that matter) interface in that a COM interface specifies a contract between the implementer and the user. A COM interface was abstract and could not be instantiated. Its importance was the contract that it specified. A **delegate** is similar, but it only specifies a contract for a single function call.

To create a **delegate**, you first need to define what the **delegate** is to look like—in other words, define a **delegate** type. The code snippet in Listing 14.1 begins a simple `HelloWorld` sample with a **delegate** definition. The full source for the code in Listings 14.1–14.8 is in the `HelloWorld` directory.

LISTING 14.1 Defining a **delegate** Type

```
public delegate void HelloWorldDelegate(string message);
```

This simply defines the return type (void) and the argument(s) (one argument of type **string**) for the **delegate**. Now you implement a candidate method that has the same signature as the **delegate** type. Listing 14.2 shows a possible implementation.

LISTING 14.2 **delegate** Function

```
static private void HelloWorldProcessor(string message)
{
    Console.WriteLine(message);
}
```

This method simply takes the supplied argument and prints it on the **Console**. The **delegate** is constructed in Listing 14.3.

LISTING 14.3 **delegate** Construction

```
HelloWorldDelegate d = new HelloWorldDelegate(HelloWorldProcessor);
```

The constructor takes a single argument, which is the name of the method that the **delegate** will call. Notice that the modifiers static and private are not considered when the **delegate** type is matched with the **delegate** method. If the return type, number of arguments, or type of arguments is varied in `HelloWorldProcessor`, then the compiler generates an error:

```
HelloWorld.cs(22): Method 'DelegatesAndEvents.HelloWorld.
➥HelloWorldProcessor(string)'
does not match delegate
'void DelegatesAndEvents.HelloWorld.HelloWorldDelegate(string)'
```

Varying the modifiers, such as static and private, does not affect the **delegate** creation. This gives a warm feeling that at least at compile time, type safety is checked.

In Listing 14.4, you call the **delegate**.

LISTING 14.4 delegate Invocation

```
d("Hello World!");
```

It should be noted that the function `d` does not exist. When the compiler sees this statement, it turns it into the following IL code:

```
IL_000e:  ldstr      "Hello World!"
IL_0013:  callvirt   instance void DelegatesAndEvents.
➥HelloWorld/HelloWorldDelegate::Invoke(string)
```

This can be verified using the `ILDASM` tool that ships with the SDK. If you expand the Main method of the `HelloWorld` application (HelloWorld.exe), you will see code like this. Notice that this Invoke takes the same number of arguments (one), the same type of arguments (string), and returns the same type (void), as the **delegate**.

Through the magic of **Reflection** (you will learn more about this in Chapter 17, "Reflection"), you can see which method has been assigned to the **delegate** in question. More precisely, you can get an instance of **MethodInfo**, which tells you about the method associated with the **delegate**. You can also obtain the **Target**, which is the instance of the object with which the **delegate** was created. A **delegate** associated with a static method has no Target. This topic is brought up to illustrate the idea of a **Target**. The call would look like Listing 14.5.

LISTING 14.5 delegate Information

```
Console.WriteLine("Method: {0}", d.Method);
Console.WriteLine("Target: {0}", d.Target);
```

This simple code snippet prints the method that is associated with the **delegate** along with the name of the instance of which the method is a part. If the method is static, then no instance is available and nothing is printed. For more information on **MethodInfo**, refer to Chapter 17.

It is more interesting when a **delegate** is defined on an instance of a class. Listing 14.6 shows the class and a **delegate** being associated with a method in the class. The complete source for this code snippet is in `HelloWorld.cs`. Some of the relevant lines from this source file have been extracted to illustrate the concepts so that the lines in Listing 14.6 will not be identical to those in `HelloWorld.cs`.

LISTING 14.6 delegate on an Instance Method

```
class DelegateClass
{
    public void HelloWorldProcessor(string message)
    {
        Console.WriteLine("DelegateClass: {0}", message);
    }
. . .
}
. . .
HelloWorldDelegate d;
DelegateClass dc = new DelegateClass();
d = new HelloWorldDelegate(dc.HelloWorldProcessor);
d("Hello World!");
```

Now when you request information about the **delegate** as in Listing 14.5, an object is returned from **Target**. This object is a reference to the instance of the class implementing the **delegate** method. When a **delegate** is constructed, two pieces of information are passed to the **Delegate** class: the method identification and an identifier for the class instance of which the method is a part. When a **delegate** that is associated with an instance is invoked, all of the accessible member fields and methods associated with that instance are available to the **delegate** method. In the `DelegateClass` in Listing 14.6, you could have a private member variable that counts the number of times the method was called. However, unlike a static method, the instance data can be used to maintain state.

Although it is called a **delegate**, in reality, when the compiler sees this keyword, it translates **delegate** to a wrapper class that is derived from **MulticastDelegate**. You can verify this with the ildasm tool. The output for this application looks like Figure 14.1.

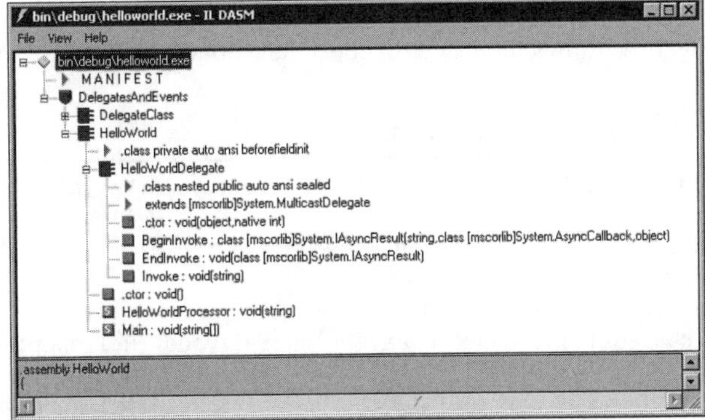

FIGURE 14.1
`HelloWorldDelegate` *exposed.*

For now, that means you have not only all of the members in the **`Delegate`** class, but you also have all of the members in the **`MulticastDelegate`** class. This means you can build a chain of **`delegate`**s, each associated with a different (or the same) method. Listing 14.7 shows one example of how this might be done.

LISTING 14.7 Using **`MulticastDelegate`** Methods

```
HelloWorldDelegate d;
DelegateClass dc = new DelegateClass();
d = new HelloWorldDelegate(HelloWorldProcessor);
d += new HelloWorldDelegate(dc.HelloWorldProcessor);
d += new HelloWorldDelegate(dc.A);
d += new HelloWorldDelegate(dc.B);
d += new HelloWorldDelegate(dc.C);
d("Multicast Hello World!");
```

This set of statements builds a list of `HelloWorldDelegates`. One of the methods associated with the **`delegate`**s is static, and the rest are methods of the `DelegateClass`.

If you were to call the **`Delegate`** class member properties **`Method`** and **`Target`**, you would only get the information associated with the last member of the chain. To access each of the **`delegate`**s in the chain, you must use the **`GetInvocationList`** member of the **`MulticastDelegate`** class. Getting information about each of the **`delegate`**s then looks like Listing 14.8.

LISTING 14.8 Getting at Each **`delegate`** in a Chain

```
Delegate [] list = d.GetInvocationList();
foreach(Delegate item in list)
{
    Console.WriteLine("Method: {0}", item.Method);
    Console.WriteLine("Target: {0}", item.Target);
}
```

To round out this overview of **delegate**s, you need to look at a couple of late-binding methods. Listing 14.9 shows the usage of these late-bound methods.

LISTING 14.9 Late-Bound **delegate** Methods

```
d = (HelloWorldDelegate)Delegate.CreateDelegate(typeof(HelloWorldDelegate),
                                                dc, "HelloWorldProcessor");
d.DynamicInvoke(new object [] {"Late-Bound Hello World!"});

// Late binding on a static method
d = (HelloWorldDelegate)Delegate.CreateDelegate(typeof(HelloWorldDelegate),
                                                typeof(HelloWorld),
                                                "HelloWorldProcessor");
d.DynamicInvoke(new object [] {"Late-Bound static Hello World!"});
```

Listing 14.9 shows two kinds of late-bound calls: one that is bound to a method of a class, and one that is bound to a static method. For these methods to be useful, you have to imagine a scripting type of environment where just **Type**s are known. From this **Type**, you can obtain a list of the methods in the type, the argument count, the return type, and so on. Both of these methods rely on the static method **CreateDelegate** to create a **delegate** from the specified **Type** and method name. All of this relies on the classes in the **System.Reflection** namespace, which will be covered in Chapter 17. Just remember that these **delegate** methods exist.

Comparing delegates

delegates can be compared. A **delegate** overrides the equality operator (==) and the (!=) operator. These two operators in turn rely on the **Equals** method that is an overridden method for the **delegate** class. Similar to the way strings can be compared by value and not by reference, the **Delegate** class compares the value of the **delegate** rather than the reference. For a **delegate**, the value consists of the values exposed by the **Method** and **Target** properties seen in Listings 14.5 and 14.8. If the **Method** and **Target** properties are the same, then the **delegate**s are considered to be equal. Two different instances will obviously have different **Target**s, so delegates defined on different instances will be considered different. In addition, if a delegate is defined as static, it will always be different from an instance delegate because the Target for a static delegate is essentially always null. A couple of examples will help to clarify the concept. The source code for this sample illustrated in Listings 14.10–14.14 is in the DelegateEquality directory.

LISTING 14.10 Comparing Static Methods

```
DelegateCallback ad = new DelegateCallback(ACallback);
DelegateCallback bd = new DelegateCallback(BCallback);
DelegateCallback cd = new DelegateCallback(ACallback);
Console.WriteLine("static {0} == {1} {2}", ad.Method, bd.Method, ad == bd);
Console.WriteLine("static {0} == {1} {2}", ad.Method, ad.Method, ad == ad);
Console.WriteLine("static {0} == {1} {2}", ad.Method, cd.Method, ad == cd);
```

Listing 14.10 shows a simple comparison of the **`Method`** properties. Assuming that `ACallback` and `BCallback` are both static methods, the first **`Console.WriteLine`** will print that the equality comparison is **`false`**, and the second will print **`true`**. This is as expected (they are either the same or they are different). The third case shows that **`delegate`** comparison is a value comparison and not just a reference comparison. Notice that even though `ad` and `cd` are different objects, comparing them for equality results in **`true`**. This is because both of the methods refer to `ACallback`. Listing 14.11 shows instance methods being compared.

LISTING 14.11 Comparing Instance Methods

```
A a1 = new A();
B b1 = new B();
C c1 = new C();

ad = new DelegateCallback(a1.ACallback);
bd = new DelegateCallback(a1.BCallback);
Console.WriteLine("instance {0}.{1} == {2}.{3} {4}",
➥ad.Target, ad.Method, bd.Target, bd.Method, ad == bd);
cd = new DelegateCallback(a1.ACallback);
Console.WriteLine("instance {0}.{1} == {2}.{3} {4}",
➥ad.Target, ad.Method, cd.Target, cd.Method, ad == cd);
```

The first comparison returns **`false`** because the **`Target`** and **`Method`** properties are both different. The second comparison returns **`true`** because the **`Target`** and **`Method`** properties are the same even though the **`delegate`** objects are different. Listing 14.12 shows a comparison in which only the **`Target`** property is different.

LISTING 14.12 Comparing Instance Methods

```
A a2 = new A();

bd = new DelegateCallback(a2.ACallback);
Console.WriteLine("instance {0}.{1} == {2}.{3} {4}",
➥ad.Target, ad.Method, bd.Target, bd.Method, ad == bd);
```

The comparison shown in Listing 14.12 will return **false**. Even though the **Method** properties are the same, the **Target** properties are different (defined on different instances of the same class). Listing 14.13 shows a comparison of two **delegate** chains.

LISTING 14.13 Comparing **delegate** Chains

```
DelegateCallback dd = ad;
dd += bd;
dd += cd;

DelegateCallback ed = ad;
ed += bd;
ed += cd;
Console.WriteLine("chain {0} == {1} {2}", dd.Method, ed.Method, dd == ed);
```

This comparison returns **true** because both chains contain the same type and number of **delegates**. Listing 14.14 shows what happens when the order is changed.

LISTING 14.14 Comparing **delegate** Chains with Different Orders

```
ed = cd;
ed += bd;
ed += ad;
Console.WriteLine("chain {0} == {1} {2}", dd.Method, ed.Method, dd == ed);
```

Notice that this comparison returns **false**. This is because even though the same **delegates** are used to build the chain, they are in a different order from the first **delegate** chain.

It is sometimes important to be able to compare delegates because of chains, as shown in Listing 14.14. You could set up a chain of delegates to notify various processes or computers of activities of which you want others to be aware. You could even set up a rudimentary “chat” that notifies others of your messages. In all of these scenarios, you will want to remove **delegates** from the chain, or you might want to see which **delegates** are set up. A comparison is needed to remove a particular **delegate** and to pick out a particular **delegate** from a chain.

Removing delegates

Now that you have some understanding of how **delegates** are compared, you can move on to how **delegates** are removed from a **delegate** chain. A **delegate** chain is simply an array of **delegates**. To remove a **delegate** from the chain, the chain is traversed and the first **delegate** that equals the **delegate** passed as an argument to **Remove** will be removed. Some examples best illustrate the concepts regarding **delegate** removal. The full source code for the code illustrated in Listings 14.15–14.17 is in the DelegateRemoval directory.

LISTING 14.15 Listing **delegates** in a **delegate** Chain

```
DelegateCallback ad = new DelegateCallback(ACallback);
DelegateCallback bd = new DelegateCallback(BCallback);
DelegateCallback cd = new DelegateCallback(CCallback);

DelegateCallback dd = ad;
dd += bd;
dd += cd;

Delegate [] da = dd.GetInvocationList();
foreach(Delegate d in da)
{
    Console.WriteLine("{0} {1}", d.Target, d.Method);
}
```

Listing 14.15 simply shows the process of building a **delegate** chain and then retrieving the contents. Notice that because you are using static callbacks, the **Target** property is null for each of the **delegate**s. Listing 14.16 shows the removal of a single **delegate** from the list.

LISTING 14.16 Removing a **delegate** from a **delegate** Chain

```
dd = (DelegateCallback)Delegate.Remove(dd, cd);
da = dd.GetInvocationList();
foreach(Delegate d in da)
{
    Console.WriteLine("{0} {1}", d.Target, d.Method);
}
```

Here the chain is searched for the cd **delegate** and it is removed. A **delegate** chain is immutable, much like many of the objects within the .NET Framework (**string** being a prime example). Because of this immutability, a new **delegate** chain is constructed and returned from the **Remove** method. The listing will show all but the cd **delegate** in the chain. Listing 14.17 shows the effect of placing duplicate **delegate**s in a chain.

LISTING 14.17 Removing Duplicates from a **delegate** Chain

```
dd += cd;
dd += cd;
dd = (DelegateCallback)Delegate.Remove(dd, cd);
da = dd.GetInvocationList();
```

LISTING 14.17 Continued

```
foreach(Delegate d in da)
{
    Console.WriteLine("{0} {1}", d.Target, d.Method);
}
```

The output on the **Console** will show that only one of the cd **delegate**s in the chain is removed. The chain is searched until either a match is found (the **delegate** is equal) or the end of the chain is reached. If a match is found, then processing is terminated. Duplicates are not removed—just the first **delegate** found. A workaround for this problem is presented in Listing 14.18.

LISTING 14.18 Removing a Chain from a **delegate** Chain

```
Console.WriteLine("Merging a chain on the list");
DelegateCallback ed = cd;
ed += cd;
dd += ed;
da = dd.GetInvocationList();
foreach(Delegate d in da)
{
    Console.WriteLine("{0} {1}", d.Target, d.Method);
}
Console.WriteLine("Removing a chain from the list");
dd = (DelegateCallback)Delegate.Remove(dd, ed);
da = dd.GetInvocationList();
foreach(Delegate d in da)
{
    Console.WriteLine("{0} {1}", d.Target, d.Method);
}
```

This code snippet first merges two chains to form one chain. The **delegate** that is specified to be removed is actually a chain, too; therefore, when that chain is found in the **delegate** chain, the entire chain is removed. In this case, both duplicate and **delegate**s are removed.

Cloning delegates

delegates implement the **ICloneable** interface so that a **delegate** can be copied. The copy will be a deep copy so that each copy can exist independently, and changes to one will not affect changes in the other. Listing 14.19 shows a simple illustration. The full source for this code is in the DelegateClone directory.

LISTING 14.19 Cloning **delegates**

```
DelegateCallback ad = new DelegateCallback(ACallback);
DelegateCallback bd = new DelegateCallback(BCallback);
DelegateCallback cd = new DelegateCallback(CCallback);

DelegateCallback dd = ad;
dd += bd;
dd += cd;

DelegateCallback ed = dd;

Console.WriteLine("Original list");
Delegate [] da = dd.GetInvocationList();
foreach(Delegate d in da)
{
    Console.WriteLine("{0} {1}", d.Target, d.Method);
}
Console.WriteLine("Copied list");
da = ed.GetInvocationList();
foreach(Delegate d in da)
{
    Console.WriteLine("{0} {1}", d.Target, d.Method);
}

dd = (DelegateCallback)Delegate.Remove(dd, cd);
da = dd.GetInvocationList();
Console.WriteLine("Original list (after Remove)");
foreach(Delegate d in da)
{
    Console.WriteLine("{0} {1}", d.Target, d.Method);
}
da = ed.GetInvocationList();
Console.WriteLine("Copied list");
foreach(Delegate d in da)
{
    Console.WriteLine("{0} {1}", d.Target, d.Method);
}
```

Listing 14.19 shows a simple **delegate** chain constructed and copied to another **delegate**. The contents of each chain are output to the console to illustrate that the copy indeed took place. Then, one member of the original **delegate** chain is removed. Again, the contents of both **delegate** chains are printed to illustrate that changes to one chain did not affect the other.

Serializing delegates

Delegates implement the ISerializable interface so that the **Delegate** class can be persisted in a serialized form. Serialization is a topic that will be developed more fully in Chapter 17, but for now just note that the class can be persisted to a file, either as text (**SoapFormatter**) or as a binary image (**BinaryFormatter**). The **BinaryFormatter** produces considerably less data than the **SoapFormatter**, but it is proprietary to Microsoft and it is not very readable. Your application might require the **BinaryFormatter**, but this chapter will focus on the SoapFormatter. Changing from one formatter to another is simple.

Listing 14.20 shows a **delegate** being serialized to a file "static-delegate.xml" and then deserialized from that same file into a new object. The complete source code for Listings 14.20 and 14.22 is in the DelegateSerialize directory.

LISTING 14.20 Serializing **delegates**

```
DelegateCallback ad = new DelegateCallback(ACallback);

Console.WriteLine("{0} {1}", ad.Target, ad.Method);

Stream streamWrite = File.Create("static-delegate.xml");
SoapFormatter soapWrite = new SoapFormatter();
soapWrite.Serialize(streamWrite, ad);
streamWrite.Close();

Stream streamRead = File.OpenRead("static-delegate.xml");
SoapFormatter soapRead = new SoapFormatter();
DelegateCallback bd = (DelegateCallback)soapRead.Deserialize(streamRead);

Console.WriteLine("{0} {1}", bd.Target, bd.Method);
Console.WriteLine("Equals {0}", ad == bd);
ad();
bd();
streamRead.Close();
```

This sample creates a **delegate** and then serializes the **delegate** to a file called "static-delegate.xml" using the **SoapFormatter** class. At that point, the file is opened back up and the **delegate** is deserialized to form the object again. After the object is created, it is compared to the original, and both **delegate**s are exercised to make sure they work. Listing 14.21 shows what the content of "static-delegate.xml" looks like.

LISTING 14.21 A Serialized **delegate**

```
- <SOAP-ENV:Envelope xmlns:xsi="http://www.w3.org/2001/XMLSchema-instance"
➥xmlns:xsd="http://www.w3.org/2001/XMLSchema"
➥xmlns:SOAP-ENC="http://schemas.xmlsoap.org/soap/encoding/"
➥xmlns:SOAP-ENV="http://schemas.xmlsoap.org/soap/envelope/"
➥SOAP-ENV:encodingStyle="http://schemas.xmlsoap.org/soap/encoding/"
➥xmlns:a1="http://schemas.microsoft.com/clr/ns/System">
-   <SOAP-ENV:Body>
-     <a1:DelegateSerializationHolder id="ref-1">
        <DelegateType id="ref-2">
             DelegatesAndEvents.DelegateCallback
           </DelegateType>
        <DelegateAssembly id="ref-3">
             DelegateSerialize, Version=1.0.583.5888,
➥Culture=neutral, PublicKeyToken=null
           </DelegateAssembly>
        <Target xsi:type="xsd:ur-type" xsi:null="1" />
        <TargetTypeAssembly href="#ref-3" />
        <TargetTypeName id="ref-4">
             DelegatesAndEvents.DelegateSerialization
           </TargetTypeName>
    <MethodName id="ref-5">
             ACallback
           </MethodName>
      </a1:DelegateSerializationHolder>
    </SOAP-ENV:Body>
  </SOAP-ENV:Envelope>
```

The serialization of the **delegate** contains everything that is needed to reconstitute the **delegate**, as was evidenced by the code that exercised the deserialized **delegate**.

Of course, this was for a **delegate** associated with a static method. Using a class instance to build a **delegate** is similar. One note, however: **delegate** is already marked as being "serializable"; if you are using an instance method; then the class that implements the object needs to be marked **Serializable** as well. Listing 14.22 shows a sample serializing a **delegate** that is associated with an instance method.

LISTING 14.22 Serializing an Instance **delegate**

```
A a = new A();
ad = new DelegateCallback(a.ACallback);

Console.WriteLine("{0} {1}", ad.Target, ad.Method);
streamWrite = File.Create("instance-delegate.xml");
soapWrite = new SoapFormatter();
soapWrite.Serialize(streamWrite, ad);
streamWrite.Close();
```

LISTING 14.22 Continued

```
streamRead = File.OpenRead("instance-delegate.xml");
soapRead = new SoapFormatter();
bd = (DelegateCallback)soapRead.Deserialize(streamRead);

Console.WriteLine("{0} {1}", bd.Target, bd.Method);
Console.WriteLine("Equals {0}", ad == bd);
ad();
bd();
streamRead.Close();
```

You can see that this code produces a file that is only a little different from the static case in Listing 14.21. This file is shown in Listing 14.23.

LISTING 14.23 A Serialized Instance **delegate**


```
- <SOAP-ENV:Envelope xmlns:xsi="http://www.w3.org/2001/XMLSchema-instance"
➥xmlns:xsd="http://www.w3.org/2001/XMLSchema"
➥xmlns:SOAP-ENC="http://schemas.xmlsoap.org/soap/encoding/"
➥xmlns:SOAP-ENV="http://schemas.xmlsoap.org/soap/envelope/"
➥SOAP-ENV:encodingStyle="http://schemas.xmlsoap.org/soap/encoding/"
➥xmlns:a2="http://schemas.microsoft.com/clr/nsassem
➥/DelegatesAndEvents/DelegateSerialize"
➥xmlns:a1="http://schemas.microsoft.com/clr/ns/System">
-   <SOAP-ENV:Body>
-     <a1:DelegateSerializationHolder id="ref-1">
        <DelegateType id="ref-3">
             DelegatesAndEvents.DelegateCallback
           </DelegateType>
        <DelegateAssembly id="ref-4">
             DelegateSerialize, Version=1.0.583.5888, Culture=neutral,
➥PublicKeyToken=null
           </DelegateAssembly>
        <Target href="#ref-5" />
        <TargetTypeAssembly href="#ref-4" />
        <TargetTypeName id="ref-6">
             DelegatesAndEvents.A
           </TargetTypeName>
        <MethodName id="ref-7">
            ACallback
          </MethodName>
      </a1:DelegateSerializationHolder>
      <a2:A id="ref-5" />
    </SOAP-ENV:Body>
  </SOAP-ENV:Envelope>
```


Other than a few naming changes to reflect the class name, the only real difference is the line `<a2:A id="ref-5"/>`. If this class had fields in addition to the callback, then those fields would be reflected here. No field is associated with this class, so the field information in the serialization is blank.

Just as a test of comparing **delegate**s, the line `Console.WriteLine("Equals {0}", ad == bd);` in Listing 14.22 prints `Equals false`. This is because the **Target** members of the **delegate**s are different.

Asynchronous delegates

From Figure 14.1, you can see that every **delegate** not only derives from **MulticastDelegate**, but also that several methods in addition to the **Delegate** and **MulticastDelegate** methods are available. When the compiler encounters the **delegate** keyword, it creates a class that extends **MulticastDelegate** and adds the following methods:

- **BeginInvoke**
- **EndInvoke**
- **Invoke**

If you try to call the **Invoke** method directly from a **delegate**, you will receive the compile time error `Invoke cannot be called directly on a delegate`. Because each **delegate** can have a different signature and it is desirable to have a type safe interface, the compiler does some things automatically for you. The first thing that the compiler does is discover the number of arguments, the types of the arguments, and the return type and use that information to build the **Invoke** and **BeginInvoke** methods. These methods will be different for every different **delegate** that is defined. The signature of **Invoke** will be identical to the **delegate** declaration. If the **delegate** declaration has three arguments, then the **Invoke** method of the wrapper class will have three arguments. With **BeginInvoke**, the situation is similar to **Invoke** except two extra arguments are appended to the argument list, an **AsyncCallback delegate**, and a state object. The second thing that the compiler does with regards to **delegate**s is that when it sees a **delegate** variable in the form of a function call, it transforms that sequence to a call to the **Invoke** method. You have already seen how the compiler expands this in Listing 14.4 and the related discussion. This section only discusses the **BeginInvoke** and **EndInvoke** methods.

Unlike **Invoke**, **BeginInvoke** and **EndInvoke** can be directly called from the **delegate**. **BeginInvoke** returns immediately on calling the function. It queues up a request to call the **delegate**. **EndInvoke** is like many of the other asynchronous callback implementations in that calling it returns the result of the **delegate** operation, or in other words, the return variable.

Armed with this information, try to rework one of the previous threading samples to use the asynchronous callback mechanism of the **Delegate** class. Because it is so visual, choose the DiningPhilosophers sample. Reviewing the code for the Dining Philosophers problem from Chapter 11, "Threading," and the associated discussion would be helpful at this point.

The Dining Philosophers Problem Using delegates (Revisited)

The first problem that you might come across when converting this sample to use asynchronous callbacks is that no handle is returned from **BeginInvoke** that you can use to stop an asynchronous process like you can with a **Thread** (using **Abort**). The finest grain control available seems to be at the point where the **delegate** completes its work and the callback is called. You might choose to use a variable to decide whether a philosopher should start thinking, eating, and so on. The code that illustrates this is shown in Listing 14.24.

LISTING 14.24 Recycling a Dining Philosopher

```
private void Recycler(IAsyncResult iar)
{
    StateHandler sh = (StateHandler)iar.AsyncState;
    sh.EndInvoke(iar);
    if(allStop != 0)
    {
        Thread.Sleep(r.Next(1000));
        sh.BeginInvoke(cb, sh);
    }
    else
    {
        // You are done eating and thinking
        BeginInvoke(colorChangeDelegate, new object[] {Color.White});
        BeginInvoke(onPhilosopherLeave, new object[] {this, EventArgs.Empty});
    }
}
```

If the allStop flag is non-zero, then the philosopher is still at the table contending for resources. Otherwise, another request is not queued, and the UI is changed to indicate this. The result of this decision is that cleanup does not happen immediately. You eventually see all of the philosophers' blocks turn white—just not all at once as in the threading version.

The next decision is how to start everything. This is relatively easy because not much changed between starting a thread and invoking an asynchronous callback. The process is kick-started with a call to each philosopher's `Start` method. Listing 14.25 shows this process.

LISTING 14.25 Starting Up

```
    public DiningPhilosopher(Mutex rightChopstick, Mutex leftChopstick)
    {
        chopsticks = new Mutex[2];
        chopsticks[0] = rightChopstick;
        chopsticks[1] = leftChopstick;

        colorChangeDelegate = new ColorChangeDelegate(ColorChange);
        onPhilosopherLeave = new EventHandler(OnPhilosopherLeave);
        stateHandler = null;
        startThinkingTime = 0;
        stopThinkingTime = 0;
        r = new Random();
        cb = new AsyncCallback(Recycler);
        stateHandler = new StateHandler(OnStateChange);
    }
. . .
        public void Start()
    {
        BeginInvoke(colorChangeDelegate, new object[] {Color.Blue});
        startThinkingTime = Environment.TickCount;
        stateHandler.BeginInvoke(cb, stateHandler);
    }
. . .

private void OnStart(object sender, System.EventArgs e)
{
    DiningPhilosopher.AllStart();
    foreach(Control b in Controls)
    {
        if(b is DiningPhilosopher)
        {
            ((DiningPhilosopher)b).Start();
        }
    }
}
```

The first two methods are extracted from the `DiningPhilosopher` control. The first is a constructor that shows how the callback and the **`delegate`** are set up for each control. The second method changes the control to reflect that it is "thinking" (blue), caches the current time stamp, and then queues up a request for an asynchronous callback. The second `OnStart` method is on the main form and is invoked as a result of clicking the `Start` button. This shows how the `Start` method of each control is invoked.

On startup, each control queues a call to `OnStateChanged`, which is shown in Listing 14.26.

LISTING 14.26 State Change

```
private void OnStateChange()
{
        int elapsed = 0;
        if(WaitHandle.WaitAll(chopsticks, 100, false))
        {
            // Eating
            BeginInvoke(colorChangeDelegate, new object[] {Color.Green});
            // Eat for a random amount of time (maximum of 1 second)
            Thread.Sleep(r.Next(1000));
            // Put down the chopsticks
            chopsticks[0].ReleaseMutex();
            chopsticks[1].ReleaseMutex();
            // Start to think
            BeginInvoke(colorChangeDelegate, new object[] {Color.Blue});
            startThinkingTime = Environment.TickCount;
        }
        else
        {
            stopThinkingTime = Environment.TickCount;
            elapsed = stopThinkingTime - startThinkingTime;
            if(elapsed > 0 && elapsed <= 100)
            {
                BeginInvoke(colorChangeDelegate,
➥new object[] {Color.BlueViolet});
            }
. . .
            else
            {
                BeginInvoke(colorChangeDelegate, new object[] {Color.Red});
            }
        }
    }
```

This function has two purposes. First, it waits for a maximum of 100 milliseconds for the chopsticks to become available. If they are available, then the color of the button turns green to indicate that the philosopher is eating. The philosopher eats for a random amount of time and then puts down his chopsticks. To indicate that the philosopher is thinking again, the button turns blue. If waiting for the chopsticks causes a timing out, then the color is changed to reflect how long it has been since the philosopher has eaten (in 100 millisecond increments). A large section of the code in this listing has been removed for brevity.

On return from `OnStateChanged`, the callback `Recycler` is called. This routine, as shown in Listing 14.26, just restarts everything again if the `allStop` variable so indicates. The final output looks identical to the output shown in Figure 11.7, so it will not be repeated here.

Now you have a version of the `DiningPhilosopher` application that does not explicitly create or start up any threads. If you are suspicious because it seems that you are getting something for nothing, you are right. Try running this application and the Task Manager at the same time. You are likely to see something like Figure 14.2.

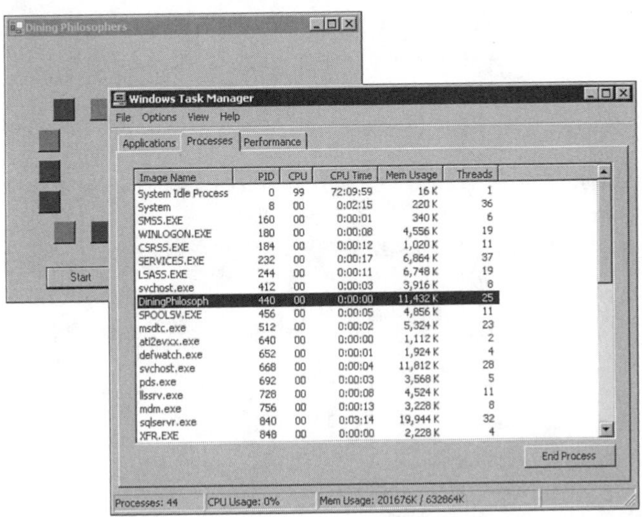

FIGURE 14.2
`DiningPhilosophers` *—Look Ma, no threads?*

How does this happen? It appears that just as many threads are in the "threading" version, yet the program never explicitly created a thread. The answer again lies in what is being done for you. **`BeginInvoke`** gets its asynchronous behavior from the **`ThreadPool`**. In essence, every **`BeginInvoke`** call translates into a call to **`ThreadPool.QueueUserWorkItem`**. A new thread is created for each **`DiningPhilosopher`**—or is there? Remember that the **`ThreadPool`** had a finite set of **`Thread`**s available for each process. Currently, the **`ThreadPool`** contains 25 **`Thread`**s, so if a process hangs onto 25 or more **`Thread`**s from the **`ThreadPool`**, then another **`Thread`** in the process might have to block waiting for a **`Thread`** to become free. To verify that this is what is happening, I wrote a small application that allows the user to start a number of the `DiningPhilosopher` applications. The application looks like Figure 14.3.

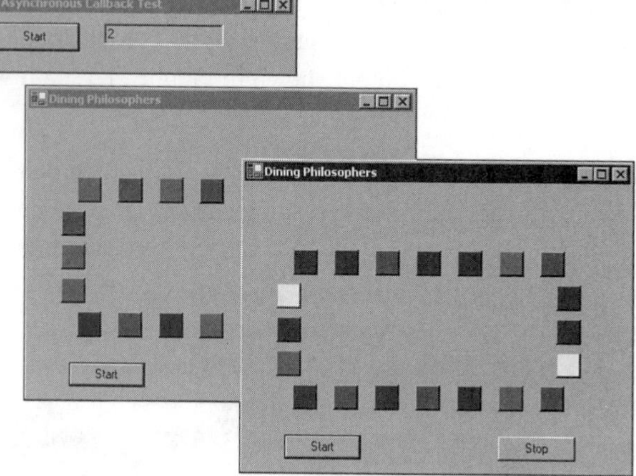

FIGURE 14.3
`ThreadPool` *test.*

Now when the Task Manager is run, the output looks like Figure 14.4.

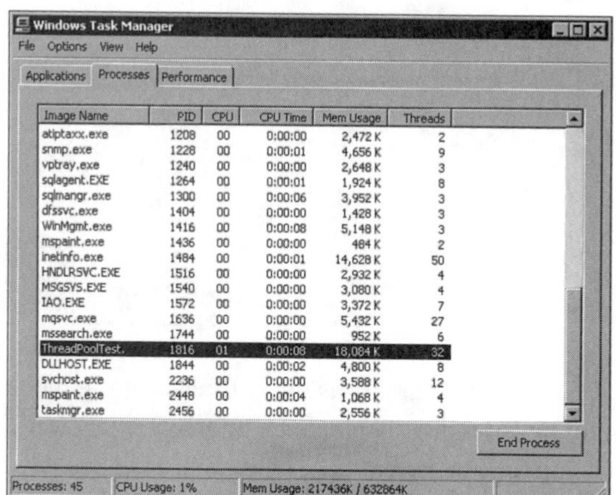

Image Name	PID	CPU	CPU Time	Mem Usage	Threads
atiptaxx.exe	1208	00	0:00:00	2,472 K	2
snmp.exe	1228	00	0:00:01	4,656 K	9
vptray.exe	1240	00	0:00:00	2,648 K	3
sqlagent.EXE	1264	00	0:00:01	1,924 K	8
sqlmangr.exe	1300	00	0:00:06	3,952 K	3
dfssvc.exe	1404	00	0:00:00	1,428 K	3
WinMgmt.exe	1416	00	0:00:08	5,148 K	3
mspaint.exe	1436	00	0:00:00	484 K	2
inetinfo.exe	1484	00	0:00:01	14,628 K	50
HNDLRSVC.EXE	1516	00	0:00:00	2,932 K	4
MSGSYS.EXE	1540	00	0:00:00	3,080 K	4
IAO.EXE	1572	00	0:00:00	3,372 K	7
mqsvc.exe	1636	00	0:00:00	5,432 K	27
mssearch.exe	1744	00	0:00:00	952 K	6
ThreadPoolTest.	1816	01	0:00:08	18,084 K	32
DLLHOST.EXE	1844	00	0:00:02	4,800 K	8
svchost.exe	2236	00	0:00:00	3,588 K	12
mspaint.exe	2448	00	0:00:04	1,068 K	4
taskmgr.exe	2456	00	0:00:00	2,556 K	3

FIGURE 14.4
`ThreadPool` *test with Task Manager.*

Notice that 40 **`Threads`** (20 philosophers and 2 applications) do not exist—the **`Thread`** count topped out at 31. If you were to add another `DiningPhilosopher` application, the number of **`Threads`** would still be 31 (or possibly 32). Again, this is because **`BeginInvoke`** uses one of the **`Thread`**s from the **`ThreadPool`**, and the **`ThreadPool`** holds 25 **`Threads`** per process. I have created *N* **`AppDomain`**s with an application running within each **`AppDomain`** so the **`AppDomain`**s must live with this cap and share the **`ThreadPool`** with the other **`AppDomain`**s.

Not only does this give insight into how asynchronous callbacks should be used, but it also further emphasizes the point made in Chapter 11: **`ThreadPool.QueueUserWorkItem`** should be used to accomplish short tasks. Hanging onto a **Thread** allocated from the **ThreadPool** could cause the application to seem slow and sluggish because of the contention for a central resource (that is, **Thread**s from the **ThreadPool**).

events Make Working with delegates Easier

Particularly for UI code, **event**s are the primary means of notification. Button clicks, mouse over, list expansion, and so on all use **event**s to notify the application of the occurrence of an event. **event**s are based on **delegate**s, so many of the same principles apply to **event**s that apply to **delegate**s. **Event**s are so similar to **delegate**s that the benefits of **event**s are not readily apparent. Maybe a couple of examples will help you appreciate an **event**.

Beginning events

The first sample shows how an **event** can be used to notify an application that something has changed. For this sample, the change is incrementing and decrementing an integer. After each modification, the registered **event**s are called. A portion of the code is shown in Listings 14.27 and 14.28. The full source is in the BeginningEvents directory. Define the **delegate** and the class that is to handle the **event**(s), starting with Listing 14.27.

LISTING 14.27 Beginning **events**—ChangedClass

```
public enum ChangeType {Add, Subtract}
public class ChangedClass
{
    // An event that clients can use to be notified whenever the
    // elements of the list change:
    public delegate void ChangeHandler(ChangeType type, int count);
    public event ChangeHandler Changed;

    private int count;
    public ChangedClass()
    {
        count = 0;
    }
    // Invoke the Changed event; called whenever list changes:
    protected void OnChanged(ChangeType type, int count)
    {
        if (Changed != null)
            Changed(type, count);
    }
    public void Add()
```

LISTING 14.27 Continued

```
    {
        Interlocked.Increment(ref count);
        OnChanged(ChangeType.Add, count);
    }
    public void Subtract()
    {
        Interlocked.Decrement(ref count);
        OnChanged(ChangeType.Subtract, count);
    }
}
```

Listing 14.27 shows the **delegate** declaration and the definition of the **event** that uses the **delegate**. The **delegate** declaration is just a declaration of the type and signature of the callback. In contrast, the **event** is a definition of a variable that occupies space in memory. The **delegate** that is associated with the **event** can take on just about any form. The types of arguments, number of arguments, and return types of the **delegate** used for an **event** are completely arbitrary. The rest of the class defines methods that cause the **event** to be raised and one method, `OnChanged`, which raises the **event**. Separate **events** could have been defined for `Add` and `Subtract` rather than having an **enum** define the type of change, but this will keep things simple. After everything is in place, all that remains is to test it. Listing 14.28 shows one possible test driver for the class defined in Listing 14.27.

LISTING 14.28 Beginning **events**—Test Driver

```
class Test
{
    private static void Changed(object sender, EventArgs e)
    {
        Console.WriteLine("Changed {0} {1} fired",
                            ((ChangedEventArgs)e).Value,
                            ((ChangedEventArgs)e).Type);
    }
    private static void Modified(object sender, EventArgs e)
    {
        Console.WriteLine("Modified {0} {1} fired",
                            ((ChangedEventArgs)e).Value,
                            ((ChangedEventArgs)e).Type);
    }
    public static void Main()
    {
        // Create a new list:
        ChangedClass changed = new ChangedClass();
        changed.Changed += new EventHandler(Changed);
        changed.Changed += new EventHandler(Modified);
```

LISTING 14.28 Continued

```
        changed.Add();
        changed.Add();
        changed.Changed -= new EventHandler(Modified);
        changed.Add();
        changed.Add();
        changed.Subtract();
        changed.Subtract();
        changed.Subtract();
        // Delegate [] da = changed.Changed.GetInvocationList();
    }
}
```

For demonstration purposes, two methods were added to the **delegate/event** chain: `Changed` and `Modified`. After calling a few methods, the `Modified` method is removed, leaving just the `Changed` method for the remainder of the test case. The output of this program looks like that shown in Figure 14.5.

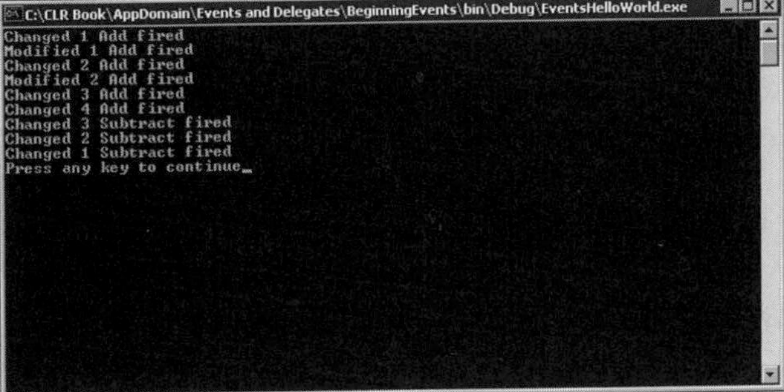

FIGURE 14.5
Beginning **event***s.*

Notice in Figure 14.5 that each modification to the class (`Add`, `Subtract` methods being called) results in an **event** being raised and each of the registered **event** handlers being called.

From this sample, what does an **event** give you that just a raw **delegate** does not? One of the benefits of using an **event** can be seen by uncommenting the last line of Listing 14.28. Because an **event** is based on a **delegate**, you should be able to get the list of the **delegate**s in the chain. If this line is uncommented, the compiler generates the following error:

```
BeginningEvents.cs(65): The event 'DelegatesAndEvents.ChangedClass.Changed'
➥can only appear on the left hand side of += or -= (except when used
➥from within the type 'DelegatesAndEvents.ChangedClass')
```

One of the benefits of using the **event** keyword is that even though the **event** is **public**, the compiler restricts access to the **event** to adding or removing **event** handlers only. The other benefit is related and can be seen from running ILDASM on the assembly produced from the code in Listings 14.27 and 14.28. Figure 14.6 shows the pertinent output of this tool.

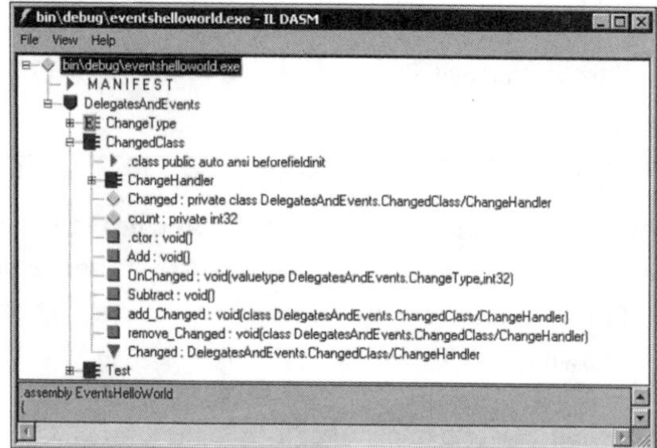

FIGURE 14.6
Running ILDASM *on Beginning Events.exe.*

Notice that as a result of the **event** keyword, two methods were added: add_Changed and removed_Changed. Looking at the IL generated for just add_Changed will give you some idea what is going on with these two methods. Listing 14.29 shows the generated IL code for the add_Changed routine.

LISTING 14.29 IL Code for add_Changed

```
.method public hidebysig specialname instance void
        add_Changed(class DelegatesAndEvents.ChangedClass/ChangeHandler
➥ 'value') cil managed synchronized
{
  // Code size       24 (0x18)
  .maxstack  8
  IL_0000:  ldarg.0
  IL_0001:  ldarg.0
  IL_0002:  ldfld class DelegatesAndEvents.ChangedClass/ChangeHandler
➥DelegatesAndEvents.ChangedClass::Changed
  IL_0007:  ldarg.1
  IL_0008:  call class [mscorlib]System.Delegate
➥[mscorlib]System.Delegate::Combine(class [mscorlib]System.Delegate,
➥class [mscorlib]System.Delegate)
  IL_000d:  castclass  DelegatesAndEvents.ChangedClass/ChangeHandler
  IL_0012:  stfld class DelegatesAndEvents.ChangedClass/ChangeHandler
➥DelegatesAndEvents.ChangedClass::Changed
  IL_0017:  ret
} // end of method ChangedClass::add_Changed
```

From the listing, you can see that `Changed` is calling the **`Combine`** member of the **`delegate`** that is associated with the **`event`**. `add_Changed` is how an **`event`** handler is added to a chain. `remove_Changed` calls the **`delegate`** method **`Remove`** to remove a **`delegate`** from a chain. You do not call these methods directly; instead, you use the `+=` and `-=` operators.

Another result of using the **`event`** keyword is that the public **`event`** is made private and only the add and remove methods are exposed. Looking at Figure 14.6, you can see that although the **`event`** `Changed` was declared public, the compiler turned it into a private field (denoted by the light-blue diamond). The green upside down triangle indicates the **`event`**, which is public.

Microsoft events

As was seen in the previous example, the **`delegate`** associated with an **`event`** can assume virtually any form. Because **`event`**s are used so frequently within the framework (particularly within the **`System.Windows.Forms`** namespace), Microsoft has adopted a convention that all **`event`**s use a particular form of **`delegate`** called appropriately the **`EventHandler`**. The **`EventHandler delegate`** looks like this:

```
public delegate void EventHandler (object sender, EventArgs e);
```

The first argument to the **`delegate`** is the sender. Typically, this is set to the **`object`** that raised the **`event`**. The second argument is an **`EventArgs`** class that contains the information that is to be passed to the **`delegate`**. The **`EventArgs`** class can be **`EventArgs.Empty`**, which indicates that no information is to be passed to the **`delegate`**, or it can be a class that is derived from **`EventArgs`**, which encapsulates the information that is to be passed to the **`delegate`**.

The `BeginningEvents` sample has been reworked to use the **`EventHandler delegate`** and **`EventArgs`**. This code is illustrated in Listings 14.30–14.32. The full source of this sample can be found in the `EventHandler` directory. Listing 14.30 defines the class, derived from **`EventArgs`**, which will be used to pass information to the **`delegate`**.

LISTING 14.30 Argument Class

```
public enum ChangeType {Add, Subtract}

public class ChangedEventArgs : EventArgs
{
    private ChangeType _type;
    private int _value;
    public ChangedEventArgs(ChangeType _type, int _value)
    {
        this._type = _type;
        this._value = _value;
    }
```

LISTING 14.30 Continued

```
    public ChangeType Type
    {
        get
        {
            return _type;
        }
    }
    public int Value
    {
        get
        {
            return _value;
        }
    }
}
```

This listing just defines a class that can be used to pass the type of change that took place (Add, Subtract), as well as the current counter value. It is important to note that with **events** and the **EventHandler delegate**, the arguments that are passed to the **delegate** are in the form of this class. As long as it is derived from EventArgs, the class can take on virtually any form. Listing 14.31 shows a class that encapsulates the event handler. This class will receive all of the notifications.

LISTING 14.31 Changed Class

```
public class ChangedClass
{
    // An event that clients can use to be notified whenever the
    // elements of the list change:
    public event EventHandler Changed;
    private int count;
    public ChangedClass()
    {
        count = 0;
    }
    // Invoke the Changed event; called whenever list changes:
    protected void OnChanged(EventArgs e)
    {
        if (Changed != null)
            Changed(this, e);
    }
    public void Add()
    {
        Interlocked.Increment(ref count);
        OnChanged(new ChangedEventArgs(ChangeType.Add, count));
    }
```

LISTING 14.31 Continued

```
    public void Subtract()
    {
        Interlocked.Decrement(ref count);
        OnChanged(new ChangedEventArgs(ChangeType.Subtract, count));
    }
}
```

This class is not much different from the sample using a custom **delegate**. The **delegate** is no longer explicitly defined. Because you are now using the **EventHandler** **delegate**, the definition of that **delegate** has already been declared elsewhere. In addition, the **event** is raised with the ChangedEventArg class. Listing 14.32 illustrates a program that uses the code in Listings 14.30 and 14.31.

LISTING 14.32 Test Driver

```
class Test
{
    private static void Changed(object sender, EventArgs e)
    {
        Console.WriteLine("Changed {0} {1} fired",
                          ((ChangedEventArgs)e).Value,
                          ((ChangedEventArgs)e).Type);
    }
    private static void Modified(object sender, EventArgs e)
    {
        Console.WriteLine("Modified {0} {1} fired",
                          ((ChangedEventArgs)e).Value,
                          ((ChangedEventArgs)e).Type);
    }
    // Test the EventHandler class:
    public static void Main()
    {
        // Create a new list:
        ChangedClass changed = new ChangedClass();
        changed.Changed += new EventHandler(Changed);
        changed.Changed += new EventHandler(Modified);
        changed.Add();
        changed.Add();
        changed.Changed -= new EventHandler(Modified);
        changed.Add();
        changed.Add();
        changed.Subtract();
        changed.Subtract();
        changed.Subtract();
    }
}
```

Except for the changes required for the new **delegate**, the test driver works the same as it did before. The output from running this sample is identical to the custom version, not using **EventHandler**.

Summary

delegates are used throughout the framework, so they are important. You should incorporate a **delegate** into your design in the following cases:

- A single method is called. Unlike an interface, a **delegate** specifies a single method's signature.
- A class needs to have multiple implementations of a method. Take, for instance, the `qsort` example given at the beginning of the chapter. You could very well imagine allowing a `compare` **delegate** to be passed to the `qsort` routine so that different objects could be sorted.
- You need to have an event-like model for processing in your application. In other words, if your application is designed so that it is more readily implemented using an asynchronous event model, then you should consider **delegate**s and **event**s.
- The caller does not need to know with which object the callback is implemented. Because all of this information is encapsulated within the **delegate** class, the user is safely shielded from the details, and all of the benefits of encapsulation are realized.
- For security or other reasons, an implementation might want to create different implementations for different clients or users. It might be that Alice will get a **delegate** that has full access rights to all accounts, whereas Bob will get a **delegate** that can access only a restricted set of accounts.
- It is necessary to easily combine, merge, and remove methods. The methods of the **MulticastDelegate** provide unparalleled ease of use for this type of function pointer manipulation.
- An interface is more useful if a group of methods best describes a process.
- An interface is also more useful if a need for inheritance and a need to easily cast to obtain different functionality exist.
- An interface might be best if only one implementation in a class is typical.

CHAPTER 15

Using Managed Exceptions to Effectively Handle Errors

In This Chapter

The .NET Framework in conjunction with the CLR eliminates a large class of errors either at runtime through automatic garbage collection and type checking or at compile time through type checking, access checks, and so on. However, a class of errors still remains that can only be handled and detected at runtime. For example, the CLR cannot know that you want to access a file that does not exist until you attempt to access it. Errors will always exist due to misunderstanding the API, security constraints, and programming logic error. What is important is how those errors are handled. The only method of handling errors in the CLR and .NET Framework is through exceptions.

This chapter gives you a good foundation on how to best use and handle exceptions. Because the .NET Framework is multilingual, it is important to understand how exceptions present themselves in many different languages. It is also important to understand how exceptions are handled in a multithreaded environment or even a multi-`AppDomain` environment.

Error Handling with Exceptions

Why does .NET take such a Draconian stance on error handling? With C++, several methods were available for handling errors, exceptions being among them. VB had an error-handling scheme that was remarkably similar to exceptions. The list goes on; each language had its own method of dealing with errors. Indeed, that was the problem. Each language had one or more ways of handling errors. One of the goals of the .NET platform was to create a unified environment where all languages were "equal." For a language to interoperate seamlessly with another language, the error-handling schemes must be the same. If the error handling tried to be all things to all languages, then every time a new language or even a new error-handling scheme was introduced, the CLR and .NET Framework would need to be redone. One scheme had to be decided on, and using exceptions seemed to be the best choice for two reasons:

- Exceptions are hard to ignore.
- Exceptions allow a programmer to decide easily the proper context in which to handle the error.

Difficulty in Avoiding Exceptions

A compelling reason to adopt exceptions as a means to handle errors is that exceptions are harder to ignore than the traditional error code return. The designer of an API must return an error code hoping that the user of the API will read the error code and do the right thing. If the user is lazy or under a schedule constraint for reading the documentation, he might just ignore the values returned. Depending on the API, ignoring the return code could leave some latent bug in the code waiting to become more apparent. Usually by the time the bug is noticed, the cause of the error has long since been forgotten. Finding the source of the problem is the key to solving it.

If the programmer is not diligent about checking *all* of the error codes, errors could creep in. These kinds of errors are time-consuming to fix and make the code that much harder to maintain. Of course, exceptions can also be ignored, but if they are ignored and an unhandled exception handler is not present, the program crashes, giving a visible sign that something is wrong. A programmer can also get around handling the error by "handling" the exception in a generic sense and doing nothing. However, exceptions make handling errors easier because the code for handling the error is isolated and apart from the error-free code. In addition, testing for return codes for each function call can add extra lines of code, especially if the types of errors are the same among a group of function calls.

Proper Context for Handling Errors

Often when an error occurs, the code that is to handle the error does not have enough information or background to know how to best handle the error. For example, if a file is not found, one possible way to handle that error is to create it.

Exceptions Overview

At the base of all exception classes is `System.Exception`, which derives from `System.Object`.

> **Note**
>
> It is possible to throw a `System.Object` directly from `System.Object`, but doing so is not consistent with how exceptions are used in the CLR. In addition, the C# compiler doesn't allow it.

Most (if not all) of the exception classes derived from `System.Exception` do not add functionality, but they do provide a type so that errors can be filtered and handled in the correct context as discussed previously. Many classes are derived directly from `System.Exception`. A couple of classes that derive directly from `System.Exception` are `IOException` and `WebException`. `IOException` is thrown when an I/O error occurs (usually the result of an operation performed in the `System.IO` namespace). `WebException` is thrown when an error occurs when accessing the network using `WebRequest` or `WebResponse`. Many other classes derive directly from `System.Exception`, but the two most important are `ApplicationException` and `SystemException`.

One of the more interesting classes of exceptions derived from **SystemException** is the **ExternalException** class. The **COMException** class is derived from **ExternalException**. When CLR interop turns HRESULTS into exceptions, it builds a **COMException**. If you are using P/Invoke to interop with Win32 and the API returns a Win32 error, then it is turned into a **Win32Exception,** which is also derived from **ExternalException**. These Win32 errors are like ERROR_FILE_NOT_FOUND and ERROR_ACCESS_DENIED. Unmanaged Structured Exception Handling (SEH) exceptions are turned into an **SEHException**, which is also derived from **ExternalException**.

Exceptions can be split into two basic categories: runtime-based exceptions and object-based exceptions. These could be loosely referred to as those exceptions that are explicitly thrown (object-based exceptions) and those that are not (runtime-based exceptions).

The runtime throws a **SystemException** when the runtime has detected an error such as divide-by-zero, overflow, array-bounds check, or accessing a null pointer. The runtime-based exceptions are usually derived from the **SystemException** class. Many exception classes are derived from **SystemException**. Some of these exceptions are thrown as a result of a catastrophic failure such as **ExecutionEngineException** (thrown due to a failure in the CLR) and **StackOverflowException** (thrown due to execution stack overflow, probably because of deep or unbounded recursion). These exceptions in general should not be caught, and it is not good programming practice to throw a **SystemException**. A prime example of a runtime-based exception would be a **DivideByZeroException**. The **DivideByZeroException** is thrown when an attempt is made to divide an integral or decimal value by zero. (Note that floating-point numbers never generate exceptions.) These types of exceptions are like those thrown by the Win32 Structured Exception Handling mechanism. Listing 15.1 shows some unmanaged code that generates these types of faults. The code for this sample is in the SEHException directory.

LISTING 15.1 Catching SEH Exceptions

```
void SEHExceptions()
{
    __try
    {
        int a = 0;
        int b = 1;
        int c = b/a;
        std::cout << "The result is: " << c << std::endl;
    }
    __except( EvalException(GetExceptionCode(), GetExceptionInformation()) )
    {
        std::cout << "Caught exception" << std::endl;
    }
```

LISTING 15.1 Continued

```
    __try
    {
        int *p = 0;
        std::cout << "The value is: " << p[1] << std::endl;
    }
    __except( EvalException(GetExceptionCode(), GetExceptionInformation()) )
    {
        std::cout << "Caught exception" << std::endl;
    }
}
```

The sample in Listing 15.1 generates two exceptions: a divide-by-zero exception (which corresponds to a managed **DivideByZeroException**) and an access violation exception (the equivalent in managed code would be a **NullReferenceException**). Listing 15.2 shows how this would be done with regular exception handling.

LISTING 15.2 Catching EH Exceptions

```
class custom_exception : public std::exception
{
public:
    explicit custom_exception(const std::string& _message) : message(_message)
    {
    }

    virtual ~custom_exception()
    {
    }

    virtual const char *what()
    {
        return (message.c_str());
    }

private:
    // The message
    std::string message;
};


void EHExceptions()
{
    try
    {
        int a = 0;
        int b = 1;
        int c = b/a;
        std::cout << "The result is: " << c << std::endl;
    }
```

LISTING 15.2 Continued

```
    catch(std::exception)
    {
        std::cout << "Caught EH exception " << std::endl;
    }
    catch(...)
    {
        std::cout << "Default caught EH exception " << std::endl;
    }

    try
    {
        int *p = 0;
        std::cout << "The value is: " << p[1] << std::endl;
    }
    catch(std::exception)
    {
        std::cout << "Caught EH exception " << std::endl;
    }
    catch(...)
    {
        std::cout << "Default caught EH exception " << std::endl;
    }
    try
    {
        throw custom_exception("This is a test");
    }
    catch(custom_exception& e)
    {
        std::cout << "Caught custom exception: " <<  e.what() << std::endl;
    }
}
```

In addition to the two runtime exceptions shown in Listing 15.1, Listing 15.2 also shows the definition and throwing of a custom exception.

The output for the code in Listing 15.1 and Listing 15.2 (both `SEH` exceptions and `EH` exceptions) is shown in Figure 15.1.

FIGURE 15.1
Catching managed exceptions.

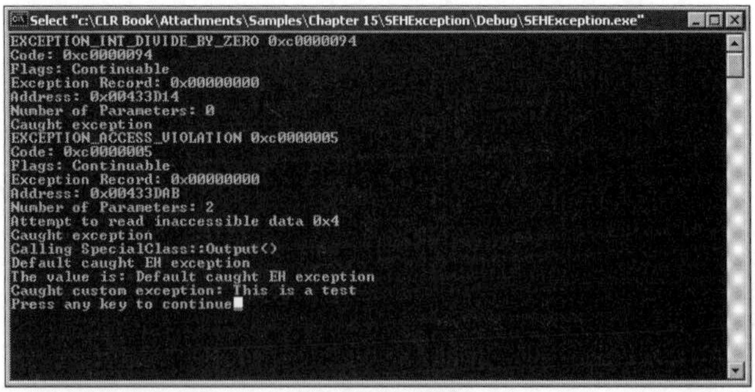

This sample shows how one would catch runtime-based exceptions in unmanaged code. It is important to understand where exceptions came from to appreciate what the CLR and the .NET Framework adds to handling exceptions. One significant advantage to using managed code is that the runtime-based exceptions are merged with the object-based exceptions. You might argue that EH or C++ exception handling does merge `SEH` and `EH` because you can catch divide by zero errors and access violations (null reference). However, a large gap exists in the functionality and information that is available with each of the exception-handling schemes. For example, with `SEH`, you can get a snapshot of the CPU registers at the time of the exception. With `SEH`, you can also retrieve the address where the exception occurred. No single unifying exception-handling scheme exists. With managed runtime-based exceptions, a single exception handling scheme is available that is quite powerful.

Object-based exceptions are exceptions that are generated by the .NET Framework classes to indicate various errors in casting, security, argument type, and so on. Some of the major exceptions in the two categories are listed next:

Following are the runtime-based exceptions:

- `ArithmeticException`—Represents a class of exceptions. Currently `DivideByZeroException`, `NotFiniteNumberException`, and `OverflowException` are derived from this exception.
- `DivideByZeroException`—Thrown when an integer is divided by zero. For example

  ```
  int a = 1;
  int b = 0;
  int c = a/b;
  ```
- `NotFiniteNumberException`—Thrown when a floating-point number is positive infinity, negative infinity, or Not-a-number (NaN). Applications in C# will not throw this exception. This exception is thrown for languages that do not support infinity and Not-a-number values. This exception is derived from `ArithmeticException`.
- `OverflowException`—Derived from `ArithmeticException` this exception is thrown at runtime when an attempt is made to write a value that is larger than that largest possible value on the receiving object. For example:

  ```
  byte a = 0;
  int b = 900;
  checked {
      a = (byte)b;
  }
  ```

- `ExecutionEngineException`—This error is a fatal error that should never occur. It is usually the result of corrupted or missing data when trying to execute code.
- `StackOverflowException`—Thrown when the call stack has filled up usually due to deep or unbounded recursion. For example

```
static void StackOverflow()
{
    StackOverflow();
}
. . .
StackOverflow();
```

- `NullReferenceException`—Thrown when access to an object that has a null value is attempted. For example

```
object o = null;
o.ToString();
```

The object-based exceptions are as follows:

- `TypeLoadException`—The online documentation indicates that this exception is thrown when the CLR cannot find the assembly or the type within the assembly, or it cannot load the type. You might get a `FileNotFoundException` for assemblies that cannot be found (using `Assembly.Load`) and a null **`Type`** for types that cannot be found.
- `IndexOutOfRangeException`—This is thrown when the runtime detects that an array is indexed improperly. For example:

```
arr[arr.Length + 10];
```

- `InvalidCastException`—This is thrown when the runtime cannot cast from one form of the execution to another. For example:

```
int n = 5;
object o = n;
string s = (string)o;
```

- `InvalidOperationException`—This is thrown when a method's call is invalid for the object's current state. For example:

```
foreach(int i in a)
{
    Console.WriteLine("Enum: {0}", i);
    if(i == 4)
        a.Remove(4);
}
```

- `MissingFieldException`—Normally if you try to access a field that is not defined, you get a compile-time error. You get a `MissingFieldException` if you modify one assembly and remove a field that is referenced in another assembly without recompiling and linking the assemblies as a unit. This exception occurs when the method that accesses the missing field is JITd (just-in-time compiled) so the exception can be generated without information as to where in a method from which this exception is generated.

- `MissingMethodException`—Similar to `MissingFieldException`, this exception is thrown when an assembly is modified independent of a dependent assembly. Also, like `MissingFieldException`, this exception is thrown when the method that references the missing method is JITd.
- `SecurityException`—This exception is thrown as the result of a failed security check. Listing 15.3 shows an example of this type of exception. Chapter 16 provides more details on security issues.

LISTING 15.3 Illustration of a `SecurityException`

```
[DllImport("user32.dll")]
public static extern int MessageBox(int hWnd, string text,
                                    string caption, uint type);

static void SecretMethod()
{
    // Create a security permission object to describe the
    // UnmanagedCode permission:
    SecurityPermission perm =
        new SecurityPermission(SecurityPermissionFlag.UnmanagedCode);

    // Deny the UnmanagedCode from our current set of permissions.
    // Any method that is called on this thread until this method
    // returns will be denied access to unmanaged code.
    perm.Deny();
    MessageBox(0, "Hello from my secret method. Shhh . . .", "Top Secret", 0);
}
. . .
try
{
    SecretMethod();
}
catch(Exception e)
{
    // Dump interesting exception information
    Console.WriteLine (e.ToString());
}
```

This is not an exhaustive list of all of the exceptions that can be thrown, but it is meant to show the types of exceptions that could be runtime-based or object-based exceptions.

The user-defined exception could be considered a third type or category of exception. Although nothing specifically denies a programmer from deriving from any of the exception classes (they are not sealed in C# terminology), it is highly recommended that the user-defined exceptions derive from the **ApplicationException** class.

When a custom exception is required for your application, you should derive that custom exception from **ApplicationException**. It is strongly recommended that a custom exception class not be derived directly from the **Exception** class. This would only make the application harder to understand and maintain. The **Exception** class is the base class for a huge range of exceptions. Consider the problem if you were trying to guess a particular animal and you were only told that it was a mammal rather than a cat or dog. Putting your application custom exceptions in the **ApplicationException** category narrows the list of errors that could have caused the exception.

Now you know that exceptions are good and return codes are bad. You also know about some of the exception types that can be thrown and have a general idea of the source of exceptions.

C# Exceptions

C# allows a programmer almost all of the functionality provided by the CLR. To demonstrate exception handling in a C# environment, look at the next example that generates exceptions of various types. Because the code is rather long, the listing has been split into small sections. The full source for Listings 15.4–15.8 is in the `BasicExceptions` directory. Listing 15.4 shows an example of how C# code can be used to catch a **DivideByZeroException**.

LISTING 15.4 Catching a Divide-By-Zero Exception

```
// Try a divide by zero
try
{
    int x = 0;
    x = 1/x;
}
catch(DivideByZeroException e)
{
    // Dump interesting exception information
    Console.WriteLine (e.ToString());
}
```

When the exception is caught, the output looks like this:

```
System.DivideByZeroException: Attempted to divide by zero.
 at Exceptions.BasicExceptions.Main(String[] args) in basicexceptions.cs:line 32
```

When an exception is converted to a string, the type of exception is first (`System.DivideByZeroException`), followed by a descriptive message, followed by a stack trace. In this case, not much stack exists because the code for this sample is all contained in **Main**. For cases in which a more complicated call-stack exists, this information can be invaluable in debugging. Listing 15.5 illustrates catching another runtime type of exception: a null reference exception.

LISTING 15.5 Catching a Null Reference Exception

```
// Try an access violation
try
{
    Object o = null;
    Console.WriteLine(o.ToString());
}
catch(NullReferenceException e)
{
    Console.WriteLine (e.ToString());
}
```

When this part of the code executes, the output looks like this:

```
System.NullReferenceException: Value null was found where an instance of an
➥object was required.
   at Exceptions.BasicExceptions.Main(String[] args) in basicexceptions.cs:
➥line 46
```

Although the CLR and the compiler are pretty smart when it comes to avoiding and detecting errors, sometimes the CLR has no choice but to throw an exception. When the runtime encounters an object that is null and it tries to call a member function from a null instance, it throws an exception. This is not what happens under unmanaged code. Take for instance a class:

```
class SpecialClass
{
public:
    void Output()
    {
        std::cout << "Calling SpecialClass::Output()" << std::endl;
    }
};
```

What would you expect to happen with this code?

```
__try
{
    SpecialClass *p = 0;
    p->Output();
}
```

```
__except( EvalException(GetExceptionCode(), GetExceptionInformation()) )
{
    std::cout << "Caught exception" << std::endl;
}
```

Unfortunately, the `Output()` member function is called on the null instance with no exception thrown at all.

Most of the time you spend writing exception code will probably be spent either developing custom exception classes or catching and interpreting exceptions thrown by the .NET Framework. Listing 15.6 illustrates the definition and usage of a custom exception class.

LISTING 15.6 Catching a Custom Exception

```
// Custom exception class derived from ApplicationException
class CustomException : ApplicationException
{
    public CustomException(String msg) : base(msg)
    {
    }
}
. . .
// Try custom exception
try
{
    throw new CustomException("I am throwing a custom exception");
}
catch(CustomException e)
{
    Console.WriteLine (e.ToString());
}
```

The first part of this listing illustrates the definition of a custom exception class derived appropriately from **`ApplicationException`**. Notice that no new functionality is added after creating this new exception class. In fact, as has already been noted, most all of the exception classes in the .NET Framework are defined much like this one. New functionality does not need to be added as a new type. The type is caught or filtered out. It is by type that a routine can decide whether it is in the best context to handle the exception.

The next section of code in Listing 15.6 illustrates throwing and catching this custom exception. Remember that all of the samples presented in this section are merely showing the concept of how to use exceptions. In the real world, this throw would be many levels deep in the call stack or this whole set of `try/catch` blocks could be nested in another set of `try/catch` blocks. The output for this section of code looks like this:

```
Exceptions.CustomException: I am throwing a custom exception
 at Exceptions.BasicExceptions.Main(String[] args) in basicexceptions.cs:line 59
```

Notice that it is possible to pass rich error information back to the user with exceptions. This is where the custom message is passed and the construction of the object is displayed. The type of exception is also shown. Much information is available in a custom exception with little work on the part of the programmer. However, this extra information does not come free. Constructing an instance of an exception class is expensive, as you will see later in this chapter. Exceptions are meant to handle exceptional conditions; using them for anything else will jeopardize the performance of your application.

Listing 15.7 illustrates an exception thrown by the framework. An **InvalidCastException** has been chosen to represent all of the other types of exceptions that can be thrown by the framework. This is probably not the best example, but it is one of the easiest to illustrate.

LISTING 15.7 Catching an Object-Based Exception

```
// Try an object-based exception (InvalidCast)
try
{
    int n = 5;
    Object o = n;
    string s = (string)o;
}
catch(InvalidCastException e)
{
    Console.WriteLine (e.ToString());
}
```

When the integer n is boxed into an **object**, the instance of the object class knows its type. If an attempt is made to unbox the original value via a cast to a type that is different, an exception is thrown. The output after catching this exception is shown next:

```
System.InvalidCastException: Exception of type System.InvalidCastException
➥was thrown.
   at Exceptions.BasicExceptions.Main(String[] args) in basicexceptions.cs:
➥line 74
```

This could have been an exception thrown as a result of a **File.Open** called for a file that could not be found, or a result of trying to shrink an **ArrayList**, or any number of cases that cause the framework classes to throw an exception. This is the way that errors are communicated and handled within the .NET Framework. If in doubt, put a set of try/catch blocks around your code. Doing so will make your code more readable and the application more stable and manageable.

One concept that has not been covered so far is how a programmer can gracefully handle the case when the exception is not thrown. This is the reason for the **finally** clause in the **try/catch** blocks. Perhaps you open a file and read from it. If an error exists, you want to report the error and close the file. If no error is present, then you still want to be able to close the file; otherwise, you have a resource leak. Listing 15.8 shows an example of opening a file, reading the contents, and closing the file. If an error exists, it will be reported and the file will be closed. The code within the **finally** block will be executed no matter what happens.

LISTING 15.8 Using **finally**

```
StreamReader streamReader = null;
try
{
    FileStream stream = File.OpenRead(@"..\..\BasicExceptions.cs");
    streamReader = new StreamReader(stream, Encoding.ASCII);
    streamReader.BaseStream.Seek(0, SeekOrigin.Begin);
    string s = streamReader.ReadToEnd();
    // Console.WriteLine(s);
}
catch(Exception e)
{
    // Dump interesting exception information
    Console.WriteLine ("There has been an error:\n{0}", e.ToString());
}
finally
{
    Console.WriteLine ("Closing the file");
    if(streamReader != null)
        streamReader.Close();
}
```

If an exception is present, the catch block does not execute. If many catch blocks exist and an exception is not thrown, none of the catch blocks are executed. When you need to have a guarantee that a given code block will be executed, regardless of whether an exception is thrown, then **finally** is the way to go. In fact, **try/finally** is a perfect idiom and valid syntax when you want to ignore an error and execute a section of code upon exiting the **try** block, no matter how that exit occurs. Even though the **finally** block is guaranteed to execute, it has not caught an exception. If you just have **try/finally** and an exception is thrown while in the **try** block, your **finally** block will be executed, but the exception that is thrown has not been handled. If it is not handled, it could end up as an unhandled exception.

It is recommended that a custom exception should derive from **ApplicationException**. In addition, it is useful for your application to partition the errors into several sets of exceptions. This gives you a "divide and conquer" approach to debugging what went wrong when something does go wrong. Listing 15.9 shows a contrived example showing how you can set up **try/catch** to handle many errors at once.

LISTING 15.9 Filtering Exceptions

```
class Custom1Exception : ApplicationException
{
    public Custom1Exception(String msg) : base(msg)
    {
    }
}
class Custom2Exception : ApplicationException
{
    public Custom2Exception(String msg) : base(msg)
    {
    }
}
class Custom3Exception : ApplicationException
{
    public Custom3Exception(String msg) : base(msg)
    {
    }
}
class Custom4Exception : ApplicationException
{
    public Custom4Exception(String msg) : base(msg)
    {
    }
}
. . .
Console.WriteLine("\nFiltering exceptions\n");
try
{
    Random r = new Random();
    switch(r.Next(4) + 1)
    {
        case 1:
            throw new Custom1Exception("I am throwing a Custom1Exception");
        case 2:
            throw new Custom2Exception("I am throwing a Custom2Exception");
        case 3:
            throw new Custom3Exception("I am throwing a Custom3Exception");
        case 4:
            throw new Custom4Exception("I am throwing a Custom4Exception");
    }
}
catch(Custom1Exception e)
{
    Console.WriteLine ("There has been a Custom1Exception error.\n{0}",
➥e.ToString());
}
catch(Custom2Exception e)
{
    Console.WriteLine ("There has been a Custom2Exception error.\n{0}",
➥e.ToString());
}
```

LISTING 15.9 Continued

```
catch(Custom3Exception e)
{
    Console.WriteLine ("There has been a Custom3Exception error.\n{0}",
➥e.ToString());
}
catch(Custom4Exception e)
{
    Console.WriteLine ("There has been a Custom4Exception error.\n{0}",
➥e.ToString());
}
```

Notice that in this example, you don't need to specify a local variable for the instance of the exception that is caught. You only need to be interested in the type of exception that is thrown; here, you don't need any of the additional information that is contained in the exception class.

In a real-world application, you will want to build several different custom exception classes so that when an exception is thrown, you can quickly narrow down the cause. You might want to consider deriving the custom exceptions from `SocketException`, `IOException`, or `ArithmeticException`, or any other of the predefined exception classes that match the domain in which an error could occur. For example, you could derive a set of exception classes that derive from `SocketException` and are thrown by your application when your application accesses a socket. Again, portioning your error domain into a manageable set goes a long way toward helping you to maintain and debug your application.

If you have a relatively complex algorithm, you might find it useful to nest exception handling. This is handled nicely within C#. Listing 15.10 shows an example of a nested set of handlers.

LISTING 15.10 Nested **try/catch** Blocks

```
Console.WriteLine("\nNested exceptions\n");
try
{
    // Try a divide by zero
    try
    {
        int x = 0;
        x = 1/x;
    }
    catch(DivideByZeroException e)
    {
        // Dump interesting exception information
        Console.WriteLine (e.ToString());
```

LISTING 15.10 Continued

```
        throw;
    }
}
catch(DivideByZeroException e)
{
    // Dump interesting exception information
    Console.WriteLine (e.ToString());
}
```

The listings so far have shown what happens when an exception is handled explicitly. Listing 15.11 shows how you can protect your code from unhandled exceptions with a last-ditch unhandled exception handler. If the exception reaches the top of the stack and it still has not found an appropriate handler, it is an unhandled exception. You can protect your code from crashing by installing an unhandled exception handler, as shown in Listing 15.11.

LISTING 15.11 Unhandled Exceptions

```
Thread.GetDomain().UnhandledException +=
    new UnhandledExceptionEventHandler(UnhandledExceptionHandler);
. . .
// Try to divide by zero and see where it gets you.
int y = 0;
y = 1 / y;
. . .
public static void UnhandledExceptionHandler(object sender,
                                            UnhandledExceptionEventArgs args)
{
    Console.WriteLine("Unhandled Exception!");
    Console.WriteLine("Sender: {0}", sender.ToString());
    Console.WriteLine("Type: {0}", args.ExceptionObject.GetType().ToString());
    Console.WriteLine("IsTerminating: {0}", args.IsTerminating);
}
```

The first section of this code shows how to register to be notified when an unhandled exception is thrown. The **UnhandledException** member of **AppDomain** is an **Event**. Remember **Event**s? When an unhandled exception is generated and an **Event** handler has been registered, the **AppDomain** agrees to call each of the **Event** handler routines before the **AppDomain** shuts down. The **Event** handler has no means to recover; in fact, the **IsTerminating** member will indicate that the CLR is shutting down (the **AppDomain** is unloading). Any code after the unhandled exception is generated (here, after `y = 1/y;`) will not be executed. The output of this section of code looks like this:

```
Unhandled Exception!
Sender: Name: BasicExceptions.exe
```

```
There are no context policies.
Type: System.DivideByZeroException
IsTerminating: True
```

After this **Event** handler has been called, the **AppDomain** is well on in its winding down phase and cannot be stopped or reversed from the **Event** handler. The **Event** handler is just a means of notification.

This main function has been sprinkled with many `try/catch` blocks. You might have wondered about the overhead involved in setting up all of the `try/catch` blocks. Throwing an exception requires some overhead; however, unlike VC++, the code is relatively unaffected by exceptions that are never thrown. Other than the incremental cost of more code, virtually no overhead is involved with many `try/catch` blocks.

Note

It is possible that you are running in this code, and when an unhandled exception occurs, you get a dialog that prompts you for a debugger to use to help find the error. For these examples, just select No. This feature is called Just-In-Time Debugging and might be useful for a variety of problems; in this context, however, it can be ignored.

VC++ Exceptions

Handling managed exceptions in VC++ is basically the same as C#. VC++ using managed extensions exposes some features of exceptions that are not available in C#. Those differences will be illustrated later. Listing 15.12 shows how to define and use a custom exception class. The full source for this sample can be found in `C++Exceptions\BasicExceptions`.

LISTING 15.12 Basic Managed VC++ Exceptions

```
__gc class MyException : public System::ApplicationException
{
public:
    MyException() : System::ApplicationException()
    {
    }
    MyException(System::String __gc *msg) : System::ApplicationException(msg)
    {
    }
};
```

LISTING 15.12 Continued

```
void ThrowMyException()
{
    throw new MyException(new System::String("This exception is thrown from
➥ThrowMyException"));
}

int wmain(void)
{
    try
    {
        ThrowMyException();
    }
    catch (MyException *e)
    {
        Console::WriteLine("Caught exception");
        Console::WriteLine(e->ToString());
    }
    __finally
    {
        Console::WriteLine("Finally");
    }
        Console::WriteLine("Almost done");
    return 0;
}
```

The first section of code defines a class that will be the exception class appropriately derived from **ApplicationException**. Although it is not required, a default constructor and a constructor that allows the user to define an error message have been defined. If the default constructor is used, the message associated with the event is `Error in the application`, which is not very descriptive. However, the constructor that takes a **string** argument allows the message that is associated with this exception to be much more descriptive. In the next section, the function that throws the exception is called and the exception is caught and displayed. The output of this code looks like this:

```
Caught exception
MyException: This exception is thrown from ThrowMyException
   at ThrowMyException() in basicexceptions.cpp:line 23
   at wmain() in basicexceptions.cpp:line 31
Finally
Almost done
```

The `__finally` block was added to illustrate how managed VC++ is different from unmanaged VC++ in one aspect. Two rules seem to exist with unmanaged VC++ exceptions. The first rule is that each function can only have one type of exception-handling scheme. If the function uses SEH (`__try`/`__except`), then you cannot also use EH (`try`/`catch`) in the same function. The second rule is that the `__finally` block is associated with a __try. You cannot have __finally and __except both associated with the same __try. Managed VC++ and this sample seem to violate both of those rules. Notice from the output that __finally is associated with the set of try/catch blocks and not with the "final" code to be executed when the function is about to return.

In Listing 15.13, you can see that with C++, "any" exception can be specified with the ellipses. This is basically telling the compiler that you want to catch any exception and you don't care to have a lot of information about it.

LISTING 15.13 Catching a General VC++ Exception

```
try
{
    ThrowMyException();
}
catch (...)
{
    Console::WriteLine("Caught general exception");
}
__finally
{
    Console::WriteLine("General exeption finally");
}
```

Although this might appear to be the most general case, many unmanaged exceptions are actually turned into **SEHException**s that are derived from **Exception**; therefore, a **catch** block that is filtering on **Exception** would handle this exception. This point is illustrated in the next sample (mixed.cpp), starting with Listing 15.14.

One more sample should solidify some basic understanding of exception handling with managed VC++.

This is another long sample, so it has been split into several listings. The full source for Listing 15.14 can be found in C++Exceptions\Mixed. First you will look at a custom exception class that is not derived from any of the managed exception classes. It is not possible to translate what is done in Listing 15.14 with C# because the compiler generates an error indicating that the exception is not derived from System.Exception:

```
The type caught or thrown must be derived from System.Exception
```

Listing 15.14 shows the definition of a possible VC++ exception that is not derived from any exception class.

LISTING 15.14 Custom Unmanaged VC++ Exceptions

```
struct UnmanagedException
{
    UnmanagedException(int e) : err(e)
    {
    }
    int Error()
    {
        return err;
    }
private:
    int err;
};
. . .
   // Throw an exception that is not based on
   // System.Exception so it is an unmanaged exception
   UnmanagedException *e = new UnmanagedException(10);
   throw (e);
. . .
catch (UnmanagedException* u)
{
    Console::WriteLine(S"\nCaught an unmanaged exception\n");
    std::cout << u->Error() << std::endl;
}
```

The first section of this code shows the definition of an unmanaged exception class. This exception class is probably more complex than it needs to be for this sample, but it uses "proper" encapsulation for the single private member, `err`. Obviously, this class could have whatever functionality the user needs for the exception class to have. The main thing to notice about this exception class is that it does not derive from any of the .NET Framework exception classes; therefore, it does not have the core functionality built into those classes. However, this simple class is easy to construct, and throwing and catching such a class will be relatively fast.

The next section of this listing shows the code that would throw this exception. This is nothing new; just construct the class and **`throw`** it.

The last section of this listing shows the exception being caught. Because this class is not derived from any of the managed exceptions, it is considered an unmanaged exception. When this section of the code executes, it generates the following output:

```
Caught an unmanaged exception
10
```

It is interesting to try an experiment and comment out the **catch** block for this exception and recompile the project. Now when the unmanaged exception is thrown, the managed exception catches it because it is identified as an **SEHException**, which is derived from **Exception**. You would have expected that because this is an unmanaged exception and the explicit filter for this exception is commented out, **catch(…)** would be the only match for this exception. However, because it is turned into an **SEHException**, this is not the case.

The rest of the exceptions that are generated in this sample are managed exceptions that are generated as a result of integer divide-by-zero, null reference exception, stack-overflow, and so on. You have seen all of these before.

The interesting case for this sample is in the following throw:

```
// Unspecified
throw;
```

Because a type is not associated with this exception, it is treated somewhat special by the runtime. It is turned into an SEHException. Look at the output for this exception:

```
System.Runtime.InteropServices.SEHException: External component has thrown an
➥exception.
   at _CxxThrowException(Void* , _s__ThrowInfo* )
   at ExceptionGenerator(Int32 i) in mixed.cpp:line 55
   at main() in mixed.cpp:line 65
```

The hard part of exceptions with VC++ is remembering whether the code was compiled with /CLR (managed). If it was compiled with /CLR, then the code is run in a managed environment and everything is much like C#. However, in a managed environment, certain constructs (such as **__finally**) are specific to VC++.

In addition, much of the filtering and SEH exception handling functionality that are part of traditional SEH exceptions is disabled or defaults to an effective no-action when running in a managed environment (/CLR). You can have a **__try/__except** block and pass an expression that evaluates to true in the **__except** block. This basic level of user filtering is available from VC++ with managed extensions. However, you can only have one **__except** block, and it cannot be combined with any other exception scheme in the function. The **__try/__except** keywords are primarily associated with unmanaged code; as such, they are outside the scope of this book. A simple example of using this construct has been included in the mixed.cpp file, but for further detail, see the SDK documentation on SEH exceptions.

VB Exceptions

Exceptions are relatively new to VB; therefore, many VB programmers will take a little while to get used to the syntax and the idea behind exceptions. VB's `On Error GoTo XXX` resembles current exception handling.

Basic VB Exceptions

Listings 15.15 and 15.16 illustrate the basics of VB exception handling. This code sample follows the form of the VC++ sample shown earlier in that an `ExceptionGenerator` throws or causes various exceptions based on an integer selector that is passed as an argument. This sample illustrates a custom exception, a divide-by-zero exception, a stack overflow exception, and a **`FileNotFoundException`**. The full source for this sample can be found in the `VBExceptions\BasicExceptions` directory. Listing 15.15 shows the essential parts of generating and catching a custom exception.

LISTING 15.15 VB Custom Exception

```
'Create a custom exception type called MyException. What makes
' it an exception is that it inherits from System.ApplicationException
Public Class MyException
    Inherits System.ApplicationException

    'Define the three standard constructors for an ApplicationException
    Public Sub New()
        MyBase.New()
    End Sub

    Public Sub New(ByVal Message As String)
        MyBase.New(Message)
    End Sub

    Public Sub New(ByVal Message As String, ByVal Inner As Exception)
        MyBase.New(Message, Inner)
    End Sub

End Class
. . .
    Sub ThrowMyException()
        Throw New MyException("This exception is thrown from ThrowMyException")
    End Sub
. . .
Case 0
    ' Custom Exception
    ThrowMyException()
```

The first section of this code shows how a custom exception class is defined. First, notice that it is derived from **ApplicationException**. Second, most of the code is defining constructors to handle various types of construction. No new functionality is added to **ApplicationException**, yet it is still a valid custom exception. VB is like C# in that it does not support an exception class that is not at least derived from **System.Exception**. If you try to use a custom exception that is not derived from **System.Exception**, the compiler will issue an error:

```
The argument to Throw must derive from System.Exception.
```

The next section of code shows the exception class being constructed and thrown. Here, the second constructor (New(ByVal Message As String)) is being used to build the exception class.

Finally, the case in the `Select` statement that calls the function is illustrated. Catching the exception that is thrown is common to all of the exceptions in this sample; this is shown more explicitly in Listing 15.16 if you want to look ahead.

The next exceptions are so similar to exceptions that are already illustrated that this chapter will cover them quickly. To generate a `DivideByZeroException`, the following code is used:

```
Case 1
    ' DivideByZero
    a = 0
    b = 1
    c = b \ a
```

To generate a `StackOverflowException`, initiate an infinite recursion, repeatedly calling itself until the stack overflows:

```
Case 2
    ' StackOverflow
    ExceptionGenerator(2)
```

To test a **FileNotFoundException**, the exception is thrown directly. The **FileStream** class in the **System.IO** namespace would typically throw the **FileNotFoundException**. Here you are concerned only with the exception, so it is thrown directly.

```
Case 3
    ' Overflow
    Throw New FileNotFoundException("Testing")
```

Each of these exceptions is handled in the same way as shown in Listing 15.16.

LISTING 15.16 Catching VB Exceptions

```
Sub Main()
    Dim i As Integer
    For i = 0 To 3 Step 1
        Try
            ExceptionGenerator(i)
        Catch e As Exception
            Console.WriteLine("Exception Caught")
            Console.WriteLine(e.ToString())
        Finally
            Console.WriteLine()
        End Try
    Next
End Sub
```

The output from this sample is much the same as the C# or C++ code samples. The **ToString()** method of an exception creates a string that includes the name of the exception, a customizable message, and a stack trace.

Advanced VB Exceptions

In the sample shown in Listing 15.16, when an SEH exception is caught, the argument to `__except` is an expression or a function that evaluates to one of three values that determines whether the exception can be handled with the current `__except` block. If multiple `__except` blocks were in the sample and `EvalException` returned `EXCEPTION_CONTINUE_SEARCH`, the next `__except` block would be evaluated to see if it was a candidate to handle the exception. This process would continue until all of the `__except` blocks had been searched. If none of the `__except` blocks accepted the exception, then the exception would be considered unhandled.

VB exposes a feature that is similar to SEH with the `When` clause of the `Catch` statement. The statement associated with the `When` clause must evaluate to a Boolean `true` or `false`. If the `When` clause evaluates to `false`, then the next `Catch` block is evaluated, and so on. Listing 15.17 shows a sample that illustrates this feature. The complete code for this sample is in the directory `VBExceptions\AdvancedExceptions`.

LISTING 15.17 Filtering VB Exceptions

```
Dim i As Integer
For i = 0 To 1 Step 1
    Try
        Throw New MyException("This exception is thrown from Main")
    Catch e As MyException When i = 0
        Console.WriteLine("MyException Caught")
        Console.WriteLine(e.ToString())
```

LISTING 15.17 Continued

```
    Catch e As Exception
        Console.WriteLine("Exception Caught")
        Console.WriteLine(e.ToString())
    Finally
        Console.WriteLine()
    End Try
Next
```

As can be seen from the code, the set of **Try/Catch** blocks is executed twice. The first time when the index variable i is 0, MyException is caught. The second time around, the index variable i is no longer zero, so the **When** clause is false and the search for a suitable exception handler continues to the next block. Because MyException is derived from **ApplicationException**, which ultimately derives from **Exception**, the next block is also of the correct type, and the second time around, the exception is caught in this block. The output from this sample looks like this:

```
MyException Caught
AdvancedExceptions.MyException: This exception is thrown from Main
   at AdvancedExceptions.AdvancedExceptions.Main() in AdvancedExceptions.vb:
➥line 9
Exception Caught
AdvancedExceptions.MyException: This exception is thrown from Main
   at AdvancedExceptions.AdvancedExceptions.Main() in AdvancedExceptions.vb:
➥line 9
```

Because of the **When** clause, each of the available exception handlers handle the same exception.

To illustrate another feature of VB exception handling, Listing 15.18 shows how the same functionality as shown in Listing 15.17 can be achieved with a non-local **goto**. The source to this listing is also a part of the sample code in VBExceptions\AdvancedExceptions.

LISTING 15.18 VB Exceptions Filtering and **goto**

```
        i = 0
        Try
retry:
            Throw New MyException("This exception is thrown from Main")
        Catch e As MyException When i = 0
            Console.WriteLine("MyException Caught")
            Console.WriteLine(e.ToString())
            i = i + 1
            Goto retry
```

LISTING 15.18 Continued

```
        Catch e As Exception
            Console.WriteLine("Exception Caught")
            Console.WriteLine(e.ToString())
        Finally
            Console.WriteLine()
        End Try
```

On entering the **try** block the first time, the variable `i` is 0; therefore, like the sample in Listing 15.17, `MyException` is caught in the first **catch** block. After printing information about the exception that is caught, `i` is incremented and execution is transferred back up to the **try** block via the **goto** statement. This is not supported or legal in C#. Trying to do this will result in a compiler error:

```
No such label 'retry' within the scope of the goto statement
```

In other words, any non-local **goto** is blocked in C#—not just in **try/catch** blocks; therefore, VB offers at least two features that are not exposed with C# when it comes to handling exceptions. Another rule that is enforced with C# is that you cannot leave the body of a **finally** clause. In other words, you cannot use **goto** or **return**, which cause the execution path to leave a **finally** clause. Because C# limits the scope of a label, it is not possible to jump into a **try** block.

Cross Language Exceptions

One of the most exciting new features of the CLR and a managed environment is that not only can programs built with different languages interact, but they can also seamlessly share exceptions. When you think about what an exception is and how it needs to be processed (walking stack, continuing execution in a different stack frame, and so on), this interoperability is pretty amazing.

You have seen many examples of how to build an exception class and throw that exception in a number of different languages. Now you will concentrate on the language interoperability when it comes to exceptions thrown under the control of the CLR. Listing 15.19 shows exceptions caught from three different languages. The complete source for this sample is in the `CrossLanguage` directory. The source for each language-specific class that throws an exception is in subdirectories below the `CrossLanguage` directory. The listing is taken from the `CrossLanguage.cs` file in the `CrossLanguage` directory.

Note

The Perl code is based on the ActiveState implementation of PerlNet. You should consult `http://www.ActiveState.com` for the latest version of Perl, VisualPerl, and PerlNet and follow the installation instructions given for each of the packages. The Perl assembly for this sample is generated from the command line using the supplied Makefile. The DLL is included with the source, so you should not need to regenerate it; however, if you do, change to the directory where you have installed the Perl portion of this sample and type `nmake -f Makefile`. That will recompile the package into an Assembly that the .NET Framework can use. PerlNet is not included as one of the languages included with Visual Studio .NET. If this fails to work, make sure that your PATH environment variable includes the Visual Studio tools (where nmake resides), and make sure that your PATH includes the directory where the Perl compiler was installed. That is the most likely source of the problem.

LISTING 15.19 Cross Language Exceptions

```
static void Main(string[] args)
{
    Console.WriteLine("\nVB exception\n");
    // Throw an exception from VB
    try
    {
        VBExceptionClass vbe = new VBExceptionClass();
        vbe.ExceptionGenerator();
    }
    catch(Exception e)
    {
        Console.WriteLine("Caught a VB exception " + e.ToString());
    }
    Console.WriteLine("\nVC++ exception\n");

    // Throw an exception from VC++
    try
    {
        CPPExceptionClass vcppe = new CPPExceptionClass();
        vcppe.ExceptionGenerator();
    }
    catch(Exception e)
    {
        Console.WriteLine("Caught a VC++ exception " + e.ToString());
    }
```

LISTING 15.19 Continued

```
    Console.WriteLine("\nPerl exception\n");
    // Now try something from Perl
    using (WordCount obj = new WordCount())
    {
        // Set 'Text' property
        obj.Text = "To be or not to be?";
        // Get 'Text' property
        Console.WriteLine("Text is '{0}'", obj.Text);
        // Calling 'Count' for a word not in 'Text' throws an exception
        try
        {
            String word = "test";
            Console.WriteLine("{0} appears {1} times", word, obj.Count(word));
        }
        catch (Exception e)
        {
            Console.WriteLine(e.ToString());
        }
    }
}
```

First, a VB class is instantiated and a method is called on that instance that throws an exception. Next, a VC++ class is instantiated and a method is called on that instance that throws an exception. Finally, a Perl "class" is instantiated, some methods are called on that class, and the text in the class is searched for the word *test*. When *test* is not found in the `Text` property of the class, an exception is thrown.

Throwing the exception in VB looks like this:

```
Throw New CustomVBException("This VB exception is thrown from
➥ExceptionGenerator")
```

Throwing the exception from VC++ looks like this:

```
throw new CustomCPPException(new System::String("This C++ exception is thrown
➥from ExceptionGenerator"));
```

In Perl, an exception is generated with the module `dies`:

```
die "Word '$word' not found" unless defined $self->{Count}->{$word};
```

The details of how the exceptions are generated should be familiar to you by now, but if you need a review, look through the source and see if you understand what is going on.

The output for this sample is shown in Listing 15.20.

LISTING 15.20 P/Invoke Exceptions

```
VB exception

Caught a VB exception VBException.CustomVBException: This VB exception is
➥thrown from ExceptionGenerator
   at VBException.VBExceptionClass.ExceptionGenerator() in
➥VBException.vb:line 4
   at CrossLanguage.CrossLanguageException.Main(String[] args) in
➥crosslanguage.cs:line 20

VC++ exception

Caught a VC++ exception CPPExceptions.CustomCPPException: This C++ exception
➥is thrown from ExceptionGenerator
   at CPPExceptions.CPPExceptionClass.ExceptionGenerator() in
➥cppexceptions.cpp:line 11
   at CrossLanguage.CrossLanguageException.Main(String[] args) in
➥crosslanguage.cs:line 32

Perl exception

Text is 'To be or not to be?'
PerlRuntime.PerlException: Word 'test' not found
   at unknown in WordCount.pm:line 56
```

P/Invoke Exceptions

Chapter 7, "Leveraging Existing Code—P/Invoke," dealt with calls into unmanaged code using P/Invoke. Next, you will look specifically at what happens to exceptions that are generated from the unmanaged code.

If an exception is generated in unmanaged code, it is caught and translated to an appropriate managed exception and rethrown. The only exception would be when no appropriate managed exception exists to which to convert. You have already seen that throwing an unspecified exception such as the following

```
Throw;
```

results in an `SEHException`. In fact, any exception that is thrown that cannot be translated to its managed counterpart results in an `SEHException`.

A sample in the `UnmanagedException` directory raises four different exceptions from unmanaged code: divide-by-zero, null-reference, string, and a custom exception based on `std::exception`. The output of the sample looks like this:

```
Divide-by-zero

System.DivideByZeroException: Attempted to divide by zero.
   at UnmanagedException.NativeMethods.DivideByZero()
   at UnmanagedException.UnmanagedExceptionTest.Main(String[] args) in
➥unmanagedexception.cs:line 30

Memory Access

System.NullReferenceException: Value null was found where an instance of an
➥object was required.
   at UnmanagedException.NativeMethods.MemoryAccess()
   at UnmanagedException.UnmanagedExceptionTest.Main(String[] args) in
➥unmanagedexception.cs:line 40

Fail

System.Runtime.InteropServices.SEHException: External component has thrown an
➥exception.
   at UnmanagedException.NativeMethods.Fail()
   at UnmanagedException.UnmanagedExceptionTest.Main(String[] args) in
➥unmanagedexception.cs:line 50

Custom

System.Runtime.InteropServices.SEHException: External component has thrown an
➥exception.
   at UnmanagedException.NativeMethods.Custom()
   at UnmanagedException.UnmanagedExceptionTest.Main(String[] args) in
➥unmanagedexception.cs:line 60
```

Notice that the first two types of exceptions can be translated directly to a managed counterpart. With the last two types of exceptions, a managed counterpart could not be found, so the default **SEHException** is thrown.

COM Exceptions

You would not expect an exception here. One of the core principles behind COM is that exceptions cannot cross COM method boundaries. Here, unlike the unmanaged exceptions of the previous section, no exceptions are thrown in unmanaged code. Where are the exceptions coming from? As you saw in Chapter 8, "Using COM/COM+ in Managed Code," to call a COM component in managed code, a wrapper must be constructed to form an interop layer between the managed code and unmanaged code. As far as exceptions are concerned, the returned HRESULT from the COM method is turned into an exception by this interop layer. This translation is not unlike that which was occurring when code was imported like this:

```
#import "msxml3.dll"
```

When the compiler sees this statement, it generates a .tli and a .tlh file that is automatically compiled as part of the project. Within these files are the following types of code:

```
inline _bstr_t IXMLDOMNode::GetnodeName ( ) {
    BSTR _result;
    HRESULT _hr = get_nodeName(&_result);
    if (FAILED(_hr)) _com_issue_errorex(_hr, this, __uuidof(this));
    return _bstr_t(_result, false);
}
```

If the COM method call `FAILED`, then `com_issue_errorex` is called, which generates a `com_error` exception. In addition to translating this `HRESULT` to an exception, the rich error information (if available, that is, the interface `ISupportErrorInfo` is implemented) is read and incorporated into the exception.

The COM interop layer performs a similar translation from `HRESULT`'s to exceptions as was done with `#import`. The one important difference is that you cannot circumvent the translation from `HRESULT`'s to exceptions. In other words, a `raw_interface_only` flag does not exist, so that the exception is not generated. Return codes do not exist in the managed world.

The following sample includes an in-process COM component that has two methods, both of which always fail. The first method just returns a `FAILED HRESULT`. The second method returns a `FAILED HRESULT` as well, but it also fills in the rich error information with a call to the ATL method `Error`. Listing 15.21 shows the implementation of these two methods. The full source for this sample is in the `COMException` and the `COMException\COMError` directories.

LISTING 15.21 COM Failures

```
STDMETHODIMP CCOMFault::Fail(void)
{
    return HRESULT_FROM_WIN32(ERROR_ACCESS_DENIED);
}

STDMETHODIMP CCOMFault::FailWithErrorInfo(void)
{
    HRESULT hr = HRESULT_FROM_WIN32(ERROR_NOT_SUPPORTED);
    Error("This is a description of the error", __uuidof(ICOMFault), hr);
    return hr;
}
```

The output of this sample looks like this:

```
Fail

System.UnauthorizedAccessException: Access is denied.
   at COMError.CCOMFault.Fail()
   at COMException.COMExceptionTest.Main(String[] args) in comexception.cs:
➥line 21

FailWithErrorInfo

System.Runtime.InteropServices.COMException (0x80070032): This is a
➥description of the error
   at COMError.CCOMFault.FailWithErrorInfo()
   at COMException.COMExceptionTest.Main(String[] args) in comexception.cs:
➥line 30
```

Notice that the first case encoded a `Win32` error code into the `FAILED HRESULT` and the interop layer translates that to an appropriate managed exception. With the second call, a **`COMException`** is thrown and the rich error information is made available as part of the exception.

Remote Exceptions

Another area where you might not expect an exception is in another **`AppDomain`**. **`AppDomain`**s are isolated so that a failure in another **`AppDomain`** will not affect another **`AppDomain`**. This is still true, but with exceptions, the CLR works hard to make sure the user sees the exceptions.

The following sample in the `AppDomainFault` directory creates another **`AppDomain`** and causes the current thread to enter the newly created **`AppDomain`**. It does this by creating a local instance of an object that is supported by that **`AppDomain`** and calling a method on that object. The object class is shown in Listing 15.22.

LISTING 15.22 `AppDomain` Exceptions

```
public class Fault : MarshalByRefObject
{
    public void DivideZero()
    {
        Console.WriteLine("In the application domain: {0} thread {1}",
➥Thread.GetDomain().FriendlyName, Thread.CurrentThread.GetHashCode());
        Console.WriteLine("Generating a fault . . . ");
```

LISTING 15.22 Continued

```
        int a = 0;
        int b = 1;
        int c = b/a;

        Console.WriteLine("Fault never occured.");
    }
}
```

As can be seen in the code, this **AppDomain** just causes a **DivideByZeroException**. The creation of the **AppDomain**, the invocation of the faulty method, and catching the resulting exception are shown in Listing 15.23.

LISTING 15.23 Creating a Faulty **AppDomain**

```
static void Main(string[] args)
{
    // Set ApplicationBase to the current directory
    AppDomainSetup info = new AppDomainSetup();

    info.ApplicationBase = "file:\\\\" + System.Environment.CurrentDirectory;

    // Create an application domain with null evidence
    AppDomain dom = AppDomain.CreateDomain("RemoteDomain", null, info);

    // Load the assembly HelloWorld2 and instantiate the type
    BindingFlags flags = (BindingFlags.Public | BindingFlags.Instance |
➥BindingFlags.CreateInstance);
    ObjectHandle objh = dom.CreateInstance("Fault", "InterAppDomain.Fault",
➥ false, flags, null, null, null, null, null);
    if (objh == null)
    {
        Console.WriteLine("CreateInstance failed");
        return;
    }

    // Unwrap the object
    Object obj = objh.Unwrap();
    // Cast to the actual type
    Fault f = (Fault)obj;

    Console.WriteLine("In the application domain: {0} thread {1}",
➥Thread.GetDomain().FriendlyName, Thread.CurrentThread.GetHashCode());

    try
    {
        // Invoke the method
        f.DivideZero();
    }
```

LISTING 15.23 Continued

```
    catch(Exception e)
    {
        Console.WriteLine(e.ToString());
    }
    // Clean up by unloading the application domain
    AppDomain.Unload(dom);
}
```

Most of the code in this listing is taken up with the creation of the **AppDomain**, and not exceptions. Finally, at the end of the listing, you see a familiar set of `try/catch` blocks. You are expecting an exception here. The output of this sample looks like this:

```
In the application domain: AppDomainFault.exe thread 58
In the application domain: RemoteDomain thread 58
Generating a fault . . .
System.DivideByZeroException: Attempted to divide by zero.

ServerStackTrace:
   at InterAppDomain.Fault.DivideZero() in fault.cs:line 14
   at System.Runtime.Remoting.Messaging.StackBuilderSink.PrivateProcessMessage
➥(MethodBase mb, Object[] args, Object server, Int32 methodPtr, Boolean
➥fExecuteInContext, Object[]& outArgs)
   at System.Runtime.Remoting.Messaging.StackBuilderSink.SyncProcessMessage
➥(IMessage msg, Int32 methodPtr, Boolean fExecuteInContext)

Exception rethrown at [0]:
   at System.Runtime.Remoting.Proxies.RealProxy.HandleReturnMessage(Imessage
➥reqMsg, IMessage retMsg)
   at System.Runtime.Remoting.Proxies.RealProxy.PrivateInvoke(MessageData&
➥msgData, Int32 type)
   at InterAppDomain.Fault.DivideZero() in fault.cs:line 9
   at AppDomainTest.InterAppDomain.Main(String[] args) in appdomainfault.cs:
➥line 47
```

From this output, you can see where you are about to generate a fault (Generating a fault…). The next line is a message from the creator of the **AppDomain** indicating that the **DivideByZeroException** was caught followed by a stack trace showing how the exception got there.

The first line in the stack shows where the exception was raised (fault.cs:line 14). Then you see that the exception was rethrown after it reached the **AppDomain** boundary (Exception rethrown at [0]:). Finally, you see the root cause of this fault is the call to `Fault.DivdeByZero()`(at `AppDomainTest.InterAppDomain.Main...` in appdomainfault.cs: line 47). In the end, after a lot of work done by the CLR, calling a method on another **AppDomain** looks like a call to the same method in the current **AppDomain** (which is the point).

Thread and Asynchronous Callback Exceptions

What happens if an exception occurs in another thread of the current **AppDomain** or in an asynchronous callback? Two samples will illustrate what happens when an exception occurs in an asynchronous callback or in another thread.

Asynchronous Callback Exceptions

At first, you might not consider exceptions in the context of an asynchronous callback. However, when you try it, it seems that there is a bug because it does not seem to work as you planned. Perhaps you were under the false impression that asynchronous callbacks simply use the **ThreadPool**, and the **ThreadPool** is a simple collection of **Thread**s. It is more complex than that. The following sample application will help you understand what is happening with exceptions and asynchronous callbacks in general. Listings 15.24–15.25 illustrate the important aspects of this sample. The full source for this sample is in the `ThreadExceptions\AsyncCallback` directory.

LISTING 15.24 Setting the Delegate for the Asynchronous Callback

```
static int WorkerThatThrowsException()
{
    Console.WriteLine("Inside WorkerThatThrowsException on thread {0}",
➥AppDomain.GetCurrentThreadId());
    throw new ApplicationException("Exception raised in
➥WorkerThatThrowsException");
    Console.WriteLine("Inside WorkerThatThrowsException about to return the
➥answer");
    return 0;
}
. . .
static void UnprotectedEndInvokeCallback(IAsyncResult iar)
{
    Console.WriteLine("Inside EndInvokeCallback on thread {0}",
➥AppDomain.GetCurrentThreadId());
    WorkerDelegate wd = (WorkerDelegate)iar.AsyncState;
    int result = wd.EndInvoke(iar);
    Console.WriteLine("Inside EndInvokeCallback the answer was {0}", result);
}
. . .
WorkerDelegate wd = new WorkerDelegate(WorkerThatThrowsException);
wd.BeginInvoke(new AsyncCallback(UnprotectedEndInvokeCallback), wd);
```

This first listing registers a callback called `UnprotectedEndInvokeCallback`. This callback illustrates the *wrong* way of handling an asynchronous callback if exceptions are expected. The output is shown next:

```
Inside Main on thread 2052
Inside WorkerThatThrowsException on thread 1072
Inside UnprotectedEndInvokeCallback on thread 1072
```

Clearly, the delegate `WorkerThatThrowsException` throws an exception, but where does it go? It seems that an exception was thrown because the **`Console`** output after the exception is thrown does not appear. Unhandled exception handlers have not been installed, so by all rights, this sample should pop up a dialog box indicating an unhandled exception. The callback routine was then changed to wrap the `EndInvoke` call with a set of **`try/catch`** blocks thanks to the advice from the `DOTNET@DISCUSS.DEVELOP.COM mailing list`. Now the routine (renamed to `EndInvokeCallback`) looks like what is shown in Listing 15.25.

LISTING 15.25 Modified Delegate for the Asynchronous Callback

```
static void EndInvokeCallback(IAsyncResult iar)
{
    Console.WriteLine("Inside EndInvokeCallback on thread {0}",
➥AppDomain.GetCurrentThreadId());
    WorkerDelegate wd = (WorkerDelegate)iar.AsyncState;
    try
    {
        int result = wd.EndInvoke(iar);
        Console.WriteLine("Inside EndInvokeCallback the answer was {0}",
result);
    }
    catch (Exception e)
    {
        Console.WriteLine("Caught exception in EndInvokeCallback:");
        Console.WriteLine(e.ToString());
    }
}
. . .
wd.BeginInvoke(new AsyncCallback(EndInvokeCallback), wd);
```

By wrapping a **`try/catch`** around the `EndInvoke`, the exception could be caught. The output looks like this:

```
Caught exception in EndInvokeCallback:
System.ApplicationException: Exception raised in WorkerThatThrowsException

ServerStackTrace:
   at ThreadExceptions.ExceptionHandlers.WorkerThatThrowsException() in
➥asynccallback.cs:line 13
```

```
   at System.Runtime.Remoting.Messaging.StackBuilderSink.PrivateProcessMessage
➥(MethodBase mb, Object[] args, Object server, Int32 methodPtr,
➥Boolean fExecuteInContext, Object[]& outArgs)
   at System.Runtime.Remoting.Messaging.StackBuilderSink.AsyncProcessMessage
➥(IMessage msg, IMessageSink replySink)

Exception rethrown at [0]:
   at System.Runtime.Remoting.Proxies.RemotingProxy.EndInvokeHelper
➥(Message reqMsg, Boolean bProxyCase)
   at System.Runtime.Remoting.Proxies.RemotingProxy.Invoke(Object NotUsed,
➥MessageData& msgData)
   at ThreadExceptions.WorkerDelegate.EndInvoke(IAsyncResult result)
   at ThreadExceptions.ExceptionHandlers.EndInvokeCallback(IAsyncResult iar)
➥in asynccallback.cs:line 23
```

This output looks remarkably similar to the output associated with Listing 15.23. This is because the same mechanisms are involved. If an asynchronous callback is expected to throw an exception, then be sure to wrap the call to **EndInvoke** with **try/catch** or the exception will silently disappear.

Thread Exceptions

This sample is largely a repeat of the previous sample with the difference being that a **Thread** is explicitly started to do the work that throws an exception. This sample illustrates the point that the **UnhandledException** event is indeed an **AppDomain** wide property. The exception raised in this **Thread** is not caught anywhere, so it ends up with the **UnhandledException** event. The sample that is partially listed in Listing 15.26 illustrates the use of the **UnhandledException** event. The full source for this sample is available at ThreadExceptions\Thread.

LISTING 15.26 Using **UnhandledException**

```
static void ExceptionFilter(object o, UnhandledExceptionEventArgs e)
{
    Console.WriteLine("Inside ExceptionFilter on thread: {0} IsTerminating:
{1}",
        AppDomain.GetCurrentThreadId(), e.IsTerminating);
}
static void ThreadStartCallback()
{
    Console.WriteLine("Inside ThreadStartCallback on thread {0}",
➥AppDomain.GetCurrentThreadId());
    int result = WorkerThatThrowsException();
    Console.WriteLine("Inside ThreadStartCallback the answer is {0}", result);
}
static int WorkerThatThrowsException()
```

LISTING 15.26 Continued

```
{
    Console.WriteLine("Inside WorkerThatThrowsException on thread {0}",
➥AppDomain.GetCurrentThreadId());
    throw new ArgumentException();
    Console.WriteLine("Inside WorkerThatThrowsException about to return the
➥answer");
    return 0;
}

. . .
AppDomain.CurrentDomain.UnhandledException += new
        UnhandledExceptionEventHandler(ExceptionFilter);

WorkerDelegate wd = new WorkerDelegate(WorkerThatThrowsException);
ThreadStart ts = new ThreadStart(ThreadStartCallback);
Thread t = new Thread(ts);
t.Start();
```

This sample first registers a callback in with the **`UnhandledException`** event of the current **`AppDomain`**. Next, a delegate is created and the **`Thread`** that will be doing the work is created and started. The only work that is done is to throw an **`ArgumentException`** in `WorkerThatThrowsException`. Because no exception handlers are available, the callback for unhandled exceptions is called. The output for this sample looks like this:

```
Inside Main on thread 1716
Inside ThreadStartCallback on thread 336
Inside WorkerThatThrowsException on thread 336
Inside ExceptionFilter on thread: 336 IsTerminating: False
```

Summary

When used properly, exceptions can add to an application's stability and robustness. The .NET Framework and the CLR have made exception handling mandatory, but at the same time, exceptions have never been easier to use and extend. In the interest of better exception and error handling, the following guidelines should prove beneficial:

- Because it is so easy to handle and generate exceptions, great care should be taken to make sure you know when *not* to rely on exceptions. If, for example, an object can be tested for an invalid condition (such as null) to avoid having an exception raised, then do so. Suppose that you have an object that must be closed to free up the resources it was using, but closing an already closed object resulted in an exception. You would be faced with the following choices:

```
if(conn.State != ConnectionState.Closed)
    conn.Close();
```

```
        or
    try {
      conn.Close();
    }
    catch(InvalidOperationException ex) {
      //Do something with the error or ignore it.
    }
```

The second method requires little processing when the exception is not generated (the connection is not already closed). The first method would be preferred if it was found that the connection was already closed most of the time. (Avoid the creation of an exception instance.)

This might involve redesigning (or designing) your class so that you can avoid an exception. Take, for instance, the **FileStream** class:

```
class FileRead {
    void Open() {
        string file = "myfile.txt";
        if(!File.Exists(file))
            return;
        FileStream stream = File.Open(file, FileMode.Open);
        int b = 0;

        // ReadByte returns -1 at EOF
        while ((b = stream.ReadByte()) != -1) {
            // Do something.
        }
    }
}
```

This class has been designed so that the exception that will be raised if an attempt to open a file that does not exist or the user does not have permission to look can be avoided.

- Throw exceptions in rare, *exceptional*, conditions. Remember that constructing an exception, although it provides invaluable information, is not cheap. You could have code like this:

```
int sum = 0;
int [] array = new int[]{1,2,3,4,5};
i = 0;
try
{
    while(true)
    {
        sum += array[i++];
    }
}
catch(Exception e)
{
}
```

However, this code is relying on exceptions for flow control, and that is not recommended. It would work and the compiler wouldn't generate a warning, but it would be considered bad programming practice.

- If you have multiple catch blocks, order the exception handlers in order of most specific to least specific.
- As the catch block for an exception becomes less specific, it might be harder to decide what to do with the exception. Remember that it might be appropriate to just rethrow the exception. This can only be done inside of a catch block. It is done by specifying a throw with no expression, like this

```
throw;
```

- All of the exception classes defined in the .NET class libraries are named with the word "Exception" at the end of the class name—for instance, `ApplicationException`, `SystemException`, and `FileNotFoundException`. To make your code more readable, it is recommended that your custom exception classes also follow this convention.
- If a user-defined exception could possibly cross **`AppDomain`** boundaries or if the exception is to be passed remotely, then make sure that the metadata associated with the class (the Assembly) is available in each **`AppDomain`** in which the exception is referenced. If this is not the case, then another exception **`FileNotFoundException`** could be generated. Making sure the assembly is available might require modification of the search path (`Appbase` property or **`AppDomain.BaseDirectory`**) for assemblies in the **`AppDomain`** or installation of the assembly in the global assembly cache (GAC).
- Do not define user-defined exceptions based on the **`Exception`** class. Use the class **`ApplicationException`** as a base for all user-defined exceptions.
- Use the exception classes in the library whenever possible and when using the predefined exception classes it makes clear the error that has occurred. If the application is littered with generic **`Exception`**s being thrown, it is hard to determine the error or exception that has occurred. At the same time, having too many user-defined exceptions can also make the code hard to read.
- In C# and C++, make sure that at least three constructors are defined for each user-defined exception. These three allow a specific error message to be assigned on construction, an inner exception to be assigned to an exception (in the case of multiple exceptions), and both an error message and an inner exception. The definition should look like this:

```
public class CustomException : ApplicationException {
    CustomException() {… }
    CustomException(string message) {… }
    CustomException(string message, Exception inner) {… }
}
```

- Use a localized description string for exceptions, especially if users will see this exception description.
- Use correct grammar and punctuation for exception messages.
- Throw an **`InvalidOperationException`** if the object's state is not appropriate for the operation at hand.
- If any of the arguments are out of range or otherwise invalid, throw an **`ArgumentException`**.
- When deciding on where to throw an exception, remember that the stack trace that is built for you begins where the exception is thrown rather than where the exception was created.
- Throw exceptions rather than return `HRESULTS` or other types of error codes.
- Make it so that throwing an exception has no side effects. Clean up intermediate results when throwing exceptions.
- Supply and use helper functions to help build an exception where appropriate. This is especially true if building an exception is especially complex or if the operations that are required to build an exception are repeated often.

CHAPTER 16

.NET Security

In This Chapter

A secure application is a prime concern to most corporate decision makers. In a memo to Microsoft employees, Bill Gates said, "When we face a choice between adding features and resolving security issues, we need to choose security." As reported by CNET News.com (`http://news.com.com/2100-1001-816880.html?tag=st.vid.nws.rl.2100-1001-816880`), Bill Gates further stated, "Our products should emphasize security right out of the box." The article at CNET News.com quoted Bill Gates as saying this new initiative is "trustworthy computing," and it is to have the "highest priority" for the company. In today's computing environment, security is crucial and is likely only to increase in importance as time goes on.

A secure program has numerous aspects. A programmer might think of a secure program as being one that is robust and not easily crashed. Customers who purchase your software might think that a secure program is one that does not corrupt their data. Companies might be concerned about how secure the licensing mechanism is. They want to make sure that the software can't be easily copied, resulting in lost revenue. The software might be responsible for handling sensitive data that only a certain set of users should have the capability to view. A secure program adequately protects data as well as authorizes and authenticates the users of that data.

The .NET Framework addresses each of these aforementioned security issues. This chapter discusses how the .NET Framework protects you from a "program gone wild." It details how code access security can provide a fine-grained level of security that prevents a program from being used in ways that you did not intend. It briefly touches on how the data that your software handles can be encrypted (using the built-in cryptography classes) or hidden (using isolated storage).

Note

Chapter 6, "Publishing Applications," is related to this chapter. That chapter discusses how you can ensure that the software running under your name is indeed yours. You are encouraged to read or reread that chapter.

Two Different, Yet Similar Security Models

The .NET Framework provides two basic models for security: code access based security and role-based security. Code access security describes what the code has permission to do and to which resources it has access. Role-based security controls who has permission to run the code and what they are allowed to do. The CLR supports both of these models using a similar infrastructure. By understanding some of the concepts that are common to both models, you should be able to understand the models better individually.

Permissions

Three types of permissions exist:

- Code access permission
- Identity permission
- Role-based security permission

Code Access Permission

Code access permission refers to a class derived from **`System.Security.CodeAccessPermission.`** This means that each permission class has a common set of methods: **`Demand`**, **`Assert`**, **`Deny`**, **`PermitOnly`**, **`IsSubsetOf`**, **`Intersect`**, and **`Union`**.

Each permission class designates a right to either access a particular resource or to perform a particular operation. All permissions are requested or demanded by the code; ultimately, the permission that is granted to the code is up to the CLR to decide. The CLR makes the decision to grant a particular permission based on evidence (which is assigned to the code when it enters the runtime environment) and policy (which is dictated by the user, machine, or enterprise policy files). Table 16.1 lists the code access permission classes that are available as part of the .NET Framework SDK.

> **Note**
>
> Evidence and policy are discussed later in this chapter.

TABLE 16.1 Code Access Permissions

Permission Class Name	*Namespace*	*Right Represented*
`DirectoryServicesPermission`	**`.DirectoryServices`**	Code access to DirectoryServices classes
`DnsPermission`	**`.Net`**	Domain Name System (DNS) Server access
`EnvironmentPermission`	**`.Security.Permissions`**	Environment variable access

TABLE 16.1 Continued

Permission Class Name	*Namespace*	*Right Represented*
`EventLogPermission`	`.Diagnostics`	Event log services access
`FileDialogPermission`	`.Security.Permissions`	File or directory access through a File dialog box
`FileIOPermission`	`.Security.Permissions`	File or directory access permissions
`IsolatedStorageFilePermission`	`.Security.Permissions`	Private virtual file system access and usage
`MessageQueuePermission`	`.Messaging`	Messaging access
`OleDbPermission`	`.Data.OleDb`	Database access using OLE DB
`PerformanceCounterPermission`	`.Diagnostics`	Performance counter access
`PrintingPermission`	`.Drawing.Printing`	Printer access
`ReflectionPermission`	`.Security.Permissions`	Metadata access through Reflection APIs
`RegistryPermission`	`.Security.Permissions`	Registry access
`SecurityPermission`	`.Security.Permissions`	SecurityPermissionFlag access
`ServiceControllerPermission`	`.ServiceProcess`	Service controller access
`SocketPermission`	`.Net`	Connection and Transport address access
`SqlClientPermission`	`.Data.SqlClient`	SQL database access
`UIPermission`	`.Security.Permissions`	User interface and Clipboard access
`WebPermission`	`.Net`	HTTP Internet resource access

Identity Permission

These permissions represent a means of identifying code by where it came from, who wrote it, and how much it is trusted. Identity permissions, such as code access permissions, are derived from **`System.Security.CodeAccessPermission`**. Table 16.2 lists the identity permissions that are part of the .NET Framework.

TABLE 16.2 Identity Permissions

Permission Class Name	*Namespace*	*Identity Description*
`PublisherIdentityPermission`	`.Security.Permissions`	Permission to act as the software publisher through a certificate.
`SiteIdentityPermission`	`.Security.Permissions`	Permission for the Web site from which the code originates.
`StrongNameIdentityPermission`	`.Security.Permissions`	Permission to access code with a strong name.
`UrlIdentityPermission`	`.Security.Permissions`	Permission for the URL from which the code originates.
`ZoneIdentityPermission`	`.Security.Permissions`	Permission for the zone from which the code originates. The zone is based on IE options.

Role-Based Permission

Role-based permission is based on a single class, **`PrincipalPermission`**. This class can be used to determine if a user has a specified identity or is a member of a specified role. A role can be part of the operating system (a member of a group for example), it can be completely specified by the application, or it can be a role that is integrated with COM+.

Type Safety

Type safety is not typically thought of as a security issue. However, type safety plays an important role in runtime security. Type-safe code accesses memory in a well-defined and allowable fashion. If the code can be verified as type safe, then it can be safely isolated from other code in the system or from other code in the same process. When code is verifiably type safe, it is guaranteed not to stray from its allocated memory space. To be backward compatible with legacy C code, C++ allows references to memory (pointers) to take on any value. With verifiably type-safe code, all memory access is tightly controlled and cannot cause other code in the system to crash or malfunction. `PEVerify` (in `Program Files\Microsoft Visual Studio .NET\FrameworkSDK\bin`) is a tool that verifies code for type safety. Ideally, you want to run this tool on your code and receive the following output:

```
All Classes and Methods in propertiescs.exe Verified
```

However, when PEVerify is run against code marked as unsafe as shown in Listing 16.1 the output of Listing 16.2 results.

LISTING 16.1 Unsafe C# Code

```
unsafe static void StringAddress(string s)
{
    fixed(char *p = s)
    {
        Console.WriteLine("0x{0:X8}", (uint)p);
    }
}
```

This simple code takes in a string and prints the address that is associated with the string. PEVerify finds numerous errors in this code. It reports numerous errors, most of which are in Listing 16.2.

LISTING 16.2 Errors from PEVerify Against Unsafe Code

```
. . .
[IL]: Error: [unsafe.exe : CLRUnleashed.Unsafe::StringAddress]
➥[local variable #0x00000000] ELEMENT_TYPE_PTR cannot be verified.
[IL]: Error: [unsafe.exe : CLRUnleashed.Unsafe::StringAddress]
➥[offset 0x00000002] [opcode ldloc.1] initlocals must be set for
➥verifiable methods with one or more local variables.
[IL]: Error: [unsafe.exe : CLRUnleashed.Unsafe::StringAddress]
➥[offset 0x00000003] [opcode conv.i] [found objref 'System.String']
➥Expected numeric type on the stack.
[IL]: Error: [unsafe.exe : CLRUnleashed.Unsafe::StringAddress]
➥[offset 0x0000000A] [opcode stloc.0] [found Int32]
➥ [expected address of Int16] Unexpected type on the stack.
. . .
[IL]: Error: [unsafe.exe : CLRUnleashed.Unsafe::StringAddress]
➥[offset 0x00000011] [opcode conv.u4] [found address of Int16]
➥Expected numeric type on the stack.
16 Errors Verifying unsafe.exe
```

To make sense of these errors, you need to look at the IL code that the C# compiler generated. This is because PEVerify refers addresses and terms that are more readily apparent in from the IL code. ILDasm can provide the output shown in Listing 16.3.

LISTING 16.3 ILDasm Listing for the Unsafe C# Code in Listing 16.1

```
.method private hidebysig static void  StringAddress(string s) cil managed
{
  // Code size       31 (0x1f)
```

LISTING 16.3 Continued

```
  .maxstack  2
  .locals ([0] char* p,
           [1] string pinned CS$00000520$00000000)
  IL_0000:  ldarg.0
  IL_0001:  stloc.1
  IL_0002:  ldloc.1
  IL_0003:  conv.i
  IL_0004:  call       int32 [mscorlib]System.Runtime.CompilerServices.
➥RuntimeHelpers::get_OffsetToStringData()
  IL_0009:  add
  IL_000a:  stloc.0
  IL_000b:  ldstr      "0x{0:X8}"
  IL_0010:  ldloc.0
  IL_0011:  conv.u4
  IL_0012:  box        [mscorlib]System.UInt32
  IL_0017:  call       void [mscorlib]System.Console::WriteLine(string,
                                                              object)
  IL_001c:  ldnull
  IL_001d:  stloc.1
  IL_001e:  ret
} // end of method Unsafe::StringAddress
```

Now you can see what `PEVerify` is complaining about:

- `ELEMENT_TYPE_PTR cannot be verified`. This is in reference to the `char* p` local variable. As stated earlier, these pointers can take on any value; therefore, they cannot be verified.
- `Initlocals must be set for verifiable methods with one or more local variables`. When a method is marked as unsafe, one of the side effects is that the local variables are not initialized. Because these variables can randomly take on any value, this cannot be verified. Even though this is in reference to ldloc.1, which is initialized with the previous two instructions, PEVerify flags this as an uninitialized variable.
- `Expected numeric type on the stack`. Here an attempt is made to convert the string on the stack to an integer. This is a correct function, but it is not type safe.
- `Expected numeric type on the stack`. This time the verification detects the address of an Int16 (char *p) on the stack rather than a simple numeric type that it was expecting. The tool is simply reporting the type mismatch.

`PEVerify` does a thorough job of verifying code even for this simple code example. If you are concerned about type safety, run your code against `PEVerify`. Note that VC++ with managed extensions is not verifiable; as such, `PEVerify` simply reports that it is a bad PE header.

If you stay away from unsafe code or at least isolate unsafe code, your code is verifiably type safe, which goes a long way toward making your code secure.

Note

All of the verification that `PEVerify` provides happens automatically as the JIT compiler converts your IL code to native code. You would normally only concern yourself with `PEVerify` if you were writing a compiler or if you just wanted to see if your code was verifiably type-safe.

Security Policy

Security policy is a set of rules governing the permissions that code is allowed to have. The administrator sets the policy and the runtime enforces it. All code is given evidence by the runtime host. This evidence, along with policy from the enterprise, machine, and user levels, determines what permissions are granted to code. Remember the following formula:

```
Evidence + Policy + Assembly Permission Requests = Permission Granted to Code
```

Security Policy Levels

Three levels of security policy are specified in XML configuration files. In order, they are as follows:

- Enterprise—The security policy at this level is described by an XML file at `%runtime install path%\Config\Enterprisesec.config`, where `%runtime install path%` is where you have installed the runtime. Typically, this is something like `\Windows\Microsoft.Net\Framework\v1.0.xxxx`. This file contains a list of code groups, permission sets, and policy assemblies. When managed code is started, the runtime uses the policy that is described at this level as the starting point for deciding what permissions the code should be granted. A domain controller distributes this XML file throughout a domain of computers. A domain administrator then dictates the policy described in this file.
- Machine—The security policy at this level is described by an XML file at `%runtime install path%\Config\security.config`. The machine level is the second level of the policy. It is only possible for the machine policy to restrict the permission set that would be granted managed code after evaluating the policy at the enterprise level. The format of this file is identical to the format of the file that describes the enterprise policy.

- User—An XML file describes the security policy at this level at `%USERPROFILE%\Application Data\Microsoft\CLR Security Config\v1.0.xxxx\Security.config`. `%USERPROFILE%` points to `\Documents and Settings\your name`. It is only possible for the user policy to restrict the permission set that would be granted managed code after evaluating the policy at the machine and enterprise levels. The format of this file is identical to the format of the files that describe the machine and enterprise policies.

A fourth security policy level is set by the developer in the code. This is the **`AppDomain`** security policy level and it cannot be changed through any of the configuration files. After the assembly is built, the policy is fixed and users or administrators cannot directly change it.

Security Policy Administration Tools

Although each level of the policy is an editable XML file and it is possible to manually edit any of the files, it is strongly recommended that these files only be modified with either the .NET Framework Configuration tool (mscorcfg.msc) or the Code Access Security Policy tool (caspol.exe). Your first choice should be the .NET Framework Configuration tool, which is shown in Figure 16.1.

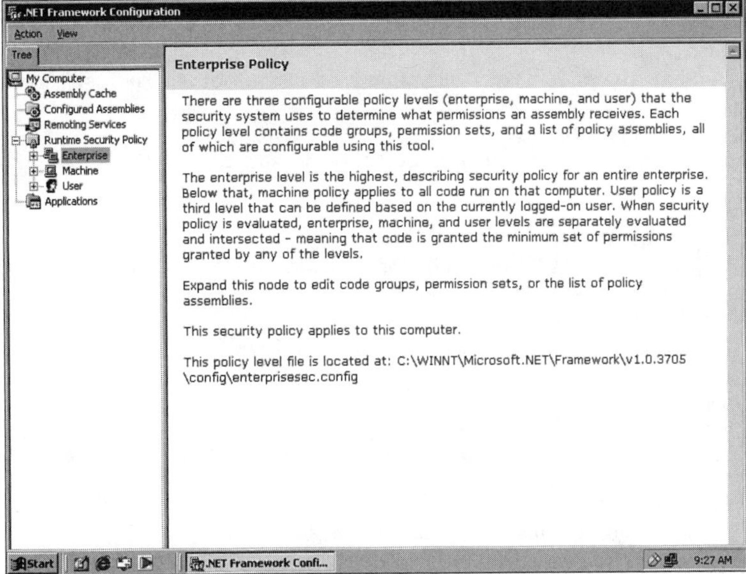

FIGURE 16.1
.NET Framework Configuration tool.

If you frequently administer the security for .NET applications, place the .NET Framework Configuration tool on your desktop as a shortcut, as shown in Chapter 6,

Figure 6.5. Look at the tree on the left pane of Figure 16.1. To illustrate using this tool to administer runtime security, the Runtime Security Policy node has been expanded. If you have the configuration tool up and running, you can expand the Runtime Security Policy node. You can see three nodes for Enterprise, Machine, and User policy. You can expand each of these nodes and modify the corresponding policy file in a consistent way that is much less likely to inadvertently corrupt a security policy file. The top-level node (Enterprise, Machine, and User) gives you a brief help description of that policy level as well as the full path to the policy file that will be modified by changing or adding information below that node.

If the .NET Framework Configuration tool does not provide you with enough flexibility, then use the Code Access Security Policy tool (caspol.exe). `Caspol` is a command-line utility that is primarily intended for scripting .NET security policy. Invoking `caspol` with no arguments provides a usage list that should give you an idea of the available options. Listing 16.4 shows some of the options that are available for `caspol`.

LISTING 16.4 Caspol Usage

```
Usage: caspol <option> <args> ...

caspol -m[achine]
    Modifier that makes additional commands act on the machine level

caspol -u[ser]
    Modifier that makes additional commands act on the user level

caspol -en[terprise]
    Modifier that makes additional commands act on the enterprise level

caspol -cu
caspol -customuser <path>
    Modifier that makes additional commands act on the custom user level

caspol -a[ll]
    Set all policy levels as the active levels

caspol -ca
caspol -customall <path>
    Modifier that makes additional commands act on all levels as a custom user

caspol -l[ist]
    List code groups & permission sets

caspol -lg
caspol -listgroups
    List code groups
```

LISTING 16.4 Continued

```
caspol -lp
caspol -listpset
    List permission sets

caspol -lf
caspol -listfulltrust
    List full trust assemblies

caspol -ld
caspol -listdescription
    List code group names and descriptions

caspol -ap
caspol -addpset { <named_xml_file> | <xml_file> <name> }
    Add named permission set to policy level

caspol -cp
caspol -chgpset <xml_file> <pset_name>
    Change named permission set in active level

caspol -rp
caspol -rempset <pset_name>
    Remove a named permission set from the policy level

caspol -af
caspol -addfulltrust <assembly_name>
    Add full trust assembly to policy level

caspol -rf
caspol -remfulltrust <assembly_name>
    Remove a full trust assembly from the policy level

caspol -rg
caspol -remgroup <label|name>
    Remove code group at <label|name>

caspol -cg
caspol -chggroup <label|name> {<mship>|<pset_name>|<flag>}+
    Change code group at <label|name> to given membership,
    permission set, or flags

caspol -ag
caspol -addgroup <parent_label|name> <mship> <pset_name> <flag>
    Add code group to <parent_label|name> with given membership,
    permission set, and flags

caspol -rsg
caspol -resolvegroup <assembly_name>
    List code groups this file belongs to
```

LISTING 16.4 Continued

```
caspol -rsp
caspol -resolveperm <assembly_name>
    List permissions granted to this file

caspol -s[ecurity] { on | off }
    Turn security on or off

caspol -e[xecution] { on | off }
    Enable/Disable checking for "right-to-run" on code execution start-up

caspol -pp
caspol -polchgprompt { on | off }
    Enable/Disable policy change prompt

caspol -r[ecover]
    Recover the most recently saved version of a level

caspol -rs
caspol -reset
    Reset a level to its default state

caspol -f[orce]
    Enable forcing save that will disable caspol functionality

caspol -b[uildcache]
    Build the security policy cache file.

caspol -?
caspol /?
caspol -h[elp]
    Displays this screen


where "<mship>" can be:
  -allcode                All code
  -appdir                 Application directory
  -custom <xml_file>      Custom membership condition
  -hash <hashAlg> {-hex <hashValue>|-file <assembly_name>}
                          Assembly hash
  -pub {-cert <cert_file_name> | -file <signed_file_name> | -hex <hex_string>}
                          Software publisher
  -site <website>         Site
  -strong -file <assemblyfile_name> {<name> | -noname}
          {<version> | -noversion}
                          Strong name
  -url <url>              URL
  -zone <zone_name>       Zone, where zone can be:
                                MyComputer
                                Intranet
```

LISTING 16.4 Continued

```
                                    Trusted
                                    Internet
                                    Untrusted

where "<flag>" can be any combination of:
  -exclusive {on|off}
                              Set the policy statement Exclusive flag
  -levelfinal {on|off}
                              Set the policy statement LevelFinal flag
  -n[ame] <name>
                              Code group name
  -d[escription] <desc>
                              Code group description
```

Details of the command-line arguments for `caspol` can be found at `ms-help://MS.VSCC/MS.MSDNVS/cptools/html/cpgrfcodeaccesssecuritypolicyutilitycaspolexe.htm`.

Modifying Security Policy Evaluation

You can restrict policy as you move from the highest level (enterprise) to the lowest level (user). For most cases, this is true, although in two cases the preceding level has the ultimate say in the policy. This is if a `LevelFinal` or `Exclusive` attribute is attached to a code group.

The `LevelFinal` attribute excludes any policy from being evaluated below the current level. For example, if this attribute was applied to a code group at the machine level, then the user policy would have no effect on the code that is a member of the code group marked with `LevelFinal`. By marking a code group with `LevelFinal`, you guarantee that any assembly in this code group will never have less than a certain set of permissions. This attribute is put in place to ensure that lower levels will not be able to restrict code permissions to the level that it no longer runs properly.

Note

Application domain security policy is always evaluated regardless of the `LevelFinal` attribute.

The `Exclusive` attribute marks a code group as the sole determining factor for policy at the current level. Normally, if an assembly could belong to several code groups, the intersection of the permission sets determines policy. If a code group is marked as

`Exclusive`, none of the other code group matches are considered for the current policy level. This attribute modifies the normal policy evaluation only for the current level. Policy is still evaluated as normal below the current level. If an assembly matches more than one code group that is marked `Exclusive`, the assembly will not be allowed to execute.

If you are using the .NET Framework Configuration tool to administer the security policy, you will not see the terms `LevelFinal` or `Exclusive`. Rather, you will see two check boxes with a textual description of these attributes. Figure 16.2 shows what the check boxes look like with the Configuration tool.

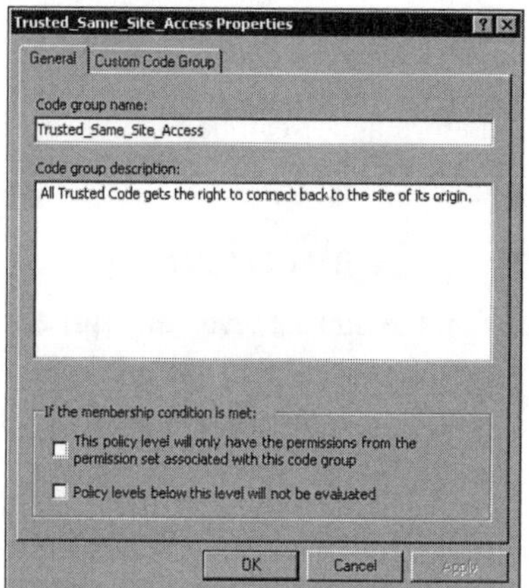

FIGURE 16.2
A code group viewed with the .NET Framework Configuration tool.

The check box labeled Policy Levels Below This Level Will Not Be Evaluated corresponds to the `LevelFinal` attribute. The other check box (This Policy Level Will Only Have the Permissions from the Permission Set Associated with This Code Group) in the group corresponds to the `Exclusive` attribute. To see the dialog box shown in Figure 16.2, select one of the code groups, right-click on the code group, and select Properties.

Code Groups

When the host of the runtime loads code, the host collects evidence about the code and presents this evidence to the runtime with the code to be executed. A code group is a set of code that has a membership criteria based on certain kinds of evidence. Code can be classified based on the following kinds of evidence:

- Application Directory—The application's installation directory.
- Hash—The cryptographic hash of an assembly. The hash uniquely identifies a particular assembly.

- Publisher—The Authenticode signature of the signer of the code.
- Site—The site of origin of the code, such as `www.microsoft.com`.
- Strong Name—The complete strong name of the assembly. This includes the public key token, the version, and so forth. See Chapter 6 for a detailed description of strong names. Technically, the Strong Name condition includes the public key, and optionally the name and version portions of the assembly name. You cannot specify culture as part of the Strong Name membership condition.
- URL—The URL of the origin of the code.
- Zone—The zone of the origin of the code based on the zones defined by Microsoft Internet Explorer.

You can see what the membership criteria for a particular code group is by using the .NET Framework Configuration tool and selecting the properties of an existing code group. Doing so gives you an idea of how a code group is defined and how you can define your own code group. Currently, the membership criteria for the Restricted_Zone Code Group is based on zone evidence. You can view the other possible membership criteria by selecting the drop-down list, as shown in Figure 16.3.

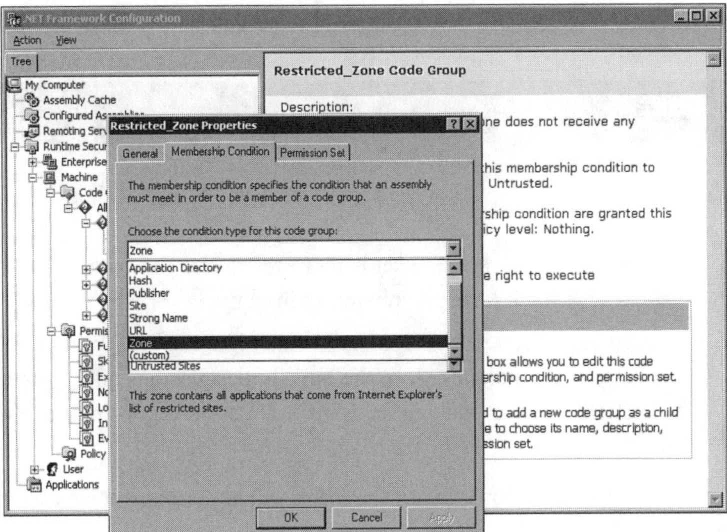

FIGURE 16.3
Code group membership condition.

From this drop-down list, you can see the evidence that was presented earlier. You can start to imagine how to create a code group that is specific to your application or applications with membership criteria from the evidence shown in Figure 16.3.

After a code group has a membership criteria defined, a permission set can be assigned to that code group. The .NET Framework installs with the following permission sets:

- FullTrust—This permission set is almost equivalent to turning security off. It allows unrestricted access to any of your computer's resources. Ensure that only assemblies that you fully trust receive this permission set.
- SkipVerification—This permission set grants the right for software to bypass verification. As discussed earlier, type safety plays a critical role in the overall security of code. By running tools such as PEVerify, you can get an idea of what kinds of type safety problems your code could have. If you have already run PEVerify on your code, you might want to allow the code to skip the equivalent verification that happens at JIT time to allow your code slightly faster startup times.
- Execution—This permission set includes the **`SecurityPermission`** with the **`SecurityPermissionFlag`** set to Execution.
- Nothing—This permission set denies permission to any resource, including the permission to execute.
- LocalIntranet—This permission set details a set of permissions that is appropriate for an application running from an intranet. More permission is given to this permission set because it is assumed that the intranet is more secure than the Internet.

> **Note**
>
> The default permissions are detailed in Table 16.3.

- Internet—This permission set is more restrictive than the LocalIntranet permission set because the Internet is inherently insecure.
- Everything—This permission set is much like the FullTrust permission set. This permission set includes all of the built-in permissions and gives unrestricted access to each. It does not include the SkipVerification flag as part of the Security permission.

Again using the drop-down list to see the possible permission set assignments, you can see a list that looks like Figure 16.4.

You can see the possible permission sets that are available by expanding the Permission Sets node of the tree in the left pane of the .NET Framework Configuration tool.

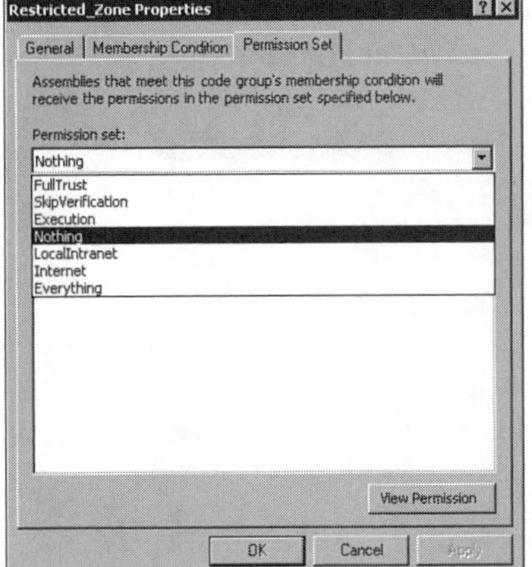

FIGURE 16.4
Code group permission set.

Note that you can define your own permission set—you are not restricted to the default permissions. Using the configuration tool, it is easy to create a new permission set. Select the top level Permission Sets node and click the Create New Permission Set hyperlink in the right pane of the tool and follow the instructions. As you start to define a new permission set, you will be asked to give the permission set a name and a description, as shown in Figure 16.5.

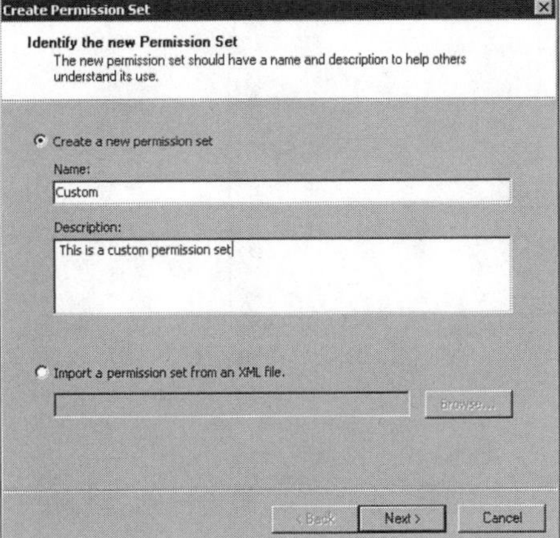

FIGURE 16.5
Start to Define a New Permission Set.

Notice that if you have another means to create the permission set, you can import the permission set description from an XML file.

After giving the permission set a name and description, you are prompted to add built-in permissions to the permission set, as shown in Figure 16.6.

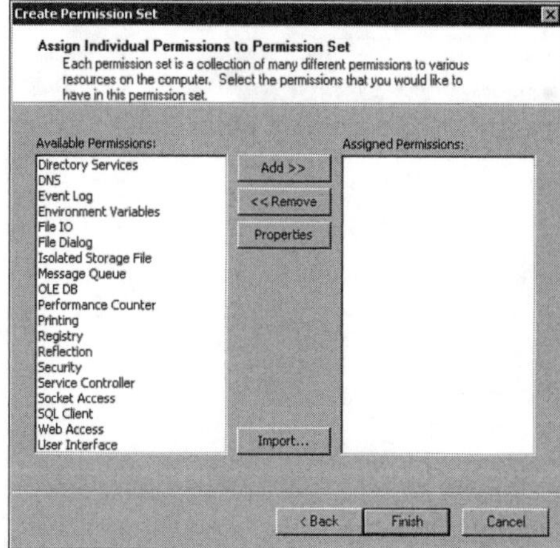

FIGURE 16.6
Adding new permissions to a permission set.

Each permission that is added to the permission set has a different set of criteria. Figure 16.7 shows how adding a **`SecurityPermission`** presents you with a dialog box listing the possible **`SecurityPermissionFlags`**.

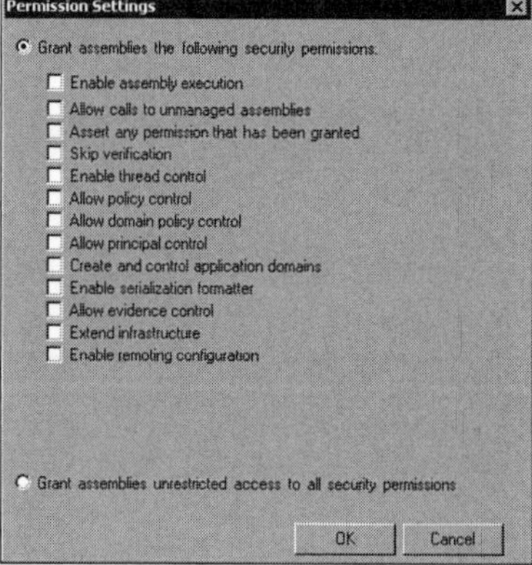

FIGURE 16.7
Adding a **`SecurityPermission`** *to a new permission set.*

On the other hand, adding a **`FileIOPermission`** prompts you for a list of files or directories and the associated access permission. Figure 16.8 shows the dialog box for adding a **`FileIOPermission`**.

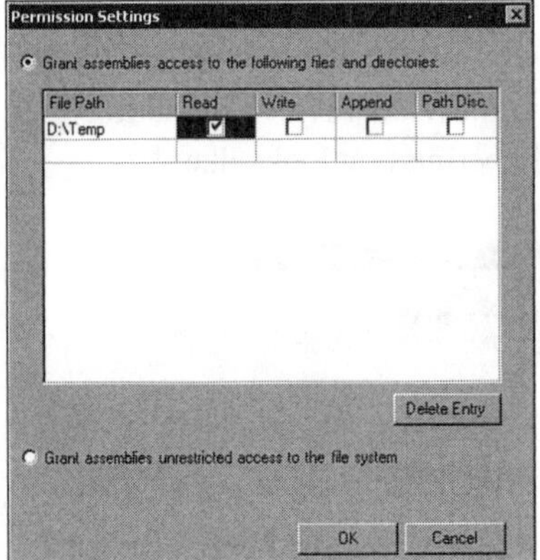

FIGURE 16.8
Adding a **FileIOPermission** *to a new permission set.*

As shown in Figure 16.8, you must specify **FileIOPermission** by indicating that you only want read access to the `D:\Temp` directory. By specifying read access to the directory, you are implicitly granting read access to all of the files contained within that directory.

Using the .NET Framework Configuration tool, you can select the Internet Zone code group and see that it has the Internet Permission Set assigned to it. (Select Properties by right-clicking on the Internet Zone code group or select the Internet Zone code group and click the Edit Code Properties hyperlink in the right pane.) Figure 16.9 shows what this looks like.

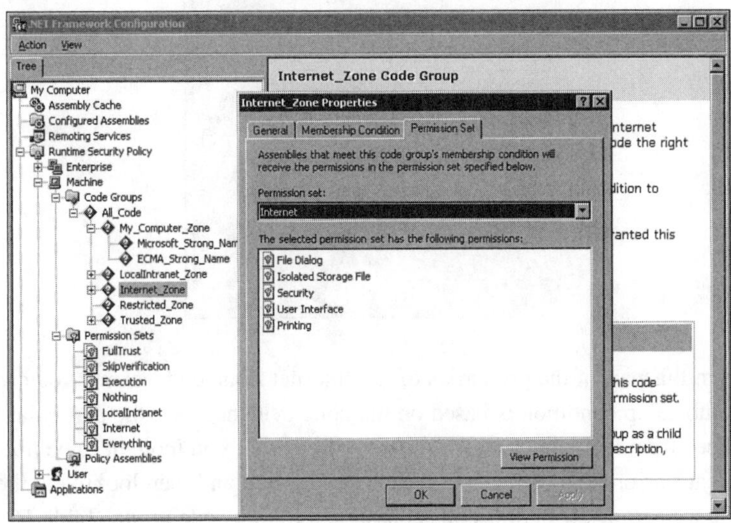

FIGURE 16.9
Internet Zone code group permission set properties.

You can select any of the permissions and look at the permission that is added to the permission set. For example, you can look at the Isolated Storage File permission by selecting this permission and then selecting the View Permission button. Figure 16.10 shows what the default Isolated Storage File permission looks like.

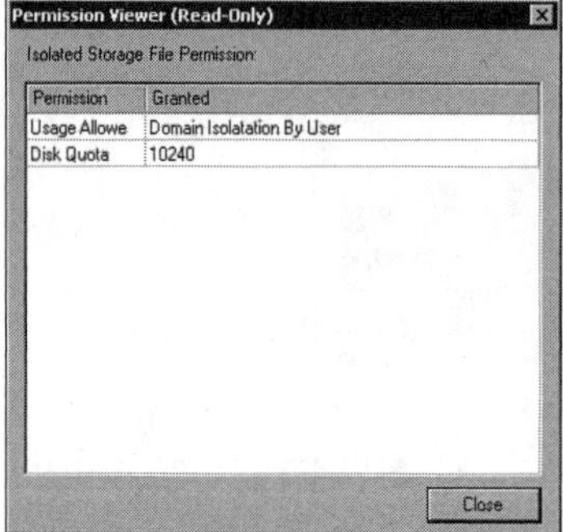

FIGURE 16.10
Internet Zone code group permission for Isolated Storage File.

Looking at the Internet Zone code group, you would expect the code to originate from the Internet. You can verify this by selecting the Membership Condition tab for the Internet Zone code group. You then see what is shown in Figure 16.11.

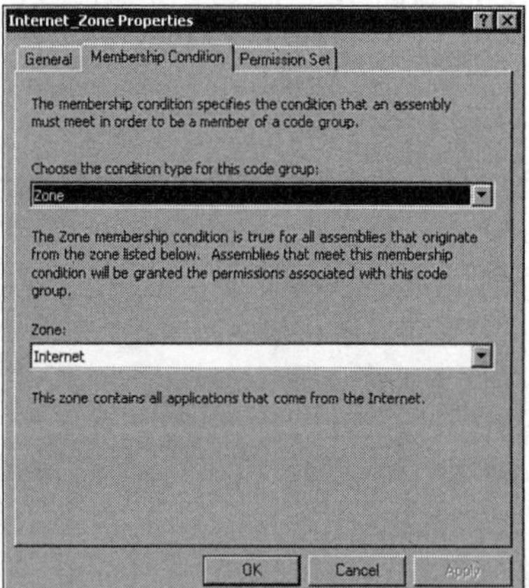

FIGURE 16.11
Internet Zone code group membership condition.

From this part of the properties of the Internet Zone code group, you can see that the membership condition is based on the zone evidence, and the particular zone that it comes from is the Internet. You just verified what you thought to be true all along. If you repeat this process of looking at each code group and then looking at the permissions that are part of the permission set assigned to that code group, Table 16.3 is the result.

TABLE 16.3 Default Permissions

Permission	*Local Intranet Permission Set* *Local Intranet Zone Code Group*	*Internet Permission Set* *Internet Code Group and Trusted Zone Code Group*
`DnsPermission`	Unrestricted	—
`EventLogPermission`	Instrument	—
`FileDialogPermission`	Unrestricted	Open (read-only access to a file)
`FileIOPermission`	Read (custom code group to directory share of origin)	—
`IsolatedStoragePermission`	AssemblyIsolationByUser (unrestricted quota)	DomainIsolationByUser (10240 bytes)
`PrintingPermission`	DefaultPrinting	SafePrinting
`ReflectionPermission`	ReflectionEmit, No Member Access, No Type Access	—
`SecurityPermission`	Execution, Assertion	Execution
`UIPermission`	Unrestricted	SafeTopLevelWindows, OwnClipboard
`WebPermission`	Connect (custom code group to site of origin)	Connect (custom code group to site of origin)

The My Computer Zone code group, the Microsoft Strong Name code group, and the ECMA Strong Name code group are not mentioned because they have the Full Trust permission set; therefore, they have unrestricted access to everything. Also not listed are the All Code code group or the Restricted Zone code group; these code groups are assigned the Nothing permission set and have no permission to access resources or perform operations.

Policy Assemblies

The security system uses policy assemblies during evaluation of a policy level. A *policy assembly* defines a custom security object such as a custom permission or a custom membership condition. You have already seen a couple custom code groups included under the Local Internet code group, the Internet Zone code group, and the Trusted Zone code group. These three code groups allow connection or read directory access to the site where the code originated. These custom code groups require special algorithms to determine membership. They are special or custom because they do not rely on the specific evaluation of a predetermined set of conditions for membership.

You can see the policy assemblies that are currently installed with the .NET Framework Configuration tool. By clicking on the Policy Assemblies node, you are presented with a screen that looks like Figure 16.12.

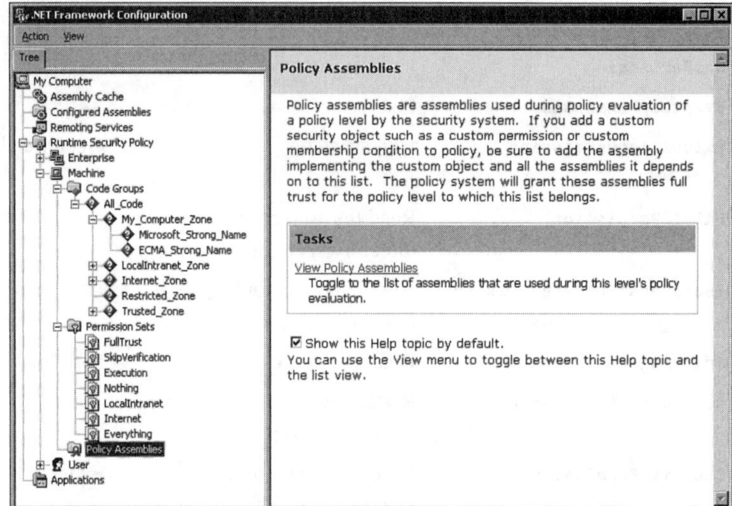

FIGURE 16.12
Policy assemblies from the .NET Framework Configuration tool.

Clicking on the `View Policy Assemblies` hyperlink or selecting the Properties menu item to view the policy assemblies (as opposed to using the Help screen) results in a listing of all policy assemblies that are installed on the computer. One such listing of policy assemblies is shown in Figure 16.13.

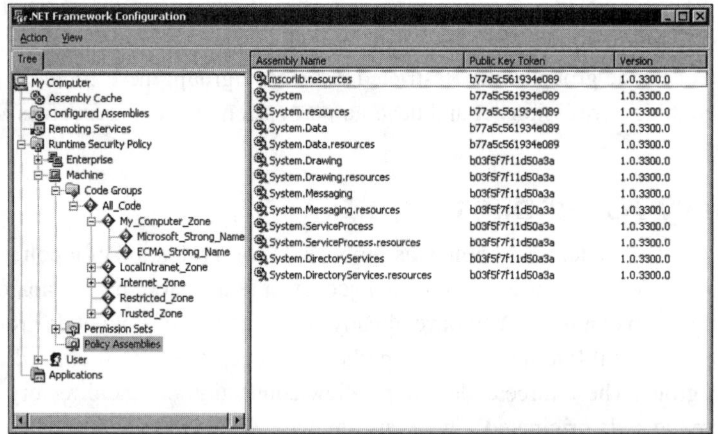

FIGURE 16.13
A list of the policy assemblies.

These policy assemblies will become important as you learn about defining custom permissions.

Principal

A *principal* represents the identity of a user who is logged into the system. Within the .NET Framework, three kinds of principals exist:

- **`GenericPrincipal`**—This class of users can stand for any user/role mapping.
- **`WindowsPrincipal`**—This class represents the Windows user.
- Custom Principal—This class extends the notion of user and role by inheriting from **`IPrincipal`**.

Authentication

Authentication is the process of verifying the identity of a principal by looking at some credentials and validating them against a known authority. Many algorithms are available to authenticate a principal: basic, digest, Passport, NTLM, or Kerberos. One of the properties of a **`WindowsPrincipal`** is the type of authentication that is used and the principal's authentication status. After a principal is authenticated, the .NET Framework can reliably use the information that the **`Principal`** object provides to make decisions (role-based security).

Authorization

After a principal has been authenticated, authorization takes over and determines what this particular principal is authorized to do. This is the task of role-based security.

Role-Based Security

You can litter your code with hard-coded **`if-then`** statements for each possible user or group of users in your system and respond to users differently in the code. However, when you add or remove a user, you have to rewrite the code. This might be a good quick solution for a small system, but for any practical application, you need to find a different way. The .NET Framework abstracts the username and password (authentication) along with the context in which the user is running into a **`Principal`** and an **`Identity`** object.

`Principal` and `Identity` Objects

A **`Principal`** object in the .NET Framework implements the **`IPrincipal`** interface. Two classes in the .NET Framework implement the **`IPrincipal`** interface: the **`WindowsPrincipal`** class and the **`GenericPrincipal`** class. Both classes contain a property value that returns an **`Identity`** object (an object that implements the **`IIdentity`** interface). The **`WindowsPrincipal`** class returns a **`WindowsIdentity`** object from the **`Identity`** property. The **`GenericPrincipal`** class returns a **`GenericIdentity`** object from its **Identity** property. **Principal** and **Identity** objects can be likened to user and group concepts, where an **Identity** is more closely associated with the concept of a user. A **Principal** object encapsulates both an **Identity** and a role. The .NET Framework grants rights to a **Principal** based on its **Identity** or role.

At a minimum, an **Identity** object encapsulates a name and an authentication type. You will rarely see an **Identity** without an associated **Principal**; the two objects usually occur in pairs. **Identity** is either associated with a Windows user account (**WindowsIdentity**) or it is not (**GenericIdentity** and custom **Identity** objects).

Creating WindowsPrincipal and WindowsIdentity Objects

Listing 16.5 shows how to get the **Identity** associated with the current logged on user or the user who is executing the program that contains these APIs. The complete source for this file is in the Principal directory.

LISTING 16.5 Printing WindowsIdentity Information

```
WindowsIdentity wi = WindowsIdentity.GetCurrent();
Console.WriteLine("My name is: {0}", wi.Name);
Console.WriteLine("Authentication type: {0}", wi.AuthenticationType);
Console.WriteLine("Anonymous: {0}", wi.IsAnonymous);
Console.WriteLine("Authenticated: {0}", wi.IsAuthenticated);
Console.WriteLine("Guest: {0}", wi.IsGuest);
Console.WriteLine("System: {0}", wi.IsSystem);
Console.WriteLine("My token is: {0}", wi.Token);
```

The **WindowsIdentity** contains a static method that returns the current user. After you obtain the Identity object, you can obtain the name of the user and the authentication that were used to verify that the user really is who he says he is. You can see from the other properties whether the user is indeed authenticated, and in a general way, you can determine who the user is (System, Guest, and so on). This Identity is, as the name implies, based on the Windows OS idea of the user, and it relies on Windows to perform the authentication. By using **WindowsIdentity**, you can assume that the token is a Windows Security token. You can use this token to get even more information about the logged on user. Keith Brown wrote a wonderful COM component that dumps token information in the form of HTML. Using COM Interop (see Chapter 8, "Using COM/COM+ from Managed Code"), you can use this COM component to dump the token information. Listing 16.6 shows the lines of code used to call this COM component. This component writes information about the token in the form of HTML, which can be viewed with Internet Explorer.

LISTING 16.6 Dumping Token Information

```
Console.WriteLine("My token is: {0}", wi.Token);
// Dump the token information
ITokDump2 itd = new TokDumpClass();
StreamWriter file = new StreamWriter("tokendump.htm");
file.Write(itd.DumpThisToken((int)wi.Token, 0x177));
file.Close();
// Display the token info
Process.Start("tokendump.htm");
```

The HTML output looks something like Figure 16.14.

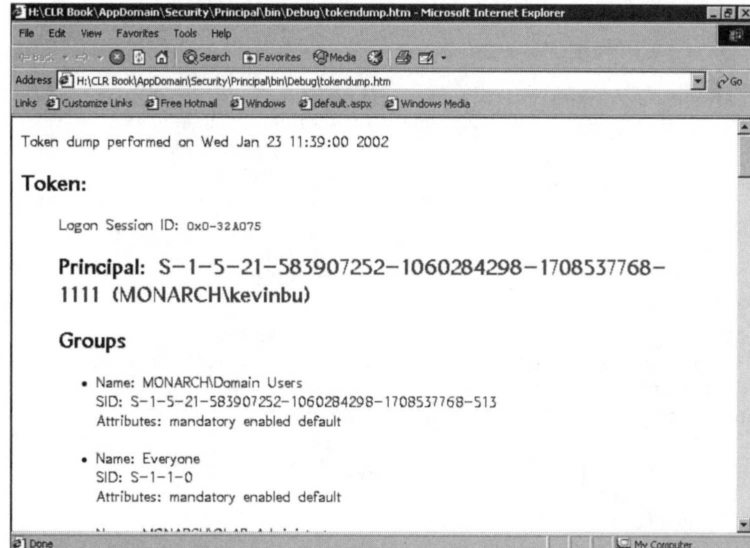

FIGURE 16.14
Windows token dump.

The converted `TokenDump` program is included in the `TokenDump` directory. The token is only a valid Windows NT Security token when you are assured that the **`Identity`** is a **`WindowsIdentity`**. For a **`GenericIdentity`** or for a custom identity, the token's meaning is up to the implementation.

After you dump the token information, look to see if a particular user is a member of a role. You can determine if a user is in a role by calling the **`IsInRole`** method that is part of the **`IPrincipal`** interface. The **`IsInRole`** method of **`IPrincipal`** takes a string that describes the particular role. The **`WindowsPrincipal`** class implements two overloaded methods. One of the overloaded methods takes an integer role identifier. The other takes one of the enumerated values for a typical role in a Windows system, **`WindowsBuiltInRole`**.

Impersonating

Using **WindowsIdentity**, you can impersonate another user on the system (assuming that you know that person's password). An overloaded constructor for **WindowsIdentity** takes a token as an argument. This token corresponds to the Windows NT Security Token—the same token that you learned how to pull information from in Listing 16.6 and Figure 16.14. No wrapper exists in the .NET Framework to obtain a Windows NT Security Token that corresponds to another user, so you have to revert to using the unmanaged calls. Use the Win32 function `LogonUser`. Listing 16.7 shows how to use this call to log in as another user. The complete source associated with this listing can be found in the `WindowsImpersonation` directory.

LISTING 16.7 Log On As Another User

```
[DllImport("advapi32.dll", SetLastError=true)]
public static extern bool LogonUser(string lpszUsername,
                                    string lpszDomain,
                                    string lpszPassword,
                                    int dwLogonType,
                                    int dwLogonProvider,
                                    out IntPtr phToken);
. . .
// The Windows NT user token.
IntPtr token;
// Get the user token for the specified user, machine,
➥and password using the unmanaged LogonUser method.
bool loggedOn = NativeMethods.LogonUser(
    // Username.
    impersonateUser.Text,
    // Computer name.
    impersonateDomain.Text,
    // Password.
    impersonatePassword.Text,
    // Logon type = LOGON32_LOGON_NETWORK_CLEARTEXT.
    (int)LogonType.LOGON32_LOGON_NETWORK_CLEARTEXT,
    // Logon provider = LOGON32_PROVIDER_DEFAULT.
    (int)LogonProvider.LOGON32_PROVIDER_DEFAULT,
    // The user token for the specified user is returned here.
    out token);
```

The output from a successful `LogonUser` attempt is the token of the logged on user. You can take this token and create a **WindowsIdentity** class to impersonate the user. Listing 16.8 shows how to do this.

LISTING 16.8 Impersonating a User

```
private WindowsImpersonationContext impersonationContext;
. . .
Debug.WriteLine("New identity created:");
WindowsIdentity loggedonUser = new WindowsIdentity(userToken);
Debug.WriteLine(loggedonUser.Name);
Debug.WriteLine(string.Format("0x{0:X8}", loggedonUser.Token));

// Impersonate the user.
impersonationContext = loggedonUser.Impersonate();
```

The **WindowsImpersonationContext** saves the current user context. That way, when you need to return to yourself, you just need to call the **Undo** method on the **WindowsInpersonationContext** class object.

A simple application has been put together that allows you to impersonate other users for whom you know the password. The complete source is in the `WindowsImpersonate` directory. Initially, characteristics of the user who started the application will be displayed on the left portion of the application. These characteristics include the username, the token associated with this user, the authentication used, and whether the user is an administrator. After you have filled in the form on the right portion of the application (machine, username, and password), you can try to log in. If you have successfully logged in, the button will change its label to *Impersonate*. Clicking on the Impersonate button causes you to impersonate the user who was logged on. After a successful impersonation, the button changes to Revert. When you click Revert, the screen is restored to the original user. The initial screen should look something like Figure 16.15.

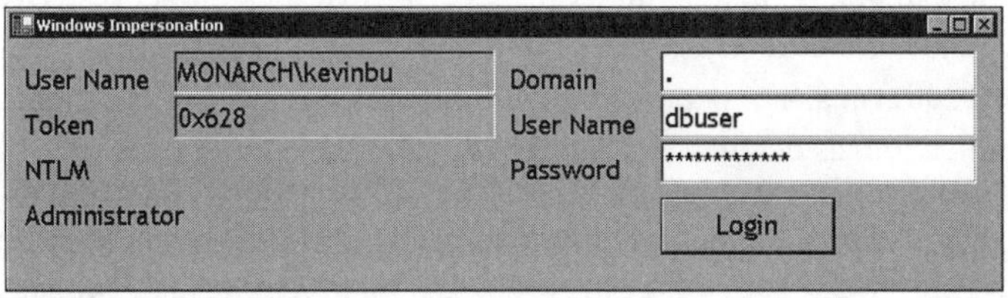

FIGURE 16.15
Windows impersonation.

Creating GenericPrincipal and GenericIdentity Objects

Using **WindowsIdentity** and **WindowsPrincipal** is great for an all-Windows environment. The authentication is handled for you, you can take advantage of the detailed security structure that is available on a Windows platform, and the tools to administer the users are already in place. The problem is that in a highly distributed environment, depending on Windows security might be impractical. Building tools to administer the users of your system who are integrated with the Windows security could be a daunting task. These are some of the reasons that **GenericPrincipal** and **GenericIdentity** objects were created. A **GenericIdentity** is not tied to Windows security. It is only associated with a username that is user definable. You can construct a **GenericIdentity** for any valid **string**. Creating a **GenericPrincipal** is similar in that it takes a **GenericIdentity**; however, it also takes an array of strings that are completely arbitrary, describing the roles to be associated with this identity. First, you construct the **GenericIdentity**:

```
GenericIdentity identity = new GenericIdentity("Kevin");
```

Next, construct a **GenericPrincipal** object to be associated with the **Identity** that was just created, along with an array that describes the roles to be associated with the identity.

```
string [] roles = new string[]{"President", "Manager", "Worker"};
GenericPrincipal principal = new GenericPrincipal(identity, roles);
```

Using **GenericIdentity** and **GenericPrincipal**, you can build any authentication that you need to. You can read the usernames from a database and have a table that maps roles to users. The role that is associated with a particular user becomes dynamic. At the same time, you still have the encapsulation that you desire for each user and the security context in which the user should operate.

Replacing a Principal Object

Every **Thread** that is running under the CLR has various properties. Two properties describe the culture to be associated with a thread: **CurrentCulture** and **CurrentUICulture**. These properties will be very essential in building an internationalized application, as detailed in Chapter 18, “Globalization/Localization.” Another property of threads that is specifically used for security is the **CurrentPrincipal** property. If you have **SecurityPermission** with the **ControlPrincipal** set, then you can modify the **Thread**’s **Principal**. The **Principal** with which you replace the **Thread**’s **CurrentPrincipal** will be the **Principal** against which **PrincipalPermision** security checks will be carried out.

If you want to make security decisions based on Windows accounts, the **WindowsPrincipal** is already defined when you log in. You might need to set the **Principal** policy so that you have access to the current user information as follows:

```
// Set principal policy so that you have permission
// to get current user information.
AppDomain.CurrentDomain.SetPrincipalPolicy(PrincipalPolicy.WindowsPrincipal);
```

```
// Get the current principal and put it into a
// principal object.
WindowsPrincipal MyPrincipal = (Thread.CurrentPrincipal as WindowsPrincipal);
```

Source for code that performs much the same function as above can be found in the `\Program Files\Microsoft Visual Studio .NET\FrameworkSDK\Samples\QuickStart\howto\samples\security\windowsidentitycheck\cs` directory as part of the SDK samples.

In this case, **`WindowsPrincipal`** is a bit different from **`GenericPrincipal`**, where you do not explicitly set a policy.

`PrincipalPermission` is the only permission object that is involved in role-based security. Typically, you construct this permission specifying a username and a role (both strings). If the **`CurrentPrincipal`** (as specified by the static **`Thread.CurrentPrincipal`** property) matches the identity and role that the permission specifies, then **`Demand`**ing the permission will succeed. If the **`Identity`** (user) or the role is not part of the **`CurrentPrincipal`**, then a security exception is thrown and the permission is **`Demand`**ed. Listing 16.9 shows an example of constructing and using the **`PrincipalPermission`** class. Source corresponding to this listing can be found in the `GenericPrincipal` directory.

LISTING 16.9 Constructing and Using the **`PrincipalPermission`** Class

```
PrincipalPermission perm = new PrincipalPermission(name, role);
. . .
private bool CheckAuthorization(PrincipalPermission perm)
{
    bool result = false;
    try
    {
        perm.Demand();
        result = true;
    }
    catch(Exception)
    {
        result = false;
    }
    return result;
}
```

The permission is constructed, a routine is called with the permission as an argument, and the **`Demand`** method is called on the permission. **`Demand`** tells the runtime that to continue, the permission must be associated with the permission object (in this case, **`PrincipalPermission`**). One of two things can happen when a **`Demand`** is made on a permission. First, the permission can be granted, in which case the call just falls to the next statement. Second, if the permission has not been granted, then a security exception is thrown.

This programmatic access to the security permissions is called *imperative security*. With imperative security, the programmer creates the permission and calls methods on the created permission to determine whether the permission has been granted. Because of the dynamic nature of this application, imperative security seems to be a better fit than its companion declarative security. Declarative security will be discussed later in this chapter in the section "Code Access Security."

As a final example for this section, a sample application has been built that demonstrates many of the principles explored in this section. The application is in the `GenericPrincipal` directory. When it first comes up, it looks like Figure 16.16.

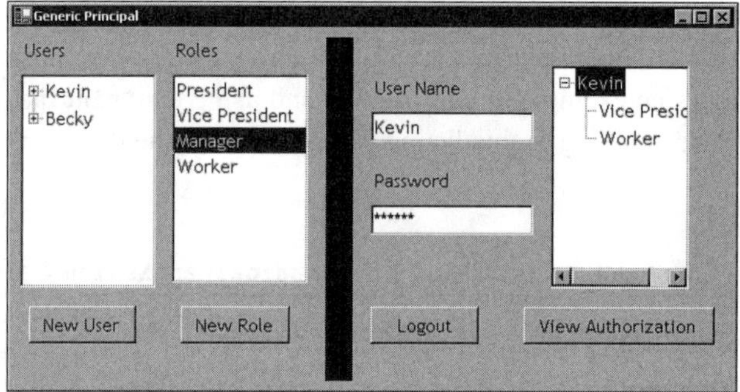

FIGURE 16.16
`GenericPrincipal` application.

You will have to use some imagination when you run this application. The application is meant to illustrate what in a real application would be two separate tasks and applications. The side to the left the vertical black bar is the user database. Here, an administrator builds a list of users and a list of roles. A new user is created by clicking on the New User button, and a new role is created by clicking on the New Role button. The association between a user and a role is done by dragging a role from the right list box and dropping it on one of the users in the left tree view. So far, no security objects are involved. The basics are in place to illustrate how to add users and roles. Security objects are not used.

The right side is meant to simulate a user logging into your system. When the user logs in, the username and password are compared against the database to make sure this is a valid user. This is *authentication*. You can make the authentication much more secure and robust, but the idea is that you have a hook on which to put your favorite authentication scheme. Again, security objects are not used. If the user database is persistent and encrypted, you might need to use some of the cryptography classes.

Next, if the username and password check out and the user is authenticated, a **GenericIdentity** is constructed based on the logged on user. In addition, a **GenericPrincipal** is constructed based on the **GenericIdentity** and the roles that are associated with this user. Then, the **IPrincipal** interface that is associated with the **GenericPrincipal** just constructed is assigned to the **CurrentPrincipal** of the current **Thread**.

At this point, the Authorization View button should appear enabled. Clicking this button causes a **PrincipalPermission** to be constructed for each of the roles in the database, and a **Demand** is made to see if the current **Thread**'s **Principal** meets the criteria in the constructed permission. If the permission has been granted, the role is added to the tree on the right. If the permission has not been granted, no action is taken. The end result is that the tree on the right should match the corresponding user tree node on the left. There has been no prevision made in this code to allow for multiple users to log on.

Code Access Security

Code access security is based on the grant of the permissions that are listed in Tables 16.1 and 16.2. Through an established policy and evidence that is associated with code, a set of permissions is established that could be granted to the code. The code either attempts an operation or requests that a permission be granted. If the permission is granted, you can assume that an access or use of a resource will succeed, at least with respect to security. Each of the permissions that is listed in Tables 16.1 and 16.2 has the following methods inherited from **CodeAccessPermission**:

- **Assert**—The CLR does a stack walk to determine whether every caller in the chain has the appropriate permission. This prevents the scenario of less privileged code calling more privileged code and indirectly having access to resources that it would not otherwise have access to. Using less trusted code to call highly trusted code to perform what otherwise would be an unauthorized action is known as a *luring attack*. The CLR prevents luring attacks by walking the stack to make sure that all callers of this method have the requisite permission. It can be costly to walk the stack to evaluate a permission. **Assert** tells the CLR to stop the stack walk at the point in the call stack that the **Assert** was issued. The primary reason that you would want to use **Assert** is performance. By using **Assert**, you avoid the costly stack walk. The problem is that this potentially opens a security hole in your application, so use **Assert** carefully. After **Assert** is issued, you open your application to a luring attack. You can issue a **Demand** for the permission, which ensures that your code has the permission (or an exception is thrown), followed by an **Assert** indicating that a stack walk is no longer necessary. (**Demand** makes sure your application has the required permission.) If you combine the use of **Demand** followed by **Assert**, you can have the benefits of the **Assert** without the associated security hole. Because of the potential security hole, a permission is associated with using **Assert**. If you cannot **Assert**, it is possible that you are not being granted **SecurityPermission** with the **SecurityPermissionFlag Assertion** set.

- **Demand**—This call forces a **SecurityException** if permission has not been granted to the resource that the permission protects. Calling this method means that you are about to access a resource that the permission is supposed to protect. If you use the **System.IO.File** class to access a file, this class will **Demand FileIOPermission** before accessing the file system. If you access the file system via P/Invoke (P/Invoke is covered in Chapter 7), you should specifically **Demand FileIOPermission** because the unmanaged code will not. Another scenario in which you would use **Demand** is coupled with **Assert**, as described earlier. If the **Demand** for a particular resource succeeds, you can call **Assert** to avoid repeated security checks on callers of a method.
- **Deny**—Sometimes an assembly might want to have less permission than it has been granted. For example, your code might need to take certain actions to limit liability. This is the purpose of the **Deny** method. Calling **Deny** on a permission explicitly denies access to the resource that the permission describes. Note that **Deny** is only applicable to the stack frame that has called **Deny** and below (assuming that the stack grows downward). For example, the following illustrates the automatic reverting of **Deny**:

```
AttemptToUseResource()
{
    // Use resource
}
DenyResource()
{
    perm.Deny();
    AttemptToUseResource();
}
UseResource()
{
    DenyResource();
    AttemptToUseResource();
}
```

  The call to AttemptToUseResource that occurs from DenyResource fails because of the **Deny** call. The call to AttemptToUseResource that occurs after the call to DenyResource succeeds because the stack frame has popped off the **Deny**.
- **Intersect**—This creates and returns a permission that is the intersection of the current permission and the permission that is passed as an argument.

- **PermitOnly**—This method is similar to **Deny**. Deny causes a stack walk to fail for access to a particular resource. **PermitOnly** specifies the only condition under which a stack walk succeeds; it fails for any other case.
- **RevertAll**—This static call explicitly reverts code permissions back to their original state. It has companion static methods that revert only specific cases: **RevertAssert**, **RevertDeny**, and **RevertPermitOnly**.
- **Union**—This allows the union of one or more permissions. This call creates a union of the current permission and the permission that is passed as an argument. You can create a union of more than two permissions by repeatedly calling **Union**.

Imperative Security

As was done with **PrincipalPermission**, each **CodeAccessPermission** derived permission class can be instantiated and programmatically manipulated. Listing 16.10 illustrates using imperative security when calling unmanaged code, first denying the permission to call unmanaged code. The complete source for this sample is in the `CodeAccessSecurity\Security1` directory. For code that is running on the local machine, imperative security is not required to use P/Invoke. This is simply an illustration of how to control and use a specific permission.

LISTING 16.10 Calling Unmanaged Code by Using Imperative Security to Deny Permission

```
private static void CallUnmanagedCodeWithoutPermission()
{
    // Create a security permission object to describe the
    // UnmanagedCode permission:
    SecurityPermission perm =
       new SecurityPermission(SecurityPermissionFlag.UnmanagedCode);

    // Deny the UnmanagedCode from the current set of permissions.
    // Any method that is called on this thread until this method
    // returns will be denied access to unmanaged code.
    perm.Deny();

    try
    {
        Console.WriteLine("Attempting to call unmanaged code without
➥permission.");
        NativeMethods.MessageBox(0, "Hello World!", "", 0);
        Console.WriteLine("Called unmanaged code without permission.
➥Whoops!");
    }
    catch (SecurityException)
    {
```

LISTING 16.10 Continued

```
        Console.WriteLine("Caught Security Exception attempting to
➥call unmanaged code.");
    }
}
```

Listing 16.11 shows how to call unmanaged code by asserting that the permission is granted. The complete source for this sample is in the CodeAccessSecurity\Security1 directory.

LISTING 16.11 Calling Unmanaged Code Using Imperative Security to Assert Permission

```
private static void CallUnmanagedCodeWithPermission()
{
    // Create a security permission object to describe the
    // UnmanagedCode permission:
    SecurityPermission perm =
       new SecurityPermission(SecurityPermissionFlag.UnmanagedCode);

    // Verify that you can be granted all the permissions that you will need.
    perm.Demand();

    // Check that you have permission to access unmanaged code.
    // If you don't have permission to access unmanaged code, then
    // this call will throw a SecurityException
    perm.Assert();

    try
    {
        Console.WriteLine("Attempting to call unmanaged code with
➥permission.");
        NativeMethods.MessageBox(0, "Hello World!", "", 0);
        Console.WriteLine("Called unmanaged code with permission.");
    }
    catch (SecurityException)
    {
        Console.WriteLine("Caught Security Exception attempting to
➥call unmanaged code. Whoops!");
    }
    // Technically this call is not required but it is good practice
    // to keep an Assert alive on as long as is needed.
    CodeAccessPermission.RevertAssert();
}
```

Both samples in Listings 16.10 and 16.11 use imperative security. The next section illustrates how to do the same with declarative security.

Declarative Security

Declarative security uses attributes that are typically attached to methods, classes, and assemblies. Use declarative security when it is known ahead of time what permission is needed or can be denied. Because a runtime cost of constructing the permission objects doesn't exist, declarative security is in most cases faster than imperative security. Listing 16.12 shows how to create a method to deny access permission to unmanaged code. Compare this with the imperative security version in Listing 16.10. The complete source for this sample is in the `CodeAccessSecurity\Security2` directory.

LISTING 16.12 Calling Unmanaged Code Using Declarative Security to Deny Permission

```
// The security permission attached to this method will deny the
// UnmanagedCode permission from the current set of permissions for
// the duration of the call to this method:
[SecurityPermission(SecurityAction.Deny, Flags =
   SecurityPermissionFlag.UnmanagedCode)]
private static void CallUnmanagedCodeWithoutPermission()
{
    try
    {
        Console.WriteLine("Attempting to call unmanaged code without
➥permission.");
        NativeMethods.MessageBox(0, "Hello World!", "", 0);
        Console.WriteLine("Called unmanaged code without permission.
➥Whoops!");
    }
    catch (SecurityException)
    {
        Console.WriteLine("Caught Security Exception attempting to
➥call unmanaged code.");
    }
}
```

Listing 16.13 shows how to create a method to **`Assert`** access permission to unmanaged code. Compare this with the imperative security version in Listing 16.11. The complete source for this sample is in the `CodeAccessSecurity\Security2` directory.

LISTING 16.13 Calling Unmanaged Code Using Declarative Security to Assert Permission

```
// The security permission attached to this method will force a
// runtime check for the unmanaged code permission whenever
// this method is called. If the caller does not have unmanaged code
// permission, then the call will generate a Security Exception.
```

LISTING 16.13 Continued

```
[SecurityPermission(SecurityAction.Demand, Flags =
     SecurityPermissionFlag.UnmanagedCode)]
 [SecurityPermission(SecurityAction.Assert, Flags =
   SecurityPermissionFlag.UnmanagedCode)]
private static void CallUnmanagedCodeWithPermission()
{
    try
    {
        Console.WriteLine("Attempting to call unmanaged code with
➥permission.");
        NativeMethods.MessageBox(0, "Hello World!", "", 0);
        Console.WriteLine("Called unmanaged code with permission.");
    }
    catch (SecurityException)
    {
        Console.WriteLine("Caught Security Exception attempting to
➥call unmanaged code. Whoops!");
    }
}
```

Notice that the code for declarative security is easier to read and has somewhat fewer lines of code involved.

Creating Your Own Code Access Permissions

To implement your own custom permission, you need to perform the following steps:

1. Design your custom permission. Don't just gloss over this step. Ensure that this permission does not overlap another permission. Consider performance implications of your custom permission. What about dependencies that your permission introduces? What is the overhead of the permission? Have you implemented declarative security?
2. Implement your design. You can create a custom permission in two ways. The first way is to derive your class from **CodeAccessPermission**. This allows you to leverage the code in **CodeAccessPermission**, which implements many of the methods of **IPermission**. If you go this route, you need to derive your class from **CodeAccessPermission** and **IUnrestrictedPermission**. Implementing **IUnrestrictedPermission** is relatively easy because it only has one method to implement: **IsUnrestricted**. This method simply returns a value that indicates whether unrestricted access to the resource is allowed. Deriving from **CodeAccessPermission**, you need to override the following methods:

   Copy—Creates a duplicate of the current permission object.

   Intersect—Returns an intersection with the passed permission.

IsSubsetOf—Returns `true` if passed permission includes everything allowed. This is indirectly called by demand and essentially grants or denies access to the resource.

FromXml—Builds a permission object from XML.

ToXml—Converts the permission to XML.

The other method to build your own permission class is to derive directly from **IPermission** and **IUnrestrictedPermission**. This is the hard way, but it probably will result in the lowest overhead for your permission. By directly deriving from **IPermission**, you can avoid the stack walk that occurs in the **CodeAccessPermission** implementation that might not be appropriate with certain permissions.

3. Make policy aware of your custom permission.
4. Add the assembly to the list of trusted assemblies.
5. Tell security policy what code should be granted to your custom permission.

Implementing the Design of a Custom Permission

Rather than going into a detailed explanation of what is involved in building a custom permission, a sample custom permission has been put together. The implementation is in `CustomPermission\DayPermission` directory. This custom permission protects a resource by time. The permission can be created so that it is valid for a number of days in the week. For example, this custom permission can be created so that it is only valid on Monday and Wednesday.

> **Note**
>
> This section describes the process that is involved in creating a custom permission. The process of creating a custom permission is valid regardless of the algorithm used to determine the permission. However, I would not recommend creating and using permissions that depend on the current time. Many optimizations occur in the .NET Framework that make the performance of security features (primarily stack walks) acceptable. Because of these optimizations, it is not guaranteed that permissions based on time will always function as expected.

Two things have to occur for the permission to allow access to the resource. First, the code that is accessing the resource needs to have been granted the permission for the days required. Second, the current day of the week needs to match that in the permission. If either of these two conditions is false, then a **Demand** throws a **SecurityException**.

Listing 16.14 shows some of the constructors that are required to implement this permission.

LISTING 16.14 Constructors in a Custom Permission

```
private bool unrestricted = false;
private ArrayList dayList = new ArrayList();

public DayPermission(PermissionState state)
{
    unrestricted = (state == PermissionState.Unrestricted);
}

public DayPermission(DayOfWeek day)
{
    dayList.Add(day);
}

public DayPermission(ArrayList days)
{
    foreach(DayOfWeek day in days)
        dayList.Add(day);
}
```

Implementing **ToXml** and **FromXml** is relatively straightforward because the **SecurityElement** class takes care of most of the hard work. **Copy** performs a deep copy of the elements in the permission. **IsSubsetOf** makes a comparison with a target permission and returns true whether they are the same or not (at least one completely contains the other). The **Intersect** and **Union** methods are the reasons for using an **ArrayList** rather than just a value for a single day. If one permission object specifies Monday and the other specifies Tuesday, what is the intersection of the two? The intersection is the null set, which cannot be represented unless you implement a representation for the null set. The same logic holds for the **Union** method.

Making Security Policy Aware of Your Custom Permission

If you make a mistake and corrupt the security policy file, you can usually restore it to the default state with `caspol -user -rs` or `caspol -rs` (to restore the machine-level security policy file).

To make the security policy aware of a custom permission, you need to create an XML file that describes your permission. When creating a custom permission, make it serializable so that this support is already in your custom permission assembly. Listing 16.15 shows some simple code to write out the serialized XML description of a custom permission class.

LISTING 16.15 Code to Output the XML Description of a Custom Permission

```
using System.IO;
using System.Security.Permissions;

class CustomPermission
{
   public static void Main()
   {
       CustomPermission perm =
           new CustomPermission(PermissionState.Unrestricted);
   NamedPermissionSet pset =
       new NamedPermissionSet("MyPermissionSet", PermissionState.None);
   pset.Description = "Permission set containing my custom permission";
   pset.AddPermission(perm);
   StreamWriter file = new StreamWriter("mypermissionset.xml");
   file.Write(pset.ToXml());
   file.Close();
   }
}
```

When code shown in Listing 16.15 is run, it outputs an XML file (`mypermisionset.xml`) that looks like Listing 16.16.

LISTING 16.16 XML Description of a Custom Permission Set

```
<PermissionSet class="System.Security.NamedPermissionSet"
               version="1"
               Name="MyPermissionSet"
               Description="Permission set containing my custom permission">
   <IPermission class="CLRUnleashed.CustomPermission,
                CustomPermission,
                Version=1.0.0.0,
                Culture=neutral,
                PublicKeyToken=03c1ed2f02a88ea9"
                version="1"
                Unrestricted="True"/>
</PermissionSet>
```

Now you can take the XML file shown in Listing 16.6 and import it into a security policy using the following command-line utility:

```
caspol -user -addpset mypermissionset.xml
```

This command adds the permission set to the user level. You could substitute `-machine` or `-enterprise` depending on for which level you will be using the new permission.

Notice that this command adds a full named permission set. You can also add just the permission by extracting the XML portion of the tag `<IPermission . . . />` and manually inserting that into an existing named permission set. Of course, this involves directly editing the XML file, but it avoids creating a new permission set.

Adding Your Custom Permission Assembly to the List of Assemblies That Are Fully Trusted

You need to add the assembly that implements the custom permission to the list of assemblies that have full trust. You can see the list using the command line:

```
caspol -listfulltrust
```

To add the assembly that implements the custom permission, use the following command line:

```
caspol -addfulltrust mypermissionset.dll
```

> **Note**
>
> Before this is done, it is a good idea to add the affected assemblies to the GAC. The security policy system needs to be able to locate the policy assemblies at runtime.

Now you can view the list of fully trusted assemblies using `caspol -listfulltrust`. You should see your assembly on the list.

> **Note**
>
> If your custom permission assembly A uses classes from assemblies B and C, then B and C need to be added to the policy assembly list. In addition, any assemblies used by B and C need to be added to the list (and so on). Especially note that for permissions written in VB, the VB runtime assemblies need to be added to the policy assembly list.

Adding a Code Group or Modifying a Code Group to Grant the Newly Formed Permission

Adding a code group is probably easier using the .NET Framework Configuration Tool because you can browse for the code for which you want to have the additional permission. Following is the `caspol` command line to add a new code group that uses the new permission set:

```
caspol -addgroup -user -allcode -strong <strong_file_path>
➥MyPermissionSet
➥-name Test_Code -Description "Test security code group"
```

Isolated Storage

Isolated storage allows an assembly or application domain to have a reserved space in the file system to store sensitive yet persistent data. This is not completely secure, but portions of the .NET Framework Security use isolated storage to access and manipulate items in the store in a secure manner. After you obtain an isolated storage file (a store), you can use standard I/O facilities to read and write files and directories within the store. You don't have to worry about any other application corrupting your data because each application (application domain or assembly) accesses only its area in isolated storage. Listing 16.17 shows a sample of how to use isolated storage.

LISTING 16.17 Using Isolated Storage

```
static void Main(string[] args)
{
    IsolatedStorageFile isf = IsolatedStorageFile.GetUserStoreForAssembly();
    // Print some statistics about the store
    Console.WriteLine(string.Format(
➥"Assembly Identity: {0}", isf.AssemblyIdentity));
    Console.WriteLine(string.Format("Current Size: {0}", isf.CurrentSize));
    Console.WriteLine(string.Format("Maximum Size: {0}", isf.MaximumSize));
    Console.WriteLine(string.Format("Scope: {0}", isf.Scope));
    // This code checks to see if the file already exists.
    string[] fileNames = isf.GetFileNames("TestStore.txt");
    foreach (string file in fileNames)
    {
        if(file == "TestStore.txt")
        {
            Console.WriteLine("The file already exists!");
            Console.WriteLine("Type \"StoreAdm /REMOVE\" at the command
➥line to delete all Isolated Storage for this user.");

            // Exit the program.
            isf.Close();
            return;
        }
    }

    writeToFile(isf);

    Console.WriteLine("The file \"TestStore.txt\" contains:");

    // Call the readFromFile and write the returned string to the
    // console.

    Console.WriteLine(readFromFile(isf));
```

LISTING 16.17 Continued

```
    // Exit the program.
    isf.Close();
}

// This method writes "Hello Isolated Storage" to the file.
private static void writeToFile(IsolatedStorageFile isoStore)
{
    // Declare a new StreamWriter.
    StreamWriter writer = null;

    // Assign the writer to the store and the file TestStore.
    writer = new StreamWriter(new IsolatedStorageFileStream("TestStore.txt",
➥FileMode.CreateNew,isoStore));

    // Have the writer write "Hello Isolated Storage" to the store.

    writer.WriteLine("Hello Isolated Storage");

    writer.Close();

    Console.WriteLine("You have written to the file.");

}
```

The `readFromFile` function has been omitted because the implementation is similar to `writeToFile`.

To use **`IsolatedStorage`**, call one of two static functions:

- **`GetUserStoreForAssembly`**—This returns an **`IsolatedStorageFile`** that is specific to the calling assembly.
- **`GetUserStoreForDomain`**—This returns an **`IsolatedStorageFile`** that is specific to the calling application domain.

After you have an **`IsolatedStorageFile`**, you can use it to create an **`IsolatedStorageFileStream`**. After you have a stream, you can use any of the IO facilities that takes a stream to read and write to the store.

You can administer the isolated storage with a utility called `storeadm`. After you run the program associated with Listing 16.17, invoke `storeadm /list` to get the following output:

```
Record #1
[Assembly]
<System.Security.Policy.Url version="1">
   <Url>file://D:/IsolatedStorage.exe</Url>
</System.Security.Policy.Url>

        Size : 1024
```

If you call `storeadm` with no arguments, you get a usage report that provides some of the options that you need to administer the store. One of the most useful options is `storeadm /remove`, which allows you to remove the store completely.

Using .NET Cryptography

Cryptography in the .NET Framework breaks down to the following areas:

- Hashing—This involves creating a byte array that uniquely defines a set of data. For example, you can create a hash of a file. Then in the future, if you suspect that the file has changed, you can simply compare the original hash with a new hash to see if the file has been altered.
- Symmetric encryption—This involves a set of data that is encrypted with a key or password and decrypted with the same key or password. This is the traditional form of encryption in which a single key unlocks the data.
- Asymmetric encryption—Asymmetric encryption involves two keys: a public key and a private key. What is encrypted with one key can only be decrypted with the other. Typically, a server encrypts data with a private key and a client decrypts the data with a public key. The public key can be distributed because it only holds the key to decrypting the data. Asymmetric encryption is much slower than symmetric encryption; therefore, it is typically only used to pass encrypted keys for symmetric encryption.

The .NET Framework has classes that support all of these aspects of cryptography. These classes are mostly wrappers around the `CryptAPI` method calls that make using cryptography much easier.

Three applications have been developed to show how to use .NET cryptography to hash a set of data and how to encrypt a set of data. The first application hashes two user-supplied strings and compares the hash values to see if the strings are equivalent. Figure 16.17 shows what the application looks like.

FIGURE 16.17
Hashing two strings.

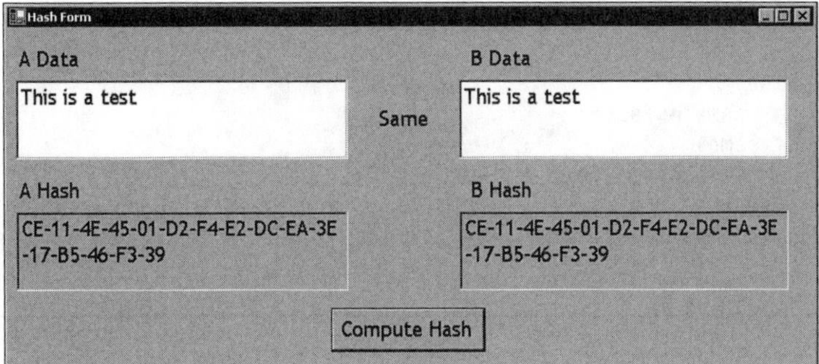

The complete source for this application is in the `Cryptography\Hash` directory.

Listing 16.18 shows how the hash is computed for the strings.

LISTING 16.18 Computing a Hash

```
private void OnComputeHash(object sender, System.EventArgs e)
{
    // Convert A to byte array
    Byte[] data1ToHash = ConvertStringToByteArray(adata.Text);
    // Convert B to byte array
    Byte[] data2ToHash = ConvertStringToByteArray(bdata.Text);

    // Create hash value from String 1 using MD5
    // instance returned by Crypto Config system
    byte[] hashvaluea = ((HashAlgorithm)
➥CryptoConfig.CreateFromName("MD5")).ComputeHash(data1ToHash);

    ahash.Text = BitConverter.ToString(hashvaluea);

    // Create hash value of String 2 using directly
    // created instance of the MD5 class
    byte[] hashvalueb =
➥(new MD5CryptoServiceProvider()).ComputeHash(data2ToHash);
    bhash.Text = BitConverter.ToString(hashvalueb);

    // Memberwise compare of hash value bytes
    bool same = true;
    if(hashvaluea.Length == hashvalueb.Length)
    {
        int i = 0;
        do
        {
            if(hashvaluea[i] != hashvalueb[i])
            {
                same = false;
                break;
            }
            i++;
        }
        while(i < hashvaluea.Length);
    }
    else
        same = false;
    if(same)
        comparison.Text = "Same";
    else
        comparison.Text = "Different";

}
```

First, each **string** needs to be converted to a **byte** array using the static function **ConvertStringToByteArray**. Next, the hash is computed for the **byte** array. Two operations are happening here: the algorithm is retrieved by a name that will be used to hash the **byte** array, and the hash is computed using **ComputeHash**. The hash is converted to a displayable string using **Bitconverter.ToString**. Then the two hash values are compared. If the hash values differ in length, they are different. If they are the same length, then each **byte** of the hashed **string** must be the same for the **string**s to be the same. This is not practical for **string**s that a user can type, but if a **byte** array could be formed representing the content of a file, then clearly comparing the hash values is preferable to a **byte**-by-**byte** comparison of the file's contents.

The next application uses hashing in a more practical, real-world sample. This application is a read-only messenger application. The complete source is in the `Messenger` directory. This application implements a portion of the RFC for MSN Messenger (which is included in the application directory). The application only signs on to the Messenger services and listens for messages sent to it. The application as is does not allow for responding or initiating a conversation. You can read the RFC and enhance this application to include more functionality as needed. This application was primarily developed to show a possible application for hashing. Listing 16.19 shows a portion of the authentication code that is used for Messenger authentication.

LISTING 16.19 Encrypting a File

```
// Request Security Package

. . .
// Send Initial Authentication Userid

. . .

// Parse MD5 Hash Check Response
// Format: USR 5 MD5 S 989048851.1851137130

. . .
// str3 = MD5 Hash Check
str3 = str3.Trim();
str2 = str3 + _password;

// Obtain MD5 Hash

MD5CryptoServiceProvider md5 = new MD5CryptoServiceProvider();
byte[] md5hash = md5.ComputeHash(Encoding.UTF8.GetBytes(str2));
str1 = GetByteString(md5hash);

tid = Convert.ToString(MessengerForm.GetNextTrialID());
str2 = "USR " + tid + " MD5 S " + str1;
SendNSData(str2);
str1 = ReceiveNSData();
```

The protocol for getting authorization from a Messenger server is as follows:

1. Request the security package and send the user handle (e-mail address).
2. Append the password to the hash value that was sent back.
3. Hash the concatenated string.
4. Send the hash of the concatenated string back to the server for verification and authorization.

By forming a hash, you don't have to send the password or an encrypted form of the password across the wire. Because the hash is formed from the string passed to you plus the password, the value sent will be different every time.

> **Note**
>
> Occasionally while debugging this messenger application, the messenger server might become "confused." This can be due to timing problems with setting breakpoints at certain parts of the code and because of improper or no response to some of the requests that the server sends. For five minutes or so, you might not be able to log on using this application or MSN Messenger. Be patient. Eventually the server will right itself and allow you to log in again. If this is intolerable, then you might just want to read the code and the RFC and recognize that .NET Cryptography can easily be used to provide a hashing function. For the more adventuresome, you will undoubtedly want to enhance this code to add functionality and make it more robust.

Next, an application that encrypts a file is built.

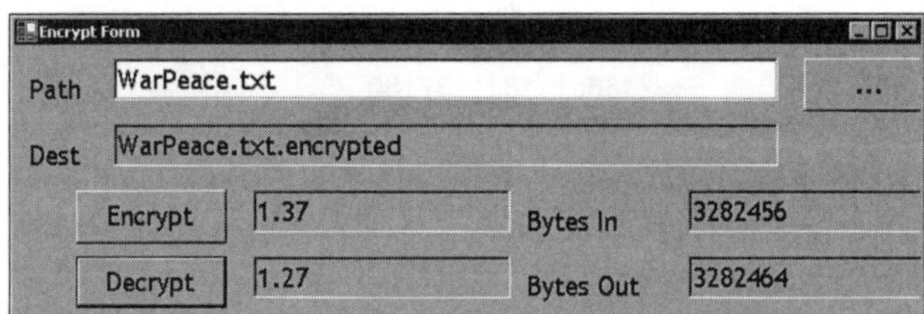

FIGURE 16.18
Encrypting a file.

Listing 16.20 shows that a file can be encrypted with the default encryption algorithm.

LISTING 16.20 Encrypting a File

```
private void OnEncrypt(object sender, System.EventArgs e)
{
    // Create the file streams to handle the input and output files.
    FileStream fin = new FileStream(filePath.Text,
➥FileMode.Open, FileAccess.Read);
    FileStream fout = new FileStream(encryptedPath.Text,
➥FileMode.OpenOrCreate, FileAccess.Write);
    fout.SetLength(0);

    // Create variables to help with read and write.
    // This is intermediate storage for the encryption.
    byte[] bin = new byte[fileChunkSize];
    // This is the total number of bytes written.
    long rdlen = 0;
    // This is the total length of the input file.
    long totlen = fin.Length;
    // This is the number of bytes to be written at a time.
    int len;

    Debug.WriteLine("Encrypting...");
    DateTime start = DateTime.Now;

    // Creates the default implementation
    //DES instance with random key
    DESCryptoServiceProvider des = new DESCryptoServiceProvider();
    fileKey = des.Key;
    fileIV = des.IV;

    //Create DES Encryptor from this instance
    ICryptoTransform desencrypt = des.CreateEncryptor();

    //Create Crypto Stream that transforms file stream using des encryption
    CryptoStream encStream = new
➥CryptoStream(fout,desencrypt,CryptoStreamMode.Write);

    //Read from the input file; then encrypt and write to the output file.
    while(rdlen < totlen)
    {
        len = fin.Read(bin, 0, fileChunkSize);
        encStream.Write(bin, 0, len);
        rdlen = rdlen + len;
    }
    fileSize.Text = Convert.ToString(rdlen);
    encStream.Close();
    fout.Close();
    fin.Close();
    DateTime stop = DateTime.Now;
    TimeSpan elapsed = stop - start;
    encryptTime.Text = string.Format("{0:F}",
➥(double)elapsed.TotalMilliseconds / 1000.0);
    decryptButton.Enabled = true;
}
```

The first portion of this code that deals with cryptography is the line that creates a **DESCryptoServiceProvider**. Only one constructor exists; therefore, to modify the default behavior, you need to use the properties of the class to modify the specific instance that is created. Notice that the key and the initialization vector are stored so that they can be used to decrypt the file. An encryptor interface is created and an encryption stream is associated with the created encryptor. After the encryption stream is created, the decrypted file can be processed much like any other stream in the system. In this sample, the stream is simply written out to disk and the elapsed time for decryption is recorded.

Listing 16.21 shows that a file can be decrypted with the default encryption algorithm using the same key and initialization vector that were used during the encryption process.

LISTING 16.21 Decrypting a File

```
private void OnDecrypt(object sender, System.EventArgs e)
{
    // Create the file streams to handle the input and output files.
    FileStream fin = new FileStream(encryptedPath.Text,
➥FileMode.Open, FileAccess.Read);
    FileStream fout = new FileStream(filePath.Text + ".decrypted",
➥FileMode.OpenOrCreate, FileAccess.Write);

    // Create variables to help with read and write.
    // This is intermediate storage for the encryption.
    byte[] bin = new byte[fileChunkSize];
    // This is the total number of bytes written.
    long rdlen = 0;
    // This is the total length of the input file.
    long totlen = fin.Length;
    // This is the number of bytes to be written at a time.
    int len;

    DateTime start = DateTime.Now;
    Debug.WriteLine("Decrypting...");

    // Creates the default implementation, which is RijndaelManaged.
    //DES instance with random key
    DESCryptoServiceProvider des = new DESCryptoServiceProvider();
    //create DES Encryptor from this instance
    ICryptoTransform desdecrypt = des.CreateDecryptor(fileKey, fileIV);

    //Create Crypto Stream that transforms file stream using des encryption
    CryptoStream decStream = new CryptoStream(fout, desdecrypt,
➥CryptoStreamMode.Write);

    //Read from the input file; then encrypt and write to the output file.
    while(rdlen < totlen)
```

LISTING 16.21 Continued

```
    {
        len = fin.Read(bin, 0, fileChunkSize);
        decStream.Write(bin, 0, len);
        rdlen = rdlen + len;
    }
    encryptedSize.Text = Convert.ToString(rdlen);
    decStream.Close();
    fout.Close();
    fin.Close();
    DateTime stop = DateTime.Now;
    TimeSpan elapsed = stop - start;
    decryptTime.Text = string.Format("{0:F}",
➥(double)elapsed.TotalMilliseconds / 1000.0);
}
```

This code is almost identical to Listing 16.20 with the exception that now a decryptor is created using the cached key and initialization vector. Like Listing 16.20, a stream is created and the decrypted file is written out to the decrypted file. You can manually compare (using `windiff`, for example) the output of the decryption process with the original file to prove to yourself that the encryption/decryption process does not change the file content.

Summary

This chapter provided a brief overview of the security services that are available within the .NET Framework. You learned about powerful features that can make your application more secure. You saw how type safety plays a key role in securing your application. You also discovered how to use the two different security models in the .NET Framework: role-based security and code-based security. You learned how to build a custom permission class and how to integrate it with the .NET Framework. You briefly walked through how to use isolated file storage to secure your data.

You also learned how to use some of the classes that are available to encrypt and hash your data. The first application simply showed how to use the cryptography classes to hash two strings and then compared the hash values to determine the equivalence of the strings. The next application was a little more practical in that it used the cryptography classes to hash a modified password to avoid sending the password or even an encrypted form of the password over the open wire. This application illustrated the basic authentication used for MSN Messenger V1.0 as specified by the RFC. The last application used the cryptography classes to encrypt and decrypt a file using a standard symmetric algorithm.

CHAPTER 17

Reflection

In This Chapter

One of the key distinctions between the Microsoft managed environment and the previous unmanaged environment is that the managed environment has a rich and extensible set of metadata that is associated with the code that is running. Of course, this metadata would not be much good if you could not easily access it. The classes that give access to the metadata of a running program are in the `System.Reflection` namespace.

The `System.Reflection` namespace contains classes that allow the programmer to obtain information about the application that is running and to dynamically add types, values, and objects to a running application. It is also possible to query a given `Assembly` for a type and obtain information about the metadata associated with that `Assembly`. Remember: An `AppDomain` provides an isolated runtime environment. An `AppDomain` consists of one or more assemblies, that when loaded, form the source for execution instructions. Assemblies contain types and values.

This chapter and the `System.Reflection` namespace is about retrieving information about these types and values and dynamically creating assemblies that contain those types and values. You will learn about attributes and how they can be used in a running program to alter the execution and behavior of that program. Microsoft has provided a means of extending attributes so that it is possible to build a custom attribute that your program can use to dynamically change the program's behavior. This chapter shows you how to build and use those custom attributes. This chapter also looks at dynamically generating code at runtime. The concept of code that generates code has long been exclusively part of languages like Lisp and Scheme. Now, the .NET Framework brings this capability to all languages that participate in it. This chapter also covers serialization, which is an important consumer of the reflection services provided by the CLR and the .NET Framework.

Note

Now would be a good time to review the Common Type System (CTS) from Chapter 2, "The Common Language Runtime—The Language," and the Assembly from Chapter 4, "The Assembly." These two chapters show how metadata is statically part of an `Assembly`. This chapter uses the information that is outlined in those chapters so that you can learn how to dynamically read, modify, and generate types and values that are part of any `Assembly`.

Using Reflection to Obtain Type Information

Reflection is used in the process of obtaining type information at runtime. Much like an **AppDomain** provides a runtime environment or home for a **Thread**, the **Assembly** provides an overall wrapper around the type information associated with an application.

This section illustrates the information that is available through reflection about an **Assembly**. Although the type is the root of all reflection operations, the **Assembly** is the home for types. This chapter looks at the assembly and its associated **Assembly** class first, and then comes back to type and its associated class **Type**. Next, it specifically looks at that **Type** class. The **Type** class allows the programmer to obtain, at runtime, specific metadata about a particular type. Finally, the chapter goes into some detail about attributes. Attributes allow a programmer to add metadata to a given type. Custom attributes allow the programmer to extend the attribute model to user-defined metadata. The CLR and the .NET Framework use attributes extensively. For attributes to be fully useful, they must be discoverable at runtime. Custom attributes are discovered and read at runtime by using reflection technology.

Note

Value types and reference types were first introduced in Chapter 2 (particularly note Figure 2.1). Three categories of value types, built-in value types, user-defined value types, and enumerations exist. Reference types break down into classes, user-defined classes, boxed-value types, delegates, pointers, and interfaces.

Obtaining Type Information from an Assembly at Runtime by Using Reflection

The **Assembly** class provides the programmer with a good deal of information about the underlying code. Of course, the Assembly class would not provide all of this information without the services provided by the classes in the **System.Reflection** namespace. To demonstrate some of the functionality offered by the **Assembly** class, look at the example assembly in Listing 17.1. This is the code that will be "reflected" upon. As many different types as possible were included in this sample so that you could easily see what information is available at runtime using the reflections services. If you want to modify this or the associated test source, the complete source is included in `AssemblySample` and `AssemblySample\SubAssembly`.

LISTING 17.1 An Assembly `TypeSampler`

```
using System;

namespace TypeSampler
{
    // User-defined value type.
    public struct MyStruct
    {
        public int a;
        public int b;
    }

    public enum Sample { Sample1, Sample2, Sample3};

    // Interfaces
    public interface IMyInterface
    {
        // Method returns an array
        string [] MyInterfaceMethod();
    }
    public interface IYourInterface
    {
        void YourInterfaceMethod(MyDelegate callback);
    }

    // Delegate
    public delegate void MyDelegate(string msg);

    // Class
    public class MyClass: IMyInterface, IYourInterface
    {
        // Fields
        private int myInt;
        private string myString;
        private Sample mySample;

        // Constructor
        public MyClass()
        {
            myInt = 0;
            myString = "unknown";
        }
        // Method
        public MyStruct MyMethod(int a, int b)
        {
            MyStruct ms = new MyStruct();
            ms.a = a;
            ms.b = b;
            return ms;
        }
```

LISTING 17.1 Continued

```
        // Interface implementations
        public string [] MyInterfaceMethod()
        {
            string [] returnArray = new string[]
➥{"This","is","returned", "from", "MyMethod",
➥ "in", "IMyInterface"};
            return returnArray;
        }

        public void YourInterfaceMethod(MyDelegate yourCallback)
        {
            yourCallback("Hello, You!");
        }

        // Property
        public int MyInt
        {
            get
            {
                return myInt;
            }
            set
            {
                myInt = value;
            }
        }

        // Another property
        public string MyString
        {
            get
            {
                return myString;
            }
        }

        // Yet another property
        public Sample MyEnum
        {
            get
            {
                return mySample;
            }
            set
            {
                mySample = value;
            }
        }
    }
}
```

The main purpose of this assembly is to provide samples of most of the types available. Except for boxed value types and pointer types, this chapter does cover all of the types in this assembly. After compiling the assembly library, you run code, part of which is found in Listing 17.2. This listing shows how all of the type information included in the source is available at runtime.

LISTING 17.2 Listing the Types in an Assembly

```
try
{
    Assembly a = Assembly.Load("SubAssembly");
    Console.WriteLine("Listing all of the types for {0}", a.FullName);
    Type [] types = a.GetTypes();
    foreach(Type t in types)
    {
        Console.WriteLine("Type: {0}", t);
    }
}
catch(Exception e)
{
    Console.WriteLine(e.ToString());
}
```

To "reflect" on an **Assembly**, you must first load it. This listing introduces two **Assembly** methods. The first is the **Load** method. This method loads an Assembly based on its display name. For those of you with a strong background in Windows programming, this might take some getting used to. This is not the name of the DLL, even if it is a DLL in which the **Assembly** is contained. It is the name of the assembly. Actually, the preceding code loads an **Assembly** based on a display name that is only partially specified. The full display name of the Assembly would be of the following form:

```
Name <,Culture = CultureInfo> <,Version = Major.Minor.Build.Revision>
➥ <,SN = StrongName> <,PK = PublicKeyToken> '\0'
```

All of the information in <> is optional. Only the `Name` portion of the display name is supplied. CultureInfo is an RFC 1766 format-defined culture. If Culture is specified as `iv`, "", or `neutral`, it is known as the *default* or *invariant culture*. An invariant culture is culture insensitive. It is associated with the English language but not with a country. This is the default for assemblies that are created with Visual Studio .NET.

Note

The Culture associated with an assembly is an important part of globalization and internationalization. These topics are covered in more detail in Chapter 18, "Globalization/Localization."

The **Version** string calls out a Major, Minor, Build, and Revision number. If you want to load a specific version of an **Assembly**, then you would specify the version information along with the assembly name. Wild-card characters are accepted for each of the **Version** numbers. For example, "Version = 1.0.*", specifies that you want version 1.0 and will take any Build or Revision number.

You can specify a strong name with SN. This is a hexadecimal-encoded value representation of the low-order 64 bits of the hash value of the public key that is assigned to the assembly. The default is to create an assembly without a strong name; the value in that case would be null.

The PK portion of the Assembly name is a hexadecimal representation of the public key of a public/private key pair. If the full public key is known and is specified, then the SN can be ignored because the full public key is a superset for the strong name.

Note

Details of strong names and public/private key pairs have already been provided in Chapters 6, "Publishing Applications," and 16, ".NET Security."

With this new information about the display name, the following supply correct arguments to the static **Load** method of the **Assembly** class:

```
Assembly a = Assembly.Load("SubAssembly");
Assembly a = Assembly.Load("SubAssembly, Version=1.*");
Assembly a = Assembly.Load("SubAssembly, Version=1.0.597.2662");
Assembly a = Assembly.Load("SubAssembly, Culture=iv");
Assembly a = Assembly.Load("SubAssembly, Culture=\"\"");
Assembly a = Assembly.Load("SubAssembly, SN=d8d19842315c20be");
```

Note that besides the Name of the assembly, all of the other portions of the display name are optional and only serve to disambiguate a specific assembly among a group of possible choices. If only one assembly exists, then just specifying the Name is all that is required.

Because all of this is rather complicated, Microsoft has provided an **AssemblyName** class that encapsulates the Name, Culture, Version, and strong name. It might be easier in your application to build a proper **AssemblyName** and then call the overloaded static **Load** method that takes an **AssemblyName** object as a parameter. You can encode the assembly information in a **string** or build an **AssemblyName** object—they both achieve the same result.

If you can't get used to an assembly name, you can also use the **LoadFrom** method. This method takes the path or filename to the .DLL or .EXE. As an alternative to **Load**, you could retrieve an Assembly with the following statement:

```
Assembly a = Assembly.LoadFrom(@"..\..\SubAssembly\bin\debug\SubAssembly.dll");
```

What about errors? As with all .NET APIs, errors are handled with exceptions. **Load** and **LoadFrom** can throw an **ArgumentNullException** if the string reference passed is null. These methods also throw **ArgumentException** if the string length is zero. If the assembly cannot be found (in the case of **Load**) or if the file specified by the path does not exist (in the case of **LoadFrom**), these methods throw **FileNotFoundException**. If the file has been tampered with and this file is signed, then **Load** and **LoadFrom** throw **FileLoadException**. **LoadFrom** requires appropriate permission to determine the current working directory if executing locally, and permission to load a path preceded by `"file:\\"`. Otherwise, a security exception will be thrown.

After obtaining the **Assembly**, the short sample obtains an array of **Type** contained in the **Assembly** with the **GetTypes** method. You should only be concerned with the **Type** names that you can see, so you iterate through the array and print the types that are contained in the **Assembly**. This is obtaining the type information at runtime, which is what reflection is all about. For this sample, the output looks like this:

```
Listing all of the types for
SubAssembly, Version=1.0.597.7307, Culture=neutral, PublicKeyToken=null
Type: TypeSampler.MyStruct
Type: TypeSampler.Sample
Type: TypeSampler.IMyInterface
Type: TypeSampler.IYourInterface
Type: TypeSampler.MyDelegate
Type: TypeSampler.MyClass
```

The full display name is printed out followed by the **Type**s defined in the **Assembly**. You can see the user-defined value type `MyStruct`; the enumerator type Sample; the two interfaces, `IMyIterface`, and `IYourInterface`; the delegate `MyDelegate`; and the user-defined class `MyClass`.

After you have an **Assembly**, you can retrieve most of the information that is encapsulated in the **Assembly**. Table 17.1 lists some of the more interesting properties and methods of an **Assembly**.

TABLE 17.1 Assembly Methods and Properties

Method or Property	*Description*

`CreateInstance`	This method in its simplest form takes a single string argument as the name of the type to create an instance of. This method is important later in the chapter when late binding is discussed.
	Example:
	`TypeSampler.MyClass mc = (TypeSampler.MyClass)`
	`a.CreateInstance("TypeSampler.MyClass");`
	The problem with this example is that the object must be defined to call it. If the assembly can be referenced to define the class, then has it not already been early bound? You could call it this way, but typically this much information is not available for late-binding. The following is a more real-world
	Example:
	`Object mc =`
	`a.CreateInstance("TypeSampler.MyClass");`
	`mc.InvokeMember(. . .);`
	or bypassing this call entirely
	`Type mct =`
	`    a.GetType("TypeSampler.MyClass");`
	`object obj = Activator.CreateInstance(mct);`
	`MethodInfo mi = mct.GetMethod("MyMethod");`
	`object[] params = new object[2];`
	`Params[0] = 1;`
	`Params[1] = 2;`
	`mi.Invoke(obj, params);`
	Again, refer to the late-binding section later in this chapter.

`GetAssembly`	This static method returns an **`Assembly`** given a **`Type`**. If, for example, you wanted to find out where the type **`double`** is defined, use the following code:
	`a = Assembly.GetAssembly(typeof(double));`
	`Console.WriteLine(a.FullName);`
	An alternative to this would be
	`a = typeof(double).Assembly;`
	`Console.WriteLine(a.FullName);`

TABLE 17.1 Continued

Method or Property	*Description*

	This code will output the full display name for the mscorlib **Assembly**, or
	`a = Assembly.GetAssembly(typeof`
	`➥(TypeSampler.MyClass));`
	`Console.WriteLine(a.FullName);`
	The full display name here would point to the `SubAssembly` **Assembly**.

`GetCallingAssembly`	This returns the **Assembly** that called the assembly that is calling this method. You need to think about the definition alone. Look at some sample code:
	`MyClass()`
	`{`
	`    myString =`
	`Assembly.GetCallingAssembly().FullName;`
	`}`
	`. . .`
	`public string MyString`
	`{`
	`    get`
	`    {`
	`        return myString;`
	`    }`
	`}`
	Look now at the method in `MyClass`:
	`string MyGetCallingAssemblyMethod()`
	`  {`
	`    return`
	`Assembly.GetCallingAssembly().FullName;`
	`}`
	Finally, look at the following code that exercises this functionality:
	`Assembly a = Assembly.Load("SubAssembly");`
	`TypeSampler.MyClass mc =`
	`➥(TypeSampler.MyClass)a.CreateInstance`
	`➥("TypeSampler.MyClass");`

TABLE 17.1 Continued

<table>
<tr><th>Method or Property</th><th>Description</th></tr>
<tr><td></td><td><pre>Console.WriteLine(Assembly.GetCallingAssembly().
➥FullName);
Console.WriteLine(mc.MyString);
Console.WriteLine(mc.MyGetCallingAssemblyMethod);</pre>
Forget about the convoluted CreateInstance call. Why not just early bind? This sequence of calls will return a reference to the mscorlib assembly (the construction occurs from mscorlib in the “late” bind sample) and two references to the assembly in which this code resides. If you were to replace the CreateInstance call with the following:
<pre>TypeSampler.MyClass mc =
  new TypeSampler.MyClass();</pre>
then all three Console.WriteLine calls would output references to the assembly that is running this code.</td></tr>
<tr><td>GetCustomAttributes</td><td>This returns an array of objects that are instances of the custom attribute classes associated with this assembly.
Example:
<pre>Object [] attributes =
a.GetCustomAttributes(true);
foreach(object o in attributes)
{
    Console.WriteLine(o);
}</pre>
On a default project (a project created by Visual Studio before a user modifies it), this code would print some lines that looked like this:
<pre>System.Reflection.AssemblyKeyNameAttribute
System.Reflection.AssemblyKeyFileAttribute
System.Reflection.AssemblyDelaySignAttribute
System.Reflection.AssemblyTrademarkAttribute
System.Reflection.AssemblyCopyrightAttribute
System.Reflection.AssemblyProductAttribute
System.Reflection.AssemblyCompanyAttribute
System.Reflection.AssemblyConfigurationAttribute
System.Reflection.AssemblyDescriptionAttribute
System.Reflection.AssemblyTitleAttribute
System.Diagnostics.DebuggableAttribute</pre></td></tr>
</table>

TABLE 17.1 Continued

Method or Property	*Description*
	Note that this is not all of the custom attributes in the assembly. These are only the assembly level attributes. If custom attributes are associated with a type in the assembly, then you can obtain those attributes from the **`Type.GetCustomAttributes`** method. Don't confuse these attributes with the attributes that are returned from **`Type.Attributes`**, which are access-level attributes—*not* custom attributes.
`GetEntryAssembly`	The static method returns the **`Assembly`** that contains the entry point. Typically in C#, this is the **`Assembly`** that contains `Main()`.
`GetExportedTypes`	This function returns the types that are public only, as opposed to `GetTypes` that return all assembly-level types.
`GetLoadedModules`	This returns an array of **`Module`**s that are loaded as part of the assembly. This method, as opposed to `GetModules`, returns a list of all of the **`Module`**s that are currently loaded. It is possible with a delay-loaded **`Module`**(s) that not all of the **`Module`**(s) associated with an **`Assembly`** are currently loaded.
`GetManifestResourceNames`	This returns an array of names of the resources in the assembly.
`GetModules`	This returns an array of **`Module`**s that are part of this assembly. This would only be different from **`GetLoadedModules`** if a **`Module`** is delay-loaded on an as-needed basis. This method returns all of the **`Module`**(s) associated with an **`Assembly`**.
`GetName`	This method allows the programmer to retrieve an **`AssemblyName`** instance associated with this assembly. Using the **`AssemblyName`** class allows you to retrieve just the Version or just the Name without having to parse the full display name returned by the **`FullName`** property.
`GetReferencedAssemblies`	This returns an array of **`AssemblyName`** instances for each referenced assembly. For a simple case, this might just return a reference to the mscorlib.
`GetSatelliteAssembly`	The method returns a satellite Assembly that corresponds to the **`CultureInfo`** passed as an argument. Satellite assemblies will be covered in more detail in Chapter 18. For now, consider a satellite assembly to be roughly equivalent to an unmanaged resource assembly. It contains localized resources as opposed to a regular assembly, which uses non-localized resources and a fixed culture.

TABLE 17.1 Continued

Method or Property	*Description*

`GetTypes`	Return an array of the **`Type`**s at the assembly level. The following code prints the type names that are exposed at the assembly level.
	`Type [] types = a.GetTypes();`
	`foreach(Type t in types)`
	`{`
	`    Console.WriteLine("Type: {0}", t);`
	`}`
	A corresponding **`GetType`** returns a single Type based on a type name passed as an argument.

`IsDefined`	This returns true or false if the passed **`Type`** is defined in the assembly.
`Load`	**`Load`** and **`LoadFrom`** have been discussed at length previously. They allow a user to load a specific assembly based on the criteria passed as arguments. These functions return an **`Assembly`** referring to the loaded assembly or they throw an exception if an error exists.
`CodeBase`	This property returns the full path to where the assembly was specified originally. On a simple assembly, the string returned from this property. For a simple assembly, this path looks like this: `file:///F:/as/bin/Debug/SubAssembly.DLL`
`EntryPoint`	This property returns a **`MethodInfo`** object that describes the entry point of the **`Assembly`**. Typically, this is `Main()` in C#. If this property is called on an assembly that does not have an entry point, null is returned (nothing in VB).
`Evidence`	This property returns an **`Evidence`** object, which is a collection of XML specifications for what security policies affect this assembly.
`FullName`	This property returns a string of the full display name for the assembly.
`GlobalAssemblyCache`	This property returns true if the assembly is loaded in the global assembly cache. It returns false otherwise.
`Location`	This property returns the location of the file containing the assembly. For a simple assembly, it looks like this: `f:\as\bin\debug\subassembly.dll` Consider this in contrast to the **`CodeBase`** format.

Using the Type Class

After you have a **Type**, you are set to drill down further into the characteristics of the instance of the **Type**. Listing 17.2 shows the **Type**s that were visible at the **Assembly** level. Rather than build another table of methods and properties, it would be good to look at some code. Listings 17.3–17.6 show source code that is contained in the `ListTypes` subdirectory. You will be extracting type information from an assembly that contains the same code as in Listing 17.1, so refer back to that listing to get a feel for the kind of type information that should be expected. Notice that you will be listing information about the program that is running. The first listing (Listing 17.3) is familiar in that you just obtain all of the **Type**s in the **Assembly**.

LISTING 17.3 Listing the Types in an Assembly

```
// Load an assembly using its filename.
Assembly a = Assembly.GetExecutingAssembly();
// Get the type names from the assembly.
Type [] types = a.GetTypes ();
foreach (Type t in types)
```

Listing 17.3 shows that you get the **Assembly** from **GetExecutingAssembly**. This method returns the Assembly that is associated with the currently running code. With that **Assembly**, you get an array of **Type**s that are visible in the **Assembly**. With that array, you start up a loop to process each of the **Type**s. In Listing 17.4, you start processing each type.

LISTING 17.4 Getting Member Information for Each Type

```
MemberInfo[] mmi = t.GetMembers();
// Get and display the DeclaringType method.
Console.WriteLine("\nThere are {0} members in {1}.",
                  mmi.Length, t.FullName);
Console.WriteLine("{0} is {1}", t.FullName,
            (t.IsAbstract ? "abstract " : "") +
            (t.IsArray ? "array " : "") +
            (t.IsClass ? "class " : "") +
            (t.IsContextful ? "context " : "") +
            (t.IsInterface ? "interface " : "") +
            (t.IsPointer ? "pointer " : "") +
            (t.IsPrimitive ? "primitive " : "") +
            (t.IsPublic ? "public " : "") +
            (t.IsSealed ? "sealed " : "") +
            (t.IsSerializable ? "serializable " : "") +
            (t.IsValueType ? "value " : ""));
Console.WriteLine ("// Members");
```

Filtering out all of the output with the exception for that generated that specifically pertains to the assembly types in Listing 17.2 leaves you with the following:

```
There are 6 members in ListTypes.MyStruct.
ListTypes.MyStruct is public sealed value
There are 13 members in ListTypes.Sample.
ListTypes.Sample is public sealed serializable value
There are 1 members in ListTypes.IMyInterface.
ListTypes.IMyInterface is abstract interface public
There are 1 members in ListTypes.IYourInterface.
ListTypes.IYourInterface is abstract interface public
There are 16 members in ListTypes.MyDelegate.
ListTypes.MyDelegate is class public sealed serializable
There are 16 members in ListTypes.MyClass.
ListTypes.MyClass is class public
There are 6 members in ListTypes.ListTypesMain.
ListTypes.ListTypesMain is class
```


Notice that the types obtained through reflection are the same **`Type`**s that were shown in Listing 17.1. The only addition is that you call **`GetMembers`** on each **`Type`**. In addition, you can tell the access level of the type along with some other characteristics. It is interesting to note that `MyStruct` is **`sealed`**, which supports the rule that structs cannot be a base class for anything else. Also note that the two interfaces are **`abstract`**. (Again, this is consistent with the idea of an interface. The interesting part is that it is not explicitly marked as abstract.) Finally, note that `Sample` and `MyDelegate` are serializable. You don't have private types (yet), so all of the **`Type`**s are **`public`**.

This function returns an array of **`MemberInfo`** objects that describe each of the members of the type. Both of the interfaces have a member count of 1. Each of the interfaces have only one member function, so that makes sense. However, the rest of the **`Type`**s seem to have too many members. `MyStruct` has 6 members, yet there are only 2 integer fields. `Sample` has 13 members, but it has only 3 enumerated values. `MyDelegate` does not seem to have members, yet 16 members show up. Finally, `MyClass` has 16 members, but only 10 show up. Listing 17.5 shows how to list the information in the **`MemberInfo`** class.

LISTING 17.5 Getting Member Information of Each Type

```
public static void PrintMembers(MemberInfo [] ms)
{
    foreach (MemberInfo m in ms)
    {
        if(m is ConstructorInfo)
        {
            Console.WriteLine ("{0}{1}{2}", "     ", m,
➥(((MethodBase)m).IsConstructor ? "constructor" : ""));
            Console.WriteLine ("{0} A member of {1}", "     ",
➥((ConstructorInfo)m).DeclaringType);
```

LISTING 17.5 Continued

```
            Console.WriteLine ("{0} Calling Convention {1}", "     ",
➥((ConstructorInfo)m).CallingConvention);
            ParameterInfo [] pi = ((ConstructorInfo)m).GetParameters();
            Console.WriteLine ("{0} There are {1} parameter(s).", "     ",
➥pi.Length);
            foreach (ParameterInfo p in pi)
            {
                Console.WriteLine ("{0}  {1} {2}", "     ",
➥p.ParameterType,p.Name);
            }
        }
        else if(m is MethodInfo)
        {
            Console.WriteLine ("{0}{1}", "     ", m);
            Console.WriteLine ("{0} A member of {1}", "     ",
➥((MethodInfo)m).DeclaringType);
            Console.WriteLine ("{0} Calling Convention {1}", "     ",
➥((MethodInfo)m).CallingConvention);
            ParameterInfo [] pi = ((MethodInfo)m).GetParameters();
            Console.WriteLine ("{0} There are {1} parameter(s).", "     ",
➥pi.Length);
            foreach (ParameterInfo p in pi)
            {
                Console.WriteLine ("{0}  {1} {2}", "     ",
➥p.ParameterType, p.Name);
            }
            Console.WriteLine ("{0} Returns {1}", "     ",
➥((MethodInfo)m).ReturnType);
        }
        else if(m is FieldInfo)
        {
            Console.WriteLine ("{0}{1}", "     ", m);
            // Get the MethodAttribute enumerated value
            FieldAttributes fieldAttributes = ((FieldInfo)m).Attributes;
            Console.Write ("{0} ", "     ");
            if((fieldAttributes & FieldAttributes.FieldAccessMask) ==
➥FieldAttributes.Private)
                Console.Write("Private ");
            if((fieldAttributes & FieldAttributes.FieldAccessMask) ==
➥FieldAttributes.Public)
                Console.Write("Public ");
            if((fieldAttributes & FieldAttributes.FieldAccessMask) ==
➥FieldAttributes.Assembly)
                Console.Write("Assembly ");
            if((fieldAttributes & FieldAttributes.FieldAccessMask) ==
➥FieldAttributes.FamANDAssem)
                Console.Write("FamANDAssem ");
            if((fieldAttributes & FieldAttributes.FieldAccessMask) ==
➥FieldAttributes.Family)
```

LISTING 17.5 Continued

```
                Console.Write("Family ");
            if((fieldAttributes & FieldAttributes.FieldAccessMask) ==
➥FieldAttributes.FamORAssem)
                Console.Write("FamORAssem ");
            if((fieldAttributes & FieldAttributes.FieldAccessMask) ==
➥FieldAttributes.FamORAssem)
                Console.Write("FamORAssem ");
            if((fieldAttributes & FieldAttributes.HasDefault) != 0)
                Console.Write("HasDefault ");
            if((fieldAttributes & FieldAttributes.HasFieldMarshal) != 0)
                Console.Write("HasFieldMarshal ");
            if((fieldAttributes & FieldAttributes.HasFieldRVA) != 0)
                Console.Write("HasFieldRVA ");
            if((fieldAttributes & FieldAttributes.InitOnly) != 0)
                Console.Write("InitOnly ");
            if((fieldAttributes & FieldAttributes.Literal) != 0)
                Console.Write("Literal ");
            if((fieldAttributes & FieldAttributes.NotSerialized) != 0)
                Console.Write("NotSerialized ");
            if((fieldAttributes & FieldAttributes.PinvokeImpl) != 0)
                Console.Write("PinvokeImpl ");
            if((fieldAttributes & FieldAttributes.PrivateScope) != 0)
                Console.Write("PrivateScope ");
            if((fieldAttributes & FieldAttributes.RTSpecialName) != 0)
                Console.Write("RTSpecialName ");
            if((fieldAttributes & FieldAttributes.SpecialName) != 0)
                Console.Write("SpecialName ");
            if((fieldAttributes & FieldAttributes.Static) != 0)
                Console.Write("Static ");
            Console.WriteLine (((FieldInfo)m).FieldType);
            Console.WriteLine ("A member of {0}", ((FieldInfo)m).DeclaringType);
            Console.WriteLine ("{0} {1}", "     ",
➥Attribute.GetCustomAttribute(m, typeof(Attribute)));
        }
        else if(m is PropertyInfo)
        {
            Console.WriteLine ("{0}{1}", "     ", m);
            Console.WriteLine ("{0} CanRead: {1}", "     ",
➥((PropertyInfo)m).CanRead);
            Console.WriteLine ("{0} CanWrite: {1}", "     ",
➥((PropertyInfo)m).CanWrite);
            Console.WriteLine ("{0} IsSpecialName: {1}", "     ",
➥((PropertyInfo)m).IsSpecialName);
            Console.WriteLine ("{0} Member of: {1}", "     ",
➥((PropertyInfo)m).DeclaringType);
            Console.WriteLine ("{0} Member type: {1}", "     ",
➥((PropertyInfo)m).MemberType);
            Console.WriteLine ("{0} Name: {1}", "     ",
➥((PropertyInfo)m).Name);
```

17

REFLECTION

LISTING 17.5 Continued

```
            Console.WriteLine ("{0} Property type: {1}", "      ",
➥((PropertyInfo)m).PropertyType);
            Console.WriteLine ("{0} Reflected type: {1}", "      ",
➥((PropertyInfo)m).ReflectedType);
            if(((PropertyInfo)m).GetGetMethod() != null)
            {
                Console.WriteLine ("{0} Get: {1}", "      ",
➥((PropertyInfo)m).GetGetMethod());
                Console.WriteLine ("{0}      Return type {1}",
➥"      ", ((PropertyInfo)m).GetGetMethod().ReturnType);
            }
            if(((PropertyInfo)m).GetSetMethod() != null)
            {
                Console.WriteLine ("{0} Set: {1}", "      ",
➥((PropertyInfo)m).GetSetMethod());
                Console.WriteLine ("{0}      Return type {1}", "      ",
➥((PropertyInfo)m).GetSetMethod().ReturnType);
            }
        }
        else
        {
            Console.WriteLine ("{0}{1}", "      ", m);
        }
    }
    Console.WriteLine();
}
```

One of the questions was that the structure `MyStruct` was listed as having six members when clearly only two members existed. Looking at the output for this **`Type`** shows where the extra members show up.

```
There are 6 members in ListTypes.MyStruct.
ListTypes.MyStruct is public sealed value.
     Int32 a
      Public System.Int32
      A member of ListTypes.MyStruct
     Int32 b
      Public System.Int32
      A member of ListTypes.MyStruct
     Int32 GetHashCode()
      A member of System.ValueType
      Calling Convention Standard, HasThis
      There are 0 parameter(s).
      Returns System.Int32
     Boolean Equals(System.Object)
      A member of System.ValueType
      Calling Convention Standard, HasThis
      There are 1 parameter(s).
       System.Object obj
```

```
 Returns System.Boolean
System.String ToString()
 A member of System.ValueType
 Calling Convention Standard, HasThis
 There are 0 parameter(s).
 Returns System.String
System.Type GetType()
 A member of System.Object
 Calling Convention Standard, HasThis
 There are 0 parameter(s).
 Returns System.Type
```


Here you see that the first two members of `MyStruct` are the integer fields that you know about: fields `a` and `b`. The rest of the fields are member methods that a **`struct`** inherits when it is declared. The members **`GetHashCode`**, **`Equals`**, and **`ToString`** are all inherited from **`System.ValueType`**. The final method, **`GetType`**, comes from **`System.Object`**. The extra four members are there because of inheritance.

The structure has been completely dissected, and any information about the structure (metadata) can be obtained through reflection. This was done by obtaining an array of **`MemberInfo`** objects describing each member. You obtain specific information about a particular member by first obtaining the proper derived type. You then cast the **`MemberInfo`** object to the proper derived type and call the specific methods of the derived type.

The **`MemberInfo`** object is the base class for a few classes, as is illustrated in the following simple hierarchy:

```
Object
    MemberInfo
        EventInfo
        FieldInfo
        MethodBase
            ConstructorInfo
            MethodInfo
        PropertyInfo
        Type
```

Therefore, **`GetMembers`** returns an array of **`MemberInfo`** objects, but depending on the member, it might actually be an **`EventInfo`**, **`FieldInfo`**, **`MethodBase`**, **`PropertyInfo`**, or **`Type`** object. The code in `PrintMembers` uses the following construct:

```
if(m is MethodInfo)
```

to determine if the member of the array is one of the specific objects. After the specific object has been determined, you have to call the methods on that object to obtain the information desired. Following is the output for the Sample enumeration:

```
There are 13 members in ListTypes.Sample.
ListTypes.Sample is public sealed serializable value
// Members
     Int32 value__
      Public RTSpecialName SpecialName System.Int32
      A member of ListTypes.Sample
     ListTypes.Sample Sample1
      Public HasDefault Literal Static ListTypes.Sample
      A member of ListTypes.Sample
     ListTypes.Sample Sample2
      Public HasDefault Literal Static ListTypes.Sample
      A member of ListTypes.Sample
     ListTypes.Sample Sample3
      Public HasDefault Literal Static ListTypes.Sample
      A member of ListTypes.Sample
     System.String ToString(System.IFormatProvider)
      A member of System.Enum
      Calling Convention Standard, HasThis
      There are 1 parameter(s).
       System.IFormatProvider provider
      Returns System.String
     System.TypeCode GetTypeCode()
      A member of System.Enum
      Calling Convention Standard, HasThis
      There are 0 parameter(s).
      Returns System.TypeCode
     System.String ToString(System.String, System.IFormatProvider)
      A member of System.Enum
      Calling Convention Standard, HasThis
      There are 2 parameter(s).
       System.String format
       System.IFormatProvider provider
      Returns System.String
     Int32 CompareTo(System.Object)
      A member of System.Enum
      Calling Convention Standard, HasThis
      There are 1 parameter(s).
       System.Object target
      Returns System.Int32
     Int32 GetHashCode()
      A member of System.Enum
      Calling Convention Standard, HasThis
      There are 0 parameter(s).
      Returns System.Int32
     Boolean Equals(System.Object)
      A member of System.Enum
      Calling Convention Standard, HasThis
      There are 1 parameter(s).
       System.Object obj
      Returns System.Boolean
```

```
System.String ToString()
 A member of System.Enum
 Calling Convention Standard, HasThis
 There are 0 parameter(s).
 Returns System.String
System.String ToString(System.String)
 A member of System.Enum
 Calling Convention Standard, HasThis
 There are 1 parameter(s).
  System.String format
 Returns System.String
System.Type GetType()
 A member of System.Object
 Calling Convention Standard, HasThis
 There are 0 parameter(s).
 Returns System.Type
```


Again, you see the first four members that you expect. The first member is the integer that holds the value, and the next three are the different values of the enumerator. The next eight members are inherited from the Enum class. The last member, **GetType**, is inherited from **System.Object**.

The properties of the remaining types in the ListTypes namespace will not be shown in this chapter because the output is not what is important. What is important is the process of using reflection to query an **Assembly** for a **Type** and listing the properties of that **Type**.

A **Type** can be queried one other way. Rather than using the general **GetMembers** method and relying on runtime type information to get the category of member that is to be retrieved, you can use many methods (such as **GetProperties**) to query directly for a specific category of member. Look at the code in Listing 17.6.

LISTING 17.6 Getting Property Information

```
PropertyInfo [] pi;
pi = t.GetProperties (BindingFlags.Instance |
                      BindingFlags.NonPublic |
              BindingFlags.Public);
Console.WriteLine ("// Instance Properties");
PrintMembers (pi);
```

Here you can specify that you are just interested in properties (**GetProperties**) of a **Type**. You can also specify what kind of property that you are interested in with the **BindingFlags**. The preceding code specifies flags that will match instance, non-public, and public properties. That is basically saying that you want all properties (instance, public, protected, or private). As you can see, the **BindingFlags** has a **FlagsAttribute** so that the enumerated values can be combined (ORd together). The **BindingFlags** that specifically apply to retrieving information are as follows:

- DeclaredOnly
- FlattenHierarchy
- IgnoreCase
- IgnoreReturn
- Instance
- NonPublic
- Public
- Static

If the code associated with Listing 17.6 is compiled and run, then you get output that looks like this:

```
There are 16 members in ListTypes.MyDelegate.
ListTypes.MyDelegate is class public sealed serializable
// Instance Properties
     System.Reflection.MethodInfo Method
      CanRead: True
      CanWrite: False
      IsSpecialName: False
      Member of: System.Delegate
      Member type: Property
      Name: Method
      Property type: System.Reflection.MethodInfo
      Reflected type: ListTypes.MyDelegate
      Get: System.Reflection.MethodInfo get_Method()
           Return type System.Reflection.MethodInfo
     System.Object Target
      CanRead: True
      CanWrite: False
      IsSpecialName: False
      Member of: System.Delegate
      Member type: Property
      Name: Target
      Property type: System.Object
      Reflected type: ListTypes.MyDelegate
      Get: System.Object get_Target()
           Return type System.Object


There are 16 members in ListTypes.MyClass.
ListTypes.MyClass is class public
```

```
// Instance Properties
     Int32 MyInt
      CanRead: True
      CanWrite: True
      IsSpecialName: False
      Member of: ListTypes.MyClass
      Member type: Property
      Name: MyInt
      Property type: System.Int32
      Reflected type: ListTypes.MyClass
      Get: Int32 get_MyInt()
           Return type System.Int32
      Set: Void set_MyInt(Int32)
           Return type System.Void
     System.String MyString
      CanRead: True
      CanWrite: False
      IsSpecialName: False
      Member of: ListTypes.MyClass
      Member type: Property
      Name: MyString
      Property type: System.String
      Reflected type: ListTypes.MyClass
      Get: System.String get_MyString()
           Return type System.String
     ListTypes.Sample MyEnum
      CanRead: True
      CanWrite: True
      IsSpecialName: False
      Member of: ListTypes.MyClass
      Member type: Property
      Name: MyEnum
      Property type: ListTypes.Sample
      Reflected type: ListTypes.MyClass
      Get: ListTypes.Sample get_MyEnum()
           Return type ListTypes.Sample
      Set: Void set_MyEnum(ListTypes.Sample)
           Return type System.Void
```

In the preceding output listing, only certain portions of the total output listing have been selected for illustration purposes. The first portion of the output shows the instance properties for `MyDelegate`. The second portion of the output shows the instance properties for `MyClass`. You might want to comment or uncomment various portions of the source code to retrieve specific information; listing all of the information that can be reflected on can be rather large. This is identical to the output that you received from **`GetMembers`**. Now you are able to retrieve the information that you want.

The following **Type** methods accept **BindingFlags** and allow a finer grain retrieval of **Type** information:

- GetMembers
- GetEvents
- GetConstructor
- GetConstructors
- GetMethod
- GetMethods
- GetField
- GetFields
- GetEvent
- GetProperty
- GetProperties
- GetMember
- FindMembers

In addition to the small code snippet in Listing 17.6, source code is also available for many of the preceding methods in the ListTypes directory.

Obtaining and Using Attributes at Runtime Using Reflection

One particular property of **Type** that might have been glossed over was that returned by **Attribute.GetCustomAttribute**. This is how you can programmatically (that is, at runtime) find attributes associated with a type. For example, you can use the **XmlSerializer** class to serialize MyClass. The default behavior is to serialize each member as a separate element. However, you can use attributes to modify this default behavior. An example of using attributes to modify the default serialization behavior is illustrated by the code in Listing 17.7.

LISTING 17.7 Adding Attributes to a Field

```
// Class
public class MyClass: IMyInterface, IYourInterface
{
    // Fields
    [XmlAttribute]
    private int myInt;
    [XmlAttribute]
```

LISTING 17.7 Continued

```
    private string myString;
    [XmlAttribute]
    private Sample mySample;
```

The process of serialization is discussed in depth a little later. The following illustrates how the serialization code could query each field of a structure at runtime to see how it should serialize the object. Listing 17.8 shows how to query a particular field for an attribute.

LISTING 17.8 Querying Fields of a Type

```
FieldInfo [] fi;
// Instance Fields
fi = t.GetFields (BindingFlags.Instance |
                  BindingFlags.NonPublic |
          BindingFlags.Public);
Console.WriteLine ("// Instance Fields");
PrintMembers (fi);
```

The portion of the PrintMembers method that keys on custom attributes looks like Listing 17.9.

LISTING 17.9 Retrieving Custom Attributes

```
if(Attribute.GetCustomAttribute(m, typeof(Attribute)) != null)
        Console.WriteLine ("{0} {1}", "     ",
➥Attribute.GetCustomAttribute(m, typeof(Attribute)));
```

Running the code in Listings 17.7–17.9 produces the following output:

```
ListTypes.MyClass is class public
// Instance Fields
     Int32 myInt
      Private System.Int32
      System.Xml.Serialization.XmlAttributeAttribute
      A member of ListTypes.MyClass
     System.String myString
      Private System.String
      System.Xml.Serialization.XmlAttributeAttribute
      A member of ListTypes.MyClass
     ListTypes.Sample mySample
      Private ListTypes.Sample
      System.Xml.Serialization.XmlAttributeAttribute
      A member of ListTypes.MyClass
```

Notice that the [XmlAttribute] associated with each of the fields is picked up. The **Attribute.GetCustomAttibute** or **Attribute.GetCustomAttributes** static methods allow a programmer access to the custom attributes associated with a member or assembly. A serialization engine obviously uses these attributes at runtime to change its behavior. Using reflection, the programmer has the same facilities available that a serialization engine has to modify a program's behavior using attributes. Although printing the attributes is informative, it is not probably what you would do in a real application. These methods return an instance of the custom attribute. Instead of printing the attribute, you could do the following:

```
Attribute attrib = Attribute.GetCustomAttribute(m, typeof(Attribute));
XmlAttributeAttribute xmlAttrib = attrib as XmlAttributeAttribute;
```

Alternatively, a **GetCustomAttributes** method exists in the **MemberInfo** class, so it is available to all of the classes that are derived from **MemberInfo**. If you prefer these methods, you would change the preceding code to the following:

```
Attribute attrib = m.GetCustomAttribute(typeof(Attribute), true);
XmlAttributeAttribute xmlAttrib = attrib as XmlAttributeAttribute;
```

Now you can treat [XmlAttribute] as a class and call its methods, get/set properties, and so on. Note the convention that is recommended for all custom attributes is as follows: [Name] translates to a class NameAttribute.

Custom attributes are used throughout the .NET Framework. They allow the functionality of the **Type** to be significantly altered. Using the available attributes expands the usefulness of a **Type** and causes it to be more fully integrated with the rest of the framework. Attributes can be used to provide additional documentation information, define which fields participate in serialization, indicate that a **Type** will participate in a transaction, and so on.

Listing the functionality of each attribute would not be very productive. To get an idea of the number of attributes, pull up the online documentation for the Attribute class hierarchy and look at the many derived classes. Just remember two rules:

- All custom attributes are enclosed in [].
- The custom attribute applies to the type immediately following the custom attribute. Only comments and white space can fall between a custom attribute and the type to which it is to apply.

Customizing Metadata with User-Defined Attributes

In addition to using attributes that are part of the .NET Framework, it is also possible to define your own attributes. Defining your own attributes is easy. The code for Listings

17.10–17.12 is in the `CustomAttribute` directory. Listing 17.10 demonstrates some of the characteristics of a simple user-defined attribute.

LISTING 17.10 User-Defined Custom Attributes

```
class HelloAttribute : Attribute
{
    public HelloAttribute()
    {
        Console.WriteLine("Constructing Hello");
    }
}

[Hello]
class MyClass
{
    public MyClass()
    {
        Console.WriteLine("Constructing MyClass");
        Object [] attributes = typeof(MyClass).GetCustomAttributes(true);
        foreach(Attribute attrib in attributes)
        {
            Console.WriteLine(attrib);
        }
    }
}

class CustomAttributesMain
{
    static void Main(string[] args)
    {
        MyClass m = new MyClass();
    }
}
```


This sample demonstrates building a simple user-defined attribute. It consists of the definition of the attribute (`HelloAttribute`), a class to which the attribute is applied, and an entry point for the sample (Main). In a real application, all three of these parts would most likely be in separate assemblies. Following are some key observations about this simple sample:

- The user-defined attribute is actually a class. This is a concept that is key in understanding how to use and define attributes. Anything that can be done in a class can be done in a user-defined attribute.
- All custom attributes must be derived from Attribute or they will not be recognized as an Attribute.

- The name of the attribute is `[Hello]`, yet the implementation of the attribute is in the class `HelloAttribute`. This is a convention for all attributes. When the compiler sees Hello as an attribute, it will append the word Attribute to the name and search for a class that implements the attribute. Following this convention will make it easy for the compiler to resolve the attribute to an implementation.

Notice the output from this sample:

```
Constructing MyClass
Constructing Hello
CustomAttributes.HelloAttribute
```

`HelloAttribute` is not instantiated until it is referred to or used. Here, `MyClass` wants to see if it has an attribute associated with it. It is only then that the constructor for `HelloAttribute` is called.

Now you will learn how to pass information from the attribute to the implementation of the attribute and eventually to the class that has been "attributed." Listing 17.10 will be modified slightly so that you can pass a string to the attribute. The result is Listing 17.11.

LISTING 17.11 User-Defined Custom Attributes with an Argument

```
class HelloAttribute : Attribute
{
    private string message;
    public HelloAttribute(string message)
    {
        this.message = message;
        Console.WriteLine("Constructing Hello");
    }
    public string Message
    {
        get
        {
            return message;
        }
    }
}

[Hello("Hello World!")]
class MyClass
{
    public MyClass()
    {
        Console.WriteLine("Constructing MyClass");
        Object [] attributes = typeof(MyClass).GetCustomAttributes(true);
        foreach(Attribute attrib in attributes)
```

LISTING 17.11 Continued

```
        {
            HelloAttribute ha = attrib as HelloAttribute;
            if(ha != null)
            {
                Console.WriteLine(ha.Message);
            }
        }
    }
}

class CustomAttributesMain
{
    static void Main(string[] args)
    {
        MyClass m = new MyClass();
    }
}
```


Now the output looks like this:

```
Constructing MyClass
Constructing Hello
Hello World!
```

Using reflection, the message reaches the class to which the attribute was applied. Multiple arguments could be passed to the attribute, such as [Hello(A, B, C)]. The implementation of the attribute class would need to add a constructor: `HelloAttribute (typea A, typeb B, typec C)`. `Typea`, `typeb`, and `typec` would specify the types required for each of the arguments. The compiler would do all of the same compile-time checking of the arguments specified in the attribute and those declared for the implementation class constructor.

All of the parameters that have been discussed so far with respect to attributes are "positional" arguments. They must occur in the order that the constructor specifies and have compatible types with the constructor arguments. It is possible to specify "optional" or "named" arguments, which would need to follow any of the positional arguments. An example of an optional or named argument to an attribute is illustrated in Listing 17.12.

LISTING 17.12 User-Defined Custom Attributes with a Named Argument

```
class HelloAttribute : Attribute
{
    private int id;
    private string message;
    public HelloAttribute(string message)
```

LISTING 17.12 Continued

```
    {
        id = 0;
        this.message = message;
        Console.WriteLine("Constructing Hello");
    }
    public int Id
    {
        get
        {
            return id;
        }
        set
        {
            Console.WriteLine("Setting ID");
            id = value;
        }
    }
    public string Message
    {
        get
        {
            return message;
        }
    }
}

[Hello("Hello World!", Id=123)]
class MyClass
{
    public MyClass()
    {
        Console.WriteLine("Constructing MyClass");
        Object [] attributes = typeof(MyClass).GetCustomAttributes(true);
        foreach(Attribute attrib in attributes)
        {
            HelloAttribute ha = attrib as HelloAttribute;
            if(ha != null)
            {
                Console.WriteLine("Message: {0}", ha.Message);
                Console.WriteLine("Id: {0}", ha.Id);
            }
        }
    }
}

class CustomAttributesMain
{
    static void Main(string[] args)
```

LISTING 17.12 Continued

```
    {
        MyClass m = new MyClass();
    }
}
```

Now the output looks like this:

```
Constructing MyClass
Constructing Hello
Setting ID
Message: Hello World!
Id: 123
```


The `HelloAttribute` object is constructed using the fixed arguments that would be supplied to a constructor. Next, the positional or named arguments are matched with a property of the implementing class, and that property is set using the data in the attribute. This is why positional arguments must come first; otherwise, the object could not be properly constructed.

If you wanted to have more than one attribute, you might be tempted to just do the following:

```
[Hello("Hello World!")]
[Hello("Hello World, again!")]
class MyClass
```

If you do this, however, you get a compiler error:

```
CustomAttributes.cs(37): Duplicate 'Hello' attribute
```

To change this behavior, you need **`AttributeUsageAttribute`**. This attribute has the following convention:

```
[AttributeUsage(
validon (AttributeTargets.XXX),
AllowMultiple=bool,
InHerited=bool
)]
```

The `validon` argument is an `AttributeUsage` enumerator called `AttributeTargets`. It has the following enumerator values:

- `All`
- `Assembly`
- `Class`
- `Constructor`

- `Delegate`
- `Enum`
- `Event`
- `Field`
- `Interface`
- `Method`
- `Module`
- `Parameter`
- `Property`
- `ReturnValue`
- `Struct`

To achieve the desired functionality (have multiple attributes), you would change the following lines on the class that implements that attribute:

```
[AttributeUsage(AttributeTargets.All, AllowMultiple=true)]
class HelloAttribute : Attribute
```

Now instead of a compiler error, you get the following output:

```
Constructing MyClass
Constructing Hello
Constructing Hello
Message: Hello World, again!
Message: Hello World!
```

Notice that the attributes are retrieved in a LIFO (last-in-first-out) manner. This is the way it is, but you should not depend on ordering for multiple attributes.

As part of the `AttributeUsage` attribute, you can specify where this attribute is valid. So far, all of the attributes have been placed on a class. If that is not the way you want your attribute to be used, then change `AttributeUsage` as follows:

```
[AttributeUsage(AttributeTargets.Class, AllowMultiple=true)]
```

Now if the user tries to apply the attribute to a field, the compiler generates an error message:

```
CustomAttributes.cs(41): Attribute 'Hello' is not valid on this declaration
➥type. It is valid on 'class' declarations only.
```

With attributes and reflection, the possibilities are limitless. Attributes are a truly groundbreaking feature.

Using Reflection to Serialize Types

One of the most prominent uses for reflection is serialization. Serialization is the process of turning an object into a stream of bytes that can be stored or transferred “elsewhere” and then used to reconstruct the object. You obviously cannot take an existing object and directly transfer it to another machine and expect it to work. Certain addresses and handles only correspond to memory on one machine or, for that matter, one process. In the past, MFC had a facility whereby an object could serialize and deserialize itself. The programmer decided which fields needed to be serialized through the code. Using reflection, it was possible to assist the programmer in serializing an object. The programmer no longer needed to depend on intimate knowledge of an object’s format to serialize it. In addition, if the object changed, it would automatically serialize in a correct manner without the need to change the code that references it.

Although an object can be serialized in many formats, the predominant format used for objects that are to be passed between disparate systems is XML. (Remoting opens the possibility of transferring data as a binary stream, which is much faster, but it is not very portable or compatible with other machines.) XML is the format that this chapter will primarily focus attention toward in discussing serialization.

The .NET Framework uses two types of serialization (binary serialization and SoapRpc serialization used with ASP.NET and Web applications have been excluded): one used for remoting and one used for “manual” serialization directly to XML. Although both of these serialization methods use XML as the underlying format, remoting uses a specific dialect of XML known as Simple Object Access Protocol (SOAP).

Serialization Used in Remoting

To demonstrate SOAP serialization that is used in remoting (refer to Chapter 13, “Remoting”), consider the following code in Listings 17.13–17.15. The full source for this sample is in `Serialization\Vehicle\VehicleSoap` and is part of the solution in `Serialization\Vehicle`.

LISTING 17.13 Building a Vehicle List

```
public class VehicleBuilder
{
    public Vehicle Vehicle(string licenseNumber)
    {
        if (licenseNumber == "0")
        {
            Vehicle v = new Car();
            v.licenseNumber = licenseNumber;
```

LISTING 17.13 Continued

```
                v.make = DateTime.Now;
                return v;
            }
            else if (licenseNumber == "1")
            {
                Vehicle v = new Bike();
                v.licenseNumber = licenseNumber;
                v.make = DateTime.Now;
                return v;
            }
            else
            {
                return null;
            }
        }
}
```

This is simply a utility class that allows you to easily build a vehicle based on the license number passed in ("0" is for a car, "1" is for a bike). Listing 17.14 shows the actual implementation of vehicle, car, and bike.

LISTING 17.14 Defining a Vehicle

```
[Serializable]
public abstract class Vehicle
{
    public string licenseNumber;
    public DateTime make;
}

[Serializable]
public class Car : Vehicle
{
}

[Serializable]
public class Bike : Vehicle
{
}
```

Notice that all that is needed to serialize the object is to indicate that the object is serializable with the **[Serializable]** attribute. Vehicle is abstract to show that the serialization services can deal with polymorphism. That is all you have to do. Listing 17.15 shows a possible test.

LISTING 17.15 Testing Serialization

```
public class VehicleSerializationTest
{
    public static int Main(string[] args)
    {
        VehicleBuilder vb = new VehicleBuilder();
        Vehicle [] va = new Vehicle[2];
        va[0] = vb.Vehicle("0");
        va[1] = vb.Vehicle("1");
        // Create an instance of the Soap Serializer class;
        // specify the type of object to serialize.
        Stream stream = File.Create("out.xml");
        SoapFormatter soap = new SoapFormatter();
        soap.Serialize(stream, va);
        stream.Close();
        stream = File.OpenRead("out.xml");
        va = (Vehicle [])soap.Deserialize(stream);
        stream.Close();
        Console.WriteLine("The first item is: {0}", va[0]);
        Console.WriteLine("The second item is: {0}", va[1]);
        return 0;
    }
}
```


The first task is to build up an array of `Vehicles`. Because of the license number passed in the first (va[0]), `Vehicle` is a `Car` and the second is a `Bike`. Next, you open up (Create) a file called `out.xml`. Using the **`SoapFormatter`** class, you serialize the `Vehicle` **`Array`** out to the file. It is not important, but it is interesting to look at what the format of the output file looks like:

```
<SOAP-ENV:Envelope xmlns:xsi="http://www.w3.org/2001/XMLSchema-instance"
➥xmlns:xsd="http://www.w3.org/2001/XMLSchema"
➥xmlns:SOAP-ENC="http://schemas.xmlsoap.org/soap/encoding/"
➥xmlns:SOAP-ENV="http://schemas.xmlsoap.org/soap/envelope/"
➥SOAP-ENV:encodingStyle="http://schemas.xmlsoap.org/soap/encoding/"
➥xmlns:a1="http://schemas.microsoft.com/clr
➥/nsassem/VehicleSerialization/VehicleSoap">
  <SOAP-ENV:Body>
    <SOAP-ENC:Array SOAP-ENC:arrayType="a1:Vehicle[2]">
        <item href="#ref-3"/>
        <item href="#ref-4"/>
    </SOAP-ENC:Array>
    <a1:Car id="ref-3">
        <licenseNumber id="ref-5">0</licenseNumber>
        <make>2001-08-21T17:46:22.1585-05:00</make>
    </a1:Car>
    <a1:Bike id="ref-4">
        <licenseNumber id="ref-6">1</licenseNumber>
        <make>2001-08-21T17:46:22.1585-05:00</make>
```

```
    </a1:Bike>
  </SOAP-ENV:Body>
</SOAP-ENV:Envelope>
```

From this file, you can see that it created a `Vehicle` array with two `Vehicles` in it (arrayType="a1:Vehicle[2]"). SOAP creates two items referring to "#ref-3" and "#ref-4." Notice that "#ref-3" refers to a `Car` and "#ref-4" refers to a `Bike` (id="ref-3" and id="ref-4" respectively).

Go back to the sample in Listing 17.15. After the `Vehicle` array is serialized, then the file is immediately opened again and **`SoapFormatter`** deserializes the contents of the file, producing the `Vehicle` array again. Finally, each item is printed to the Console to verify that it was properly deserialized. The output looks like this:

```
The first item is: VehicleSerialization.Car
The second item is: VehicleSerialization.Bike
```

You got back exactly what you put in.

The next example shows how the serializer can descend multiple levels of an object graph. Portions of the code will be shown in Listings 17.16 and 17.17. The full source for this sample is in `Serialization\Multilevel\MultilevelSoap` and is part of the solution in `Serialization\Multilevel`. You start out with a definition of the classes involved in Listing 17.16.

LISTING 17.16 A Family Organization

```
[Serializable]
public class Person
{
    public string name;
    public double age;
}

[Serializable]
public class Marriage
{
    public Person husband;
    public Person wife;
}

[Serializable]
public class Family
{
    public Marriage couple;
    public Person [] children;
}
```

As you can see, this organization nests one class in another. This will test to see if you can maintain this structure when serializing and deserializing. Listing 17.17 shows the test used to exercise this serialization.

LISTING 17.17 Building and Testing a Family Organization

```
public static int Main(string[] args)
{
    Person me = new Person();
    me.age = 43;
    me.name = "Kevin Burton";

    Person wife = new Person();
    wife.age = 50;
    wife.name = "Becky Burton";

    Marriage marriage = new Marriage();
    marriage.husband = me;
    marriage.wife = wife;

    Family family = new Family();
    family.couple = marriage;

    family.children = new Person[4];
    family.children[0] = new Person();
    family.children[0].age = 20;
    family.children[0].name = "Sarah";
    family.children[1] = new Person();
    family.children[1].age = 18;
    family.children[1].name = "Ann Marie";
    family.children[2] = new Person();
    family.children[2].age = 17;
    family.children[2].name = "Mike";
    family.children[3] = new Person();
    family.children[3].age = 13;
    family.children[3].name = "Rose";
    Stream stream = File.Create("out.xml");
    SoapFormatter soap = new SoapFormatter();
    soap.Serialize(stream, family);
    stream.Close();

    Console.WriteLine(family.couple.husband.name);
    Console.WriteLine(family.couple.wife.name);
    foreach(Person p in family.children)
    {
        Console.WriteLine(p.name);
    }

    Console.WriteLine("----------");
```

LISTING 17.17 Continued

```
    stream = File.OpenRead("out.xml");
    soap = new SoapFormatter();
    family = (Family)soap.Deserialize(stream);
    stream.Close();
       Console.WriteLine(family.couple.husband.name);
    Console.WriteLine(family.couple.wife.name);
    foreach(Person p in family.children)
    {
        Console.WriteLine(p.name);
    }

    return 0;
}
```

The serialized output looks like this:


```
SOAP-ENV:Envelope xmlns:xsi="http://www.w3.org/2001/XMLSchema-instance"
➥xmlns:xsd="http://www.w3.org/2001/XMLSchema"
➥xmlns:SOAP-ENC="http://schemas.xmlsoap.org/soap/encoding/"
➥xmlns:SOAP-ENV="http://schemas.xmlsoap.org/soap/envelope/"
➥SOAP-ENV:encodingStyle="http://schemas.xmlsoap.org/soap/encoding/"
➥xmlns:a1="http://schemas.microsoft.com/clr/nsassem/MultiLevel/
➥MultiLevelSoap">
<SOAP-ENV:Body>
  <a1:Family id="ref-1">
    <couple href="#ref-3"/>
    <children href="#ref-4"/>
  </a1:Family>
  <a1:Marriage id="ref-3">
    <husband href="#ref-5"/>
    <wife href="#ref-6"/>
  </a1:Marriage>
  <SOAP-ENC:Array id="ref-4" SOAP-ENC:arrayType="a1:Person[4]">
    <item href="#ref-7"/>
    <item href="#ref-8"/>
    <item href="#ref-9"/>
    <item href="#ref-10"/>
  </SOAP-ENC:Array>
  <a1:Person id="ref-5">
    <name id="ref-11">Kevin Burton</name>
    <age>43</age>
  </a1:Person>
  <a1:Person id="ref-6">
    <name id="ref-12">Becky Burton</name>
    <age>50</age>
  </a1:Person>
  <a1:Person id="ref-7">
    <name id="ref-13">Sarah</name>
    <age>20</age>
```

```
  </a1:Person>
  <a1:Person id="ref-8">
    <name id="ref-14">Ann Marie</name>
    <age>18</age>
  </a1:Person>
  <a1:Person id="ref-9">
    <name id="ref-15">Mike</name>
    <age>17</age>
  </a1:Person>
  <a1:Person id="ref-10">
    <name id="ref-16">Rose</name>
    <age>13</age>
  </a1:Person>
</SOAP-ENV:Body>
</SOAP-ENV:Envelope>
```


The output from the program looks like this:

```
Kevin Burton
Becky Burton
Sarah
Ann Marie
Mike
Rose
----------
Kevin Burton
Becky Burton
Sarah
Ann Marie
Mike
Rose
```

As was expected, what you put in is what you got out.

XML Serialization

To demonstrate XML serialization, or more precisely, serialization using **`System.Xml.Serialization`**, you will use the same classes that you used in the previous section. To start out, you will look at how the `Vehicle` class is serialized. Compare this implementation with the implementation described in Listings 17.13–17.15. Portions of the code will be shown in Listings 17.18–17.20. The full source to this sample is in `Serialization\Vehicle\VehicleXml` and is part of the solution in `Serialization\Vehicle`.

You will begin by generating a `Vehicle` array. No changes are required to the `VehicleBuilder` class, so for this sample, assume that you are using the same code as in Listing 17.13. Listing 17.18 shows how little is changed from the previous section.

LISTING 17.18 Vehicles Marked for Serialization

```
[XmlInclude(typeof(Car)), XmlInclude(typeof(Bike))]
public abstract class Vehicle
{
    public string licenseNumber;
    public DateTime make;
}

public class Car : Vehicle
{
}

public class Bike : Vehicle
{
}
```

If you did not want to serialize an abstract class, you could have just removed the `[Serializable]` attribute from the classes and that would be all that needed to be done. As it is, you need to add an `[XmlInclude]` attribute; otherwise, the **`XmlSerializer`** gets confused when trying to serialize a `Vehicle` array. Listing 17.19 shows the test program.

LISTING 17.19 Testing Vehicle Serialization with **`XmlSerializer`**

```
public static int Main(string[] args)
{
    VehicleBuilder vb = new VehicleBuilder();
    Vehicle [] va = new Vehicle[2];
    va[0] = vb.Vehicle("0");
    va[1] = vb.Vehicle("1");

    // Create an instance of the XmlSerializer class;
    // specify the type of object to serialize.
    XmlSerializer serializer =
        new XmlSerializer(typeof(Vehicle[]));
    StreamWriter streamWriter = new StreamWriter("out.xml");
    serializer.Serialize(streamWriter, va);
    streamWriter.Close();

    StreamReader streamReader = new StreamReader("out.xml");
    va = (Vehicle [])serializer.Deserialize(streamReader);
    streamReader.Close();

    Console.WriteLine("The first item is: {0}", va[0]);
    Console.WriteLine("The second item is: {0}", va[1]);

    return 0;
}
```

Just like before, you create a `Vehicle` array first. Then instead of using a **`SoapFormatter`**, you use **`XmlSerializer`**. The Vehicle array is serialized to "out.xml". This file now looks like this:

```
<?xml version="1.0" encoding="utf-8"?>
<ArrayOfVehicle xmlns:xsi="http://www.w3.org/2001/XMLSchema-instance"
➥xmlns:xsd="http://www.w3.org/2001/XMLSchema">
  <Vehicle xsi:type="Car">
    <licenseNumber>0</licenseNumber>
    <make>2001-08-21T22:04:59.2750080-05:00</make>
  </Vehicle>
  <Vehicle xsi:type="Bike">
    <licenseNumber>1</licenseNumber>
    <make>2001-08-21T22:04:59.2750080-05:00</make>
  </Vehicle>
</ArrayOfVehicle>
```

This is a little more readable than the SOAP version, but the same information is contained here. It has been said that programmatic types dominate serialization in **`System.Runtime.Serialization`**, which is used by remoting. In other words, the serialization scheme used for **`System.Runtime.Serialization`** is more centered in CLR types than in XML types if a conflict exists. With serialization using **`System.Xml.Serialization`**, the focus is more on XML types. A little of that bias can be seen in the requirement to use `[XmlInclude]` when serializing an abstract class. More importantly, using the attributes associated with **`System.Xml.Serialization`** gives the programmer a great deal of flexibility in mapping between CLR types and XML types.

This mapping is achieved by using an optional tool called the XML Schema Design Tool (xsd.exe). If the preceding vehicle class was put into a library (VehicleLibrary.dll), then you could run xsd.exe on the library like this:

```
xsd VehicleLibrary.dll
```

This would generate a file 'schema0.xsd' that looks like this:

```
<?xml version="1.0" encoding="utf-8"?>
<xs:schema elementFormDefault="qualified"
➥xmlns:xs="http://www.w3.org/2001/XMLSchema">
  <xs:element name="Vehicle" nillable="true" type="Vehicle" />
  <xs:complexType name="Vehicle" abstract="true">
    <xs:sequence>
      <xs:element minOccurs="0" maxOccurs="1" name="licenseNumber"
➥type="xs:string" />
      <xs:element minOccurs="1" maxOccurs="1" name="make"
➥type="xs:dateTime" />
    </xs:sequence>
  </xs:complexType>
```

```
  <xs:complexType name="Automobile">
    <xs:complexContent mixed="false">
      <xs:extension base="Vehicle" />
    </xs:complexContent>
  </xs:complexType>
  <xs:complexType name="Bicycle">
    <xs:complexContent mixed="false">
      <xs:extension base="Vehicle" />
    </xs:complexContent>
  </xs:complexType>
  <xs:element name="Car" nillable="true" type="Car" />
  <xs:element name="Bike" nillable="true" type="Bike" />
</xs:schema>
```

This schema can be used to validate the XML coming into the system and that was generated by **XmlSerializer**. Because the sample that is shown both generates the XML and generates the schema as well, it is difficult to show the significance.

Suppose that the XML document must have the tags "Car" and "Bike" changed to "Automobile" and "Bicycle." In that case, you would just need to modify the Vehicle class:

```
[XmlType("Automobile")]
public class Car : Vehicle
{
}

[XmlType("Bicycle")]
public class Bike : Vehicle
{
}
```

Now the XML that is generated by the XmlSerializer looks like this:

```
<?xml version="1.0" encoding="utf-8"?>
<ArrayOfVehicle xmlns:xsi="http://www.w3.org/2001/XMLSchema-instance"
➥xmlns:xsd="http://www.w3.org/2001/XMLSchema">
  <Vehicle xsi:type="Automobile">
    <licenseNumber>0</licenseNumber>
    <make>2001-08-21T23:04:57.6792592-05:00</make>
  </Vehicle>
  <Vehicle xsi:type="Bicycle">
    <licenseNumber>1</licenseNumber>
    <make>2001-08-21T23:04:57.6792592-05:00</make>
  </Vehicle>
</ArrayOfVehicle>
```

If the xsd.exe tool were run on the same library, it would generate the following:

```
<?xml version="1.0" encoding="utf-8"?>
<xs:schema elementFormDefault="qualified"
➥xmlns:xs="http://www.w3.org/2001/XMLSchema">
  <xs:element name="Vehicle" nillable="true" type="Vehicle" />
  <xs:complexType name="Vehicle" abstract="true">
    <xs:sequence>
      <xs:element minOccurs="0" maxOccurs="1" name="licenseNumber"
➥type="xs:string" />
      <xs:element minOccurs="1" maxOccurs="1" name="make"
➥type="xs:dateTime" />
    </xs:sequence>
  </xs:complexType>
  <xs:complexType name="Automobile">
    <xs:complexContent mixed="false">
      <xs:extension base="Vehicle" />
    </xs:complexContent>
  </xs:complexType>
  <xs:complexType name="Bicycle">
    <xs:complexContent mixed="false">
      <xs:extension base="Vehicle" />
    </xs:complexContent>
  </xs:complexType>
  <xs:element name="Automobile" nillable="true" type="Automobile" />
  <xs:element name="Bicycle" nillable="true" type="Bicycle" />
</xs:schema>
```

Now the schema will properly validate XML documents coming into the system, and you will generate proper XML documents. (If this requirement were imposed on you, it would be likely that the external source or destination of the document would already have a schema that you would use to generate classes.) Notice that the class names (in other words, the CLR types) have not changed. The other XML attributes allow for similar flexibility in mapping CLR types to XML types.

Late Binding to an Object Using Reflection

When the compiler encounters a reference when building an assembly, it loads the referenced assemblies and uses them to resolve all of the unresolved types. However, if you don't have the reference at compile time, you will not be able to call methods. You have just seen that with the classes in **System.Reflection**, you can dissect any assembly and find the methods and types in the assembly. It turns out that **System.Reflection** provides a means whereby a call can be made to a method in an assembly that is not known at compile time. This process is known as *late binding*.

It might be difficult to understand the usefulness of late binding at first, but some applications are not possible without a means of late binding. What if you wanted to provide feedback to third-party software? You don't know and don't want to know what the company will be doing with this feedback, but you want to provide a means whereby you can effectively notify them. You don't know ahead of time how many notifications you will have to set up. One solution would be to have a certain directory in which the third-party software would reside. You indicate to the developers of this third-party software that if they want to receive this notification, they will have to provide a function `OutputMessage` that takes as a single argument a string that contains the notification message. Now all you have to do is scan the directory and find out which of the software modules (probably DLLs) have an `OutputMessage` method defined and call the method. Using reflection, Listing 17.20 shows how this might be done with the .NET Framework. The complete source for this sample is in the `LateBinding` directory. Also included are two subprojects that build the required "first.dll" and "second.dll." If you need to use a directory other than the two directories supplied, or if you don't want to use debug mode, you will need to change the source so that it can locate the two DLLs.

LISTING 17.20 Late Binding Client

```
static void Main(string[] args)
{
    Assembly first = Assembly.LoadFrom(@"..\..\First\bin\debug\first.dll");
    Assembly second = Assembly.LoadFrom(@"..\..\Second\bin\debug\second.dll");
    Assembly [] assemblies = new Assembly[] { first, second };
    foreach(Assembly a in assemblies)
    {
        Type[] types = a.GetTypes();
        foreach(Type t in types)
        {
            try
            {
                object o = Activator.CreateInstance(t);
                MethodInfo m = t.GetMethod("OutputMessage");
                m.Invoke(o, new object [] {"This is my message"});
            }
            catch(Exception e)
            {
                Console.WriteLine(e);
            }
        }
    }
}
```

Notice that directory scanning code has not been included for clarity. An Assembly array is available that you can scan for the `OutputMessage` method. The key portion of the code is the three lines beginning with the **Activator.CreateInstance** call. The **Activator.CreateInstance** creates an instance of the type specified. Here that type will be the class containing the OutputMessage method. A search is performed for the OutputMessage method within the **Type**. The return for this scan is an instance of the **MethodInfo** class that corresponds to the OutputMessage method. The method is then called with a single string argument.

As you can imagine, late binding is pretty slow compared to compiled early bound code, but in some cases, the flexibility provided by late binding more than justifies the extra CPU cycles.

Dynamic Generation of Code

Up to this point, the reflection services have been used to read type information at runtime. It is also possible to have your code build code. Dynamically building and running code is used in a number of different places throughout the .NET Framework. Two such examples are the **Regex** (regular expression) class and the **XmlSerializer** class. The tools are available for you to generate your own code by using code.

This section first discusses a simple "Hello World!" sample in which a single function can generate code for all of the languages supported. This function builds a code tree and then hands the tree over to the code generation APIs. This section will then delve into a more real-world sample where you gain improvement over the brute force method of multiplying matrixes. Finally, this section will discuss Reflection.Emit and dynamically generating IL code.

Code Document Object Model (CodeDom)

The complete source for this sample is located in CodeCom\GenerateCode. The source that is presented here is shown in Listings 17.21–17.26.

LISTING 17.21 CodeProvider Initialization

```
public static void HelloWorldCode(CodeDomProvider provider, StreamWriter output)
{
    // Generate code
    ICodeGenerator cg = provider.CreateGenerator(output);
    CodeGeneratorOptions op = new CodeGeneratorOptions();
```

The function takes two generic arguments. The first is a **CodeDomProvider**, which is the base class for all **CodeDomProviders**. Currently, only two CodeDomProviders exist: one for VB (VBCodeProvider) and one for C# (CsharpCodeProvider). Eventually, many other languages will be supported. If you pass a `VBCodeProvider` to this method, then VB code will be generated. If you pass `CsharpCodeProvider`, then C# code will be generated. The output Stream argument is a generic Stream for the destination of the generated code. You will generate some comments and wrap a namespace around the code. The code listing continues with Listing 17.22.

LISTING 17.22 Comments and Namespace

```
// Generate the comments at the beginning of the function
CodeCommentStatement comment =
➥new CodeCommentStatement("Code to generate Hello World");
cg.GenerateCodeFromStatement(comment, output, op);
comment = new CodeCommentStatement("First generate the namespace.");
cg.GenerateCodeFromStatement(comment, output, op);

// The namespace
CodeNamespace codeNamespace = new CodeNamespace("HelloWorld");
// The namespace
CodeNamespaceImport import = new CodeNamespaceImport("System");
codeNamespace.Imports.Add(import);
```

Some comments are inserted at the beginning of the file, and a namespace is wrapped around the code. Notice that these classes are all generic in nature, making it easy to generate code in many different languages.

LISTING 17.23 Main Entry Point

```
// The class is named with a unique name
CodeTypeDeclaration mainClass = new CodeTypeDeclaration("HelloWorldMain");

// Add the class to the namespace
codeNamespace.Types.Add(mainClass);

// Set up the Main function
CodeEntryPointMethod main = new CodeEntryPointMethod();

CodeParameterDeclarationExpression param =
    new CodeParameterDeclarationExpression("System.String []", "args");

comment = new CodeCommentStatement("Output the greeting on the Console");
main.Statements.Add(comment);
```

This section of code generates an entry point for the generated code. In C#, this should look something like this: "`void Main(`*`strings[] args`*`)`". The listing continues with a variable declaration that will contain the message to be written. Next, you declare a variable to hold the message in Listing 17.24.

LISTING 17.24 Declare a Variable

```
CodeVariableDeclarationStatement variable =
➥new CodeVariableDeclarationStatement(typeof(string), "message",
➥new CodePrimitiveExpression("Hello World!"));
main.Statements.Add(variable);
```

A string variable called `message` is declared and initialized to "Hello World!". In Listing 17.25, you finish things up and generate the code.

LISTING 17.25 Call `Console.WriteLine` to Output a Message to the Console

```
CodeVariableReferenceExpression[] arg = new CodeVariableReferenceExpression[1];
arg[0] = new CodeVariableReferenceExpression(variable.Name);
CodeMethodReferenceExpression type = new CodeMethodReferenceExpression();
type.MethodName = "Console";
CodeMethodInvokeExpression methodCall =
➥new CodeMethodInvokeExpression(type,"WriteLine",arg);
main.Statements.Add(methodCall);

mainClass.Members.Add(main);

cg.GenerateCodeFromNamespace(codeNamespace, output, op);

}
```

Here, you pass the variable message to **`Console.WriteLine`**, effectively writing "Hello World!" to the Console. After this last bit of code is generated, the **`GenerateCodeFromNamespace`** method on **`ICodeGenerator`** interface is called to generate the code for the tree that you have just constructed.

The code that drives this function is in the Main entry point for the sample. Listing 17.26 shows a portion of this code.

LISTING 17.26 Generating Code and Executing the Code

```
static void Main(string[] args)
{
    CSharpCodeProvider csprovider = new CSharpCodeProvider();
    string filename = "HelloWorld";
    Stream s = File.Open(filename + ".cs", FileMode.Create);
    StreamWriter t = new StreamWriter(s);

    GenerateCode.HelloWorldCode(csprovider, t);
    t.Close();
    s.Close();
```

LISTING 17.26 Continued

```
    GenerateCode.CompileAndExecute(csprovider, filename + ".cs",
➥filename + "cs.exe ");

    VBCodeProvider vbprovider = new VBCodeProvider();
    s = File.Open(filename + ".vb", FileMode.Create);
    t = new StreamWriter(s);
    GenerateCode.HelloWorldCode(vbprovider, t);

    t.Close();
    s.Close();
    GenerateCode.CompileAndExecute(vbprovider, filename + ".vb",
➥filename + "vb.exe ");
}
```

This listing illustrates driving code generation for two different languages. As soon as the interface (**CodeProvider**) is available for other languages, this function could be extended. The methodology is similar in each section (CSharp and VB). First, a file is created that contains the source to be compiled. Next, the code is generated, and then the code is compiled and executed. Listings 17.27 and 17.28 show the code that is generated for this sample.

LISTING 17.27 C# Generated Code

```
// Code to generate Hello World! and "any" language
// First generate the namespace.
namespace HelloWorld {
    using System;


    public class HelloWorldMain {

        public static void Main() {
            // Output the greeting on the Console
            string message = "Hello World!";
            Console.WriteLine(message);
        }
    }
}
```

Listing 17.28 shows the VB code.

LISTING 17.28 VB-Generated Code

```
'Code to generate Hello World! and "any" language
'First generate the namespace.
Imports System
```

LISTING 17.28 Continued

```
Namespace HelloWorld

    Public Class HelloWorldMain

        Public Shared Sub Main()
            'Output the greeting on the Console
            Dim message As String = "Hello World!"
            Console.WriteLine(message)
        End Sub
    End Class
End Namespace
```


Except for syntax differences, the code looks the same. That is the point.

Compiling Code for Multiple Languages

Just as you can generate code for multiple languages, you can also compile code for all languages for which you have a specific implementation of the **CodeProvider** interface. Again, a short example will help you realize how to accomplish this. This sample will be illustrated in Listings 17.29–17.31. The full source for this sample is in the `CodeDom\HelloWorld` directory. Listing 17.29 shows the common code used to compile VB and C# code.

LISTING 17.29 Building a Generic Function to Compile and Run Code

```
public static void CompileAndRun(CodeDomProvider provider,
➥string source, string target)
{
    // Now use the CodeProvider interface
    CompilerParameters param = new CompilerParameters(null, target, true);
    param.GenerateExecutable = true;
    ICodeCompiler cc = provider.CreateCompiler();
    CompilerResults cr = cc.CompileAssemblyFromSource(param, source);
    System.Collections.Specialized.StringCollection output = cr.Output;
    foreach(string s in output)
    {
        Console.WriteLine(s);
    }

    if(cr.Errors.Count != 0)
    {
        CompilerErrorCollection es = cr.Errors;
        foreach(System.CodeDom.Compiler.CompilerError e in es)
        {
            Console.WriteLine(e.ToString());
        }
        }
```

Here you just build up the compiler parameters (in this case, just two). The first compiler parameter is the name of the file (assembly) to which to output the compiled results. The second compiled parameter is a flag indicating that you want a standalone executable as opposed to a library. Based on the passed in `CodeDomProvider`, you create an `ICodeCompiler` interface. This interface compiles the code and generates the errors if any exist. If errors are present, then you print them. If no errors are present, then you move on to the code in Listing 17.30.

LISTING 17.30 Running Generically Compiled Code

```
    else
    {
        // Set ApplicationBase to the current directory
        AppDomainSetup info = new AppDomainSetup();
        info.ApplicationBase = "file:\\\\" +
System.Environment.CurrentDirectory;
        // Create an application domain with null evidence
        AppDomain dom = AppDomain.CreateDomain("HelloWorld", null, info);
        dom.ExecuteAssembly(target);
        // Clean up by unloading the application domain
        AppDomain.Unload(dom);
    }
}
```

This is standard boilerplate code that creates an `AppDomain` and loads and runs the compiled code in that `AppDomain`. The driver for this routine simply generates the source and creates the `CodeDomProvider`. This is illustrated in Listing 17.31.

LISTING 17.31 Driver for Testing Various `CodeDom` Compilers

```
static void Main(string[] args)
{
    string target = "HelloWorld.exe ";
    string [] source = new string[1];
    source[0] =
@"using System;

namespace HelloWorld
{
    /// <summary>
    /// Summary description for HelloWorldMain.
    /// </summary>
    class HelloWorldMain
    {
        static void Main(string[] args)
        {
            Console.WriteLine(""Hello World!"");
```

LISTING 17.31 Continued

```
        }
    }
}";
    CSharpCodeProvider cscp = new CSharpCodeProvider();
    Compiler.CompileAndRun(cscp, source[0], target);

    source[0] =
@"Imports System
Namespace SimpleHelloWorld
    Public Class SimpleHelloWorld
        'Run the application
        Shared Sub Main()
            Console.WriteLine(""Hello World from VB!"")
        End Sub
    End Class
End Namespace

";
    VBCodeProvider vbscp = new VBCodeProvider();
    Compiler.CompileAndRun(vbscp, source[0], target);
}
```


This code initializes a string with the source to be compiled, creates a **CodeDomProvider**, and passes that information to the compiler code shown in Listings 17.29–17.31. The result looks like this:

```
Hello World!
Hello World from VB!
```

This is a convenient method for dynamically generating and compiling code in a generic fashion.

A specialized compiler is available only in the **Microsoft.CSharp** namespace that allows the user to compile multiple sources at a time. Instead of a single string containing the source, an array of strings is passed to the interface to be compiled. This is handy, but so far, only a C# version of it is available.

Matrix Multiplication

Now you will generate some code that actually does some work. The **Regex** class uses dynamically generated code to increase performance, and so does **XmlSerializer**. In the managed code world, a large body of code is being generated that uses templates to the extreme. The idea is that the compiler is used to help optimize the code. Why can't the same thing be done with managed code?

Eric Gunnerson presented a great example of how dynamically generated code can rival the performance of a custom solution with his polynomial evaluation code. Presented next is a matrix multiplication scheme that shows similar performance gains. The source for the code presented in Listings 17.32–17.35 is located in the `CodeDom\MatrixMultiplication` directory.

Just for reference, Listing 17.32 shows the brute force method of multiplying two matrixes.

LISTING 17.32 Brute Force Matrix Multiplication

```
public override double [,] Multiply()
{
    // Initialize the result array
    for(int i = 0; i < A.GetLength(0); i++)
        for(int j = 0; j < B.GetLength(1); j++)
            C[i,j] = 0.0;

    // Loop over the rows of A
    for(int i = 0; i < A.GetLength(0); i++)
        // Loop over the columns of A and rows of B
        for(int j = 0; j < A.GetLength(1); j++)
        {
            // Loop over the columns of B
            for(int k = 0; k < B.GetLength(1); k++)
                C[i,k] += A[i,j] * B[j,k];
        }
    return C;
}
```

The code for Listing 17.32 performs reasonably well. It will be used as a baseline for measuring how this multiplication can be improved. On my machine, Table 17.2 shows some performance numbers for multiplying two square N x N matrixes.

TABLE 17.2 Direct Matrix Multiplication

N	*Multiplications/Second*
10	3,200
20	450
50	30
100	4

These were respectable results. Now see if you can improve things with some dynamically generated code. You would mainly be focusing on unrolling the loops involved with matrix multiplication. You could apply other algorithms such as Strassen's divide and conquer algorithm, but to show the benefits of dynamic code generation, just focus on loop unrolling.

Listing 17.33 shows how to generate code at runtime to multiply two arrays. This listing builds on the information presented in the previous section on **CodeDom**.

LISTING 17.33 Matrix Multiplication Using Dynamic Code Generation

```
private void GenerateCode()
{
    string filename = "mmf";
    Stream s = File.Open(filename + ".cs", FileMode.Create);
    StreamWriter t = new StreamWriter(s);

    // Generate code in C#
    CSharpCodeProvider provider = new CSharpCodeProvider();
    ICodeGenerator cg = provider.CreateGenerator(t);
    CodeGeneratorOptions op = new CodeGeneratorOptions();

    // Generate the comments at the beginning of the function
    CodeCommentStatement comment =
➥new CodeCommentStatement("Matrix Multiplication (Fixed)");
    cg.GenerateCodeFromStatement(comment, t, op);

    // The class is named with a unique name
    string className = "__MatrixMultiplyFixed";
    CodeTypeDeclaration matrixClass = new CodeTypeDeclaration(className);
    // The class implements IPolynomial
    matrixClass.BaseTypes.Add("MatrixMultiplication.IMatrixMultiply");

    // Set up the Multiply function
    CodeMemberMethod multiplyMethod = new CodeMemberMethod();
    multiplyMethod.Name = "Multiply";
    multiplyMethod.Parameters.Add(
➥new CodeParameterDeclarationExpression("double [,]", "A"));
    multiplyMethod.Parameters.Add(
➥new CodeParameterDeclarationExpression("double [,]", "B"));
    multiplyMethod.Parameters.Add(
➥new CodeParameterDeclarationExpression("double [,]", "C"));
    // workaround for bug below...
    multiplyMethod.ReturnType = new CodeTypeReference("public void");
    // BUG: This doesn't generate "public"; it just leaves
    // the attribute off of the member...
    multiplyMethod.Attributes |= MemberAttributes.Public;
    StringBuilder str = new StringBuilder();

    str.Append("{");
    // Loop over the rows of A
    for(int i = 0; i < A.GetLength(0); i++)
```

LISTING 17.33 Continued

```
    {
        // Loop over the columns of A and rows of B
        for(int j = 0; j < A.GetLength(1); j++)
        {
            // Loop over the columns of B
            for(int k = 0; k < B.GetLength(1); k++)
                C[i,k] += A[i,j] * B[j,k];
        }
        str.Append("{");
        for(int j = 0; j < B.GetLength(1); j++)
        {
            if(j < A.GetLength(0) - 1)
                str.Append(string.Format("{0},\r\n",C[i,j]));
            else
                str.Append(string.Format("{0}",C[i,j]));
        }
        if(i < A.GetLength(0) - 1)
            str.Append("},\r\n");
        else
            str.Append("}");
    }
    str.Append("}");
    CodeSnippetTypeMember variable = new CodeSnippetTypeMember(
➥string.Format(
➥"static readonly double [,] result = new double[{0},{1}]\r\n{2};",
➥A.GetLength(0), B.GetLength(1), str.ToString()));
    matrixClass.Members.Add(variable);

    CodeAssignStatement assignment = new CodeAssignStatement();
    assignment.Left = new CodeVariableReferenceExpression("C");
    assignment.Right = new CodeVariableReferenceExpression("result");
    multiplyMethod.Statements.Add(assignment);

    matrixClass.Members.Add(multiplyMethod);
    cg.GenerateCodeFromType(matrixClass, t, op);

    t.Close();
    s.Close();

    // Now use the CodeProvider interface
    CSharpCodeProvider cscp = new CSharpCodeProvider();
    CompilerParameters param = new CompilerParameters(null, null, true);
    param.GenerateInMemory = true;
    param.IncludeDebugInformation = false;
    param.CompilerOptions = "/optimize+";
    param.ReferencedAssemblies.Add("MatrixMultiplication.exe ");
    ICodeCompiler cc = cscp.CreateCompiler();
```

LISTING 17.33 Continued

```
    CompilerResults cr = cc.CompileAssemblyFromFile(param, filename + ".cs");
    System.Collections.Specialized.StringCollection output = cr.Output;
    foreach(string outputSting in output)
    {
        Console.WriteLine(outputSting);
    }

    if(cr.Errors.Count != 0)
    {
        CompilerErrorCollection es = cr.Errors;
        foreach(System.CodeDom.Compiler.CompilerError e in es)
        {
            Console.WriteLine(e.ToString());
        }
    }
    else
    {
        matrixMultiplyInterface =
➥(IMatrixMultiply)cr.CompiledAssembly.CreateInstance(className);
    }
}
```


This code is not unlike the simple code that generated the "Hello World" message in Listings 17.21–17.26. Now see how it performs. The performance numbers have been compiled in Table 17.3.

TABLE 17.3 Fixed Matrix Multiplication

N	*Multiplications/Second*
10	10,876,658
20	10,794,473
50	10,976,948
100	10,638,297

Wow! The results seem to be independent of the size of the array. And talk about fast! As you suspected, this is too good to be true. Essentially, the two matrixes were multiplied and the results were statically recorded. Now whenever a user asks to multiply those two matrixes, you can just return the static result array. The code that is generated looks like that in Listing 17.34.

LISTING 17.34 Fixed Matrix Multiplication-Generated Code

```
public class __MatrixMultiplyFixed : MatrixMultiplication.IMatrixMultiply {

    static readonly double [,] result = new double[10,10]
{{1.88956889330368,
1.30658585741975,
1.31508360075735,
. . .
1.43246374777113,
1.80918436134982,
1.19113607833798}};
    public void Multiply(double [,] A, double [,] B, double [,] C) {
        C = result;
    }
}
```

If you have a computationally intense function or expression to evaluate, and you only need to evaluate it once and use the results many times, this might be one method to employ. You can achieve the same result with a global static variable and possibly a flag, but this is just another means to an end.

Listing 17.35 shows the code to dynamically generate code to multiply two matrixes, unrolling the loop to increase performance.

LISTING 17.35 Matrix Multiplication Unrolling Loops at Runtime

```
private void GenerateCode()
{
    string filename = "mml";
    Stream s = File.Open(filename + ".cs", FileMode.Create);
    StreamWriter t = new StreamWriter(s);

    // Generate code in C#
    CSharpCodeProvider provider = new CSharpCodeProvider();
    ICodeGenerator cg = provider.CreateGenerator(t);
    CodeGeneratorOptions op = new CodeGeneratorOptions();

    // Generate the comments at the beginning of the function
    CodeCommentStatement comment = new CodeCommentStatement(
➥"Matrix Multiplication (Loop)");
    cg.GenerateCodeFromStatement(comment, t, op);

    // The class is named with a unique name
    string className = "__MatrixMultiplyLoop";
    CodeTypeDeclaration matrixClass = new CodeTypeDeclaration(className);
    // The class implements IPolynomial
    matrixClass.BaseTypes.Add("MatrixMultiplication.IMatrixMultiply");
```

LISTING 17.35 Continued

```
    // Set up the Multiply function
    CodeMemberMethod multiplyHelperMethod = new CodeMemberMethod();
    multiplyHelperMethod.Name = "_Multiply";
    multiplyHelperMethod.Parameters.Add(
➥new CodeParameterDeclarationExpression(typeof(double [,]), "A"));
    multiplyHelperMethod.Parameters.Add(
➥new CodeParameterDeclarationExpression(typeof(double [,]), "B"));
    multiplyHelperMethod.Parameters.Add(
➥new CodeParameterDeclarationExpression(typeof(int), "i"));
    multiplyHelperMethod.Parameters.Add(
➥new CodeParameterDeclarationExpression(typeof(int), "j"));
    multiplyHelperMethod.ReturnType = new CodeTypeReference(typeof(double));
    {
        CodeBinaryOperatorExpression plus;
        CodeBinaryOperatorExpression lastplus;
        plus = new CodeBinaryOperatorExpression();
        plus.Operator = CodeBinaryOperatorType.Add;
        CodeMethodReturnStatement returnStatement =
➥new CodeMethodReturnStatement(plus);
        CodeBinaryOperatorExpression multiply;
        multiply = new CodeBinaryOperatorExpression();
        multiply.Operator = CodeBinaryOperatorType.Multiply;
        multiply.Right = new CodeSnippetExpression("A[i,0]");
        multiply.Left = new CodeSnippetExpression("B[0,j]");
        plus.Left = multiply;
        lastplus = plus;
        for(int k = 1; k < A.GetLength(1); k++)
        {
            multiply = new CodeBinaryOperatorExpression();
            multiply.Operator = CodeBinaryOperatorType.Multiply;
            multiply.Right = new CodeSnippetExpression(
➥string.Format("A[i,{0}]",k));
            multiply.Left = new CodeSnippetExpression(
➥string.Format("B[{0},j]",k));
            if(k < A.GetLength(1) - 1)
            {
                plus = new CodeBinaryOperatorExpression();
                plus.Operator = CodeBinaryOperatorType.Add;
                lastplus.Right = plus;
                plus.Left = multiply;
            }
            else
            {
                lastplus.Right = multiply;
            }
            lastplus = plus;
        }
        multiplyHelperMethod.Statements.Add(returnStatement);
    }
    matrixClass.Members.Add(multiplyHelperMethod);
```

LISTING 17.35 Continued

```
    // Set up the Multiply function
    CodeMemberMethod multiplyMethod = new CodeMemberMethod();
    multiplyMethod.Name = "Multiply";
    multiplyMethod.Parameters.Add(
➥new CodeParameterDeclarationExpression(typeof(double [,]), "A"));
    multiplyMethod.Parameters.Add(
➥new CodeParameterDeclarationExpression(typeof(double [,]), "B"));
    multiplyMethod.Parameters.Add(
➥new CodeParameterDeclarationExpression(typeof(double [,]), "C"));
    // workaround for bug below...
    multiplyMethod.ReturnType = new CodeTypeReference("public void");
    // BUG: This doesn't generate "public"; it just leaves
    // the attribute off of the member...
    multiplyMethod.Attributes |= MemberAttributes.Public;
    // Loop over the rows of A
    for(int i = 0; i < A.GetLength(0); i++)
    {
        // Loop over the columns of B
        for(int j = 0; j < B.GetLength(1); j++)
        {
            CodeAssignStatement assignment = new CodeAssignStatement();
            assignment.Left = new CodeArrayIndexerExpression(
                              new CodeVariableReferenceExpression("C"),
                    new CodePrimitiveExpression(i),
                              new CodePrimitiveExpression(j));
            assignment.Right = new CodeMethodInvokeExpression(
                              null,
                              "Multiply",
                              new CodeVariableReferenceExpression("A"),
                new CodeVariableReferenceExpression("B"),
                new CodePrimitiveExpression(i),
                              new CodePrimitiveExpression(j));
            multiplyMethod.Statements.Add(assignment);
        }
    }

    matrixClass.Members.Add(multiplyMethod);
    cg.GenerateCodeFromType(matrixClass, t, op);

    t.Close();
    s.Close();

    string target = "mml.dll";
    // Now use the CodeProvider interface
    CSharpCodeProvider cscp = new CSharpCodeProvider();
    CompilerParameters param = new CompilerParameters(null, null, true);
    param.GenerateInMemory = true;
    param.IncludeDebugInformation = false;
    param.CompilerOptions = "/optimize+";
```

LISTING 17.35 Continued

```
    param.ReferencedAssemblies.Add("MatrixMultiplication.exe ");
    ICodeCompiler cc = cscp.CreateCompiler();
    CompilerResults cr = cc.CompileAssemblyFromFile(param, filename + ".cs");
    System.Collections.Specialized.StringCollection output = cr.Output;
    foreach(string outputSting in output)
    {
        Console.WriteLine(outputSting);
    }
    if(cr.Errors.Count != 0)
    {
        CompilerErrorCollection es = cr.Errors;
        foreach(System.CodeDom.Compiler.CompilerError e in es)
        {
            Console.WriteLine(e.ToString());
        }
    }
    else
    {
        matrixMultiplyInterface =
➥(IMatrixMultiply)cr.CompiledAssembly.CreateInstance(className);
    }
}
```

This code still uses **CodeDom** to build the matrix multiplication code, but the code generation has been fixed so that the matrix multiplication occurs with every matrix. This code truly unrolls the loops when doing a matrix multiplication.

A sample of the code that this code generates is shown in Listing 17.36.

LISTING 17.36 Matrix Multiplication with Unrolled Loops

```
// Matrix Multiplication (Loop)
public class __MatrixMultiplyLoop : MatrixMultiplication.IMatrixMultiply {

    private System.Double _Multiply(System.Double[,] A, System.Double[,] B,
➥int i, int j) {
        return ((B[0,j] * A[i,0])
                    + ((B[1,j] * A[i,1])
                    + ((B[2,j] * A[i,2])
                    + ((B[3,j] * A[i,3])
                    + ((B[4,j] * A[i,4])
                    + ((B[5,j] * A[i,5])
                    + ((B[6,j] * A[i,6])
                    + ((B[7,j] * A[i,7])
                    + ((B[8,j] * A[i,8])
                    + (B[9,j] * A[i,9]))))))))));
    }
```

LISTING 17.36 Continued

```
    public void Multiply(System.Double[,] A, System.Double[,] B,
➥System.Double[,] C) {
        C[0, 0] = _Multiply(A, B, 0, 0);
        C[0, 1] = _Multiply(A, B, 0, 1);
        C[0, 2] = _Multiply(A, B, 0, 2);
. . .
        C[9, 7] = _Multiply(A, B, 9, 7);
        C[9, 8] = _Multiply(A, B, 9, 8);
        C[9, 9] = _Multiply(A, B, 9, 9);
    }
}
```

Table 17.4 shows the performance of this dynamically generated code.

TABLE 17.4 Matrix Multiplication With Unrolled Loops

N	*Multiplications/Second*
10	8,260
20	1,080
50	67
100	5

Comparing these results with Table 17.2, you can see that until you get to multiplying two 100 × 100 matrixes, unrolling the loops seems to increase performance about two fold.

Note

In putting these samples together, I ran into some obstacles that under normal circumstances would only occur because the code was being generated by code.

For instance, one problem I ran into was that the line lengths became too long as I generated code. The C# compiler limits the line length to 2,046 characters. I would not normally type 2,046 characters on a line, so this case would most likely occur only with code generating code. This is a line-length limit, not a statement length limit. I can break the 2,046 characters into two lines (not two statements) to make the compiler happy again.

Another problem that I ran into was that when generating the last sample that unrolled the loops, I initially put all of the code into one method. When I got to run the 100 × 100 matrix multiplication test, I noticed that the code file that was generated was tens of megabytes in size, and it exhausted my machine's virtual memory to compile it. In addition, even when multiplying smaller arrays, the dynamically generated code ran almost twice as slow as the brute force method.

I wanted to see why the generated code was so big. Multiplying two 100 × 100 matrixes with the loops unrolled would have 10,000 statements each with 100 multiplication terms in it. I had to think of a better way.

My solution was to create a helper function that performed the multiplication for each term. I still had 10,000 statements, but each statement called a function. That function had 100 multiplication terms in it. This reduced the size of the code generated for a 100 × 100 multiplication to about 450Kb and increased performance as well.

The moral of the story is that the CLR is not friendly toward large methods. Even though I had the extra overhead of calling a function, it dramatically increased the performance of the overall function.

Dynamically generating code, although somewhat difficult to work with, is a valid way to increase the performance of certain classes of functions.

Without reflection, it would not be possible to generate and run code as was done in the previous examples. Reflection can be used to examine and to generate type information at runtime.

Directly Generating IL (`Reflect.Emit`)

The idea behind **`Reflect.Emit`** is much the same as with the `CodeDom` model. With **`Reflection.Emit`**, you are just generating code at a much lower level code (IL) than with the **`CodeDom`**. A simple Hello World sample is included in Listing 17.37. The full source is in the `Emit` directory.

LISTING 17.37 Using `Reflection.Emit` to Generate a Hello World Program

```
static Type GenerateCode()
{
    AppDomain currentDomain = AppDomain.CurrentDomain;

    // Create new assembly in the current AppDomain
    AssemblyName assemblyName = new AssemblyName();
    assemblyName.Name = "HelloAssembly";
    // Create AssemblyBuilder
    AssemblyBuilder assemblyBuilder = currentDomain.DefineDynamicAssembly(
➥assemblyName, AssemblyBuilderAccess.Run);
```

LISTING 17.37 Continued

```
    // Create ModuleBuilder
    ModuleBuilder moduleBuilder =
➥assemblyBuilder.DefineDynamicModule("HelloModule");
    // Create TypeBuilder
    TypeBuilder typeBuilder =
➥moduleBuilder.DefineType("HelloClass", TypeAttributes.Public);
    // Create MethodBuilder
    MethodBuilder methodBuilder = typeBuilder.DefineMethod("HelloWorld",
➥MethodAttributes.Public, null, null);
    // Create MSIL generator
    ILGenerator msil = methodBuilder.GetILGenerator();
    // Generate code
    msil.EmitWriteLine("Hello World!");
    msil.Emit(OpCodes.Ret);
    // Return created type
    return typeBuilder.CreateType();
}
static void Main(string[] args)
{
    try
    {
        Type t = GenerateCode();
        object o = Activator.CreateInstance(t);
        MethodInfo mi = t.GetMethod("HelloWorld");
        Console.WriteLine(mi.Invoke(o, null));
    }
    catch(Exception e)
    {
        Console.WriteLine(e);
    }
}
```

The code creates an Assembly called `HelloAssembly` in the current **`AppDomain`**. Notice that a culture, version, or signing information is not assigned to this **`Assembly`** that would make the **`AssemblyName`** a "full" **`AssemblyName`**. An **`AssemblyBuilder`** is created with an access permission of Run. The other possibilities are `RunAndSave` and `Save`. The **`AssemblyBuilder`** is used to create a **`ModuleBuilder`**, the **`ModuleBuilder`** is used to create a **`TypeBuilder`**, and the **`TypeBuilder`** is used to create a **`MethodBuilder`**. **`MethodBuilder`** can create **`ILGenerator`**. With the **`ILGenerator`**, you can emit IL code. For this sample, you just emit enough code to return "Hello World!" from the "HelloWorld" method. After all of the IL code is emitted, a **`Type`** can be created and returned. With this **`Type`**, you can do a late-bound call on the "HelloWorld" method and print the string that is returned.

Reflection.Emit obviously has enormous possibilities for dynamically generating code. It is potentially easier to use than `CodeDom` and has less overhead. Of course, you need to know IL, which might make it harder to use this class. The RegEx and Jscript libraries are built upon **Reflection.Emit** to boost performance much the same as with the matrix multiplication sample that was illustrated, with the added bonus that using **Reflection.Emit** has lower overhead.

Summary

Reflection is a good way to browse for information about any particular piece of code. This chapter showed examples of how virtually anything about the code can be discovered through reflection. It looked at attributes and how they can be used and customized to extend and enhance any application. This chapter also discussed late-binding and how it is implemented under .NET and some possible applications for late-binding. It examined one of the key consumers of the reflection services: serialization. The two types of serialization that are used by the .NET Framework and implemented by the CLR were explored. Finally, this chapter discussed some methods of dynamically generating code by having code generate code. Without reflection, the CLR would be crippled indeed.

Summary

CHAPTER 18

Globalization/ Localization

IN THIS CHAPTER

A recent Aberdeen study (go to `http://www.info-edge.com/product_detail.asp?sku1=17026&` or `http://www.aberdeen.com/ab_company/hottopics/web_globalization/`) indicated that by 2003, more than 60% of all Internet users will be from outside North America. Many U.S. companies today derive more than half of their revenue from international sales. For most software providers, international sales are the foremost vehicle for future sales growth. In addition, with the advent of the Internet and in general global communication, it is increasingly becoming "expected" that software "talk" in a native language. Although English-only software was tolerated in the past, it will not be so in the future.

This chapter looks at the various tools and facilities that are provided in the .NET Framework to build an international application. The CLR lies at the heart of all of these services.

International Application Basics

The .NET Framework provides extensive support for building international applications. Building an international application requires that the developer extract all of the aspects of the application that are specific to cultural conventions. Examples of culture-dependent information include language, number formatting, currency formatting, date and time formatting, and reading order (right-to-left, left-to-right). The code that is being developed should make no assumptions of a particular locale or cultural convention. Listing 18.1 looks at how *not* to develop an international application. The code for this localized application is available in the `NotLocalizable` directory.

LISTING 18.1 A Provincial Application

```
string [] lines = new string[4];

lines[0] = "Hello.";
DateTime now = DateTime.Now;
lines[1] = "How are you?";
lines[2] = string.Format("{0}/{1}/{2}", now.Month, now.Day, now.Year);
lines[3] = "Goodbye.";

textBox.Lines = lines;
```

Your marketing department thinks so highly of this code that they have sold it into French, German, Chinese, and Japanese markets. The problem is that an implicit assumption has been made about the character set. As it turns out in the .NET Framework, a **`string`** is internally represented with the Unicode character set, so it is not such a problem. However, the programmer who is developing this code implicitly assumed an ASCII character set. Undoubtedly, he has made more serious assumptions about the character set elsewhere in the code where the conversion is not so automatic. Another problem is that all of these phrases must be translated into the appropriate language. The translator is not a programmer, and he would not understand what needs to be translated by reading the code. This is a problem. You would have to work one on one with the translator to identify where the strings are that you want to translate. The second problem is that now you immediately don't have just one application—you have four. Each application would have its own source and would need to be compiled and maintained separately. Finally, all of these languages have different conventions with regard to formatting the date. Few translators will be able to read the code and understand that you have formatted a date, and be able to make suggestions on how it best could be done. As it stands, the application looks like Figure 18.1.

FIGURE 18.1
Output of a provincial application.

From this simple sample, you can see which portions of the application are specific to a given locale. This application is not localizable because the cultural conventions and language have not been separated from the application. This application has not been internationalized.

It is best to tackle the immediate problem of language translation first because you know how to handle that. For example, Table 18.1 illustrates translations of some simple phrases from English to French, German, Japanese, and Chinese. The English phrase is in the left column and the translated phrase is in the right one.

TABLE 18.1 English Phrase Translations

English Phrase	*Translation*
	French
Hello.	`Bonjour.`
Goodbye.	`Au revoir, Adeiu.`

TABLE 18.1 Continued

English Phrase	*Translation*
How are you?	Comment allez-vous? Ça va?
	German
Hello.	Guten Tag.
Goodbye.	Auf Wiedersehen.
How are you?	Wie geht's?
	Japanese
Hello.	今日は
Goodbye.	さよなら
How are you?	お元気ですか？
	Chinese
Hello.	你好
Goodbye.	再见
How are you?	你好吗?

Now that the phrases are translated, you need a mechanism whereby you can put this information into a file and have the application read the translated string. Doing this is the subject of this chapter, but as a teaser, Listing 18.2 shows some of what the code might look like in a truly localized application. The code for this localized application is available in the `LocalizedApplication` directory.

LISTING 18.2 A Localized Application

```
ResourceManager rm = new ResourceManager("LocalizedApplication.Strings",
➥ Assembly.GetExecutingAssembly());

// Default
lines[0] = "---- Default ----";
```

LISTING 18.2 Continued

```
lines[1] = rm.GetString("hello");
lines[2] = rm.GetString("greeting");
lines[3] = now.ToLongDateString();
lines[4] = rm.GetString("goodbye");
. . .
Thread.CurrentThread.CurrentCulture = new CultureInfo("zh-CN");
Thread.CurrentThread.CurrentUICulture = Thread.CurrentThread.CurrentCulture;
// Chinese
lines[20] = "---- Chinese ----";
lines[21] = rm.GetString("hello");
lines[22] = rm.GetString("greeting");
lines[23] = now.ToLongDateString();
lines[24] = rm.GetString("goodbye");
```

Now the application can easily display any or all of the languages. Notice that all of the strings are retrieved with the same code, and the date string is formatted using the same method call. These lines of code could easily be put into a method or function, making the program easy to maintain and understand. The output looks like Figure 18.2.

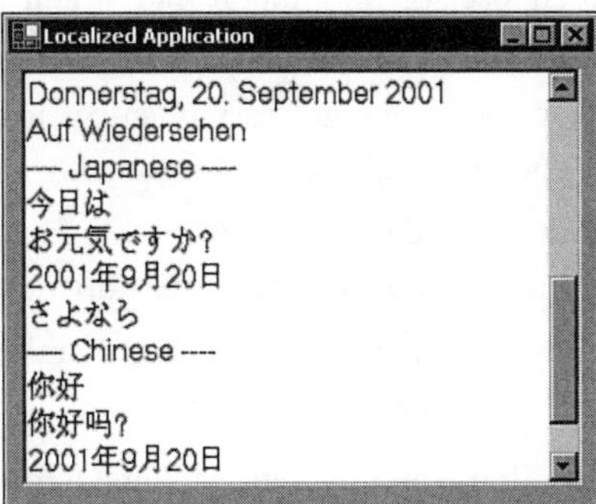

FIGURE 18.2
Output of a localized application.

This has been a simple sample of the process of localizing an application. As you can imagine, as the application grows larger, this process is that much harder. Make all but the simplest applications localizable. Extract the cultural conventions and language-dependent strings from the code early. Retrofitting internationalization is hard at best and nearly impossible at worst.

Now that you have an idea of what is involved in building an international application, this chapter will look at some of the details and tools that are available from the CLR and the .NET Framework to aid in this process.

The Road to an International Application

Building an international application, although not that difficult, does take some forethought and planning, but the payoff can be enormous. Following are some of the reasons why you would want to go to the extra trouble it takes to build an international application:

- For many companies, more than half of current profits are generated in international markets.
- Even the users of the English version of the software might have second thoughts about using the software if it has not embraced other languages and cultures. Internationalizing an application has a way of giving a certain amount of credibility to the software. Code is often better designed and better made if it adheres to a framework that demands localizability.
- Because of fierce competition, more international users have a choice. All other things being equal, users will choose software that respects their local customs and language.
- The European Common Market will have regulatory practices in place to make sure that software adapts to a country's culture and language.
- After the initial framework is in place, the actual cost of internationalizing an application is minor when considered over the life of the software.
- Communicating in a native language and adopting local cultural conventions is fundamental to building respect and trust that is key to success in today's market.

Now that you know the reasons for building an international application, how should you go about doing so? Remember that internationalization is the process of extracting all cultural/regional conventions and language dependencies from the software. An application can become internationalized to a certain degree:

- The absolute bare minimum requirement for an application to be considered internationalized is the removal of any character-set and cultural dependencies (such as date and number format). Because the default character set of a string within the .NET Framework is 16-bit Unicode, most applications meet this requirement out of the box. It is possible to add code as was done in Listing 18.1 (the date format in this sample is hard-coded for a U.S. style date), but it does take a certain amount of effort to break the rules.

- At the next level, all user-visible strings are moved out of the software and into a language and country-dependent resource file. Java calls these `ResourceBundles`. The Visual Studio 6 environment built binary resource files that ended in a .res suffix from .rc source files. The .NET Framework binary resource is named with a .resources suffix, and it is created either from an XML .resx file or a .txt file that contains key/value pairs to be entered into a string table.
- At the third level, an application can decide to support non-Western languages such as Chinese, Japanese, and Korean. This requires a commitment up front to either Unicode or multibyte character encoding. This level of internationalization increases the storage cost of string-related data because now all character data requires more than one character to represent and store the data. Additional time is required to develop such an application because further consideration must be given to sorting, indexing, and manipulating the string data. Some languages such as Thai require special algorithms to even break a sentence into words.

  In addition, some non-Western languages, such as Arabic, have an added complexity in that they read from right-to-left. This requirement can be difficult for a programmer who is not used to this convention.
- The highest degree at which an application can be internationalized is for the application to support many different character encodings at once. This would mean that an application could display Chinese and English at the same time. Internationalization would mean that provision should be provided so that an application can support multiple encodings at a time.

As will be seen further in this chapter, the .NET Framework and the CLR supply support for all of these degrees of internationalization. After the application is internationalized, it needs to be localized to be a true international application.

When localizing an application, the following must be taken into account:

- Time can be represented as a 24-hour clock or a 12-hour clock. Separators can be either the common colon or a single period. (Italy uses the period convention).
- A date can be represented in many different ways. You can use different separators, different orders, different abbreviations for months, and even different calendars. For instance, in the Thai Buddhist calendar, the year 2001 is the year 2544. The Hijri calendar, used in many Arabic-speaking countries, has 12 months in a year, but each month is not the same length as in the Gregorian calendar. In addition, the Hijri calendar recognizes one era A.H. (referencing Mohammed's migration from Mecca), so 2001 becomes 1422.

- Number formatting also has several different conventions. Some cultures have a convention that uses a period instead of a comma to separate the thousands (1000000 becomes 1.000.000,00). Negative numbers can also be represented in many different ways.
- Every country has a different currency symbol.
- Word order varies between countries.
- Some languages do not have a word separator character.
- Collation sequences differ from country to country.
- Oriental languages do not have capitalization. Rules for capitalization differ from country to country.
- The rules of hyphenations (including what to hyphenate and where) can differ from country to country.
- Spelling, grammar, and punctuation can vary from language to language.
- Particular care must be taken when phrases are combined to form messages. Make sure that the combination is grammatically and culturally correct. One area where this would occur would be in the building of an error message.
- Translation of phrases can rarely be done literally.

In all but the simplest of localization projects, it is recommended that a known, trusted professional translator be used to assist in the localization. This is especially true if you are not comfortable with the language and the culture/region that you are trying to address.

To extract the cultural dependencies, you need an object or class to encapsulate those cultural dependencies. The CLR and the .NET Framework use the `CultureInfo` class for this purpose.

Using the `CultureInfo` Class

As the name implies, the `CultureInfo` class holds culture-specific information such as language, regional dialect, country/region, calendar, and cultural conventions. `CultureInfo` encapsulates information that is required by culture-specific operations such as sorting, string comparison, character type information, and date and number formatting. This class extends and encapsulates a "locale" that was used to describe languages and cultures with VBScript, C++, and VB.

A specific `CultureInfo` object is completely described by a string that is of the format <languagecode>-<country>. The details of the format of this string are based on RFC 1766.

Note

RFC 1766 specifies the culture string to be of the following form:

<languagecode>-<country/regioncode>

<languagecode> is a lowercase two-letter code derived from ISO 639-1, and <country/regioncode> is an uppercase two-letter code derived from ISO 3166. For example, English is `en`, Spanish is `es`, German is `de`, and Chinese is `zh` for the <languagecode>.

One source for RFC 1766 is `http://www.faqs.org/rfcs/rfc1766.html`.

RFC 1766 has been copied and made available many other places besides the preceding URL. This document references ISO 639 and ISO 3166. The essence for ISO 639 can be obtained at `http://www.oasis-open.org/cover/iso639a.html`.

ISO 639 lists the language codes for each of the recognized languages. The official copy of the document is at `http://www.iso.ch/iso/en/CatalogueDetailPage.CatalogueDetail?CSNUMBER=4766`, but it must be purchased. The ISO 3166 lists country codes. One source for these country codes is at `http://www.unicode.org/unicode/onlinedat/countries.html`.

A neutral culture is associated with a language but not a specific country. Therefore, `en` would specify English, but not a specific country. A complete specification `en-US` would specify English in the United States, `en-GB` would be English in Great Britain, and `en-CA` would be English in Canada.

An invariant culture is a culture that is associated with a language but not with any particular country. Anywhere a culture is required, the invariant culture can be used except for sorting. An invariant culture should be used only for processes that produce or consume culture-independent results, such as system services.

The CLR relies on operating system support for various cultures. The support for the culture and language must be installed for support to be available. This support is not intrinsic to the CLR or the .NET Framework, and it is not installed by default when your operating system is installed. Under Windows 2000, Control Panel → Regional Options → General tab, you will see language settings, as shown in Figure 18.3.

If you have checked support for all languages and then run the code in Listing 18.3, you can see the languages and cultures for which you have support. The complete source for this application is in the `CultureList` directory.

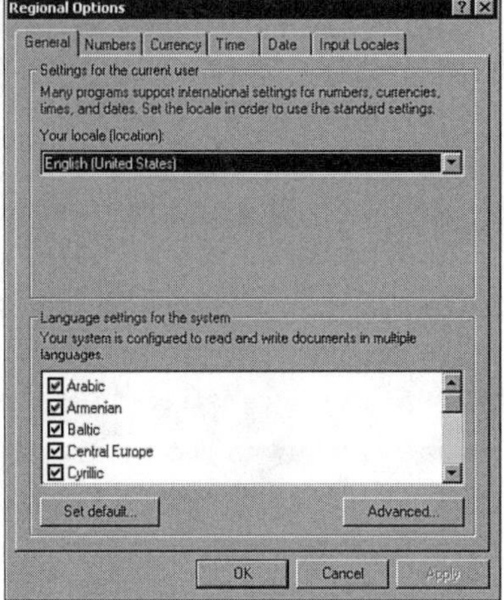

FIGURE 18.3
Installed language support.

LISTING 18.3 Programmatically Listing Supported Cultures

```
using System;
using System.Globalization;

namespace CLRUnleashed
{
    class CultureList
    {
        public static void Main(String[] args)
        {
            CultureInfo[] cia =
CultureInfo.GetCultures(CultureTypes.SpecificCultures);
            foreach(CultureInfo ci in cia)
            {
                Console.WriteLine(ci);
            }
        }
    }
}
```

From Listing 18.3, you can see which languages and cultures are currently supported. From this list, some notable missing components include the following:

- `en-UK` seems to have been superseded by `en-GB`.
- `ko-KP` (North Korea) is not supported.
- `bo-cn` (Tibetan) is not supported.

Given the great amount of information contained in a `CultureInfo` object, you can understand how a line had to be drawn somewhere. Table 18.2 shows the supported cultures. Because support for additional languages and cultures will undoubtedly be added, you should check to see which cultures are supported with the code that is provided in Listing 18.3. Table 18.2 should be taken as an example of some of the specific cultures that are currently supported.

TABLE 18.2 Installed/Supported Cultures

Culture Code	*Language – Country*	*Culture Code*	*Language – Country*
af-ZA	Afrikaans – South Africa	de-AT	German – Austria
ar-AE	Arabic – United Arab Emirates	de-CH	German – Switzerland
ar-BH	Arabic – Bahrain	de-DE	German – Germany
ar-DZ	Arabic – Algeria	de-LI	German – Liechtenstein
ar-EG	Arabic – Egypt	de-LU	German – Luxembourg
ar-IQ	Arabic – Iraq	es-HN	Spanish – Honduras
ar-JO	Arabic – Jordan	el-GR	Greek – Greece
ar-KW	Arabic – Kuwait	en-AU	English – Australia
ar-LB	Arabic – Lebanon	en-BZ	English – Belize
ar-LY	Arabic – Lybia	en-CA	English – Canada
ar-MA	Arabic – Morocco	en-CB	English – Caribbean
ar-OM	Arabic – Oman	en-GB	English – Great Britain
ar-QA	Arabic – Qatar	en-IE	English – Ireland
ar-SA	Arabic – Saudi Arabia	en-JM	English – Jamaica
ar-SY	Arabic – Syria	en-NZ	English – New Zealand
ar-TN	Arabic – Tunisia	en-PH	English – Philippines
ar-YE	Arabic – Yemen	en-TT	English – Trinidad Tobago
be-BY	Byelorussian – Belarus	en-US	English – US
bg-BG	Bulgarian – Bulgaria	en-ZA	English – South Africa
ca-ES	Catalan – Spain	en-ZW	English – Zimbabwe
cs-CZ	Czech – Czech Republic	es-AR	Spanish – Argentina
cy-az-AZ	Azeri (Latin) – Azerbaijan	es-BO	Spanish – Bolivia
cy-sr-SP	Serbian (Cyrillic) – Serbia	es-CL	Spanish – Chile
cy-uz-UZ	Uzbek (Latin) – Uzbekistan	es-CO	Spanish – Columbia
da-DK	Danish – Denmark	es-CR	Spanish – Costa Rica

TABLE 18.2 Continued

Culture Code	*Language – Country*	*Culture Code*	*Language – Country*
es-DO	Spanish – Dominican Republic	id-ID	Indonesian – Indonesia
es-EC	Spanish – Ecuador	is-IS	Icelandic – Iceland
es-ES	Spanish – Spain	it-CH	Italian – Switzerland
es-GT	Spanish – Guatemala	it-IT	Italian – Italy
es-MX	Spanish – Mexico	ja-JP	Japanese – Japan
es-NI	Spanish – Nicaragua	ka-GE	Georgian – Georgia
es-PA	Spanish – Panama	kk-KZ	Kazakh – Kazachstan
es-PE	Spanish – Peru	kn-IN	Kannada – India
es-PR	Spanish – Puerto Rico	kok-IN	Konkani – India
es-PY	Spanish – Paraguay	ko-KR	Korea – South Korea
es-SV	Spanish – El Salvador	ky-KZ	Kirghiz – Kazakhstan
es-UY	Spanish – Uruguay	lt-az-AZ	Azeri (Cyrillic) – Azerbaijan
es-VE	Spanish – Venezuela	lt-LT	Lithuanian – Lithuania
et-EE	Estonian – Estonia	lt-sr-SP	Serbian (Latin) – Serbia
eu-ES	Basque – Spain	lt-uz-UZ	Uzbek (Cyrillic) – Uzbekistan
fa-IR	Persian – Iran	lv-LV	Latvian – Latvia
fi-FI	Finnish – Finland	mk-MK	Macedonian – Macedonia
fo-FO	Faeroese – Faeroe Islands	mn-MN	Mongolian – Mongolia
fr-BE	French – Belgium	mr-IN	Marathi – India
fr-CA	French – Canada	ms-BN	Malay – Brunei Darussalam
fr-CH	French – Switzerland	ms-MY	Malay – Malaysia
fr-FR	French – France	nb-NO	Norwegian (Bokmål) – Norway
fr-LU	French – Luxembourg	nl-BE	Dutch – Belgium
fr-MC	French – Monaco	nl-NL	Dutch – Netherlands
gl-ES	Galician – Spain	nn-NO	Norwegian (Nynorsk) – Norway
gu-IN	Quechua – India	pa-IN	Punjabi – India
he-IL	Hebrew – Israel	pl-PL	Polish – Poland
hi-IN	Hindi – India	pt-BR	Portuguese – Brazil
hr-HR	Croatian – Croatia	pt-PT	Portuguese – Portugal
hu-HU	Hungarian – Hungary		
hy-AM	Armenian – Armenia		

TABLE 18.2 Continued

Culture Code	*Language – Country*	*Culture Code*	*Language – Country*
ro-RO	Romanian – Romania	th-TH	Thai – Thailand
ru-RU	Russian – Russian Federation	tr-TR	Turkish – Turkey
sa-IN	Sanskrit – India	tt-TA	Tatar – Tatarstan
sk-SK	Slovak – Slovakia	uk-UA	Ukrainian – Ukraine
sl-SI	Slovenian – Slovenia	ur-PK	Urdu – Pakistan
sq-AL	Albanian – Albania	vi-VN	Vietnamese – Vietnam
sv-FI	Swedish – Finland	zh-CN	Chinese – PRC
sv-SE	Swedish – Sweden	zh-HK	Chinese – Hong Kong
sw-KE	Swahili – Kenya	zh-MO	Chinese – Macau
syr-SY	Syriac – Syria	zh-SG	Chinese – Singapore
ta-IN	Tamil – India	zh-TW	Chinese – Taiwan
te-IN	Telugu – India	div-MV	Dhivehi – Maldives

If you're curious, that totals 136 cultures that are installed and supported. When an application starts up, it acquires a culture from the default culture that is part of the user preferences. What if you were at a company that wanted to support 50 of these cultures in their application? You would want to test each of the cultures to make sure that they work, which would require 50 PCs each with a specific language and locale associated with it. It turns out that a better way is available.

It is not completely accurate to say that the application acquires a culture. Every **Thread** has a culture associated to it—specifically, a **CultureInfo** object. Therefore, it is possible for an application to have one **AppDomain** and several **Thread**s, each with different **CultureInfo** objects associated with them. To get/set the **CultureInfo** object associated with a Thread, you use the **CurrentCulture** property. To get a property use the following:

```
CultureInfo ci = Thread.CurrentThread.CurrentCulture;
```

To associate a **CultureInfo** object with a Thread, use this:

```
Thread.CurrentThread.CurrentCulture = new CultureInfo(c);
```

Here, `c` is a string variable that has one of the values taken from Table 18.2.

A neutral culture is a super-set to a specific culture. A neutral culture is associated with a language and no-specific country. This is only possible if all of the countries associated with the language do not require specific modifications to the language as to render it non-neutral. For example, notice that a neutral Chinese culture does not exist. That is because some of the countries listed as speaking Chinese use a modified written language, creating a simplified version and a traditional version. Table 18.3 lists the current neutral cultures.

TABLE 18.3 Neutral Cultures

Neutral Culture	*Language*	*Neutral Culture*	*Language*
af	Afrikaans	it	Italian
ar	Arabic	ja	Japanese
az	Azeri	ka	Georgian
be	Byelorussian	kk	Kazakh
bg	Bulgarian	kn	Kannada
ca	Catalan	ko	Korean
cs	Czech	kok	Konkani
da	Danish	ky	Kirghiz
de	German	lt	Lithuanian
div	Dhivehi	lv	Latvian
el	Greek	mk	Macedonian
en	English	mn	Mongolian
es	Spanish	mr	Marathi
et	Estonian	ms	Malay
eu	Basque	nl	Dutch
fa	Persian	no	Norwegian
fi	Finnish	pa	Punjabi
fo	Faeroese	pl	Polish
fr	French	pt	Portuguese
gl	Galician	ro	Romanian
gu	Quechua	ru	Russian
he	Hebrew	sa	Sanskrit
hi	Hindi	sk	Slovak
hr	Croatian	sl	Slovenian
hu	Hungarian	sq	Albanian
hy	Armenian	sv	Swedish
id	Indonesian	sw	Swahili
is	Icelandic	syr	Syriac

TABLE 18.3 Continued

Neutral Culture	*Language*	*Neutral Culture*	*Language*
ta	Tamil	ur	Urdu
te	Telugu	uz	Uzbek
th	Thai	vi	Vietnamese
tr	Turkish	zh-CHS	Chinese – Simplified
tt	Tatar	zh-CHT	Chinese – Traditional
uk	Ukrainian		

A **Thread** cannot be assigned a neutral culture. Trying to do so results in an exception being thrown:

```
System.NotSupportedException: Culture "fr" is a neutral culture. It can not
➥be used in formatting and parsing and therefore cannot be set as the
➥thread's current culture.
   at System.Globalization.CultureInfo.CheckNeutral(CultureInfo culture)
   at System.Threading.Thread.set_CurrentCulture(CultureInfo value)
   at LocalizedApplication.LocalizedApplicationForm..ctor() in
➥localizedapplication.cs:line 39
```

If a **Thread** cannot be assigned a neutral culture, what good is a neutral culture? As it turns out, a neutral culture is important for an application when loading a language-specific resource, as you will see next. If you really do not care to which country a specific culture is assigned, then use the static **CultureInfo.CreateSpecificCulture** method like this:

```
Thread.CurrentThread.CurrentCulture = CultureInfo.CreateSpecificCulture("fr");
```

As the preceding exception indicates, the **CurrentCulture** is associated with formatting and parsing string data. If you need to format a date properly, it will use the culture information contained in the **CurrentCulture** property of the thread that is performing the format. Formatting numbers, currency, time, and sorting all use the **CurrentCulture** property to determine how the operation should be performed.

After the **CultureInfo** object is associated with the current thread, you use the **CultureInfo** object indirectly via calls to date formatting, number formatting, and so on. Specific calls retrieve date formatting information, number formatting information, calendar information, and so on. However, typically, you would just call the formatting or parsing function, and that function would look up the culture and do the right thing.

Using the RegionInfo Class

In direct contrast to the **CultureInfo** class, the **RegionInfo** class holds data that is not dependent on user preferences or settings. This class contains information such as whether the region uses metric units, what the name of the region is, what the English name of the region is, what the name of the currency symbol is, and so on. If you have constructed a **RegionInfo** class based on Saudi Arabia, and your operating system has set the English language as its default, then the **DisplayName** of the region will always be Saudi Arabia.

Using Resources in Your Application

Resources are repositories for data that your application requires. In the end, all resources end up as binary `.resources` files, which are then embedded into the running executable. You can see the resources that your application has available to it by looking at the compiled application or library with the tool *ildasm*. If resources are embedded into your application, then these resources would show up as a .mresource in the manifest of the **Assembly**. Figure 18.4 shows how the output might look.

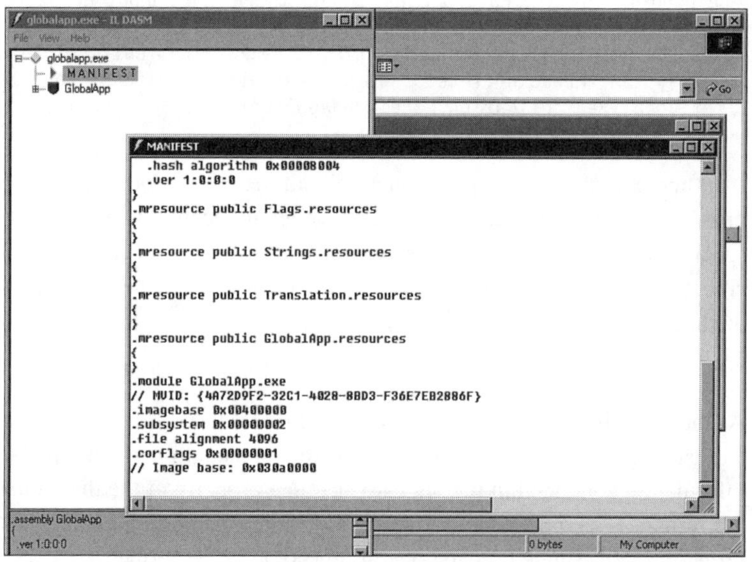

FIGURE 18.4
Looking for resources in an application.

Notice that the .mresource is declared as being *public*. This means that these resources are visible to other assemblies. Resources can also be private, as shown in Figure 18.5.

A *private resource* is a resource that is not visible to other assemblies. You can create a private resource by directly using the assembly linker al. The option to use when embedding assemblies is `/embed`. The `/embed` option takes a comma-delimited string as an argument of the following form:

```
/embed:<filename>[,<name>[,Private]
```

FIGURE 18.5
Private resources.

```
MANIFEST
.assembly GlobalApp.resources
{
  .hash algorithm 0x00008004
  .ver 1:0:0:0
  .locale = (65 00 6E 00 2D 00 55 00 53 00 00 00 )          // e.n.-.U.S..
}
.mresource private 'Flags.en-US.resources'
{
}
.mresource private 'Translation.en-US.resources'
{
}
.module GlobalApp.resources.dll
// MVID: {444694DD-D9B0-48F7-8A39-FF21C813D5B6}
.imagebase 0x00400000
.subsystem 0x00000003
.file alignment 4096
.corflags 0x00000001
// Image base: 0x030a0000
```

The last argument is optional and it makes a resource private. Finally, resources can be linked in rather than embedded into an assembly. A linked resource means that rather than have the entire resource embedded in the assembly, a reference to the .resources file is available. Figure 18.6 shows how a linked resource might look.

FIGURE 18.6
Linked resources.

```
MANIFEST
.assembly GlobalApp.resources
{
  .hash algorithm 0x00008004
  .ver 1:0:0:0
  .locale = (65 00 6E 00 2D 00 55 00 53 00 00 00 )          // e.n.-.U.S..
}
.file nometadata 'flags.en-US.resources'
    .hash = (B6 1D 9F 6D 30 49 D2 14 25 21 51 D4 D6 2F B4 75  // ...m0I..%!(
             B3 9E B2 60 )                                    // ...`
.file nometadata 'translation.en-US.resources'
    .hash = (ED B5 8F 1A 46 58 9A F6 BE B6 45 BE 22 96 7B C0  // ....FX....
             F9 34 F1 52 )                                    // .4.R
.mresource private 'Flags.en-US.resources'
{
  .file 'flags.en-US.resources' at 0x00000000
}
.mresource private 'Translation.en-US.resources'
{
  .file 'translation.en-US.resources' at 0x00000000
}
.module GlobalApp.resources.dll
// MVID: {D94428C8-1F7F-426E-9AA0-CB3EEF620510}
.imagebase 0x00400000
```

This would result in a significantly smaller assembly, but now the .resources file(s) must be included as part of the distribution. The .resources file(s) becomes a dependency that must be resolved at runtime.

To add embedded or linked resources to an assembly, you use the al tool supplied as part of the .NET SDK. This tool is called the Assembly Linker, and it is installed by default in the runtime installation directory (for example, `\Windows\Microsoft.NET\Framework\v1.x.x.xxxx`). If you want to embed a binary .resources file into your assembly, the command line would look something like this:

```
al /out:GlobalApp.resources.dll /c:en-US /v:1.0.0.0
➥/embed:Flags.en-US.resources,Flags.en-US.resources,Private
➥/embed:Translation.en-US.resources,Translation.en-US.resources,Private
```

To link a resource, you modify the command line only slightly:

```
al /out:GlobalApp.resources.dll /c:en-US /v:1.0.0.0
➥/embed:Flags.en-US.resources,Flags.en-US.resources,Private
➥/embed:Translation.en-US.resources,Translation.en-US.resources,Private
```

Notice that each of these two options can occur multiple times on a command line, thus creating multiple resources in an assembly.

Now you can put a binary .resources file into the assembly. How is the .resources file generated? A .resources file is compiled using the resgen utility. This utility takes in either a plain text .txt file or an XML .resx file.

The text file contains simple name/value pairs like this:

```
hello=Hello
goodbye=Goodbye
greeting=How are you?
```

Compiling this source with resgen would result in three resource strings. (For example, the application could query for the resource string `greeting` and have "How are you?" returned.) Only strings can be included in this source form of a resource.

A .resx resource file is more complicated because it includes a schema or a definition of the type and format of the tags that follow first. If you were to include the same resource information as described in the preceding paragraph, the .resx file would look like Listing 18.4.

LISTING 18.4 A Sample .resx File

```
<?xml version="1.0" encoding="utf-8" ?>
<root>
    <xsd:schema id="root" targetNamespace="" xmlns=""
➥xmlns:xsd=http://www.w3.org/2001/XMLSchema
➥xmlns:msdata="urn:schemas-microsoft-com:xml-msdata">
        <xsd:element name="root" msdata:IsDataSet="true">
            <xsd:complexType>
                <xsd:choice maxOccurs="unbounded">
                    <xsd:element name="data">
                        <xsd:complexType>
                            <xsd:sequence>
                                <xsd:element name="value" type="xsd:string"
➥minOccurs="0" msdata:Ordinal="1" />
                                <xsd:element name="comment" type="xsd:string"
➥minOccurs="0" msdata:Ordinal="2" />
```

LISTING 18.4 Continued

```
                        </xsd:sequence>
                        <xsd:attribute name="name" type="xsd:string" />
                        <xsd:attribute name="type" type="xsd:string" />
                        <xsd:attribute name="mimetype"
➥type="xsd:string" />
                    </xsd:complexType>
                </xsd:element>
                <xsd:element name="resheader">
                    <xsd:complexType>
                        <xsd:sequence>
                            <xsd:element name="value" type="xsd:string"
➥minOccurs="0" msdata:Ordinal="1" />
                        </xsd:sequence>
                        <xsd:attribute name="name" type="xsd:string"
➥use="required" />
                    </xsd:complexType>
                </xsd:element>
            </xsd:choice>
        </xsd:complexType>
    </xsd:element>
</xsd:schema>
<resheader name="ResMimeType">
    <value>text/microsoft-resx</value>
</resheader>
<resheader name="Version">
    <value>1.0.0.0</value>
</resheader>
<resheader name="Reader">
    <value>System.Resources.ResXResourceReader</value>
</resheader>
<resheader name="Writer">
    <value>System.Resources.ResXResourceWriter</value>
</resheader>
<data name="hello">
    <value>Hello</value>
    <comment>Hello</comment>
</data>
<data name="goodbye">
    <value>Goodbye</value>
    <comment>Goodbye</comment>
</data>
<data name="greeting">
    <value>How are you?</value>
    <comment>greeting</comment>
</data>
</root>
```

This is a lot of overhead just to encapsulate three strings! The key portion of the file is in the last few lines, where you see the following lines:

```
<data name="hello">
    <value>Hello</value>
    <comment>Hello</comment>
</data>
<data name="goodbye">
    <value>Goodbye</value>
    <comment>Goodbye</comment>
</data>
<data name="greeting">
    <value>How are you?</value>
    <comment>greeting</comment>
</data>
```

However, this format has structure, and the .resx file can contain more than just strings. To get over the overhead, Visual Studio .Net automates the production of .resx files. In addition, two classes, **ResXResourceReader** and **ResXResourceWriter**, allow a programmer to build .resx files. In fact, a tool called resxgen is shipped with the .NET SDK that takes in an image file (.bmp, .jpg, .ico, and so on) and creates a .resx file that contains the image. This tool uses the **ResXResourceWriter** class to do the bulk of its work.

Accessing .NET Resources

After resources are embedded or linked into an assembly, they can be accessed with the **ResourceSet**, **ResourceReader**, or **ResourceManager** classes.

This section will first look at **ResourceSet** so you can get some appreciation for what **ResourceManager** adds in functionality.

Assuming the same resource strings as described in Listings 18.3 and 18.4, the following code will retrieve the named resources from the resource file.

```
ResourceSet rs = new ResourceSet(a.GetManifestResourceStream(s));
Debug.WriteLine(rs.GetString("hello"));
Debug.WriteLine(rs.GetString("goodbye"));
Debug.WriteLine(rs.GetString("greeting"));
rs.Close();
```

The argument to the **ResourceSet** constructor is a stream returned by the **Assembly** a. A **ResourceSet** can take a filename or an **IResourceReader** interface. The next three lines retrieve the named resource strings from the set. The problem with **ResourceSet** is that a specific resource file must be specified to read in a resource. In a running environment, using **ResourceSet** does not offer much more than reflection in getting the resources. **ResourceSet** is meant as a tool for reading .resources files; it is not a general solution that meets the requirements for an international application. **ResourceSet** is the base class for the **ResXResourceReader** class; therefore, it is important for reading resources, but it is not culturally aware. What about **ResourceReader**?

You can look at the resources in an **Assembly**. Listing 18.5 illustrates how this can be done.

LISTING 18.5 Listing Resources in an Assembly

```
Assembly a = Assembly.LoadFrom(@"ja\LocalizedApplication.resources.dll");
foreach(string s in a.GetManifestResourceNames())
{
    Debug.WriteLine(s);
    ManifestResourceInfo ri = a.GetManifestResourceInfo(s);
    if(ri.FileName != null)
        Debug.WriteLine("File name: " + ri.FileName);
    if(ri.ReferencedAssembly != null)
        Debug.WriteLine("Assembly: " + ri.ReferencedAssembly.GetName());
    Debug.WriteLine("Location: " + ri.ResourceLocation);
    Stream rs = a.GetManifestResourceStream(s);
    ResourceReader rr = new ResourceReader(rs);
    IDictionaryEnumerator ren = rr.GetEnumerator();
    //Go through the enumerator, printing out the key and value pairs.
    while (ren.MoveNext())
    {
        Debug.WriteLine(string.Format("Name: {0}", Convert.ToString(ren.Key)));
        Debug.WriteLine(string.Format("Value: {0}",
➥Convert.ToString(ren.Value)));
    }
}
```


The added benefit of **ResourceReader** is that you can enumerate through the resources. With **ResourceSet**, you had to know ahead of time what the names of the resources were.

The original goal was to build a localized application. How does all of this apply? The **ResourceManager** class relies heavily on the notion of satellite assemblies. Before you learn about the features of the **ResourceManager** class, you need to understand satellite assemblies.

Putting It All Together with Satellite Assemblies

Satellite assemblies are assemblies that have no code—just data. They are roughly equivalent to resource DLLs in the unmanaged world. A satellite assembly can be created on the command line with the al tool. You have already seen the creation of a satellite assembly in the discussion of the differences between embed and link. The command line is repeated here for clarity:

```
al /out:GlobalApp.resources.dll /c:en-US /v:1.0.0.0
➥/embed:Flags.en-US.resources,Flags.en-US.resources,Private
➥/embed:Translation.en-US.resources,Translation.en-US.resources,Private
```

The key point to notice from this command line is that no code or files are referencing code—just resources and the output. Also notice that a version and a culture are specified ("1.0.0.0" and "en-US" respectively).

The **ResourceManager** is a class that provides convenient access to culture-specific resource information at runtime. For most cases, this class queries the **Thread.CurrentUICulture** for the culture that is to be used for the search. **Thread.CurrentUICulture**, like **Thread.CurrentCulture**, is a property that can be assigned to or retrieved. Typically in an international application, it is advisable to set both of these properties to the same **CultureInfo** object. Just remember that **CurrentUICulture** is used almost exclusively by the **ResourceManager** class to look for appropriate culture-specific resources, whereas **CurrentCulture** is used by the runtime in formatting, parsing, and sorting.

It is possible to retrieve resources without setting the culture for the thread. You can retrieve a **ResourceSet** that is particular to a specific culture. For example:

```
ResourceSet rmrs = rm.GetResourceSet(new CultureInfo("ja-JP"), true, true);
Debug.WriteLine(rmrs.GetString("hello"));
Debug.WriteLine(rmrs.GetString("goodbye"));
Debug.WriteLine(rmrs.GetString("greeting"));
```

This would retrieve the named resources from the resource set built for the Japanese culture regardless of what **CurrentUICulture** is set to. This method provides no "fallback" if the specified resource does not exist.

To effectively use this class, some structure must be in place. For each culture that is to be supported, a subdirectory (relative to the current working directory of the application) must exist that has the same name as the culture, and the satellite assembly should be placed in that directory. For example, if you are expecting to support Japanese, then you need to have a directory called `ja-JP` in which you include a satellite assembly that has a name of the form <application name>.resources.dll, where <application name> is the main assembly name of the application. In addition, you need to make sure that the version as recorded in the main assembly is the same as the version in the satellite assembly.

Note

The version restriction can be modified with **`SatelliteContractVersionAttribute`** or publisher policy configuration. If you want to change the main assembly version number, then place a line like this:

[SatelliteContractVersion("<satellite-version>")]

where <satellite-version> is a string specifying the version used to load satellite assemblies. Without this attribute, the version of the main assembly is used. Notice that you cannot specify a single assembly. All assemblies must be versioned in unison. Refer to Chapter 6, "Publishing Applications," to see how to construct a publisher policy.

A **`ResourceManager`** object is constructed with a line like the following:

```
ResourceManager rm = new ResourceManager("LocalizedApplication.Strings", a);
```

The string that is passed as the first argument is the "base-name" of the resources. If you are unsure what to put there, look at the satellite assemblies with ildasm. You should see something like Figure 18.7.

FIGURE 18.7
Resource base name.

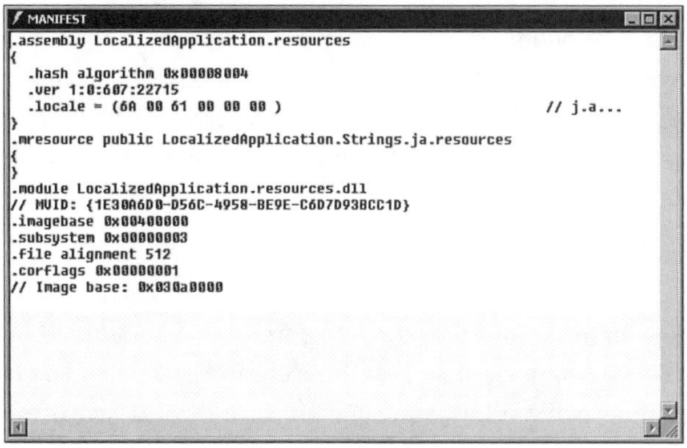

```
MANIFEST
.assembly LocalizedApplication.resources
{
  .hash algorithm 0x00008004
  .ver 1:0:607:22715
  .locale = (6A 00 61 00 00 00 )                          // j.a...
}
.mresource public LocalizedApplication.Strings.ja.resources
{
}
.module LocalizedApplication.resources.dll
// MVID: {1E30A6D0-D56C-4958-BE9E-C6D7D93BCC1D}
.imagebase 0x00400000
.subsystem 0x00000003
.file alignment 512
.corflags 0x00000001
// Image base: 0x030a0000
```

Notice on the `.mresource` line the name of the file preceding the culture ("ja") and the suffix (".resources"). This is the base name of the resources, and it is what is used as an argument to the constructor of **`ResourceManager`**. The last argument is the Assembly to which the **`ResourceManager`** is tied. For most cases, you can get the Assembly with the following line:

```
Assembly a = Assembly.GetExecutingAssembly();
```

After a **ResourceManager** is constructed, calls can be made to the **GetObject** or **GetString** methods. This is where the culture-aware features of **ResourceManager** start to kick in. Calling **GetObject** or **GetString** results in a search for an assembly that matches the **CurrentUICulture** of the **Thread** calling these methods. If the matching satellite assembly has not been loaded, then the subdirectory that matches the culture string is searched for the satellite DLL. If the directory does not exist or the satellite assembly cannot be loaded, then a neutral culture is tested.

For example, if the specific culture was "ja-JP," then the neutral culture is "jp." What if you wanted to support all English speaking countries and cultures with a single resource? This can be done by building a single satellite DLL and placing it in an "en" subdirectory with a culture assigned to it as "en." Now when a thread set up with "en-GB" or "en-AU" cultures (Great Britain and Australia respectively) the thread retrieves resources from the "en" subdirectory, a resource for a specific culture does not exist.

If neither a neutral culture nor a specific culture matches the culture in **CurrentUICulture**, then the satellite loading process is said to "fallback." An application should place resources of the same name as the satellite assemblies in the main assembly. This allows for a default resource if no resource seems to be available.

A Sample Using the Hard Way (Manual)

The manual process of building an internationalized application has been described. It is important that you understand the process involved in building such an application before you go to the "wizard-generated code" of the IDE. Visual Studio .NET allows the automation of many of the tasks outlined so far, but underneath it is doing the same work. When something goes wrong, you will need to understand why it went wrong and how to fix it. This understanding will not come from automatically generated code.

The following sample simply showcases some of the features that have been described. Ideally, the strings in the application should be translated and placed in a satellite assembly. As it is, this application shows a flag for each of the selected languages and displays some of the culture-specific information contained in the **CultureInfo** class. Only one string has been translated. (The translations are from `http://www.trigeminal.com/samples/provincial.html`, put together by Michael Kaplan). If you want to add more translations, additional strings can be added easily. The application looks like Figure 18.8.

The complete source for Listings 18.6–18.8 is located in the Localization directory. The first listing shows a portion of the commands used to build the satellite assemblies.

FIGURE 18.8
Localization showcase.

LISTING 18.6 Building Resource Assemblies

```
. . .
resxgen /i:united-nations.bmp /o:Flags.resx /n:flag
resgen flags.resx flags.resources
resgen globalapp.resx globalapp.resources
resgen strings.resx strings.resources
resgen translation.txt translation.resources

cd bo-CN
del /s *.resx
..\resxgen /i:tibet.bmp /o:Flags.bo-CN.resx /n:flag
resgen flags.bo-CN.resx flags.bo-CN.resources
resgen translation.bo-CN.txt translation.bo-CN.resources
al /out:GlobalApp.resources.dll /c:bo-CN /v:1.0.0.0
➥/embed:Flags.bo-CN.resources,Flags.bo-CN.resources,Private
➥/embed:Translation.bo-CN.resources,Translation.bo-CN.resources,Private

cd ..\de-AT
del /s *.resx
..\resxgen /i:austria.bmp /o:Flags.de-AT.resx /n:flag
resgen flags.de-AT.resx flags.de-AT.resources
resgen translation.de-AT.txt translation.de-AT.resources
al /out:GlobalApp.resources.dll /c:de-AT /v:1.0.0.0
➥/embed:Flags.de-AT.resources,Flags.de-AT.resources,Private
➥/embed:Translation.de-AT.resources,Translation.de-AT.resources,Private

cd ..\de-LU
del /s *.resx
..\resxgen /i:luxembourg.bmp /o:Flags.de-LU.resx /n:flag
resgen flags.de-LU.resx flags.de-LU.resources
resgen translation.de-LU.txt translation.de-LU.resources
al /out:GlobalApp.resources.dll /c:de-LU /v:1.0.0.0
➥/embed:Flags.de-LU.resources,Flags.de-LU.resources,Private
➥/embed:Translation.de-LU.resources,Translation.de-LU.resources,Private
. . .
```

For each supported culture (language and country), a .resx is generated that represents the flag. The generated flag .resx file is compiled with resgen into a .resources file, and the translated text in the .txt file is compiled into a .resources file. Finally, the satellite assembly is created, embedding the .resources files that were just created. For many cultures (like with this application), this is quite a process.

After a language/culture has been selected in the application, the code in Listing 18.7 starts:

LISTING 18.7 Retrieving Information from the Satellite Assemblies

```
LanguageIdentifier li = (LanguageIdentifier)languageSelection.SelectedItem;
Text = "GlobalApp " + li.Message;
Thread.CurrentThread.CurrentUICulture = new CultureInfo(li.CultureString);
Thread.CurrentThread.CurrentCulture = Thread.CurrentThread.CurrentUICulture;
ResourceManager rm = new ResourceManager("Flags", this.GetType().Assembly);
flagImage.Image = (System.Drawing.Image)rm.GetObject("flag");
rm = new ResourceManager("Translation", this.GetType().Assembly);
translatedText.Text = (string)rm.GetObject("question");
```

The first line extracts the `LanguageIdentifier` object. This is just a simple object that encapsulates the string that is to be displayed on the `ComboBox` and the culture string associated with it. Next, you set the **`CurrentUICulture`** and the **`CurrentCulture`** properties of the current thread based on the selected language. Then, a **`ResourceManager`** object is constructed and the "flag" and the translated "question" resources are retrieved. Other than the name of an audio file (used to say the translated phrase in the selected language if available), that is about all that is contained in the satellite assembly. Listing 18.8 shows how different information is formatted specific to the culture selected.

LISTING 18.8 Using CultureInfo for Formatting

```
DateTime now = DateTime.Now;
time.Text = now.ToLongTimeString();
date.Text = now.ToLongDateString();
double d = 1000000.0;
floatNumber.Text = String.Format("{0:N}", d);
currencyNumber.Text = String.Format("{0:C}", d);
// Region Info
RegionInfo ri = new RegionInfo(ci.LCID);
metric.Text = Convert.ToString(ri.IsMetric);
countryName.Text = ri.DisplayName;
```

These simple lines of code perform culture-specific formatting of the data. Notice in the output that even in languages that are similar, the region has different conventions on formatting date, time, and currency. In addition, notice that the text is displayed differently for right-to-left languages. Besides the display, try editing the translated line for any of the Arabic languages. Pressing the right arrow key causes the caret to move left; the left arrow key causes the caret to move right. If you insert some English into the phrase, then the cursor will behave like expected for a Western language, only while in the inserted text.

The last few lines of Listing 18.8 show some of the information contained in the **`RegionInfo`** class.

A Sample Using Visual Studio .NET

One of the problems with trying to do without Visual Studio .NET is that building the UI becomes very hard. Simply resizing the dialog box or moving one of the controls becomes a trial-and-error process. It is possible to build all of the satellite assemblies by hand and still use Visual Studio to build the UI. This is a little better, but it means you are constantly switching between Visual Studio and the command line to build the application. With Visual Studio .NET, building a localized application consists of the following steps:

- Start with a fresh solution and build the UI as you would normally.
- After the UI has been built, change the Localizable property of the Form to True, shown in Figure 18.9. It is important that the UI essentially be "complete" when starting the localization process. As you select each language, specific files will be generated based on the default. If this default changes, then corresponding changes will need to be made to each of the generated files. If you have generated files for many languages, this process could be tedious and error prone. The default is the resource that will be used in the fallback mode.

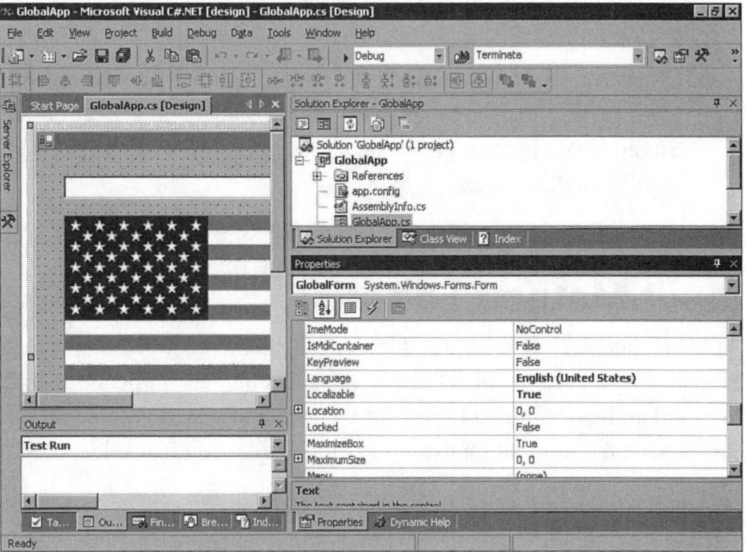

FIGURE 18.9
Selecting localizable in Visual Studio .NET.

- Select a language/culture to which you want to localize. The Language/Culture property can be seen just above the Localizable property in Figure 18.9. If this property is selected, a list of possible cultures to select will be presented. You just need to pick one.
- Assume that you chose "Spanish (Mexico)" in the previous step. This will cause a .resx file to be generated with the same name as your application with the culture name es-MX embedded in the name. As you add bitmaps, strings, and so on, they will be added to the generated .resx file. Figure 18.10 shows what your directory might look like after selecting a few languages.

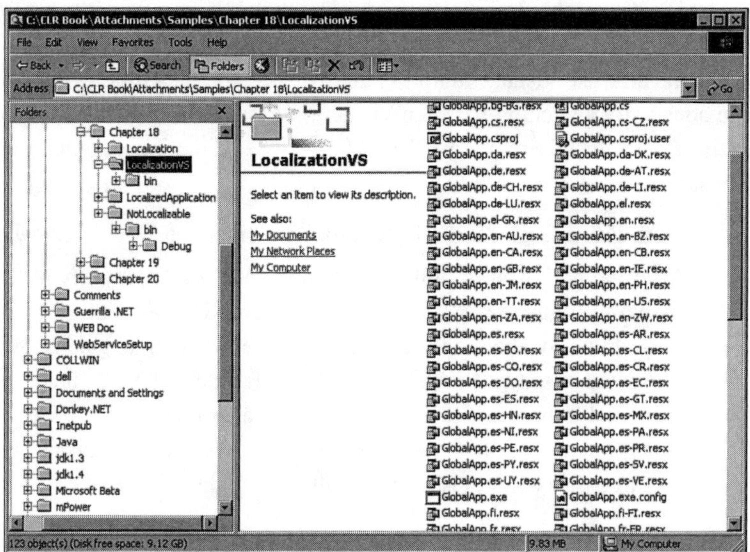

FIGURE 18.10
Generated files after selecting many languages.

- When you are satisfied, build the project. You will see as part of the build process a `Building satellite assemblies...` status line appear during the build. Visual Studio is taking each of the .resx files, creating the appropriate directory, and placing the satellite assembly in it.
- Repeat the previous two steps for each culture that you want to support.

Input Method Editor(s)

Although not directly related to the CLR, it should be noted that standard methods are available for inputting non-Western characters into an application. To do this, you need to install an Input Method Editor for the locale in which you are interested. Figure 18.11 shows what the installation dialog box looks like. You just select the locale in the IME that you want to install. You do not need to reboot. Now the EN in the bottom-right corner of your screen has meaning. Selecting it shows the input methods that are available.

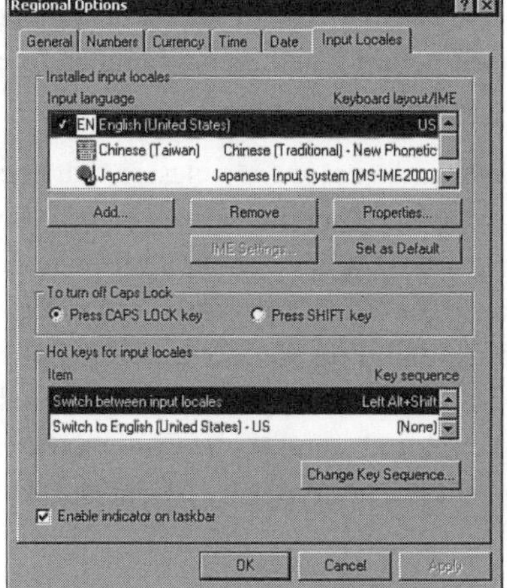

FIGURE 18.11
Installing input method editors.

After these editors are installed, you can use them to write messages in another language like that shown in Figure 18.12.

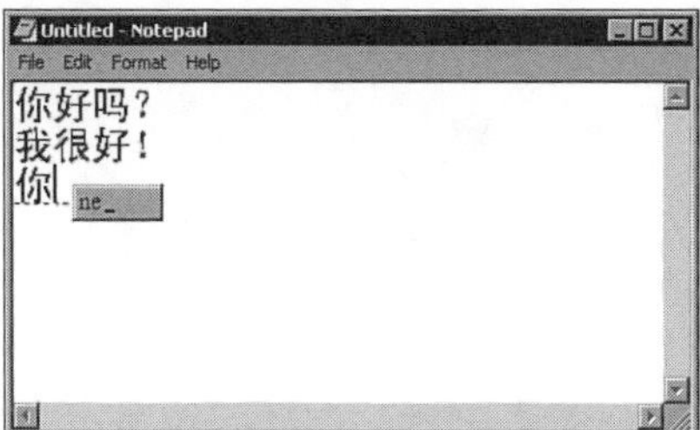

FIGURE 18.12
Using an IME.

This figure shows a Chinese IME that allows you to input the Romanized sound of the character. Numerous other IMEs do handwriting analysis to detect the character, map the keyboard to specific characters, and so on. Almost all of the supported languages have an IME that allows the input of non-Western characters from a standard keyboard and mouse.

Summary

This chapter laid the foundation for building an international application. It is important to start the design of an international application early on in the development process.

Retrofitting code for localization and globalization is difficult. You discovered the differences between the many different file formats that are common with an international application. You learned some of the standards that the .NET Framework supports as far as specifying cultural identity. You also learned how to use the **ResourceManager** class along with satellite assemblies to make building and maintaining an international application that much easier.

In addition, you explored **CultureInfo** and **RegionInfo** classes that encapsulate a great deal of cultural information. You learned that each thread can be assigned a **CultureInfo** and that all operations that might have cultural differences rely on the thread's **CurrentCulture** and **CurrentUICulture** properties. You discovered what Visual Studio .NET brings to the table as far as building an international application. The Visual Studio makes it much easier to build and support an international application. Finally, you took a slight detour and explored some of the OS-specific tools (IMEs), which are available input characters that are not typically associated with the standard keyboard.

CHAPTER 19

Debugging .NET Applications

IN THIS CHAPTER

Debugging in any environment is an art. It requires a thorough understanding of the environment and the tools available. With the CLR, you are able to devote more time to the application and less time to "programming details." When a problem arises, you need to understand as much as possible about certain key features of the CLR to be able to diagnose and solve the problem.

When I took one of my first programming classes, I had to build a traffic signal. The traffic signal was to run through the sequence of green, yellow, and red. It also had to take input from a crossing signal so that the sequence could be altered somewhat to take into account a pedestrian who wanted to cross. What I remember about that project is how much time I spent worrying about how I was going to archive and retrieve my program (from cartridge tape), interpreting the cryptic error messages that the assembler returned, and figuring out how I was going to move blocks of assembly code in case the function took more statements than I had accounted for. I spent little time on the problem of sequencing the lights and a lot of time on the "mechanics" of the environment. Debugging in such an environment usually meant making sure I had not moved the code to the wrong place, that all of the references to the moved code had been correctly updated, and that I was testing the correct bit. Memory was simply a place where the code was not. I relied heavily on interrupt service routines for timing and scheduling.

The next generation found me dynamically allocating memory, but I was still limited by the amount of physical memory that was available. DOS extenders allowed more memory to be addressed, but there was still a fixed size of physical memory of which the programmer was aware as the software was developed. Although many of the problems associated with the "assembly" era were abstracted away from the programmer, memory was still an issue. The programmer had to be aware not only of how much memory his program used, but in general, he had to be aware of how much memory the system was using.

With the advent of virtual memory, the programmer worried less about how much memory was installed or available. It became common to not even check the return of `malloc` or `new` (in C or C++ code) because it was assumed that more memory was always available. The programmer now had to be concerned with page faults and swap space. Typically, a program did not run out of memory—it just got slower as more time was spent swapping portions of the program to disk. While the programmer worried proportionately less about memory, advances were also being made in scheduling of the CPU.

It was possible for an errant program to "take over" the CPU. If my program did not play nicely in the sandbox and spin in a tight loop, your program was affected. With preemptive multitasking, one program was less likely to affect the operation of the whole system. The operating system also made it appear as if many processes were running in parallel.

After it was possible for every process to be run "at the same time," the programmer wanted finer grained control over how his program was scheduled. Threads essentially became a unit of scheduling over which the programmer had control.

With each new generation or paradigm shift, the problems of the previous generation remained, although they were largely abstracted away from the programmer. The tools available to debug a program also changed as well. The tools had to give the programmer the information that was specific to the environment. With physical memory and interrupts, good tools would allow the programmer to see how much memory was used up and how often and which interrupt service routines were being executed. With virtual memory and threads, terms such as working set size, thread count, and CPU usage became important.

With the CLR and the .NET Framework, concepts such as type, value, assembly, and application domain become important. To effectively debug in this environment, the tools must reflect information and statistics about these new concepts. That is the focus of this chapter: to familiarize you with the tools that are available to glean information from the system about these new terms. After you understand these tools and facilities, you can combine them as the art of debugging.

Providing Feedback to the User

I read about a "debug" session where the software that guided a missile was being tested. A great deal of effort had been put into making sure that the appropriate notification or feedback was in place when an error was detected. However, when the missile was launched and nothing was reported, it could not be determined if the test was successful because adequate provision had not been made for progress or "success" events.

Alternatively, I was in a meeting with a pilot going over some of the details about some software that had been developed to control the plane. His one comment about the initial phase of this design was that there were "too many red lights." What he meant was that a red light should indicate a truly exceptional event, one that demanded his attention right now. If this was not the case, a pilot tended to ignore the red light. He said this was a major factor in the crash of a plane that was being tested because the wrong red light had been ignored.

In developing software, you must walk an equally fine line between providing enough feedback and providing too much.

Trace and Debug Statements

Printing and logging messages has been part of debugging probably since the first program was written. When developing an application, the programmer must know what is going on to successfully debug the program. To this end, the **Trace** and **Debug** classes were developed. These classes, found in the **System.Diagnostics** namespace, replace the `Debug.Print` method that was used in VB applications. They provide a method to log messages. The default place where these messages are logged is on the debugging output window in Visual Studio .NET. These classes default to writing the output to OutputDebugString that is detailed in the Platform SDK or MSDN documentation. In the simplest form, you can write a message like this:

```
Trace.WriteLine("This is a trace message.");
```

or this:

```
Debug.WriteLine("This is a debug message.");
```

Notice that these are static methods. You don't need to instantiate a class to call these methods. They look remarkably like the **Console.WriteLine** methods, and, in fact, they are similar. The major difference is that the **Trace** and **Debug** methods do not take any formatting specifications. You could always do the formatting on-the-fly, like this:

```
Debug.WriteLine(string.Format("This is the {0}th debug message.", count));
```

These methods can be indented so that messages reflect a tree hierarchy and make reading the messages a little easier:

```
void foo()
{
    Debug.WriteLine("I am in foo.");
}
Debug.WriteLine("Calling foo.");
Debug.Indent();
foo();
Debug.Unindent();
Debug.Writeline("Foo has returned.");
```

This would result in the following output:

```
Calling foo.
    I am in foo.
Foo has returned.
```

Debug has been used here, but you could just as easily use **Trace**. The two classes have identical methods. What is the difference? Both of these methods are conditionally compiled. **Trace** is enabled when the **TRACE** macro is defined. **Debug** is enabled when the **DEBUG** macro is defined.

Note

You can define these macros in several ways. For C#, adding `/d:TRACE` or `/d:DEBUG` to the compiler command line will enable **`Trace`** or **`Debug`** respectively. For VB, the syntax is slightly different: `/d:TRACE=True` and `/d:DEBUG=True`. With Managed Extensions for C++, you must enclose the **`Trace`** and **`Debug`** methods with `#ifdef TRACE...#endif` to get the same functionality. In Visual Studio .NET **`Trace`** is enabled by default for both release and debug builds (see Figure 19.1), whereas **`Debug`** is only enabled in the debug build. Of course, you can always change this convention by changing the compiler options or explicitly putting `#define TRACE` or `#define DEBUG` at the top of a C# source file.

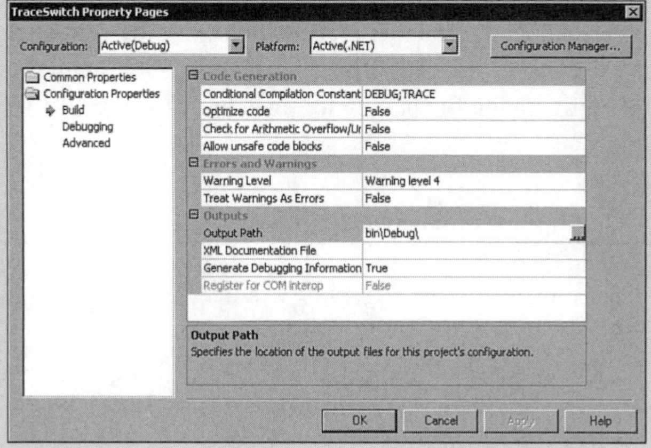

FIGURE 19.1
`Debug` *and* **`Trace`** *conditional compilation.*

You can also supply a category name to the output:

```
Debug.WriteLine("This is a test", "Foo");
```

This will produce output similar to the following:

```
Foo: This is a test
```

In addition to this compile time control over the output of **`Trace`** and **`Debug`**, these classes also have methods that allow runtime control of the output.

Both **`Trace`** and **`Debug`** have **`WriteIf`** and **`WriteLineIf`** methods. **`WriteIf`** is like Write, and **`WriteLineIf`** is like WriteLine in that they write a string without a carriage return and line feed and with one respectively. In addition, the …If versions not only write the message string, but they also accept a **`bool`** value or an expression that evaluates to a

bool that determines whether the message should be written. The following is exactly equivalent to **WriteLine**:

```
Debug.WriteLineIf(true, "This is a test.");
```

In a real application, you can supply any expression to control the output of the message. The following will only generate a message when a is greater than 5:

```
Debug.WriteLineIf(a > 5, "The variable 'a' is greater than 5.");
```

What if you wanted to easily turn on tracing on an application that has shipped? With the methods and APIs presented already, you could put flags in the registry or some custom file. This need has already been anticipated.

On startup, every application looks in the directory in which it was started for a configuration file. For an application called "TraceSwitch.exe", the configuration file would be "TraceSwitch.exe.config". It is here that custom application settings are stored. Specific settings in the configuration file pertain to "switches." Listing 19.1 shows a possible configuration file.

LISTING 19.1 Configuration Switches

```
<configuration>
  <system.diagnostics>
    <switches>
      <add name="MySwitch" value="3" />
      <add name="YourSwitch" value="1" />
    </switches>
  </system.diagnostics>
</configuration>
```

Listing 19.1 shows two switches being defined called `"MySwitch"` and `"YourSwitch"`. Each switch has been given a default value. The values that are acceptable for the **Trace** class are shown in Table 19.1.

TABLE 19.1 TraceLevel enum Values

TraceLevel enum	*Value*
Off	0
Error	1
Warning	2
Info	3
Verbose	4

Listing 19.2 shows you how to take advantage of the configuration settings.

Note

The full source of the code snippet in Listing 19.2 is in the `TraceSwitch` directory in a file called `TraceSwitch.cs`.

LISTING 19.2 Using Switches That Are Configured in a Configuration File

```
TraceSwitch ts1 = new TraceSwitch("MySwitch", "My debugging switch");
TraceSwitch ts2 = new TraceSwitch("YourSwitch", "Your debugging switch");

Trace.WriteLineIf(ts1.Level == TraceLevel.Info, "My output");
Trace.WriteLineIf(ts1.TraceError, "My error output");
Trace.WriteLineIf(ts1.TraceWarning, "My warning output");
Trace.WriteLineIf(ts1.TraceInfo, "My info output");

Trace.WriteLineIf(ts2.Level == TraceLevel.Error, "Your output");
Trace.WriteLineIf(ts2.TraceError, "Your error output", "Category");
```

Each switch is constructed by name and given a brief description that is used for informational purposes only. The name is compared against the switch names in the configuration file. If a match occurs between the switch name and the switch name in the configuration file, then the switch is assigned to the value specified in the configuration file. If no match is found, the switch defaults to Off. Changing the value in the configuration file can change the logging output of your program.

As you can see from Listing 19.2, the level of the switch can be directly compared to one of the enumerated values to form the **`bool`** expression that is required by the **`WriteLineIf`** or **`WriteIf`** methods. As an added convenience, the **`TraceSwitch`** classes have accessors that return true if the level set is greater than the level of the accessor. If the level of the switch is set to **`Warning`**, then not only will the **`TraceWarning`** method return **`true`**, but the **`TraceError`** method will return **`true`** also. Listing 19.2 illustrates the use of these accessors.

What if four levels are not enough, or you want to change the behavior of the accessors? For that, you can derive your own **`Switch`** class. Listing 19.3 shows a partial listing of a custom switch class. The full source for this listing is in the `TraceSwitch` directory.

LISTING 19.3 Defining a Custom Switch Class

```
// The possible values for the new switch.
public enum CustomTracingSwitchLevel
```

LISTING 19.3 Continued

```
{
  Off = 0,
  ShowStopper = 1,
  Critical = 2,
  Severe = 3,
  Annoying = 4,
  Success = 5
}
public class CustomTracingSwitch : Switch
{
  public CustomTracingSwitch(string displayName, string description) :
➥ base(displayName, description)
  {
  }
  public bool ShowStopper
  {
    get
    {
      return SwitchSetting >= (int)CustomTracingSwitchLevel.ShowStopper;
    }
  }
  public bool Critical
  {
    get
    {
      return SwitchSetting >= (int)CustomTracingSwitchLevel.Critical;
    }
  }
```

This custom class is used in much the same way that **TraceSwitch** is used. Following is an example of how to use this custom class:

```
CustomTracingSwitch cs = new CustomTracingSwitch("CustomSwitch",
➥ "Custom debugging switch");
Trace.WriteLineIf(cs.Annoying, "Custom error output", "Custom category");
```

The line in the configuration file that pertains to this switch is as follows:

```
<add name="CustomSwitch" value="4" />
```

Everything is just about the same as using the built-in **TraceSwitch** class.

You have substantial flexibility in specifying which messages are output. How do you specify where the output goes?

The output of the **Trace** and **Debug** classes goes to the debugger by default. Specifically, the output goes to `OutputDebugString`. Using the **TraceListener** class, the output can be redirected almost anywhere. Adding the following lines to a program directs the output of **Trace** and **Debug** classes to **System.Console.Out**:

```
TextWriterTraceListener myWriter = new
      TextWriterTraceListener(System.Console.Out);
Trace.Listeners.Add(myWriter);
```

As you can see, these lines add the **TraceListener** (**TextWriterTraceListener** is derived from **TraceListener**). Therefore, the output will still go to the debugger output window; you have just added an additional destination for the trace messages. What you have just done programmatically, you can also do with the configuration file. Listing 19.4 shows an example.

LISTING 19.4 TraceListener Configuration

```
<configuration>
  <system.diagnostics>
    <trace autoflush="true" indentsize="4">
      <listeners>
        <add name="debugOut" type="System.Diagnostics.DefaultTraceListener" />
        <add name="fileOut"
➥type="System.Diagnostics.TextWriterTraceListener"
➥initializeData="trace.log" />
        <add name="eventLogOut"
➥type="System.Diagnostics.EventLogTraceListener"
➥initializeData="TestTrace" />
        <remove name="debugOut" />
      </listeners>
    </trace>
    <switches>
      <add name="MySwitch" value="3" />
      <add name="YourSwitch" value="1" />
      <add name="CustomSwitch" value="4" />
    </switches>
  </system.diagnostics>
</configuration>
```

Here you have created listeners for the debugger (**DefaultTraceListener**), output to a file (**TextWriterTraceListener**), and output to the Event Log (**EventLogTraceListener**). These are currently the three classes that are derived from **TraceListener** that are available as part of the SDK. You can always build a class derived from **TraceListener** yourself.

Listing 19.5 shows how to programmatically add a custom **TraceListener** to your list of **TraceListener**s. This **TraceListener** accumulates all of the **Trace** output from the program and mails it to the address on the constructor. Naturally, you will want to change the e-mail address.

> **Note**
>
> The complete source for Listings 19.5 and 19.6 is located in the TraceSwitch directory in the TraceSwitch.cs file.

LISTING 19.5 Adding a Custom **TraceListener**

```
CustomTraceListener ctl = new CustomTraceListener
➥("first.last@mycompany.com");
Trace.Listeners.Add(ctl);
```

Listing 19.6 shows a portion of the implementation of this custom **TraceListener**.

LISTING 19.6 Implementing a Custom **TraceListener**

```
public class CustomTraceListener : TraceListener
{
  private Queue messageList;
  private StringBuilder message;
  private string mailTo;

  public CustomTraceListener(string to)
  {
    messageList = Queue.Synchronized(new Queue());
    mailTo = to;
  }
  public override void Close()
  {
    // The listener is closed
    Flush();

    MailMessage mailMessage = new MailMessage();
    mailMessage.To = mailTo;
    mailMessage.Subject = "Trace listing";
    mailMessage.BodyFormat = MailFormat.Text;

    while (messageList.Count > 0 )
      mailMessage.Body += messageList.Dequeue() + "\r\n";

    mailMessage.Body += "\r\n";
    SmtpMail.Send(mailMessage);
  }
  public override void Flush()
  {
    // The listener is flushed
    if(message != null)
    {
      messageList.Enqueue(message);
```

LISTING 19.6 Continued

```
        message = null;
    }
}
. . .
  public override void Write(string s)
  {
    // Write an appendable message
    if(message == null)
      message = new StringBuilder();
    message.Append(s);
  }
. . .
  public override void WriteLine(string s)
  {
    Flush();
    // Write a message line
    messageList.Enqueue(s);
. . .
```

This class is straightforward. All of the **Write** and **WriteLine** methods from **TraceListener** have been overwritten. For the **Write** methods, the message is appended to the end of the last **Write** message using the **StringBuilder** class. When a **WriteLine** method is called, the results are "flushed" from the **Write** calls and then the message passed in is queued. The **Flush** method and the **Close** methods of the **TraceListener** class are overridden. For **Flush**, the results from previous **Write** method calls, if any, are "flushed." The **Close** method actually does the work after it "flushes" the **Write** results. Then the mail message is built. The To field is set to be the same as that passed in on the constructor for the listener. The format and the subject are set appropriately. Then for every line that has been cached in the **Queue**, a line is built in the **Body** of the **MailMessage**. Finally, the message is sent. What if all of the information that you need to debug an application for an angry customer could be delivered to your desk?

John Robbins wrote a full-featured **TraceListener** class and a **TraceSwitch** class in his Bugslayer Column in the February 2001 issue of *MSDN Magazine*. His implementation of a `TraceListener` class allowed for one class to handle output for many different types of output. His class handles the case where an interactive user does not exist (as in a service). It has been reproduced in the `TraceListener\Bugslayer` directory mainly because his original implementation was for Beta 1 of the .NET Framework. The necessary modifications have been made, and it has put together as a solution for Visual Studio .NET.

This section will now focus on the method by which these classes are able to magically appear and reappear based on compile time switches.

At the heart of **Trace** and **Debug** (at least for C#) is the **ConditionalAttribute**.

> **Note**
>
> Not all languages that are supported by the CLR support this attribute in the same way. For example, you might have noticed that you have to take special care to enable or disable **Trace** and **Debug** calls with VC++. This is primarily because VC++ does not support the **ConditionalAttribute** in the same way that C# does.

This attribute is available to be used in any application whose language supports attributes. The compiler recognizes **ConditionalAtrribute**. If the **ConditionalAttribute** is encountered, the compiler makes sure that the method that is associated with this **attribute** is never called. This is a subtle point that might or might not be important in your application. Look at this example:

```
[Conditional("DEBUG")]
static void WriteDebugOutput()
{
  Console.WriteLine("This is debugging information");
}
```

This simple code has a **ConditionalAttribute** associated with it. Somewhere else in the code, you can make a call to this method:

```
WriteDebugOutput();
```

If DEBUG is defined, it is as if the **ConditionalAttribute** were absent and the call were being made to the WriteDebugOutput function. What is interesting is when DEBUG is not defined. It turns out that the code for WriteDebugOutput is present, but the calls to this implementation are removed if DEBUG is not defined. You can see this by using ILDASM on code that was compiled without DEBUG being defined. This is shown in Figure 19.2.

You can see from the main output that the method is still present, and clicking on the method shows that the code (along with the **ConditionalAttribute**) is still intact. Now look at Figure 19.3 with DEBUG defined.

At the end of code shown in Figure 19.3, you see the call to the function, as expected (the IL code instruction is call, and the method being called is WriteDebugOutput). To change this behavior, you need to compile the code and make sure that DEBUG is not defined. The resulting assembly looks like Figure 19.4.

The call to the function disappeared. The compiler noticed that the function had a **ConditionalAttribute** associated with it and the "condition" was not met; therefore, the compiler removed all calls to that method. The method will never be called. This means that it will never be referenced and it will never be turned into native code by the Just-In-Time (JIT) compiler. Notice also that the **Trace** statements are still present because in a release build, using the default Visual Studio .NET settings TRACE is defined.

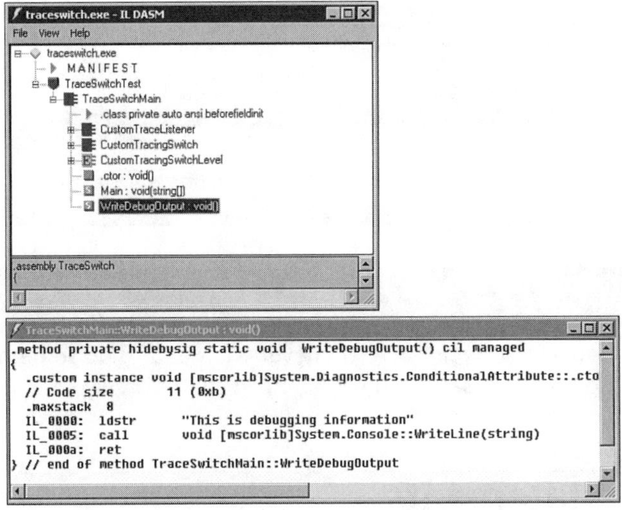

FIGURE 19.2
Code with a `Conditional` `Attribute`.

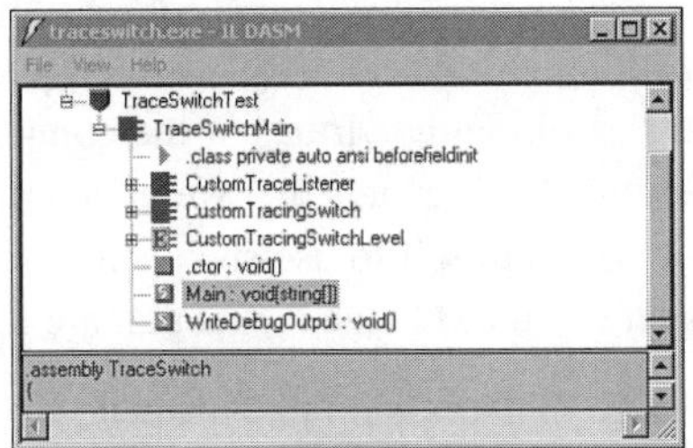

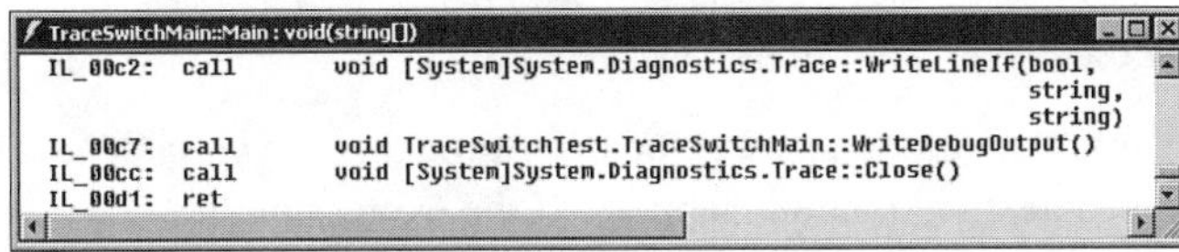

FIGURE 19.3
Conditional Compilation Output with DEBUG *Defined*

The net effect is that you can conditionally compile code. When the symbol passed to the constructor of the **ConditionalAttribute** is not defined, all calls to that method are removed and only the overhead of the code implementing the method remains (which should be minor).

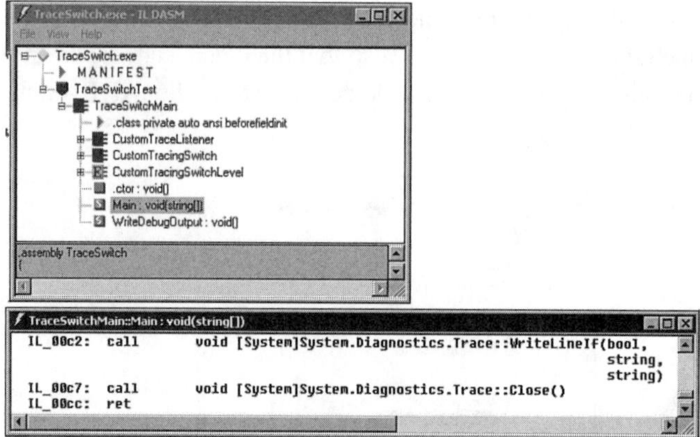

FIGURE 19.4
Conditional compilation output with DEBUG *not defined.*

> **Note**
>
> Use the **ConditionalAttribute** whenever you need to do something other than print a diagnostic message and you want to conditionally compile that code.

Assert Statements

I read an article in the *IEEE Spectrum Magazine* that I have not been able to locate since. In that article, the author, in a tongue-in-cheek way, was complaining about fault-tolerant computers. In essence, he was extolling the virtues of the computer that crashed horribly when there was a bug. He felt that having bugs that were "tolerated" in a computer was intolerable. He just could not bring himself to use such a computer. The software version of fault intolerance is the **Assert** and **Fail** statements that are a part of **Trace** and **Debug**.

With an **Assert**, you can specify an expression that evaluates to a **bool**. This would look like this:

```
Trace.Assert(a < 5, "a is less than 5");
```

This line would throw up a message box any time that the variable a is less than 5. If that expression is **true**, then nothing happens. If the expression is **false**, then a message box is thrown up indicating the line in the source of the assertion failure along with any optional message that can be passed to the **Assert** method. In the message box, the user has the option to Abort (stop the program), Retry (break in to the debugger), or Ignore (continue the program as if the **Assert** had not happened). **Fail** is similar to **Assert** except that a **bool** isn't available to pass to **Fail**. **Fail** always throws up a message box.

Fail("Error") is functionally equivalent to **Assert(false, "Error")**. Of course, because **Assert** and **Fail** are members of the **Trace** and **Debug** classes, they can be conditionally compiled out.

Trace.Fail or **Debug.Fail** should be considered alternatives to the VB **Stop** statement.

```
#If DEBUG Then
   Stop
#Else
   ' Don't stop
#End If
```

Event Logging

You have already seen at least a sample of using the Event Log with the **EventLogTraceListener** derived from **TraceListener**. Messages (events) can be added to the Event Log without using the **EventLogTraceListener**.

Reading the Event Log

All of the Event Log activity in .NET can be controlled with the **EventLog** class. The **EventLog** class is used to read and write to the Event Log. First, look at an example of how you can use this class to read the Event Log. Listing 19.7 shows how to use the **EventLog** class to read from the Event Log. This listing shows all of the entries from the "Application" log on the local machine (".").

Note

The complete source for this sample is in the `EventLogging` directory in the `EventLogging.cs` file.

LISTING 19.7 Displaying the Application Log

```
EventLog myApplicationLog = new EventLog("Application",".");
foreach(EventLogEntry entry in myApplicationLog.Entries)
{
  Console.WriteLine("\tEntry: " + entry.Message);
}
```

The first argument of the constructor is the name of the log. It is named "Application" here, but this is just for clarity because log filenames can be no longer than eight characters. Three special logs are on all servers: Application, System, and Security. All applications and services use the `Application` log. Device drivers use the `System` log. The system generates success and failure audit events in the `Security` log when security auditing is turned on.

Listing 19.7 just displayed the messages. No particular order is implied when enumerating through the messages like this. You can impose your own order by incorporating the TimeGenerated, TimeWritten, and Index into your listing.

The last argument to the constructor is the name of the machine. The convention here is that "." signifies the local machine.

As you iterate through the **`Entries`** for this **`EventLog`**, only print out the **`Message`** property of each **`Entry`**. Numerous other properties exist, such as **`TimeWritten`**, **`TimeGenerated`**, **`MachineName`**, **`EntryType`**, **`UserName`**, **`EventID`**, and **`CategoryNumber`**.

Writing to the Event Log

When using the **`EventLogTraceListener`**, all of the events generated are placed in the `Application` log. This is fine for a small number of applications. A better approach would be to create a separate log for an individual application or group of applications that originated from a single company. Listing 19.8 shows the steps necessary to create a custom Event Log. The complete source associated with this listing is in the `EventLogging` directory in the `EventLogging.cs` file.

LISTING 19.8 Creating a Custom Event Log

```
const string log = "MyEventLog";
const string source = "EventLoggingSource";
. . .

//Create an EventLog instance and assign its source.
EventLog myLog = new EventLog(log, ".", source);
```

When creating a new log, it is assumed that you will want to write to it. To write to the Event Log, you have to declare a source name. If you don't specify a source, the first write operation to the Event Log generates an exception:

```
An unhandled exception of type 'System.ArgumentException' occurred
➥in system.dll
Additional information: Source property was not set before writing
➥to the Event Log.
```

A source name can be any arbitrary string, but it must be defined. If the source does not exist then the first Write to the Event Log will create the source.

After the Event Log has been created and a source has been registered, you are ready to write to the log. Listing 19.9 shows an example of writing an entry to the log.

LISTING 19.9 Writing Messages to the Log

```
myLog.WriteEntry("Writing information to the event log.");
myLog.WriteEntry("Writing an error to the event log.",
➥EventLogEntryType.Error);
myLog.WriteEntry("Writing a warning to the event log.",
➥EventLogEntryType.Warning);
myLog.WriteEntry("Writing a success audit to the event log.",
➥EventLogEntryType.SuccessAudit);
myLog.WriteEntry("Writing a failure audit to the event log.",
➥EventLogEntryType.FailureAudit);
myLog.WriteEntry("Writing to the event log with an ID.",
➥EventLogEntryType.Error, 1, 2);
```

Figure 19.5 shows a view of the log that has been created. Note that the application in the **EventLogging** directory stops on a **Console.ReadLine** so that the user can open the event viewer and see the events created. After the events have been created and the user enters a character, the log is deleted.

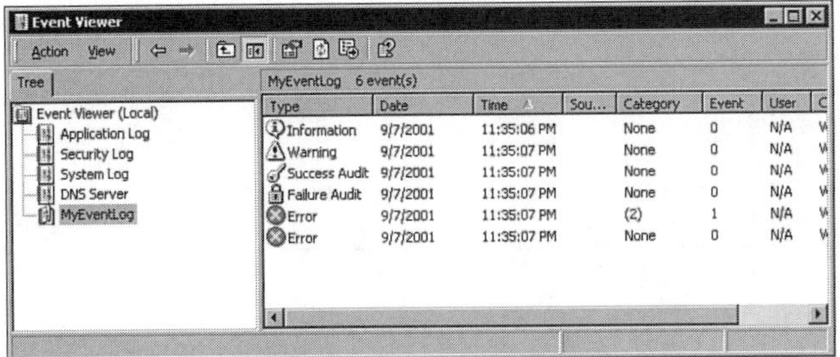

FIGURE 19.5
Writing to the Event Log.

Several overloaded **WriteEntry** methods exist. Each method either has default values for an "entry" or allows for filling a value for the "entry." For example, the last call in Listing 19.9 not only writes a value for the message, but the second argument is also the type of message. An Event Log entry can have one of the following types:

- `Error`
- `FailureAudit`
- `SuccessAudit`
- `Information`
- `Warning`

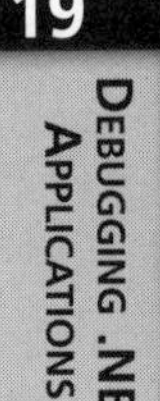

Note

An example of every type of event has been included in Listing 19.9, and the results can be seen in Figure 19.5.

The next argument in the sample is the event identifier. This is an application-specific identifier for a particular event. It is intended that this identifier be used to map a specific string that can be used to describe details about the error or event. The source and the event identifier uniquely identify an event.

The final argument is a category ID. The category ID is also an application-specific identifier that can be used to sort a list of events and otherwise give more detailed information about the event.

In the application that you have been following, Listing 19.10 shows how to remove the log and the event source after the user presses Enter.

LISTING 19.10 Removing a Log

```
Console.ReadLine();
myLog.Close();
EventLog.DeleteEventSource("EventLoggingSource");
EventLog.Delete("MyEventLog");
```

Setting Up Event Notification

It is possible to set up a process that "listens" for events from a particular source. Setting up an event source that can act as a notification is identical to the process involved in just writing to the Event Log. I have written an event source that acts as a source for an event that can be configured via a simple dialog box. This dialog box looks like Figure 19.6.

FIGURE 19.6
An event source.

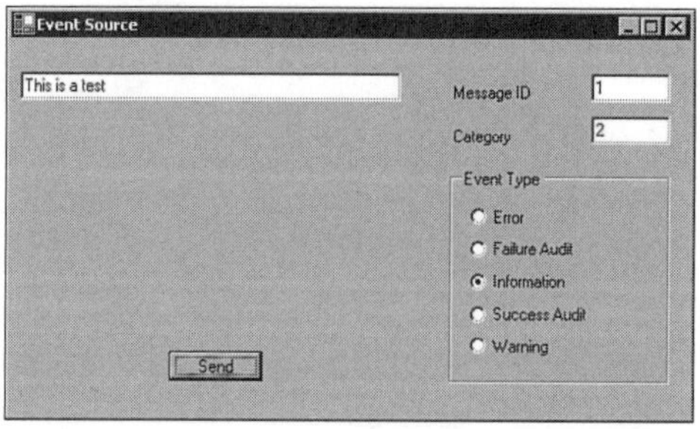

This event source just writes an event that is configurable by the user to the Event Log. The details of writing to the Event Log are identical to that discussed in the previous section.

Note

The complete source for this application is in the `EventSourceSink` directory. A `Source` directory and a `Sink` subdirectory contain individual projects for the `Source` and `Sink` projects respectively.

For purposes of this discussion, the `Sink` project is the most interesting. The key difference in setting up an event sink is the addition of the following line:

```
this.eventLog.EntryWritten +=
➥new System.Diagnostics.EntryWrittenEventHandler(this.OnEntryWritten);
```

This line registers an event that will be called each time an event is written to the log. When an event is written to the log, the `OnEntryWritten` method is called. This method is shown in Listing 19.11.

LISTING 19.11 Writing Messages to the Log

```
private void OnEntryWritten(object sender,
➥System.Diagnostics.EntryWrittenEventArgs e)
{
  DateTime time = e.Entry.TimeGenerated;
  string entryType = e.Entry.EntryType.ToString();
  string message = e.Entry.Message;
  string id = Convert.ToString(e.Entry.EventID);
  string cat = Convert.ToString(e.Entry.CategoryNumber);
  messageListBox.Items.Add(time + " " + entryType + " " +
➥message + " " + id + " " + cat);
}
```

The routine is simple. All of the information that was written to the Event Log is contained in **`EntryWrittenEventArgs`**. For this sample, this information is added to the **`ListBox`**. The resulting application looks like Figure 19.7.

As each event is written to the log, the `OnEntryWritten` method is called in the `Sink` application and the information is added to the contents of the **`ListBox`**. Figure 19.8 illustrates passing the same information to the sink and the Event Log.

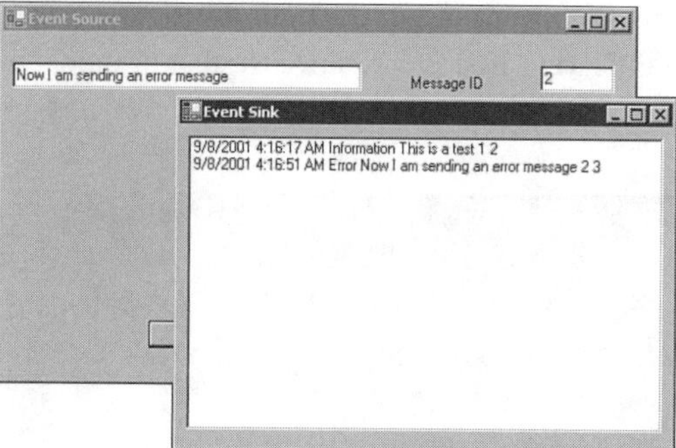

FIGURE 19.7
An event sink.

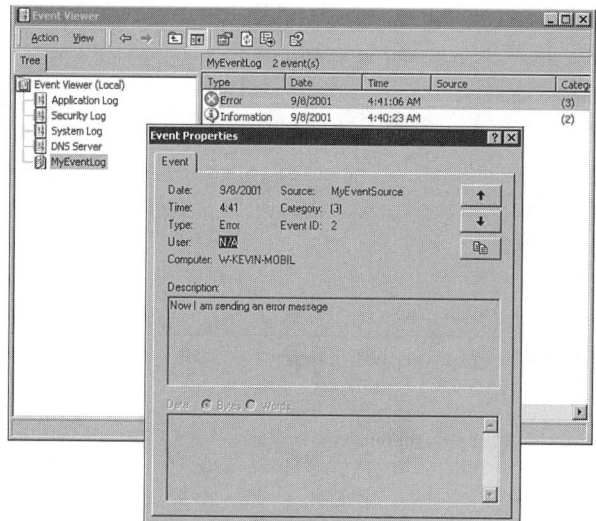

FIGURE 19.8
The Event Log for the source/sink sample.

Providing Feedback from an ASP.NET Page

ASP.NET uses the CLR and the .NET Framework to help generate useful error and trace information that can be used to debug an application. This information can be dynamically turned on and off. Turning on this debugging information on an ASP.NET page is as simple as adding `trace="true"` to a `Page` directive like this:

```
<%@ Page language="c#" trace="true" %>
```

Note

This section assumes that the reader has some familiarity with ASP.NET for this discussion to be the most useful.

The complete source for this ASP.NET page is in the `ASPTrace` directory. Some initial setup is required so that this sample works as advertised. The main work is to create a virtual directory that points to the location of this page source. First, you need to invoke the Internet Services Manager, right-click Default Web Site, and select New - Virtual Directory. This brings up the dialog box shown in Figure 19.9.

FIGURE 19.9
Configuring a new virtual directory.

When you have the wizard up, click on the Next button to begin adding a virtual directory. For an alias, specify ASPTrace. When the wizard prompts for the physical directory, enter the directory in which the ASPTrace sample was installed. Now Internet Information Services should look like Figure 19.10.

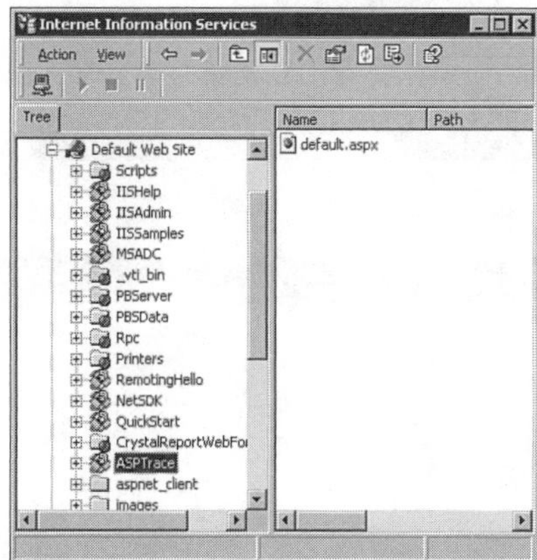

FIGURE 19.10
Virtual directories in the Internet Information Services.

Now when you specify `http://localhost/ASPTrace/default.aspx` as a URL for your browser, this sample will be run. With the trace turned on, this page shows a complete set of statistics that are acquired while generating the page, as shown in Figure 19.11.

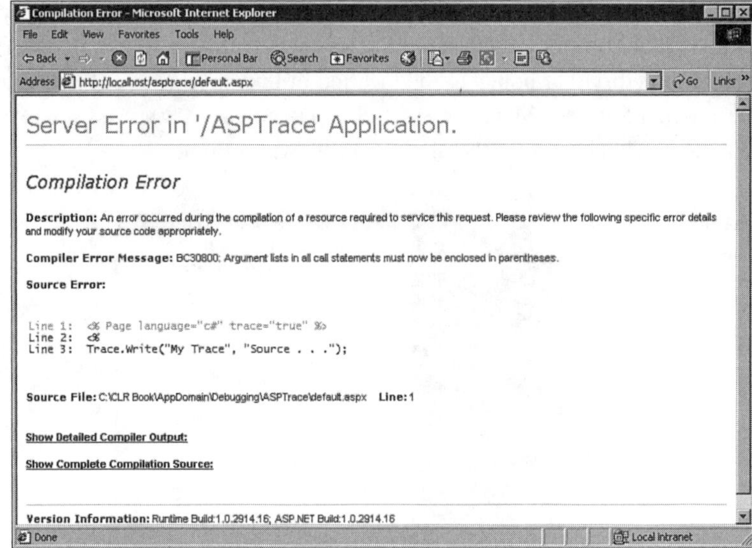

FIGURE 19.11
A faulty ASP.NET page.

A syntax error exists on the page. As you can see, ASP.NET generates detailed error information that allows you to quickly determine the problem with a given Web page. After the problem is corrected, the ASP.NET page looks like Figure 19.12.

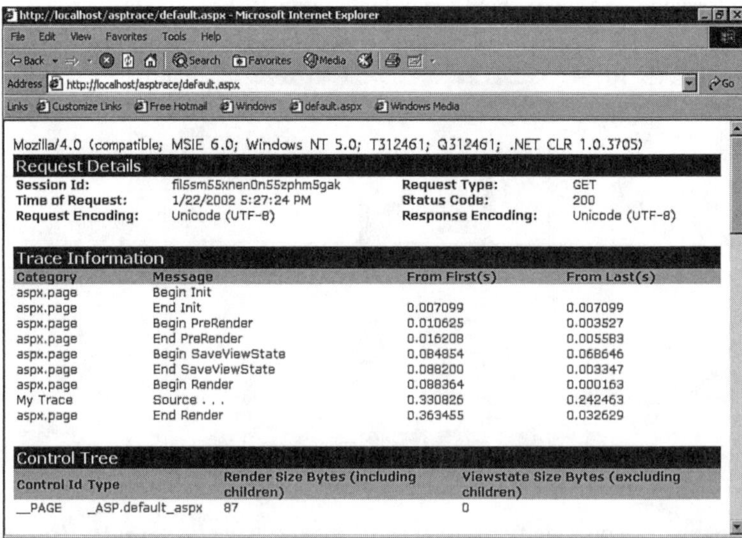

FIGURE 19.12
Trace statistics on an ASP.NET page.

Toward the end of the Trace Information shown in Figure 19.12 is a category called My Trace. Where did this come from? Looking at the source for the page, you see code that looks like Listing 19.12.

LISTING 19.12 Generating Custom Trace Information on an ASP.NET Page

```
<%
    Trace.Write("My Trace", "Source . . .");
    HttpRequest r;
    r = this.Request;
    HttpResponse rs;
    rs = this.Response;
    rs.Write(r.ServerVariables["HTTP_USER_AGENT"]);
%>
```

When tracing is turned off (trace="false" or the attribute is removed), this Web Page simply echoes the HTTP_USER_AGENT server variable to the caller. You can ignore most of Listing 19.12 for the purposes of debugging. The line `Trace.Write...` is where the trace information is generated for Figure 19.11. Unlike the **`Trace`** and **`Debug`** classes, the first argument specifying a category is neither optional nor numeric, and its output is directed to the caller's Web page. Other than that difference, this function behaves identically to the similar statements with the **`Trace`** and **`Debug`** classes. Gone are the days when "Response.Write" statements had to be sprinkled throughout the code to diagnose a problem.

Using the `ErrorProvider` Class

One way to debug an application is to prevent bad data from being entered into the application. Although this might sound like a simple enough procedure, correct user validation is often a critical feature that is overlooked. (Only one example is supplied here using a specific error validation method.) Look at other means of validating input, and don't assume anything about input data. There are as many ways to validate user input as there are different types of user input. One particularly interesting feedback mechanism that can be used to provide the user of an application information about what is wrong with the input provided is the **`ErrorProvider`** class.

One common approach to validation is a message box popping up to indicate the reason for a failed validation. This is not only intrusive, but after the message box is dismissed, the error often remains. A better solution is to use the **`ErrorProvider`** class. This class puts a small icon next to the offending input. When the user hovers over the icon, a familiar ToolTip provides details about why this input was not correctly validated. Although originally developed for validating input records from a database, this class can be used in an application that has no association with a database.

Validating User Input and the **ErrorProvider**

To use the **ErrorProvider** class, you can add it to a form or construct it manually. In this sample, the latter was chosen. The following code shows how the **ErrorProvider** class is instantiated and initialized for use in an application.

```
private ErrorProvider errorProvider;
. . .
errorProvider = new ErrorProvider();
```

An event handler is registered to handle the validating event. In the body of the event handler, part of which is shown in Listing 19.13, you can see how the **ErrorProvider** class can be used. The complete source for this sample is in the `Validation` directory.

LISTING 19.13 Validating User Input in an Event Handler

```
private void OnRangeValidating(object sender,
➥System.ComponentModel.CancelEventArgs e)
{
  TextBox t = sender as TextBox;
  try
  {
    int x = Int32.Parse(t.Text);
    if(x > 0 && x <= 10)
      errorProvider.SetError(t, "");
    else
    {
      errorProvider.SetError(t, string.Format(
➥"Invalid range. {0} is not between 1 and 10", x));
      throw new ArgumentOutOfRangeException(t.ToString(),
➥x, "Enter a numbr from 1 to 10");
    }
  }
```

This event handler first casts the sender **object** to a **TextBox**. Although in this sample, this is the only source for the event, you could develop measures that are more defensive. Such measures would depend on what you are defending against. You might suspect an error in the parse routine, the text might change while it is being parsed in a multi-threaded environment, and the parser might have a problem that causes it to modify more than just the variable that is the target of the operation. However, for the purposes of this sample, leave out that code. The content of the **TextBox** is parsed for an integer and compared to the range 1 to 10. If it is in the range, the error is cleared. If the number is out of range, the error is recorded and an exception is thrown that indicates the error. The exception is raised to indicate that the user input is invalid. Calling **SetError** initializes the ToolTip with the string passed as the second argument. The first argument is a reference to the control, and it is passed to the **SetError** so that the icon that indicates an error can be correctly placed. When the input is determined to be invalid, the sample ends up looking like Figure 19.13.

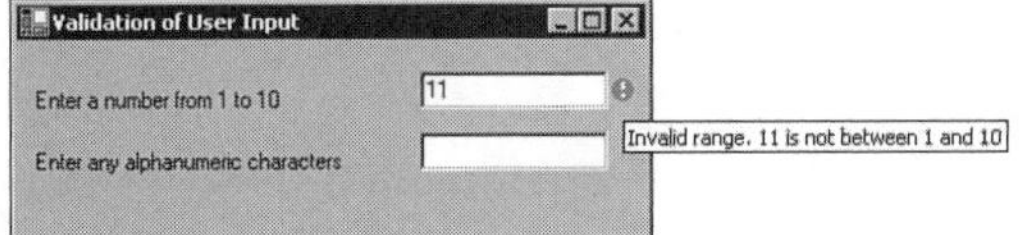

FIGURE 19.13
Using **ErrorProvider** *with user input.*

Validating Database Input and the ErrorProvider

Database applications are outside of the scope of this book. The information is only provided here to illustrate how this debugging technique can be applied to a database application. It is assumed that you have some database application experience to fully appreciate the code in this section.

To validate data that is retrieved as a record set from a database can be challenging because no clear way exists to provide feedback to the user. A message box could be popped up with each invalid entry, but that would be annoying to the user and possibly cause the application to become unusable. (What if 1,000 records were read in and 500 had validation errors?) One of the original intentions for the **ErrorProvider** class was to indicate invalid entries in a database. A small sample has been put together that uses the Northwind database (shipped as a sample database in almost all SQL Server installations). In this sample, the `Employees` table is read. An "error" indicator has been placed next to all those employees who have 9 or more years of service. For those employees, the error indicator simply "reminds" the user that these employees deserve a raise. Listing 19.14 shows how you can use this class to indicate exceptional or error conditions on database data. The complete source for this listing is in the `ValidatingData` directory.

LISTING 19.14 Validating Data in a Database

```
private void OnLoadData(object sender, System.EventArgs e)
{
  errorProvider = new ErrorProvider();
  errorProvider.ContainerControl = this;
  errorProvider.BlinkRate = 200;

  string select = "SELECT EmployeeID, LastName, FirstName, Title, BirthDate,
➥HireDate, Notes FROM Employees";
  SqlDataAdapter cmd = new SqlDataAdapter(select, sqlNorthwindConnection);
  Employees ds = new Employees();
  cmd.Fill(ds, "Employees");
```

LISTING 19.14 Continued

```
  employeesDataGrid.SetDataBinding(ds, "Employees");

  errorProvider.DataSource = ds;
  errorProvider.DataMember = "Employees";

  foreach (DataRow row in (ds.EmployeesTable.Rows))
  {
    DateTime hd = Convert.ToDateTime(row["HireDate"]);
    TimeSpan seniority = DateTime.Now - hd;
    if (seniority.TotalDays/365.25 > 9)
    {
      row.RowError = "Is this employee due for a raise?";
      row.SetColumnError("HireDate", string.Format("This employee is has been
➥working for us for {0:F0} years.", seniority.TotalDays/365.25));
    }
  }
}
```

The only difference in setting up the **ErrorProvider** is that different properties are set. For a database application, the **ContainerControl**, **DataSource**, and **DataMember** properties must be set. The **ContainerControl** is the control that contains the control with which the data is associated. For this sample, the **DataGrid** control is contained in the main dialog box. The **DataSource** is the class that is used to cache the results from the data query. For this sample, the **DataGrid** contains only one table, so the **DataMember** is the name given to that member.

Now when the **ErrorProvider** is properly associated with the database control, it can be used to provide feedback to the user about invalid data in the database. This feedback is specifically indicated with the **RowError** and **SetColumnError** methods of the **DataRow** class. The resulting output looks like Figure 19.14.

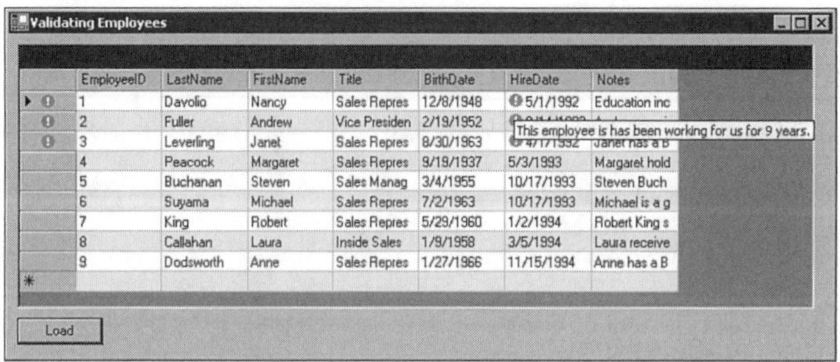

FIGURE 19.14
Using ErrorProvider *with database input.*

A user can be notified of error conditions in many different ways. The method that you choose is highly dependent on your application. If you ship your applications with a guarantee of no bugs, then error feedback is unnecessary. However, it is possible that a bug might creep into the software before it ships. If this is a possibility, then you must pay careful attention to make sure sufficient information is provided if an error occurs. Customers are usually willing to help gather information about a problem as long as there is information to gather. If there is no information to gather about an error, then customers quickly become concerned that the problem will not be resolved. Their concerns might be justified. It is essential that error and debugging information are designed into the application early.

Using a Debugger

As part of Visual Studio .NET, two debuggers are available: DbgClr and Devenv. DbgClr is almost identical to the debugger associated with the Visual Studio Development Environment except that it provides a read-only view of a particular project. With DbgClr, it is not possible to use edit-and-continue, and it is not possible to modify the source, recompile, and run from the same tool like it is with the debugger associated with Visual Studio .NET (devenv.exe). These differences aside, the functionality is just about the same for each of the tools. DbgClr might be faster than Devenv simply because not as much overhead is associated with DbgClr. DbgClr doesn't have a compiler, editor, and so on built in like Devenv does.

Any programmer who has used either the debugger associated with Visual Basic or the debugger associated with previous versions of Visual Studio should find most of the features familiar. The following sections highlight some of the added features of the debugger(s) that are a part of the Visual Studio .NET suite of tools.

Setting Breakpoints

You can set breakpoints just as you do with Visual Studio 6. You simply highlight the line on which the breakpoint should be set, right-click, and select Insert Breakpoint. You can also select New Breakpoint and specified options to be applied to the breakpoint, such as Hit Count and Condition, before setting the breakpoint.

One special note is Visual Studio .NET makes a clear distinction between debugging managed code and debugging unmanaged code. If your application includes both managed code and unmanaged code and the main project uses managed code, then to step into or set breakpoints in the source of unmanaged code, you need to specifically enable this feature. Figure 19.15 shows where you can enable debugging unmanaged code.

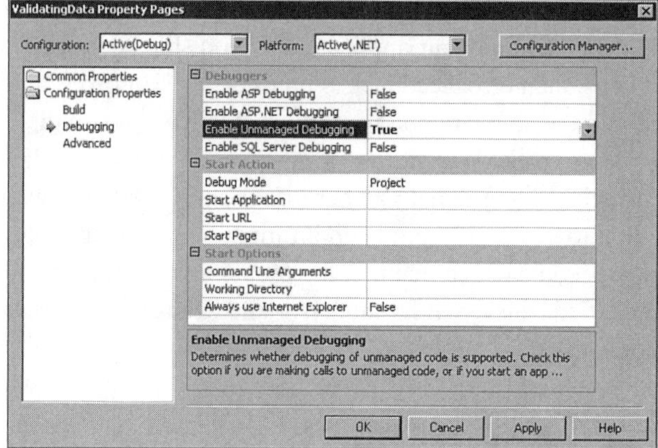

FIGURE 19.15
Enable unmanaged code debugging.

After this Enable Unmanaged Debugging option has been set to True, you can freely debug both unmanaged and managed code. Without this option, calls into unmanaged code are skipped.

Stepping Through Your Code

One particularly useful option that a debugger provides is the ability to single step through your code. This is supported with Visual Studio .NET. The main difference is that now you can debug an application that consists of multiple languages. For example, your main assembly is written in C# and you reference or link in code that was compiled with Visual Basic. As you step through the code with a debugger, you can step into code written in either Visual Basic or C#. You can set breakpoints in either the Visual Basic source code or the C# source code, and the program will stop when that point in your execution path has been reached. In other words, debugging an application that is composed of multiple languages can happen just as easily as if the whole project were written in one language.

Status Information

Much of the information about your application is provided. This is particularly important when multiple AppDomains, threads, or processes exist. With the debugger, you can switch into the context of any AppDomain, thread, or process easily. Look at the toolbar in Figure 19.16, which shows a debugging of the ThreadPoolTest sample introduced in Chapter 14, "`Delegates` and `Events`."

The same toolbar is shown, this time with the thread information selected in Figure 19.17.

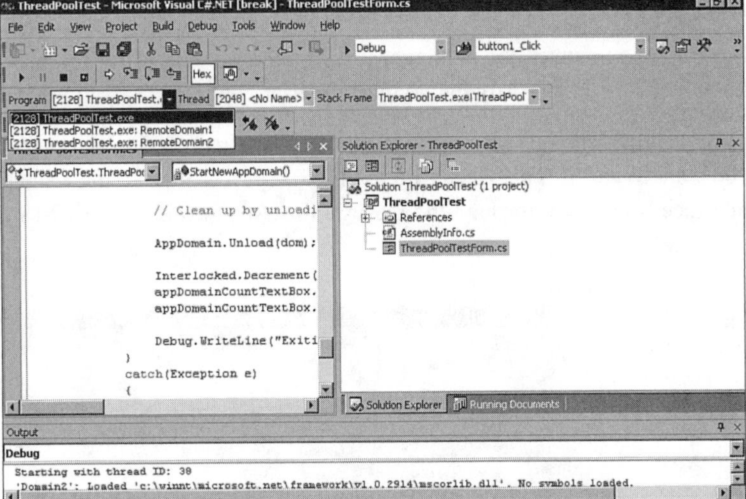

FIGURE 19.16
Application AppDomain information.

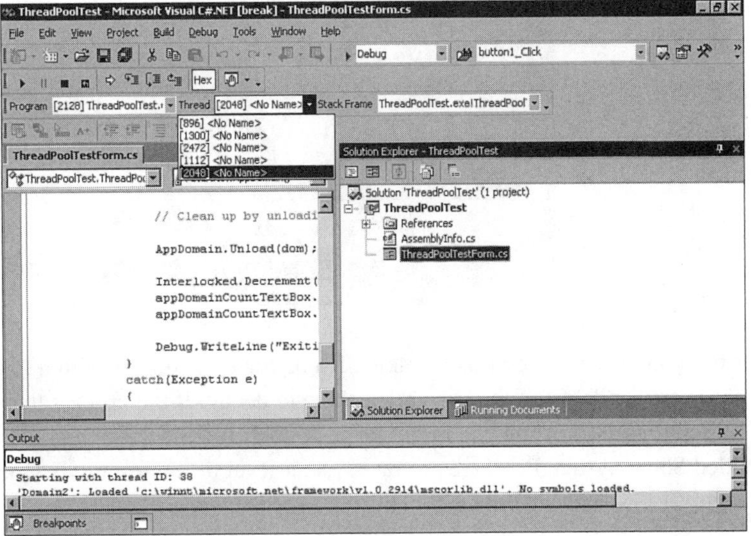

FIGURE 19.17
Application thread information.

By selecting any of the input provided in these drop-down menus, the user can move to that particular context. Selecting a particular thread changes the debugger to show the current line in the source that the particular thread is executing. Something similar happens when a particular **`AppDomain`** is selected. Note that you are still actually selecting a thread context, but if that context is currently in another **`AppDomain`**, then the drop-down list shows the friendly name of the **`AppDomain`** that is currently hosting the particular thread.

Attaching to a Running Process

It is possible to attach the debugger to a running process. After the debugger is attached, that process is temporarily halted until the user continues it from the debugger.

To attach the debugger to a running process, you first need to select the process to which you want to attach. The Visual Studio .NET IDE provides an interface to do this. This interface is accessed through the Debug\Processes menu. Figure 19.18 shows this interface.

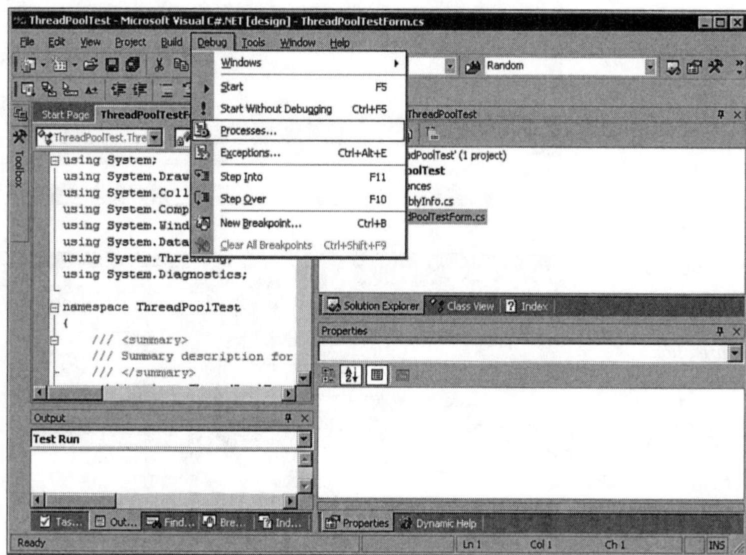

FIGURE 19.18
Selecting a process to which to attach.

After you have selected this menu item, a dialog box appears with a list of all of the processes available on the current machine to debug. If the process that you want to debug is a service, then you might need to select the check box in the lower-left corner titled Show System Processes so that system-level processes are included in the list. Figure 19.19 shows what a typical list of processes might look like.

As you can see from this figure, not only do you get a listing of available processes, but you also can see which processes are .NET applications and which are not. Select ThreadPoolTest.exe, which is a .NET application. A dialog box appears prompting you to input the types of applications that you want to debug. You want to debug both Common Language Runtime programs and Native (unmanaged) programs. Because this is the default, you don't have to do anything here. Just click OK. Figure 19.20 shows what this dialog box looks like.

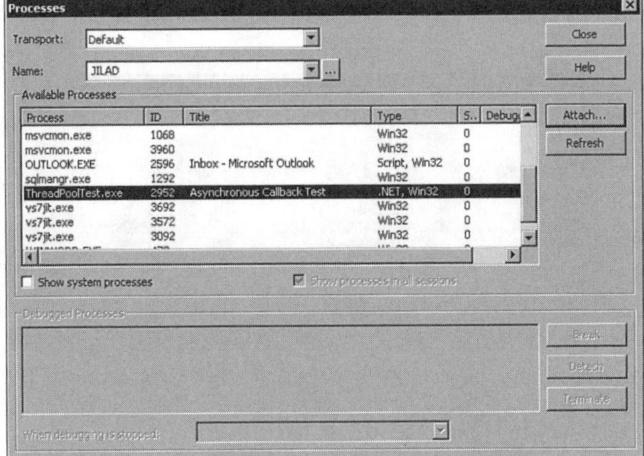

FIGURE 19.19
Selecting a process from a list of processes.

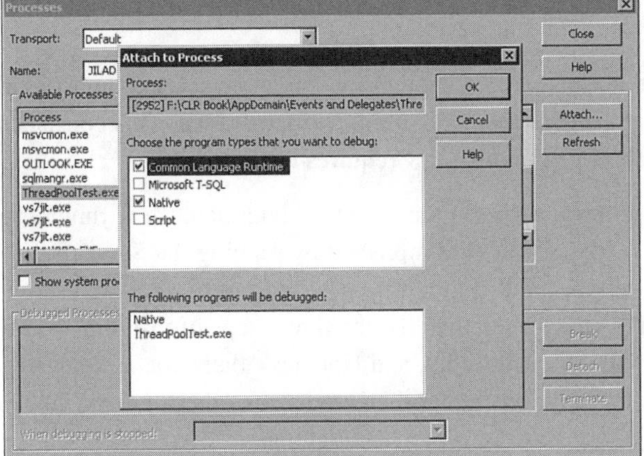

FIGURE 19.20
Selecting the program types to debug.

After you click OK, the process is attached to the debugger and you are returned to the original process listing dialog box (as shown in Figure 19.19). However, this time is refreshed to indicate that you have attached to the process (see Figure 19.21).

After the process has been successfully attached to the debugger, the window shown in Figure 19.21 can be dismissed. If you load a source page associated with the program being debugged, you will be able to set breakpoints and single step through the program just as if you had started up with the debugger.

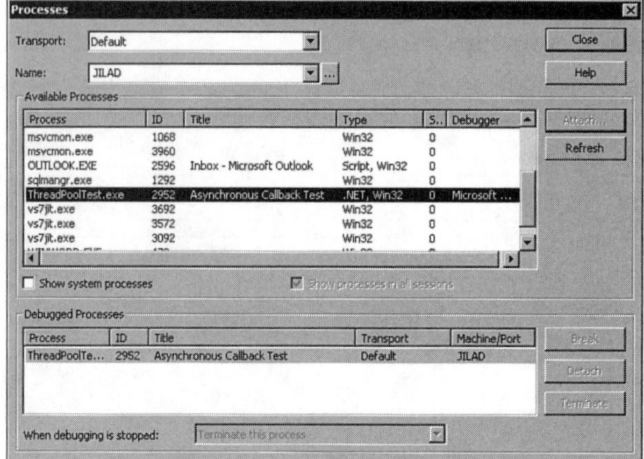

FIGURE 19.21
Showing the process that has been attached to the debugger.

Remote Debugging

It is possible to debug a process on another machine. To do this, you essentially follow the same steps as attaching to a process on the local machine. Remote debugging requires some setup first, however.

For the process to run at all on another machine, the machine must at least have the redistributable portion of the .NET Framework installed. This consists mostly of the DLLs and executables that the CLR requires to run.

You also have to make sure that the remote debug manager is running on the remote machine. This is most easily accomplished by running the Server Setup on the CD that was used to install the SDK. In the lower-left corner of the initial setup screen when you installed the SDK (the screen that had the three steps of installing the Windows Component Update, Visual Studio, and Updates), there was a small hyperlink, Server Setup. If you clicked on this rather than any of the other options, you would have installed the required files for remote debugging.

When you have completed both of these steps successfully, you should be able to go to the Services icon of the administrative tools and see that the Machine Debug Manager (mdm.exe) is running. The Services tool should look like Figure 19.22.

The specific properties of this service should look like Figure 19.23.

Of primary importance is that the service is started. The service should be configured to start automatically. If the service is configured to start manually, you will need to remember to start it before each debug session.

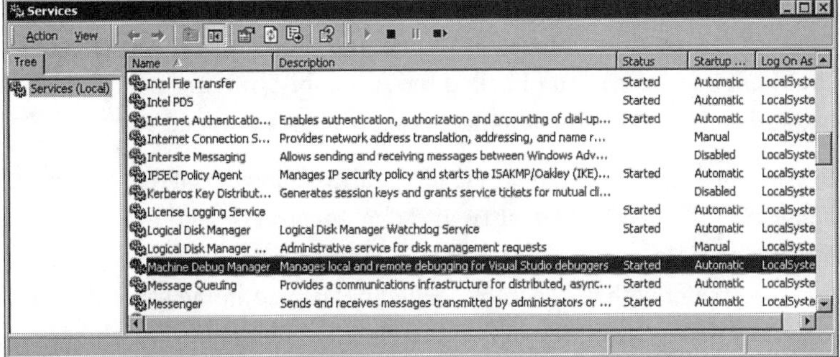

FIGURE 19.22
Machine Debug Manager.

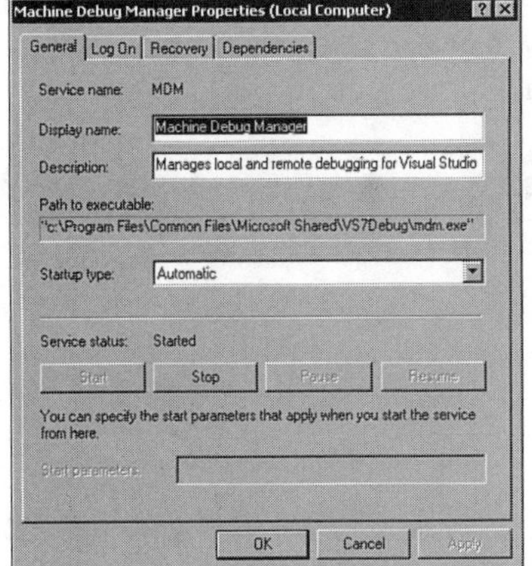

FIGURE 19.23
Machine Debug Manager service properties.

When this initial setup is complete, you can attach to a process on a remote machine exactly as you attached to a process on the local machine. A portion of the dialog box allows you to set the machine name from where the process list is to come. You can specify the machine name of any machine that has been properly set up. After a process has been attached on the remote machine, debugging proceeds exactly as described previously in the "Attaching to a Running Process" section.

Determining Assembly Load Failures

With managed code and the CLR, an assembly might not load properly. This usually is the result of an assembly being in the incorrect location or having been renamed, or because of a version or culture mismatch. For whatever reason, it can be annoying when the application will not run because of this error. It is often difficult to trace down the cause of this error. (Compare this to the old problem that was encountered when a DLL could not be found.) A tool called the Assembly Binding Log Viewer (fuslogvw.exe) can help diagnose a problem when an assembly does not load correctly.

In Chapter 14, you saw an application called ThreadPoolTest.exe that created an **AppDomain**, loaded an **Assembly** into that **AppDomain**, and ran it. (It specifically loaded the DiningPhilosopers.exe assembly.) Part of the requirement for this application was that the assembly that was to be loaded be located in the same directory as the main assembly. Go to that directory and rename the DiningPhilosophers.exe assembly to dp.exe. Now as far as the application is concerned, the DiningPhilosophers.exe assembly does not exist. When you run the application and click Start, you get a failure because the assembly cannot be found. If you invoke fuslogvw.exe (invoke it from a Command Prompt window as fuslogvw), you will see something like Figure 19.24.

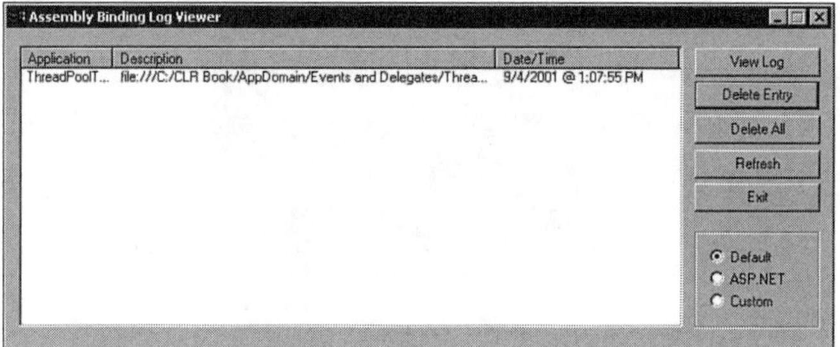

FIGURE 19.24
Looking at assembly binder failures.

A failure was recorded for the ThreadPoolTest.exe process. If you select the far left column and click the button View Log, you will see a detailed report of the failure, as shown in Figure 19.25.

From this report, you can see that the reason for the failure was "The system cannot find the file specified." You already know that because you caused the error. When the load failure is not so obvious, it is nice to know that this tool exists to tell you why.

You can cause successes to be logged in addition to failures by modifying the registry with the following line:

```
Windows Registry Editor Version 5.00
[HKEY_LOCAL_MACHINE\SOFTWARE\Microsoft\Fusion]
"ForceLog"=dword:00000001
```

Changing this entry back to 0 or "false" returns the logging behavior to the default of logging failures only.

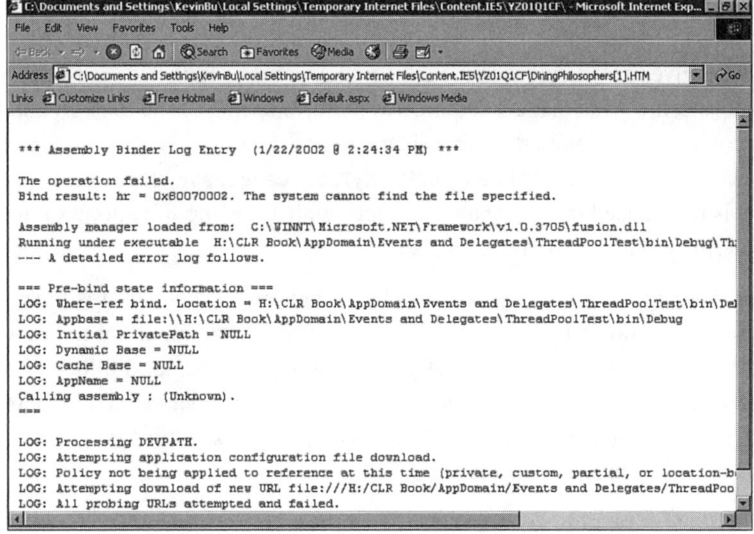

FIGURE 19.25
Detailed report of an assembly binder failure.

It is possible to add another entry, “LogPath”, to this registry entry. With this setting, you can select the Custom radio box for the fuslogvw.exe application. The log entries will be displayed for this path. It is recommended that the default be used because with the “Custom” log path, the user becomes responsible for cleaning the log entries; in the default location, the system handles the cleaning task. Following is a registry sample showing how to set a custom log entry:

```
Windows Registry Editor Version 5.00
[HKEY_LOCAL_MACHINE\SOFTWARE\Microsoft\Fusion]
"LogPath"="D:\\FusLog"
```

An entry exists for ASP.NET. If you suspect that the assembly binder failure is a part of ASP.NET, then this radio button should be selected. Normally, the default contains log entries for everything but ASP.NET.

Building Your Own Debugger

When all else fails, you can build your own debugger. Before .NET, this option was rarely considered because of the deep understanding that was required of the specific compiler, the executable format, machine-dependent assembly instructions, and so on. With the .NET Framework, a well-documented debugging API is available.

The documentation for the debugging API is in two documents: in `\Program Files\Microsoft Visual Studio .NET\FrameworkSDK\Tool Developer`

Guidelines\docs\Debug.doc and \Program Files\Microsoft Visual Studio .NET\FrameworkSDK\Tool Developer Guidelines\docs\DebugRef.doc. The first document gives an overview of the debugging process and the second goes into detail about the specific APIs that are required to perform specific functions. In addition, source is provided for a command-line debugger cordbg.exe in \Program Files\Microsoft Visual Studio .NET\FrameworkSDK\Tool Developer Guidelines\Samples\debugger. It is reproduced in the cordbg directory with a few modifications so that you can compile it with Visual Studio .NET as a solution.

Although you might never need to build your own debugger, it is nice to know that it is possible to do so with relatively little work. It is also important to know how a basic debugger is put together so that you can appreciate the possibilities and limitations of the debugger that you choose to use. The APIs that are documented in Debug.doc and DebugRef.doc are the same APIs that companies like Numega are using to build tools to help you debug your application.

Cordbg is not a toy debugger that is only useful for illustrating the debugging API. It is a powerful debugger that can be used to do serious debugging work. To get an overview of the functionality of the debugger, invoke cordbg. Then type h or help at the command prompt. Listing 19.15 shows some of the commands available. Complete documentation on this sample is available at ms-help://MS.VSCC/MS.MSDNVS/cptools/html/cpgrfruntimedebuggercordbgexe.htm.

LISTING 19.15 Cordbg Commands

```
Usage: h[elp] [<command> ...]
Displays debugger command descriptions. If no arguments
are passed, a list of debugger commands is displayed. If
one or more command arguments is provided, descriptions
are displayed for the specified commands. The ? command
is an alias for the help command.

The following commands are available:

ap[pdomainenum]     Display appdomains/assemblies/modules in the current
➥process
a[ttach]            Attach to a running process
as[sociatesource]   Associate a source file with a breakpoint or stack frame
b[reak]             Set or display breakpoints
con[t]              Continue the current process
ca[tch]             Stop on exception, thread, and/or load events
dis[assemble]       Display native disassembled instructions
del[ete]            Remove one or more breakpoints
du[mp]              Dump the contents of memory
d[own]              Navigate down from the current stack frame pointer
```

LISTING 19.15 Continued

```
de[tach]              Detach from the current process
ex[it]                Kill the current process and exit the debugger
f[unceval]            Function evaluation
g[o]                  Continue the current process
h[elp]                Display debugger command descriptions
i[n]                  Step into the next source line
ig[nore]              Ignore exception, thread, and/or load events
k[ill]                Kill the current process
l[ist]                Display loaded modules, classes, or global functions
m[ode]                Display/modify various debugger modes
ns[ingle]             Step over the next native instruction
n[ext]                Step over the next source line
news[tr]              Create a new string via function evaluation
newobjnc              Create a new object via function evaluation, no
➥constructor
newo[bj]              Create a new object via function evaluation
o[ut]                 Step out of the current function
pro[cessenum]         Display all managed processes running on the system
p[rint]               Print variables (locals, args, statics, etc.)
pa[th]                Set or display the source file search path
q[uit]                Kill the current process and exit the debugger
regd[efault]          Change the JIT debugger
r[un]                 Start a process for debugging
re[sume]              Resume a thread
rem[ove]              Remove one or more breakpoints
reg[isters]           Display CPU registers for current thread
ref[reshsource]       Reload a source file for display
<                     Read and execute commands from a file
su[spend]             Suspend a thread
ss[ingle]             Step into the next native instruction
so                    Step over the next source line
si                    Step into the next source line
s[tep]                Step into the next source line
sh[ow]                Display source code lines
set                   Modify the value of a variable (locals, statics, etc.)
setip                 Set the next statement to a new line
stop                  Set or display breakpoints
t[hreads]             Set or display current threads
>                     Write commands to a file
uw[here]              Display an unmanaged stack trace (Win32 mode only)
ut[hreads]            Set or display unmanaged threads (Win32 mode only)
uc[lear]              Clear the current unmanaged exception (Win32 mode only)
u[p]                  Navigate up from the current stack frame pointer
?                     Display debugger command descriptions
wt                    Track native instruction count and display call tree
wr[itememory]         Write memory to target process
w[here]               Display a stack trace for the current thread
x                     Display symbols matching a given pattern
```

If you are using this debugger, you probably want to know detailed information about the processes involved. You are probably using this debugger because the standard debugger does not display the information that you require. This debugger naturally has all of the same features that the UI debuggers have, although it is not as visual or easy to use. However, cordbg has some features that are not available in the standard UI debugger. Some of these features are "modes" with cordbg. These modes are shown in Listing 19.16.

LISTING 19.16 Cordbg Commands

```
AppDomainLoads=0          AppDomain and Assembly load events are not
➥displayed
ClassLoads=0              Class load events are not displayed
DumpMemoryInBytes=0       Memory is dumped in DWORDS
EnhancedDiag=0            Suppress display of diagnostic information
HexDisplay=1              Numbers are displayed in hexadecimal
ILNatPrint=0              Offsets will be IL xor native-relative
ISAll=0                   All interceptors are skipped
ISClinit=0                Class initializers are skipped
ISExceptF=0               Exception filters are skipped
ISInt=0                   User interceptors are skipped
ISPolicy=0                Context policies are skipped
ISSec=0                   Security interceptors are skipped
JitOptimizations=0        JIT's will produce debuggable (non-optimized) code
LoggingMessages=0         Managed log messages are suppressed
ModuleLoads=0             Module load events are not displayed
SeparateConsole=0         Debuggees share cordbg's console
ShowArgs=1                Arguments will be shown in stack trace
ShowModules=1             Module names will be included in stack trace
ShowStaticsOnPrint=0      Static fields are not included when displaying
➥objects
ShowSuperClassOnPrint=0   Super class names are not included when
➥displaying objects
UnmanagedTrace=0          Unmanaged debug events are not displayed
USAll=0                   Unmapped stop locations are skipped
USEpi=0                   Epilogs are skipped, returning to calling method
USPro=0                   Prologs are skipped
USUnmanaged=0             Unmanaged code is skipped
Win32Debugger=0           CorDbg is not the Win32 debugger for all processes
```

The primary mode to call attention to is the "`JitOptimizations`" mode. With this mode set to "0" when a function is encountered, the JIT will not optimize the code at all, thus producing "debuggable" code. If JIT optimizations are "1" or "enabled," then the JIT will optimize the code as it encounters each function. This could produce inline code. In addition, variables might only be associated with registers, which could be hard to debug as you try to associate the code generated with the high-level code that was the source. Using this option can reveal many unexpected problems and inconsistencies with your code as long as you are fluent with the native instruction set. Take a look at Listing 19.17, which shows a sample debug session with the "Hello World!" sample in Chapter 11, "Threading."

LISTING 19.17 Debugging `ThreadHelloWorld`

```
017:                    Thread t = new Thread(new ThreadStart(ThreadEntry));
(cordbg) sh
012:            {
013:                    Console.WriteLine("Hello Threading World!");
014:            }
015:            static void Main(string[] args)
016:            {
017:*                   Thread t = new Thread(new ThreadStart(ThreadEntry));
018:                    t.Name = "Hello World Thread";
019:                    t.Priority = ThreadPriority.AboveNormal;
020:                    t.Start();
021:                    t.Join();
022:            }
(cordbg) wt
      19         ThreadHelloWorldTest::Main
      16          Thread::set_Name
       4         String::Equals
       9          Thread::set_Name
       5         Debugger::.cctor
      19        Thread::set_Name
       7         ThreadHelloWorldTest::Main
      35        Thread::Start
[thread 0x300] Thread created.
Hello Threading World!
[thread 0x300] Thread exited.
       7        ThreadHelloWorldTest::Main

     121 instructions total
(cordbg)
```

The debugging output shows a clear trace of all of the calls made by this application. The call to set the **`Priority`** property and the call to **`Join()`** have been reduced to an inline call and show up as `ThreadHelloWorldTest::Main`. Notice that the number of native instructions executed is printed in the first column so that an idea of the cost of the method call can be gauged. If the JitOptimizations mode is turned off (set to zero), compare the output in Listing 19.18.

LISTING 19.18 Debugging `ThreadHelloWorld` with JitOptimizations Turned Off

```
(cordbg) wt
      13         ThreadHelloWorldTest::Main
       8          Thread::.cctor
      17           LocalDataStoreMgr::.ctor
       7            ArrayList::.ctor
       8           Object::.ctor
      10          ArrayList::.ctor
       7           LocalDataStoreMgr::.ctor
      19           Hashtable::.cctor
      33              Hashtable::.ctor
       8             Object::.ctor
      28              Hashtable::.ctor
      41             Hashtable::GetPrime
      23              Hashtable::.ctor
      10             Hashtable::set_hcp
       3              Hashtable::.ctor
      10             Hashtable::set_comparer
      18          Hashtable::.ctor
       4           LocalDataStoreMgr::.ctor
       8          Object::.ctor
       6         LocalDataStoreMgr::.ctor
       9         Thread::.cctor
       9          Thread::.ctor
       8         Object::.ctor
      11        Thread::.ctor
       5         ThreadHelloWorldTest::Main
      20          Thread::set_Name
      10           String::op_Inequality
      15          String::Equals
       8         String::op_Inequality
       7          Thread::set_Name
       9          Debugger::.cctor
       7         Debugger::get_IsAttached
      22        Thread::set_Name
       4         ThreadHelloWorldTest::Main
      16        Thread::set_Priority
       3         ThreadHelloWorldTest::Main
       8          Thread::Start
       3           CallContext::get_SecurityData
      16          Thread::get_CurrentThread
       3           CallContext::get_SecurityData
      13            Thread::GetLogicalCallContext
       5             LogicalCallContext::.cctor
      12              Type::.cctor
       8               Missing::.cctor
       7                Missing::.ctor
```

LISTING 19.18 Continued

```
       8              Object::.ctor
       5             Missing::.ctor
       9            Missing::.cctor
      17             Type::.cctor
      12            Type::GetTypeFromHandle
       8             Type::.cctor
      12            Type::GetTypeFromHandle
       8             Type::.cctor
      12            Type::GetTypeFromHandle
      11             Type::.cctor
       7              __Filters::.ctor
       8             Object::.ctor
       5            __Filters::.ctor
      50            Type::.cctor
      12           Type::GetTypeFromHandle
      10           LogicalCallContext::.cctor
       9            LogicalCallContext::.ctor
       8           Object::.ctor
       5          LogicalCallContext::.ctor
       8         Thread::GetLogicalCallContext
       3          CallContext::get_SecurityData
      13           LogicalCallContext::get_SecurityData
       7            CallContextSecurityData::.ctor
       8           Object::.ctor
       5          CallContextSecurityData::.ctor
       8         LogicalCallContext::get_SecurityData
       3        CallContext::get_SecurityData
       3         Thread::Start
       7        CallContextSecurityData::get_Principal
[thread 0x134] Thread created.
      13       Thread::Start
Hello Threading World!
[thread 0x134] Thread exited.
      10       ThreadHelloWorldTest::Main

     823 instructions total
(cordbg)
```

Optimization has not hidden many of the calls, and you can get a better idea of what is involved in running your program.

When an unhandled exception is thrown, it might be clearer to see the exception with cordbg. If the TraceSwitch sample is run on a computer that does not have an e-mail account set up, an exception is generated when an attempt is made to generate a message. With cordbg, the output looks like Listing 19.19.

LISTING 19.19 Catching an Unhandled Exception with Cordbg

```
(cordbg) g
Warning: couldn't load symbols for c:\winnt\assembly\gac\system.xml\
➥1.0.2411.0__b77a5c561934e089\system.xml.dll
This is debugging information
Warning: couldn't load symbols for c:\winnt\assembly\gac\system.web\
➥1.0.2411.0__b03f5f7f11d50a3a\system.web.dll
First chance exception generated: (0x00beab38)
➥<System.Runtime.InteropServices.COMException>
First chance exception generated: (0x00bee638)
➥<System.Reflection.TargetInvocationException>
First chance exception generated: (0x00bf5f7c) <System.Web.HttpException>
Unhandled exception generated: (0x00bf5f7c) <System.Web.HttpException>
  _httpCode=0x00000000
  _errorFormatter=<null>
  _className=<null>
  _exceptionMethod=<null>
  _exceptionMethodString=<null>
  _message=(0x00bf5ed8) "Could not access 'CDO.Message' object"
  _innerException=(0x00bee638) <System.Reflection.TargetInvocationException>
  _helpURL=<null>
  _stackTrace=(0x00bf5fc4) array with dims=[84]
  _stackTraceString=<null>
  _remoteStackTraceString=<null>
  _remoteStackIndex=0x00000000
  _HResult=0x80004005
  _source=<null>
  _xptrs=0x00000000
  _xcode=0xe0434f4d

[007f] mov         eax,dword ptr [ebp-20h]
(cordbg)
```

It's more apparent what the cause of the failure was. First, you can look at the message of the exception along with any of the other properties to see what this exception was. In addition, you can see a stack trace so you can link the exception to the code. Listing 19.20 shows the stack trace information available from cordbg.

LISTING 19.20 Getting Stack Trace Information on an Exception

```
 (cordbg) w
Thread 0x430 Current State:Normal
0)* system.web!LateBoundAccessHelper::CallMethod +007f
➥[no source information available]
                obj=(0x00bea5ec) <System.__ComObject>
                methodName=(0x00bea470) "Send"
                args=(0x00beab28) array with dims=[0]
1) system.web!CdoSysHelper::Send +06d8 [no source information available]
```

LISTING 19.20 Continued

```
                message=(0x00be98a8) <System.Web.Mail.MailMessage>
2) system.web!System.Web.Mail.SmtpMail::Send +006e
➥[no source information available]
                message=(0x00be98a8) <System.Web.Mail.MailMessage>
3) traceswitch!CustomTraceListener::Close +00c3 in traceswitch.cs:51
4) system!System.Diagnostics.TraceInternal::Close +004d
➥[no source information available]
5) system!System.Diagnostics.Trace::Close +0009
➥[no source information available]
6) traceswitch!TraceSwitchTest.TraceSwitchMain::Main +019e in
➥traceswitch.cs:190
                args=(0x00ba18fc) array with dims=[0]
(cordbg)
```

Cordbg offers some enticing features. What is exceptional is that you have source for this debugger and you have documentation on the APIs that the source is using.

Outlining the Startup Phase of Cordbg

The basic steps for starting a debug session are outlined in Figure 19.26.

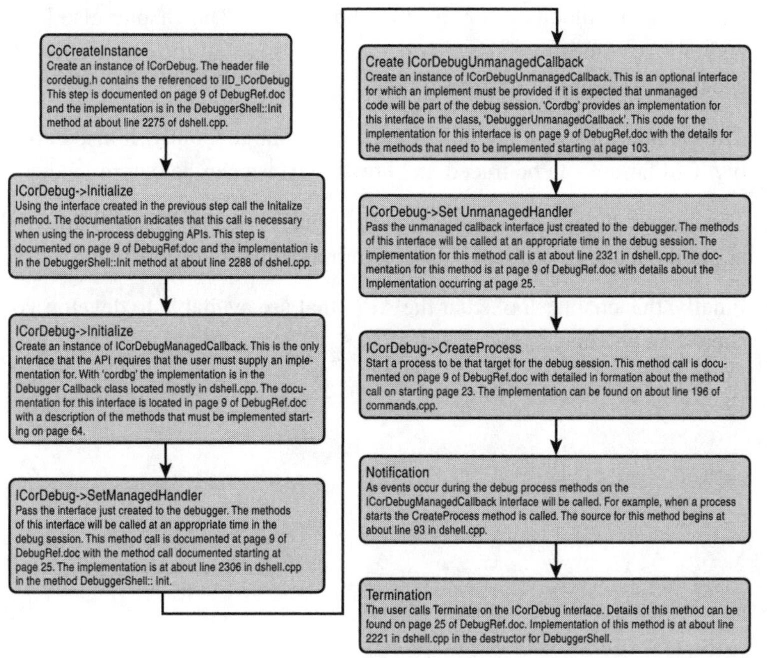

FIGURE 19.26
Essentials of the debugging API calls.

As can be seen from the figure, you just need to instantiate the `ICorDebug` interface, provide an `ICorDebugManagedCallback` implementation, create the process, and respond to the events. After a process has been created, the cordbg application simply reads commands until a quit is read in.

```
// Read commands from the user prompt
while (!shell->m_quit)
   shell->ReadCommand();
```

If you were to build a debugger based on these APIs, you would follow the same steps.

To correctly accomplish these tasks, a considerable amount of code needs to be developed for the user interface, but having these interfaces available for developing a debugger has made the task much easier and more portable.

Summary

This chapter presented a broad range of tools and techniques that can be used to debug a managed application running under the CLR.

It outlined the new **`Trace`** and **`Debug`** classes and the supporting classes that can be used to determine the state of a running program. It also looked at various ways that these classes can be modified for specific applications. The chapter also looked at the **`Assert`** and **`Fail`** methods that allow a programmer to signal the occurrence of an exceptional event that requires user intervention.

The chapter looked at the process of loading an assembly. It also explored how an assembly load failure can be traced and how the cause can be determined.

The chapter also looked at the debugger that is part of Visual Studio .NET. You learned about the features that can help determine the cause of most bugs or problems.

Finally, this chapter looked at the APIs that are available to develop your own debugger, should that be necessary.

CHAPTER 20

Profiling .NET Applications

IN THIS CHAPTER

Profiling is the process of collecting information about something so that you can come to a conclusion. You're probably aware of what is called *racial profiling*. The issue is that police or government officials gather information about a particular race to form or support an opinion that is held about that race. Many problems result from this approach, but one key to this analogy is that data collected can be used to support rather than form an opinion. Unlike racial profiling, software profiling is good and is encouraged. When profiling software, the developer collects data about the application (memory use, CPU usage, and so on) and forms an opinion as to why the application performs the way it does. Without the data, a developer is left to guess as to the causes of a particular problem. Probably worse yet is that the data might be incomplete and used to support a preconceived notion about the operation of the application.

After an application works, it is inevitable that it needs to be tuned. The application might require too much memory, be too slow, require too many resources, and so on. For all but the most trivial applications, programmers are notoriously wrong about the cause of program bottlenecks. Often, these wrong hunches cause the programmer to invest a great deal of effort in optimizing code that has little or no effect on the overall performance of the application. With the CLR taking over many of the tasks that traditionally have plagued programmers, it is even harder to determine the causes for a program's poor performance. With managed code, it is even more necessary to use proper tools to fine-tune an application.

This chapter first reviews some of the traditional tools that are available for profiling. These tools provide substantial information and should not be dismissed just because they are not .NET tools. Next, the chapter explores performance counters, which provide an easy-to-use, extensible view into your .NET application. Finally, the chapter looks at the interface that is provided so that you can build your own profile tool.

Traditional Tools Used in Profiling a .NET Application

The tools that existed pre-.NET still can be used to profile some of the characteristics of a .NET application. A .NET application still needs memory and it still needs the services of the CPU on which it is running. These tools provide information about the usage of generic resources such as these. Before you look at the specific tools (such as .NET performance counters and a custom profiler API) that are available for .NET applications, you need to review what is and has been available for any application.

Obtaining a Snapshot of Memory Usage with memsnap

This tool provides a snapshot of memory (and some resource) usage. It comes as part of Visual Studio .NET in `Microsoft Visual Studio .NET\Common7\Tools\Bin\WinNT`. If this utility is not in the directory specified, then you probably failed to install the Platform SDK (which is not installed by default). It is a command-line utility and it writes the snapshot to memsnap.log unless you specify a specific log file. Invoking `memsnap` with no arguments or `-?` gives this usage help output, as in Listing 20.1.

LISTING 20.1 memsnap Usage

```
memsnap [-t] [-g] [-?] [<logfile>]
memsnap logs system memory usage to <logfile>
<logfile> = memsnap.log by default
-t   Add tagging information (time (GMT), date, machinename)
-g   Add GDI and USER resource counts
-?   Gets this message
memsnap - Creates a memsnap.log file that contains a snap-shot of the memory
usage. Each subsequent usage appends to the memsnap.log file.
```

If you have a managed application running like ThreadPoolTest.exe of Chapter 14, "`Delegates` and `Events`," the log file looks like Listing 20.2.

LISTING 20.2 memsnap Output

```
Process ID          Proc.Name Wrkng.Set PagedPool  NonPgdPl  Pagefile
➥     Commit   Handles   Threads
00000000              (null)     16384          0         0         0
➥          0         0         1
00000008              System    212992          0         0     24576
➥      24576        114         38
. . .
0000B09C     ThreadPoolTest.  10821632      33868      8332   4116480
➥    4116480        119         4
0000B0A8         Memsnap.Exe    962560      13824      2016    434176
➥     434176         20         1
```

If you start an instance of the DiningPhilosophers.exe application, look at `memsnap`:

```
Process ID          Proc.Name Wrkng.Set PagedPool  NonPgdPl  Pagefile
➥     Commit   Handles   Threads
0000B09C     ThreadPoolTest.  14708736      46736     12232   6963200
➥    6963200        443         27
```

If you start three instances of the DiningPhilosophers.exe applications, you see the following:

```
Process ID         Proc.Name Wrkng.Set PagedPool  NonPgdPl  Pagefile
➥     Commit   Handles   Threads
0000B09C     ThreadPoolTest.  21106688     63760     15716  16670720
➥  16670720      1391        38
```

Because 20 threads should exist per application, this just confirms the limit that the **ThreadPool** places on the number of threads that it allocates, as discussed in Chapter 11, "Threading." If you stop all of the applications and return back to just the small ThreadPoolTest.exe form, you see the following:

```
Process ID         Proc.Name Wrkng.Set PagedPool  NonPgdPl  Pagefile
➥     Commit   Handles   Threads
0000B09C     ThreadPoolTest.  15237120     51916      9528   9191424
➥   9191424       286         8
```

As you can see from the output, most of the threads have been returned to the pool, some of the memory has been reclaimed from the `Pagefile`, and `the Working Set` is somewhat smaller.

Obtaining Processor Usage Information with pstat

This function provides much of the same information as `memsnap` except that it also provides a dump of process-specific information including memory on standard output. This tool is located in the same place as `memsnap` (`Microsoft Visual Studio.NET\Common7\Tools\Bin\WinNT`). The output is substantial, so you might want to invoke `pstat` like this:

```
pstat |more
```

or

```
pstat >pstat.log
```

The first bit of information that this utility prints is basic system information, as shown in Listing 20.3.

LISTING 20.3 pstat Usage

```
Pstat version 0.3:  memory: 261424 kb  uptime:  0  1:10:09.603

PageFile: \??\D:\pagefile.sys
    Current Size: 393216 kb  Total Used:  34464 kb   Peak Used  35384 kb

 Memory: 261424K Avail:  48256K  TotalWs: 245064K InRam Kernel: 3464K P:70456K
 Commit: 217564K/ 103000K Limit: 632712K Peak: 251296K  Pool N:10816K P:89728K
```

This shows how much RAM is available, how long the computer has been up, basic information about the `PageFile` that you have for your system, and system-wide memory information. In addition, a section is available where process-specific information is printed.

```
   User Time    Kernel Time    Ws   Faults  Commit Pri Hnd Thd Pid Name
. . .
  0:00:06.489   0:00:00.500 14860     9201    8948  8  282   6 45212
➥ ThreadPoolTest.
```

This is the same information as `memsnap`, with the exception that here you can see how much time was spent in kernel and user mode. A more detailed output is available for each of the processes. For the ThreadPoolTest.exe process, the output looks like Listing 20.4.

LISTING 20.4 `pstat` Report of Thread Status for a Process

```
pid:b09c pri: 8 Hnd:  282 Pf:   9201 Ws:  14860K ThreadPoolTest.
 tid pri Ctx Swtch StrtAddr    User Time   Kernel Time  State
 b098  10       1156 77E97CC6  0:00:00.871  0:00:00.050 Wait:UserRequest
 b0a0   8          1 77E87532  0:00:00.000  0:00:00.000 Wait:UserRequest
 b0a4  10        375 77E87532  0:00:00.110  0:00:00.050 Wait:UserRequest
 79c    8          8 77E87532  0:00:00.000  0:00:00.000 Wait:LpcReceive
 150    8       3118 77E87532  0:00:00.000  0:00:00.000 Wait:DelayExecution
 20c    8          8 77E87532  0:00:00.010  0:00:00.000 Wait:UserRequest
```

Detailed information is available about each of the six threads that is running in the process. You can see a thread ID, a priority, the number of context switches, the start address of the thread, how much time the thread has spent in user mode and kernel mode, and what the current state of the thread is. If you were to start the `DiningPhilosophers` application, you would see detail on more threads. At the end of the output from `pstat` is a detailed table of the drivers and system services that are loaded and running on the system.

Profiling Memory Usage with `vadump`

Also located in `Microsoft Visual Studio .NET\Common7\Tools\Bin\WinNT`, `vadump` reports memory usage information about a particular process. To use this tool, you first must obtain the process ID of the process. You might not know that process ID, so you will have to use `pview` or the `Task Manager` to get the hex ID of each process. You can activate the Task Manager from the Start Toolbar by right-clicking on the toolbar and selecting `Task Manager`. After the `Task Manager` comes up, you can select the Processes tab to view the processes and the associated IDs. `pview` is a program found in `Microsoft Visual Studio .NET\Common7\Tools\Bin\WinNT`. Start `pview` from a command line (assuming that you have the preceding path in your PATH environment variable). `pview` lists each process with its ID in parentheses. You then need to convert this hex version of the process ID to decimal. (You can use the calculator in Accessories to do this conversion.) Notice that `Task Manager` displays process IDs as decimal, so conversion is not necessary. The usage report for `vadump` is shown in Listing 20.5.

LISTING 20.5 vadump Usage

```
vadump -\?
Usage:
 Dump the address space:
    vadump [-sv] -p decimal_process_id

 Dump the current workingset:
    vadump -o [-mpsv] [-l logfile] -p decimal_process_id

 Dump new additions to the workingset (Stop with ^C):
    vadump -w [-crv] [-l logfile] -p decimal_process_id

       -c Include code faults faulting PC summary
       -m Show all code symbols on page
       -o Workingset snapshot w/ summary
       -r Print info on individual faults
       -s Summary info only
       -t Include pagetable info in summary
       -w Track new working set additions
       -v Verbose
```

If you invoke `vadump` with all of the defaults, you get output that is split into three sections. The first section is an address map for the process. It looks like Listing 20.6.

LISTING 20.6 vadump Address Map

```
Address: 00000000 Size: 00010000
    State Free

Address: 00010000 Size: 00001000
    State Committed
    Protect Read/Write
    Type Private

Address: 00011000 Size: 0000F000
    State Free

Address: 00020000 Size: 00001000
    State Committed
    Protect Read/Write
    Type Private
```

LISTING 20.6 Continued

```
Address: 00021000 Size: 0000F000
    State Free

Address: 00030000 Size: 000F4000 RegionSize: 100000
    State Reserved
    Type Private

Address: 00130000 Size: 00001000
    State Committed
    Protect Read Only
    Type Mapped

Address: 00131000 Size: 0000F000
    State Free

Address: 00140000 Size: 00061000 RegionSize: 100000
    State Committed
    Protect Read/Write
    Type Private

Address: 00240000 Size: 00006000 RegionSize: 10000
    State Committed
    Protect Read/Write
    Type Private

Address: 00250000 Size: 00001000 RegionSize: 10000
    State Committed
    Protect Read/Write
    Type Mapped
. . .
```

The next section describes how to obtain the memory that is associated with each DLL. Listing 20.7 shows a partial output of the `vadump` utility. Because you are using this tool to profile a .NET application, you can see how much memory each of the DLLs is responsible for. If the section under mscoree.dll includes some huge numbers, then you cannot fix this problem because the problem is with the CLR. Large memory usage in the main portion of the code (ThreadPoolTest) is something that you have a better chance of affecting.

LISTING 20.7 vadump DLL Memory Usage

```
Total  Image Commitment 37752832
    READONLY:             9662464
    READWRITE:            1425408
    WRITECOPY:            1576960
    EXECUTEREAD:         25088000
```

LISTING 20.7 Continued

```
Total ThreadPoolTest.exe Commitment     20480
    READONLY:                 12288
    EXECUTEREAD:               8192

Total ntdll.dll Commitment   692224
    READONLY:                196608
    READWRITE:                16384
    WRITECOPY:                 4096
    EXECUTEREAD:             475136

Total mscoree.dll Commitment   126976
    READONLY:                 16384
    READWRITE:                 8192
    WRITECOPY:                 4096
    EXECUTEREAD:              98304
```

A summary report, as shown in Listing 20.8, offers important information about an application. Specifically, for this .NET application, you can see how much of a memory resource hog this application will be.

LISTING 20.8 vadump Summary

```
Dynamic Reserved Memory 49557504

PageFaults:                  6720
PeakWorkingSetSize       14942208
WorkingSetSize           13570048
PeakPagedPoolUsage          57524
PagedPoolUsage              51696
PeakNonPagedPoolUsage       15984
NonPagedPoolUsage           13984
PagefileUsage             6762496
PeakPagefileUsage         8273920
```

If you add a flag to turn on verbose mode, you get an address map of where each of the DLLs associated with the process were loaded, as in Listing 20.9.

LISTING 20.9 vadump Verbose

```
vadump -v -p 3932
Symbols loaded: 00400000 : 00408000  ThreadPoolTest.exe
Symbols loaded: 77f50000 : 77ff9000  ntdll.dll
Symbols loaded: 60280000 : 6029f000  mscoree.dll
Symbols loaded: 77dd0000 : 77e5a000  ADVAPI32.dll
. . .
```

LISTING 20.9 Continued

```
Symbols loaded: 5f060000 : 5f246000  system.windows.forms.dll
Symbols loaded: 5f250000 : 5f502000  system.windows.forms.dll
Symbols loaded: 5e4b0000 : 5e61a000  system.dll
Symbols loaded: 5e620000 : 5e7d4000  system.dll
Symbols loaded: 61260000 : 612a8000  MSCORJIT.DLL
Symbols loaded: 516f0000 : 51758000  diasymreader.dll
Symbols loaded: 5ec00000 : 5ec70000  system.drawing.dll
Symbols loaded: 5ec70000 : 5ed34000  system.drawing.dll
Symbols loaded: 6b180000 : 6b321000  gdiplus.dll
Symbols loaded: 5fa10000 : 5fb32000  system.xml.dll
Symbols loaded: 77120000 : 771ab000  OLEAUT32.DLL
. . .
(regular output)
```

Listing 20.9 shows the output of `vadump` for the same `ThreadPoolTest` application. Notice that from the output of this tool, you can see not only what DLLs are loaded, but also where they are placed. You can immediately see that this is a managed (.NET) application. You can see DLLs such as mscoree.dll and system.windows.forms.dll loaded into the address space.

Like most other traditional tools, `vadump` mainly provides information about the process memory and how it is allocated and used.

Detailed Execution Profile of a .NET Application Using `profile`

`profile` is also located in `Microsoft Visual Studio .NET\Common7\Tools\Bin\WinNT`. From the output of `profile`, you can obtain a count of the number of functions called in each DLL that is loaded as part of the process. The output of `profile` is somewhat cryptic, but it can be useful for low-level analysis of a running process.

Invoking `profile` like this

```
profile DiningPhilosophers.exe
```

leads to output like Listing 20.10.

LISTING 20.10 `profile` Output

```
78,ntdll.dll,Total
1,ntdll.dll,RtlMultiByteToUnicodeN (77f81ff0)
5,ntdll.dll,RtlEnterCriticalSection (77f821d6)
1,ntdll.dll,RtlConsoleMultiByteToUnicodeN (77f822c5)
1,ntdll.dll,allmul (77f827c0)
. . .
```

LISTING 20.10 Continued

```
6,ntdll.dll,RtlFreeHeap (77fcb633)
9,mscoree.dll,Total
2,mscoree.dll,GetHostConfigurationFile (602834be)
6,mscoree.dll,CoInitializeCor (6028390b)
1,mscoree.dll,StrongNameFreeBuffer (60286e6e)
38,KERNEL32.DLL,Total
3,KERNEL32.DLL,LocalAlloc (77e86568)
3,KERNEL32.DLL,LocalFree (77e865f3)
3,KERNEL32.DLL,InterlockedIncrement (77e86659)
1,KERNEL32.DLL,InterlockedDecrement (77e8666a)
. . .
1,KERNEL32.DLL,IsProcessorFeaturePresent (77e8ddf1)
1,KERNEL32.DLL,SetEnvironmentVariableW (77e8dea0)
4,KERNEL32.DLL,GetEnvironmentVariableA (77e9fb75)
1,KERNEL32.DLL,FindVolumeMountPointClose (77ea0877)
2,RPCRT4.DLL,Total
1,RPCRT4.DLL,RpcBindingSetAuthInfoExW (77d5959c)
1,RPCRT4.DLL,I_RpcServerUseProtseqEp2W (77d5abe3)
```

As you can see, the output is difficult to understand. The first number is the number of times that the function in the specified DLL was called. The second field gives the name of the DLL. The third field is either the total number of calls associated with this DLL (in which case it is "Total"), or it is the name of the function within the DLL that was called. The last field is the address of the function in the DLL. The problem with this output is that it does not list managed method calls.

Monitoring Page Faults with `pfmon`

This tool is also located in `Microsoft Visual Studio .NET\Common7\Tools\Bin\WinNT`. `Pfmon` outputs information about the number of page faults that your process or application generates. One possible way to invoke this tool is as follows:

```
pfmon -n traceswitch.exe
```

With the `-n` switch, the tool outputs all of its information to a file pfmon.log. When this tool is used to monitor the page faults for a .NET application, traceswitch.exe (introduced in the last chapter), the log file looks like Listing 20.11.

LISTING 20.11 `pfmon` Output

```
SOFT: GlobalMemoryStatus : GlobalMemoryStatus
SOFT: 602812e1 : 6029afb0
HARD: 602812e1 : 6029afb0
SOFT: ReleaseSemaphore+0x2b : ReleaseSemaphore+0x0000002B
```

LISTING 20.11 Continued

```
SOFT: SetFileTime+0x86 : SetFileTime+0x00000086
SOFT: VerifyVersionInfoW+0x3b : VerifyVersionInfoW+0x0000003B
SOFT: StrongNameErrorInfo+0x10a8 : StrongNameErrorInfo+0x000010A7
SOFT: CorValidateImage : CorValidateImage
SOFT: DllCanUnloadNow+0x319 : DllCanUnloadNow+0x00000318
HARD: CorValidateImage+0x6b : 004000a8
SOFT: RtlFindCharInUnicodeString+0x405 : 004032a0
HARD: RtlIsValidHandle+0xfe : 00402000
SOFT: RtlDosApplyFileIsolationRedirection_Ustr+0x1cb :
➥ RtlCaptureContext+0x0000FCA0
SOFT: GetDateFormatW+0x5ae : GetDateFormatW+0x000005AD
SOFT: SetErrorMode+0x94 : SetErrorMode+0x00000093
SOFT: CorExeMain : CorExeMain
SOFT: CreateConfigStream+0xc98 : CreateConfigStream+0x00000C98
SOFT: 60291262 : 60291262
SOFT: CreateActCtxW+0xa3a : CreateActCtxW+0x00000A3A
SOFT: 60290f8a : 60290f8a
SOFT: CreateConfigStream : CreateConfigStream
SOFT: 602932b9 : 602932b8
SOFT: RegQueryInfoKeyW : AllocateLocallyUniqueId+0x00000229
SOFT: RegEnumValueW : CommandLineFromMsiDescriptor+0x0000057A
SOFT: CommandLineFromMsiDescriptor+0x3f3 :
➥CommandLineFromMsiDescriptor+0x000003F2
SOFT: RtlAddRefActivationContext+0x2c : 00410000
SOFT: wcsrchr+0xde : 60c5400c
SOFT: RtlFindCharInUnicodeString+0x405 : 60c36424
SOFT: RtlFindCharInUnicodeString+0x456 : 60a61000
. . .
PFMON: Total Faults 3241  (KM 366 UM 3241 Soft 2974, Hard 267, Code 960,
➥ Data 2281)
```

A page fault occurs when a thread addresses memory that is not in the main working-set. The page that contains the address is brought into the current working-set, and some pages might be removed from the current working set. The presence of many page faults indicates that the process is accessing a wide range of addresses that are probably not contiguous. If your process has many page faults, it is probably *thrashing*, a term indicating that a large portion of the time allocated to your application is spent paging memory to and from disk. When this occurs, performance decreases. A simple fix is to change your program to access memory in a more linear fashion.

Monitoring Process Timing, Memory, and Thread Count with `pview`

`pview` is located in `Microsoft Visual Studio .NET\Common7\Tools\Bin\WinNT`. `pview` presents a graphical display of processes on your system. It provides all of the information available from the previous command-line tools, but in a dialog-type user interface. When you invoke pview.exe, you get a dialog box that looks like Figure 20.1. Notice that this figure highlights information about a .NET application, `ThreadPoolTest.exe`.

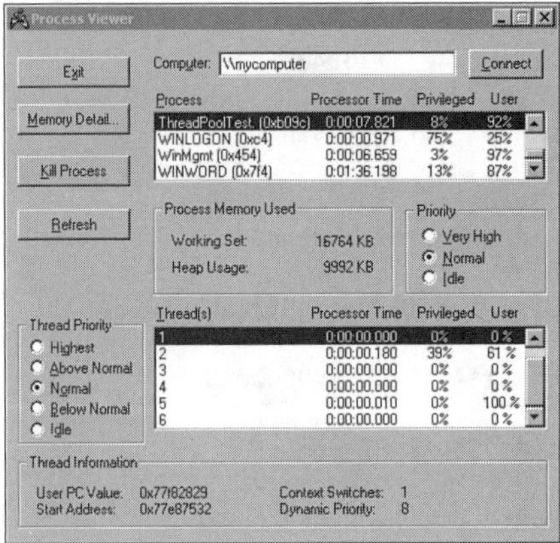

FIGURE 20.1
`pview` *process view.*

You can highlight each of the threads listed for each process and get the start address of the thread, the current address location of the thread, the number of context switches, and the priority. If you highlight a process and select the Memory Detail button, you will get a dialog box that looks like Figure 20.2.

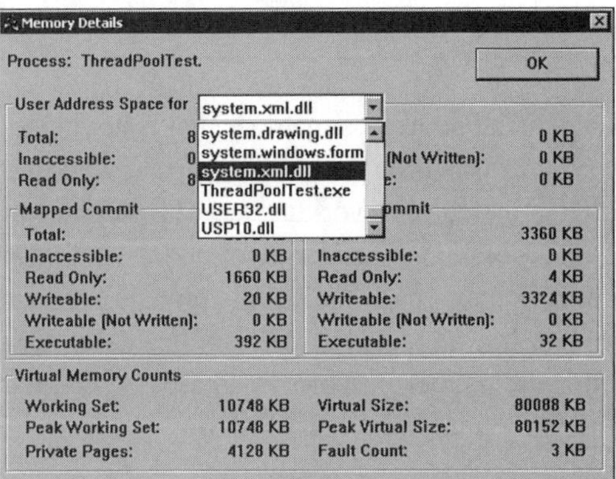

FIGURE 20.2
`pview` *memory detail.*

This dialog box contains much information, but notice that the DLLs that would have specific interest for a managed process are shown in the drop-down list. `pview` incorporates much of the same information that is obtained from `vadump` and `pstat` into a compact graphical form.

Task Manager

The `Task Manager` is always available by right-clicking on the toolbar. On Windows 2000 machines, three tabs exist: Applications, Processes, and Performance. With Windows XP, a fourth tab titled Networking has been added. If you need to monitor network activity, the Networking tab can be useful. It shows a graphical view of network utilization. If your application uses the network heavily, the Network tab offers a quick check to see if the bottleneck in your program is the network. Figure 20.3 shows what the `Task Manager` looks like.

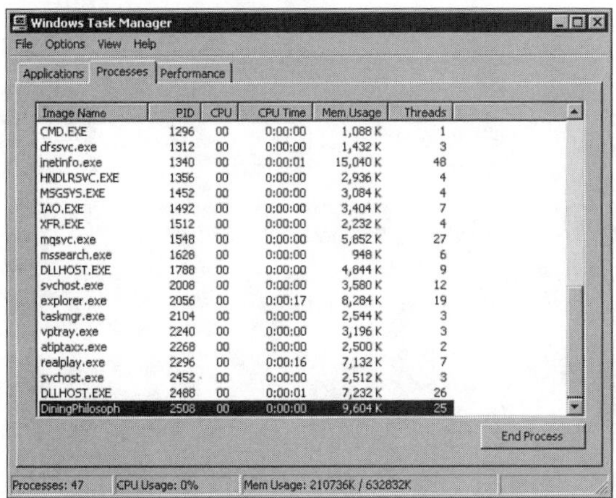

FIGURE 20.3
Monitoring a .NET application with `Task Manager`.

The Processes tab shows information about each process running on your system. By default, the process identifier, CPU usage, CPU time, memory usage, and thread count are displayed. However, as can be seen in Figure 20.4, other types of information can also be displayed. Depending on the information you need to gather about your application, you might be interested in some of this information. For example, if you are concerned that thread pooling is not working, you can turn on the option to list the number of threads in a process and see if the thread count goes too high.

Monitoring System-Wide Information with `perfmtr`

`perfmtr` is located in `Microsoft Visual Studio .NET\Common7\Tools\Bin\WinNT`. `perfmtr` provides a console view of the processes running on your system. By default, invoking `perfmtr` like this:

```
perfmtr
```

The output is similar to Figure 20.5, which monitors the CPU usage for the system.

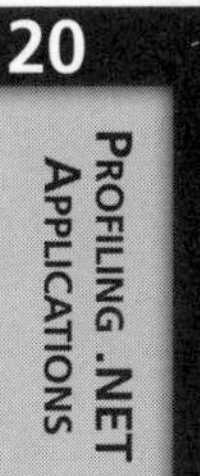

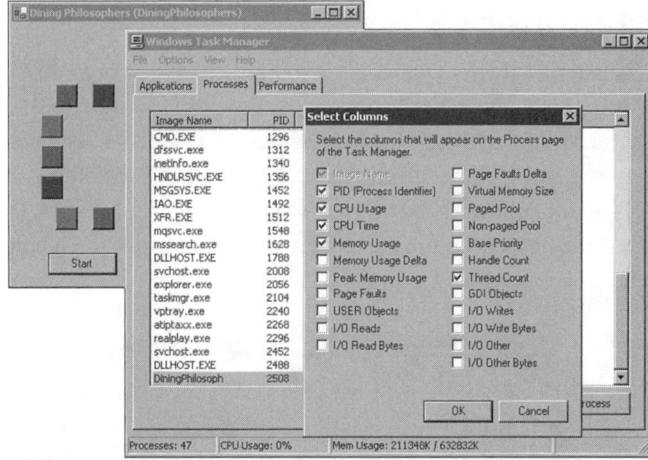

FIGURE 20.4
Task Manager process view options.

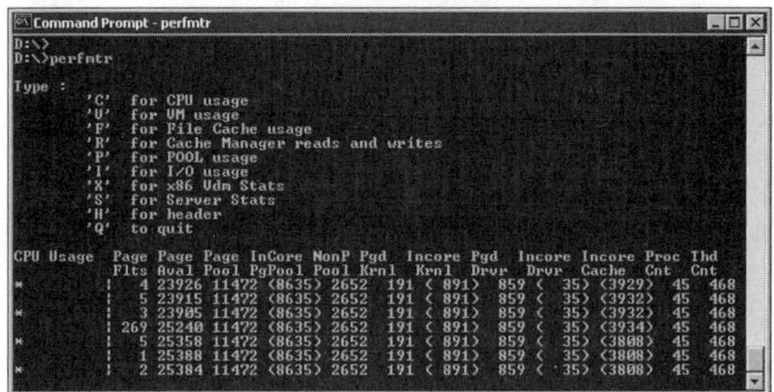

FIGURE 20.5
Monitoring system-wide CPU usage with `perfmtr`.

Other system-wide status information is available by entering the appropriate letter as indicated when the tool is first invoked. For example, "C" causes `permtr` to do a continuous dump of CPU usage, "V" provides a dump of virtual memory, and "H" causes file cache information to be monitored. See Figure 20.5 for all of the options, or invoke the tool on your own. `Permtr` provides system information, and it would only be useful in profiling an application if this information was used as a baseline.

Profiling the Profiler with `exctrlst`

This last tool leads us into the next section. `exctrlst` shows the performance counters that have been installed. This tool shows the tools that are available through the Performance Monitor. When you run this tool, you get a dialog box that looks like Figure 20.6.

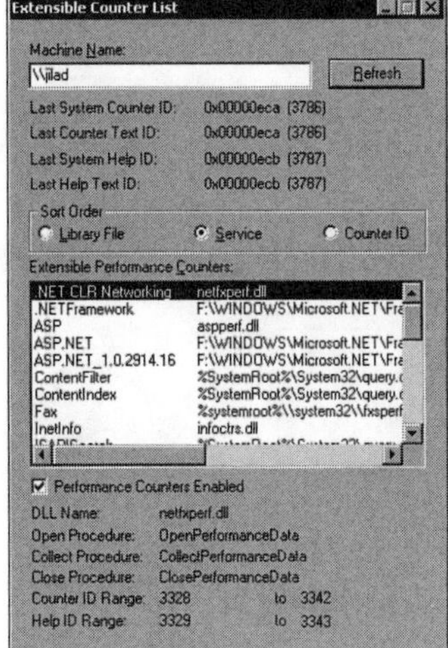

FIGURE 20.6
Performance counter information.

With this tool, you can see which DLL is associated with each of the performance categories. You can use this information along with some of the tools outlined earlier to determine whether a significant bottleneck exists due to the profile process. If the performance counter caused the application to crash, you could either debug it (if it was your performance counter) or send the information to those responsible for the performance counter to help them diagnose the problem.

Although `Exctrlst` does not indicate the exact counters that are available, it does indicate that the Performance Monitor has been extended and additional counters are available. It also shows the counter range that is used.

Using the Performance Monitor and `PerformanceCounters` to Profile .NET Applications

The .NET Framework has made it even easier to use and monitor performance counters. Even creating a custom performance counter is simple.

Bringing up the Performance Monitor and clicking on the Add button on the toolbar (the button with the '+' symbol on it) provides a list of the Performance Counters available (In Windows 2000, Performance Monitor can be found under Administrative

Tools/Performance. In Windows XP, the Administrative Tools have been moved to the Control Panel, so you will have to bring up the Control Panel to open the Performance Monitor). Figure 20.7 shows the counters categories that have been added specifically to support .NET applications.

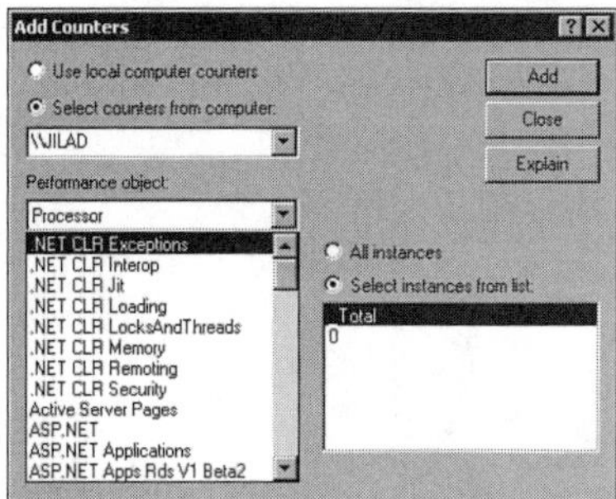

FIGURE 20.7
.NET performance counters.

As an example of using the .NET-specific performance counters, you will now see how to monitor JIT activity (Just-In-Time compilation, in case you have forgotten). The `ThreadPoolTest` application, presented in Chapter 14, has a way to control and visualize JIT activity. Figure 20.8 shows the Performance Monitor collecting data on an instance of `ThreadPoolTest`.

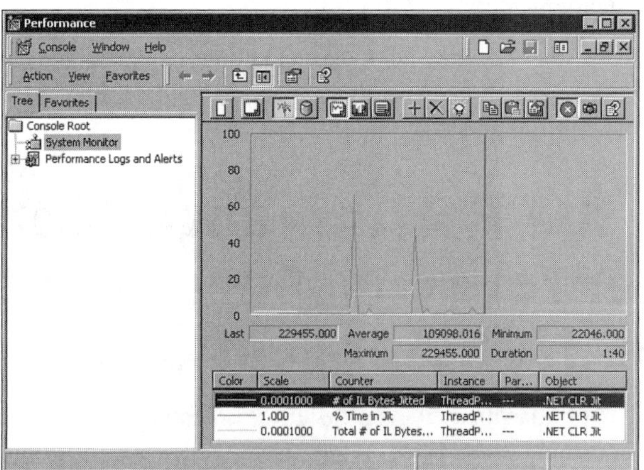

FIGURE 20.8
JIT counters.

As can be seen from Figure 20.8, two spikes indicated significant JIT activity. At the peak of each of these spikes, the total number of JITd bytes increased. Each of these spikes correspond to an invocation of a new instance of `DiningPhilosophers.exe` in the application `ThreadPoolTest`. It would be hard to devise another way of obtaining this kind of information without using performance counters. Many other .NET Framework-specific performance counters are available to provide this kind of specific information about your .NET application.

A list of the counters available is shown in Table 20.1.

TABLE 20.1 .NET Performance Counters

Category	*Description / Counter*
Exception Performance Counters (.NET CLR Exceptions)	Describes the performance counters that provide information about the exceptions thrown by an application.
	# of Exceps Thrown
	# of Exceps Thrown / Sec
	# of Filters / Sec
	# of Finallys / Sec
	Throw to catch depth / Sec
Interop Performance Counters (.NET CLR Interop)	Describes the performance counters that provide information about an application's interaction with COM components, COM+ services, and external type libraries.
	# of CCWs
	# of marshalling
	# of stubs
JIT Performance Counters (.NET CLR JIT)	Describes the performance counters that provide information about code that has been just-in-time (JIT) compiled.
	# of IL bytes JITted
	# of IL methods JITted
	% Time in JIT
	IL bytes JITted / sec
	Standard JIT failures
	Total # of IL bytes JITted
Loading Performance Counters (.NET CLR Loading)	Describes the performance counters that provide information about assemblies, classes, and application domains that are loaded.
	Bytes in Loader Heap
	Current AppDomains

TABLE 20.1 Continued

Category	*Description / Counter*
	Current Assemblies
	Current classes loaded
	Rate of AppDomains
	Rate of AppDomains unloaded
	Rate of Assemblies
	Rate of classes loaded
	Rate of load failures
	Total # of load failures
	Total AppDomains
	Total AppDomains unloaded
	Total Assemblies
	Total classes loaded
Lock and Thread Performance Counters (.NET CLR Locks AndThreads)	Describes the performance counters that provide information about managed locks and threads that an application uses.
	# of current logical threads
	# of current physical threads
	# of current recognized threads
	# of total recognized threads
	Contention tate / sec
	Current queue length
	Queue length / sec
	Queue length peak
	Rate of recognized threads / sec
	Total # of contentions
Memory Performance Counters (.NET CLR Memory)	Describes the performance counters that provide information about the garbage collector.
	# Bytes in all heaps
	# GC handles
	# Gen 0 collections
	# Gen 1 collections

TABLE 20.1 Continued

Category	*Description / Counter*
	# Gen 2 collections
	# Induced GC
	# of pinned objects
	# of sink blocks in use
	# Total committed bytes
	# Total reserved bytes
	% Time in GC
	Allocated bytes/second
	Finalization survivors
	Gen 0 heap size
	Gen 0 promoted rules/sec
	Gen 1 heap size
	Gen 1 promoted bytes/sec
	Gen 2 heap size
	Large object heap size
	PromotedFinalization - memory from Gen 0
	Promoted finalization - memory from Gen 1
	Promoted memory from Gen 0
	Promoted memory from Gen 1
Networking Performance Counters (.NET CLR Networking)	Describes the performance counters that provide information about data that an application sends and receives over the network.
	Bytes received
	Bytes sent
	Connections established
	Datagrams received
	Datagrams sent
Remoting Performance Counters (.NET CLR Remoting)	Describes the performance counters that provide information about the remoted objects that an application uses.
	Channels
	Context proxies

TABLE 20.1 Continued

Category	*Description / Counter*
	Context bound Classes loaded
	Context bound Objects alloc / sec
	Contexts
	Remote calls / sec
	Total remote calls
Security Performance Counters (.NET CLR Security)	Describes the performance counters that provide information about the security checks that the common language runtime performs for an application.
	# Link time checks
	% Time in RT checks
	Stack walk depth
	Total runtime checks

Samples have been put together to demonstrate the use of the performance counters described in Table 20.1. These samples are included in the source for this chapter. For the most part, each category of counter is illustrated by a single executable program along with an `.msc` file, which describes the counters to be used. You can double-click on the `.msc` file and double-click on the .exe file to see the performance counters in action. Some of the files will need to be edited to bring them in line with your environment (different server, different network adapter, and so on). When this is the case, a comment will be included on each of these categories. Most of the files can be built with something like `csc filename.cs`. For convenience, a batch file called `build.bat` has been included that compiles all of the performance counter samples.

The first category that I will look at is the .NET CLR Exceptions category. Listing 20.12 illustrates throwing exceptions every half-second (exception.cs).

LISTING 20.12 Throwing Exceptions

```
private void ThrowException()
{
    throw new ApplicationException("Throwing an exception from
➥ThrowException");
}
. . .
while(true)
```

LISTING 20.12 Continued

```
{
    try
    {
        ThrowException();
    }
    catch(ApplicationException)
    {
        TimeSpan ts = new TimeSpan(Environment.TickCount);
        Console.WriteLine("{0}", ts.ToString());
    }
    // Every half a second I throw an exception.
    Thread.Sleep(500);
}
```

With this code, the Performance Monitor setup file (exception.msc) looks at two counters. The first, # of Exceps Thrown, steadily increases as the graph progresses because an unending number of exceptions are being thrown. The second counter is a rate, # of Exceps Thrown/sec. Because an exception is thrown once every half second, the rate remains constant at two exceptions per second. To stop the application, simply press Enter in the console window created for the application.

The next counter that fits into this category is # of Finallys/sec. Listing 20.13 illustrates a finally block (finally.cs).

LISTING 20.13 Returning from a Function Via Finally

```
private void FinallyFunction()
{
    try
    {
        TimeSpan ts = new TimeSpan(Environment.TickCount);
        throw new ApplicationException(string.Format("{0} . . .",
➥ts.ToString()));
    }
    finally
    {
        Console.WriteLine("finally");
    }
}
```

Loading the Performance Monitor file (finally.mcs) sets up only one counter. The results from this performance counter are much like the rate for the code associated with Listing 20.12. Here, the FinallyFunction is called every half second, and every time it is called, the finally block is guaranteed to be called. The result is a constant rate of two finallys per second.

Another category is .NET CLR JIT. Listing 20.14 shows the driver for the sample that drives the JIT Performance Counters (jit.cs).

LISTING 20.14 JIT in a Loop

```
while(true)
{
    Type t = GenerateCode();
    object o = Activator.CreateInstance(t);
    MethodInfo mi = t.GetMethod("HelloWorld");
    mi.Invoke(o, null);
    Thread.Sleep(500);
}
```

The Performance Monitor file (jit.mcs) loads five counters. When the sample is running, you should see the # of IL Bytes JITted, # of Methods JITted, and Total # of Bytes JITted steadily ramping up. This is because the loop creates a new method (albeit the same method) each time around the loop. Therefore, the entire method is jitted each trip around the loop. The last two counters, % Time in JIT and IL Bytes JITted/sec, are relatively constant because they are basically a rate, and the rate is throttled at a JIT every half second.

The next category, .NET CLR Loading, is best demonstrated with an application that has been introduced already, `ThreadPoolTest.exe`. This sample spawns multiple copies of the `DiningPhilosophers` sample, each in its own **`AppDomain`**. To run this test, double-click on `loading.mcs` and then run the `ThreadPoolTest` sample. Notice that each time you click to start a new instance of `DiningPhilosophers`, the number of **`AppDomains`**, classes, and assemblies increase. When you exit one of these instances, they decrease again.

The next category is .NET CLR LocksAndThreads. To demonstrate the logical, physical threads, and contention (locks), three samples have been included. Listing 20.15 shows an example of starting a series of 10 threads and then waiting for each to finish (pthread.cs).

LISTING 20.15 Starting Physical Threads

```
static void WorkerThread()
{
    Thread.Sleep(r.Next(1000));
}
static void TestThread()
{
    try
```

LISTING 20.15 Continued

```
    {
        while(true)
        {
            Thread [] t = new Thread[10];
            for(int i = 0;i < 10;i++)
            {
                t[i] = new Thread(new ThreadStart(WorkerThread));
                t[i].Start();
            }
            for(int i = 0;i < 10;i++)
            {
                t[i].Join();
            }
            Thread.Sleep(5000);
        }
    }
    catch(Exception e)
    {
        Console.WriteLine("TestThread aborting: {0}", e.Message);
    }
}
```

The corresponding Performance Monitor file (`pthread.msc`) loads two counters: # of current logical Threads and # of current physical Threads. Notice that every five seconds, an additional 10 threads are started, and the logical and physical thread count are the same.

Next, look at the logical threads (`lthread.cs`). The thread pool is being used. Listing 20.16 shows what is being done to get a logical thread.

LISTING 20.16 Starting Threads from the Thread Pool

```
void WorkerThread(Object number)
{
    int id = (int)number;
    // Sleep for 1 second to simulate doing work
    Thread.Sleep(1000);
    // Signal that the async operation is now complete.
    TimeSpan ts = new TimeSpan(Environment.TickCount);
    Console.WriteLine("{0} {1}", id, ts);
    asyncEvents[id].Set();
}
void TestThread()
{
    try
```

LISTING 20.16 Continued

```
    {
        while(true)
        {
            Console.WriteLine("Start ---------------");
            for(int i = 0;i < threadCount;i++)
            {
                ThreadPool.QueueUserWorkItem(new WaitCallback(WorkerThread),
➥ i);
            }
            Console.WriteLine("End ---------------");
            for(int i = 0;i < threadCount;i++)
            {
                asyncEvents[i].WaitOne();
                asyncEvents[i].Reset();
            }
        }
    }
    catch(Exception e)
    {
        Console.WriteLine("TestThread aborting: {0}", e.Message);
    }
}
```

For this sample, the `threadCount` is 100. One hundred work-units have been allocated that might or might not happen simultaneously. Looking at the Performance Monitor (`lthread.mcs`), you can see a constant two physical threads and the number of logical threads, ramping up to 28 and then remaining constant. The thread pool is doing some work to keep the number of threads that are running at any given time down.

Contention (`contention.cs`) is also looked at, as shown in Listing 20.17.

LISTING 20.17 Starting Contending Threads

```
private void WorkerThread()
{
    Monitor.Enter(this);
    Thread.Sleep(r.Next(1000));
    Monitor.Exit(this);
}
private void TestThread()
{
    try
    {
        while(true)
        {
            Thread [] t = new Thread[10];
            for(int i = 0;i < 10;i++)
```

LISTING 20.17 Continued

```
            {
                t[i] = new Thread(new ThreadStart(WorkerThread));
                t[i].Start();
            }
            for(int i = 0;i < 10;i++)
            {
                t[i].Join();
            }
            Thread.Sleep(5000);
        }
    }
    catch(Exception e)
    {
        Console.WriteLine("TestThread aborting: {0}", e.Message);
    }
}
```

Ten threads are started, but each has to wait while the thread ahead of it does some work (in this case, it sleeps for 1 second). Using several counters, this contention can be illustrated with the Performance Monitor (`contention.mcs`). This sample file monitors three counters (# of current logical Threads, # of current physical Threads, and Total # of Contentions). Notice that the count of threads allocated is steadily increasing, but the number of contentions is also steadily increasing.

Another Performance Monitor category is .NET CLR Memory. Two samples have been together to illustrate the counters in this category. One of the counters available is the number of pinned objects encountered when doing a garbage collection scan. The easiest way to illustrate this counter is to pin an object and initiate a garbage collection cycle. Listing 20.18 shows how to do this (gcpinned.cs).

LISTING 20.18 Forcing a Pinned Object

```
unsafe void PinnedThread()
{
    byte [] ba1 = new byte[100];
    byte [] ba2 = new byte[100];
    byte [] ba3 = new byte[100];
    byte [] ba4 = new byte[100];
    for(int i = 0; i < ba1.Length; i++)
    {
        ba1[i] = (byte)(i % 256);
        ba2[i] = (byte)(i % 256);
        ba3[i] = (byte)(i % 256);
        ba4[i] = (byte)(i % 256);
    }
```

LISTING 20.18 Continued

```
    fixed(byte *p1 = ba1,p2 = ba2, p3 = ba3, p4 = ba4)
    {
        asyncEvent.WaitOne();
    }
}
void TestThread()
{
    Thread t;
    asyncEvent = new ManualResetEvent(false);
try
    {
        while(true)
        {
            asyncEvent.Reset();
            t = new Thread(new ThreadStart(PinnedThread));
            t.Start();

            Thread.Sleep(500);

            // Performing a GC promotes the object's generation
            GC.Collect();

            asyncEvent.Set();
            t.Join();

            Thread.Sleep(500);
            // Performing a GC promotes the object's generation
            GC.Collect();

            Thread.Sleep(500);
        }
    }
    catch(Exception e)
    {
        Console.WriteLine("TestThread aborting: {0}", e.Message);
    }
}
```

In the worker thread, an object is pinned and then you must wait for a signal to unpin the object(s). The resulting Performance Monitor output shows that a pinned object was encountered. The Performance Monitor setup loads one counter, # of Pinned Objects. This single counter now reads 1 when the code `gcpinned.exe` is run, indicating that one pinned object was encountered during GC.

Next, look at the generational garbage collector. Listing 20.19 shows how to move allocated objects through the generations of the garbage collector (`gcgen.cs`).

LISTING 20.19 Moving Through the Generations of the Garbage Collector (GC)

```
TestObj [] toa = new TestObj[10];
while(true)
{
    for(int i = 0; i < toa.Length; i++)
        toa[i] = new TestObj("TestObj" + i.ToString());

    // Performing a GC promotes the object's generation
    GC.Collect();

    GC.Collect();

    GC.Collect();

    // Destroy the strong reference to this object
    for(int i = 0; i < toa.Length; i++)
        toa[i] = null;

    GC.Collect(0);
    GC.WaitForPendingFinalizers();

    GC.Collect(1);
    GC.WaitForPendingFinalizers();

    GC.Collect(2);
    GC.WaitForPendingFinalizers();
    Thread.Sleep(500);
}
```

Ten objects are allocated, and a GC is forced to collect cycle to move the objects from one generation to the next. The objects are set to null and collected, which frees memory associated with these objects. The associated `gcgen.msc` sets up counters to illustrate the collection as well as the induced collection (because a normal cycle would take a long time).

.NET CLR Networking is the next category to explore. You will probably need to do a little work to get this sample set up. Listing 20.20 shows some code to test a TCP connection.

LISTING 20.20 TCP Networking

```
Socket s = null;
try
{
    IPHostEntry host = Dns.GetHostByName(server);
    s = new Socket(host.AddressList[0].AddressFamily,
                   SocketType.Stream, ProtocolType.Tcp);
```

LISTING 20.20 Continued

```
    IPEndPoint remoteEP = new IPEndPoint(host.AddressList[0], port);
    s.Connect(remoteEP);
    Console.WriteLine("Connected to {0}", server);
    byte[] writeBuffer = new byte[16384];
    byte[] readBuffer = new byte[16384];
    int nTransmitted;
    int nReceived;
    int nTotalReceived;
    while(true)
    {
        nTransmitted = s.Send(writeBuffer, 0,
                              writeBuffer.Length,
                              SocketFlags.None);
        nReceived = 0;
        nTotalReceived = 0;
        while(nTotalReceived < nTransmitted)
        {
            nReceived = s.Receive(readBuffer, nReceived,
                                  nTransmitted - nTotalReceived,
                                  SocketFlags.None);
            nTotalReceived += nReceived;
        }
    }
}
catch(Exception e)
{
    Console.WriteLine("TestThread aborting: {0}", e.Message);
}
finally
{
    if(s != null)
        s.Close();
}
```

If you look at the source for this listing (`tcp.cs`), you will notice that it has a hardcoded name in it. You need to change that name to a server on your network that supports the echo protocol. This protocol echoes all of the bytes sent to it. Using this service makes it so that you don't have to set up a server process, which is much easier.

The second change you probably need to make is to the Performance Monitor setup file. You need to select a network adapter that corresponds to your system. To do this, just double-click on `tcp.mcs` and from the Performance Monitor application, change the settings and save the file back out to `tcp.mcs` (overwriting the old file). Now you will be able to see the number of bytes coming in (received) and the number of bytes going out (sent).

The next category is .NET CLR Remoting. The samples here might require some modification to fit your environment. The default configuration is for the client and the server to run from `localhost`. If that is okay, then you just need to bring up two command windows and run the server in one window and the client in the other. Make sure that you start the server first. Otherwise, you will generate an exception on the first method call on the client. Listing 20.21 shows how the server is implemented (`remserver.cs`).

LISTING 20.21 Remoting Server

```
public class Sample
{
  public static int Main(string [] args)
  {

    TcpChannel chan = new TcpChannel(8085);
    ChannelServices.RegisterChannel(chan);
    RemotingConfiguration.RegisterWellKnownServiceType(Type.GetType(
➥"RemotingSamples.HelloServer,remobject"), "SayHello",
➥WellKnownObjectMode.SingleCall);
      System.Console.WriteLine("Hit <enter> to exit...");
      System.Console.ReadLine();
      return 0;
  }
}
```

Listing 20.22 shows the client (`remclient.cs`) for this remoting test sample.

LISTING 20.22 Remoting Client

```
public static int Main(string [] args)
{
    try
    {
        TcpChannel chan = new TcpChannel();
        ChannelServices.RegisterChannel(chan);
        HelloServer obj = (HelloServer)Activator.GetObject(
➥typeof(RemotingSamples.HelloServer),
➥"tcp://localhost:8085/SayHello");
        while(true)
        {
            Console.WriteLine(obj.HelloMethod(
➥"The client says hello."));
            Thread.Sleep(500);
        }
    }
    catch(Exception e)
```

LISTING 20.22 Continued

```
    {
        System.Console.WriteLine("Could not locate server");
        Console.WriteLine(e);
    }
    return 0;
}
```

Both the client and the server need to know about the object that is passed from the client to the server. Listing 20.23 shows this object (`remobject.cs`).

LISTING 20.23 Remoting Object

```
public class HelloServer : MarshalByRefObject
{
  public HelloServer()
  {
      Console.WriteLine("HelloServer activated");
  }

  public String HelloMethod(String name)
  {
      Console.WriteLine("Hello.HelloMethod : {0}", name);
      return "I received your greeting: " + name;
  }
}
```

Two Performance Monitor setup files have been built: `remserver.msc` and `remclient.msc`. Both of these tell you the same thing, but you might want to monitor either the client or the server. A counter keeps track of the number of contexts. These counters should be a constant two. One counter, Remote Calls/sec, should be constant at 2 (2 per second or 1 every half-second) because of the **`Thread.Sleep(500)`** call. The last counter, Total Remote Calls, keeps track of the total number of remote calls made. This should be a steadily increasing ramp function, where the slope is the rate of remote calls, which is two per second.

Finally, a sample is provided to illustrate the security counters on the security category, .NET CLR Security. Not many counters are available, but building a sample that exercises these counters is difficult. To fully exercise these counters, you might need to edit the source for some of these tests. Five counters are listed. Three demonstrations are available that exercise most of these five counters. Listing 20.24 illustrates how the stack is walked to perform a security check (security.cs).

LISTING 20.24 Walking the Stack for Security

```
public static void CopyFile(String srcPath, String dstPath, bool stackCheck)
{
    // Create a file permission set indicating all of this method's intentions.
    FileIOPermission fp = new FileIOPermission(FileIOPermissionAccess.Read,
                                               Path.GetFullPath(srcPath));
    fp.AddPathList(FileIOPermissionAccess.Write |
                    FileIOPermissionAccess.Append,
                    Path.GetFullPath(dstPath));

    // Verify that we can be granted all the permissions we'll need.
    fp.Demand();

    // Assert the desired permissions here.
    if(!stackCheck)
        fp.Assert();
. . .
}
void RecurseSecurityCheck(int i)
{
    if(i > 0)
        RecurseSecurityCheck(i - 1);
    else
    {
        // No stack walk
        // CopyFile(".\\Security.exe ", ".\\Security.copy.exe ", false);
        // Stack walk required
        CopyFile(".\\Security.exe ", ".\\Security.copy.exe ", true);
    }
}
void TestThread()
{
    try
    {
        while(true)
        {
            RecurseSecurityCheck(50);
            Thread.Sleep(100);
        }
    }
    catch(Exception e)
    {
        Console.WriteLine("TestThread aborting: ", e.Message);
    }
}
```

Notice that the RecurseSecurityCheck is called until the stack is of the size specified, and then the CopyFile routine is called. As shown in Listing 20.24, the stack check variable is true, so the `fp.Assert()` call is not executed. This means that the code will walk the stack to make sure that all contexts have the permission to execute the file operation. If `fp.Assert()` is allowed to be executed, then it turns off the stack walk and assumes that everyone in the call tree has the proper permission. The Performance Counters verify this. If you run the code as in Listing 20.24, then a counter is monitored called Stack Walk Depth, which has a steady value of 52. Fifty of those frames are due to the recursive call that is made before calling `CopyFile`. If the Assert is allowed to run, then the Stack Walk Depth is no longer 52 but 1.

Next, look at the counter, # Link Time Checks. To exercise this counter, modify the `CopyFile` routine used previously as (`secattrib.cs`):

```
[FileIOPermissionAttribute(SecurityAction.LinkDemand, Unrestricted=true)]
public static void CopyFile(String srcPath, String dstPath)
```

The Performance Monitor (`secattrib.mcs`) shows the same numbers as before. It is still walking the stack, and a steadily increasing number of runtime checks are occurring, but the # Link Time Checks is 1. This is because when this routine was jitted, a security check was required by the attribute. If you change LinkDemand to Assert, no stack-walk will exist.

You might want to exercise the # Link Time Checks a little more. To do so, you can add the following lines to the `jit.cs` code:

```
PermissionSet ps = new PermissionSet(PermissionState.Unrestricted);
EnvironmentPermission cp = new EnvironmentPermission
➥(PermissionState.Unrestricted);
ps.AddPermission(cp);
methodBuilder.AddDeclarativeSecurity(SecurityAction.LinkDemand, ps);
```

This forces a security check each time a method is JITted. Because this code continually submits code to be JITted, you should see # Link Time Checks steadily increase (`seclink.mcs`).

Programmatic Access to the Performance Counters

It has always been somewhat of a chore to add performance monitoring to an application. In 1998, Jeffrey Richter wrote a detailed article on PerfMon.exe in the August 1998 issue of *MSJ*. In this article, he not only provided a good overview of the Performance Monitor application (PerfMon.exe), but he also showed how to add custom performance counters to your application. This information is still relevant and would be a good review of performance counters in general. You can find it at `http://www.microsoft.com/msj/defaultframe.asp?page=/msj/0898/performance.htm`.

Ken Knudsen proposed building a COM component to ease the task in the February 2000 issue of *MSDN Magazine*. You can read about it at `http://www.microsoft.com/MSJ/0200/comperf/comperf.asp`.

The Performance Monitor is an application that allows you to easily visualize performance counters. However, the Performance Monitor might not address specific requirements that must be met by your application. You might want to build a custom performance monitoring application, or you might want to incorporate certain performance counters into your application. The .NET Framework provides a powerful set of classes to support monitoring performance counters. A simple application can be found in the `PerformanceMonitor` directory. The application illustrates the usage of some of these classes. When the application starts, it looks like Figure 20.9.

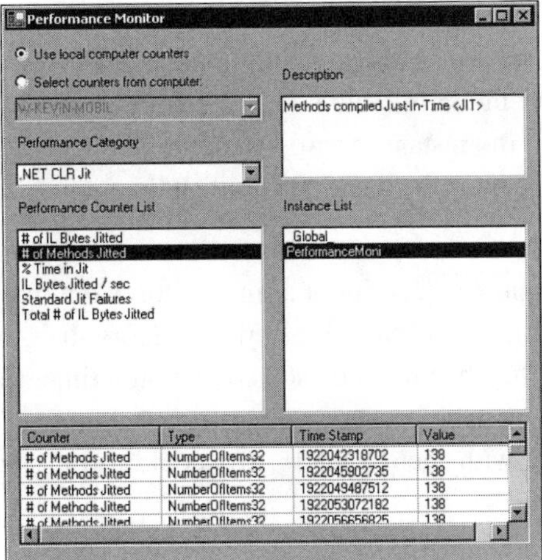

FIGURE 20.9
Performance Monitor application.

This application lists performance counter categories that are available for the computer on which it is run. It also shows which instances and counters are associated with each category. Selecting a particular counter or instance starts a timer, which reads the value from the selected counter every second. How is this done?

> **Note**
>
> All of the performance monitor classes are in the **`System.Diagnostics`** namespace.

You need a list of the performance counter categories. **GetCategories** is a static function within the **PerformanceCounterCategory** class that retrieves the performance counter categories available on the local machine. An overloaded method takes a single string argument specifying the machine for which a category list is required. Using **GetCategories** is as simple as Listing 20.25.

LISTING 20.25 Getting a Listing of the Performance Counter Categories

```
PerformanceCounterCategory [] pcc  =
➥PerformanceCounterCategory.GetCategories();
foreach(PerformanceCounterCategory p in pcc)
{
    categoryList.Items.Add(p.CategoryName);
```

In Listing 20.25, an array of the performance categories was retrieved, and the name of the category was added to a **ListBox**. Although getting the name of the categories is interesting, it is not the only method available within the **PerformanceCounterCategory** class. You also need to retrieve the instances associated with the category and the specific counters associated with the category. You can accomplish this in two ways.

The first method of drilling down into a performance counter category is the most efficient if you are dealing with whole categories at a time. It turns out that if you use the **ReadCategory** method, a snapshot is taken of the entire category. It is more efficient to read the category in bulk like this than to read each counter at a time. Calling the **ReadCategory** method returns an **InstanceDataCollectionCollection**. If you want to just list the counters associated with each category, you could form a loop like that shown in Listing 20.26.

LISTING 20.26 Getting a Listing of the Counters in Each Performance Counter Category

```
InstanceDataCollectionCollection dcc = p.ReadCategory();
ICollection keys = dcc.Keys;
foreach(string key in keys)
{
    Debug.WriteLine(string.Format("{0} {1}", p.CategoryName, key));
}
```

Listing 20.26 simply reads all data associated with the category and prints the category name and a counter associated with it. You need to find out about each instance associated with the counter and that data for the counter. Listing 20.27 shows how you can enumerate through each instance to get the data associated with the instance.

LISTING 20.27 Getting a Listing of the Instances and Data in Each Performance Counter Category

```
InstanceDataCollectionCollection dcc = p.ReadCategory();
. . .
ICollection values = dcc.Values;
foreach(InstanceDataCollection value in values)
{
    Debug.Indent();
    ICollection vvs = value.Values;
    foreach(InstanceData vv in vvs)
    {
        Debug.WriteLine(string.Format("{0} {1}", vv.InstanceName, vv.RawValue));
    }
    Debug.Unindent();
}
```

An instance can be associated with each counter. For example, if you were looking at the thread counters, the name of the category for monitoring CLR threads would be .NET CLR LocksAndThreads. A counter in that category would be # of current physical Threads. Because each process can have many threads and multiple processes can exist, each process is recognized as an instance in performance counter lingo. Listing 20.27 shows how to move through each instance in the collection and prints the current value for that instance. In a real application, you would need to correlate the enumeration of the instance data with the counters that are part of the Keys, as shown in Listing 20.26. Also, note that not all counters are simply a count. Many types of counters exist, and a real application would need to handle each of the different kinds of counters. The following list presents some of the more common types of counters:

- AverageTimer32—This counter measures the time it takes on average to complete an operation or process. An average counter always has an AverageBase counter associated with it.
- CounterTimer—This is a percentage counter that measures the average time that a component is active.
- ElapsedTime—This is a difference counter that measures the total time between when a component of process was started and the current time.
- NumberOfItems32—This is an instantaneous counter that measures the most recently observed value.
- RateOfCountsPerSecond32—This is a difference counter that measures the average number of operations completed during each second of the sample interval.
- SampleCounter—This is an average counter that measures the average number of operations completed in one second. When a counter of this type is sampled, a one or a zero is returned. The counter data is the number of ones that were sampled.

The sample application `PerformanceMonitor` doesn't use the methods described in Listings 20.26 and 20.27. This is primarily because for this application, you don't need to get the performance data from a whole category at once. This application used a different approach, as described in the following paragraph.

In the Performance Monitor application, when the user selects a performance category (initialized during startup), **`PerformanceCounterCategory`** is reconstructed and a method is called to get the instances associated with the category (**`GetInstanceNames`**). This method returns an array of strings that are associated with the category that is selected. This array of strings is used to fill the instance **`ListBox`** with the name of each instance. Not all categories have instances associated with them. If instances are not present, then you can construct an array of counters based on a single instance. In contrast, if multiple instances exist, try to construct an array of **`PerformanceCounter`**s based on the first instance, assuming that the same number of counters exist for each instance. The code to do this is part of the `PerformanceMonitor` sample. A code snippet from this application is shown in Listing 20.28.

LISTING 20.28 Getting a Listing of the Instances and Data Associated with a Performance Counter Category

```
PerformanceCounterCategory pcc;
if(computerList.Enabled)
    pcc = new PerformanceCounterCategory((string)cb.SelectedItem,
                                          (string)computerList.SelectedItem);
else
    pcc = new PerformanceCounterCategory((string)cb.SelectedItem);
string [] instanceNames = pcc.GetInstanceNames();
foreach(string s in instanceNames)
{
    instanceList.Items.Add(s);
}
if(instanceNames.Length > 0)
{
    // Get the counters for the last instance (they should all be the same)
    PerformanceCounter [] pca = pcc.GetCounters(instanceNames[0]);
    foreach(PerformanceCounter pc in pca)
    {
        counterList.Items.Add(pc.CounterName);
    }
}
else
{
    PerformanceCounter [] pca = pcc.GetCounters();
    foreach(PerformanceCounter pc in pca)
    {
        counterList.Items.Add(pc.CounterName);
    }
}
```

After the user selects either a counter or an instance, a timer is started, which reads the **PerformanceCounter** every second. The code to accomplish this is shown in Listing 20.29.

LISTING 20.29 Obtaining a Current PerformanceCounter

```
PerformanceCounterCategory pcc = new
PerformanceCounterCategory((string)categoryList.SelectedItem);
PerformanceCounter pc;
if(instanceList.SelectedIndex == -1 &&
   instanceList.Items.Count > 0)
{
    instanceList.SelectedIndex = 0;
}
if(computerList.Enabled)
    pc = new PerformanceCounter(pcc.CategoryName,
                                (string)lb.SelectedItem,
                                (string)instanceList.SelectedItem,
                                (string)computerList.SelectedItem);
else
    pc = new PerformanceCounter(pcc.CategoryName,
                                (string)lb.SelectedItem,
                                (string)instanceList.SelectedItem);
counterHelp.Text = pc.CounterHelp;
currentPerformanceCounter = pc;
timer.Enabled = true;
```

This code creates a new **PerformanceCounter** based on the selections that the user has made for the category, counter, instance, and computer. The code that is executed when an instance is selected is similar. The last line of Listing 20.29 enables the timer. After this timer is enabled, it fires an event every second. The handler for this event looks at the current **PerformanceCounter** and reads various property values from the current instance. A portion of this code is shown in Listing 20.30.

LISTING 20.30 Reading the Current PerformanceCounter

```
ListViewItem item = new ListViewItem(currentPerformanceCounter.CounterName);
CounterSample sample = currentPerformanceCounter.NextSample();
item.SubItems.Add(Convert.ToString(currentPerformanceCounter.CounterType));
item.SubItems.Add(Convert.ToString(sample.TimeStamp));
item.SubItems.Add(Convert.ToString(sample.RawValue));
samples.Items.Add(item);
```

This code creates an item to put into the **ListView** and populates the item with the name of the counter, the type of counter, a time stamp for the sample, and the raw value for the sample.

Adding a Custom Counter Category Using the Server Explorer

The Performance Monitor architecture is also extensible. You can add your own performance counter. The .NET Framework makes adding your own performance counter much easier. You can add a custom performance counter in two ways. The first method is to use the Server Explorer that is part of Visual Studio .NET. The second method is to add it programmatically, as discussed in the section "Adding a Counter Programmatically."

The Server Explorer tab of Visual Studio .NET brings new functionality to the developer's desktop. You can look at event logs, message queues, performance counters, services, and databases. The Performance Counter portion alone provides a list of the performance counter categories, performance counters, and performance counter instances. To create a new performance counter category, right-click on the Performance Counter node of the Server Explorer, and you will be presented with a pop-up menu that looks like Figure 20.10.

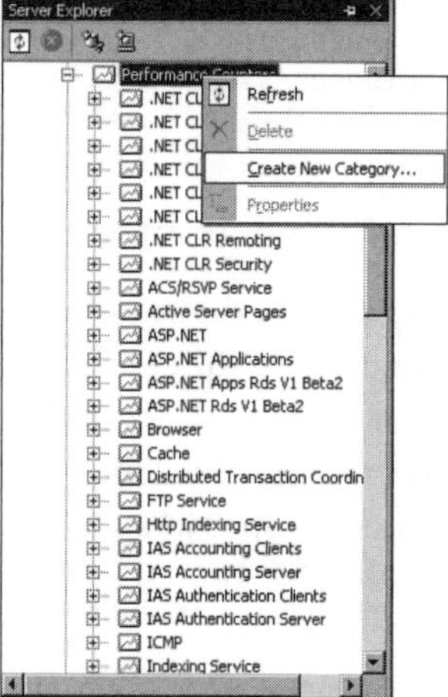

FIGURE 20.10
Adding a performance counter category by using the Server Explorer.

To demonstrate adding a custom performance counter, you can add a counter whose purpose is to count the number of times a "Hello World" method has been called.

To create a custom performance counter category, select the Create New Category menu item shown in Figure 20.10. After you have selected this menu item, you will be presented with a form similar to Figure 20.11.

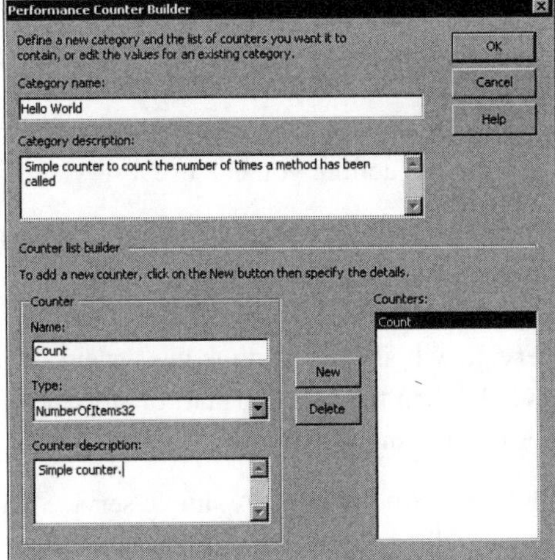

FIGURE 20.11
New performance counter category form.

As you can see from Figure 20.11, the form is already partially filled in. The goal is to create a Hello World performance counter category that has just one performance counter in it called Count. You could add any number of counters to this category, but one counter is sufficient. After you click the OK button for this form, a new performance category is created, as shown in Figure 20.12.

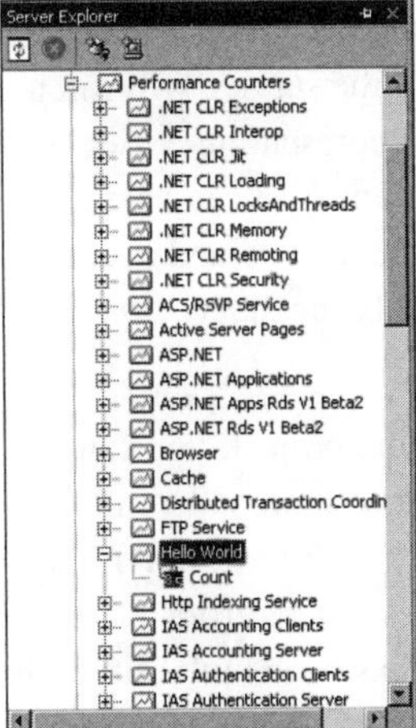

FIGURE 20.12
The Hello World performance category.

Your new performance counter category joins the ranks of all of the other performance counter categories. You can do anything with this performance counter category that you can do with those categories that predated your own.

Building a Service to Write to the Custom `PerformanceCounter`

Now that you have a new performance counter, you need a program to modify it so that you can see it in action. To perform this action, you can use a service.

Building a service with Visual Studio .NET or even services in general have not yet been discussed. As you are probably well aware, a *service* is a process that can be configured to be manually or automatically started by the system. If the service is configured to automatically start, then the service will start every time the system reboots. If the service is configured to start manually, then the user can start or stop the service from the Server Explorer or the Services control snap-in.

Building a service is easy with Visual Studio .NET. A simple service solution has been included in the `HelloWorldService` directory. A new C# project has been started, and the Windows Service Wizard has been used to help build the service. Two components have been added: a performance counter, and a timer to modify the custom performance counter created in the previous section.

From the same "design" window where the timer and performance counter components were dragged, an "installer" has been added to the project by right-clicking on the Design window and selecting the Add Installer menu item. This adds a `ProjectInstaller.cs` file that has a design and code window. From the code window, you can see that two components are present: a **`ServiceProcessInstaller`** and a **`ServiceInstaller`**. You can set the account that the service will run under when started, or optionally, choose a username and password representing a user account. In this case, the service will run under the **`LocalSystem`** account. You can change the properties of the **`ServiceInstaller`** component to give the service a name and a startup type (among other properties). Here, the service is named `HelloWorldService`, and the startup type is **`Manual`**.

Now that you have a project installer as part of the project, you can build the project. The build will create a HelloWorldService.exe. From a command window, you can install the service using the installutil.exe utility that comes with the .NET Framework SDK. For the sample to work, you will need to install this service. From a command window, navigate to where the `HelloWorldService.exe` file has been built (either the `Release` or `Debug` subdirectory of `bin` in the project). At that point, install the service with `installutil HelloWorldService.exe`. If the service installs correctly, you should see something like Listing 20.31.

> **Note**
>
> Make sure that your environment variables are set correctly, or you will find that none of the preceding commands work. You can use a file called vcvars32.bat that is located in `Microsoft Visual Studio .NET\Common7\Tools` to set up your variables properly.

LISTING 20.31 Installing a Service

```
>installutil HelloWorldService.exe
Microsoft (R) .NET Framework Installation utility
Copyright (C) Microsoft Corp 2001. All rights reserved.

Running a transacted installation.

Beginning the Install phase of the installation.
See the contents of the log file for the HelloWorldService.exe assembly's
➥progress.
The file is located at HelloWorldService.InstallLog.
Call Installing. on the HelloWorldService.exe assembly.
Affected parameters are:
   assemblypath = HelloWorldService.exe
   logfile = HelloWorldService.InstallLog
Installing service HelloWorldService...
Service HelloWorldService has been successfully installed.
Creating EventLog source HelloWorldService in log Application...

The Install phase completed successfully, and the Commit phase is beginning.
See the contents of the log file for the HelloWorldService.exe assembly's
➥progress.
The file is located at HelloWorldService.InstallLog.
Call Committing. on the HelloWorldService.exe assembly.
Affected parameters are:
   assemblypath = HelloWorldService.exe
   logfile = HelloWorldService.InstallLog

The Commit phase completed successfully.

The transacted install has completed.
```

Using the Services snap-in or the Server Explorer allows you to see the new service. You can see what it will look like in the Services snap-in with Figure 20.13.

FIGURE 20.13
The newly created HelloWorldService.

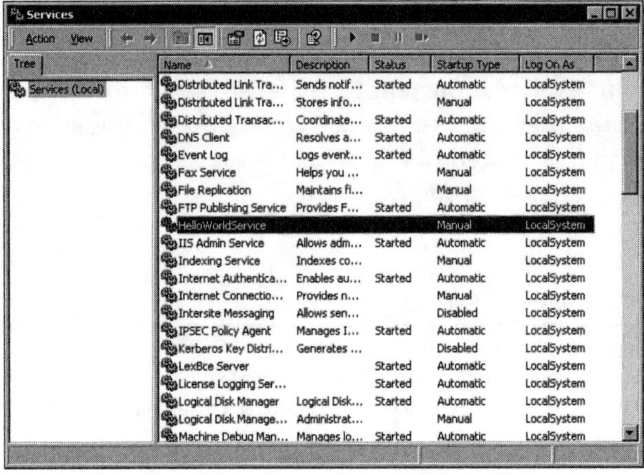

You can right-click on this service to bring up properties of the service. You can also start or stop the service from this snap-in. In addition, you can start or stop the service from the Server Explorer by right-clicking on the service. You can also view properties and see the current running status of the service. A square red block in the lower-left corner of the icon next to the service name indicates that the service is stopped. A green triangle indicates that the service is started. The services portion of the Server Explorer looks like Figure 20.14.

FIGURE 20.14
The newly created HelloWorldService as viewed by the Server Explorer.

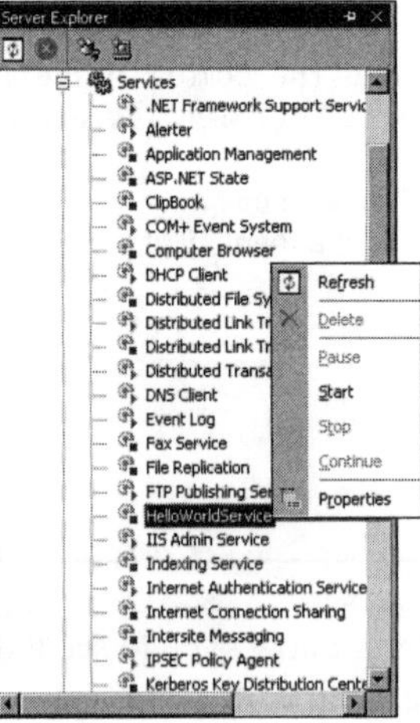

After you start the service, the timer is configured to fire every 100 milliseconds. At that interval, you simply increment the custom performance counter. To accomplish this, you set the appropriate properties on the timer, as well as the performance counter components that you added to the service design window. You also add the code in Listing 20.32 to perform the modification of the counter.

LISTING 20.32 Modifying the Performance Counter

```
private void OnTimer(object sender, System.Timers.ElapsedEventArgs e)
{
    performanceCounter.Increment();
}
```

Monitoring the Custom Performance Counter

Now that you have added the new performance counter and built the service, you can monitor the performance counter with the Performance Monitor or programmatically. If you choose to use the Performance Monitor, you will need to select the counter that you want to monitor, as shown in Figure 20.15.

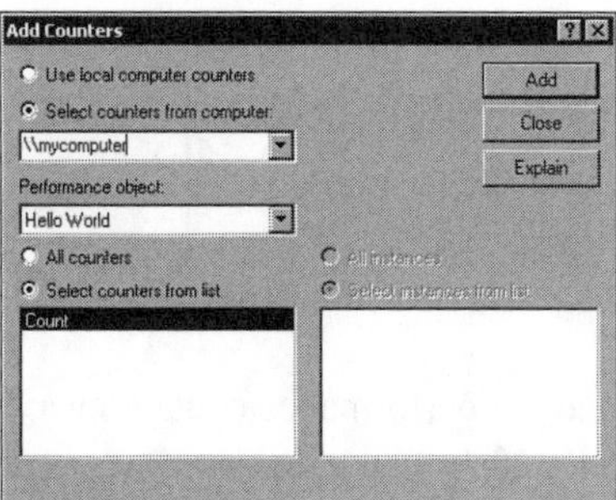

FIGURE 20.15
Selecting the HelloWorld performance counter.

After you have selected the counter, the graph will display the value of the counter at regular intervals, producing a graph that looks like Figure 20.16.

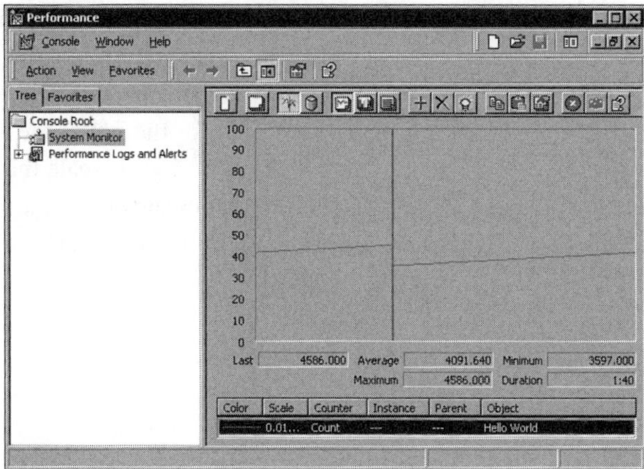

FIGURE 20.16
Monitoring the HelloWorld performance counter.

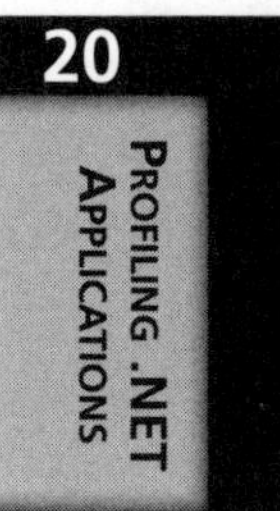

As you increment the counter, you should see a steadily increasing graph, as shown in Figure 20.16.

You can also monitor the performance counter programmatically. Using the same tool that was associated with Listings 20.28–20.30, you can monitor the current value of the custom performance counter. After you have selected the performance counter category and performance counter, you should see something like Figure 20.17.

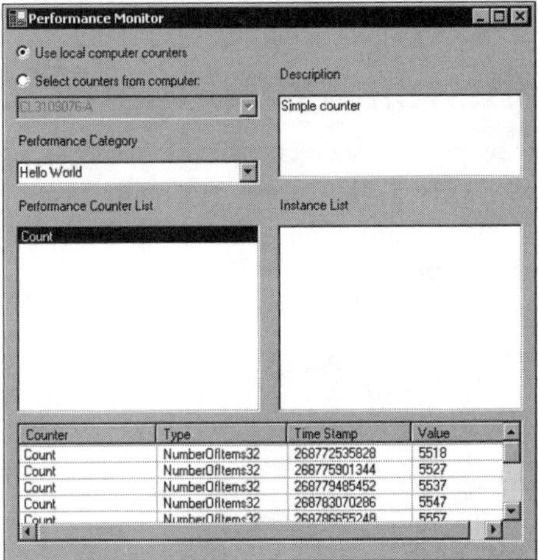

FIGURE 20.17
Programmatically monitoring the HelloWorld performance counter.

Remember to have the timer set to read the performance counter every second with this application. As you can see from Figure 20.16, the value increases by 10 with each new display. This indicates that all is working correctly because the performance counter was incremented to 10 times per second (a 100-millisecond interval).

Adding a Counter Programmatically

Instead of using the Server Explorer to create a custom performance counter, you can programmatically create the counter as well. You might want to do this for a custom application that needs to create and destroy performance counters or an application that has a specialized need to have the counter exist only for the life of the application. Many different scenarios can be devised in which it is just easier to create the counter programmatically. A simple application has been devised that creates the same counter that was made using the Server Explorer. The critical portion of this sample is shown in Listing 20.33.

LISTING 20.33 Programmatically Creating a Custom Performance Counter

```
CounterCreationDataCollection CounterDatas =
➥new CounterCreationDataCollection();
// Create the counters and set their properties.
CounterCreationData cdCounter = new CounterCreationData();
cdCounter.CounterName = "Count";
cdCounter.CounterHelp = "Simple counter";
cdCounter.CounterType = PerformanceCounterType.NumberOfItems32;
// Add counter to the collection.
CounterDatas.Add(cdCounter);
// Create the category and pass the collection to it.
PerformanceCounterCategory.Create("Hello World",
                                  "Hello World performance category",
                                  CounterDatas);
```

Using Custom Profiling APIs

Like the debugging APIs that the .NET Framework supports, an interface is available that can be used to profile .NET applications. The primary documentation for the profiling interface is in the *Tools Developers Guide* in a file called Profiling.doc. The API consists of two COM interfaces: `ICorProfilerCallback` and `ICorProfilerInfo`. To build a profiler, the programmer must implement the methods that are part of `ICorProfilerCallback`. The profiler is implemented as an in-process COM DLL. This DLL implements the `ICorProfilerCallback` interface. `ICorProfilerInfo` is an interface that is implemented in the CLR and queried for during the initialization of the profiler.

The SDK ships with two sample profilers that illustrate what is involved in building a profiler for managed code. Each of the samples is included in the `profiler` directory because the projects have been modified so that you can use Visual Studio .NET to compile and run the profilers. A General Code Profiler can be found in the `gcp_profiler` directory, and a Hot Spots Tracker can be found in the `hst_profiler` directory. These projects have been copied into `gcp` and `hst` directories respectively, and they have been modified so that they can be compiled with Visual Studio .NET.

Each of the samples follows the same setup process. After the code has been compiled and the resulting DLL properly linked, all you need to do is run a simple batch file called EnableProfiler.bat from a Command Prompt window. This batch file registers the COM DLL and sets two environment variables:

- Cor_Enable_Profiling—This environment variable is set to a non-zero value to turn on profiling.
- Cor_Profiler—This environment variable is set to the CLSID or ProdID of the COM component that implements the `ICorProfilerCallback` interface.

Running any managed process under this environment will result in the CLR doing the equivalent of `CoCreateInstance` to instantiate the CoClass that implements the `ICorProfilerCallback` interface. After an instance of the interface has been created, the CLR calls the `Initialize` method of this interface. The implementation of the `Initialize` method is responsible for setting flags to indicate the events to receive. These flags and the implementation of the various methods in the `ICorProfilerCallback` are what differentiate one profiler from another. The `Initialize` method is also where the profiler should query for `ICorProfilerInfo` so that additional information can be obtained from the CLR about the profiling process. When the process is finished, the CLR will call the Shutdown method of `ICorProfilerCallback`.

General Code Profiler

The General Code Profiler (GCP) sets the flags for the events for which it is to listen for, as shown in Listing 20.34.

LISTING 20.34 General Code Profiler Event Flags

```
m_dwEventMask = (DWORD) (    COR_PRF_MONITOR_CLASS_LOADS
                           | COR_PRF_MONITOR_MODULE_LOADS
                           | COR_PRF_MONITOR_ASSEMBLY_LOADS
                           | COR_PRF_MONITOR_APPDOMAIN_LOADS
                           | COR_PRF_MONITOR_JIT_COMPILATION
                           | COR_PRF_MONITOR_EXCEPTIONS
                           | COR_PRF_MONITOR_THREADS
                           | COR_PRF_MONITOR_CODE_TRANSITIONS
                           | COR_PRF_MONITOR_ENTERLEAVE
                           | COR_PRF_MONITOR_CACHE_SEARCHES
                           | COR_PRF_DISABLE_INLINING );
```

Specifically, notice that the following are not defined (refer to corprof.h and to page 58 of Profiling.doc):

```
COR_PRF_MONITOR_FUNCTION_UNLOADS
COR_PRF_MONITOR_GC
COR_PRF_MONITOR_OBJECT_ALLOCATED
COR_PRF_MONITOR_REMOTING
COR_PRF_MONITOR_CCW
COR_PRF_MONITOR_REMOTING_COOKIE
COR_PRF_MONITOR_REMOTING_ASYNC
COR_PRF_MONITOR_SUSPENDS
COR_PRF_MONITOR_CLR_EXCEPTIONS
COR_PRF_ENABLE_REJIT
COR_PRF_ENABLE_INPROC_DEBUGGING
COR_PRF_ENABLE_JIT_MAPS
COR_PRF_DISABLE_OPTIMIZATIONS
     COR_PRF_ENABLE_OBJECT_ALLOCATED
```

As you can see from the previous list of options that the GCP does not use, many profiling options can be associated with a profiling application.

This sample profiler records the information as the events are called. Most functions follow the same format. Look at Listing 20.35, which illustrates the implementation of the method `AppDomainCreationFinished` (defined in ProfilerGCP.h, which is part of the source for this profiler).

LISTING 20.35 GCP `AppDomainCreationFinished` Callback Implementation

```
HRESULT ProfilerCallback::AppDomainCreationFinished(AppDomainID appDomainID,
                                                    HRESULT hrStatus)
{
    _ASSERT_( SUCCEEDED( hrStatus ) );
    try
    {
         AddAppDomain( appDomainID );
    }
    catch ( BaseException *exception )
    {
       exception->ReportFailure();
       delete exception;
       Failure();
    }
    return S_OK;
} // ProfilerCallback::AppDomainCreationFinished
```

The way that each of the callbacks records an event is to enter it into a table. The GCP has a series of tables in ProfilerHelper.h. The tables look like Listing 20.36.

LISTING 20.36 GCP Tables

```
// tables
SList<ClassInfo *, ClassID> *m_pClassTable;
SList<ThreadInfo *, ThreadID> *m_pThreadTable;
SList<ModuleInfo *, ModuleID> *m_pModuleTable;
SList<FunctionInfo *, FunctionID> *m_pFunctionTable;
SList<AssemblyInfo *, AssemblyID> *m_pAssemblyTable;
SList<AppDomainInfo *, AppDomainID> *m_pAppDomainTable;
```

When the profile session is complete and the Shutdown method has been called, GCP dumps the contents of the tables in a routine `DumpTables()`, as shown in Listing 20.37.

LISTING 20.37 DumpTables in GCP

```
void PrfInfo::DumpTables()
{
    // dump thread table
    if ( m_pThreadTable != NULL )
    {
        wprintf( L"*** THREAD TABLE ***\n" );
        m_pThreadTable->Dump();

        wprintf( L"\n" );
        wprintf( L"\n" );
    }

    // dump AppDomain table
    if ( m_pAppDomainTable != NULL )
    {
        wprintf( L"*** APP_DOMAIN TABLE ***" );
        m_pAppDomainTable->Dump();

        wprintf( L"\n" );
        wprintf( L"\n" );
    }


    // dump Assembly table
    if ( m_pAssemblyTable != NULL )
    {
        wprintf( L"*** ASSEMBLY TABLE ***\n" );
        m_pAssemblyTable->Dump();

        wprintf( L"\n" );
        wprintf( L"\n" );
    }

    // dump module table
    if ( m_pModuleTable != NULL )
    {
        wprintf( L"*** MODULE TABLE ***\n" );
        m_pModuleTable->Dump();

        wprintf( L"\n" );
        wprintf( L"\n" );
    }

    // dump class table
    if ( m_pClassTable != NULL )
    {
        wprintf( L"*** CLASS TABLE ***\n" );
        m_pClassTable->Dump();
```

LISTING 20.37 Continued

```
        wprintf( L"\n" );
        wprintf( L"\n" );
    }

    // dump function table
    if ( m_pFunctionTable != NULL )
    {
        wprintf( L"*** FUNCTION TABLE ***\n" );
        m_pFunctionTable->Dump();

        wprintf( L"\n" );
        wprintf( L"\n" );
    }
} // PrfInfo::DumpTables
```

Earlier it was said that you could invoke any managed process in the profile environment. That's not completely true. Here, due to the implementation using wprintf, only **Console** applications will properly display the output of the profiler. The output from a managed application looks like Listing 20.38.

LISTING 20.38 Output from the GCP

```
This is debugging information
CLR Profiler General Code Profiler Sample
AppDomain ID NOT FOUND in AppDomain Table
*** THREAD TABLE ***

THREAD ID: 0x0013eb88
    HANDLE: 0x000000ac
    WIN32 ID: 0x00000890

THREAD ID: 0x0013ef18
    HANDLE: 0x000000d4
    WIN32 ID: 0x000007bc

*** APP_DOMAIN TABLE ***
APPDOMAIN ID: 0x60c3c568
    NAME: mscorlib.dll
    PROCESS ID: 0x00000788

APPDOMAIN ID: 0x00139de0
    NAME: DefaultDomain
    PROCESS ID: 0x00000788

APPDOMAIN ID: 0x60c3d9b8
    NAME: EE Shared Assembly Repository
    PROCESS ID: 0x00000788
```

LISTING 20.38 Continued

```
*** ASSEMBLY TABLE ***

ASSEMBLY ID: 0x00142e78
    NAME: mscorlib
    MODULE ID: 0x00143438
    APPDOMAIN ID: 0x60c3d9b8


ASSEMBLY ID: 0x0014e838
    NAME: TraceSwitch
    MODULE ID: 0x0014e978
    APPDOMAIN ID: 0x00139de0


ASSEMBLY ID: 0x00151880
    NAME: System
    MODULE ID: 0x00152200
    APPDOMAIN ID: 0x00139de0


ASSEMBLY ID: 0x001644a8
    NAME: System.Xml
    MODULE ID: 0x00157740
    APPDOMAIN ID: 0x00139de0


ASSEMBLY ID: 0x0016b298
    NAME: System.Web
    MODULE ID: 0x00169dd0
    APPDOMAIN ID: 0x00139de0
*** MODULE TABLE ***
. . .
*** CLASS TABLE ***
. . .
CLASS ID: 0x003750a0
    NAME: TraceSwitchTest.TraceSwitchMain
    TOKEN: 0x02000002
    MODULE ID: 0x0014e978
. . .
*** FUNCTION TABLE ***
. . .
FUNCTION ID: 0x00375078
    NAME: TraceSwitchTest.TraceSwitchMain::WriteDebugOutput
    TOKEN: 0x06000001
    CLASS ID: 0x003750a0
    MODULE ID: 0x0014e978
    CODE SIZE: 40 bytes
    START ADDRESS: 0x03641bf8
```

LISTING 20.38 Continued

```
    Dumping Enter-Leave event counters
        Enter Counter:     1
        Left Counter:      1
        TailCall Counter: 0
        Unwind Counter:    0
. . .
```

This profiler builds a list based on each event called. Other than just confirming that certain classes and functions were instantiated and executed, this sample does not do much. In Listing 20.38, the profiler is used to profile some code, `TraceSwitch`, which was introduced in the previous chapter. As you can see from the output, the method `WriteDebugOutput` was called once and exited once. In addition, the address of the function is recorded. None of the other profiling tools that have been introduced thus far can give you this kind of information about a managed process. Until profilers for managed code are commercially available, these profiling APIs might be your only choice.

Windows General Code Profiler

Many of the principles that were developed in the previous section were used to create a more user-friendly profiler by providing a graphical user interface for profiling. This profiler has been named WinGCP because it takes much of the information provided by the GCP profiler presented earlier and formats it into a more presentable Windows UI.

To use the profiling API, you have to profile the .NET application completely devoid of managed code. A user interface could have been developed using MFC, but it would have been a difficult task. A method was needed to completely separate the UI from the function. One way of accomplishing this is to separate the UI and the profiler with a socket connection.

Profiling proceeds as with the GCP described earlier. When the process that is being profiled finishes, the GCP dumps all of the information out to the console or file. With WinGCP, you can dump the information in an XML format to a memory stream, open up a socket, and output the data to the UI server. Listing 20.39 captures the important points about the data transfer from the client (the profiler) to the server (the UI).

LISTING 20.39 Output and Connection from WinGCP

```
std::wostringstream out;
out << L"<?xml version=\"1.0\"?>" << std::endl;
out << L"<profile>" << std::endl;
// dump Thread table
```

LISTING 20.39 Continued

```
for(ConstantThreadIterator it = m_threadTable.begin();
    it != m_threadTable.end();
    ++it)
{
       it->second.Dump(out);
}
     // dump AppDomain table
for(ConstantAppDomainIterator it = m_appDomainTable.begin();
    it != m_appDomainTable.end();
    ++it)
{
       it->second.Dump(out);
}
. . .
SOCKET socket = WSASocket(AF_INET, SOCK_STREAM, 0, NULL, 0, 0);
if (socket == INVALID_SOCKET)
{
    return;
}
std::string server;
char *lpserver = getenv("COR_PROFILER_SERVER");
if(lpserver == NULL)
    server = "localhost";
else
    server = lpserver;

SOCKADDR_IN sin;
sin.sin_family = AF_INET;
sin.sin_addr.s_addr = inet_addr(server.c_str());
if(sin.sin_addr.s_addr == INADDR_NONE)
{
    LPHOSTENT lpHost = ::gethostbyname(server.c_str());
    if(lpHost != NULL)
    {
        sin.sin_addr.s_addr =
            ((LPIN_ADDR)lpHost->h_addr)->s_addr;
    }
    else
    {
        ::closesocket(socket);
        socket = INVALID_SOCKET;
        return;
    }
}

char *lpport = getenv("COR_PROFILER_SERVER_PORT");
int port = 8085;
if(lpserver != NULL)
    port = atoi(lpport);
```

LISTING 20.39 Continued

```
sin.sin_port = htons((u_short)port);

if (::WSAConnect(socket, (LPSOCKADDR) &sin,
➥sizeof (SOCKADDR_IN), NULL, NULL, NULL, NULL) != 0)
{
    ::closesocket(socket);
    socket = INVALID_SOCKET;
    return;
}
// Send the date
long lTotalBytes;
long nBytes = lTotalBytes = ::send(socket,
                                   (LPCSTR)out.str().c_str(),
                                   out.str().length() * sizeof(wchar_t), 0);
while(lTotalBytes < out.str().length()*sizeof(wchar_t))
{
    nBytes = ::send(socket,
                    (LPCSTR)out.str().c_str() + lTotalBytes,
                    (out.str().length() * sizeof(wchar_t)) - lTotalBytes, 0);
    lTotalBytes += nBytes;
}
::closesocket(socket);
socket = INVALID_SOCKET;
```

When the managed process has exited, the information is transferred from the client (profiler) to the server (the UI). The first part of Listing 20.39 shows the beginning of formatting the output as XML. Following the dump of the profile statistics to an XML stream, the server and the server port are found using the environment variables `COR_PROFILER_SERVER` and `COR_PROFILER_SERVER_PORT`. Then a connection is created to the server, and the profile statistics are written out to the server.

Listing 20.40 shows how the server or user interface portion of `WinGCP` sets up and starts the client process.

LISTING 20.40 WinGCP Server Setting Up and Starting the Profile Client

```
ProcessStartInfo psi;
if(arguments.Text.Length > 0)
    psi = new ProcessStartInfo(pathToFile.Text, arguments.Text);
else
    psi = new ProcessStartInfo(pathToFile.Text);
psi.EnvironmentVariables.Add("DBG_PRF_LOG", "1");
psi.EnvironmentVariables.Add("Cor_Enable_Profiling", "1");
psi.EnvironmentVariables.Add("COR_PROFILER", "{01568439-E2BA-4434-8ACC-
816239E8B8B5}");
// psi.EnvironmentVariables.Add("COR_PROFILER_SERVER_PORT", "8085");
```

LISTING 20.40 Continued

```
// psi.EnvironmentVariables.Add("COR_PROFILER_SERVER", "localhost");
psi.UseShellExecute = false;
int pos = pathToFile.Text.LastIndexOf("\\");
psi.WorkingDirectory = pathToFile.Text.Substring(0, pos);
Process p = Process.Start(psi);
```

Notice that this is the only part of the application that is dependent on the server and the client both residing on the same machine. With a little imagination, you could easily adapt this code using remoting so that the client profiler could run on virtually any machine. The server just listens for the results back from the client (see Listing 20.41).

LISTING 20.41 WinGCP Server Listening for Results

```
listeningClient = new TcpListener(8085);
listeningClient.Start();
try
{
    bool continueProcessing = true;
    while(continueProcessing)
    {
        Socket s = listeningClient.AcceptSocket();
        NetworkStream ns = new NetworkStream(s);
        XmlTextReader channel = new XmlTextReader(ns);
        profileInfoInterface.ProcessData(channel);
    }
}
catch(Exception e)
{
    // SocketException when listeningClient.Stop is called
    // during an AcceptSocket.
    // "A blocking operation was interrupted by a call to
    // WSACancelBlockingCall"
    Debug.WriteLine(e);
}
finally
{
    listeningClient.Stop();
}
```

In this thread, the server listens for the data coming from the client, decodes the XML stream, and then displays the results to the user in the dialog box. By separating the presentation from the data, WinGCP enhances the original GCP visually. In addition, the original GCP can now can be used to profile non-console applications (Windows apps).

The cracking of the XML message and the display of the results are not shown for the purpose of keeping this presentation as compact as possible. The complete source for this application is in the `WinGCP` directory.

Finding Frequently Accessed Code with the Hot Spots Tracker

As a final example of using the profiling API, this section will discuss the Hot Spots Tracker (HST) that is part of the Framework SDK. You can find the original source in `\Program Files\Microsoft Visual Studio .NET\FrameworkSDK\Tool Developers Guide\Samples\profiler\hst_profiler` or see the slightly modified version in the `hst` directory of the samples for this book. This profiling tool illustrates how changing some of the events to which the profiling tool listens can greatly affect the profiler implementation.

The HST supports even fewer flags than GCP did, as evidenced in Listing 20.42.

LISTING 20.42 Flags for the HST Profiler

```
m_dwEventMask = (DWORD)(COR_PRF_MONITOR_THREADS |
                        COR_PRF_DISABLE_INLINING |
                        COR_PRF_MONITOR_SUSPENDS |
                        COR_PRF_MONITOR_ENTERLEAVE |
                        COR_PRF_MONITOR_EXCEPTIONS |
                        COR_PRF_MONITOR_CODE_TRANSITIONS);
```

In many ways, this profiler provides more useful profiling information than the GCP profiler. The HST tracks the time spent in each function. When a function is entered, the `Enter` method is called. The `Enter` method looks like Listing 20.43.

LISTING 20.43 HST Implementation for the `Enter` Method

```
void ProfilerCallback::Enter( FunctionID functionID )
{
    ///////////////////////////////////////////////////////////////////////////
    TimeTracker timer( static_cast<PrfInfo *>( g_pCallbackObject ) );
    ///////////////////////////////////////////////////////////////////////////

    try
    {
        g_pCallbackObject->UpdateCallStack( functionID, PUSH );
    }
    catch ( BaseException *exception )
    {
        exception->ReportFailure();
        delete exception;

        g_pCallbackObject->Failure();
    }

} // ProfilerCallback::Enter
```

LISTING 20.43 Continued

```
/* public */
void ProfilerCallback::Leave( FunctionID functionID )
{
    ///////////////////////////////////////////////////////////////////////////
    TimeTracker timer( static_cast<PrfInfo *>( g_pCallbackObject ) );
    ///////////////////////////////////////////////////////////////////////////

    try
    {
        g_pCallbackObject->UpdateCallStack( functionID, POP );
    }
    catch ( BaseException *exception )
    {
        exception->ReportFailure();
        delete exception;

        g_pCallbackObject->Failure();
    }

} // ProfilerCallback::Leave
```

The `Enter` callback method calls `UpdateCallStack` with a `PUSH`, and the `Leave` callback method calls `UpdateCallStack` with a POP. The `TimerTracker` simply adds a time stamp to the class so that it can be calculated later how long this function was executed.

This profiler also has a `DumpTables` method, which is implemented in Listing 20.44.

LISTING 20.44 HST Implementation of `DumpTables`

```
void PrfInfo::DumpTables()
{
    //
    // Dump the thread table if you actually performed profiling
    //
    if ( BASEHELPER::FetchEnvironment( LOG_ENVIRONMENT ) != 0xFF
➥ /* don't log anything */ )
    {
        if ( (m_pThreadTable != NULL) &&
             (m_dwEventMask != (DWORD)COR_PRF_MONITOR_NONE) )
    {
            LOG_TO_FILE( ("Thread ID;Function;Times Called;Exclusive
➥Time;Inclusive Time;Callee Time;Suspended Time;Profiler Time\n\n") )
            m_pThreadTable->Dump();
        }
    }

} // PrfInfo::DumpTables
```

This function prints a header and calls the Dump method for the Thread table, which is reproduced in Listing 20.45.

LISTING 20.45 HST Implementation of Dump

```
void FunctionTimingInfo::Dump()
{
    HRESULT    hr;
    ULONG argCount = 0;
    BOOL bIsStatic = FALSE;
    WCHAR functionName[MAX_LENGTH];
    WCHAR returnTypeStr[MAX_LENGTH];
    WCHAR functionParameters[10 * MAX_LENGTH];


    //
    // The intention is to dump the data into a semi-colon delimited list. The
    // data can then be imported into a spreadsheet and analyzed. The format
    // is essentially comprised of
    //
    //        thread ID
    //       function name and parameters
    //       times called
    //       exclusive time
    //       inclusive time
    //       callee time
    //          suspended time
    //       profiler time
    //
    hr = BASEHELPER::GetFunctionProperties( g_pPrfInfo->m_pProfilerInfo,
                                            m_id,
                                            &bIsStatic,
                                            &argCount,
                                            returnTypeStr,
                                            functionParameters,
                                            functionName );
    if ( SUCCEEDED( hr ) )
    {
        //
        // Dump thread ID, return type, function name, and function
        // parameters; note, function parameters are separated by a
        // '+' sign.
    //
    LOG_TO_FILE( ("0x%08x;", m_win32ThreadID) )
    if ( bIsStatic == TRUE )
            LOG_TO_FILE( ("static ") )

       if ( returnTypeStr[0] != NULL )
            LOG_TO_FILE( ("%S ", returnTypeStr) )
```

LISTING 20.45 Continued

```
        if ( functionName[0] != NULL )
            LOG_TO_FILE( ("%S(", functionName) )

    if ( argCount > 0 )
        {
            WCHAR *parameter;
            WCHAR *separator = L"+";
            //
            // Parse and dump parameters
            //
            parameter = wcstok( functionParameters, separator );
            while ( parameter != NULL )
            {
                LOG_TO_FILE( (" %S", parameter) )
         parameter = wcstok( NULL, separator );
                if ( parameter != NULL )
                    LOG_TO_FILE( (",") )
            } // while
        }
        LOG_TO_FILE( (" );") )

        //
        // Dump statistics
        //
        double exclusiveTime;


        // to compute exclusive time for the function, subtract the callee
        // time, suspended time, and profiler time from the inclusive time
        exclusiveTime = ( ((double)m_inclusiveTime.QuadPart /
➥(double)g_frequency.QuadPart) -
                        ( ((double)m_calleeTime.QuadPart /
➥(double)g_frequency.QuadPart)    +
                             ((double)m_suspendedTime.QuadPart /
➥(double)g_frequency.QuadPart) +
                             ((double)m_profilerTime.QuadPart /
➥(double)g_frequency.QuadPart) ) );

        LOG_TO_FILE( ("%d;%f;%f;%f;%f;%f\n",
                      m_timesCalled,
                      exclusiveTime,
                      ((double)m_inclusiveTime.QuadPart /
➥(double)g_frequency.QuadPart),
                     ((double)m_calleeTime.QuadPart /
➥(double)g_frequency.QuadPart),
                     ((double)m_suspendedTime.QuadPart /
➥(double)g_frequency.QuadPart),
                     ((double)m_profilerTime.QuadPart /
➥(double)g_frequency.QuadPart)) )
```

LISTING 20.45 Continued

```
    }
    else
            LOG_TO_FILE( ("Unable to Retreive Information about the
➥Function Name, Parameters and Return Type\n") )

} // FunctionTimingInfo::Dump
```

The HST profiler can be used with any managed process because the output is written to a file. The LOG_TO_FILE macro determines how the profile information is output.

```
#define LOG_TO_FILE( message ) BASEHELPER::LogToFile message;
```

This function opens the file output.log.

```
stream = ((count == 1) ? fopen( "output.log", "w" ) :
                         fopen( "output.log", "a+" ));
```

When you use this profiler, you get output that looks like Listing 20.46.

LISTING 20.46 HST Output

```
Thread ID;Function;Times Called;Exclusive Time;Inclusive Time;Callee Time;
➥Suspended Time;Profiler Time

0x000009c8;UNMANAGED FRAME( );1542;115.476832;162.039139;45.721695;0.000000;
➥0.840613
0x000009c8;System.ComponentModel.EventHandlerListSystem.ComponentModel.
➥Component::get_Events( );87;0.000835;0.022671;0.001297;0.000000;
➥0.020539
0x000009c8;System.ComponentModel.ISite System.ComponentModel.Component::
➥get_Site( );30;0.000251;0.010837;0.000000;0.000000;0.010586
0x000009c8;void System.ComponentModel.Component::Dispose( );4;0.003515;
➥0.887392;0.882895;0.000000;0.000982
0x000009c8;void System.ComponentModel.Component::Dispose( bool );4;0.000172;
➥0.003737;0.001866;0.000000;0.001699
0x000009c8;bool System.ComponentModel.Component::get_DesignMode( );7;0.000073;
➥0.021668;0.000000;0.000000;0.021595
. . .
0x000009c8;void ThreadPoolTest.ThreadPoolTestForm::InitializeComponent( );
➥1;0.017098;2.809657;2.792239;0.000000;0.000320
0x000009c8;static void ThreadPoolTest.ThreadPoolTestForm::Main( );
➥1;0.006464;158.332578;158.325792;0.000000;0.000322
0x000009c8;void ThreadPoolTest.ThreadPoolTestForm::OnStart( Object );
➥1;0.004145;0.306971;0.302464;0.000000;0.000361
. . .
0x000009c8;void System.Threading.Thread::.ctor( System.Threading.ThreadStart );
➥1;0.000217;0.000777;0.000215;0.000000;0.000345
0x000009c8;void System.Threading.Thread::Start( );
➥1;0.002435;0.015568;0.012785;0.000000;0.000348
```

Because this file is neatly delimited by semi-colons, you can import it into an Excel spreadsheet and sort based on columns. This was done in Figure 20.18.

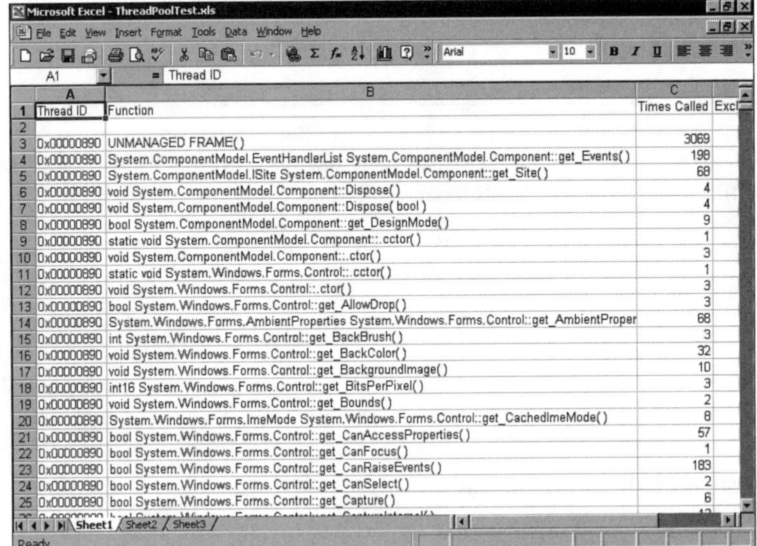

	A	B	C
1	Thread ID	Function	Times Called
2			
3	0x00000890	UNMANAGED FRAME()	3069
4	0x00000890	System.ComponentModel.EventHandlerList System.ComponentModel.Component::get_Events()	198
5	0x00000890	System.ComponentModel.ISite System.ComponentModel.Component::get_Site()	68
6	0x00000890	void System.ComponentModel.Component::Dispose()	4
7	0x00000890	void System.ComponentModel.Component::Dispose(bool)	4
8	0x00000890	bool System.ComponentModel.Component::get_DesignMode()	9
9	0x00000890	static void System.ComponentModel.Component::.cctor()	1
10	0x00000890	void System.ComponentModel.Component::.ctor()	3
11	0x00000890	static void System.Windows.Forms.Control::.cctor()	1
12	0x00000890	void System.Windows.Forms.Control::.ctor()	3
13	0x00000890	bool System.Windows.Forms.Control::get_AllowDrop()	3
14	0x00000890	System.Windows.Forms.AmbientProperties System.Windows.Forms.Control::get_AmbientProper	68
15	0x00000890	int System.Windows.Forms.Control::get_BackBrush()	3
16	0x00000890	void System.Windows.Forms.Control::get_BackColor()	32
17	0x00000890	void System.Windows.Forms.Control::get_BackgroundImage()	10
18	0x00000890	int16 System.Windows.Forms.Control::get_BitsPerPixel()	3
19	0x00000890	void System.Windows.Forms.Control::get_Bounds()	2
20	0x00000890	System.Windows.Forms.ImeMode System.Windows.Forms.Control::get_CachedImeMode()	8
21	0x00000890	bool System.Windows.Forms.Control::get_CanAccessProperties()	57
22	0x00000890	bool System.Windows.Forms.Control::get_CanFocus()	1
23	0x00000890	bool System.Windows.Forms.Control::get_CanRaiseEvents()	183
24	0x00000890	bool System.Windows.Forms.Control::get_CanSelect()	2
25	0x00000890	bool System.Windows.Forms.Control::get_Capture()	6

FIGURE 20.18
Importing HST output data into an Excel spreadsheet.

Summary

This chapter explored some of the tools available to help you determine where performance bottlenecks in an application are. Some of the traditional tools that are available for determining memory and threading information were discussed. Next, the chapter showed how to use `PerformanceCounter`s and how to build custom `PerformanceCounter`s. Finally, the APIs that are available for building a custom profiling application were explored.

Appendixes

PART IV

IN THIS PART

APPENDIX A

C# Basics

In This Appendix

This appendix should fill in any holes that remain in your understanding of C#. Because most of the examples in this book are written in C#, it has been assumed that you have experience in many aspects of C# programming. Perhaps some of the programming constructs caught you by surprise because it had been assumed that that construct was general knowledge. This appendix will give you the basics of C# so that you can read and understand the examples throughout the book. If a particular construct confuses you, you can turn to this appendix for a brief explanation of the construct or syntax. This allows for a common base of understanding from which the ideas behind the CLR can be better communicated. If you are unfamiliar with C# and this brief appendix is not enough to bring you up to speed, try reading Eric Gunnerson's book *A Programmer's Introduction to C#.*

Building a Program with C#

One of your first tasks in learning C# is to create a C# program. Listing A.1 shows a simple C# program that simply prints a message to the **Console**.

LISTING A.1 Simple C# Program

```
using System;
namespace Hello
{
    class HelloMain
    {
        static void Main(string[] args)
        {
            Console.WriteLine("Hello!");
        }
    }
}
```

First, notice that a **namepace** encloses the entire program. This is strictly not required. If the namespace is taken out, leaving the class `HelloMain`, the program would still compile and run. However, it is a good idea to get in the habit of enclosing your programs with a namespace. This prevents conflicts with other modules and libraries.

Classes can only exist directly in a namespace. You cannot put methods or fields directly under a namespace. A namespace only specifies an extra qualifying "name" for the classes contained in the namespace. Look, for example, at Listing A.2.

LISTING A.2 Namespace Example

```
namespace Hello
{
    class Write
    {
        static void OutputLine(string line)
        {
            System.Console.WriteLine(line);
        }
    }
}
```

The long form of the method `OutputLine` would be `Hello.Write.OutputLine`. If you were to include **`using Hello;`**, you could shorten the call to the method to `Write.OutputLine`. You cannot include a class in a **`using`** statement; it is just to shorten namespace specifications.

After the namespace is the class definition. In Listing A.1, notice that only one method is in the class, and it is not only static, but it is the entry point for the program. When the CLR loads a C# program, it looks for a static `Main` method, and that is where the program begins execution. In the previous paragraph explaining Listing A.2, you saw how any static method could be called. You call static method with `class type.method`. (In Listing A.2, the class type is `Hello.Write` and the method is `OutputLine`.)

The only task that the `Main` method performs is to write a message out to the **`Console`**. Because `using System;` was used in Listing A.1, you don't have to specify `System.Console.WriteLine`—just `Console.WriteLine`. The only time that this could be confusing is if you wanted to look up documentation on this method or the **`Console`** class; you would need to know that the **`Console`** class is part of the **`System`** namespace.

To compile and run this program, you just need to run the C# compiler like this:

```
csc hello.cs
```

> **Note**
>
> A complete description of the command-line options for the C# compiler is part of the SDK, "C# Compiler Options," at `ms-help://MS.VSCC/MS.MSDNVS/cscomp/html/vcrefCompilerOptions.htm`.

Now add a method to this class so that you can modify the program, as in Listing A.3.

LISTING A.3 Adding a Simple Method to the `Hello` Program

```
using System;
namespace Hello
{
    class HelloMain
    {
        static void Output(string message)
        {
            Console.WriteLine(message);
        }
        static void Main(string[] args)
        {
            Output("Hello!");
        }
    }
}
```

Now another function or method exists, and it is also static. Static methods can only call static methods and reference static fields in the class. Non-static methods and fields will be covered in more detail when C# objects are discussed.

Now you can organize the "output" functions into a library. Listing A.4 shows the output function in a class by itself.

LISTING A.4 A "Library" of Functions

```
using System;
namespace Hello
{
    public class Output
    {
        public static void OutputLine(string message)
        {
            Console.WriteLine(message);
        }
    }
}
```

Listing A.5 shows how to call a method into this library.

LISTING A.5 Calling a Function into a Library

```
namespace Testing
{
    class HelloMain
    {
        static void Main(string[] args)
```

LISTING A.5 Continued

```
        {
            Output.OutputLine("Hello!");
        }
    }
}
```

Figure A.1 shows two different ways to compile and link this program with multiple modules.

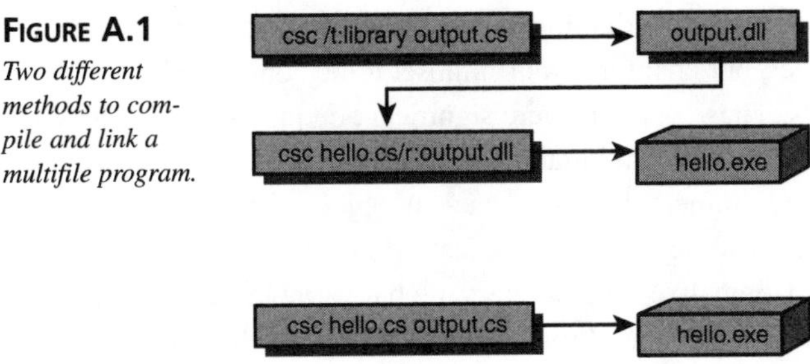

FIGURE A.1
Two different methods to compile and link a multifile program.

The first method shown in Figure A.1 shows a two-step process. First, you create the library (in this case, it is called `output.dll`), and next, you compile and link in that library. You would use this method to distribute or use a library. Assume that `output.dll` was your library. You could build the library as in the first step, distribute this library to your customers, and instruct them to link in your library using the second step. On the other hand, if you are a consumer and you want to use the library, you would link in the library that you obtained from a third party using the second step. The second method requires that you have source for both the caller and the callee modules. You would use this method if you were only interested in organizing your code into functional modules and you were not interested in distributing this code as a library.

Object-Oriented Programming with C#

Back in the late 1980s and early 1990s is when I first became aware of a new paradigm in the programming community. For years, I had learned about "structured programming." Using C or FORTRAN, it was easy to understand that structure made a program easier to understand, build, and modify. To be able to explain the operation of a program in a step-by-step, flowchart fashion seemed to be the best way to program.

Then, along came languages like Smalltalk, Lisp, and Scheme, which encouraged a more "unconventional" view of a program. These languages taught that the data was not only the most important consideration in developing a program, but it was also the one item that was most likely to change. You could write an elegant structured program that multiplied two matrices of integers. Perhaps later you are told that the data changed and you need to multiply two matrices of floating point values. You would need to write a new routine to do the multiplication. It's important that you're not more focused on the procedure or the code than on the data. Thus, objects are born. An object is the data that describes a real-world concept or "object."

Object-oriented programming is merely "orienting" or focusing on the object instead of the program. It is no silver bullet, but changing your mindset to be "object-oriented" yields some significant benefits. These benefits were significant enough that C++ was created so that the many C programmers could take advantage of object-oriented features. The problem was that programmers wanted to have an object-oriented program, but they were unwilling to give up some of the non-object-oriented features to which they had become accustomed. Things like void pointers, global variables, and C type casting were too pervasive to force a change. Programmers would use objects when they were convenient to use them, a fallback on "easier" procedural programming when deadlines loomed close. With C++, it was easier to write bad programs than good programs.

C# Objects

Everything in C# is an **`Object`**.

> **Note**
>
> One exception to this generalization does exist. In an unsafe context, pointer types are not objects because they do not derive from **`System.Object`**.

Because everything is an **`Object`**, everything has four base methods:

- Equals—Method to determine if two instances are equal
- GetHashCode—Method to uniquely identify an **`Object`**
- GetType—Method for obtaining the type of the **`Object`**
- ToString—Method for converting the **`Object`** to a string

Would you expect the following to compile?

```
Console.WriteLine("{0} {1}", 1.ToString(), 1.GetType());
```

It not only compiles, but it also outputs this:

```
1 System.Int32
```

The following

```
Console.WriteLine("{0} {1}", 1.23.ToString(), 1.23.GetType());
```

outputs this

```
1.23 System.Double
```

To really prove the point, you could try the following:

```
Console.WriteLine("{0} {1} {2} {3}",
                  1.23.ToString(),
                  1.23.GetType(),
                  1.23.GetType().BaseType,
                  1.23.GetType().BaseType.BaseType);
```

This outputs the following:

```
1.23 System.Double System.ValueType System.Object
```

Just a few layers down, even a basic floating point value is an object. Two types of objects exist: value objects and class objects. These two types are mainly differentiated by the way that they are stored in memory and how they are passed as arguments to methods or functions.

Value Type Objects

Two types of value objects are used and supported by C#: built-in types such as System.Int32 and System.Double, and user-defined types.

Built-In Value Types

C# has a rich set of built-in value types. The built-in types are listed in Table A.1.

TABLE A.1 Built-In Value Types

Category	*C# Data Type*	*Description*	*Size*	*Range*
Integer	Byte	An 8-bit unsigned integer.	8	0 to 255
	sbyte	An 8-bit signed integer. Not CLS compliant.	8	–128 to 127

TABLE A.1 Continued

Category	*C# Data Type*	*Description*	*Size*	*Range*
	short	A 16-bit signed integer.	16	–32768 to 32767
	int	A 32-bit signed integer.	32	–2147483648 to 2147483647
	long	A 64-bit signed integer.	64	–9223372036854775808 to 9223372036854775807
	ushort	A 16-bit unsigned integer. Not CLS compliant.	16	0 to 65535
	uint	A 32-bit unsigned integer. Not CLS compliant.	32	0 to 4294967295
	ulong	A 64-bit unsigned integer. Not CLS compliant.	64	0 to 18446744073709551615
Floating point	float	A single-precision (32-bit) floating-point number. 7 digits of precision.	32	–3.402823E+38 to 3.402823E+38
	double	A double-precision (64-bit) floating-point number. 15–16 digits of precision.	64	–1.79769313486232E+308 to to 1.79769313486232E+308
Logical	bool	A Boolean value (true or false).	1	true (1), false(0)
Other	char	A Unicode (16-bit) character.	16	0 to 65535
	decimal	A 96-bit decimal value. 28–29 bits of precision.	128	–79228162514264337593543950335 to 79228162514264337593543950335
	enum	A user-defined name for a list of values.	—	Depends on the base type. Valid base types are byte, sbyte, short, ushort, int, uint, long, and ulong. Default is int.

Listing A.6 shows some examples of using these built-in value types.

LISTING A.6 Using Built-In Value Types

```
byte a = 2;
sbyte b = -2;
short c = 0x1FFF;
int d = -1234;
long e = 49;
ushort f = 0xFFFE;
uint g = 4294967294;
ulong h = 18446744073709551614;
float i = -1.0F;
float j = 1.0e2F;
double k = 10.8;
double l = 1234.5678D;
bool m = true;
char n = 'A';
char o = '\x456';
char p = '\u0924';
decimal q = 90.45M;
```

Enumerated types require a definition like the examples in Listing A.7.

LISTING A.7 Defining an Enumeration Type

```
enum Cars
{
    Ford,
    Chevrolet,
    Buick,
    Dodge
}
enum Boats : byte
{
    Sail,
    Yacht,
    Speed,
    Fishing
}
enum Motorcycle : long
{
    Honda = 1,
    Yamaha,
    Kawasaki,
    BMW
}
```

After an enumeration type is defined, it can be used in `switch` statements, `if` statements, and other flow control, as in Listing A.8.

LISTING A.8 Using an Enumeration Type

```
Boats eb = Boats.Sail;
switch(eb)
{
    case Boats.Sail:
        Console.WriteLine("Sail boat");
    break;
}

if(eb == Boats.Sail)
{
    Console.WriteLine("Sail boat");
}
```

Finally, a number of operations can be performed with enumeration types. Listing A.9 gives an example of some of these operations.

LISTING A.9 Operations That Are Available on an Enumeration Type

```
Boats b = Boats.Sail;

// Print the string name of the enum
Console.WriteLine("{0}", b);

// Print the value and name for each enum
foreach(byte i in Enum.GetValues(b.GetType()))
{
    Console.WriteLine("Boat Value: {0} -> {1}",
                      i,
                      Enum.GetName(b.GetType(), i));
}

// Iterate through each of the string names for the enum
foreach(string s in Enum.GetNames(b.GetType()))
{
    Console.WriteLine("Enum: {0}", s);
}

// Try to get a enum with a particular name
b = (Boats)Enum.Parse(typeof(Boats), "Fishing", true);
Console.WriteLine("Parse enum: {0}", b);

// See if a value is represented in the enum
if(Enum.IsDefined(typeof(Boats), (byte)3))
{
    Console.WriteLine("The value is 3 is defined for Boats");
}
```

Listing A.10 shows what the output for these operations would look like.

LISTING A.10 Output for Enumeration Operations

```
Sail
Boat Value: 0 -> Sail
Boat Value: 1 -> Yacht
Boat Value: 2 -> Speed
Boat Value: 3 -> Fishing
Enum: Sail
Enum: Yacht
Enum: Speed
Enum: Fishing
Parse enum: Fishing
The value is 3 is defined for Boats
```

Value types are stored on the stack of a running program.

When a value type is boxed, it inherits from **System.ValueType**, and methods and properties of that class can be used to describe the particular value type. Boxing is simply the conversion of a value type to a class or reference type. Unboxing is the reverse operation. Boxing and unboxing are C#'s support for the IL **box** and **unbox** instructions.

User-Defined Value Types

It is also possible to define your own value type. When defining your own value type, you use a **struct**. Unlike C++ where the difference between a **struct** and a **class** is primarily member default access permissions, C# makes a larger distinction between a **struct** and a class. Following are some of the differences between a **struct** and a reference type or a **class**.

- A **struct** is allocated on the stack and passed as an argument by value.
- A **struct** cannot derive from a **struct**. A **struct** can only derive from an **interface**.
- A **struct** cannot have an explicit parameterless constructor otherwise known as a default constructor.

When an object is defined as a **struct**, it assumes value semantics. It is created on the stack and passed by value when given as an argument to a function. A **struct** in C# is **sealed**; therefore, it cannot be used as a base for inheritance. A simple structure that represents the data members for the representation of a complex number is shown in Listing A.11.

LISTING A.11 A Complex Value

```
struct Complex
{
    public double real;
    public double imag;
}
```

In a real application, you could add methods so that this object has more utility. Listing A.11 only shows the data, and it is not a functional object. For example, if you have a `Complex` value and want to print the value, you have code that looks like Listing A.12.

LISTING A.12 Using the Default `ToString` Method

```
Complex cn = new Complex();
cn.real = 1.0;
cn.imag = 0.0;
Console.WriteLine("{0}", cn);
```

Listing A.12 prints the following:

```
Testing.Complex
```

This is not what was expected. To show the actual values associated with this object, you must override the default **`ToString`** method. The resulting structure looks like Listing A.13.

LISTING A.13 Printing a Complex Value

```
struct Complex
{
    public double real;
    public double imag;
    public override string ToString()
    {
        return (string.Format("({0}, {1}i)", real, imag));
    }
}
```

Listing A.12 outputs the following:

```
(1, 0i)
```

This is probably more what you had in mind.

It is generally not good practice to make fields public as in Listings A.11 and A.13. This violates one of the key principles of object-oriented programming: encapsulation. To support encapsulation, C# introduces the concept of an *accessor*. An *accessor* is a set of

read or write methods that allows access to the fields in your object. If only a read accessor is defined, then the object is read-only. If both a read and write accessor are defined, then that field is read-write. The `Complex` **`struct`** to take advantage of accessors results in a `Complex` value that looks like Listing A.14.

LISTING A.14 Adding Accessors to the Complex Value

```
struct Complex
{
    double real;
    double imag;
    public override string ToString()
    {
        return (string.Format("({0}, {1}i)", real, imag));
    }
    public double Real
    {
        get
        {
            return real;
        }
        set
        {
            real = value;
        }
    }
    public double Imaginary
    {
        get
        {
            return imag;
        }
        set
        {
            imag = value;
        }
    }
}
```

Accessing the member values of this user-defined type requires a slight modification to the code that was directly accessing the fields. Changing Listing A.12 to use accessors becomes Listing A.15.

LISTING A.15 Using Accessors Instead of Direct Field Access

```
Complex cn = new Complex();
cn.Real = 1;
cn.Imaginary = 0;
```

In Listing A.15, what looks like a field access is actually turned into an access to the field via a method call.

To compare two `Complex` objects, add the code shown in Listing A.16 to your user-defined value type.

LISTING A.16 Comparing Complex Objects

```
public static bool operator==(Complex a, Complex b)
{
    if(a.real == b.real &&
       a.imag == b.imag))
    {
        return(true);
    }
    else
    {
        return(false);
    }
}
public static bool operator!=(Complex a, Complex b)
{
    return(!(a == b));
}
public override bool Equals(object o)
{
    Complex b = (Complex)o;
    return(this == b);
}
public override int GetHashCode()
{
    return(real.GetHashCode() ^ imag.GetHashCode());
}
```

The last two methods, **`Equals`** and **`GetHashCode`**, are overrides strictly for interoperation with the rest of the .NET Framework. They are not required to compare objects; however, if they are not defined as a pair, the compiler generates a warning message.

If you want to add two `Complex` objects, then you would add the code from Listing A.16 to Listing A.17.

LISTING A.17 Adding Complex Objects

```
public static Complex operator+(Complex a, Complex b)
{
Complex r = new Complex();
r.real = a.real + b.real;
r.imag = a.imag + b.imag;
return(r);
}
```

To negate a `Complex` value, you need to build a unary operator. Listing A.18 shows how this is done.

LISTING A.18 Negating a Complex Object

```
public static Complex operator-(Complex a)
{
    Complex r = new Complex();
    r.real = -a.real;
    r.imag = -a.imag;
    return(r);
}
. . .
Complex cnn = -cn;
Console.WriteLine("{0}", cnn);
. . .
(-1, 0i)
```

You get the idea. You could make many improvements to this object to make it easier to use. You could add methods to subtract, divide, and multiply two complex numbers. You could add a constructor that takes real and imaginary arguments so that you don't have to assign the fields individually. You could add methods to return the magnitude and phase corresponding to the real and imaginary values. You could add error handling. The list could go on and on. No matter how many methods and properties you add to this object, it is still a lightweight value type object because the memory required for an individual instance is that required for two 64-bit floating-point values. This is a perfect example of the kind of object that is suited for a value type. Custom value type objects are supposed to be relatively small. Contrast that with an object that looks like Listing A.19.

LISTING A.19 A Large Object

```
struct BigObject
{
    long value1;
    long value2;
    long value3;
    long value4;
    long value5;
    long value6;
    long value7;
. . .
}
```

If this object were passed often as an argument, it could be a detriment to performance because each of the fields would have to be pushed on to the stack during the call and popped off of the stack in the called function. An object like this probably should be a reference type or class.

Strings Act Like Value Types

The **string** class is technically a reference type for the following reasons:

- It is not boxed or unboxed.
- It does not derive from **ValueType** when boxed.
- It is allocated from the heap.
- It is passed to a method by reference.
- It is a class (**System.String**).
- It is immutable. (You cannot change the value of the string without reallocating a new string.)

A string acts like a value type. (It has value semantics.) Listing A.20 shows some of the operations that can be performed with a **string**.

LISTING A.20 String Operations

```
static void Main(string[] args)
{
    string s = "This is a test";
    // Output each character in the string
    foreach(char c in s)
    {
        Console.WriteLine("Char: {0}", c);
    }
    // Output each character in the string using string indexing
    for(int i = 0; i < s.Length; i++)
    {
        Console.WriteLine("Char: {0}", s[i]);
    }
    // Output each word in the string (word delimited by space)
    foreach(string sub in s.Split())
    {
        Console.WriteLine("Word: {0}", sub);
    }
    // Convert the whole string to upper-case
    string us = s.ToUpper();
    Console.WriteLine(us);
    // Convert the whole string to lower-case
    string ls = s.ToLower();
    Console.WriteLine(ls);
    // Insert a string so the new string reads: This is a new test
    string ins = s.Insert(s.IndexOf("test"), "new ");
    Console.WriteLine(ins);
    // Replace a string so the new string reads: This is another test
    string rs = s.Replace("a", "another");
```

LISTING A.20 Continued

```
    Console.WriteLine(rs);
    // Find a substring starting where 'a' is and 6 characters after that
    string ss = s.Substring(s.IndexOf("a"), 6);
    Console.WriteLine(ss);
}
```

A common operation with strings is concatenation. It enables you to do what is illustrated in Listing A.21.

LISTING A.21 String Operations

```
String a = "This is";
String b = " a test";
String c = a + b;
```

The resulting string will be what you expect ("This is a test"), but you should avoid this because a more efficient means can perform this function with the **`StringBuilder`** class in the **`System.Text`** namespace. Listing A.22 shows how to do this.

LISTING A.22 Concatenating Strings with **`StringBuilder`**

```
using System.Text;
. . .
String astr = "This is";
String bstr = " a test";
StringBuilder sb = new StringBuilder();
sb.Append(astr);
sb.Append(bstr);
```

Reference Type Objects

Reference types are everything that is not a value type in a safe managed environment. This includes classes, interfaces, delegates, and arrays.

Arrays

C# supports arrays of any type. The class that supports arrays is defined in the abstract base class **`System.Array`**. There are three types of arrays: single dimensional, multidimensional, and jagged.

Listing A.23 shows an example of some of the operations available with a C# single dimension array.

LISTING A.23 Single Dimension Array Operations

```
static void Single()
{
    // Declare an array
    int [] a = new int[10];
    for(int i = 0; i < a.Length; i++)
        a[i] = i;
    // Initialize and declare in one statement
    int [] b = new int [] {0, 1, 2 ,3 ,4 ,5, 6, 7, 8, 9};
    Console.WriteLine("{0} {1} {2}", a.Equals(b),
                                     a.Length, b.Length);
    // Copy two elements from 'a' starting at index 5 to
    // 'b' starting at 0.
    Array.Copy(a, 5, b, 0, 2);
    foreach(int i in b)
        Console.WriteLine("{0}", i);
    // Create an array of strings
    string [] c = new string [] {"Monday",
                                 "Tuesday",
                                 "Wednesday",
                                 "Thursday",
                                 "Friday",
                                 "Saturday",
                                 "Sunday"};
    // Iterate through the array of strings
    foreach(string s in c)
        Console.WriteLine("{0}", s);
}
```

The first thing you might notice about C# arrays is the order of the [], known as the *rank specifier*. This is different from C++, so it might take you a little time to get used to the syntax. The compiler reminds you with an error like this if you forget the syntax:

```
array.cs(10,10): error CS0650: Syntax error, bad array declarator. To declare a
        managed array the rank specifier precedes the variable's identifier
```

The other feature of arrays that might take some getting used to is the declaration. You can declare an array with this:

```
int [] array;
```

You can initialize the array declaration with a size:

```
int [] array = new int [10];
```

You can also initialize an array with values and a size:

```
int [] array = new int [] { 1, 2, 3, 4, 5};
```

You can't declare an array of a specific size without new:

```
// Error !!!
int [10] array;
```

Again, this is just a convention that is valid with C++ but not valid with C#.

Listing A.24 shows an example of some of the operations available with a C# multi-dimensional array.

LISTING A.24 Multi-Dimensional Array Operations

```
static void Multiple()
{
    // Declare a multi-dimensional array
    int [,] a = new int[5,5];
    for(int i = 0; i < a.GetLength(0); i++)
        for(int j = 0; j < a.GetLength(1); j++)
            a[i,j] = i * a.GetLength(1) + j;
    // Initialize and declare in one statement
    int [,] b = new int [,] {{0, 0, 0, 0, 0},
                             {1, 1, 1, 1, 1},
                             {2, 2, 2, 2, 2},
                             {3, 3, 3, 3, 3},
                             {4, 4, 4, 4, 4}};
    Console.WriteLine("{0} {1} dimensions {2}x{3} {4}x{5}", a.Equals(b),
                                                           a.Rank,
                                                           a.GetLength(0),
                                                           a.GetLength(1),
                                                           b.GetLength(0),
                                                           b.GetLength(1));
    // When copying between multi-dimensional arrays, the array
    // behaves like a long one-dimensional array, where the rows
    // (or columns) are conceptually laid end to end. For example,
    // if an array has three rows (or columns) with four elements
    // each, copying six elements from the beginning of the array
    // would copy all four elements of the first row (or column)
    // and the first two elements of the second row (or column).
    Array.Copy(a, 5, b, 5, 5);
    for(int i = 0; i < a.GetLength(0); i++)
    {
        for(int j = 0; j < a.GetLength(1); j++)
        {
            Console.Write("{0}", b[i,j]);
        }
        Console.WriteLine();
    }
    // Create a two-dimensional array of strings
    string [,] c = new string [,]{{"0 - Monday",
                                   "0 - Tuesday",
                                   "0 - Wednesday",
```

LISTING A.24 Continued

```
                                        "0 - Thursday",
                                        "0 - Friday",
                                        "0 - Saturday",
                                        "0 - Sunday"},
                                       {"1 - Monday",
                                        "1 - Tuesday",
                                        "1 - Wednesday",
                                        "1 - Thursday",
                                        "1 - Friday",
                                        "1 - Saturday",
                                        "1 - Sunday"}};
    // Iterate through the array
    foreach(string s in c)
            Console.WriteLine(s);
    int [,,,] d = new int [5,5,5,5];
    Console.WriteLine("{0} dimensions", d.Rank);
}
```

With multi-dimensional arrays, you might have trouble getting used to some of the syntax. When referencing an element within a multi-dimensional array, notice that the syntax is [1,2] to access the second row and the third element. This is unlike the [1][2] syntax that you might be used to. Notice, however, that it is easy to retrieve the number of dimensions in a given array (**Rank**) and to retrieve the number of elements in a given dimension (**GetLength**).

Listing A.24 shows only two-dimensional arrays. You could extend all of the features of a two-dimensional array to n-dimensional arrays.

A jagged array allows each row of an array to have different lengths (hence, the word *jagged*). Listing A.25 shows an example of some of the operations available with a C# jagged array.

LISTING A.25 Jagged Array Operations

```
static void Jagged()
{
    // Declare a multi-dimensional array
    int [][] a = new int[5][];
    for(int i = 0; i < a.Length; i++)
        a[i] = new int [i + 1];
    for(int i = 0; i < a.Length; i++)
    {
        for(int j = 0; j < a[i].Length; j++)
        {
            a[i][j] = i;
        }
```

LISTING A.25 Continued

```
        }
        foreach(int [] ia in a)
        {
            foreach(int i in ia)
                Console.Write("{0}", i);
            Console.WriteLine();
        }
        // Initialize and declare in one statement
        int [][] b = {new int [] {0},
                      new int [] {1, 1},
                      new int [] {2, 2, 2},
                      new int [] {3, 3, 3, 3},
                      new int [] {4, 4, 4, 4, 4}};
        foreach(int [] ia in b)
        {
            foreach(int i in ia)
                Console.Write("{0}", i);
            Console.WriteLine();
        }
    }
```

A jagged array is literally an array of arrays. Figure A.2 shows conceptually how the array looks.

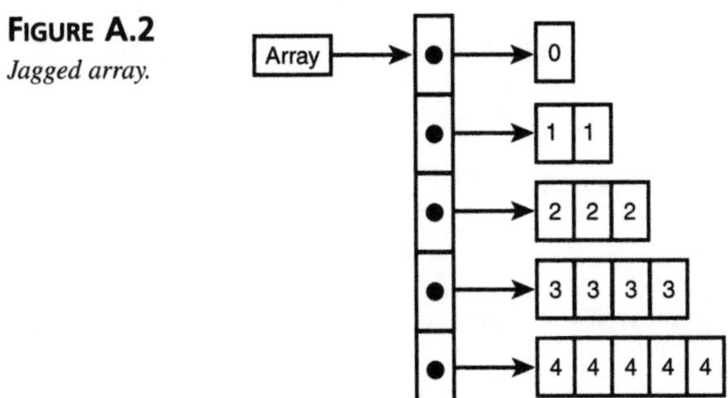

FIGURE A.2
Jagged array.

When working with a jagged array, you need to avoid the temptation to think of it as a two-dimensional array. Again, it is an array of arrays.

Interface

An interface is like an abstract class with all the members abstract. It contains no data—just a signature of methods that should be implemented in the class that is derived from the interface. Unlike an abstract class, a class can derive from multiple interfaces. Listing A.26 shows some simple uses of interfaces.

LISTING A.26 Interface Usage

```
using System;
namespace Testing
{
    interface ICommunicate
    {
        void Speak(string s);
        void Listen(string s);
        void Read(string s);
        void Write(string s);
    }
    interface ITravel
    {
        void Walk();
        void Car();
        void Train();
        void Plane();
    }
    class Activities: ICommunicate, ITravel
    {
        // ICommunicate
        public void Speak(string s)
        {
            Console.WriteLine("I said, \"{0}\".", s);
        }
        public void Listen(string s)
        {
            Console.WriteLine("I heard you say, \"{0}\".", s);
        }
        public void Read(string s)
        {
            Console.WriteLine("I just read, \"{0}\".", s);
        }
        public void Write(string s)
        {
            Console.WriteLine("I just wrote, \"{0}\".", s);
        }
        // ITravel
        public void Walk()
        {
            Console.WriteLine("I am walking.");
        }
        public void Car()
        {
            Console.WriteLine("I riding in a car.");
        }
        public void Train()
        {
            Console.WriteLine("I riding in a train.");
        }
```

LISTING A.26 Continued

```
        public void Plane()
        {
            Console.WriteLine("I riding in a plane.");
        }
    }
    class InterfaceMain
    {
        static void Main(string[] args)
        {
            Activities a = new Activities();
            // Look for an interface that is not implemented
            try
            {
                IComparable ic = (IComparable)a;
            }
            catch(Exception e)
            {
                Console.WriteLine(e);
            }
            // Checking to see if the interface is implemented
            if(a is ICommunicate)
            {
                ICommunicate ac = (ICommunicate)a;
                ac.Speak("I said that");
                ac.Listen("I am talking to you");
                ac.Read("The quick brown fox jumped over the lazy cow.");
                ac.Write("What I did on my summer vacation.");
            }
            if(a is ITravel)
            {
                ITravel at = (ITravel)a;
                at.Walk();
                at.Car();
                at.Train();
                at.Plane();
            }
            Console.WriteLine("------------------------");
            // Checking to see if the interface is implemented
            // If it is implemented then the result is a non-null
            // interface.
            ICommunicate c = a as ICommunicate;
            if(c != null)
            {
                c.Speak("I said that");
                c.Listen("I am talking to you");
                c.Read("The quick brown fox jumped over the lazy cow.");
                c.Write("What I did on my summer vacation.");
            }
            ITravel t = a as ITravel;
```

LISTING A.26 Continued

```
            if(t != null)
            {
                t.Walk();
                t.Car();
                t.Train();
                t.Plane();
            }
        }
    }
}
```

If you had forgotten to implement one of the methods in the class that was deriving from these interfaces, you would get an error like this:

```
interface.cs(18,8): error CS0535: 'Testing.Activities' does not implement
        interface member 'Testing.ICommunicate.Read(string)'
```

The compiler helps you to use interfaces correctly.

Listing A.26 purposely repeats code so that you can see two different methods for getting at an interface. More precisely, you can see two different *safe* methods for getting at an interface. Notice the code at the beginning of **Main** where there is a cast to an interface that is not implemented. Here, you get an **InvalidCastException** because you are trying to cast to an interface that has not been implemented. If you want to deal with the exceptions, then you can simply cast the instance to the **interface** that you require. However, C# has provided two different methods that allow you to test for an interface without having an exception thrown. These two methods use the **is** and **as** operators.

The **is** operator tests for a specific **interface**. It returns **true** if the object supports that interface and **false** if it does not. This avoids having to catch an exception if the **interface** is not supported. The problem with the **is** operator is that after it is determined that the **interface** is supported, a cast still must be performed to get the **interface**. Thus, using the **is** operator usually requires two queries on the object. The **as** operator fixes this.

If the **interface** is supported by the object, then the **as** operator returns a reference to the interface. If the **interface** is not supported, then **null** is returned. This saves an extra query on the object if the test succeeds.

delegate

delegates and **event**s were covered in detail in Chapter 14, "Delegates and Events."

Class

A class defines an object. All of the other features of C# are auxiliary to and provide support for the class. It is in the class where a program becomes object oriented. Of course, simply using or defining a class does not necessarily make an object-oriented program. It is when the features of the language are used to correctly implement object-oriented principles that a program becomes object oriented. This brief overview of C# will show how C#, and in particular the class in C#, can be used to support the object-oriented tenets of encapsulation, inheritance, and polymorphism (see *Inside C#* by Tom Archer, Microsoft Press, 2001).

Encapsulation in its broadest sense is simply wrapping some feature or data. Earlier in this chapter, you saw a simple wrapping around two floating-point numbers in Listing A.11 that was called a `Complex` number. It was obvious as more features were added to that object, the two floating-point numbers became less visible, even hidden. Accessors turned the floating-point numbers into properties. At the point when the user of the object no longer has access to the internal data, the data is fully encapsulated and the programmer is free to modify the data without affecting the user. If you decided to modify the data to use two integers, two floats, or any other of a number of combinations, you could do so without affecting the user. When you can do that, your data is encapsulated.

At that point, you support the encapsulation tenet of object-oriented programming. To support encapsulation, a **`struct`** does not offer anything less in terms of features that would cause you to choose a **`class`** over a **`struct`**. A **`class`** can have accessors that follow the same syntax rules as for a **`struct`**. A **`class`** overrides **`ToString`** to support display of the object just as with a **`struct`**. A class implicitly derives from **`System.Object`** so that **`Equals`**, **`GetHashCode`**, and so on can be overridden in the same way as with a **`struct`**. In fact, you could replace the word *struct* with the word *class* in the code used to illustrate a `Complex` value type (see Listings A.11 through A.18) and the code would still compile and run.

A **`struct`** is implicitly **`sealed`**. It cannot be derived from another **`struct`** or **`class`**. If you try to create another **`struct`** derived from a **`struct`**, you get an error indicating that the base is not an **`interface`**. (A **`struct`** can derive from an interface.) If you try to derive from a **`struct`** to create a new class, you get an error like this:

```
cannot inherit from sealed class 'Testing.Complex'
```

Memory allocation is where a **`class`** and **`struct`** start to diverge. What if you had a complex number object as was illustrated in Listings A.11 through A.18 and you wanted to add a couple of properties to it so that it supported polar notation? If you either did not have access to the source or did not want to modify the source for `Complex`, you would not be able to do this. However, by applying the modifications shown in Listing A.27, this is possible.

LISTING A.27 A Polar Class

```
class Complex
{
    protected double real;
    protected double imag;
. . .
class Polar: Complex
{
    public double Magnitude
    {
        get
        {
            return Math.Sqrt(real*real + imag*imag);
        }
    }
    public double Phase
    {
        get
        {
            return Math.Atan2(imag,real);
        }
    }
}
```

Once you make `Complex` a **`class`** (and allow access to its internal data via the **`protected`** keyword), you can derive from it as shown in the `Polar` **`class`**. Now all of the functionality of the `Complex` **`class`** is available to you. You can reuse the code to implement `Complex`. More importantly, this functionality has been tested; because you are not modifying it at all, you are not breaking anything. This is kind of like the Hippocratic oath for software: "As to diseases, make a habit of two things—to help, or at least do no harm." (Hippocrates, *The Epidemics*, Bk. I, Sect. XI, tr. by W. H. S. Jones, cited in *Familiar Medical Quotations*, edited by Maurice B. Strauss, pub. by Little, Brown and Company, p. 625).

Polymorphism allows for a uniform treatment of all objects that is dependent on the object. You might want to think about that for a moment. C# uses polymorphism extensively. It is what makes something like the following possible:

```
Console.WriteLine("{0}", obj);
```

What is exceptional about polymorphism is that obj in the preceding line can be any **System.Object**. Because everything is ultimately derived from **System.Object** in C#, this is not a problem. The default might not be what you had in mind, but it will always work. To change the default implementation, the implementation for the class that defines the obj instance needs to override the **ToString** method that is part of every **System.Object**. Because the methods in **System.Object** might be too restrictive or not have the functionality that you want to expose, you can create your own polymorphic system of objects.

A classic example of polymorphism is with a graphics application and shapes. Listing A.28 shows an outline of how this would be implemented.

LISTING A.28 A Polymorphic Shape Drawing System

```
abstract class Shape
{
    public abstract void Draw();
}

class Circle: Shape
{
    double x;
    double y;
    double r;
    public Circle(double x, double y, double r)
    {
        this.x = x;
        this.y = y;
        this.r = r;
    }
    override public void Draw()
    {
        Console.WriteLine("Drawing a circle of radius {0}", r);
    }
}

class Triangle: Shape
{
    double [,] vertices;
    public Triangle(double x1, double y1,
                    double x2, double y2,
                    double x3, double y3)
    {
        vertices = new double [,] {{x1, y1},
                                   {x2, y2},
                                   {x3, y3}};
    }
```

LISTING A.28 Continued

```
override public void Draw()
    {
        Console.WriteLine("Drawing a triangle");
    }
}

class Square: Shape
{
    double x;
    double y;
    double s;
    public Square(double x, double y, double s)
    {
        this.x = x;
        this.y = y;
        this.s = s;
    }
    override public void Draw()
    {
        Console.WriteLine("Drawing a {0}x{0} square", s);
    }
}

class PolymorphicMain
{
    static void Main(string[] args)
    {
        Shape [] shapes = new Shape [] {new Circle(0,0,2),
                                        new Triangle(0,0,0,1,1,1),
                        new Square(0,0,5)};
        foreach(Shape s in shapes)
        {
            s.Draw();
        }
    }
}
```

Notice that `Main` has only an array of `Shape` objects. Each `Shape` object takes care of drawing itself. The programmer no longer needs to test for what type of object it is and draw it specifically. The programmer just calls the `Draw` method on each object in the array and each object draws itself. The output of the code in Listing A.28 looks like this:

```
Drawing a circle of radius 2
Drawing a triangle
Drawing a 5x5 square
```

Pointer Type

Value types and reference types are primarily used in a safe environment. If you have code running in an unsafe environment, then an additional type is available known as a *pointer type*. Listing A.29 shows a simple example of using a pointer type.

LISTING A.29 A Pointer Type Example

```
using System;

// csc /unsafe pointer.cs
namespace Testing
{
    class PointerMain
    {
        static unsafe void FillBuffer(byte[] buffer)
        {
            int count = buffer.Length;
            fixed(byte *p = buffer)
            {
                for(int i = 0; i < count; i++)
                {
                    p[i] = (byte)i;
                }
            }
        }
        static void Main(string[] args)
        {
            byte [] buffer = new byte[256];
            FillBuffer(buffer);
        }
    }
}
```

This simple example fills a buffer with an increasing value based on its position in the buffer.

A more useful sample would be one that performs some useful work. When processing an image, it is frequently necessary to find out where in the image the edges of an object are. One method of doing that is to process the image with an edge-finding kernel. One particularly useful set of kernels is the set of Sobel kernels. The process involved is shown in Figure A.3

This is a good example of when using a pointer type in an unsafe environment is necessary. If you want to process an image, you need to get at the data of the image. The first problem is that the only way you can get at the raw data is by retrieving a one-dimensional vector from the image. The second problem is to access the data. Each pixel or byte access needs to do at bare minimum an index operation, and when you add in the overhead associated with a managed call, this could slow things down quite a bit. A method in the **`Bitmap`** class allows the user to get at a pointer type that points to the data for the image. Listing A.30 shows a portion of the sample in the `ImageProcessing` directory that uses an unsafe pointer to find the edges of an image.

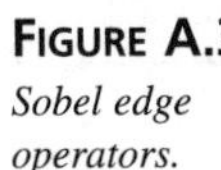

FIGURE A.3
Sobel edge operators.

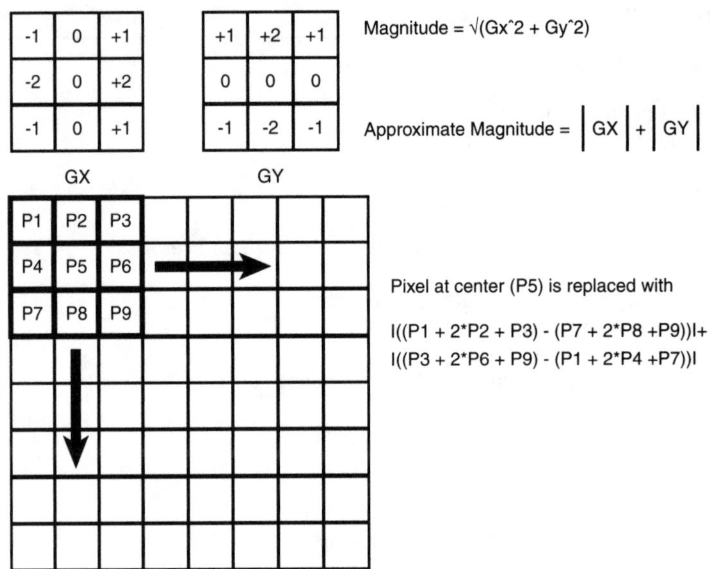

LISTING A.30 Using an Unsafe Pointer to Process an Image

```
unsafe private void OnProcess(object sender, System.EventArgs e)
{
    BitmapData data = null;
    try
    {
        data = rawImage.LockBits(new Rectangle(new Point(0,0),
                                 new Size(rawImage.Width, rawImage.Height)),
                                 ImageLockMode.ReadWrite,
                                 rawImage.PixelFormat);
        int [,] cache = new int[data.Height,data.Width];
        Byte *p1;
        Byte *p2;
        Byte *p3;
        int max, min, temp;
        max = 0;
        min = 255;
        // Find the range
        for(int i = 1; i < data.Height - 1; i++)
```

LISTING A.30 Continued

```
        {
            // Points to the center of the kernel
            p1 = (Byte *)data.Scan0.ToPointer() + ((i - 1) * data.Stride);
            p2 = (Byte *)data.Scan0.ToPointer() + (i * data.Stride);
            p3 = (Byte *)data.Scan0.ToPointer() + ((i + 1) * data.Stride);
            for(int j = 1; j < data.Width - 1; j++)
            {
                temp = (Math.Abs((*p1 + *(p1 + 1) * 2 + *(p1 + 2)) -
                                (*p3 + *(p3 + 1) * 2 + *(p3 + 2))) +
                        Math.Abs((*(p1 + 2) + *(p2 + 2) * 2 + *(p3 + 2)) -
                                (*p1 + *p2 * 2 + *p3)));
                if(temp > max)
                    max = temp;
                if(temp < min)
                    min = temp;
                cache[i,j] = temp;
                p1++;
                p2++;
                p3++;
            }
        }
        for(int i = 1; i < data.Height - 1; i++)
        {
            // Points to the center of the kernel
            p2 = (Byte *)data.Scan0.ToPointer() + (i * data.Stride) + 1;
            for(int j = 1; j < data.Width - 1; j++)
            {
                temp = (int)(((float)cache[i,j]/(float)max) * 255.0);
                *p2++ = (Byte)temp;
            }
        }
    }
    finally
    {
        rawImage.UnlockBits(data);
        image.Refresh();
    }
}
```

Basic Programming Elements of C#

After you have an understanding of the structure of an object-oriented program, the rest is pretty much just filling in the blanks. Now you can quickly go through each of the basic elements of a C# program.

abstract

I have discussed a little bit about an abstract class. You can use the **abstract** modifier to declare an **abstract** method or property. An abstract class has the following properties:

- An **abstract** class cannot be instantiated.
- A non-**abstract** class that is derived from an **abstract** class must implement all of the **abstract** methods and properties.
- An **abstract** class must provide implementations for all of the methods of an inherited interface.
- An **abstract** class can declare its "implementation" of an interface method to be abstract, thus forwarding the responsibility of implementation to the class that derives from it.

Listing A.31 shows the implementation of a basic **abstract** class.

LISTING A.31 Using **abstract**

```
using System;

namespace Testing
{
    // Abstract class
    abstract class Point
    {
        protected int x = 0;
        protected int y = 0;
        // Abstract methods
        public abstract void Increment();
        public abstract void Decrement();

        // Abstract properties
        public abstract int X
        {
            get;
        }

        public abstract int Y
        {
            get;
        }
    }

    class NewPoint: Point
    {
        public override void Increment()
```

LISTING A.31 Continued

```
        {
            x++;
            y++;
        }
        public override void Decrement()
        {
            x--;
            y--;
        }

        public override int X
        {
            get
            {
                return x;
            }
        }

        public override int Y
        {
            get
            {
                return y;
            }
        }
    }
    class AbstractMain
    {
        public static void Main()
        {
            NewPoint p = new NewPoint();
            p.Increment();
            p.Increment();
            p.Decrement();
            Console.WriteLine("x = {0}, y = {1}", p.X, p.Y);
        }
    }
}
. . .
x = 1, y = 1
I am in A
I am in B
I am in C
```

It should be noted that an **abstract** method or property is implicitly **virtual**, and **abstract** methods and properties can only be defined in an **abstract** class. The code in Listing A.31 obeys these rules.

Listing A.32 shows a short example of using **abstract** in conjunction with an **interface**.

LISTING A.32 Using **abstract** with an **interface**

```
interface IFunctions
{
    void A();
    void B();
    void C();
}
abstract class Function : IFunctions
{
    public void A()
    {
        Console.WriteLine("I am in A");
    }
    public abstract void B();
    public abstract void C();
}
. . .
class NewFunction : Function
{
    public override void B()
    {
        Console.WriteLine("I am in B");
    }
    public override void C()
    {
        Console.WriteLine("I am in C");
    }
}
. . .
NewFunction f = new NewFunction();
IFunctions i = (IFunctions)f;
i.A();
i.B();
i.C();
```

Notice that the **abstract** class either implemented the **interface** method (as in method A) or forwarded the responsibility on to the deriving class by making the **interface** method abstract (as in methods B and C).

as

This operator returns a **null** if the class is not derived from the specific class or interface. If it has in its hierarchy the class or interface, then a reference to the class or interface is returned. An example of using the **as** operator is shown in Listing A.33.

LISTING A.33 Using **as**

```
class C
{
}
class B : C
{
}
class A : B
{
}

class AsMain
{
    public static void Main()
    {
        A a = new A();
        B b = new B();
        C c = new C();
        try
        {
            B bcc = (B)c;
        }
        catch(Exception e)
        {
            Console.WriteLine(e);
        }
        B bc = c as B;
        if(bc == null)
            Console.WriteLine("C is not a B");
        B ba = a as B;
        if(ba == null)
            Console.WriteLine("A is not a B");
    }
}
```

The code of Listing A.33 outputs the following:

```
System.InvalidCastException: Specified cast is not valid.
   at Testing.AbstractMain.Main()
C is not a B
```

At first, an exception is thrown because `C` is not derived from `B` and cannot be cast to a `B` object. By using **`as`**, a **`null`** is returned to avoid having the overhead of an exception.

base

This operator is used to access members of a base class from a derived class. It can only be called from within properties or methods in a derived class. It cannot be called from a static method. Typically, it would be called from a constructor:

```
public Foo(string s) : base(s)
```

This would call the base constructor for the object with an argument of a string. This operator can also be used from a method or property:

```
base.Bar();
```

This would call the Bar method in the base class. Typically, this would be used to disambiguate a call to a base class method that has the same signature as the calling method.

break

This statement terminates the closest enclosing loop or conditional statement. Look at Listing A.34.

LISTING A.34 Using **break**

```
public static void Main()
{
    string input;
    Console.WriteLine("Starting loop.");
    while(true)
    {
        Console.Write("Input . . .");
        input = Console.ReadLine();
        if(input[0] == 'B')
            break;
    }
}
```

This program will continue to run until the user enters a string starting with `'B'`, at which point the program terminates.

Break is also used to exit a **switch** block.

A **switch** statement is an alternative to **if** when it is possible for an object to have more than two different values.

Listing A.50 shows the basic uses of a **switch** statement.

case

A **case** statement is always included as part of a **switch** statement. A **switch** statement is an alternative to **if** when it is possible for an object to have more than two different values. The **case** statement delimits the sections of code that should be executed if the match condition specified by the **case** statement occurs.

catch

See Chapter 15 "Using Managed Exceptions to Effectively Handle Errors," for examples of using **try/catch/finally** with exceptions.

checked

This operator forces an exception to be thrown if an integer overflow occurs. The opposite unchecked makes sure that the output is not checked for overflow condition. Listing A.35 shows these two operators in action.

LISTING A.35 Using **checked** and **unchecked**

```
class CheckedMain
{
    static short x = Int16.MaxValue;
    static short y = Int16.MaxValue;
    static int AddShort()
    {
        int ret = 0;
        try
        {
            ret = (short)(x + y);
        }
        catch(Exception e)
        {
            Console.WriteLine(e);
        }
        return ret;
    }
    static int AddCheckedShort()
    {
        int ret = 0;
        try
        {
            ret = checked((short)(x + y));
        }
        catch(Exception e)
        {
            Console.WriteLine("Checked:");
            Console.WriteLine(e);
        }
        return ret;
    }
    static int AddUncheckedShort()
```

LISTING A.35 Continued

```
    {
        int ret = 0;
        try
        {
            ret = unchecked((short)(x + y));
        }
        catch(Exception e)
        {
            Console.WriteLine("Unchecked:");
            Console.WriteLine(e);
        }
        return ret;
    }
    public static void Main()
    {
        Console.WriteLine("AddShort returns: {0}",
                                AddShort());
        Console.WriteLine("AddCheckedShort returns: {0}",
                                AddCheckedShort());
        Console.WriteLine("AddUncheckedShort returns: {0}",
                                AddUncheckedShort());
    }
}
```

The output for Listing A.35 is as follows:

```
AddShort returns: -2
Checked:
System.OverflowException: Arithmetic operation resulted in an overflow.
   at Testing.CheckedMain.AddCheckedShort()
AddCheckedShort returns: 0
AddUncheckedShort returns: -2
```

const

The modifier **const** specifies that the field or local variable cannot be modified. As a field in a class, it might look like this:

```
public const int c1 = 5;
```

As a local variable, it might look like this:

```
const int c1 = 5;
```

If you attempt to modify a **const** value, the compiler generates an error like this:

```
error CS0131: The left-hand side of an assignment must be a
        variable, property or indexer
```

continue

The **continue** directive forces execution to continue at the bottom of the nearest enclosing loop. Listing A.36 shows a possible usage of **continue**.

LISTING A.36 Using **continue**

```
public static void Main()
{
    string input;
    bool stop = false;
    Console.WriteLine("Starting loop.");
    while(!stop)
    {
        Console.Write("Input . . .");
        input = Console.ReadLine();
        if(input[0] != 'B')
        {
            continue;
        }
        stop = true;
    }
}
```

The line `stop = true;` is skipped until the user enters a string beginning with 'B'.

default

A **default** statement is always included as part of a **switch** statement. A **switch** statement is an alternative to **if** when it is possible for an object to have more than two different values. The **default** statement matches all cases that are not specifically specified by **case** statements.

delegate

A **delegate** wraps the signature of a function or method into a class. **delegate**s have been likened to function pointers in C or C++. After a **delegate** is defined, it can be used to reference a method or function without having to know at compile time which function or method will be invoked. The key feature of a delegate is that it is a type-safe, and secure way to reference a function or method. **delegate**s are covered in detail in Chapter 14, "**Delegate**s and **Event**s."

do

The keyword begins a **do/while** block that continually executes until the expression in **while** evaluates to **false**. Note that unlike **while**, this statement always executes the enclosing block at least once. Listing A.37 shows an example.

LISTING A.37 Using **do**

```
public static void Main()
{
    string input;
    bool stop = false;
    Console.WriteLine("Starting loop.");
    do
    {
        Console.Write("Input . . .");
        input = Console.ReadLine();
        if(input[0] == 'B')
            stop = true;
    }
    while(!stop);
}
```

else

If is a control statement that executes a statement block if the expression supplied as an argument to the **if** statement evaluates to **true**. The **if** statement has an optional **else** clause that is executed if the expression evaluates to **false**.

```
if(x > 0)
    Console.WriteLine("X > 0");
else
    Console.WriteLine("X <= 0");
```

event

An **event** wraps the functionality of a **delegate** into yet another class that only exposes two operators, the += **operator** for adding a **delegate** to an event list, and the -= **operator** for removing a **delegate** from an event list. Declaring an **event** requires two arguments. The first is the **delegate** signature for the method or function that will be added into this **event**, and the second is the name of the variable that holds the **event**.

Events are covered in detail in Chapter 14.

explicit

This modifier forces the user to do an explicit cast conversion. This is the opposite of **implicit**, which allows for a silent, automatic conversion. Listing A.38 shows a simple application using **implicit** and **explicit**.

LISTING A.38 Using **explicit** and **implicit**

```
struct Complex
{
    double real;
    double imag;
    public Complex(double real, double imag)
    {
        this.real = real;
        this.imag = imag;
    }
    public override string ToString()
    {
        return (string.Format("({0}, {1}i)", real, imag));
    }
    public static explicit operator Complex(double r)
    {
        return new Complex(r, 0);
    }
    public static implicit operator Complex(double [] n)
    {
        if(n.Length != 2)
            throw new ArgumentException();
        return new Complex(n[0], n[1]);
    }
}

class ExplicitMain
{
    static void Main(string[] args)
    {
        Complex cn = new Complex(1,0);
        Console.WriteLine("{0}", cn);
        cn = (Complex)2;
        Console.WriteLine("{0}", cn);
        double [] da = new double [] {3,0};
        cn = da;
        Console.WriteLine("{0}", cn);
    }
}
```

Notice that the conversion from **double** to `Complex` requires an explicit cast, whereas the conversion from an array of **double** to `Complex` is done implicitly. If the explicit cast is removed, then the compiler flags it as an error, indicating that no conversion can be done implicitly.

extern

Commonly used with the **DllImport** attribute, this modifier declares that a function is defined externally. There are many examples of using the **extern** directive in Chapter 7, "Leveraging Existing Code—P/Invoke."

finally

Finally is a way of stipulating that a section of code must be executed no matter how the execution path leaves the current scope.

See Chapter 15 for examples of using **try/catch/finally** with exceptions.

fixed

This statement prevents the garbage collector from relocating memory. It "pins" the memory for the duration of the associated block of statements. See Listing A.28 for an example.

for

This statement sets up a loop that first executes the statements in the initialization section. It then executes the iterator section and the statement associated with the **for** loop as long as the expression evaluates to **true**. Listing A.39 shows a simple example of using **for**.

LISTING A.39 Using **for**

```
for(int i = 0; i < 5; i++)
    Console.WriteLine("{0}", i);
```

This simple section of code simply prints the numbers 0 through 4.

foreach

This construct allows you to iterate through any collection that supports the **GetEnumerator** method that returns an enumerator. A simple example looks like Listing A.40.

LISTING A.40 Using **foreach** with an Array

```
string [] sa = new string [] { "This", "is", "a", "test" };
foreach(string s in sa)
{
    Console.WriteLine(s);
}
```

Arrays of any value support the **foreach** construct. In addition, the collections classes support the required enumerators to use in **foreach**. It is also possible to use **foreach** with user-defined classes. When building a user-defined class that can work with **foreach**, you can use two approaches. The first approach enables the user to iterate through a collection only in C#. The second approach not only allows the user to iterate through a collection with C# and **foreach**, but it also allows iteration using another language, such as VB. Listing A.41 shows the C#-specific approach.

LISTING A.41 Using **foreach** with a C# Collection

```
// Declare the collection:
public class CSharpCollection
{
    int[] items;

    public CSharpCollection()
    {
        items = new int[5] {1, 2, 3, 4, 5};
    }

    public CSharpEnumerator GetEnumerator()
    {
        return new CSharpEnumerator(this);
    }

    // Declare the enumerator class:
    public class CSharpEnumerator
    {
        int nIndex;
        CSharpCollection collection;
        public CSharpEnumerator(CSharpCollection coll)
        {
            collection = coll;
            nIndex = -1;
        }

        public bool MoveNext()
        {
            nIndex++;
            return(nIndex < collection.items.GetLength(0));
        }

        public int Current
        {
            get
            {
                return(collection.items[nIndex]);
            }
        }
```

LISTING A.41 Continued

```
    }
}
. . .
CSharpCollection col = new CSharpCollection();
Console.WriteLine("Values in the C# collection are:");
foreach (int i in col)
{
    Console.WriteLine(i);
}
```

To allow **foreach** to iterate through a custom collection, you need to follow these rules:

- You need to define the collection as part of an **interface**, **struct**, or **class**.
- The class or structure needs to define a method **GetEnumerator** that returns an Enumerator type.
- The Enumerator type returned by **GetEnumerator** needs to implement a **Current** property that returns an item of the correct type or a type that can be converted to the underlying type contained in the collection.
- The Enumerator type also must implement a **MoveNext** method that returns a **bool** of **false** when the end of the collection has been reached.

Listing A.42 shows a generic approach to iterating through collections.

LISTING A.42 Using **foreach** with a Generic Collection

```
. . .
Systems.Collections;
. . .
public class GenericCollection: IEnumerable
{
    int[] items;
    public GenericCollection()
    {
        items = new int[5] {6, 7, 8, 9, 10};
    }

    public GenericEnumerator GetEnumerator()
    {
        return new GenericEnumerator(this);
    }

    // Implement the GetEnumerator() method:
    IEnumerator IEnumerable.GetEnumerator()
    {
        return GetEnumerator();
    }
```

LISTING A.42 Continued

```
    // Declare the enumerator and implement the IEnumerator interface:
    public class GenericEnumerator: IEnumerator
    {
        int nIndex;
        GenericCollection collection;
        public GenericEnumerator(GenericCollection coll)
        {
            collection = coll;
            nIndex = -1;
        }

        public void Reset()
        {
            nIndex = -1;
        }

        public bool MoveNext()
        {
            nIndex++;
            return(nIndex < collection.items.GetLength(0));
        }

        public int Current
        {
            get
            {
                return(collection.items[nIndex]);
            }
        }

        // The current property on the IEnumerator interface:
        object IEnumerator.Current
        {
            get
            {
                return(Current);
            }
        }
    }
}
. . .
GenericCollection gencol = new GenericCollection();
Console.WriteLine("Values in the generic collection are:");
foreach (int i in gencol)
{
    Console.WriteLine(i);
}
```

For the generic approach, you need to follow all of the rules that apply to the C#-specific case. In addition, you need to implement the **IEnumerable** interface.

goto

Transfers control to a labeled statement. Unlike its C++ predecessor, this jump has some restrictions on where it can go. For example, a C# **goto** cannot jump into a statement block.

See **switch** for how to use **goto** in a **switch** statement.

if

if is a control statement that executes a statement block if the expression supplied as an argument to the **if** statement evaluates to **true**. The **if** statement has an optional **else** clause that is executed if the expression evaluates to **false**.

```
if(x > 0)
    Console.WriteLine("X > 0");
else
    Console.WriteLine("X <= 0");
```

implicit

See **explicit** for an example of how to use **explicit** versus **implicit**.

in

See **foreach**.

interface

An **interface** is a way of describing a set of methods that have no implementation. It is the responsibility of the **class** or **struct** inheriting from an **interface** to implement each of the methods described as part of the **interface**. The methods declared as members of an **interface** are implicitly **abstract**. It is an error to explicitly declare the methods **abstract**. You would use an **interface** if you wanted to guarantee that certain methods would be implemented on a certain set of your classes. You can even check to make sure that a given instance implements a particular **interface** either through a direct cast and catching an exception or by using the **as** operator. Listing A.43 (or the associated code in `interface.cs`) illustrates the usages of the **interface** keyword.

LISTING A.43 Using **interface**

```
interface ICommunicate
{
    void Speak(string s);
    void Listen(string s);
    void Read(string s);
    void Write(string s);
}
interface ITravel
{
    void Walk();
    void Car();
    void Train();
    void Plane();
}
class Activities: ICommunicate, ITravel
{
}
. . .
Activities a = new Activities();
try
{
    IComparable ic = (IComparable)a;
}
catch(Exception e)
{
    Console.WriteLine(e);
}
if(a is ICommunicate)
{
    ICommunicate ac = (ICommunicate)a;
    ac.Speak("I said that");
    ac.Listen("I am talking to you");
    ac.Read("The quick brown fox jumped over the lazy cow.");
    ac.Write("What I did on my summer vacation.");
}
if(a is ITravel)
{
    ITravel at = (ITravel)a;
    at.Walk();
    at.Car();
    at.Train();
    at.Plane();
}
Console.WriteLine("-------------------------");
ICommunicate c = a as ICommunicate;
if(c != null)
```

LISTING A.43 Continued

```
{
    c.Speak("I said that");
    c.Listen("I am talking to you");
    c.Read("The quick brown fox jumped over the lazy cow.");
    c.Write("What I did on my summer vacation.");
}
ITravel t = a as ITravel;
if(t != null)
{
    t.Walk();
    t.Car();
    t.Train();
    t.Plane();
}
```

internal

The **internal** access modifier allows access to a particular type only from files that comprise a single assembly. Other assemblies do not have access to this type. Listing A.44 shows a library created from `external.cs`. That library is being used with `internal.cs` to create a program.

LISTING A.44 Building an Application from Multiple Files

```
(internal.cs)
// csc /r:external.dll internal.cs
using System;

namespace Testing
{
    class InternalMain
    {
        static void Main(string[] args)
        {
            InternalClass ic = new InternalClass();
        }
    }
}
(external.cs)
// csc /t:library external.cs
using System;

namespace Testing
{
    public class InternalClass
    {
```

LISTING A.44 Continued

```
        public InternalClass()
        {
            Console.WriteLine("Constructing InternalClass");
        }
    }
}
```

Modify Listing A.44 to use the **internal** modifier. Now the listing looks like Listing A.45.

LISTING A.45 Building an Application from Multiple Files

```
 (external.cs)
// csc /t:library external.cs
using System;

namespace Testing
{
    internal class InternalClass
    {
        public InternalClass()
        {
            Console.WriteLine("Constructing InternalClass");
        }
    }
}
```

The compile statement from Listing A.44 of `internal.cs` fails with an error indicating that the class is not accessible.

is

Test for runtime type compatibility with a given object. See the previous section on **interface**s for examples of using this operator.

lock

See Chapter 11, "Threading," for examples of using the **lock** statement for synchronization.

namespace

The **namespace** keyword is used to create a scope for all of the members contained within the **namespace** block. When an identifier is enclosed in a namespace, it is *fully qualified.*

new

New constructs a new instance of an object.

operator

Three types of operators can be defined: unary, binary, and conversion. During the discussion of user-defined value types, a `Complex` value was defined. This value showed examples of unary and binary operators.

A conversion operator must have an additional modifier of either **explicit** or **implicit** depending on how the conversion is to take place. See **explicit** for examples of conversion operators.

Unary operators that can be overridden are as follows:

```
+ - ! ~ ++ -- true false
```

Binary operators that can be overridden are as follows:

```
+ - * / % & | ^ << >> == != > < >= <=
```

All operators are static methods.

out

Out is one of the method parameters that describes how arguments are passed to and from a method call. **Out** specifies that the called method will fill in the value for the parameter. Listing A.46 shows how to use **out**.

LISTING A.46 Using **out**

```
public static int TestOut(out int i, out int j)
{
    i = 2;
    j = 3;
    return 1;
}
public static void Main()
{
    int a;
    int b;
    int c = TestOut(out a, out b);
    Console.WriteLine("{0} {1} {2}", a, b, c);
}
. . .
2 3 1
```

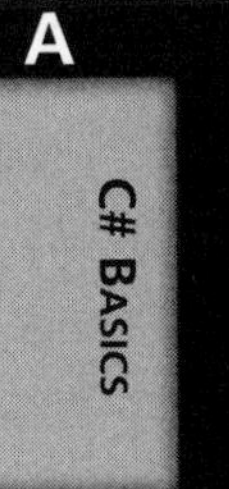

override

An **override** modifier specifies that the method overrides the method with the same signature inherited from the base class. You cannot override a non-virtual or static method. See **explicit** for an example of the syntax used with **override**.

params

Params is a method parameter that specifies a variable number of arguments. Listing A.47 shows a simple example.

LISTING A.47 Using **params**

```
class ParamsMain
{
    public static void TestParams(params string [] a)
    {
        foreach(string s in a)
            Console.WriteLine(s);
    }
    public static void Main()
    {
        TestParams("This", "is", "a", "test");
        string [] s = new string [] {"Monday",
                                     "Tuesday",
                                     "Wednesday",
                                     "Thursday",
                                     "Friday",
                                     "Saturday",
                                     "Sunday"};
        TestParams(s);
    }
}
. . .
This
is
a
test
Monday
Tuesday
Wednesday
Thursday
Friday
Saturday
Sunday
```

private

`Private` is a member access modifier. Members that are declared **`private`** are only accessible from the **`class`** or **`struct`** in which they are defined.

protected

`Protected` is a member access modifier. Members that are declared **`protected`** are accessible from the **`class`** in which they are defined as well as from the **`class`** that inherits the **`class`** in which they are defined.

public

`Public` is a member access modifier. Members that are declared **`public`** have no access restrictions.

readonly

A **`readonly`** variable can only be modified during the declaration or in the constructor of a **`class`** or **`struct`**. This differs from a **`const`** variable, which cannot be modified anywhere in the code. Listing A.48 shows how **`readonly`** can be used.

LISTING A.48 Using **`readonly`**

```
class Readonly
{
    // const int c1 = 5;
    readonly int c1;
    public Readonly()
    {
        c1 = 6;
    }
    public int Value
    {
        get
        {
            return c1;
        }
    }
}
class ReadonlyMain
{
    public static void Main()
    {
        Readonly ro = new Readonly();
        Console.WriteLine("{0}", ro.Value);
    }
}
```

If you uncomment the line where the field c1 is declared as **const**, a compile-time error is generated from the line where c1 is assigned in the constructor.

ref

Ref is similar to **out**. However, when a parameter is marked with **ref**, data will be transferred to the method as well as from the method, as in **out**.

Listing A.49 illustrates some important differences between **ref** and **out**.

LISTING A.49 Using **ref** and **out**

```
class RefMain
{
    public static int TestRef(ref int i, ref int j)
    {
        Console.WriteLine("Entering TestRef {0} {1}", i, j);
        i = 5;
        j = 6;
        return 4;
    }
    public static int TestOut(out int i, out int j)
    {
        // Console.WriteLine("Entering TestOut {0} {1}", i, j);
        i = 2;
        j = 3;
        return 1;
    }
    public static void Main()
    {
        int a;
        int b;
        int c = TestOut(out a, out b);
        Console.WriteLine("{0} {1} {2}", a, b, c);
        // int d;
        // int e;
        int d = -1;
        int e = -2;
        int f = TestRef(ref d, ref e);
        Console.WriteLine("{0} {1} {2}", d, e, f);
    }
}
```

If you remove the comments from the **Console.WriteLine** in TestOut, you get a compile-time error because **out** parameters are unassigned on entering the method. If you remove the comments from the declarations of variables d and e and comment the declarations that contain an assignment, you also get a compile-time error because **ref** parameters must be initialized.

return

A **return** causes a return from the enclosing method or function. Optionally, a return type can be supplied as an argument to this statement.

sealed

If a class is sealed, it cannot be used as a base class to construct another class. Sealed classes offer some performance benefits, so sealing a class should be considered if it is known ahead of time that this class will not be involved in inheritance hierarchies.

stackalloc

This function is similar to `_alloca` in the C runtime library. It allocates a block of memory on the stack. This function must be called in an unsafe context because it returns a pointer type. The memory allocated is not subject to garbage collection, so it is not necessary to use **fixed** to pin the memory. Listing A.50 shows how this function is used.

LISTING A.50 Using **stackalloc**

```
class StackallocMain
{
    static unsafe void FillBuffer(out int[] buffer)
    {
        buffer = new int [10];
        int count = buffer.Length;
        int *p = stackalloc int[count];
        int *t = p;
        for(int i = 0; i < count; i++)
            *t++ = i;
        t = p;
        for(int i = 0; i < count; i++)
            buffer[i] = *t++;
    }
    static void Main(string[] args)
    {
        int [] buffer;
        FillBuffer(out buffer);
        foreach(int i in buffer)
            Console.WriteLine("{0}", i);
    }
}
```

This sample simply allocates some memory, initializes the contents to an increasing integer, and copies that memory to an output buffer. Of course, the main purpose of this sample is to show the usage of **stackalloc**.

static

This keyword specifies that a member belongs to the type rather than to an instance of the type.

switch

A **switch** statement is an alternative to **if** when it is possible for an object to have more than two different values.

Listing A.51 shows the basic uses of a **switch** statement.

LISTING A.51 Using **switch**

```
enum Animals
{
    Cat,
    Worm,
    Mammal
}
class SwitchMain
{
static void AnimalOperations(Animals animal)
{
    switch(animal)
    {
        case Animals.Cat:
            Console.WriteLine("This is a Cat");
            goto case Animals.Mammal;
        case Animals.Worm:
            Console.WriteLine("Worm");
            break;
        case Animals.Mammal:
            Console.WriteLine("This is a mammal.");
            goto default;
        default:
            Console.WriteLine("This is also a vertebrate.");
            break;
    }
}
static void Main(string[] args)
{
    AnimalOperations(Animals.Cat);
    AnimalOperations(Animals.Worm);
    AnimalOperations(Animals.Mammal);
}
```

Goto statements are almost as bad in C# code as they were in C++ or C code, so it's best to avoid them. As you can see from the previous example, it is not trivial to figure out just what will be printed. Use **goto** only when necessary. It is used here just to be complete in the description of the syntax of a **switch** statement.

this

This is a reference to the enclosing object instance.

throw

See Chapter 15 for examples of using **throw** with exceptions.

try

See Chapter 15 for examples of using **try/catch/finally** with exceptions.

typeof

This operator is used to obtain a **System.Type** object for a given type. Listing A.52 shows how to use this operator.

LISTING A.52 Using **typeof**

```
class TypeofMain
{
    public static void Main()
    {
        Type t = typeof(System.String);
        Console.WriteLine("Assembly: {0}", t.Assembly);
        Console.WriteLine("Assembly Name: {0}", t.AssemblyQualifiedName);
    }
}
```

unchecked

The unchecked operator makes sure that the output is not checked for overflow condition. Listing A.35 shows an example of using both **checked** and **unchecked** operators in action.

unsafe

This keyword marks a method as potentially not type safe. In an unsafe method, type safety checks are not performed. An unsafe method does not initialize the local variable

automatically. Marking a method as unsafe enables a programmer to isolate unsafe code from safe code. Listing A.29 and Figure A.3 provide some examples of using the **unsafe** operator.

using

using has two different uses. One is to specify a namespace alias. The other is to define a scope at the end of which an object will be destroyed.

Listing A.53 shows how you can define a different alias for a namespace with **using**.

LISTING A.53 Using the **using** Directive

```
using MySystem = System;

namespace Testing
{
    using MyCompanyAlias = MyCompany.OutputFunctions;
    namespace MyCompany
    {
        namespace OutputFunctions
        {
            class OutputToConsole
            {
                public static void Line(string s)
                {
                    MySystem.Console.WriteLine("Hello!");
                }
            }
        }
    }

    class UsingMain
    {
        public static void Main()
        {
            MyCompanyAlias.OutputToConsole.Line("Hello!");
        }
    }
}
```

The common usage is to just have "**using System;**", which defines a blank namespace to be an alias to **System**, essentially prohibiting you from specifying the **System** namespace. Here, an alias is specified for **System** to be `MySystem`. Similarly, an alias has been defined to save some typing for `MyCompany.OutputFunctions`.

The other usage of **using** is to define a scope for an object lifetime. Many samples in Chapter 10, "Memory/Resource Management," show resource allocation. The sample in Listing A.54 merely shows the syntax.

LISTING A.54 Using the **using** Statement

```
class ResourceAllocation : IDisposable
{
    public ResourceAllocation()
    {
        Console.WriteLine("I am allocating a very expensive resource.");
    }
    public void Dispose()
    {
        Console.WriteLine("The very expensive resource is being reclaimed.");
    }
}
class DisposeMain
{
    public static void Main()
    {
        ResourceAllocation r = new ResourceAllocation();
        using(r)
        {
            Console.WriteLine("I am using the resource.");
        }
    }
}
```

virtual

A **virtual** modifier on a method indicates that this method is a candidate to be overridden by a class that inherits from the class that is defining the method. In Listing A.28, the abstract keyword implicitly defines a method as virtual. You can replace just the definition of the Shape class with Listing A.55.

LISTING A.55 Using the **virtual** Modifier

```
class Shape
{
    public virtual void Draw()
    {
        Console.WriteLine("Drawing a Shape");
    }
}
```

The original program compiles and runs just as before. In real life, it does not make sense to define a method to draw a `Shape` because a `Shape` is an abstract concept and should be abstract. (It could even better be an interface.) However, this sample shows the usage and syntax of the **`virtual`** modifier.

volatile

A **`volatile`** keyword indicates that the variable can be modified by the hardware, OS, or concurrently running thread. When a variable is marked as **`volatile`**, the system always reads the current value of the variable at the point it is requested. If a variable is not **`volatile`**, it is possible that the CLR might decide that it is more efficient to use a cached value instead of reading a fresh copy. In addition, a **`volatile`** variable is written immediately. Here is how you would declare a **`volatile`** field:

```
public volatile int i;
```

while

Much like the **`do`** statement covered previously, this keyword declares a loop that executes until the expression evaluates to **`false`**. Listing A.56 illustrates a **`while`** statement.

LISTING A.56 Using **`while`**

```
public static void Main()
{
    string input;
    bool stop = false;
    Console.WriteLine("Starting loop.");
    while(!stop)
    {
        Console.Write("Input . . .");
        input = Console.ReadLine();
        if(input[0] == 'B')
            stop = true;
    }
}
```

APPENDIX B

.NET Framework Class Libraries

The CLR provides a wonderful framework on which to build applications. Based on the CLR, many possibilities exist. With the .NET library, integration of the language and the library have reached a new level. So much is available within the .NET Framework Class Libraries. This appendix provides an overview of the library code that is available for you to use in your code. It does not provide an exhaustive reference for all of the classes, structs, or namespaces. This is because many of the major classes, structs, and namespaces have already been reviewed in earlier chapters of this book, and some of the classes, structs, and namespaces either require too much background information or too much explanation.

System.BitConverter

This class has a number of methods that convert from raw (unmanaged) data to managed data types. Listing B.1 shows an example of converting from a byte array to an integer (`bitconverter.cs`).

LISTING B.1 `System.BitConverter` Sample

```
static void Main(string [] args)
{
    byte [] rawData = new byte [] {1,2,3,4};
    int convertedInt = BitConverter.ToInt32(rawData, 0);
    Console.WriteLine("Raw data: {0}{1}{2}{3}",
                      rawData[0],
                      rawData[1],
                      rawData[2],
                      rawData[3]);
    Console.WriteLine("Converted data: {0} 0x{0:X}",
                      convertedInt);
}
```

The output for this application looks like this:

```
Raw data: 1234
Converted data: 67305985 0x4030201
```

System.Buffer

The Buffer class allows the programmer to perform simple manipulation of a managed type as if it were unmanaged. Essentially, the type of the data is ignored.

Listing B.2 shows an example of manipulating an integer array without respect to its type (`buffer.cs`).

LISTING B.2 **`System.Buffer`** Sample

```
public class BufferMain
{
    static void Main(string [] args)
    {
        int [] rawData = new int [] {1,2,3,4};
        Console.WriteLine("Array byte length: {0}",
                          Buffer.ByteLength(rawData));
        for(int i = 0;i < Buffer.ByteLength(rawData); i++)
        {
            if((i % 4) == 0)
                Console.WriteLine();
            Console.Write("0x{0:X} ", Buffer.GetByte(rawData, i));
        }
    }
}
```

This array contains 4 integers. Each integer requires 4 bytes of storage, so the array takes up 16 bytes. The output of the sample is shown in Listing B.3.

LISTING B.3 **`System.Buffer`** Sample Output

```
Array byte length: 16
0x1 0x0 0x0 0x0
0x2 0x0 0x0 0x0
0x3 0x0 0x0 0x0
0x4 0x0 0x0 0x0
```

System.Console

This class has already been used extensively throughout this book, but you might not be aware of a couple of points. This class allows the programmer to "redirect" the standard input, standard output, and standard error. This is how a managed application can be included as part of a Web page and the output appears on the generated Web page. In addition, it is possible for the programmer to acquire a stream associated with standard error, standard output, and standard input rather than taking the defaults in the **`Write`**, **`WriteLine`**, **`Read`**, and **`ReadLine`** methods.

System.Convert

This class converts one base type to another base type. All of the basic types are represented in each version, but that conversion might not actually occur. Three different cases exist:

- No conversion takes place. An example of this is converting a type to itself.
- If the conversion does not make sense, the **Convert** class method throws an exception (**InvalidCastException**, **FormatException**, **OverflowException**, and so on).
- The **Convert** method succeeds in making the conversion.

Listing B.4 shows an example of a conversion from a **string** read in the **Console** to a **DateTime** structure (convert.cs).

LISTING B.4 Conversion Example

```
public static void Main(String[] args)
{
    Console.Write("Input a date: ");
    string input = Console.ReadLine();
    try
    {
        DateTime date = Convert.ToDateTime(input);
        Console.WriteLine("{0}", date.ToLongDateString());
    }
    catch(Exception e)
    {
        Console.WriteLine(e);
    }
    Console.Write("Input a byte sized integer: ");
    input = Console.ReadLine();
    try
    {
        byte b = Convert.ToByte(input);
        Console.WriteLine("You entered: {0}", b);
    }
    catch(Exception e)
    {
        Console.WriteLine(e);
    }
    Console.Write("Input a number: ");
    input = Console.ReadLine();
    try
    {
        int number = Convert.ToInt32(input);
        Console.WriteLine("You entered: {0}", number);
    }
    catch(Exception e)
    {
        Console.WriteLine(e);
    }
}
```

System.DateTime

An instance of a **DateTime** structure represents a point in time specified by a date and a time. This structure offers many date manipulation methods. Listing B.5 shows an example of some of the functionality of this structure (`datetime.cs`).

LISTING B.5 DateTime Example

```
static void Main(string [] args)
{
    Console.WriteLine("Min: {0}", DateTime.MinValue);
    Console.WriteLine("Max: {0}", DateTime.MaxValue);
    DateTime date = DateTime.Now;
    Console.WriteLine("Long DateTime {0} {1}",
                      date.ToLongDateString(),
                      date.ToLongTimeString());
    Console.WriteLine("Date: {0}", date.Date);
    Console.WriteLine("Month: {0}", date.Month);
    Console.WriteLine("Day: {0}", date.Day);
    Console.WriteLine("Day of week: {0}", date.DayOfWeek);
    Console.WriteLine("Day of year: {0}", date.DayOfYear);
    Console.WriteLine("TimeOfDay: {0}", date.TimeOfDay);
    Console.WriteLine("Hour: {0}", date.Hour);
    Console.WriteLine("Minute: {0}", date.Minute);
    Console.WriteLine("Second: {0}", date.Second);
    Console.WriteLine("Millisecond: {0}", date.Millisecond);
    Console.WriteLine("Ticks: {0}", date.Ticks);
    Console.WriteLine("In one hour it will be: {0} {1}",
                      date.AddHours(1).ToLongDateString(),
                      date.AddHours(1).ToLongTimeString());
    Console.WriteLine("An hour ago it was: {0} {1}",
                      date.AddHours(-1).ToLongDateString(),
                      date.AddHours(-1).ToLongTimeString());
    Console.WriteLine("Tomorrow will be: {0} {1}",
                      date.AddDays(1).ToLongDateString(),
                      date.AddDays(1).ToLongTimeString());
    Console.WriteLine("Yesterday was be: {0} {1}",
                      date.AddDays(-1).ToLongDateString(),
                      date.AddDays(-1).ToLongTimeString());
    Console.WriteLine("Next week will be: {0} {1}",
                      date.AddDays(7).ToLongDateString(),
                      date.AddDays(7).ToLongTimeString());
    Console.WriteLine("Last week was be: {0} {1}",
                      date.AddDays(-7).ToLongDateString(),
                      date.AddDays(-7).ToLongTimeString());
    Console.WriteLine("Next month will be: {0} {1}",
                      date.AddMonths(1).ToLongDateString(),
                      date.AddMonths(1).ToLongTimeString());
    Console.WriteLine("Last month was be: {0} {1}",
                      date.AddMonths(-1).ToLongDateString(),
                      date.AddMonths(-1).ToLongTimeString());
}
```

System.Environment

Use this class to retrieve the following information:

- Command-line arguments
- Current directory
- System directory
- Exit codes
- Machine name
- Domain name
- Username
- Tick count
- Newline character sequence
- OS version
- Environment variable settings
- Contents of the call stack
- Version of the CLR
- Working set

Listing B.6 shows a sample program calling some of the environment methods and properties (environment.cs).

LISTING B.6 Environment Example

```
static void Main(string [] args)
{
    Console.WriteLine("Command line: {0}", Environment.CommandLine);
    Console.WriteLine("Directory: {0}", Environment.CurrentDirectory);
    Console.WriteLine("Exit Code: {0}", Environment.ExitCode);
    Console.WriteLine("Machine name: {0}", Environment.MachineName);
    Console.Write("NewLine: ");
    string nl = Environment.NewLine;
    foreach(byte c in nl)
    {
        Console.Write("0x{0:X} ", c);
    }
    Console.WriteLine();
    Console.WriteLine("OS Version: {0}", Environment.OSVersion);
    Console.WriteLine("Stack trace: {0}", Environment.StackTrace);
    Console.WriteLine("System directory: {0}", Environment.SystemDirectory);
    Console.WriteLine("Tick count: {0}", Environment.TickCount);
    Console.WriteLine("User domain name: {0}", Environment.UserDomainName);
```

LISTING B.6 Continued

```
    Console.WriteLine("Interactive: {0}", Environment.UserInteractive);
    Console.WriteLine("User name: {0}", Environment.UserName);
    Console.WriteLine("Version: {0}", Environment.Version);
    Console.WriteLine("Working set: {0}", Environment.WorkingSet);
    Console.WriteLine("Expand environment variables: {0}",
Environment.ExpandEnvironmentVariables("PATH=%PATH%;INCLUDE=%INCLUDE%"));
    Console.Write("Command line: ");
    string [] ca = Environment.GetCommandLineArgs();
    foreach(string s in ca)
        Console.Write("{0} ", s);
    Console.WriteLine();
    Console.WriteLine("PATH: {0}", Environment.GetEnvironmentVariable
➥("PATH"));
    IDictionary env = Environment.GetEnvironmentVariables();
    Console.WriteLine("Environment: ");
    foreach(DictionaryEntry de in env)
        Console.WriteLine("{0} {1}", de.Key, de.Value);
    Console.WriteLine("Application Data: {0}",
Environment.GetFolderPath(Environment.SpecialFolder.ApplicationData));
    Console.WriteLine("Common Application Data: {0}",
Environment.GetFolderPath(Environment.SpecialFolder.CommonApplicationData));
    Console.WriteLine("Common Program Files: {0}",
Environment.GetFolderPath(Environment.SpecialFolder.CommonProgramFiles));
    Console.WriteLine("Cookies: {0}", Environment.GetFolderPath
➥(Environment.SpecialFolder.Cookies));
    Console.WriteLine("DesktopDirectory: {0}",
Environment.GetFolderPath(Environment.SpecialFolder.DesktopDirectory));
    Console.WriteLine("Favorites: {0}", Environment.GetFolderPath
➥(Environment.SpecialFolder.Favorites));
    Console.WriteLine("History: {0}", Environment.GetFolderPath
➥(Environment.SpecialFolder.History));
    Console.WriteLine("InternetCache: {0}", Environment.GetFolderPath
➥(Environment.SpecialFolder.InternetCache));
    Console.WriteLine("LocalApplicationData: {0}",
Environment.GetFolderPath(Environment.SpecialFolder.LocalApplicationData));
    Console.WriteLine("Personal: {0}", Environment.GetFolderPath
➥(Environment.SpecialFolder.Personal));
    Console.WriteLine("ProgramFiles: {0}", Environment.GetFolderPath
➥(Environment.SpecialFolder.ProgramFiles));
    Console.WriteLine("Programs: {0}", Environment.GetFolderPath
➥(Environment.SpecialFolder.Programs));
    Console.WriteLine("Recent: {0}", Environment.GetFolderPath
➥(Environment.SpecialFolder.Recent));
    Console.WriteLine("SendTo: {0}", Environment.GetFolderPath
➥(Environment.SpecialFolder.SendTo));
    Console.WriteLine("StartMenu: {0}", Environment.GetFolderPath
➥(Environment.SpecialFolder.StartMenu));
    Console.WriteLine("Startup: {0}", Environment.GetFolderPath
➥(Environment.SpecialFolder.Startup));
    Console.WriteLine("System: {0}", Environment.GetFolderPath
```

LISTING B.6 Continued

```
➥(Environment.SpecialFolder.System));
    Console.WriteLine("Templates: {0}", Environment.GetFolderPath
➥(Environment.SpecialFolder.Templates));
    string [] ld = Environment.GetLogicalDrives();
    foreach(string s in ld)
        Console.Write("{0} ", s);

    Environment.Exit(1);
}
```

System.Guid

`System.Guid` is a structure for manipulating GUIDs. A GUID is a 128-bit integer that is used to identify objects. A GUID can be used to uniquely identify an object across machines or networks. This identifier has a low probability of being duplicated. The following sample allocates a GUID and prints it in various formats. It then allocates another GUID and compares it with the first. Listing B.7 shows an example of using this structure to manipulate two GUIDs (`guid.cs`).

LISTING B.7 GUID Example

```
static void Main(string [] args)
{
    Guid guid = Guid.NewGuid();

    Console.WriteLine("Guid: {0}", guid);
    Console.WriteLine("Guid: {0}", guid.ToString("N"));
    Console.WriteLine("Guid: {0}", guid.ToString("D"));
    Console.WriteLine("Guid: {0}", guid.ToString("B"));
    Console.WriteLine("Guid: {0}", guid.ToString("P"));
    Guid guid2 = Guid.NewGuid();

    Console.WriteLine("Equal: {0}", guid == guid2);
    Console.WriteLine("Equal: {0}", guid == guid);
}
```

The output for this code is as follows:

```
Guid: eea06edf-5f3a-47cb-bca2-374bfbed72ec
Guid: eea06edf5f3a47cbbca2374bfbed72ec
Guid: eea06edf-5f3a-47cb-bca2-374bfbed72ec
Guid: {eea06edf-5f3a-47cb-bca2-374bfbed72ec}
Guid: (eea06edf-5f3a-47cb-bca2-374bfbed72ec)
Equal: False
Equal: True
```

System.IFormatProvider

This interface provides important functionality, allowing a class that implements the methods defined in this interface to customize formatted output. The **IFormatProvider** interface provides custom formatting for **ToString**. Some custom format codes already exist for numeric data types, date and time formatting, and enumerators. You can also provide your own formatting by inheriting from the **IFormatProvider** interface and implementing the methods specified.

You might want to look in the online documentation for "Custom Numeric Format Strings" because the documentation there is much more detailed than this appendix is able to cover. Listing B.8 shows an example of formatting a double (iformatprovider.cs).

LISTING B.8 Numeric **IFormatProvider** Example

```
double d = 123.0;
Console.WriteLine("{0} \t\t-> {1} \t\t-> {2}", d, @"#####",
➥d.ToString("#####"));
Console.WriteLine("{0} \t\t-> {1} \t\t-> {2}", d, @"00000",
➥d.ToString("00000"));
d = 1234567890.0;
Console.WriteLine("{0} \t-> {1} \t-> {2}", d, @"(###) ### - ####",
➥d.ToString("(###) ### - ####"));
d = 1.2;
Console.WriteLine("{0} \t\t-> {1} \t\t-> {2}", d, @"#.##",
➥d.ToString("#.##"));
Console.WriteLine("{0} \t\t-> {1} \t\t-> {2}", d, @"0.00",
➥d.ToString("0.00"));
Console.WriteLine("{0} \t\t-> {1} \t\t-> {2}", d, @"00.00",
➥d.ToString("00.00"));
d = 1234567890.0;
. . .
```

Listing B.9 shows the output of the code in Listing B.8.

LISTING B.9 Numeric **IFormatProvider** Example Output

```
123              -> #####              -> 123
123              -> 00000              -> 00123
1234567890       -> (###) ### - ####   -> (123) 456 - 7890
1.2              -> #.##               -> 1.2
1.2              -> 0.00               -> 1.20
1.2              -> 00.00              -> 01.20
1234567890       -> #,#                -> 1,234,567,890
1234567890       -> #,,                -> 1235
```

LISTING B.9 Continued

```
1234567890       -> #,,,                    -> 1
1234567890       -> #,##0,,                 -> 1,235
0.086            -> #0.##%                  -> 8.6%
86000            -> 0.###E+0                -> 8.6E+4
86000            -> 0.###E+000              -> 8.6E+004
86000            -> 0.###E-000              -> 8.6E004
123456           -> [##-##-##]              -> [12-34-56]
1234             -> ##;(##)                 -> 1234
-1234            -> ##;(##)                 -> (1234)
```

The **DateTime** structure also has some custom format strings. Listing B.10 shows some examples (iformatprovider.cs).

LISTING B.10 **DateTime IFormatProvider** Example

```
DateTime now = DateTime.Now;
Console.WriteLine("{0} \t-> {1} \t\t-> {2}", now, @"d, M",
➥now.ToString("d, M"));
Console.WriteLine("{0} \t-> {1} \t\t-> {2}", now, @"d MMMM",
➥now.ToString("d MMMM"));
Console.WriteLine("{0} \t-> {1} \t-> {2}", now, @"dddd MMMM yy gg",
➥now.ToString("dddd MMMM yy gg"));
Console.WriteLine("{0} \t-> {1} \t\t-> {2}", now, @"h , m: s",
➥now.ToString("h , m: s"));
. . .
```

Listing B.11 shows the output from Listing B.10. Your output, of course, will differ due to time differences, time zone differences, and culture settings.

LISTING B.11 **DateTime IFormatProvider** Example Output

```
10/3/2001 1:20:11 PM    -> d, M               -> 3, 10
10/3/2001 1:20:11 PM    -> d MMMM             -> 3 October
10/3/2001 1:20:11 PM    -> dddd MMMM yy gg    -> Wednesday October 01 A.D.
10/3/2001 1:20:11 PM    -> h , m: s           -> 1 , 20: 11
10/3/2001 1:20:11 PM    -> hh,mm:ss           -> 01,20:11
10/3/2001 1:20:11 PM    -> HH-mm-ss-tt        -> 13-20-11-PM
10/3/2001 1:20:11 PM    -> hh:mm, G\MT z      -> 01:20, GMT -5
10/3/2001 1:20:11 PM    -> hh:mm, G\MT zzz    -> 01:20, GMT -05:00
```

The enum type implements an IFormatProvider interface. Listing B.12 shows the usage of the codes that enum supports (iformatprovider.cs).

LISTING B.12 **Enum IFormatProvider Example**

```
enum Letters
{
    A,
    B,
    C,
    D,
    E,
    F,
    G,
    H,
. . .
Letters c = Letters.R;
Console.WriteLine("{0} \t-> {1} \t-> {2}", c, @"G", c.ToString("G"));
Console.WriteLine("{0} \t-> {1} \t-> {2}", c, @"F", c.ToString("F"));
Console.WriteLine("{0} \t-> {1} \t-> {2}", c, @"D", c.ToString("D"));
Console.WriteLine("{0} \t-> {1} \t-> {2}", c, @"X", c.ToString("X"));
```

The output from this listing is shown in Listing B.13.

LISTING B.13 **Enum IFormatProvider Example Output**

```
R       -> G    -> R
R       -> F    -> R
R       -> D    -> 17
R       -> X    -> 00000011
```

System.Math

This provides a core set of mathematical functions along with two constants: the ratio of the circumference of a circle to its diameter (pi) and the natural logarithm base (e). Listing B.14 provides an example of using parts of the **Math** class (math.cs).

LISTING B.14 **Math Example**

```
static void Main(string [] args)
{
    Console.WriteLine("Pi: {0}", Math.PI);
    Console.WriteLine("E: {0}", Math.E);
    Console.WriteLine("sqrt(2): {0}", Math.Sqrt(2.0));
    Console.WriteLine("log(e): {0}", Math.Log(Math.E));
    Console.WriteLine("cos(pi): {0}", Math.Cos(Math.PI));
    Console.WriteLine("sin(pi): {0}", Math.Sin(Math.PI));
    Console.WriteLine("2^5: {0}", Math.Pow(2,5));
}
```

System.OperatingSystem

This class supplies information about an operating system such as the version and the platform identifier. A *platform identifier* is simply an enumerated constant that indicates the type of platform, such as Windows NT.

System.Random

This class provides an implementation of a pseudo-random number generator. **System.Random** makes it easy to generate numbers that are statistically close to random. Listing B.15 shows how to use the **Random** class (random.cs).

LISTING B.15 Random Example

```
static void Main(string [] args)
{
    Random r = new Random();
    for(int i = 0; i < 10; i++)
    {
        Console.Write("{0} {1} {2} {3} {4} {5} {6} {7} {8} {9}",
            r.NextDouble().ToString("0.0000"),
            r.NextDouble().ToString("0.0000"),
            r.NextDouble().ToString("0.0000"),
            r.NextDouble().ToString("0.0000"),
            r.NextDouble().ToString("0.0000"),
            r.NextDouble().ToString("0.0000"),
            r.NextDouble().ToString("0.0000"),
            r.NextDouble().ToString("0.0000"),
            r.NextDouble().ToString("0.0000"),
            r.NextDouble().ToString("0.0000"));
        Console.WriteLine();
    }
    for(int i = 0; i < 10; i++)
    {
        Console.Write("{0} {1} {2} {3} {4} {5} {6} {7} {8} {9}",
            r.Next(0,99).ToString("00"),
            r.Next(0,99).ToString("00"),
            r.Next(0,99).ToString("00"),
            r.Next(0,99).ToString("00"),
            r.Next(0,99).ToString("00"),
            r.Next(0,99).ToString("00"),
            r.Next(0,99).ToString("00"),
            r.Next(0,99).ToString("00"),
            r.Next(0,99).ToString("00"),
            r.Next(0,99).ToString("00"));
        Console.WriteLine();
    }
}
```

System.TimeSpan

This structure represents an interval of time. Because the number of days in months and years varies and those values change between some cultures, the longest unit of time used by **TimeSpan** is a day. Listing B.16 shows an example of using **TimeSpan** (timespan.cs).

LISTING B.16 TimeSpan Example

```
public class TimeSpanMain
{
    static void Main(string [] args)
    {
        // Allocate a TimeSpan object
        // with a given number of ticks
        TimeSpan ts = new TimeSpan(1012);
        Console.WriteLine("{0}", ts);
        // Allocate a TimeSpan object
        // with days, hours, minutes, seconds
        ts = new TimeSpan(11, 13, 46, 40);
        Console.WriteLine("{0} {1}", ts, ts.Ticks.ToString("#,#"));
    }
}
```

The output for Listing B.16 is as follows:

```
00:00:00.0001012
11.13:46:40 10,000,000,000,000
```

System.TimeZone

The **TimeZone** class encapsulates information about time zones and provides conversion utilities between local time and UTC time. Listing B.17 provides an example using **TimeZone** (timezone.cs).

LISTING B.17 TimeZone Example

```
public class TimeZoneMain
{
    static void Main(string [] args)
    {
        TimeZone tz = TimeZone.CurrentTimeZone;
        Console.WriteLine("{0} {1}", tz.DaylightName, tz.StandardName);
        DaylightTime dt = tz.GetDaylightChanges(DateTime.Now.Year);
        Console.WriteLine("Start daylight savings time {0}", dt.Start);
        Console.WriteLine("End daylight savings time {0}", dt.End);
```

LISTING B.17 Continued

```
        Console.WriteLine("Daylight savings time change {0}", dt.Delta);
        Console.WriteLine("Is daylight savings? {0}",
➥tz.IsDaylightSavingTime(DateTime.Now));
        Console.WriteLine("UTC {0}", tz.ToUniversalTime(DateTime.Now));
    }
}
```

System.Version

This structure simply provides a wrapper around arbitrary version information. Listing B.18 shows some of its functionality (`version.cs`).

LISTING B.18 **`Version`** Example

```
public class VersionMain
{
    static void Main(string [] args)
    {
        Version v1 = new Version("1.2.3.4");
        Version v2 = new Version(1,2,3,5);
        Console.WriteLine("{0} {1}", v1, v2);
        Console.WriteLine("v1 > v2? {0}", v1 > v2);
    }
}
```

System.Collections

Many general-purpose collections are implemented in the .NET Framework SDK. Most of these collections are used as base classes to customize the feature set for an application.

System.Collections.ArrayList

Unlike the **`Array`**, an **`ArrayList`** can dynamically change its size as new items are added to the collection. Listing B.19 shows an example using an **`ArrayList`** (`arraylist.cs`).

LISTING B.19 **`ArrayList`** Example

```
static void Main(string [] args)
{
    ArrayList al = new ArrayList();
    lock(al.SyncRoot)
```

LISTING B.19 Continued

```
    {
        al.Add("This");
        al.Add("is");
        al.Add("a");
        al.Add("test");
        al.Add(0);
        al.Add(1);
        Console.WriteLine("Sychronized: {0}", al.IsSynchronized);
        Console.WriteLine("Read-only: {0}", al.IsReadOnly);
        Console.WriteLine("Fixed size: {0}", al.IsFixedSize);
        Console.WriteLine("Capacity: {0}", al.Capacity);
        Console.WriteLine("Count: {0}", al.Count);
    }
    foreach(object o in al)
    {
        Console.WriteLine("{0} {1}", o, o.GetType());
    }
    al = ArrayList.Synchronized(al);
    Console.WriteLine("Sychronized: {0}", al.IsSynchronized);
}
```


Listing B.20 shows the output from Listing B.19.

LISTING B.20 `ArrayList` Example Output

```
Sychronized: False
Read-only: False
Fixed size: False
Capacity: 16
Count: 6
This System.String
is System.String
a System.String
test System.String
0 System.Int32
1 System.Int32
Sychronized: True
```

At first, some basic information is printed about the `ArrayList`. This instance is not synchronized; therefore, it is not thread-safe. You can get a thread-safe reference by calling the Synchronized method. As an alternative, you can also use **`SyncRoot`** to return a handle that a thread can call **`lock`** on to provide multiple threads synchronized access to the class.

The values in the array are printed. Notice that more than just strings are stored in the **`ArrayList`**. Because the **`ArrayList`** stores Objects, you can store integers (which are boxed on input and unboxed on output).

System.Collections.BitArray

A **BitArray** provides a means to store binary data. A **BitArray** is a collection of bools. Listing B.21 shows an example using BitArray (bitarray.cs).

LISTING B.21 **BitArray** Example

```
static void Main(string [] args)
{
    BitArray ba1 = new BitArray(8);
    ba1[0] = true;
    ba1[1] = false;
    ba1[2] = true;
    ba1[3] = false;
    ba1[4] = true;
    ba1[5] = false;
    ba1[6] = true;
    ba1[7] = false;
    foreach(bool b in ba1)
        Console.Write("{0} ", b);
    Console.WriteLine();
    BitArray ba2 = new BitArray(8);
    ba2[0] = true;
    ba2[1] = true;
    ba2[2] = true;
    ba2[3] = true;
    ba2[4] = false;
    ba2[5] = false;
    ba2[6] = false;
    ba2[7] = false;
    foreach(bool b in ba2)
        Console.Write("{0} ", b);
    Console.WriteLine();
    BitArray bar = new BitArray(ba1);
    bar.And(ba2);
    Console.WriteLine("--- And ---");
    foreach(bool b in bar)
        Console.Write("{0} ", b);
    Console.WriteLine();
    bar = new BitArray(ba1);
    bar.Or(ba2);
    Console.WriteLine("--- Or ---");
    foreach(bool b in bar)
        Console.Write("{0} ", b);
    Console.WriteLine();
    bar = new BitArray(ba1);
    bar.Xor(ba2);
    Console.WriteLine("--- Xor ---");
    foreach(bool b in bar)
        Console.Write("{0} ", b);
    Console.WriteLine();
}
```

Just to prove that it works, Listing B.22 shows the output for Listing B.21.

LISTING B.22 **`BitArray`** Example Output

```
True False True False True False True False
True True True True False False False False
--- And ---
True False True False False False False False
--- Or ---
True True True True True False True False
--- Xor ---
False True False True True False True False
```


System.Collections.Hashtable

A **`Hashtable`** provides a collection that can be indexed by association to a key. You could also call it an associative array. Listing B.23 shows an example using a **`Hashtable`** (`hashtable.cs`). This sample builds a list using integers and strings as keys. After the sample builds a list, it prints the list and accesses arbitrary members of the list based on the assigned key.

LISTING B.23 **`Hashtable`** Example

```
public class HashTableMain
{
    static void Main(string [] args)
    {
        Hashtable ht = new Hashtable();
        ht.Add("1", "First");
        ht.Add("2", "Second");
        ht.Add("3", "Third");
        ht.Add("4", "Fourth");
        ht.Add("5", "Fifth");
        ht.Add(1, "One");
        ht.Add(2, "Two");
        ht.Add(3, "Three");
        ht.Add(4, "Four");
        ht.Add(5, "Five");
        foreach(DictionaryEntry de in ht)
        {
            Console.WriteLine("{0} {1}", de.Key, de.Value);
        }
        Console.WriteLine("Contains 1: {0}", ht.Contains(1));
        Console.WriteLine("Contains 6: {0}", ht.Contains(6));
        Console.WriteLine("ContainsValue First: {0}",
ht.ContainsValue("First"));
        Console.WriteLine("ht[1]: {0}", ht[1]);
    }
}
```

System.Collections.ICollection

ICollection is an interface that defines three properties (**Count**, **IsSynchronized**, and **SynchRoot**) and one method (**CopyTo**) to copy the collection to an array. All collections in the .NET Framework derive from this interface and as such implement each of these members. Listing B.24 shows how to extract the **ICollection** interface from an **ArrayList** and use it through calls to the **ArrayList** instance (icollection.cs) instead of indirectly.

Listing B.24 ICollection Example

```
public class ICollectionMain
{
    static void Main(string [] args)
    {
        ArrayList al = new ArrayList();
        al.Add("This");
        al.Add("is");
        al.Add("a");
        al.Add("test");
        al.Add(0);
        al.Add(1);
        ICollection ic = (ICollection)al;
        lock(ic.SyncRoot)
        {
            Console.WriteLine("Sychronized: {0}", ic.IsSynchronized);
            Console.WriteLine("Count: {0}", ic.Count);
            Object [] oa = new Object [6];
            ic.CopyTo(oa, 0);
            foreach(object o in oa)
            {
                Console.WriteLine("{0} {1}", o, o.GetType());
            }
        }
    }
}
```

Of course, because it is an interface, you can inherit from it and your class can be used in the same contexts as built-in types.

System.Collections.IDictionary

Like **ICollection**, **IDictionary** is an interface that defines methods and properties for use with key-value pair collections. The following listing shows how to extract the **IDictionary** interface from a **Hashtable** and use it instead of the **Hashtable** instance. This is particularly useful if you have a collection of classes that all derive from **IDictionary** because you can take advantage of polymorphism. Listing B.25 shows how to extract the **IDictionary** interface from **Hashtable** (idictionary.cs).

LISTING B.25 **IDictionary** Example

```
public class IDictionaryMain
{
    static void Main(string [] args)
    {
        Hashtable ht = new Hashtable();
        IDictionary id = (IDictionary)ht;
        id.Add("1", "First");
        id.Add("2", "Second");
        id.Add("3", "Third");
        id.Add("4", "Fourth");
        id.Add("5", "Fifth");
        id.Add(1, "One");
        id.Add(2, "Two");
        id.Add(3, "Three");
        id.Add(4, "Four");
        id.Add(5, "Five");
        foreach(DictionaryEntry de in id)
        {
            Console.WriteLine("{0} {1}", de.Key, de.Value);
        }
        Console.WriteLine("Contains 1: {0}", id.Contains(1));
        Console.WriteLine("Contains 6: {0}", id.Contains(6));
        Console.WriteLine("id[1]: {0}", id[1]);
    }
}
```


Like **ICollection**, you should also look at your classes to see if it would make sense to derive your class from **IDictionary**.

System.Collections.IEnumerable

IEnumerable is an interface that defines a single method, **GetEnumerator**, which provides a flexible interface for enumerating the contents of a collection. Listing B.26 shows an example of using the **IEnumerable** interface (`ienumerable.cs`).

LISTING B.26 **IEnumerable** Example

```
public class IEnumerableMain
{
    static void Main(string [] args)
    {
        ArrayList al = new ArrayList();
        al.Add("This");
        al.Add("is");
        al.Add("a");
        al.Add("test");
        al.Add(0);
```

LISTING B.26 Continued

```
        al.Add(1);
        IEnumerable ienum = (IEnumerable)al;
        IEnumerator ie = ienum.GetEnumerator();
        while(ie.MoveNext())
        {
            Console.WriteLine("{0} {1}", ie.Current, ie.Current.GetType());
        }
    }
}
```

System.Collections.IList

IList is an interface that describes methods for accessing objects in a collection by using indices. Listing B.27 shows an example of how this interface can be used (ilist.cs).

LISTING B.27 **IList** Example

```
static void Main(string [] args)
{
    ArrayList al = new ArrayList();
    IList il = (IList)al;
    il.Add("This");
    il.Add("is");
    il.Add("a");
    il.Add("test");
    il.Add(0);
    il.Add(1);
    Console.WriteLine("Read-only: {0}", il.IsReadOnly);
    Console.WriteLine("Fixed size: {0}", il.IsFixedSize);
    Console.WriteLine("il[0]: {0}", il[0]);
    Console.WriteLine("il[1]: {0}", il[1]);
    Console.WriteLine("il contains \"test\": {0}", il.Contains("test"));
    Console.WriteLine("Removing \"test\" . . .");
    il.Remove("test");
    Console.WriteLine("il contains \"test\": {0}", il.Contains("test"));
    Console.WriteLine("il contains 2: {0}", il.Contains(2));
}
```

System.Collections.Queue

You will use a **Queue** if you are expecting objects to be added and removed from the container in a first-in, first-out (FIFO) basis. Listing B.28 shows an example using a **Queue** (queue.cs).

LISTING B.28 **Queue Example**

```
static void Main(string [] args)
{
    Queue q = new Queue();
    lock(q.SyncRoot)
    {
        q.Enqueue("First");
        q.Enqueue("Second");
        q.Enqueue("Third");
        q.Enqueue("Fourth");
        q.Enqueue("Fifth");
    }
    Console.WriteLine("Count: {0}", q.Count);

    foreach(object o in q)
    {
        Console.WriteLine("{0} {1}", o, o.GetType());
    }
    object obj;
    obj = q.Dequeue();
    Console.WriteLine("{0} {1}", q.Count, obj);
    obj = q.Dequeue();
    Console.WriteLine("{0} {1}", q.Count, obj);
    obj = q.Dequeue();
    Console.WriteLine("{0} {1}", q.Count, obj);
    obj = q.Dequeue();
    Console.WriteLine("{0} {1}", q.Count, obj);
    obj = q.Dequeue();
    Console.WriteLine("{0} {1}", q.Count, obj);
}
```

The output from this code is as follows:

```
Count: 5
First System.String
Second System.String
Third System.String
Fourth System.String
Fifth System.String
4 First
3 Second
2 Third
1 Fourth
0 Fifth
```

System.Collections.ReadOnlyCollectionBase

This abstract class is designed to be a base class. It provides a framework for implementing a read-only collection. Many classes in the .NET Framework derive from this class.

Listing B.29 shows an example of one of the classes that derives from this class, `ProcessThreadCollection` (`rocb.cs`).

LISTING B.29 **`ReadOnlyCollectionBase`** Example

```
static void Main(string [] args)
{
    Process [] pa = Process.GetProcesses();
    foreach(Process p in pa)
    {
        ProcessThreadCollection ptc = p.Threads;
        Console.WriteLine("Process: {0} Threads: {1}", p.ProcessName,
ptc.Count);
    }
}
```

System.Collections.SortedList

A **`SortedList`** is just that: a sorted list. Listing B.30 shows an example using the **`SortedList`** class (`sortedlist.cs`).

LISTING B.30 **`SortedList`** Example

```
static void Main(string [] args)
{
    SortedList sl = new SortedList();
    sl.Add("1", "First");
    sl.Add("2", "Second");
    sl.Add("3", "Third");
    sl.Add("4", "Fourth");
    sl.Add("5", "Fifth");
    foreach(DictionaryEntry de in sl)
    {
        Console.WriteLine("\"{0}\" {1}", de.Key, de.Value);
    }
    Console.WriteLine("Contains \"1\": {0}", sl.Contains("1"));
    Console.WriteLine("Contains \"6\": {0}", sl.Contains("6"));
    Console.WriteLine("ContainsValue \"First\": {0}",
➥sl.ContainsValue("First"));
    Console.WriteLine("sl[\"1\"]: {0}", sl["1"]);
    sl.Clear();
    sl.Add(1, "First");
    sl.Add(2, "Second");
    sl.Add(3, "Third");
    sl.Add(4, "Fourth");
    sl.Add(5, "Fifth");
    foreach(DictionaryEntry de in sl)
    {
```

LISTING B.30 Continued

```
        Console.WriteLine("{0} {1}", de.Key, de.Value);
    }
    Console.WriteLine("Contains 1: {0}", sl.Contains(1));
    Console.WriteLine("Contains 6: {0}", sl.Contains(6));
    Console.WriteLine("ContainsValue First: {0}", sl.ContainsValue("First"));
    Console.WriteLine("sl[1]: {0}", sl[1]);
}
```

System.Collections.Stack

A **Stack** is like a **Queue** in that it is optimized for adding and removing objects from the collection. With a **Stack**, however, the items are removed on a last-in, first-out basis. Listing B.31 shows an example using **Stack** (stack.cs).

LISTING B.31 **Stack** Example

```
static void Main(string [] args)
{
    Stack stack = new Stack();
    stack.Push("First");
    stack.Push("Second");
    stack.Push("Third");
    stack.Push("Fourth");
    stack.Push("Fifth");
    Console.WriteLine("Count: {0}", stack.Count);
    foreach(string s in stack)
    {
        Console.WriteLine(s);
    }
    string sobj;
    sobj = (string)stack.Pop();
    Console.WriteLine("{0} {1}", stack.Count, sobj);
    sobj = (string)stack.Pop();
    Console.WriteLine("{0} {1}", stack.Count, sobj);
    sobj = (string)stack.Pop();
    Console.WriteLine("{0} {1}", stack.Count, sobj);
    sobj = (string)stack.Pop();
    Console.WriteLine("{0} {1}", stack.Count, sobj);
    sobj = (string)stack.Pop();
    Console.WriteLine("{0} {1}", stack.Count, sobj);
}
```

The output from Listing B.31 is instructive in that you can see that items are removed from the collection in a last-in, first-out basis. Listing B.32 shows the output from Listing B.31.

LISTING B.32 **Stack** Example Output

```
Count: 5
Fifth
Fourth
Third
Second
First
4 Fifth
3 Fourth
2 Third
1 Second
0 First
```

System.Collections.Specialized

The **System.Collections.Specialized** namespace includes a number of collection classes that have been developed for specific functionality. Most of these classes are derivations from the "core" group of collection classes.

System.Collections.Specialized.BitVector32

Although **BitArray** is general and adapts well to vectors of Boolean values that are arbitrary in size, it usually results in performance cost. `BitVector32` is a class optimized for Boolean values that can fit on a 32-bit built-in type. Listing B.33 shows an example of using BitVector32 (`bitvector32.cs`).

LISTING B.33 **BitVector32** Example

```
public class BitVector32Main
{
    // Create masks for the bit vector.
    private static readonly int MaskOne = BitVector32.CreateMask();
    private static readonly int MaskTwo = BitVector32.CreateMask(MaskOne);
    private static readonly int MaskThree = BitVector32.CreateMask(MaskTwo);
    private static readonly int MaskFour = BitVector32.CreateMask(MaskThree);
    private static readonly int MaskFive = BitVector32.CreateMask(MaskFour);
    private static readonly int MaskSix = BitVector32.CreateMask(MaskFive);
    private static readonly int MaskSeven = BitVector32.CreateMask(MaskSix);
    private static readonly int MaskEight = BitVector32.CreateMask(MaskSeven);
    // Create sections for the bit vector.
    private static readonly BitVector32.Section first =
        BitVector32.CreateSection(15);
    private static readonly BitVector32.Section second =
        BitVector32.CreateSection(15, first);

    static void Main(string [] args)
    {
        BitVector32 bv = new BitVector32();
```

LISTING B.33 Continued

```
        bv[MaskEight] = true;
        bv[MaskOne] = true;
        Console.WriteLine("{0}", bv);
        bv = new BitVector32();
        bv[first] = 14;
        bv[second] = 7;
        Console.WriteLine("{0}", bv);
    }
}
```


Listing B.33 generates the following output:

```
BitVector32{00000000000000000000000010000001}
BitVector32{00000000000000000000000001111110}
```

System.Collections.Specialized.CollectionsUtil

The **CollectionUtil** class provides some useful utility functions that allow a user to obtain a case-insensitive **SortedList** or a case-insensitive **Hashtable**. Listing B.34 shows an example of using some methods in the **CollectionUtil** class (util.cs).

LISTING B.34 **CollectionsUtil** Example

```
public class CollectionsUtilMain
{
    static void Main(string [] args)
    {
        Hashtable ht = CollectionsUtil.CreateCaseInsensitiveHashtable();
        ht.Add("First", "This is the first one");
        ht.Add("Second", "This is the second one");
        ht.Add("Third", "This is the third one");
        ht.Add("Fourth", "This is the fourth one");
        ht.Add("Fifth", "This is the fifth one");
        foreach(DictionaryEntry de in ht)
        {
            Console.WriteLine("{0} {1}", de.Key, de.Value);
        }
        Console.WriteLine("Contains \"first\": {0}", ht.Contains("first"));
        Console.WriteLine("Contains \"sixth\": {0}", ht.Contains("sixth"));
        Console.WriteLine("ht[\"FIRST\"]: \"{0}\"", ht["FIRST"]);

        // Now a case-insensitive sorted list
        SortedList sl = CollectionsUtil.CreateCaseInsensitiveSortedList();
        sl.Add("First", "This is the first one");
        sl.Add("Second", "This is the second one");
        sl.Add("Third", "This is the third one");
        sl.Add("Fourth", "This is the fourth one");
        sl.Add("Fifth", "This is the fifth one");
```

LISTING B.34 Continued

```
        foreach(DictionaryEntry de in sl)
        {
            Console.WriteLine("\"{0}\" {1}", de.Key, de.Value);
        }
        Console.WriteLine("Contains \"first\": {0}", sl.Contains("first"));
        Console.WriteLine("Contains \"sixth\": {0}", sl.Contains("sixth"));
        Console.WriteLine("sl[\"FIRSTT\"]: \"{0}\"", sl["FIRST"]);
    }
}
```

To show the case insensitivity, Listing B.35 shows the output from Listing B.34.

LISTING B.35 **`CollectionsUtil`** Example Output

```
First This is the first one
Second This is the second one
Fourth This is the fourth one
Third This is the third one
Fifth This is the fifth one
Contains "first": True
Contains "sixth": False
ht["FIRST"]: "This is the first one"
"Fifth" This is the fifth one
"First" This is the first one
"Fourth" This is the fourth one
"Second" This is the second one
"Third" This is the third one
Contains "first": True
Contains "sixth": False
sl["FIRSTT"]: "This is the first one"
```

`System.Collections.Specialized.HybridDictionary`

This class does not provide new visible functionality, but it does add a possible performance feature. This class starts out building a **`ListDictionary`**-based collection while the collection is small; then, as the collection grows, it switches to a **`Hashtable`**. Listing B.36 shows an example using **`HybridDictionary`** (`hybriddictionary.cs`).

LISTING B.36 **`HybridDictionary`** Example

```
public class HybridDictionaryMain
{
    static void Main(string [] args)
    {
        HybridDictionary ht = new HybridDictionary();
        ht.Add("1", "First");
```

LISTING B.36 Continued

```
        ht.Add("2", "Second");
        ht.Add("3", "Third");
        ht.Add("4", "Fourth");
        ht.Add("5", "Fifth");
        ht.Add(1, "One");
        ht.Add(2, "Two");
        ht.Add(3, "Three");
        ht.Add(4, "Four");
        ht.Add(5, "Five");
        foreach(DictionaryEntry de in ht)
        {
            Console.WriteLine("{0} {1}", de.Key, de.Value);
        }
        Console.WriteLine("Contains 1: {0}", ht.Contains(1));
        Console.WriteLine("Contains 6: {0}", ht.Contains(6));
        Console.WriteLine("ht[1]: {0}", ht[1]);
    }
}
```


`System.Collections.Specialized.NameValueCollection`

This collection is a sorted collection of **`string`** keys and **`string`** values. Entries in this collection can be accessed either with a string (associative) or an index. The comparer and the hashtable provider are by default case insensitive. Listing B.37 shows an example of using a **`NameValueCollection`** (`namevaluecollection.cs`).

LISTING B.37 **`NameValueCollection`** Example

```
static void Main(string [] args)
{
    NameValueCollection nvc = new NameValueCollection();
    nvc.Add("First", "This is the first item");
    nvc.Add("Second", "This is the second item");
    nvc.Add("Third", "This is the third item");
    Console.WriteLine("Count: {0}", nvc.Count);
    foreach(string s in nvc)
    {
        Console.WriteLine(s);
    }
}
```

`System.Collections.Specialized.StringCollection`

This class provides a collection of **`string`**s that are stored and retrieved in a case-insensitive manner. Duplicate **`string`**s are allowed in the collection. Listing B.38 shows an example of using **`StringCollection`** (`stringcollection.cs`).

LISTING B.38 **`StringCollection`** **Example**

```
public class StringCollectionMain
{
    static void Main(string [] args)
    {
        StringCollection sc = new StringCollection();
        sc.Add("First");
        sc.Add("Second");
        sc.Add("Third");
        sc.Add("Fourth");
        sc.Add("Fifth");
        Console.WriteLine("Read-only: {0}", sc.IsReadOnly);
        Console.WriteLine("Count: {0}", sc.Count);
        foreach(string s in sc)
        {
            Console.WriteLine(s);
        }
    }
}
```

`System.Collections.Specialized.StringDictionary`

This class provides a dictionary of **`string`**s using **`string`** keys and values. **`String`**s are stored and retrieved from the collection in a case-insensitive manner. Listing B.39 shows an example of using **`StringDictionary`** (`stringdictionary.cs`).

LISTING B.39 **`StringDictionary`** **Example**

```
public class StringDictionaryMain
{
    static void Main(string [] args)
    {
        StringDictionary sd = new StringDictionary();
        sd.Add("First", "This is the first string");
        sd.Add("Second", "This is the second string");
        sd.Add("Third", "This is the third string");
        sd.Add("Fourth", "This is the fourth string");
        sd.Add("Fifth", "This is the fifth string");
        Console.WriteLine("Count: {0}", sd.Count);
        foreach(DictionaryEntry de in sd)
        {
            Console.WriteLine("{0} {1}", de.Key, de.Value);
        }
        Console.WriteLine("sd[\"First\"]: {0}", sd["First"]);
        Console.WriteLine("sd[\"Second\"]: {0}", sd["Second"]);
        Console.WriteLine("ContainsKey \"First\": {0}",
➥sd.ContainsKey("First"));
        Console.WriteLine("sd[\"FIRST\"]: {0}", sd["FIRST"]);
        Console.WriteLine("ContainsKey \"Sixth\": {0}",
```

LISTING B.39 Continued

```
sd.ContainsKey("Sixth"));
    }
}
```

Listing B.40 shows the output from Listing B.39. This output illustrates how the **StringDictionary** is case insensitive.

LISTING B.40 **StringDictionary** Example Output

```
Count: 5
third This is the third string
first This is the first string
fifth This is the fifth string
second This is the second string
fourth This is the fourth string
sd["First"]: This is the first string
sd["Second"]: This is the second string
sd["FIRST"]: This is the first string
ContainsKey "First": True
ContainsKey "Sixth": False
```


System.ComponentModel

The **System.ComponentModel** namespace along with **System.ComponentModel.Design** and **System.ComponentModel.Design.Serialization** contains many classes. Most of the classes deal with support for building (design-time) and deploying (run-time) pluggable components. Check out the following online articles on the ComponentModel:

- "Creating Designable Components for Microsoft Visual Studio .NET Designers," Shawn Burke, http://msdn.microsoft.com/library/default.asp?url=/library/en-us/dndotnet/html/pdc_vsdescmp.asp.
- "Component Programming Essentials," http://msdn.microsoft.com/library/default.asp?url=/library/en-us/cpguidnf/html/cpconcomponentprogrammingessentials.asp?frame=true.

System.ComponentModel.License

This class represents a base class that is used for all licenses. Licensing a component involves the use of the **LicenseProviderAttribute**, **LicenseProvider**, **LicenseManager**, **LicenseContext**, and **LicenseException** classes. For a simple implementation, the **LicFileLicenseProvider** class is provided with the SDK. To enable licensing in a windows control, you could follow the example in Listing B.41 (see the License solution in the License directory).

LISTING B.41 License Provider for a Class Using **LicFileLicenseProvider**

```
 [LicenseProvider(typeof(LicFileLicenseProvider))]
public class UserControl : System.Windows.Forms.UserControl
{
    private License license = null;
    private System.Windows.Forms.Label label;
    private System.ComponentModel.Container components = null;
    public UserControl()
    {
        // Add Validate to the control's constructor.
        license = LicenseManager.Validate(typeof(UserControl), this);
        // This call is required by the Windows.Forms Form Designer.
        InitializeComponent();
    }
...
protected override void Dispose( bool disposing )
{
    if( disposing )
    {
        if( components != null )
            components.Dispose();
        if (license != null)
        {
            license.Dispose();
            license = null;
        }
    }
    base.Dispose( disposing );
}
```

First, notice that the control has **LicenseProviderAttribute** applied to the class. The specific provider is specified as **LicFileLicenseProvider**. If you were to license a class, the code would be similar. Listing B.42 shows an example of licensing a control class.

LISTING B.42 License Provider for a Control Using **LicFileLicenseProvider**

```
 [LicenseProvider(typeof(LicFileLicenseProvider))]
public class UserControl : IDisposable
{
    private License license = null;
    public UserControl()
    {
```

LISTING B.42 Continued

```
        // Add Validate to the control's constructor.
        license = LicenseManager.Validate(typeof(UserControl), this);
    }
...
    public void Dispose()
    {
        if (license != null)
        {
            license.Dispose();
            license = null;
        }
    }
```


The only provider that is shipped with the .NET Framework is **`LicFileLicenseProvider`**. This class looks for a file `type-name.lic`, where `type-name` is the full name of the type being licensed. Here, it would be `LicensedControl.UserControl.lic` because the namespace is `LicensedControl` and the class name is `UserControl`. On startup the control is created as follows:

```
control = new LicensedControl.UserControl();
```

The constructor is called, and in the constructor, a call is made to validate the control. The **`LicFileLicenseProvider`** class looks for the .LIC file and reads the first line. If the first line of the file ends in `is a licensed component`, then the validation returns **`true`** and the object can be instantiated. If the file is not found or is not valid, then a **`LicenseException`** exception is thrown and the construction of the object fails.

You need to modify the license class to provide custom license verification. To do this, you need to build a class that derives from **`LicenseProvider`**. A snippet from the new class is shown in Listing B.43.

LISTING B.43 License Provider for a Class Using a Custom License Provider

```
 [LicenseProvider(typeof(TimeBombLicenseProvider))]
public class UserClass
{
    private License license = null;
    public UserClass()
    {
        // Validate the license. If this fails, the constructor
        // will not complete and the constructor will fail.
        license = (TimeBombLicenseProvider.TimeBombLicense)
➥LicenseManager.Validate(typeof(UserClass), this);
    }
```

The implementation of the `LicenseProvider` and the `License` class looks like Listing B.44.

LISTING B.44 Implementation of a Custom License Provider

```
public class TimeBombLicenseProvider : LicenseProvider
{
    protected virtual bool IsKeyValid(string key, Type type)
    {
        // Make sure that the key is not empty
        if (key != null)
        {
            DateTime now = DateTime.Now;
            // Get the dates for which this license is valid.
            int startIndex = key.IndexOf(',') + 1;
            int endIndex = key.IndexOf(',', startIndex) + 1;
            DateTime validStartTime = new DateTime(Convert.ToInt64
➥(key.Substring(startIndex, endIndex - startIndex - 1)));
            DateTime validEndTime = new DateTime(Int64.Parse
➥(key.Substring(endIndex)));

            Debug.WriteLine("Start date: " + validStartTime.ToString() +
➥" End date: " + validEndTime.ToString() + "\n" +
➥"Now: " + now.ToString());

            Debug.WriteLine(string.Format("Now is greater than start: {0}",
➥now > validStartTime));
            Debug.WriteLine(string.Format("Now is less than end: {0}",
➥now < validEndTime));
            // Make sure that "now" is in between the
            // start and end dates of the license.
            return (now > validStartTime && now < validEndTime &&➥
key.StartsWith(string.Format("{0} is a licensed component.",type.FullName)));
        }
        return false;
    }

    public override License GetLicense(LicenseContext context, Type type,
➥object instance, bool allowExceptions)
    {
        TimeBombLicense lic = null;

        Debug.Assert(context != null, "No context provided!");
        if (context != null)
        {
            // Is this control in runtime mode?
            if (context.UsageMode == LicenseUsageMode.Runtime)
            {
                // In runtime mode, retrieve the stored
                // license key from the context.
                string key = context.GetSavedLicenseKey(type, null);
```

LISTING B.44 Continued

```
                //Check if the stored license key is null
                //and call IsKeyValid to make sure the
                //license key is valid
                if (key != null && IsKeyValid(key, type))
                {
                    //If the key is valid, create a new license
                    lic = new TimeBombLicense(this, key);
                }
            }

            //if we're in design mode or
            //a suitable license key wasn't found in
            //the runtime context,
            //attempt to look for a .LIC file
            if (lic == null)
            {
(... Code to find the license file . . .)
                Debug.WriteLine("Path of license file: " + licenseFile);

                // Make sure the .LIC file exists.
                if (File.Exists(licenseFile))
                {
                    // Read the first line of the file
                    Stream licStream = new FileStream(licenseFile,
➥FileMode.Open, FileAccess.Read, FileShare.Read);
                    StreamReader sr = new StreamReader(licStream);
                    string s = sr.ReadLine();
                    sr.Close();

                    Debug.WriteLine("Contents of license file: " + s);

                    // Check to see if the key is valid
                    if (IsKeyValid(s, type))
                    {
                        lic = new TimeBombLicense(this, s);
                    }
                }

                //If we managed to create a license, put it into the context.
                if (lic != null)
                {
                    context.SetSavedLicenseKey(type, lic.LicenseKey);
                }
            }

        }
        return lic;
    }
```

An attribute has been added to specify the **LicenseProvider** as TimeBombLicenseProvider. The LicenseManager is included in the class that inherits from **License**. Here, TimeBombLicense inherits from **License**. A partial listing of this code is shown in Listing B.45.

LISTING B.45 Custom License Class

```
public class TimeBombLicense : License
{
    private TimeBombLicenseProvider owner;
    private string key;
    private DateTime validStartTime;
    private DateTime validEndTime;

    public TimeBombLicense(TimeBombLicenseProvider owner, string key)
    {
        this.owner = owner;
        this.key = key;
        int startIndex = key.IndexOf(',') + 1;
        int endIndex = key.IndexOf(',', startIndex) + 1;
        this.validStartTime = new DateTime(Convert.ToInt64(key.Substring
➥(startIndex, endIndex - startIndex - 1)));
        this.validEndTime = new DateTime(Int64.Parse
➥(key.Substring(endIndex)));
    }
. . .
```

System.ComponentModel.TypeDescriptor

The two classes **TypeDescriptor** and **TypeConverter** allow for a flexible conversion scheme between types. To take advantage of this conversion, add an attribute to your class to indicate that a converter is available. It looks something like this:

```
[TypeConverter(typeof(ComplexConverter))]
public class Complex
{
```

Then you need to implement the converter. To implement a converter, you derive a class from **TypeConverter** and implement the required virtual methods. As a minimum, you need to implement the **CanConvertFrom**, **ConvertFrom**, and **ConvertTo** methods. The implementation looks like Listing B.46 (typeconverter.cs).

LISTING B.46 Custom Type Converter

```
public class ComplexConverter : TypeConverter
{
    // CanConvertFrom of TypeConverter
    public override bool CanConvertFrom(ITypeDescriptorContext context,
                                        Type st)
    {
        if (st == typeof(string))
        {
            return true;
        }
        return base.CanConvertFrom(context, st);
    }
    // ConvertFrom of TypeConverter.
    public override object ConvertFrom(ITypeDescriptorContext context,
                                       CultureInfo culture, object value)
    {
        if (value is string)
        {
            string[] v = ((string)value).Split(new char[] {','});
            return new Complex(double.Parse(v[0]), double.Parse(v[1]));
        }
        return base.ConvertFrom(context, culture, value);
    }

    // ConvertTo of TypeConverter.
    public override object ConvertTo(ITypeDescriptorContext context,
                                     CultureInfo culture, object value,
                                     Type destinationType)
    {
        if (destinationType == typeof(string))
        {
            return ((Complex)value).Real + "," + (Complex)value).Imaginary;
        }
        return base.ConvertTo(context, culture, value, destinationType);
    }
}
```

Listing B.47 provides an example of using the conversion methods. Typically, these conversion methods are called from controls to convert from a sting in the property page of the IDE to a specific type that the component requires.

LISTING B.47 Type Conversion Using Class Derived from **TypeConverter**

```
Complex c = (Complex)TypeDescriptor.GetConverter(typeof(Complex)).
➥ConvertFromString("1.0,2.0");
string ds = (string)TypeDescriptor.GetConverter(c).ConvertToString(c);
Console.WriteLine("{0},{1} <-> {2}", c.Real, c.Imaginary, ds);
```

System.Configuration

System.Configuration is a namespace that contains classes for reading and manipulating configuration files. Listing B.48 (configuration.exe.config) shows a sample configuration file.

LISTING B.48 Application Configuration File

```
<configuration>
    <appSettings>
        <add key="Application Name" value="MyApplication" />
        <add key="Application Size" value="10X10" />
        <add key="Application Position" value="Middle" />
        <add key="Application Duration" value="Infinite" />
    </appSettings>
</configuration>
```

The code in Listing B.49 retrieves the configuration settings (configuration.cs) from the configuration file in Listing B.48.

LISTING B.49 Reading an Application Configuration File

```
public class ConfigurationMain
{
    static void Main(string [] args)
    {
        NameValueCollection nv = ConfigurationSettings.AppSettings;
        Console.WriteLine("Count: {0}", nv.Count);
        foreach(string s in nv)
        {
            Console.WriteLine("Key: {0} Value: {1}", s, nv[s]);
        }
    }
}
```

The output for Listing B.49 is shown in Listing B.50.

LISTING B.50 Reading an Application Configuration File

```
Count: 4
Key: Application Name Value: MyApplication
Key: Application Size Value: 10X10
Key: Application Position Value: Middle
Key: Application Duration Value: Infinite
```

System.Data

The **System.Data** namespace covers the classes and support for addresses' database engines.

You can see a specific example of using some of these classes in Chapter 19, "Debugging .NET Applications," in the section "Validating Database Input and the ErrorProvider."

System.Diagnostics

The **Systems.Diagnostics** namespace provides classes and support for interaction with a debugger. This support can prove invaluable in diagnosing many problems or bugs in an application.

You can find many examples of using these classes in Chapter 19 and in the previous section on `System.Collections.ReadOnlyCollectionBase` (enumerating the processes running on the system).

System.Drawing

This namespace provides classes and support for construction and display of arbitrary graphical objects.

A few examples of using classes in this namespace can be found in the `ImageProcessing` application in Appendix A, "C# Basics."

You can also find a simple example in the `Scribble` directory. You create two cached variables:

```
private Graphics graphics = null;
private Point lastPoint;
```

When you click on a mouse button, the `OnMouseDown` event handler is called, the **Graphics** object is created, and the current point is saved.

```
graphics = CreateGraphics();
lastPoint = new Point(e.X, e.Y);
```

When the mouse button is released, the **Graphics** object is destroyed.

```
graphics.Dispose();
graphics = null;
```

The OnMouseMove handler is called and a line is drawn between the last **Point** and the current **Point**. (Look at the application in the Scribble directory.) Listing B.51 shows drawing a line with each mouse movement.

LISTING B.51 Marking a Mouse Click

```
if(graphics != null)
{
    Point currentPoint = new Point(e.X, e.Y);
    graphics.DrawLine(new Pen(Color.Red), lastPoint, currentPoint);
    lastPoint = currentPoint;
}
```

System.Drawing.Drawing2D

The **System.Drawing.Drawing2D** namespace provides classes and support for two-dimensional drawing.

To demonstrate some of the capabilities in **System.Drawing.Drawing2D**, a simple application has been put together that connects points that the user inputs and allows the user to rotate the resulting image. This sample is in the Polygon directory.

Every time a mouse is clicked on the canvas, a point is drawn. (Look at the solution in the Polygon directory.) Listing B.52 shows what happens on a mouse click event.

LISTING B.52 Marking a Mouse Click

```
Graphics dc = CreateGraphics();
if(fill)
{
    fill = false;
    dc.Clear(Color.White);
    points.Clear();
}
dc.FillEllipse(Brushes.Red,
               e.X - 5, e.Y - 5,
               10, 10);
dc.DrawEllipse(new Pen(Color.Black),
               e.X - 5, e.Y - 5,
               10,10);
points.Add(new PointF(e.X, e.Y));
dc.Dispose();
```

When the user presses the C key, the points are connected. Listing B.53 shows how to connect the points.

LISTING B.53 Connecting the Points

```
Graphics dc = CreateGraphics();
dc.SmoothingMode = SmoothingMode.HighQuality;
// Build a points array
Point [] pa = new Point [points.Count + 1];
byte [] pt = new Byte [points.Count + 1];
int index = 0;
foreach(PointF p in points)
{
    pa[index] = new Point((int)p.X, (int)p.Y);
    pt[index] = (byte)PathPointType.Line;
    index++;
}
pt[0] |= (byte)PathPointType.Start;
pt[index] = (byte)PathPointType.CloseSubpath |
            (byte)PathPointType.Line;
pa[index] = pa[0];
// Build a drawing Pen
Pen pen = new Pen(Color.Red, 10);
pen.StartCap = LineCap.Round;
pen.EndCap = LineCap.Round;
pen.LineJoin = LineJoin.Round;
// Create a GraphicsPath
GraphicsPath gp = new GraphicsPath(pa, pt);
// Draw the path
dc.DrawPath(pen, gp);
// Free up the resources used
pen.Dispose();
gp.Dispose();
dc.Dispose();
fill = true;
```

When the user presses the R key, the image is rotated by 10 degrees around the center of the image. Listing B.54 shows how to use the Matrix class in `System.Drawing.Drawing2D` to rotate the drawing.

LISTING B.54 Rotating the Drawing

```
Graphics dc = CreateGraphics();
dc.SmoothingMode = SmoothingMode.HighQuality;
// Clear the canvas
dc.Clear(Color.White);
// Try to get the dimensions of the drawing surface
RectangleF bounds = dc.VisibleClipBounds;
// Find the center of the canvas
PointF point = new PointF(bounds.Location.X + bounds.Width/2.0F,
                          bounds.Location.Y + bounds.Height/2.0F);
// Create a transformation matrix
Matrix m = new Matrix();
m.RotateAt(10, point);
```

LISTING B.54 Continued

```
// Copy the points
Point [] pa = new Point [points.Count + 1];
byte [] pt = new Byte [points.Count + 1];
int index = 0;
foreach(PointF p in points)
{
    pa[index] = new Point((int)p.X, (int)p.Y);
    pt[index] = (byte)PathPointType.Line;
    index++;
}
pt[0] |= (byte)PathPointType.Start;
pt[index] = (byte)PathPointType.CloseSubpath |
            (byte)PathPointType.Line;
pa[index] = pa[0];

// Create a Pen
Pen pen = new Pen(Color.Red, 10);
pen.StartCap = LineCap.Round;
pen.EndCap = LineCap.Round;
pen.LineJoin = LineJoin.Round;

// Create a GraphicsPath
GraphicsPath gp = new GraphicsPath(pa, pt);
// Transform the points based on the matrix
gp.Transform(m);
// Draw the polygon
dc.DrawPath(pen, gp);
// Retrieve the points and copy them back
// In case there is another rotate command
PointF [] pathPoints = gp.PathPoints;
points.Clear();
foreach(PointF p in pathPoints)
{
    points.Add(p);
}
// Return resources.
pen.Dispose();
gp.Dispose();
dc.Dispose();
```

`OnPaint` has not been overridden, so a refresh or anything that causes the image to be redrawn clears the image.

System.IO

To demonstrate some of the classes available in the **`System.IO`** namespace, a `Directory` application was built in the `Directory` directory. By recursing through the directory structure, you can make use of the **Directory**, **File**, **FileInfo**, and **DirectoryInfo** classes. (This sample application is available in the `Directory` directory.) Listing B.55 shows a code snippet that initializes a tree control with drive and directory information.

LISTING B.55 Filling the `TreeControl` with File, Directory, and Drive Information

```
private void InitializeTreeControl()
{
// Initialize TreeControl.
// Populate the TreeView with data.
// First add the root node.
rootNode = new TreeNode("My Computer", (int)ImageListTypes.Computer,
(int)ImageListTypes.Computer);
directoryTree.Nodes.Add(rootNode);
TreeNodeCollection driveCollection =  rootNode.Nodes;
// Get a list of logical drives.
string [] driveNames = Directory.GetLogicalDrives();
foreach (string s in driveNames)
{
    ImageListTypes imageIndex = ImageListTypes.Computer;
    ImageListTypes selectedIndex = ImageListTypes.Computer;
    DriveType dt = (DriveType)NativeMethods.GetDriveTypeW(s);
    if (dt == DriveType.Removable)
    {
...
    }
    else
{
...
        // For each logical drive find the
        // directories and files
        PopulateTreeNode(s, driveNode.Nodes);
    }
...
}
```

Notice that it was necessary to drop down to P/Invoke to get the drive type. There doesn't seem to be a class or method to retrieve this information.

Next, the tree is populated on the level beneath. First, you get the names of the files using **Directory.GetFiles(path)**, and then you get the names of the directories using **Directory.GetDirectories(path)**. Listing B.56 shows how this is done.

LISTING B.56 Filling the Subnodes of the Tree with File and Directory Information

```
private int PopulateTreeNode(string path, TreeNodeCollection nodeCollection)
{
    try
    {
```

LISTING B.56 Continued

```
        string [] fileNames = Directory.GetFiles(path);
        foreach (string s in fileNames)
        {
            TreeNode fileNode = new TreeNode(s.Substring
➥(s.LastIndexOf(@"\")+1),
                                            (int)ImageListTypes.File,
                                            (int)ImageListTypes.File);
            fileNode.Tag = s;
            nodeCollection.Add(fileNode);
        }
        string [] dirNames = Directory.GetDirectories(path);
        foreach (string s in dirNames)
        {
            TreeNode dirNode;
            string dir = s.Substring(s.LastIndexOf(@"\")+1);
            if(dir.Equals("RECYCLER"))
                dirNode = new TreeNode(dir, (int)ImageListTypes.Recycle,
                                            (int)ImageListTypes.Recycle);
            else
                dirNode = new TreeNode(dir, (int)ImageListTypes.FolderClosed,
                                            (int)ImageListTypes.FolderOpen);
            dirNode.Tag = s;
            nodeCollection.Add(dirNode);
        }
    }
    catch(Exception e)
    {
        Debug.WriteLine(e);
        return 1;
    }
    return 0;
}
```

System.Messaging

The **System.Messaging** namespace provides classes and support for interaction with the Microsoft Message Queue (MSMQ). Many classes, structures, and enumerations are part of this namespace. The primary class that interacts with MSMQ is the **MessageQueue** class.

The **MessageQueue** class provides a compact and easy-to-use interface to Microsoft Message Queues (MSMQ). Message Queues provide a reliable means to send messages between two processes. If the receiving end is not available, then the message is stored for later retrieval.

A simple example has been put together that sends a message (`messagesend.cs`) and receives a message (`messagereceive.cs`). For this sample to work, a public queue "myQueue" needs to be added to the message queue. The functionality exists in the **`MessageQueue`** class to create a message. Potentially you could check to see if the message queue exists, and if it does not, you could create it before sending a message. Listing B.57 shows a simple example of opening an existing message queue and sending a message to it. Notice that this is completely asynchronous and returns immediately after the message is sent.

LISTING B.57 Sending a Message with **`MessageQueue`**

```
public class MessageQueueSend
{
    static void Main(string [] args)
    {
        string message = "Hello!!!";
        if(args.Length > 0)
            message = args[0];
        // Create a new instance of the class.
        MessageQueueSend myNewQueue = new MessageQueueSend();
        // Send a message to a queue.
        myNewQueue.SendMessage(message);
        return;
    }
    //**************************************************
    // Sends a message to a queue.
    //**************************************************
    public void SendMessage(string message)
    {
        string queueName = ".\\myQueue";
        if(MessageQueue.Exists(queueName))
        {
            // Connect to a queue on the local computer.
            MessageQueue myQueue = new MessageQueue();
            // Send a message to the queue.
            if (myQueue.Transactional == true)
            {
                Console.WriteLine("Sending transactional message");
                myQueue.Send("Hello!!!", new MessageQueueTransaction());
            }
            else
            {
                Console.WriteLine("Sending message");
                myQueue.Send("Hello!!!");
            }
        }
        else
```

LISTING B.57 Continued

```
        {
            Console.WriteLine("{0} does not exists.", queueName);
            MessageQueue [] mqa = MessageQueue.GetPublicQueues();
            foreach(MessageQueue m in mqa)
            {
                Console.WriteLine("Public: {0}", m.QueueName);
            }
            mqa = MessageQueue.GetPrivateQueuesByMachine(".");
            foreach(MessageQueue m in mqa)
            {
                Console.WriteLine("Private: {0}", m.QueueName);
            }
        }
        return;
    }
}
```

Listing B.58 shows how to receive a message sent using the code in Listing B.57 (`messagereceive.cs`).

LISTING B.58 Receiving a Message with **MessageQueue**

```
public class MessageQueueReceive
{
    static void Main(string [] args)
    {
        // Create a new instance of the class.
        MessageQueueReceive q = new MessageQueueReceive();
        // Receive a message from a queue.
        q.ReceiveMessage();
        return;
    }

    //*************************************************
    // Receives a message containing an Order.
    //*************************************************
    public void ReceiveMessage()
    {
        // Connect to a queue on the local computer.
        MessageQueue myQueue = new MessageQueue(".\\myQueue");
        // Set the formatter to indicate the body contains an Order.
        myQueue.Formatter = new XmlMessageFormatter(new string[]
➥{"System.String"});
        try
        {
            // Receive and format the message.
            // Wait 5 seconds for a message to arrive.
            Message myMessage =   myQueue.Receive(new TimeSpan(0,0,5));
```

LISTING B.58 Continued

```
            string messageText = (string)myMessage.Body;
            // Display message information.
            Console.WriteLine("Message received: " + messageText);
        }
        catch (MessageQueueException e)
        {
            // Handle no message arriving in the queue.
            if (e.MessageQueueErrorCode == MessageQueueErrorCode.IOTimeout)
            {
                Console.WriteLine("No message arrived in the queue.");
            }
        }
        // Handle invalid serialization format.
        catch (InvalidOperationException e)
        {
            Console.WriteLine(e.Message);
        }
        return;
    }
}
```


System.Text

The `System.Text` namespace contains classes that deal with converting from one character encoding to another. The input is assumed primarily to be Unicode. The output varies with the encoding class that is selected. Listing B.59 shows an example of using the UTF8 encoding class (`encoding.cs`).

LISTING B.59 Using UTF8 Encoding

```
byte [] encoded;
UTF8Encoding encoding = new UTF8Encoding();
Console.WriteLine("CodePage: {0}", encoding.CodePage);
Console.WriteLine("EncodingName: {0}", encoding.EncodingName);
Console.WriteLine("WindowsCodePage: {0}", encoding.WindowsCodePage);
encoded = encoding.GetBytes(japanese);
Console.WriteLine("Encoded Japanese: {0} <-> {1}",
                  japanese.Length, encoded.Length);
encoded = encoding.GetBytes(chinese);
Console.WriteLine("Encoded Chinese: {0} <-> {1}",
                  chinese.Length, encoded.Length);
encoded = encoding.GetBytes(english);
Console.WriteLine("Encoded English: {0} <-> {1}",
                  english.Length, encoded.Length);
```

This sample contains three strings: one Japanese, one Chinese, and one English. They are all stored as a .NET **string**. The UTF8 encoder takes these strings in and outputs a sequence of bytes corresponding to the UTF8 representation of these strings. Listing B.60 shows the output of Listing B.59.

LISTING B.60 UTF8 Encoding Output

```
CodePage: 65001
EncodingName: Unicode (UTF-8)
WindowsCodePage: 1200
Encoded Japanese: 7 <-> 21
Encoded Chinese: 4 <-> 12
Encoded English: 12 <-> 12
```

What was 7 Japanese characters (14 bytes) turned into 21 UTF-8 bytes? What was 4 Chinese characters (8 bytes) turned into 12 UTF-8 bytes? And what was 12 English characters (24 bytes) turned into 12 UTF-8 bytes? Clearly, for Japanese and Chinese, you cannot assume that just two bytes (16-bits) need to represent a character in UTF8. For English, the encoding actually decreased the size of the required bytes by exactly one-half.

System.Text.RegularExpressions

The **RegularExpressions** class (and the associated support classes) in .NET has taken a great stride forward in providing additional ease of use and functionality to traditional regular expression processing. Listing B.61 shows how to use one regular expression to split apart the components of a file path (`regex.cs`).

LISTING B.61 Regular Expressions and a File Path

```
public class RegexMain
{
    public static void Main(String[] args)
    {
        Regex pathregex = new Regex(@"(?<drive>[^:]:\\)?
➥((?<dir>[^\\]+)\\)*
➥(?<file>((?<base>[^.]+)[.]?(?<ext>.*)))");
        string s = @"c:\a\b\c\d\e.cs";

        if ( args.Length > 0 )
        {
            s = args[0];
        }

        Match mc = pathregex.Match(s);
```

LISTING B.61 Continued

```
        if ( mc.Success )
        {
            Console.WriteLine("Success in parsing \"{0}\" !!", s);
            Console.WriteLine("Drive: " + mc.Groups["drive"].Value);
            CaptureCollection cc = mc.Groups["dir"].Captures;
            // Print number of captures in this group.
            Console.WriteLine("Directories: {0}", cc.Count);
            // Loop through each capture in group.
            for (int i = 0; i < cc.Count; i++)
            {
                // Print capture and position.
                Console.WriteLine("{0} starts at character {1}",
                                  cc[i], cc[i].Index);
            }
            Console.WriteLine("File: " + mc.Groups["file"].Value);
            Console.WriteLine("Base: " + mc.Groups["base"].Value);
            Console.WriteLine("Extension: " + mc.Groups["ext"].Value);
        }
        else
        {
            Console.WriteLine(s + " is not a valid path address");
        }
    }
}
```

Listing B.62 shows the output from the code in Listing B.61.

LISTING B.62 Output from File Path Parsing Using Regular Expressions

```
Success in parsing "c:\a\b\c\d\e.cs" !!
Drive: c:\
Directories: 4
a starts at character 3
b starts at character 5
c starts at character 7
d starts at character 9
File: e.cs
Base: e
Extension: cs
```

System.Timers

Timers are a great addition to the library. Using **Events**, you can add a timer to a Console application. Listing B.63 shows how to implement a timer (`timer.cs`).

LISTING B.63 Timers Example

```
public class TimerMain
{
    private static long lastTickCount = 0;
    public static void OnElapsedEvent(object source, ElapsedEventArgs e)
    {
        if(lastTickCount == 0)
        {
            lastTickCount = Environment.TickCount;
            Console.WriteLine("Hello!!");
        }
        else
        {
            long currentTickCount = Environment.TickCount;
            Console.WriteLine("Hello!! {0}", currentTickCount - lastTickCount);
            lastTickCount = currentTickCount;
        }
    }
    static void Main(string [] args)
    {
        Timer timer = new Timer();
        timer.Elapsed+=new ElapsedEventHandler(OnElapsedEvent);
        // Set the Interval to 1 second.
        timer.Interval = 1000;
        timer.Enabled = true;

        Console.WriteLine("Press <enter> to quit the sample.");
        Console.ReadLine();
    }
}
```

System.Web

The **System.Web** namespace has many classes. Embedded namespaces contain yet more classes. The following demonstrates a simple application that shows the processes running on the Web server. This application does not show functionality that could not be achieved with start ASP, but it does offer a new model for developing software for the Web. Hopefully, this sample will pique your curiosity and you will search more in-depth sources to get a feel for just how extensive the Web services in the .NET Framework are.

This sample took about 10 minutes to write. The process involved starting up Visual Studio .NET and opening a new Web application project. Then a Table control was added and resized, and code was added code in Page_Load to initialize the data. Listing B.64 shows what the code behind the ASP.NET page looks like to implement a process viewer on a Web page.

LISTING B.64 Web-Based Process List

```
public class WebProcessForm : System.Web.UI.Page
{
    protected System.Web.UI.WebControls.Table ProcessTable;

    private void Page_Load(object sender, System.EventArgs e)
    {
        // Generate rows and cells.
        TableRow r = new TableRow();
        // Process ID
        TableCell c = new TableCell();
        c.Controls.Add(new LiteralControl("Process ID"));
        r.Cells.Add(c);
...
        Process [] pa = Process.GetProcesses();
        foreach(Process p in pa)
        {
            ProcessThreadCollection ptc = p.Threads;
            r = new TableRow();
            // Process ID
            c = new TableCell();
            c.HorizontalAlign = HorizontalAlign.Right;
            c.Controls.Add(new LiteralControl(p.Id.ToString()));
            r.Cells.Add(c);
...
```

The ASP.NET (.aspx) page contains the following:

```
<body MS_POSITIONING="GridLayout">
    <form id="Form1" method="post" runat="server">
        <asp:Table id="ProcessTable"
                     style="Z-INDEX: 101; LEFT: 14px;
➥POSITION: absolute; TOP: 20px"
                    runat="server"
                    Width="816px"
                    Height="360px" CellSpacing="10"
                    GridLines="Both">
</asp:Table>
    </form>
</body>
```

To use this Web page, you need to create a virtual directory that points to where you have installed the source for this appendix. All of the files are in the WebProcessViewer directory. After you have created a virtual directory, you can start up the application from Internet Explorer with the following URL:

```
http://localhost/WebProcessViewer/WebProcessForm.aspx
```

System.Windows.Forms

This is the root of most user interfaces (omitting only Web). You will likely be faced with putting together a user interface program after you have been programming for a while in a Windows environment. It has never been easier to generate a user interface.

Many details about a Windows user interface would make complete coverage here problematic. Instead, a sampler application has been put together that uses most of the controls available with Visual Studio .NET. Figure B.1 shows this program running. The complete source for this program is in the `WindowsForm` directory.

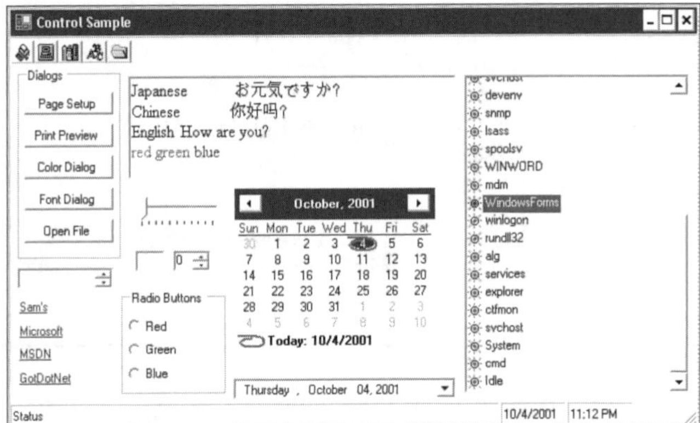

FIGURE B.1
Windows form demonstration.

You can select a date or date range using the calendar, or you can use the combo-like box to make the calendar drop down. The timer updates the time every 30 seconds so you can see how the timer works and how to use the status bar panels. The hyperlinks on the left side of the window start IE and give it a URL that corresponds to the company Web site.

If you double-click on any of the processes in the right portion of the form, you get another form detailing information about that process. This is shown in Figure B.2.

Note

To get the sample `WindowsForm` to run successfully in your environment, you need to modify two variables in `WindowsForm.cs`. Modify the variable, PRINTER, to point to the printer that you are using. In addition, modify the RTFPATH variable to `SampleText.rtf` file, which contains an example of RTF in a few different languages.

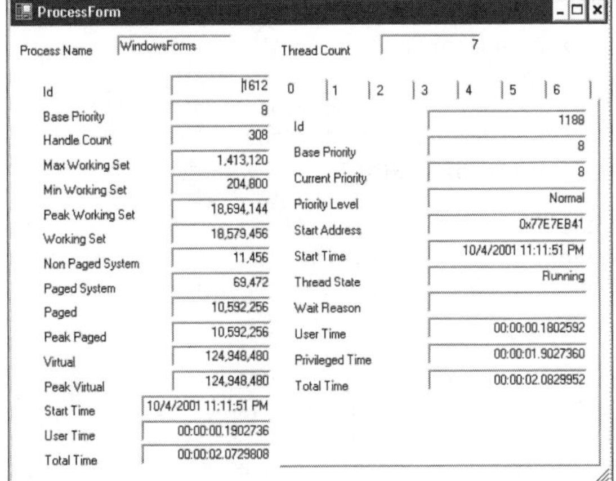

FIGURE B.2
Detailed process information.

You would do well to review the source for this application to see how to use the controls that are illustrated. Now is a good time to review the essential parts of a Windows program.

Every Windows application (using .NET) consists of three sections: declaration, initialization, and containment. Listing B.65 shows the first of these steps.

LISTING B.65 Declaration of Controls

```
public class windowsForm : System.Windows.Forms.Form
{
    private System.Windows.Forms.StatusBar statusBar;
    private System.Windows.Forms.NotifyIcon notifyIcon;
    private System.Windows.Forms.StatusBarPanel statusBarPanel1;
    private System.Windows.Forms.StatusBarPanel statusBarPanel2;
    private System.Windows.Forms.StatusBarPanel statusBarPanel3;
    private System.Windows.Forms.Button pageSetup;
    private System.Windows.Forms.GroupBox dialogGroup;
    private System.Windows.Forms.PageSetupDialog pageSetupDialog;
    private System.Windows.Forms.PrintPreviewDialog printPreviewDialog;
    private System.Windows.Forms.Button printPreview;
    private System.ComponentModel.IContainer components;
    private StreamReader streamToPrint;
...
```

After the variables are declared, you need to instantiate and initialize each one. Listing B.66 shows how this is done.

LISTING B.66 Initializing Controls

```
private void InitializeComponent()
{
    this.components = new System.ComponentModel.Container();
    System.Resources.ResourceManager resources = new
System.Resources.ResourceManager(typeof(windowsForm));
    this.statusBar = new System.Windows.Forms.StatusBar();
    this.statusBarPanel1 = new System.Windows.Forms.StatusBarPanel();
    this.statusBarPanel2 = new System.Windows.Forms.StatusBarPanel();
    this.statusBarPanel3 = new System.Windows.Forms.StatusBarPanel();
    this.notifyIcon = new System.Windows.Forms.NotifyIcon(this.components);
    this.pageSetup = new System.Windows.Forms.Button();
    this.dialogGroup = new System.Windows.Forms.GroupBox();
    this.openFileButton = new System.Windows.Forms.Button();
    this.fontButton = new System.Windows.Forms.Button();
    this.colorButton = new System.Windows.Forms.Button();
    this.printPreview = new System.Windows.Forms.Button();
    this.pageSetupDialog = new System.Windows.Forms.PageSetupDialog();
    this.printPreviewDialog = new System.Windows.Forms.PrintPreviewDialog();
    this.openFileDialog = new System.Windows.Forms.OpenFileDialog();
    this.colorDialog = new System.Windows.Forms.ColorDialog();
    this.fontDialog = new System.Windows.Forms.FontDialog();
    this.timer = new System.Windows.Forms.Timer(this.components);
    this.toolBar = new System.Windows.Forms.ToolBar();
. . .
    //
    // openFileButton
    //
    this.openFileButton.Location = new System.Drawing.Point(7, 144);
    this.openFileButton.Name = "openFileButton";
    this.openFileButton.Size = new System.Drawing.Size(88, 22);
    this.openFileButton.TabIndex = 5;
    this.openFileButton.Text = "Open File";
    this.toolTip.SetToolTip(this.openFileButton, "Open file");
    this.openFileButton.Click += new System.EventHandler(this.OnOpenFile);
    //
    // fontButton
    //
    this.fontButton.Location = new System.Drawing.Point(7, 114);
    this.fontButton.Name = "fontButton";
    this.fontButton.Size = new System.Drawing.Size(88, 21);
    this.fontButton.TabIndex = 4;
    this.fontButton.Text = "Font Dialog";
    this.toolTip.SetToolTip(this.fontButton, "Font dialog");
    this.fontButton.Click += new System.EventHandler(this.OnFontDialog);
    //
    // colorButton
    //
    this.colorButton.Location = new System.Drawing.Point(7, 83);
```

LISTING B.66 Continued

```
    this.colorButton.Name = "colorButton";
    this.colorButton.Size = new System.Drawing.Size(88, 22);
    this.colorButton.TabIndex = 3;
    this.colorButton.Text = "Color Dialog";
    this.toolTip.SetToolTip(this.colorButton, "Color dialog");
    this.colorButton.Click += new System.EventHandler(this.OnColorDialog);
    //
    // printPreview
    //
    this.printPreview.Location = new System.Drawing.Point(7, 53);
    this.printPreview.Name = "printPreview";
    this.printPreview.Size = new System.Drawing.Size(88, 22);
    this.printPreview.TabIndex = 2;
    this.printPreview.Text = "Print Preview";
    this.toolTip.SetToolTip(this.printPreview, "Print preview");
    this.printPreview.Click += new System.EventHandler(this.OnPrintPreview);
. . .
```


Finally, all of the controls are put into a collection as part of the form. This is shown in Listing B.67.

LISTING B.67 Collecting the Controls

```
this.Controls.AddRange(new System.Windows.Forms.Control[] {
      this.listView,
      this.msdnLinkLabel,
      this.gotdotnetLinkLabel,
      this.microsoftLinkLabel,
      this.samsLinkLabel,
      this.groupBox1,
      this.dateTimePicker,
      this.monthCalendar,
      this.domainUpDown,
      this.numericUpDown,
      this.trackBarValue,
      this.trackBar,
      this.richTextBox,
      this.toolBar,
      this.dialogGroup,
      this.statusBar});
```

All of this code is auto-generated as you design your application within the framework of Visual Studio .NET. When it becomes too complicated for Visual Studio .NET to figure out your intentions, the automated design mode is no longer available. That's why it is important to understand what is going on.

Property pages are handled a little differently here. To dynamically add property pages that describe each thread in each process, you must define a separate User Control that encapsulates what each page should look like. Then you just need to construct each page and add it to the tab control. This happens as a pop-up dialog box, so you can do this in the Page_Load method of your dialog box. This function is much like the initialize dialog routine in MFC and C++ and should be familiar to VB programmers. Listing B.68 shows what to do for each page.

LISTING B.68 Initializing TabPage Controls

```
private void ProcessForm_Load(object sender, System.EventArgs e)
{
    int count = 0;
    threadTabControl.SuspendLayout();
    threadTabControl.Controls.Clear();
    threadCount.Text = processThreadCollection.Count.ToString();
    foreach(ProcessThread pt in processThreadCollection)
    {
        ThreadInfoPage tp = new ThreadInfoPage();
        tp.TabName = count.ToString();
        tp.Id = pt.Id;
        tp.BasePriority = pt.BasePriority;
        tp.CurrentPriority = pt.CurrentPriority;
        tp.PriorityLevel = pt.PriorityLevel;
        tp.StartAddress = pt.StartAddress;
        tp.StartTime = pt.StartTime;
        tp.ThreadState = pt.ThreadState;
        if(pt.ThreadState == ThreadState.Wait)
            tp.WaitReason = pt.WaitReason;
        tp.UserProcessorTime = pt.UserProcessorTime;
        tp.TotalProcessorTime = pt.TotalProcessorTime;
        tp.PrivilegedProcessorTime = pt.PrivilegedProcessorTime;
        threadTabControl.Controls.Add(tp);
        count++;
    }
    threadTabControl.ResumeLayout(false);
}
```

You can get more complete details by looking at the source in the `WindowsForms` directory.

System.Xml

The model that the .NET Framework uses to read and parse XML files is somewhat of a mix between the traditional COM approach and the SAX approach. Listing B.69 shows how to read in and process an XML file (`xmlread.cs`). Two sample XML files, book-list.xml and number-list.xml, have also been included.

LISTING B.69 Reading an XML File

```
public class ReadXmlFile
{
    public static void Main(string [] args)
    {
        string document = "booklist.xml";
        ReadXmlFile readXml = new ReadXmlFile();
        if ( args.Length > 0 )
        {
            foreach(string arg in args)
                readXml.Process(arg);
        }
        else
            readXml.Process(document);
    }
    public void Process(String document)
    {
        XmlTextReader reader = null;
        try
        {
            // Load the file with an XmlTextReader.
            Console.WriteLine ("Reading file {0} ...", document);
            reader = new XmlTextReader (document);
            Console.WriteLine ("File {0} read successfully ...", document);
            // Process the supplied XML file.
            Console.WriteLine ("Processing ...");
            Console.WriteLine ();
            FormatXml(reader, document);
        }
        catch (Exception e)
        {
            Console.WriteLine ("Failed to read the file {0}", document);
            Console.WriteLine ("Exception: {0}", e.ToString());
        }

        finally
        {
            Console.WriteLine();
            Console.WriteLine("Processing of the file {0} complete.", document);
            // Finished with XmlTextReader
            if (reader != null)
                reader.Close();
        }
    }

    private static void FormatXml (XmlReader reader, string filename)
    {
        int declarationCount=0;
        int piCount=0;
        int docCount=0;
        int commentCount=0;
```

LISTING B.69 Continued

```
        int elementCount=0;
        int attributeCount=0;
        int textCount=0;
        int whitespaceCount=0;

        while (reader.Read())
        {
            switch (reader.NodeType)
            {
                case XmlNodeType.XmlDeclaration:
                    Format (reader, "XmlDeclaration");
                    declarationCount++;
                    break;
                case XmlNodeType.ProcessingInstruction:
                    Format (reader, "ProcessingInstruction");
                    piCount++;
                    break;
                case XmlNodeType.DocumentType:
                    Format (reader, "DocumentType");
                    docCount++;
                    break;
                case XmlNodeType.Comment:
                    Format (reader, "Comment");
                    commentCount++;
                    break;
...
```

Notice that after the file is read into the **`XmlReader`**, each node type is read in a node at a time. This process happens asynchronously with SAX; however, here it is still token-based processing, but it is synchronous.

`System.Xml.Xsl`

The real way to format XML is with a style sheet (.xsl file). However, style sheets do so much more with XML than parse and format. So many examples are available for using XSL to reformat XML for display (HTML) or transforming it into another XML form. For that reason, this section will show how XSL can be used to process data.

Listing B.70 shows an example of how to transform XML using an XSL style sheet. This listing corresponds to the C# code in the file, `xmltransform.cs`.

LISTING B.70 Transforming an XML File

```
public static void Main(string [] args)
{
    string xmldocument = "booklist.xml";
    string xsldocument = "total-sales.xsl";
```

LISTING B.70 Continued

```
        TransformXmlFile transformXml = new TransformXmlFile();
        if ( args.Length > 1 )
        {
            transformXml.Process(args[0], args[1]);
        }
        else
            transformXml.Process(xmldocument, xsldocument);
    }

    public void Process(string document, string xsl)
    {
        XmlReader reader = null;
        try
        {
            XPathDocument myXPathDocument = new XPathDocument (document);
            XslTransform myXslTransform = new XslTransform();
            myXslTransform.Load(xsl);
            reader = myXslTransform.Transform(myXPathDocument, null);
            while (reader.Read())
            {
                Console.WriteLine(reader.Value);
            }
        }
        catch (Exception e)
        {
            Console.WriteLine ("Exception: {0}", e.ToString());
        }
        finally
        {
            Console.WriteLine();
            Console.WriteLine("Processing of the file {0} complete.", document);
            // Finished with XmlTextReader
            if (reader != null)
                reader.Close();
        }
    }
```

First, the XML document is loaded into the **`XPathDocument`** class and the XSL document is loaded into an instance of **`XslTransform`** class. Then a call is made to the **`XslTransform.Transform`** method to transform the XML document. The Transform call returns an **`XmlReader`** stream, which is used to retrieve the transformed document. These two examples contain only one line, which is a summary of the XML document being transformed. The XSL style sheet `number-total.xsl` works with `number-list.xml` and totals the numbers that are listed as element values in the XML file. The XSL style sheet `total-sales.xsl` works with `booklist.xml` and totals the sales for each book listed in `booklist.xml`.

APPENDIX C

Hosting the Common Language Runtime

IN THIS APPENDIX

The CLR ships with several different hosts. These hosts have taken the CLR and customized its environment so that it is better suited for the application:

- ASP.NET—This host is initialized by an ISAPI filter that starts the CLR and makes sure all of the Web traffic is properly routed to the correct process.
- Internet Explorer—IE needs to recognize a special MIME type so that it can execute managed code controls from HTML pages.
- Shell Executables—When a process containing managed code starts, a small piece of unmanaged code bootstraps the managed code and runs it.

Sometimes you might want to customize the startup and initialization of the CLR for a given process. You might have certain security settings that are required for every process. Your application might require special options for managing multiple users or processes. You might want to build your own custom host for various reasons. This appendix provides you with an overview of the process of getting a custom host for the CLR up and running.

Adding a Custom Host for the Common Language Runtime

The first thing that needs to happen when writing a custom CLR host is to load and initialize the CLR. This happens through a small piece of code that takes a version and other startup information and starts the CLR. This code is known as a "shim" and it is implemented in a file called `mscoree.dll`. On startup, a process will get a pointer to an interface in this shim and through that interface initialize and start the CLR.

To get an interface to this shim, call `CorBindToRuntimeEx`. Listing C.1 shows how to make a call to this function. The complete source that is associated with this listing and the following code snippets are available in the `CustomCLR` directory for this Appendix.

LISTING C.1 Loading the CLR into the Process

```
LPWSTR pszVer = L"v1.0.2204";
LPWSTR pszFlavor = L"wks";
ICorRuntimeHost *pHost = NULL;

//
// CorBindToRuntime is the primary api host
// used to load the CLR into a process.
// In addition to version and "svr" vs "wks"
// concurrent gc, and "no
// domain neutral code ("single domain host")
// is selected.
```

LISTING C.1 Continued

```
HRESULT hr = CorBindToRuntimeEx(
                //version
                pszVer,
                // svr or wks
                pszFlavor,
                //domain-neutral"ness" and gc settings
                STARTUP_LOADER_OPTIMIZATION_SINGLE_DOMAIN |
                    STARTUP_CONCURRENT_GC,
                CLSID_CorRuntimeHost,
                IID_ICorRuntimeHost,
                (void **)&pHost);
```

The end result of calling this function is a pointer to an interface that can control the running of the CLR. Of course, if the HRESULT returned `FAILED` (or `!(SUCCEEDED)`), then the pointer is not modified. If it succeeds, then an `ICorRuntimeHost` interface is returned. This function takes three arguments that control the CLR that is loaded, the version, the CLR type, and the optimization and GC flags.

The version string is a UNICODE (two bytes per character) string specifying the version of the CLR that is to be loaded. It is of the form "vmajor.minor.build". An example of the CLR for the released version would be "v1.0.3705". This is just a suggestion to the loader as to what version should be loaded. To get the version that was actually loaded, call `GetCORVersion`. Null can be passed to `CorBindToRuntimeEx`, in which case the host is delegating the decision about which version to load (normally, this is the latest version of the CLR).

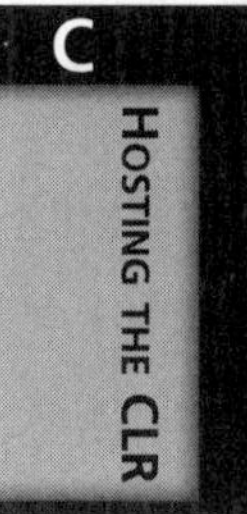

The next argument is also a UNICODE string that can have two values: "wks" or "svr," indicating a workstation or server build respectively. If "wks" is specified, it is a request to use the CLR that is implemented in `mscorwks.dll`. If "svr" is specified, it is a request to use the CLR that is implemented in `mscorsvr.dll`. These two DLLs are loaded from the directory that is specified by the version string or the version that is loaded. If `NULL` is passed as an argument, the workstation build is loaded. The workstation build is optimized for client applications. The server build is tuned to a server type of environment. For example, the server build takes advantage of multiple processors on a single machine and performs garbage collection on a separate processor in parallel with the mainline code. If only one processor exists on the machine, then specifying "svr" doesn't always revert to "wks".

The last flag specifies the mode in which the garbage collector is to run. These modes might or might not be concurrent. The flag STARTUP_CONCURRENT_GC indicates that CLR should perform garbage collection on a background thread rather than on any one of the user threads. If the flag is missing, then the CLR garbage collection is run in series with the user code and on threads that the user code has allocated. This mode of operation is less responsive than the concurrent mode, but the overall performance of the GC is better.

In addition to the GC flags, three optimization flags determine how assemblies are loaded into the application domain. These three flags are as follows:

- STARTUP_LOADER_OPTIMIZATION_SINGLE_DOMAIN—This flag specifies single domain mode. It is assumed that every domain will have a single assembly.
- STARTUP_LOADER_OPTIMIZATION_MULTI_DOMAIN—This flag specifies domain-neutral mode. If multiple assemblies are loaded into a domain, this flag allows for the static and read-only portions of the code to be shared among the assemblies loaded into the GC.
- STARTUP_LOADER_OPTIMIZATION_—This flag specifies that strong named assemblies (shared assemblies) should be loaded domain neutral.

Note that these flags are not flags in the same sense of the term used for enums. Each of these flags is mutually exclusive and cannot be combined.

The last two input arguments specify the CLSID for the class that is implementing the host interface and the IID for the host interface respectively.

When `CorBindToRuntimeEx` completes successfully, you have an `ICorRuntimeHost` interface that has the following methods you can call:

- `Start`—Starts the runtime. In general, it is not necessary to call this method because the CLR is automatically started when the first application domain is created or the first request to run managed code is received.
- `Stop`—Unloads the CLR from the process. In general, it is not necessary to call this method because the CLR is automatically shut down when the process exits. Note that when the CLR is unloaded using `Stop()`, it cannot be reinitialized into the same process.
- `CreateDomain`—Creates an application domain. The caller receives an interface pointer to an instance of **`System.AppDomain`** that can be used to further control the domain. The type of this interface pointer is **`_AppDomain`**. Compare this to the static function to create an application domain in managed space, that is, **`AppDomain.CreateDomain`**.
- `CreateDomainEx`—Extends the functionality of **`CreateDomain`** by allowing callers to pass in an **`IAppDomainSetup`** interface that contains properties used to configure the domain. Compare this to the static function to create an application domain in managed space, that is, **`AppDomain.CreateDomain`**.

- `CreateDomainSetup`—Returns an interface pointer of type **`IAppDomainSetup`**. **`IAppDomainSetup`** contains methods that allow a host to configure various aspects of a domain before it is created. The pointer returned from this method is typically passed to **`CreateDomainEx`**. Compare this function with the **`AppDomainSetup`** class with its associated members and constructors.
- `CreateEvidence`—Returns an interface pointer of type **`IIdentity`**. **`IIdentity`** allows you to create security evidence that is passed to **`CreateDomain(Ex)`**. Compare this method with the implementations of **`IIdentity`** in the **`WindowsIdentity`**, **`PassportIdentity`**, **`GenericIdentity`**, and **`FormsIdentity`**. Also look at the **`Evidence`** class in the **`System.Security.Policy`** namespace.
- `GetConfiguration`—Returns an **`ICorConfiguration`** interface that has the methods to control how the process and **`AppDomain`** interact with a debugger and customize the size of the GC heap and callbacks for thread control and **`AppDomain`** loading events.
- `GetDefaultDomain`—Returns an interface pointer to the default domain for the process. Compare this with the **`AppDomain.CurrentDomain`** property.
- `UnloadDomain`—Unloads the domain. Compare this with the **`AppDomain.Unload`** static method.
- `EnumDomains`—Returns an enumerator that a host can use to enumerate the domains in the process.
- `NextDomain`—Returns the next domain in the enumeration. This method returns `S_FALSE` when the enumeration has no more domains.
- `ResetDomain`—Resets the enumerator back to the beginning of the list.

After you have an **`ICorRuntimeHost`** interface, the CLR has been loaded in this process. You might want to see just what version of the CLR has been loaded. The version string in **`CorBindToRuntimeEx`** was just a suggestion. You can get the version of the CLR that is loaded in your process as follows:

```
wchar_t buffer[128];
DWORD dwBytes;
hr = GetCORVersion(buffer, sizeof(buffer), &dwBytes);
wprintf(L"Version %ls of the CLR loaded...\n", buffer);
```

To start running managed code, you need to get a pointer to an **`AppDomain`**. You can use the methods on the **`ICorRuntimeHost`** to create new **`AppDomain`**s and load and run assemblies into these **`AppDomain`**s. This involves many transitions between managed and unmanaged space. In addition, you need to keep track of the last **`AppDomain`** that unloads because unloading the last **`AppDomain`** also implicitly calls **`Stop`** and unloads the CLR from the process. After the CLR is unloaded from the process, it cannot be reloaded. For those reasons, you typically want to build a small stub assembly that starts and stops the **AppDomain**s to be associated with your process. To get a pointer to the default **AppDomain** for the process, you need to execute code that looks like Listing C.2.

LISTING C.2 Getting a Pointer to the Default **AppDomain**

```
//
// Get a pointer to the default domain in the process.
//
AppDomain *pDefaultDomain = NULL;
IUnknown   *pAppDomainPunk = NULL;
hr = pHost->GetDefaultDomain(&pAppDomainPunk);
hr = pAppDomainPunk->QueryInterface(__uuidof(_AppDomain),
                                    (void**) &pDefaultDomain);
```

These lines of code return an interface to the default **AppDomain** for the process. Listing C.3 shows how to load and run the managed hosting code.

LISTING C.3 Loading and Running the Managed Hosting Code

```
//
// Load the managed portion of our host into the default domain.
//
ICorRun *pMgdHost = NULL;
ObjectHandle *pObjHandle = NULL;

hr = pDefaultDomain->CreateInstance(_bstr_t("MgdHost"),
        bstr_t("ClrHost.MgdHost.HostProcessRequest"),
        &pObjHandle);
if(FAILED(hr))
    return;
printf("Managed hosting code successfully created...\n");

VARIANT v;
VariantInit(&v);
hr = pObjHandle->Unwrap(&v);

hr = v.pdispVal->QueryInterface(__uuidof(ICorRun),
                                (void**) &pMgdHost);
if(FAILED(hr))
    return;
pMgdHost->Run(_bstr_t("DiningPhilosophers"),
              _bstr_t("DiningPhilosophers.exe "));
```

The **CreateInstance** method is looking for an assembly; therefore, that assembly needs to be located so that the **AppDomain** can find it. An **AppDomain** first starts out looking for an assembly by using its base directory. This is also one of the first steps in securing your application. You should put the assembly in the same directory as specified by the **BaseDirectory** or **ApplicationBase** so that the **AppDomain** can find it.

After the host is inside managed code (in the preceding example, you enter managed code by executing the Run method), it must ensure that the **ApplicationBase** and the **ConfigurationFile** properties are set. The **ApplicationBase** is the first place that the **AppDomain** looks for assemblies. The **ConfigurationFile** property is a path to an XML configuration file that specifies settings for assembly versioning and locating types that the application accesses remotely.

If the CLR cannot find a given assembly, it raises an event `AssemblyResolve`. If the assembly for the particular host is in memory (in the case of `Reflection.Emit`) or otherwise hidden, then this event handler resolves and returns an **Assembly**. The simplicity of hooking up to this event handler is shown in Listing C.4.

LISTING C.4 Resolving an **Assembly** Reference

```
private Assembly AssemblyResolveHandler(object sender, ResolveEventArgs e)
{
    // resolve the assembly
}
. . .
ad.AssemblyResolve += new ResolveEventHandler(AssemblyResolveHandler);
```

Another possibly interesting event that can be listened to would be the event that is raised any time an **Assembly** is loaded. Listing C.5 shows hooking up to this event.

LISTING C.5 Loading an **Assembly** Event

```
private void AssemblyLoadHandler(object sender, AssemblyLoadEventArgs e)
{
    Console.WriteLine("Loading: {0}", e.LoadedAssembly.GetName().Name);
    return;
}
. . .
// Hook up a load handler
ad.AssemblyLoad += new AssemblyLoadEventHandler(AssemblyLoadHandler);
```

All of this is customization. You can (and should) add a specific security policy for a custom CLR host, special configuration, and so on. Now that you are in managed code, you can specialize many different settings.

Note

This Appendix briefly showed how you can add a custom host for the CLR. Each of the existing hosts for the CLR follows this same procedure to start up the CLR. This Appendix has shown where it is appropriate to add security and configuration information for a custom host to increase isolation and security. Now you can build your own or at least have a better idea of what is going on when you execute your next managed application. Feel free to modify and enhance the code in the `CustomCLR` directory.

APPENDIX D

The Common Language Runtime as Compared to the Java Virtual Machine

In This Appendix

Don Box once gave a talk titled "Dot Net: How, Why, and Where?" at a DevelopMentor .NET Conference. He commented, "We are moving to a world where there are basically two places [that] code runs: the JVM and the CLR" (`http://technetcast.ddj.com/tnc_play_stream.html?stream_id=604`).

If this is true, then JVM as a platform and Java as language deserve some treatment. This Appendix compares the Common Language Runtime (CLR) and the Java Virtual Machine (JVM). Many of the features and functionality of both Java and the CLR are accessed and used through a language (Java in the case of Java and the languages that support the CLI, in the case of the CLR). For this reason, this Appendix makes some comparative statements about languages on each of the two platforms.

Historical Backdrop of the War of Who Will Manage Your Code

The idea of managing code to increase a programmer's productivity and the robustness of software products has been around for some time now. It is the level of management that has increased with the CLR and the JVM. Going back to the days when you programmed on a limited budget of memory, you had to be constantly aware of the memory cost of your program, which proved to severely limit a programmer's productivity. A scheme was devised in which a programmer had to worry much less about memory because memory was now "virtual" and a programmer could almost assume that it was in limitless supply. With the CLR and the JVM, the programmer not only worries less about memory (it's no longer necessary to free memory), but the CLR and the JVM have taken over many other functions. Functions such as security, I/O, thread management, type safety, and error handling are now either handled by the environment that is managing your code or greatly assisted by that environment. The problem is that these issues are so broad that much room for interpretation exists on how best to manage code. With the advent of the CLR, managed code can now be essentially split into two camps: the JVM and the CLR. The idea of what technology can best manage your code has become arguably one of the most hotly contested technical issues of the later part of the 20th century, and the battle promises to continue for the foreseeable future.

Since the inception of Java in 1996, many programmers have given up control to reap the benefits of a managed environment. Even Visual Basic has a runtime that manages the code that is run to relieve a programmer from worrying about common tasks. The idea of managed code became so appealing that Microsoft entered the Java market with Visual J++. Microsoft incorporated a JVM as part of the operating system so that the browser could correctly run and display Web pages that had Java scripts embedded in them. This was not enough, however. Managed code still had a stigma surrounding it that it was too slow, the management could be better handled by unmanaged code, debugging was difficult, and so forth. Microsoft successfully "optimized" the JVM and Visual J++ specifically for Windows platforms. The problem was that this was in violation of the license agreement that Microsoft had with Sun Microsystems. After a long legal battle, the courts ruled in January 2001 that Microsoft was to be fined $20 million dollars and restricted from more development on an implementation of Java features after version 1.1.4, on which Visual J++ was based. Although this might seem to be a defeat to Microsoft, in the end, it might be Java's undoing. In July 2001, Microsoft announced that both Windows XP and Internet Explorer 6 would not incorporate any form of a JVM.

Note

Sun paradoxically took out a full page ad on August 9, 2001 in the *Wall Street Journal*, voicing disgust that Microsoft omitted the JVM from Windows XP. To quote from the ad, the article encouraged users to do the following:

> Demand that Microsoft include the Java platform in their XP operating system. And that PC vendors like Dell, Compaq, Gateway, IBM, and HP include the Java platform on their systems. And if Microsoft still won't do it, a free copy of the latest Java platform will be available for download at `java.sun.com`. Sure, people will have to take one extra step, but at least they'll have a choice. Which is more than Microsoft is offering.

The fear in Java camps is that users will not take the extra step to download a JVM, and sites that use Java will need to think of an alternative. Most PC users run a Windows OS. If even a percentage of those Windows users opt out of the JVM option, it could really hurt Java. The battle is just beginning to be fought, and at this point, it's unpredictable how it will turn out. What does this have to do with a JVM and CLR comparison?

This is an important issue. Those at Microsoft and Sun both want your code managed within their framework. For software development to move forward, it needs to be managed. Both the JVM and the CLR seem to be good. It would be hard to pick the CLR over a JVM or vice versa strictly on technical grounds.

In a #1 bestseller by Spencer Johnson, M.D. titled *Who Moved My Cheese?*, the author allegorically chronicles the experiences of two mice, Sniff and Scurry, and two "little people," Hem and Haw. The two mice "ignorantly" notice that the cheese is gone and immediately go on to find more cheese. Hem and Haw let their emotions rule their actions, generally feeling depressed and sorry for themselves. Hem and Haw did not start looking for new cheese until it was almost too late. The book teaches many lessons through this analogy, but the one lesson that software developers need to take from this book is to move on when it's necessary. In a way, Microsoft has moved our "cheese." It's important to understand the new world of managed code, right now represented by the CLR and the JVM, and look for the "cheese" in one of those two worlds. By looking at a comparison of the CLR and the JVM, this Appendix sets out to illustrate many of the common problems solved (in different ways) by each. It also points out how one framework solves a particular problem better than the other.

Comparing many of the features of the CLR with those of a JVM serves as a review of the topics covered throughout this book. By looking at the implementation of a particular feature in the JVM, you can see the CLR in a new light.

Java Versus .NET Languages

Note

To do a decent comparison between the CLR and a JVM, it makes sense to install Java. The discussions in this Appendix assume use of Java 1.4 of Java and the associated PDK from Sun (`http://developer.java.sun.com/developer/index.jshtml`).

Look at Listing D.1, which shows the simplest of Java programs.

LISTING D.1 Hello World in Java

```
// To compile and run
// javac -classpath . helloworld.java
// java HelloWorld
// (case is important)
class HelloWorld
{
    public static void main(String[] args)
    {
        System.out.println("Hello World from Java!");
    }
}
```

Compiling this program produces a class file called `HelloWorld.class`. To run the program, type `java HelloWorld`. With Java, you specify a class name to run. Running this program in a Windows command prompt requires that the case of the class be entered exactly as specified in the .java source. Now look at functionally of the same program in C# in Listing D.2.

LISTING D.2 Hello World in C#

```
// csc helloworld.cs
using System;

class HelloWorldMain
{
    static void Main(string [] args)
    {
        Console.WriteLine("Hello World from C#");
    }
}
```

These programs are so similar that it would be impossible to make a decision as to which was better based on this syntax alone. The story does not end here, however. Look at the same program in VB in Listing D.3.

LISTING D.3 Hello World in VB

```
Option Explicit On
Option Strict On

Imports System
'
' vbc helloworld.vb
'
Module HelloWorldVB
    Public Class HelloWorldMain
        Public Shared Sub Main()
        Console.WriteLine("Hello World from VB!")
        End Sub
    End Class
End Module
```

Now look at Listing D.4 for the same thing in JScript.

LISTING D.4 Hello World in JScript

```
// jsc helloworld.js
print ("Hello World from JScript!");
```

Note

JScript deviates from a standalone script file with respect to input and output. For a standalone script file, use `Wscript.Echo` instead of `print`.

Listing D.5 shows a Perl version.

LISTING D.5 Hello World in Perl

```
# plc helloworld.pl
print "Hello World from perl!"
```

To really make things really confusing, look at the code for the same thing in J# in Listing D.6.

LISTING D.6 Hello World in J#

```
package HelloWorld;

// jc helloworld.jsl.
public class HelloWorld
{
    public static void main(String[] args)
    {
        System.out.println("Hello World from J#!");
    }
}
```

The examples could continue to include all of the languages that the .NET Framework supports (or technically that support the .NET Framework); theoretically, the list includes all of the computer languages. For the initial release, approximately 20 languages will have compilers built to generate IL. Microsoft will be shipping at least four—C#, VB, C++, and JScript—with J# likely still in beta when Visual Studio .NET is released to manufacturing. .NET is such an important environment for building language independent applications that it is likely that languages developed in the future will also add support for .NET. Clearly, if your application is developed or will be developed in any other language than Java, then the Java platform, J2EE, is clearly a bad choice.

Java does have an intermediate form that is Java Byte Code (JBC), so theoretically, different languages could generate JBC and then Java could be considered language independent. A compiler from Queensland University Technology takes in Pascal and generates either JBC or MSIL (`http://www2.fit.qut.edu.au/CompSci/PLAS//ComponentPascal/`). Many JBC generators exist, but in the Web article "Is Java Language Neutral?" (`http://www.objectwatch.com/issue_33.htm`), Roger Sessions concludes the following:

Based on this research, I draw the following conclusions:

> 1. If there are any serious commercially supported compilers that generate JBC from non-Java languages, there are very few—probably fewer than 5.
> 2. If there is any commercial usage of non-Java JBC-emitting compilers, it is very limited. It is highly unlikely that more [than] an infinitesimal fraction of the JBC in existence today came from anything other [than] Java.
> 3. If there is any support for language neutrality in the Java runtime, it is very marginal. None of the non-Java JBC-emitting languages [indicates] that they can support the minimum features that I previously identified as necessary for true language neutrality. None, for example, seem to support either cross-language polymorphic method resolution or cross-language exception handling—features that are absolutely critical for true language neutrality.
>
> At best, the Java platform supports not true language neutrality, but rather language replacement. There is a big difference between language neutrality and language replacement.

One could argue that the .NET Framework is not multilingual but multisyntax. After all, it is just syntax that separates the many languages that are supported under .NET, is it not?

A paper by Roger Sessions titled "Java 2 Enterprise Edition (J2EE) Versus the .NET Platform: Two Visions for eBusiness" (`http://www.objectwatch.com/our_position.htm`) gives the following statement indicating that what separates the languages is more than just syntax:

> Retraining is probably the most expensive option. In my experience, there is tremendous overhead associated with retraining traditional programmers to be proficient object-oriented Java programmers. This is borne out by a recent study of the Gartner group, who concluded it costs approximately $60,000 to retrain a COBOL programmer to be a Java programmer. I believe the costs will be similar for a Visual Basic programmer. And at the end of this exercise, you have gained nothing in productivity. You will simply have a programmer who can now write the same code they could have written $60,000 ago, but can now write that code in Java. In many companies, I have seen productivity hurt by the adoption of object-oriented technologies, as work-time often gets squandered in endless and non-productive theoretical discussions about "correct" object-oriented design and analysis.

One of the languages that is syntactically the most different from the others is Perl. Assume for a moment that you need a program to count all of the words in a document. Also assume that you or one of the team members who is working for you is familiar with the syntax of Perl. You or your team member might write word counting program using the Perl code in Listing D.7.

LISTING D.7 Counting Words in Perl

```
use strict;

open(INFILE, $ARGV[0]);

my($WordCount) = 0;
my(%Words);
my($StartTime) = time();
while (<INFILE>)
{
    $_ = lc($_);
    foreach my $Word (split(/[\s\,\.\?\!'""\(\)\;\:]+/))
    {
        $WordCount++;
        $Words{$Word}++;
    }
}
close(INFILE);
```

You can test this script using the Perl interpreter:

```
perl wordcount.pl document.txt
```

When you feel that the script does what it should do, you can bring it easily into the .NET world by compiling it as a library or a standalone executable, like this:

```
plc wordcount.pl
```

or

```
plc -target="library" wordcount.pl
```

The idea is that for such a specialized task—especially if you or your staff has experience using Perl—it is trivial to bring such a task in as a library. Forcing someone to use one language might not be in the best interest of getting a solution in the customers' hands. A similar argument can be made for VJ++ and J#, VB and VB .NET, and so on.

Java Versus C#

You might say that Java is a better language. You might want to train your key programming staff on just one language, and you want it to be the "best" language. If you present it like that, you are in for a religious battle. Programmers and software engineers tend to hold the key tool of their trade, the language, near and dear. Now is a good time to compare several features, showing how they are implemented using Java and a representative language from .NET, C#.

User-Defined Types

Java has two types: primitive types and classes. Primitive types are built into the language. They are types like Boolean, integers, floating-point numbers, and characters. Classes in Java are built and ultimately consist of primitive types. .NET and C# have value types and reference types (to use .NET language). At first glance, value types are synonymous with Java's primitive types. Indeed, value types in .NET include integers, floating-point numbers, and characters (in addition to fixed-point decimal, enum, and Boolean). These entities are called value types because they are passed between methods or functions as values. If a reference is assigned to another reference, changing one of the references changes both. For an example, look at Listing D.8.

LISTING D.8 Assigning References in Java

```
class Complex {
   double real;
   double imag;
}

class ProcessComplex {
   public static void main(String[] args) {
        Complex c = new Complex();
        c.real = 1;
        c.imag = 2;
        Complex d = c;
        System.out.println("Prior to change: " + c.real + "," + c.imag);
        d.real = 30;
        d.imag = 40;
        System.out.println("After change: " + c.real + "," + c.imag);
   }
}
```

This code outputs the following:

```
Prior to change: 1.0,2.0
After change: 30.0,40.0
```

Modifying d also changes c. This is because d is a reference to c. You can port this code to C#, as shown in Listing D.9.

LISTING D.9 Assigning References in C#

```
using System;

namespace ComplexReferenceType
{
    class Complex
    {
        public double real;
        public double imag;
    }
    class ProcessComplex
    {
        public static void Main(String[] args)
        {
            Complex c = new Complex();
            c.real = 1;
            c.imag = 2;
            Console.WriteLine("Prior to change: {0},{1}", c.real, c.imag);
            d.real = 30;
            d.imag = 40;
            Console.WriteLine("After change: {0},{1}", c.real, c.imag);
        }
    }
}
```

This produces virtually the same output as the Java code:

```
Prior to change: 1,2
After change: 30,40
```

C# differs from Java in that you can change the class (reference type) to a struct (value type), and value semantics will be enforced. The Complex class then becomes the following:

```
struct Complex
{
    public double real;
    public double imag;
}
```

Now when you compile and run the C# program, you get this:

```
Prior to change: 1,2
After change: 1,2
```

Therefore, modifying d does not change c. You now have a user-defined value type that acts just like the built-in or primitive values. Having this option available is an advantage for C#.

Java passes instances of the class by reference in method calls. A quick example of Java passing by reference is shown in Listing D.10.

LISTING D.10 Passing by Reference in Java

```
class Complex {
   double real;
   double imag;
}

class ProcessComplex {
   public static void Process(Complex n) {
       System.out.println("Process: " + n.real + "," + n.imag);
       n.real = 10;
       n.imag = 20;
   }
   public static void main(String[] args) {
       Complex c = new Complex();
       c.real = 1;
       c.imag = 2;
       System.out.println("Before Process: " + c.real + "," + c.imag);
       Process(c);
       System.out.println("After Process: " + c.real + "," + c.imag);
   }
}
```

If you were to run this program, you would get the following output:

```
D:\>java ProcessComplex
Before Process: 1.0,2.0
Process: 1.0,2.0
After Process: 10.0,20.0
```

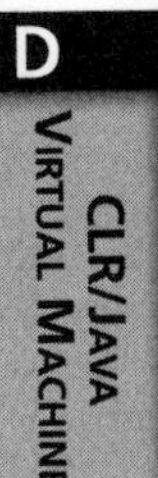

The code in the Process method modifies the passed argument. Because the instance is passed by reference, the changes made to the reference in the method persist after the method call returns.

Moving this Java code to C# yields code as shown in Listing D.11.

LISTING D.11 Passing by Reference in C#

```
using System;

namespace ComplexReferenceType
{
    class Complex
    {
        public double real;
        public double imag;
    }
    class ProcessComplex
    {
        public static void Process(Complex n)
        {
            Console.WriteLine("Process: {0},{1}", n.real, n.imag);
            n.real = 10;
            n.imag = 20;
        }
        public static void Main(String[] args)
        {
            Complex c = new Complex();
            c.real = 1;
            c.imag = 2;
            Console.WriteLine("Before Process: {0},{1}", c.real, c.imag);
            Process(c);
            Console.WriteLine("After Process: {0},{1}", c.real, c.imag);
        }
    }
}
```

If you run this program, you get the following:

```
D:\>complex
Before Process: 1,2
Process: 1,2
After Process: 10,20
```

This output is the same as the Java code. You must be passing the Complex argument by reference because modifying it in the method results in a modified argument upon returning from the method.

Again, if you modify the declaration of `Complex` to be a **`struct`** instead of a **`class`**, you get the following output:

```
D:\>complex
Before Process: 1,2
Process: 1,2
After Process: 1,2
```

.NET is flexible in the way that arguments are passed. By changing the declaration to `struct`, you create a user-defined value type. Java does not have this concept. A back-door exists for value types. If you really want to modify a value in a method, then you can explicitly pass-by-reference with a **`ref`** keyword. An example of using **`ref`** is shown in Listing D.12.

LISTING D.12 Passing a Value Type by Reference in C# Using **`ref`**

```
using System;

namespace ComplexReferenceType
{
    struct Complex
    {
        public double real;
        public double imag;
    }
    class ProcessComplex
    {
        public static void Process(ref Complex n)
        {
            Console.WriteLine("Process: {0},{1}", n.real, n.imag);
            n.real = 10;
            n.imag = 20;
        }
        public static void Main(String[] args)
        {
            Complex c = new Complex();
            c.real = 1;
            c.imag = 2;
            Console.WriteLine("Before Process: {0},{1}", c.real, c.imag);
            Process(ref c);
            Console.WriteLine("After Process: {0},{1}", c.real, c.imag);
        }
    }
}
```

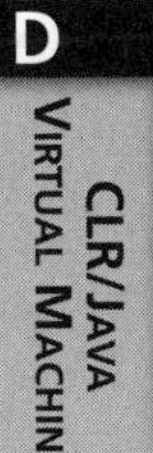

The output is identical to the output from Listing D.11. The argument is explicitly passed by reference so that any modifications to the instance are passed back to the caller.

Exceptions

Java only enforces exceptions that are checked. A *checked* exception is one that is derived from the `Exception` class but not from `RuntimeException`. Listing D.13 shows an example of Java throwing various exceptions.

LISTING D.13 Java Exception Handling

```
import java.lang.Exception;

class UserDefinedException extends Exception
{
    UserDefinedException() { super(); }
    UserDefinedException(String s) { super(s); }
}
class TestException
{
    public static void main(String[] args)
    {
        String s[] = { "divide", "null", "array", "user" };
        for (int i = 0; i < s.length; i++)
        {
            try
            {
                exceptionGenerator(s[i]);
                System.out.println("TestException \"" + s[i] +
                                   "\" didn't throw an exception");
            }
            catch (Exception e)
            {
                System.out.println("TestException \"" + s[i] +
                                   "\" threw a " + e.getClass());
                System.out.println("        with message: " + e.getMessage());
            }
        }
    }
    static int exceptionGenerator(String s) throws UserDefinedException
    {
        try
        {
            if (s.equals("divide"))
            {
                int i = 0;
                return i/i;
            }
            if (s.equals("null"))
            {
                s = null;
                return s.length();
            }
            if (s.equals("array"))
            {
                int [] ia = {1, 2 ,3 ,4};
                return ia[ia.length];
            }
            if (s.equals("user"))
                throw new UserDefinedException("UserDefinedException thrown
➥from exceptionGenerator");
```

LISTING D.13 Continued

```
            return 0;
        }
        finally
        {
            System.out.println("[exceptionGenerator(\"" + s + "\") done]");
        }
    }
}
```

If you omit the throws UserDefinedException clause from the exceptionGenerator function definition, then you get the following compile-time error:

```
D:\>javac -classpath . exception.java
exception.java:47: unreported exception UserDefinedException;
➥must be caught or declared to be thrown
    throw new UserDefinedException("UserDefinedException thrown
➥from exceptionGenerator");
```

C# supports exceptions, but it does not enforce them. The enforcement of exceptions in .NET is left up to the language. For instance, if the code in Listing D.13 is compiled with J# and the throws clause is left out, the following error is generated:

```
exception.jsl(47,5) : error J#1237: Exception 'UserDefinedException' is not
➥caught and does not appear in throws clause º8.4.4
```

If you compile and run the Java code in Listing D.13, you get the output shown in Listing D.14.

LISTING D.14 Java Exception Handling Output

```
D:\>java TestException
[exceptionGenerator("divide") done]
TestException "divide" threw a class java.lang.ArithmeticException
        with message: / by zero
[exceptionGenerator("null") done]
TestException "null" threw a class java.lang.NullPointerException
        with message: null
[exceptionGenerator("array") done]
TestException "array" threw a class java.lang.ArrayIndexOutOfBoundsException
        with message: null
[exceptionGenerator("user") done]
TestException "user" threw a class UserDefinedException
        with message: UserDefinedException thrown from exceptionGenerator
```

If the code in Listing D.13 is compiled with J#, you get the output in Listing D.15.

LISTING D.15 J# Exception Handling Output

```
D:\>exception
[exceptionGenerator("divide") done]
TestException "divide" threw a class java.lang.ArithmeticException
        with message: / by zero
[exceptionGenerator("null") done]
TestException "null" threw a class java.lang.NullPointerException
        with message: Value null was found where an instance of an object
➥was required.
[exceptionGenerator("array") done]
TestException "array" threw a class java.lang.ArrayIndexOutOfBoundsException
        with message: Exception of type System.IndexOutOfRangeException
➥was thrown.
[exceptionGenerator("user") done]
TestException "user" threw a class UserDefinedException
        with message: UserDefinedException thrown from exceptionGenerator
```

Converting Listing D.13 to C#, compiling, and running the code gives you the output shown in Listing D.16.

LISTING D.16 C# Exception Handling Output

```
D:\>exception
[exceptionGenerator("divide") done]
TestException "divide" threw a System.DivideByZeroException
        with message: Attempted to divide by zero.
[exceptionGenerator("") done]
TestException "null" threw a System.NullReferenceException
        with message: Value null was found where an instance of an object
➥was required.
[exceptionGenerator("array") done]
TestException "array" threw a System.IndexOutOfRangeException
        with message: Exception of type System.IndexOutOfRangeException
➥was thrown.
[exceptionGenerator("user") done]
TestException "user" threw a Exceptions.UserDefinedException
        with message: UserDefinedException thrown from exceptionGenerator
```

Notice that if the message for the Java code is `null`, it is replaced by a message that is common between C# and J# in the J# code. Full source for each of these samples is in `Exception.java`, `Exception.jsl`, and `Exception.cs` respectively.

Properties

Both Java and C# support properties. Java supports properties through a common get/set idiom. Listing D.17 shows an implementation of a complex number class that has two properties, each of which is read/write.

LISTING D.17 Java Properties

```
class Complex {
    private double real;
    private double imag;
    public Complex()
    {
        this.real = 0;
        this.imag = 0;
    }
    public Complex(double real, double imag)
    {
        this.real = real;
        this.imag = imag;
    }
    public double getReal()
    {
        return real;
    }
    public void setReal(double real)
    {
        this.real = real;
    }
    public double getImag()
    {
        return imag;
    }
    public void setImag(double imag)
    {
        this.imag = imag;
    }
    public String toString()
    {
        return "(" + real + "," + imag + ")";
    }
}

class ComplexPropertyMain
{
     public static void main(String[] args)
    {
        Complex c = new Complex(1,2);
        System.out.println("Complex number:     " + c);
        System.out.println("        real:       " + c.getReal());
        System.out.println("        imaginary:  " + c.getImag());
    }
}
```

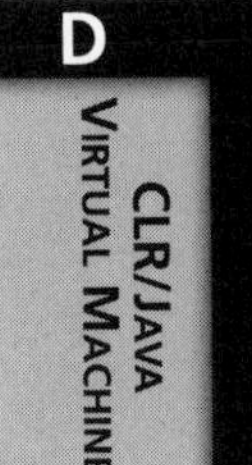

Little distinguishes a property from a method in this example, but this is how a property is defined in Java. This class will be recognized as having the properties `Real` and `Imag`

rather than having four methods that have similar semantics. J# compiles the code in Listing D.17 directly without changes. To illustrate properties in .NET, the code in Listing D.17 has been converted to the C# code in Listing D.18.

LISTING D.18 C# Properties

```
using System;

class Complex {
    private double real;
    private double imag;
    public Complex()
    {
        this.real = 0;
        this.imag = 0;
    }
    public Complex(double real, double imag)
    {
        this.real = real;
        this.imag = imag;
    }
    public double Real
    {
        get
        {
            return real;
        }
        set
        {
            real = value;
        }
    }
    public double Imag
    {
        get
        {
            return imag;
        }
        set
        {
            imag = value;
        }
    }
    public override string ToString()
    {
        return "(" + real + "," + imag + ")";
    }
}
```

LISTING D.18 Continued

```
class ComplexPropertyMain
{
    public static void Main(String[] args)
    {
        Complex c = new Complex(1,2);
        Console.WriteLine("Complex number:    " + c);
        Console.WriteLine("       real:       " + c.Real);
        Console.WriteLine("       imaginary:  " + c.Imag);
    }
}
```

Unlike Java, the property is accessed like a public member variable (that is, `c.Real` and `c.Imag`). In addition, look at the C# generated assembly with `ILDasm`, as shown in Figure D.1.

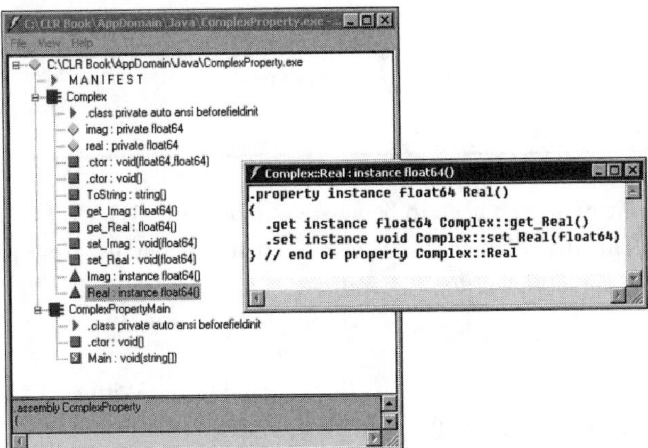

FIGURE D.1
C# generated properties.

Notice that a specific property instruction exists in IL for properties. Although having support of properties at the IL level might suggest that all languages support properties, this is not true. Support for properties is optional within the .NET Framework. C# supports properties.

Events

Java supports the idea of event notification through a listener's idiom. The vast majority of the listeners seem to be tied to graphical user interfaces such as `Swing`. Listing D.19 shows a sample of an `ActionListener` on a button.

LISTING D.19 Java Listener

```
import javax.swing.JApplet;
import javax.swing.JButton;

import java.awt.Toolkit;
import java.awt.BorderLayout;
import java.awt.event.ActionListener;
import java.awt.event.ActionEvent;

public class Button extends JApplet
                    implements ActionListener {
    JButton button;
    static int count = 0;
    public void init() {
        button = new JButton("Click Me");
        getContentPane().add(button, BorderLayout.CENTER);
        button.addActionListener(this);
    }

    public void actionPerformed(ActionEvent e) {
        button.setText("Again: " + count++);
    }
}
```

To run this application, you need to be aware that a simple HTML file contains an <APPLET> tag. This file references the class file that is generated from javac. To use this file, you use the appletviewer tool, as follows:

```
start appletviewer button.htm
```

This simple applet prompts the user to click on the button. With each click, the text on the button face updates to show the number of clicks.

To add an event in C#, you need to define a handler, as shown in Listing D.20.

LISTING D.20 C# Event Handler

```
private void OnClick(object sender, System.EventArgs e)
{
    Button b = null;
    try
    {
        b = (Button)sender;
        b.Text = "Again: " + count++;
    }
    catch(Exception ex)
    {
        Debug.WriteLine(ex);
    }
}
```

After the handler has been implemented, you add it to the list of event handlers with the following line:

```
this.button.Click += new System.EventHandler(this.OnClick);
```

The callback mechanism for Java and .NET is similar. The mechanism for .NET with events and delegates is much more flexible than that used for Java, although .NET UI components use Events extensively. Anyone who has worked on Visual J++ will immediately recognize the same concept of a delegate.

Database Access

Both the JVM and the CLR have methods and classes to access a relational database. Because of the influence of ODBC, the access methodology is similar.

Listing D.21 shows how to go about accessing a database in Java using JDBC.

LISTING D.21 Java Database Access

```
import java.lang.Exception;
import java.sql.*;
import java.util.*;
import java.lang.Class;

class TestDataBase
{
    public static void main(String[] args)
    {
        String sURL = "jdbc:odbc:Northwind";
        String sUserID = "kevinbu";
        String sPassword = "";
        String sQuery = "SELECT EmployeeID, LastName, FirstName,
➥Title FROM Employees";
        Connection con = null;
        Statement stmt = null;
        try
        {
            Class.forName("sun.jdbc.odbc.JdbcOdbcDriver");
            con = DriverManager.getConnection ( sURL,
                sUserID,
                sPassword);

            DatabaseMetaData dbmd = con.getMetaData();
            System.out.println(
                "DBMS: " +
                dbmd.getDatabaseProductName()  + ", " +
                dbmd.getDatabaseProductVersion() );
```

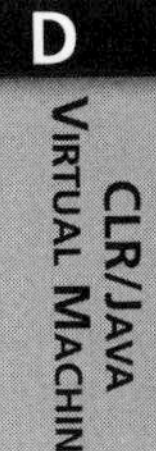

LISTING D.21 Continued

```
            System.out.println(
                "Driver: " +
                dbmd.getDriverName()  + ", " +
                dbmd.getDriverVersion() );

            stmt = con.createStatement();
        }
        catch ( SQLException SQLe)
        {
            System.err.println( "problems connecting to " +
                sURL + ":" );
            System.err.println( SQLe.getMessage() );
            System.err.println( "SQL State: " +
                SQLe.getSQLState() );

            if( con != null)
            {
                try { con.close(); }
                catch( Exception e ) {}
            }

            return;
        } // end catch
        catch ( ClassNotFoundException CSFe)
        {
            System.err.println( "Class not found exception: " +
➥CSFe.getMessage() );
        }
        try
        {
            ResultSet rs;
            ResultSetMetaData rsmd;
            rs = stmt.executeQuery( sQuery );
            rsmd = rs.getMetaData();
            int i = rsmd.getColumnCount();
            for( int ndx = 1; ndx <= i; ndx++ )
            {
                System.out.println(
                    "Column Name: " +
                    rsmd.getColumnName( ndx ) + "." );
                System.out.println(
                    "Column SQL Type: " +
                    rsmd.getColumnTypeName( ndx ) + "." );
                System.out.println(
                    "Column Java Class Equivalent: " +
                    rsmd.getColumnClassName( ndx ) + ".\n" );
            }
            while( rs.next() )
```

LISTING D.21 Continued

```
            {
                System.out.println(rs.getInt("EmployeeID") + " " +
                                   rs.getString("LastName") +  " " +
                                   rs.getString("FirstName") +  " " +
                                   rs.getString("Title"));
            } // end if( result.next() )
        }
        catch (Exception e)
        {
            e.printStackTrace();
        }
        finally
        {
. . . (cleanup) . . .
    }
}
```

The preceding example uses the JDBC-ODBC driver (look at the line containing `Class.forName`). Sun recommends that this be used as a last resort, and that more direct implementations of JDBC drivers should be used. The algorithm used to connect to the database is much the same, with the exception that ADO.NET and C# are used instead of the Java APIs.

Listing D.22 shows how the same database is accessed with C#.

LISTING D.22 C# Database Access

```
using System;
using System.Data;
using System.Data.SqlClient;
using System.Diagnostics;

namespace DataBase
{
    /// <summary>
    /// Summary description for DataBaseMain.
    /// </summary>
    class DataBaseMain
    {
        static void Main(string[] args)
        {
            SqlConnection nwindConn = new SqlConnection(
➥"Data Source=localhost;" +
➥"Integrated Security=true;" +
➥"Initial Catalog=northwind");
            SqlCommand employeesCommand = new SqlCommand(
➥"SELECT EmployeeID, LastName, FirstName, Title FROM
➥ Employees", nwindConn);
```

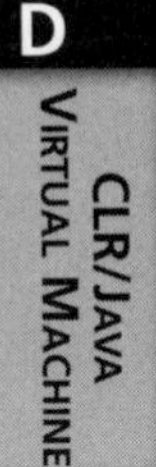

LISTING D.22 Continued

```
            try
            {
                nwindConn.Open();
                SqlDataReader myReader = employeesCommand.ExecuteReader();
                DataTable schemaTable = myReader.GetSchemaTable();
                foreach (DataRow myRow in schemaTable.Rows)
                {
                    foreach (DataColumn myCol in schemaTable.Columns)
                        Console.WriteLine(myCol.ColumnName +
                                          " = " +
                                          myRow[myCol]);
                    Console.WriteLine();
                }
                do
                {
                    Console.WriteLine("{0} {1} {2} {3}",
                                      myReader.GetName(0),
                                      myReader.GetName(1),
                                      myReader.GetName(2),
                                      myReader.GetName(3));

                    while (myReader.Read())
                        Console.WriteLine("{0} {1} {2} {3}",
                                          myReader.GetInt32(0),
                                          myReader.GetString(1),
                                          myReader.GetString(2),
                                          myReader.GetString(3));

                } while (myReader.NextResult());
                myReader.Close();
                nwindConn.Close();
            }
            catch(Exception e)
            {
                Debug.WriteLine(e);
            }
        }
    }
}
```

If you have trouble running this program, you probably need to change the "Data Source" string for the connection. You need to specify the machine from which your database is served. If you have installed .NET, you might need to put something like "<machine-name>\NETSDK", where <machine-name> is the name of your local machine. Check the permissions you have set up for the database. You might not be able to rely on Windows-integrated security.

Polymorphism

In Java, all methods are virtual, so it is easy to override the base class method. Listing D.23 shows a simple example of `Letters` and `Numbers` inheriting from a base class `Character`.

LISTING D.23 Java Inheritance

```
class Character
{
    protected String value;
    Character()
    {
        value = "null";
    }
    Character(String value)
    {
        this.value = value;
    }
    public void Output()
    {
        System.out.println("I am a character " + value);
    }
}
class Letter extends Character
{
    Letter(String value)
    {
        super(value);
    }
    public void Output()
    {
        System.out.print("I am a letter and ");
        super.Output();
    }
}
class Number extends Character
{
    Number(String value)
    {
        super(value);
    }
    public void Output()
    {
        System.out.print("I am a number and ");
        super.Output();
    }
}
```

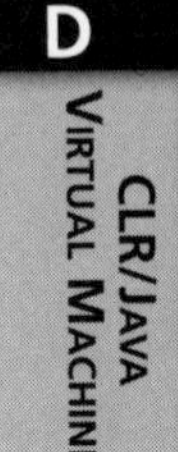

Listing D.23 Continued

```
class CharacterOutput
{
    public static void main(String[] args)
    {
        Character c [] = new Character [] { new Letter("A"),
                                            new Letter("B"),
                                            new Letter("C"),
                                            new Number("1"),
                                            new Number("2"),
                                            new Number("3") };
        // Enumerate command-line args array
        for(int i = 0; i < c.length; ++i)
            c[i].Output();
    }
}
```

In this listing, the `Output` method is overridden in the classes `Letter` and `Number`. If you were to add a new function `Output` that took a single argument, this `Output` method would have a different signature than the base class `Output` method, so it would be considered an overloaded method. Listing D.24 shows an example of an overloaded `Output` method.

Listing D.24 Java Overloading a Method

```
class Number extends Character
{
    Number(String value)
    {
        super(value);
    }
    public void Output()
    {
        System.out.print("I am a number and ");
        super.Output();
    }
    public void Output(String prefix)
    {
        System.out.print(prefix + ": ");
        Output();
    }
}
```

Of course, unless the function is declared in the base class, no inheritance exists (at least for that function). However, because the signature of the `Output` method (with an argument) is different from the signature to the `Output` method in the base class, this `Output` function is said to hide the `Output` method in the base class. Hiding can better be illustrated with field values. Listing D.25 shows how the Number class has its own value that hides the value in the base class.

LISTING D.25 Java Hiding a Field

```
class Number extends Character
{
    float value;
    Number(String value)
    {
        super(value);
    }
    public void Output()
    {
        System.out.print("I am a number and ");
        super.Output();
    }
}
```

In .NET, all methods are non-virtual by default. If you want the same functionality of the code in Listing D.23 in C#, you could start with the code in Listing D.26.

LISTING D.26 Ambiguous C# Inheritance

```
using System;
namespace Polymorphism
{
    class Character
    {
        String value;
        public Character()
        {
            value = "null";
        }
        public Character(String value)
        {
            this.value = value;
        }
        public void Output()
        {
            Console.WriteLine("I am a character {0}", value);
        }
    }
    class Letter : Character
    {
        public Letter(String value) : base(value)
```

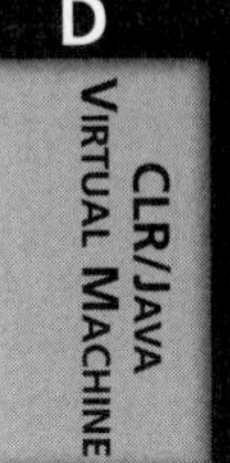

LISTING D.26 Continued

```
        {
        }
        public void Output()
        {
            Console.Write("I am a letter and ");
            base.Output();
        }
    }
    class Number : Character
    {
        public Number(String value) : base(value)
        {
        }
        public void Output()
        {
            Console.Write("I am a number and ");
            base.Output();
        }
    }

    class CharacterOutput
    {
        public static void Main(String[] args)
        {
            Character [] c = new Character [] { new Letter("A"),
                                                new Letter("B"),
                                                new Letter("C"),
                                                new Number("1"),
                                                new Number("2"),
                                                new Number("3") };
                // Enumerate command-line args array
                for(int i = 0; i < c.Length; ++i)
                    c[i].Output();
        }
    }
}
```

If you try to compile the code in Listing D.26, you get an error message like this:

```
character.cs(25,15): warning CS0108: The keyword new is required on
        'Polymorphism.Letter.Output()' because it hides inherited member
        'Polymorphism.Character.Output()'
character.cs(15,15): (Location of symbol related to previous warning)
```

At that point, heed the warning and add a **new** keyword. Now the output is this:

```
I am a character A
I am a character B
I am a character C
```

```
I am a character 1
I am a character 2
I am a character 3
```

This is not the output you want, though, because it doesn't have polymorphism. Live with the warning (by getting rid of the **new** keyword) and your output still looks the same. What is going on here? With C#, because methods are by default non-virtual, the code of Listing D.26 literally hides the Output method of the base. The keyword **new** just makes the warning go away. If you want virtual behavior, add the virtual keyword to the output method of Listing D.26. Now you get a slightly different warning:

```
character.cs(25,15): warning CS0114: 'Polymorphism.Letter.Output()' hides
        inherited member 'Polymorphism.Character.Output()'. To make the current
        member override that implementation, add the override keyword. Otherwise
        add the new keyword.
character.cs(15,23): (Location of symbol related to previous warning)
```

If you still try to run the program despite the warning, you still won't see polymorphism. You have already tried **new**, but now that the `Output` method is **`virtual`**, the warning tells you to try **`override`**. When you think about it, you do want to override the base class method with your method in the class that inherits the base class. When you explicitly add **`override`** to the `Output` method in the `Letter` class and the `Number` class, you get the desired output:

```
I am a letter and I am a character A
I am a letter and I am a character B
I am a letter and I am a character C
I am a number and I am a character 1
I am a number and I am a character 2
I am a number and I am a character 3
```

To get the behavior that you want in C#, you need to explicitly specify your intentions in the code, and the language gives you the keywords to do this. When the specification is ambiguous, you get a warning. This behavior is preferable to having to remember rules about what happens when.

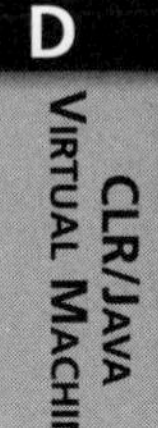

Interop with Legacy Code

One problem with adoption of a managed environment is that much of the unmanaged code either can't be rewritten or would be too costly to rewrite. Both Java and .NET have gateways that can be used so that the unmanaged code can be accessed with managed code.

Java has what is called the Java Native Interface, or JNI, that is used to interoperate with unmanaged code. Although theoretically the code underneath can be implemented in any programming language, the methods that are exposed and callable by JNI must follow the C calling convention. Legacy means C/C++ with the exposed methods in C. To build an interface that is callable from Java, you must first start with Java. For the purposes of illustration, a function will be written in C that displays a greeting and is callable from Java. That function will be able to be called from managed code. Listing D.27 shows a starting point for the Java implementation.

LISTING D.27 JNI Prompt Driver

```
class HelloWorldJni {
    public native void displayHelloWorld();

    static {
        System.loadLibrary("hello");
    }

    public static void main(String[] args) {
        new HelloWorldJni().displayHelloWorld();
    }
}
```

The two things to note about this listing are the `native` keyword and the funny looking `static` block. The `native` keyword tells Java that this method is a native legacy call, not a normal Java method. The static block is executed when the code starts running. On a Unix system, this block loads a library called hello, so on a Windows system it looks for `hello.dll`. That's not all there is to it, however. Now you have to develop the implementation of the call. Start by compiling this driver program to produce a `HelloWorldJni.class` like this:

```
javac -classpath . HelloWorldJni.java
```

You could try to run this class now, but it wouldn't be able to find the `hello.dll` file. To start to build this file, generate a signature or declaration of the function that you want to call from Java with a utility called `javah`:

```
javah HelloWorldJni
```

Like running the interpreter, `javah` takes the name of the class to get its information, not from the name of the file (at least explicitly). The tool looks in the `HelloWorldJni.class`, finds all of the native methods, and generates a declaration of how these functions will be called in Java. For this example, the generated header file (.h) looks like Listing D.28.

LISTING D.28 JNI `HelloWorldJni.h` from `javah`

```
/* DO NOT EDIT THIS FILE - it is machine generated */
#include <jni.h>
/* Header for class HelloWorldJni */

#ifndef _Included_HelloWorldJni
#define _Included_HelloWorldJni
#ifdef __cplusplus
extern "C" {
#endif
/*
 * Class:     HelloWorldJni
 * Method:    displayHelloWorld
 * Signature: ()V
 */
JNIEXPORT void JNICALL Java_HelloWorldJni_displayHelloWorld
  (JNIEnv *, jobject);

#ifdef __cplusplus
}
#endif
#endif
```

The important part of this listing is the declaration of the function `Java_HelloWorldJni_displayHelloWorld`. For this example, only one method is declared native in the Java source, so only one function is declared. The function name is split into three parts separated by _. The first part declares that this function is to be called from Java. The second part indicates that this native interface is to be called from the `HelloWorldJni` class. The last part indicates the native function to be called. After you have a declaration, you need to have an implementation. Listing D.29 shows a possible implementation of the `displayHelloWorld` function.

LISTING D.29 JNI Native Call Implementation

```
#include <jni.h>
#include "HelloWorldJni.h"
#include <stdio.h>

JNIEXPORT void JNICALL
Java_HelloWorldJni_displayHelloWorld(JNIEnv *env, jobject obj)
{
    printf("Hello world, from 'C'!\n");
    return;
}
```

If you compile this function into `hello.dll` and place it in the same place as the `HelloWorldJni.class` file, you can run the Java program:

```
java HelloWorldJni
```

and get the expected output:

```
Hello world, from 'C'
```

In its simplest form, this is how to transition from the managed world of Java to unmanaged code. What if you want to pass data to and from unmanaged code? Like Listing D.27 shows, you start with a Java driver program, with the function that you want to call declared as native. This is illustrated in Listing D.30.

LISTING D.30 JNI Prompt Driver

```
class PromptJni {

    private native String getLine(String prompt);

    public static void main(String args[]) {
        PromptJni p = new PromptJni();
        String input = p.getLine("Type a line: ");
        System.out.println("User typed: " + input);
    }
    static {
        System.loadLibrary("Prompt");
    }
}
```

Here you are declaring that a `native` function `getLine`, exists in `Prompt.dll` that you want to call from Java. This method takes a single String argument and passes back a String. You still need to compile the driver program and generate the header with `javah` as before, but the implementation is where the work is done. Listing D.31 shows a possible implementation of the `getLine` method.

LISTING D.31 JNI Prompt `getLine` Implementation

```
#include <jni.h>
#include "PromptJni.h"
#include <string>
#include <iostream>

JNIEXPORT jstring JNICALL Java_PromptJni_getLine(JNIEnv *env,
➥jobject obj, jstring prompt)
{
    std::string s;
```

LISTING D.31 Continued

```
    const char *str = env->GetStringUTFChars(prompt, 0);
    std::cout << str;
    env->ReleaseStringUTFChars(prompt, str);
    std::getline(std::cin, s);
    return env->NewStringUTF(s.c_str());
}
```

This is compiled as C++, so you have the functionality of some of the C++ libraries. However, the function, `getLine`, still has a C calling convention and none of the C++ features are exposed or can be exposed to Java.

This implementation illustrates that you need to explicitly convert data from Java to unmanaged and from unmanaged to Java. This process is called *marshaling*. You need to call `GetStringUTFChars` to convert from a Java `String` and call `NewString` to convert from unmanaged to a Java `String`. Java has many helper methods to convert to and from different types. Methods are also available so that your unmanaged code can call methods in the managed Java world.

Building a JNI interface is an involved process, and for a large project, it can be mind numbing. In addition, Java doesn't interact with COM. Many companies market products to act as a bridge between Java and COM, but this interaction is not really part of the language. One simple approach to build an interaction with COM is to build a JNI interface, as was shown earlier. The implementation of the function described by the JNI interface could call COM, thus forming an interop layer.

.NET has P/Invoke, which greatly simplifies interaction with unmanaged code. With P/Invoke, you don't need to build a special unmanaged DLL to call unmanaged code. You just need to be sure that the functions that are exported and that are to be called by .NET follow a C calling convention. If you had source, your unmanaged code would look like Listing D.32.

LISTING D.32 Possible Source for Hello World Unmanaged Function

```
#include "stdio.h"
#include "helloworld.h"

void displayHelloWorld()
{
    printf("Hello world, from 'C'!\n");
    return;
}
```

This source is not necessary, however. You just need to be sure of the calling convention. After you know it is the correct calling convention, you can treat the DLL as a black box. You do not need to know the internal implementation—just the interface definition. Now you can move to the C# code. Listing D.33 shows how to call the `displayHelloWorld` method in `helloworld.dll`.

LISTING D.33 Calling Unmanaged Code from C#

```
using System;
using System.Runtime.InteropServices;

namespace InteropTest
{
    class InteropTestMain
    {
        [DllImport("helloworld.dll")]
        public static extern void displayHelloWorld();
        static void Main(string[] args)
        {
            displayHelloWorld();
        }
    }
}
```

With the addition of two lines of code, you can call any of the methods on a DLL. This is good, but it gets better when you have to deal with functions that have arguments. Suppose that you have a function in a DLL that has an implementation like Listing D.34.

LISTING D.34 Source for `getLine`

```
#include <windows.h>
#include <string>
#include <iostream>
#include "prompt.h"

LPCSTR getLine(LPCSTR prompt)
{
    static std::string s = prompt;
    std::cout << s;
    std::getline(std::cin, s);
    return s.c_str();
}
```

Remember that you do not have to have source for this to work. In the source code, you can see the type of function with which you need to interface. This `getLine` function in

Listing D.34 takes in an argument (LPCSTR prompt) and returns an argument (LPTSTR). At this point, you should call this function from managed code (C#). Listing D.35 shows how to call this function from C#.

LISTING D.35 Calling `getLine` from C#

```
using System;
using System.Runtime.InteropServices;

namespace InteropTest
{
    class InteropTestMain
    {
        [DllImport("prompt.dll")]
        public static extern string getLine(string prompt);
        static void Main(string[] args)
        {
            string input = getLine("Type a line: ");
            Console.WriteLine("User typed: {0}", input);
        }
    }
}
```

Again, just two lines of code give you access to the `getLine` function. If you look closely at the declaration of the `getLine` function, you can see that it has already been declared by taking a **`string`** argument and returning a **`string`**. The runtime notices that it needs to convert that string to a character pointer (LPCSTR). The runtime handles all of the conversion work. Many options are available that allow simple effective communication with legacy code.

With this technology available, if you need to access legacy code, .NET presents a strong and compelling case for adopting the .NET Framework to handle this communication layer between managed and unmanaged code.

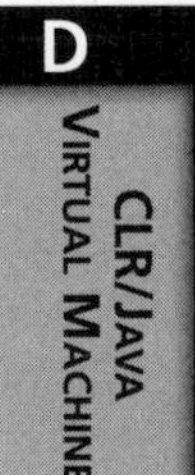

Attributes

Java *could* support attributes. They are part of the class file format (`http://java.sun.com/docs/books/vmspec/2nd-edition/html/ClassFile.doc.html#43817`), but they have not formally been supported in the language.

.NET supports attributes on classes, fields, methods, and assemblies. They are exposed differently on each of the languages, but they are useful. They are used extensively in the .NET Framework library. Listing D.36 shows one possible use of an attribute.

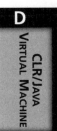

LISTING D.36 Using a Conditional Attribute in C#

```
using System;

namespace AttributeTest
{
    class AttributeMain
    {
        [Conditional("DEBUG")]
        private static void HelloWorld()
        {
            Console.WriteLine("Hello World!");
        }
        static void Main(string[] args)
        {
            HelloWorld();
        }
    }
}
```

The compiler knows about this attribute. If the macro is defined (in the case of Listing D.36, it is DEBUG), then the call to the function that is associated with the macro will happen; however, if the macro is not defined, the compiler removes all calls to the function. Listing D.37 shows the same thing in VB.

LISTING D.37 Using a Conditional Attribute in VB

```
Option Explicit On
Option Strict On

Imports System
Imports System.Diagnostics
'
' vbc /d:DEBUG=True vbattrib.vb
'
Module VBAtrribute
    Public Class VBAttributeMain
        <Conditional("DEBUG")> _
        Public Shared Sub HelloWorld()
            Console.WriteLine("Hello World from VB!")
        End Sub
        Public Shared Sub Main()
            HelloWorld()
        End Sub
    End Class
End Module
```

The continuation character (_) is important for the attribute to apply to the following function in VB.

Serialization

It is important to be able to convert an object to a series of bytes and then be able to convert that series of bytes back into an object. This must be done to transfer bytes from one machine to another via a serial connection, Ethernet, and so on. Even if this object needs to be persisted to a file on the computer's hard drive, it still needs to be serialized. Java has a fixed custom binary format to which objects are serialized. Having a custom binary format does not matter if all of the parties consuming the object are written in Java. Listing D.38 shows how to serialize a simple class consisting of a `String` and a `Date`.

LISTING D.38 Java Serialization

```
import java.io.*;
import java.lang.*;
import java.util.*;

class DateClass implements Serializable {

    private Date d;
    private String s;

    DateClass (String s, Date d) {
        this.s = s;
        this.d = d;
    }

    public static void main(String args[]) {
        Date d = new Date();
        DateClass corg = new DateClass("This is a test", d);
        DateClass cnew = null;

        // Serialize the original class object
        try {
            FileOutputStream fo = new FileOutputStream("dateclass.tmp");
            ObjectOutputStream so = new ObjectOutputStream(fo);
            so.writeObject(corg);
            so.flush();
            so.close();
        } catch (Exception e) {
            e.printStackTrace();
            System.exit(1);
        }

        // Deserialize in to new class object
        try {
            FileInputStream fi = new FileInputStream("dateclass.tmp");
            ObjectInputStream si = new ObjectInputStream(fi);
```

LISTING D.38 Continued

```
            cnew = (DateClass) si.readObject();
            si.close();
        } catch (Exception e) {
            e.printStackTrace();
            System.exit(1);
        }

        // Print out to check the correctness
        System.out.println();
        System.out.println("Printing the original class...");
        System.out.println(corg);
        System.out.println();
        System.out.println("Printing the new class...");
        System.out.println(cnew);
        System.out.println();
        System.out.println("The original and new classes should be the same!");
        System.out.println();
    }

    // Convert the class to human readable format. Useful for testing.
    public String toString() {
        StringBuffer sb = new StringBuffer();
        sb.append(s + ": ");
        sb.append(d.toString());
        return(sb.toString());
    }
}
```

This class needs to declare that it implements `Serializable` and that it is now possible to use default serialization to serialize the object. The object is stored in a file called `dateclass.tmp`. Looking at this file, you can see that this file format is indeed binary. If you had wanted to provide some special handling when serializing the object, you could have overridden the methods `writeObject` and `readObject`.

Converting Listing D.38 to C# yields the code in Listing D.39.

LISTING D.39 C# Serialization

```
using System;
using System.IO;
using System.Xml;
using System.Xml.Serialization;
using System.Text;

public class DateClass
```

LISTING D.39 Continued

```
{
    public DateTime d;
    public String s;

    public DateClass()
    {
    }
    public DateClass (String s, DateTime d)
    {
        this.s = s;
        this.d = d;
    }

    public static void Main(String [] args)
    {
        DateTime d = DateTime.Now;
        DateClass corg = new DateClass("This is a test", d);
        DateClass cnew = null;
        string filename = "dateclass.xml";

        // Serialize the original class object
        try
        {
            XmlSerializer ser = new XmlSerializer(typeof(DateClass));
            TextWriter writer = new StreamWriter(filename);
            ser.Serialize(writer, corg);
            writer.Close();
        }
        catch (Exception e)
        {
            Console.WriteLine(e);
            return;
        }

        // Deserialize into new class object
        try
        {
            XmlSerializer ser = new XmlSerializer(typeof(DateClass));
            TextReader reader = new StreamReader(filename);
            cnew = (DateClass)ser.Deserialize(reader);
            reader.Close();
        }
        catch (Exception e)
        {
            Console.WriteLine(e);
            return;
        }
```

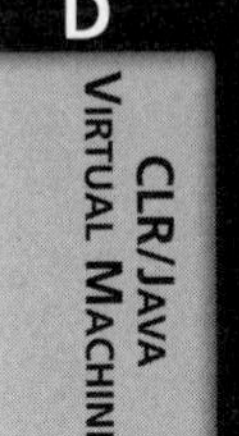

LISTING D.39 Continued

```
            // Print out to check the correctness
            Console.WriteLine();
            Console.WriteLine("Printing the original class...");
            Console.WriteLine(corg);
            Console.WriteLine();
            Console.WriteLine("Printing the new class...");
            Console.WriteLine(cnew);
            Console.WriteLine();
            Console.WriteLine("The original and new classes should be the same!");
            Console.WriteLine();
    }

    // Convert the class to human readable format. Useful for debugging
    public override string ToString()
    {
        StringBuilder sb = new StringBuilder();
        sb.Append(s + ": ");
        sb.Append(d.ToLongDateString() + " " + d.ToLongTimeString());
        return(sb.ToString());
    }
}
```

At the basic level, the C# and Java seem to have the same capability. This is only the beginning for C#, however. First, you build an XML serialization scheme. The file `dateclass.xml`, looks like Listing D.40.

LISTING D.40 DateClass Serialized to XML

```
<?xml version="1.0" encoding="utf-8" ?>
- <DateClass xmlns:xsi="http://www.w3.org/2001/XMLSchema-instance"
             xmlns:xsd="http://www.w3.org/2001/XMLSchema">
  <d>2001-10-16T12:05:50.6496833-05:00</d>
  <s>This is a test</s>
  </DateClass>
```

With attributes, you can change the token names. (The default is the name of the variable that is being serialized.) You can also add a namespace and move an element to become an attribute, among other things. The XML serialization alone has many options. You can change a few lines of code and use either a **`SoapFormatter`** or a **`BinaryFormatter`** to format the data. In Listing D.39, the code has been modified to use these classes, and the source is included in `dateclasssoap.cs`.

Versioning

.NET has versioning built in from the start. It is part of an assembly's identity—its name. Java has no loader support for versioning. It is impossible to differentiate between two different versions of Java code running on the same machine. To see how to access the version information in .NET, look at the code in Listing D.41.

LISTING D.41 Retrieving Version Information

```
using System;
using System.Reflection;

[assembly:AssemblyVersion("1.2.3.4")]#

namespace Version
{
    class VersionMain
    {
        static void Main(string[] args)
        {
            AssemblyName an = Assembly.GetExecutingAssembly().GetName();
            Console.WriteLine(an.FullName);
            Console.WriteLine(an.Name);
            Console.WriteLine(an.Version);
        }
    }
}
```

Of course, a C# program would rarely need to access this information. Versioning usually happens outside of the code. Most likely, the code will be loaded in the GAC and run side-by-side. Then the version information is part of the identity (along with the culture information) of the assembly.

Runtime Discovery of Type Information

Reflection is not new to the CLR. It is a necessary and beneficial feature. Listing D.42 is a small sample of how Java discovers runtime characteristics of code.

LISTING D.42 Java Reflection

```
import java.lang.*;
import java.lang.reflect.*;

class Reflection
{
    private int fielda;
    private float fieldb;
```

Listing D.42 Continued

```
    private String fieldc;
    Reflection()
    {
       fielda = 0;
       fieldb = 0;
       fieldc = "";
    }
    Reflection(int a, float b, String c)
    {
        fielda = a;
        fieldb = b;
        fieldc = c;
        return;
    }
    int getfielda()
    {
        return fielda;
    }
    float getfieldb()
    {
        return fieldb;
    }
    String getfieldc()
    {
        return fieldc;
    }
    int add(int a)
    {
        return a + fielda;
    }
    float add(float b)
    {
        return b + fieldb;
    }
    String add(String c)
    {
        return c + fieldc;
    }
    void Reflect()
    {
        try
        {
            System.out.println("> " + this.getClass().getName() + " methods");
            Method methods [] = this.getClass().getMethods();
            for(int i = 0; i < methods.length; i++)
            {
                System.out.print("    " + methods[i].getReturnType() + " " +
➥methods[i].getName());
```

LISTING D.42 Continued

```
                Class  p [] = methods[i].getParameterTypes();
                System.out.print("(");
                for(int j = 0; j < p.length; j++)
                    if(j != p.length - 1)
                        System.out.print(p[j] + ", ");
                   else
                        System.out.print(p[j]);
                System.out.println(") ");
            }
. . .
```

C# can do the same thing as shown in Listing D.43.

LISTING D.43 C## Reflection

```
using System;
using System.Reflection;

public class ReflectionTest
{
    private int fielda;
    private float fieldb;
    private string fieldc;
    ReflectionTest()
    {
       fielda = 0;
       fieldb = 0;
       fieldc = "";
    }
    ReflectionTest(int a, float b, String c)
    {
        fielda = a;
        fieldb = b;
        fieldc = c;
        return;
    }
    int getfielda()
    {
        return fielda;
    }
    float getfieldb()
    {
        return fieldb;
    }
    string getfieldc()
    {
        return fieldc;
    }
```

LISTING D.43 Continued

```
    int add(int a)
    {
        return a + fielda;
    }
    float add(float b)
    {
        return b + fieldb;
    }
    string add(string c)
    {
        return c + fieldc;
    }
    void Reflect()
    {
        try
        {
            Type t = GetType();
            Console.WriteLine("> " + t.BaseType.Name + " methods");
            MethodInfo [] methods = t.BaseType.GetMethods(
➥BindingFlags.NonPublic |
➥BindingFlags.Public |
➥BindingFlags.Instance);
            for(int i = 0; i < methods.Length; i++)
            {
                Console.Write("    " + methods[i].Name);
                ParameterInfo [] p = methods[i].GetParameters();
                Console.Write("(");
                for(int j = 0; j < p.Length; j++)
                    if(j != p.Length - 1)
                        Console.Write(p[j].ParameterType + ", ");
                    else
                        Console.Write(p[j].ParameterType);
                Console.WriteLine(") ");
            }
. . .
```

Look at the full source for both of these samples in `reflection.java` and `reflection.cs` respectively.

Parsing XML

.NET has XML baked into everything. It might not be as clear how Java deals with XML, especially because many XML handling classes are new to 1.4. Listing D.44 shows one way in which an XML file can be parsed with Java.

LISTING D.44 SAX Processing in Java

```
public static void main(String argv[])
{
    if (argv.length != 1) {
        System.err.println("Usage: cmd filename");
        System.exit(1);
    }

    // Use an instance of ourselves as the SAX event handler
    DefaultHandler handler = new EchoXML();
    // Use the default (non-validating) parser
    SAXParserFactory factory = SAXParserFactory.newInstance();
    try {
        // Set up output stream
        out = new OutputStreamWriter(System.out, "UTF8");

        // Parse the input
        SAXParser saxParser = factory.newSAXParser();
        saxParser.parse( new File(argv[0]), handler);

    } catch (Throwable t) {
        t.printStackTrace();
    }
    System.exit(0);
}
```

The handlers have been omitted, but you can see how the SAX engine is set up in the listing. The full source to this listing is in `EchoXML.java`. Appendix B, ".NET Framework Class Libraries," provides a simple example of using a SAX-like method of processing XML from C#.

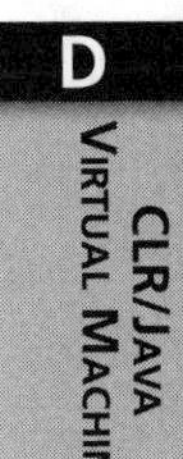

Miscellaneous Language Differences

The following list presents some simple language differences, just in case you are looking for a key feature:

- Java does not have **`foreach`** or **`goto`**.
- Java has no pointers. C# can drop down to unsafe mode.
- With C#, all types are derived from **`System.Object`**. That means that even primitive types have ToString, GetHashCode, GetType, and Equals methods available to them. In addition, collections can be made including primitive types and other types. Java does not have that option.
- Java has no operator overloading.
- Java has no preprocessor directives.

- Although the potential exists to have cross-platform IL with the CLR, it does not exist now, and Java has a clear advantage on this issue.
- Java does not have a `struct` or `enum`.
- C# adds a decimal type that Java does not have.
- C# has verbatim strings where escape characters are not interpreted.
- C# has in, out, and ref keywords to explicitly control how arguments are passed.

Web Access

Java is almost synonymous with the Web. Java applets are available that run client side and provide a dynamic UI. Java servlets and JSP pages provide data back to a client.

With .NET, it is extremely easy to build a Web service. ASP.NET provides a vehicle for server-side processing of Web requests.

GUI Client Apps

Java had AWT, which was followed up and superceded by Swing. Swing contains most of the UI controls that are needed to develop a dynamic Web page.

.NET has two UI frameworks. `System.Windows.Forms` is used for standalone clients, and `System.Web.Forms` is used for Web clients. Visual Studio .NET makes building a UI to run under either one of these UI frameworks easy.

Taking into Account Your Company and Your Employees

Technical reasons aside, one of the prime factors that you should consider in choosing one platform over another is what is right for your company. If you have a strong tradition as a user of Microsoft tools and products and do not see Linux or Sun platforms in the future, then moving to the CLR makes sense. If you need your application to run on many different platforms that Microsoft does not support yet and you are committed to the managed view, then your choice is somewhat more complex and Java should be considered. It is hardly the hard and fast rule that you were looking for, but do what is best for your company.

Tip

In summary:

- Investing in the JVM and Java certainly leverages the platform independence that Java currently enjoys. Many Java gurus, however, would caution you in relying too much on Java being completely platform independent.
- .NET and the CLR are currently tied to a Windows platform.
- .NET offers many of the same features that Java does, but many features are much more easily exploited. If you want to heavily interoperate between managed code and legacy DLLs, for instance, then consider the ease with which .NET handles this.
- Java has a big head start, but .NET has some compelling advantages that could quickly close the gap.
- Neither one of the technologies is going away any time soon.
- In the end, you need to do what is best for your company and what makes sense for your project.

Additional References

This Appendix briefly describes some of the resources that you will find useful in understanding the .NET Framework and the CLR. The resources are organized by chapter. A general section is also included that provides a list of books that contain information that is applicable to most chapters. First read the appropriate chapter, and then if you want to delve deeper or just get another opinion, turn to some of the recommended resources. Many of the recommended resources rely on online documentation that accompanies the .NET Framework. Much effort has gone into providing clear and accurate documentation for the .NET Framework, and this Appendix is a good source of reliable information.

Note

URLs that are preceded with `ms-help://` denote online documentation that is available with the .NET Framework SDK.

Chapter 2 References

This chapter discusses the elements that make up the .NET Framework and how the CLR uses those elements to provide a common computing environment.

- Rao Surapaneni, Narayana. IL "The Language of CLR"—A Platform for Cross-Language. `http://www.c-sharpcorner.com/Language/ILtheLangOfCLRbyNRS.asp`.

  A brief article about some of the cross-language features of the CLR.

- Watkins, Damien. "Handling Language Interoperability with the Microsoft .NET Framework." `http://msdn.microsoft.com/library/default.asp?url=/library/en-us/dndotnet/html/interopdotnet.asp`.

  Provides a good overview of how language interoperability is achieved using a common type system.

Chapter 3 References

This chapter provides an overview of how code is loaded and run in the CLR and the model that is used to run managed IL code by the CLR.

- "About Dynamic-Link Libraries." `ms-help://MS.VSCC/MS.MSDNVS/dllproc/dll_1tpv.htm`.

  It is useful to compare how DLL code is loaded and run in a traditional sense because many of the same principles apply to managed code.

- Pietrek, Matt. "Under the Hood—NT DLL Initialization." `ms-help://MS.VSCC/MS.MSDNVS/dnmsj99/html/hood0999.htm`.

  Similar to the previous reference, this article explains how a DLL is loaded and initialized.

Chapter 4 References

This chapter describes the architecture of the assembly and how the metadata is physically placed there.

- Partition II Metadata.doc. Program Files\Microsoft Visual Studio .NET\FrameworkSDK\Tool Developers Guide\docs\Partition II Metadata.doc.

  The reference on metadata. Most questions that you have about metadata are answered in this document.

- PEVerify Tool (peverify.exe). `ms-help://MS.VSCC/MS.MSDNVS/cptools/html/cpgrfpeverifytoolpeverifyexe.htm`.

  A detailed explanation of the options that are available to the PEVerify tool to verify your code.

- Pietrek, Matt. "Avoiding DLL Hell: Introducing Application Metadata in the Microsoft .NET Framework." `ms-help://MS.VSCC/MS.MSDNVS/dnmag00/html/metadata.htm`.

  Provides a good overview of some of the methods available for accessing metadata and why metadata is important.

- Richter, Jeffrey. "Microsoft .NET Framework Delivers the Platform for an Integrated, Service-Oriented Web." `ms-help://MS.VSCC/MS.MSDNVS/dnmag00/html/framework.htm`.

  Provides an overview of how an assembly is loaded and run.

Chapter 5 References

This chapter focuses on IL instructions.

- "Compiling to MSIL." `ms-help://MS.VSCC/MS.MSDNVS/cpguide/html/cpconmicrosoftintermediatelanguagemsil.htm`.

  Explains where IL fits when running your program.

- "ILDasm Tutorial." `ms-help://MS.VSCC/MS.MSDNVS/cptutorials/html/il_dasm_tutorial.htm`.

  Provides a good overview of the MSIL Disassembler.

- Partition III CIL.doc. Program Files\Microsoft Visual Studio .NET\FrameworkSDK\Tool Developers Guide\docs\Partition III CIL.doc.

  This is the reference on IL instructions.
- Robbins, John. "ILDASM Is Your New Best Friend." `http://msdn.microsoft.com/msdnmag/issues/01/05/bugslayer/bugslayer0105.asp`.

  Provides a good overview of ILDasm as well as an introduction to some IL instructions.

Chapter 6 References

This chapter focuses on some of the issues that surround deploying and maintaining a component.

- Mojica, Jose. "Versioning VB 6 Components with VB .NET: An Excuse to Use VB .NET Today." `http://dotnet.oreilly.com/news/complus_0801.html`.

  A good article on using .NET to version VB software.

Chapter 7 References

This chapter focuses on using the Platform Invoke services to call unmanaged code.

- "Platform Invoke Tutorial." `ms-help://MS.VSCC/MS.MSDNVS/csref/html/pinvoke_example3`.

  Provides a starting point and numerous samples on using P/Invoke.
- "P/Invoke VC++ Interop." `ms-help://MS.VSCC/MS.MSDNVS/vcmxspec/html/vcmg_PlatformInvocationServices.htm`.

  Gives some samples as well as provides some performance numbers.
- Sells, Chris. "Visual Studio .NET: Managed Extensions Bring .NET CLR Support to C++." `http://msdn.microsoft.com/msdnmag/issues/01/07/vsnet/vsnet.asp`.

  Although much of the article is devoted to other features of VC++ managed extensions, this article provides useful information on interoperating with managed code.
- "When to Use VC++ Extensions. `ms-help://MS.VSCC/MS.MSDNVS/vcmex/html/vcconfeaturesofmanagedextensionsforc.htm`.

  Provides some useful guidelines for when to use VC++ managed extensions.

Chapter 8 References

This chapter is primarily concerned with how the .NET Framework can use and call into unmanaged COM components.

- Box, Don. "House of COM: Migrating Native Code to the .NET CLR." *MSDN Magazine*. May 2001. `http://msdn.microsoft.com/msdnmag/issues/01/05/com/com0105.asp`.

  Provides a good overview of the interop services that are available from the .NET Framework.

- "COM Data Types." `ms-help://MS.VSCC/MS.MSDNVS/cpguide/html/cpconcomdatatypes.htm`.

  A large table showing the relationships between .NET data types and COM data types.

- Lewis, John R. ".NET/COM Interop." `http://www.aspzone.com/articles/john/dotNETInterop/`.

  A simple VB example of using COM interop.

- Platt, David S. ".NET Interop: Get Ready for Microsoft .NET by Using Wrappers to Interact with COM-Based Applications." `http://msdn.microsoft.com/msdnmag/issues/01/08/Interop/Interop.asp`.

  Good overview of the interop facilities that are available in .NET.

- Rao Surapaneni, Narayana. "An Insight into Code Reusability and COM Interoperability." `http://www.c-sharpcorner.com/Articles/CodeReusabilityNRS.asp`.

  A good overview and comparison of interop methods.

Chapter 9 References

This chapter focuses on how to use a .NET component from managed code as a COM object.

- "First Look—Creating COM+ components with .NET Beta2." `http://www.dotnetnut.com/kbdetail.asp?Id=28`.

  Very brief overview of creating a COM+ Component using .NET.

- Hawkins, Jonathan and Shannon Pahl. "Microsoft .NET Framework Component Services, Part 1." `http://msdn.microsoft.com/library/default.asp?url=/library/en-us/dndotnet/html/pahlcompserv.asp`.

  Gives a good overview of how to create a COM+ component using .NET and what component services are available from within a .NET component.

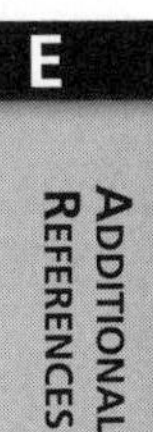

Chapter 10 References

This chapter focuses on memory and resource management within the .NET Framework.

- "Dr. GUI Garbage Collection." `http://msdn.microsoft.com/library/default.asp?url=/library/en-us/dnguinet/html/drguinet01312001.asp`.

  A good article that details some of the features of a .NET application. Included in this article is an explanation of how the .NET Framework manages memory and resources.

- Kath, Randy. "Managing Heap Memory in Win32." `http://msdn.microsoft.com/library/default.asp?url=/library/en-us/dngenlib/html/msdn_heapmm.asp`.

  A traditional view of memory and how it is managed with unmanaged code.

- Krishnan, Murali R. "Heap: Pleasures and Pains." `http://msdn.microsoft.com/library/default.asp?url=/library/en-us/dngenlib/html/heap3.asp`.

  A good article that details some of the problems and issues with a standard Win32 heap.

- Narkiewicz, Jan. "Ultimate Guide to .NET Object Cleanup, Part I, II, III." `http://www.csharptoday.com/content/articles/20020104.asp?WROXEMPTOKEN=50677ZpFz7XrGbYCKGndLmoHnE`.

  Provides an in-depth analysis of garbage collection and cleanup of objects created within the .NET Framework.

- "Programming Essentials for Garbage Collection." `http://msdn.microsoft.com/library/default.asp?url=/library/en-us/cpguidnf/html/cpconprogrammingessentialsforgarbagecollection.asp`.

  Documentation on how the system performs garbage collection and how a programmer can take advantage of some of its features.

- Richter, Jeffrey. "Garbage Collection: Automatic Memory Management in the Microsoft .NET Framework." *MSDN Magazine*, November 2000. `http://msdn.microsoft.com/msdnmag/issues/1100/gci/gci.asp`.

  Part 1 of this two-part series explains how garbage collection works and what to be aware of when designing objects that require the garbage collection services.

- Richter, Jeffrey. "Garbage Collection—Part 2: Automatic Memory Management in the Microsoft .NET Framework. *MSDN Magazine*. December 2000. `http://msdn.microsoft.com/msdnmag/issues/1200/gci2/gci2.asp`.

  Explores **`WeakReferences`** and how they can be used from within the .NET Framework. It also details how the generations are used to optimize the garbage collector and how to monitor garbage collection activity.

Chapter 11 References

This chapter deals with threading and synchronization. The following books each have excellent chapters and/or sections on threading and synchronization.

- Brain, Marshall. *Win32 System Services*. Upper Saddle River: Prentice Hall PTR, 1996.
- Peterson, James L. and Abraham Silberschatz. *Operating System Concepts*. Reading: Addison-Wesley Publishing Company, 1985.
- Richter, Jeffrey. *Advanced Windows*. Redmond: Microsoft Press, 1997.
- Troelsen, Andrew. *C# and the .NET Platform*. Berkeley: APress, 2001.

Chapter 12 References

This chapter focuses on peer-to-peer networking, or what is thought of as traditional networking. Many good sources for background material are available, so the sources have been organized into two groups.

General Networking

The following books give solid background material for networking. *Win32 System Services* and *Win32 Network Programming* provide an excellent treatise on networking on a Win32 platform. They discuss most aspects of Win32 network programming. *Unix Network Programming* is one of those classic books that is required reading to understand key technologies, such as sockets, ports, and connections.

- Brain, Marshall. *Win32 System Services*. Upper Saddle River: Prentice-Hall, 1996.
- Davis, Ralph. *Win32 Network Programming*. Reading: Addison Wesley Developers Press, 1996.
- Stevens, W. Richard. *Unix Network Programming*. Englewood Cliffs: Prentice-Hall, 1990.

System.Net Samples and Advice

This section contains links to many samples of peer-to-peer networking that should help you understand how to correctly implement a networking application.

- Bawala, Kareem. "WebRequest Class." `http://www.c-sharpcorner.com/References/ReferencesWebRequest.asp`.

  Simple sample of using the WebRequest class to get the contents of a URL.

- Farley, Bill. "Stock Quoter." http://www.c-sharpcorner.com/1/StockQuoterB.asp.

  Short example of using .NET SMTP mail facilities.
- "Get IP Address of a Host." http://www.c-sharpcorner.com/1/get_ip.asp.

  Short sample showing how to retrieve an IP address from a URL.
- Ruiz-Scougall, Jesus. "Re: .Net IO." http://discuss.develop.com/archives/wa.exe?A2=ind0008&L=DOTNET&P=R57222&m=11.

  Recommendation for using the asynchronous model.
- Singh, Pramod. "Asynchronous Request in .NET (C#)." http://www.c-sharpcorner.com/1/async_req.asp.

  Example of using the asynchronous methods.
- Suresh Raj, Gopalan. "Making GET and POST Requests on Web Pages." http://www.execpc.com/~gopalan/dotnet/webgetpost.html.

  Sample using .NET to GET and POST Web requests.

Chapter 13 References

This chapter focuses on using and extending the remoting services that the .NET Framework offers.

- Ballinger, Keith, Jonathan Hawkins, and Pranish Kumar. "SOAP in the Microsoft .NET Framework and Visual Studio .NET." http://msdn.microsoft.com/library/default.asp?url=/library/en-us/dndotnet/html/hawksoap.asp.

  Using SOAP for .NET Remoting, ASP.NET, and ATL Web Services.
- Berns, Brian. "Web Service Proxy." http://msdn.microsoft.com/library/default.asp?url=/library/en-us/dnvs600/html/webservproxwiz.asp?frame=true.

  Using the Web Service Proxy Wizard to create a proxy.
- Box, Don. "SoapSuds." http://discuss.develop.com/archives/wa.exe?A2=ind0102B&L=DOTNET&P=R2&m=8142.

  Mail message that discusses the SoapSuds tool.
- Box, Don. "A Young Person's Guide to the Simple Object Access Protocol." http://msdn.microsoft.com/msdnmag/issues/0300/soap/soap.asp.

  Article detailing SOAP and its uses.
- Green, Dan. "Dot Net Dan's Delving into .NET—Revving .NET Remoting." http://dotnetdan.com/articles/misc/mbrI.htm.

  Article showing an example remoting service.

- Noss, John and Jonathan Hawkins. "COM+ Web Services: The Check Box Route to XML Web Services." http://msdn.microsoft.com/library/default.asp?url=/library/en-us/dndotnet/html/comwscheckb.asp.

  An article detailing how to turn a COM component into Web service with no extra programming.
- Obermeyer, Piet. "Format for .NET Remoting Configuration Files." http://msdn.microsoft.com/library/default.asp?url=/library/en-us/dndotnet/html/remotingconfig.asp.

  Good article that details the configuration options for a remoting service.
- Obermeyer, Piet and Jonathan Hawkins. "Microsoft .NET Remoting: A Technical Overview." http://msdn.microsoft.com/library/default.asp?url=/library/en-us/dndotnet/html/hawkremoting.asp.

  Good overview of creating a basic remoting service.
- Obermeyer, Piet. "Side-By-Side and Versioning Considerations for .NET Remoting." http://msdn.microsoft.com/library/default.asp?url=/library/en-us/dndotnet/html/versremote.asp.

  Versioning considerations when using or programming a .NET Remoting service.
- "Remote Object Configuration." ms-help://MS.VSCC/MS.MSDNVS/cpguide/html/cpconremoteobjectschannels.htm.

  Good reference on the syntax for configuring applications that use remoting.
- "Remoting Concepts." http://msdn.microsoft.com/library/en-us/cpapndx/html/_cor_remoting_concepts.asp?frame=true.

  Head of a chain of documentation on key remoting concepts.
- Skonnard, Aaron. "SOAP: The Simple Object Access Protocol." http://www.microsoft.com/mind/0100/soap/soap.asp.

  Good article giving an overview of SOAP both as a message format and a protocol.
- Srinivasan, Paddy. "An Introduction to Microsoft .NET Remoting Framework." http://msdn.microsoft.com/library/default.asp?url=/library/en-us/dndotnet/html/introremoting.asp.

  A good overview of the different types of remoting calls and services.
- Tomescu, Mihail Catalin. "Web Services Between .NET, Java, and MS SOAP Toolkit." http://www.csharphelp.com/archives/archive53.html.

  Side-by-side comparison of SOAP servers and clients using Java and .NET.
- "Using CallContext to Transfer User Identity." ms-help://MS.VSCC/MS.MSDNVS/cpref/html/frlrfSystemRuntimeRemotingMessagingCallContextClassTopic.htm.

  A good example of using CallContext to transfer data.

Chapter 14 References

This chapter deals with `events` and `delegates` within the .NET Framework.

- Archer, Tom. *Inside C#*. Redmond: Microsoft Press, 2001.

  Provides a good explanation of `events` and `delegates`

- Grimes, Richard. ".NET Delegates: Making Asynchronous Method Calls in the .NET Environment." *MSDN Magazine*, August 2001. `http://msdn.microsoft.com/msdnmag/issues/01/08/Async/Async.asp`.

  Explains how events and delegates can be used in an asynchronous environment.

- Gunnerson, Eric. "A Programmer's Introduction to C#, Second Edition." Berkeley: Apress, 2001.

  Provides a good explanation of delegates as used in C#.

- Richter, Jeffrey. ".NET: An Introduction to Delegates." *MSDN Magazine*, April 2001. `http://msdn.microsoft.com/msdnmag/issues/01/04/net/net0104.asp`.

  Provides a brief overview of delegates.

- Richter, Jeffrey. ".NET: Delegates, Part 2." *MSDN Magazine*, June 2001. `http://msdn.microsoft.com/msdnmag/issues/01/06/net/net0106.asp`.

  Provides historical background on delegates and introduces multicast delegates.

- Richter, Jeffrey. ".NET: Implementation of Events with Delegates." *MSDN Magazine*, August 2001. `http://msdn.microsoft.com/msdnmag/issues/01/08/net/net0108.asp`.

  Discusses how events encapsulate and make using delegates easier.

Chapter 16 References

This chapter focuses on .NET security. The classes and programming models that pertain to .NET security are discussed, and various examples are given.

- "About .NET Security." `http://www.gotdotnet.com/team/clr/about_security.aspx`.

  Provides a good starting point for .NET Security documentation.

- "Cryptography Overview." `ms-help://MS.VSCC/MS.MSDNVS/cpguide/html/cpconcryptographyoverview.htm`.

  Overview of some of the classes that are available to support cryptography.

- "Custom Permissions." `ms-help://MS.VSCC/MS.MSDNVS/cpguide/html/cpconcustompermissions.htm`.

Starting point for documentation on adding a custom permission.

- "Designing Permissions." ms-help://MS.VSCC/MS.MSDNVS/cpguide/html/cpcondesigningpermission.htm.

  Detailed discussion on design decisions that need to be made before building a custom permission.

- "Designing Your Own Permissions." ms-help://MS.VSCC/MS.MSDNVS/cpguide/html/cpconcreatingyourowncodeaccesspermissions.htm.

  Step-by-step explanation on how to create a custom permission.

- Howard, Rob. "Encrypting SOAP Messages." http://msdn.microsoft.com/library/default.asp?url=/library/en-us/dnaspnet/html/asp09272001.asp?frame=true.

  An extension for adding encryption to a SOAP message.

- "Isolated Storage Overview." ms-help://MS.VSCC/MS.MSDNVS/cpguide/html/cpconisolatedstorage.htm.

  Starting point for isolated storage documentation.

- ".NET Licensing." http://www.gotdotnet.com/team/windowsforms/licensing.aspx.

  Discusses options for .NET licensing.

- "Overview of Code Access Security Model." http://msdn.microsoft.com/library/default.asp?url=/library/en-us/cpapndx/html/_cor_overview_of_the_code_access_security_model.asp.

  Good overview of the code access security model.

- Patil, Vijay Kumar. "Understanding .NET Security." http://www.c-sharpcorner.com/Tutorials/DotNetSecurityVP001.asp.

  Good overview of .NET security features.

- Persits, Peter. "Crash Course in Cryptography." http://www.15seconds.com/issue/991216.htm.

  Basic overview of cryptography terms.

- "Role-Based Security." http://msdn.microsoft.com/library/default.asp?url=/library/en-us/cpguidnf/html/cpconrole-basedsecurity.asp.

  A starting point for documentation on role-based security within .NET.

- "Securing Your Application." http://msdn.microsoft.com/library/default.asp?url=/library/en-us/cpguidnf/html/cpconsecuringyourapplication.asp.

  Good documentation of various aspects of building a secure application.

- "Security Tools." `http://msdn.microsoft.com/library/default.asp?url=/library/en-us/cpguidnf/html/cpconsecuritytools.asp`.

  A table detailing the various security tools that are available from within the .NET Framework.
- Shakil, Kamran. "Security Features in C#." `http://www.csharphelp.com/archives/archive189.html`.

  Good overview of permissions, type safety, principal, authentication, and authorization.
- "Updating Security Policy." `ms-help://MS.VSCC/MS.MSDNVS/cpguide/html/cpconupdatingsecuritypolicy.htm`.

  Explains how to update the security policy after adding a custom permission.

Appendix A References

This appendix is provided as a tutorial on the syntax and some programming of C#. Reading Appendix A should make the code samples in the book more readable. For further information on C#, the following books are useful for providing a good background in C#.

- Archer, Tom. *Inside C#*. Redmond: Microsoft Press, 2001.
- ArunGG. "C# and Its Types." `http://www.csharphelp.com/archives/archive75.html`.

  A brief overview of some of the types that C# offers.
- Bajaj, Samir. "Design Patterns: Solidify Your C# Application Architecture with Design Patterns." `http://msdn.microsoft.com/msdnmag/issues/01/07/patterns/patterns.asp`.

  Discusses some design patterns that are valid for C# and encourages you to look for more.
- Gunnerson, Eric. *A Programmer's Introduction to C#, Second Edition*. Berkeley: APress, 2001.
- Mayo, Joseph. *C# Unleashed*. Indianapolis: Sams Publishing, 2001.
- Robinson, Simon, et al. *Profesional C#*. Birmingham, UK: WROX Press, Ltd, 2001.
- Troelsen, Andrew. *C# and the .NET Platform*. Berkeley: APress, 2001.
- "Value Types." `http://msdn.microsoft.com/library/default.asp?url=/library/en-us/cpguidnf/html/cpconvaluetypes.asp?frame=true`.

  Good documentation on the value type within the .NET Framework.

Appendix B References

Because this book cannot contain a detailed explanation on every topic that could be conceived in the .NET Framework, Appendix B is sort of a catchall. It gives a brief explanation of important namespaces from within the .NET Framework library and provides some samples.

- Mitchell, Scott. "Drawing Serpinski's Triangle with ASP.NET." `http://www.4guysfromrolla.com/webtech/090201-1.shtml`.

  A good example of some of the graphics class methods that are available.

- Moryani, Barkha. "XSLT/XML/C#." `http://www.csharphelp.com/archives/archive78.html`.

  Provides an example of using the XSLT classes in .NET.

- Prosise, Jeff. "Windows Forms: A Modern-Day Programming Model for Writing GUI Applications." *MSDN*, Feb. 2001. `http://msdn.microsoft.com/library/default.asp?url=/library/en-us/dnmag01/html/winforms.asp`.

  A good overview of the Windows.Forms classes that are available.

- Tollington, Andrew D. "C# Custom Collection Implementation." `http://www.csharphelp.com/archives/archive89.html`.

  An example of creating a custom collection class that is derived from CollectionBase.

Appendix D References

Appendix D compares Java and code that is written for the .NET Framework.

- Adams, Prof. "RMI Example: Hello World Program." `http://courses.cs.vt.edu/~wwwtut/summer.97/Notes/RMIexample.html`.

  Step-by-step tutorial on how to create a sample that uses RMI.

- Banerjee, Ashish. ".NET Framework for Java Programmers." `http://www.csharphelp.com/archives/archive10.html`.

  How the CLR and J2EE compare.

- Cringely, Robert. "Making Lemonade: How Microsoft Is Using Its Own Legal Defeat to Hurt Java." `http://www.pbs.org/cringely/pulpit/pulpit20010816.html`.

  Article detailing how the legal defeat could ultimately be in Microsoft's favor.

- Driver, Mark. "Commentary: J#.Net Will Be Ignored." `http://news.cnet.com/news/0-1003-201-7475235-0.html?tag=dd.ne.dtx.nl-hed.0`.

  Article predicting that J# will be largely ignored.

- Farley, Jim. "Microsoft .NET vs. J2EE: How Do They Stack Up?" `http://java.oreilly.com/news/farley_0800.html`.

  Comparison of .NET and J2EE.

- "Java-Dependent Small Businesses to Be Left High and Dry by Recent Microsoft Windows XP, IE6 Java Boycott." `http://www.smallbiztechtalk.com/news/archives/tips081301-bn1.htm`.

  Article detailing some of the impacts that omitting the JVM with Windows XP could have on Java businesses.

- Mahoney, Matt. "Introduction to Java." `http://cs.fit.edu/~mmahoney/cse3103/java/`.

  Brief overview of some of the features available from Java as well as a history of those features.

- Rubens, Paul. "J2EE and .NET: Two Roads Diverge in XML." `http://www.internetnews.com/asp-news/article/0,,3411_868321,00.html`.

  Article that details how .NET and J2EE can and should closely interoperate using XML.

- Sullivan, Tom, et al. "Developers Ponder Java–Windows XP Split." `http://www.idg.net/crd_java_653257_103.html`.

  Article on the decision not to bundle the JVM with Windows XP.

- Surveyer, Jacques. "C# Strikes a Chord." `http://www.ddj.com/documents/s=875/ddj0065g/`.

  Make some comparisons between the languages Java and C#.

INDEX

A

B

D

E

P

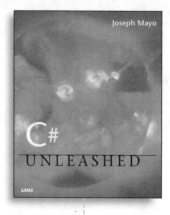

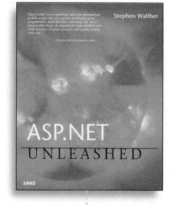